PRACTICAL GUIDE TO CORPORATE TAXATION

DOMINIC DAHER
JOSHUA ROSENBERG
STEVE JOHNSON

.CCH

a Wolters Kluwer business

Editorial Staff

Managing Editor . . . . Lynn S. Kopon, J.D., LL.M.
Production . . . . Christopher Zwirek
Index . . . . Deanna Leach

This publication is designed to provide accurate and authoritative information in regard to the subject matter covered. It is sold with the understanding that the publisher is not engaged in rendering legal, accounting, or other professional service and that the author is not offering such advice in this publication. If legal advice or other expert assistance is required, the services of a competent professional person should be sought.

ISBN: 978-0-8080-2789-8

4025 W. Peterson Ave.
Chicago, IL 60646-6085
1 800 248 3248
www.CCHGroup.com

Printed in the United States of America

We dedicate this book to our families,
without whose love and support
this work would have never been possible.

Preface

Practical Guide to Corporate Taxation is a capstone treatise that provides a comprehensive easily-understood guide to corporate tax law. *Practical Guide to Corporate Taxation* provides up-to-date comprehensive coverage of pertinent provisions of the Internal Revenue Code, relevant administrative guidance, and appropriate case law in the area of corporate taxation. Above all, *Practical Guide to Corporate Taxation* discusses corporate tax law in an easily understood practical manner.

Professor Daher (University of San Francisco School of Law and University of San Francisco School of Management), Professor Rosenberg (University of San Francisco School of Law), and Professor Johnson (Florida State University of Law) bring to life one of the most challenging areas of tax law with their expert analysis. This treatise is absolutely essential for anyone hoping to gain a better understanding of corporate income taxation.

Hereafter, this book will be updated from time to time, and new editions will be produced as significant changes in the tax law warrant. We hope *Practical Guide to Corporate Taxation* will serve as your trusted reference guide when researching corporate tax law.

Dominic Daher
Joshua Rosenberg
Steve Johnson

March 2012

About the Authors

Dominic Daher is the Director of Internal Audit and Tax Compliance for the University of San Francisco. Mr. Daher also serves as an Adjunct Professor of Accountancy in the University of San Francisco's School of Management where he teaches Federal Taxation and Advanced Federal Taxation and as an Adjunct Professor of Law in the University of San Francisco's School of Law where he teaches Federal Income Taxation, Accounting for Lawyers, and Law Practice Management: A Pathway to Success. In May 2005, Mr. Daher garnered the Outstanding Faculty of the Year Award.

Mr. Daher is a member of the National Association of College and University Business Officer's (NACUBO) Tax Council, and he regularly presents at the annual NACUBO Tax Forum. Mr. Daher serves on the editorial advisory boards for some of the leading tax and accounting publications in the country, including: *The M&A Tax Report* (CCH), *Taxation of Exempts* (WG&L), *The Exempt Organization Tax Review* (Tax Analysts), *The Tax Advisor* (AICPA), *Corporate Business Taxation Monthly* (CCH), *Internal Auditor* (The IIA), *Internal Auditing* (WG&L); and *A Guide to Federal Tax Issues for Colleges and Universites* (NACUBO). Additionally, Mr. Daher serves as the Vice President for Academic Relations and as a member of the Board of Governors for the San Francisco Chapter of the Institute of Internal Auditors; he is also a member of the Financial Accounting Standards Board's (FASB) Not-for-Profit Resource Group.

Mr. Daher is the author of over 40 published articles which deal with various aspects of federal tax law and nonprofit accounting issues, including one which has been cited in a report to the United States Congress by the National Taxpayer Advocate. Among his many other accolades, Mr. Daher is the co-author of a leading treatise on federal tax law, *The Hornbook on the Law of Federal Income Taxation* (Thomson West 2008), which has been cited in numerous decisions by various Federal Circuit Courts of Appeals. Mr. Daher's other books include: *Accounting for Not-For-Profit Organizations* (BNA 2006), *Accounting for Mergers and Acquisitions of Not-For-Profit Organizations* (BNA 2009), *Interest Expense Deductions* (BNA 2007), *Accounting for Business Combinations* (WG&L 2008), *Accounting for Business Combinations* (second edition) (WG&L 2009), *Accounting for Business Combinations* (third edition) (WG&L 2010), and *Accounting for Business Combinations* (fourth edition) (WG&L 2011).

Mr. Daher holds a Master of Laws in Taxation from New York University School of Law (where he served as the Graduate Editor of the Environmental Law Review); a Juris Doctor from Washington University School of Law (where he was the Judge Myron D. Mills Scholar); and both Master and Bachelor of Accountancy degrees from the University of Missouri-Columbia (where he was a merit scholar and graduated with honors).

Joshua Rosenberg is a Professor of Law at the University of San Francisco School of Law, where he teaches Federal Taxation and Corporate Tax, and where he has been recognized as the Outstanding Professor of the Year on three different occasions. Professor Rosenberg also teaches Corporate Tax in the Tax LL.M. program at Golden Gate University, and he has previously taught in the Tax LL.M program at New York University, as well as Boalt Hall Law School and Stanford Law School.

Professor Rosenberg has co-authored (with Lind, Schwarz and Lathrope) the leading law school texts on Corporate Tax (*Fundamentals of Corporate Taxation*, Foundation Press), Partnership Tax (*Fundamentals of Partnership Taxation*, Foundation Press), and Taxation of Business Enterprises (*Fundamentals of Business Enterprise Taxation*, Foundation Press). He has also co-authored (with Daher) the *West Hornbook Series Treatise* on The Law of Federal Income Taxation.

In addition to his books, Professor Rosenberg has published numerous articles on taxation; his articles have appeared in journals including the Stanford Law Review, the Michigan Law Review, and The California Law Review.

Steve Johnson received his J.D. from New York University School of Law in 1981. From 1981 to 1986, he was a member of the tax department of the New York City office of Willkie Farr & Gallagher, where he worked on corporate reorganizations, syndications, international transactions, business start-ups and liquidations, corporate finance, and other areas.

From 1986 to 1994, Steve was an attorney with the IRS Chief Counsel's Office, where he litigated cases in the Tax Court and Bankruptcy Court and rendered technical advice across a broad spectrum of substantive and procedural areas of taxation. He received four Superior Accomplishment awards for work in the Large Case Program and tax litigation, was the lead attorney for two national tax shelter projects, taught in the Chief Counsel's Trial Attorney Training Program, and served as a Special Assistant United States Attorney.

Since leaving the Chief Counsel's Office, Steve has taught tax law in law schools. He was a Visiting Professor of Taxation at Chicago-Kent College of Law; a tenured professor at Indiana University School of Law–Bloomington; a tenured professor, named-professorship holder, and associate dean at the William S. Boyd School of Law at the University of Nevada, Las Vegas; and a tenured University Professor at the Florida State University College of Law. Steve also visited at the University of California, Hastings College of the Law and is a member of the faculty of the Tax LL.M. program at the University of Alabama School of Law.

Among other subjects, Steve teaches Federal Income Tax, Taxation of Corporations and Partnerships, Taxation of International Transactions, Business Planning, Civil and Criminal Tax Procedure, and Advanced Issues in Taxation Seminar.

Steve has been a featured speaker at numerous tax law conferences sponsored by the American Bar Association, state and local bar and accounting groups, and law schools. He is an Associate Editor of the *ABA Section of Taxation News Quarterly* and a featured columnist for *State Tax Notes.*

Steve has authored numerous books, book chapters, and articles on federal, state, and local tax issues. His articles have been cited in decisions by the United States Supreme Court, several federal appellate courts, district courts, the Court of Federal Claims, and the Tax Court and by guidance documents issued by the IRS Chief Counsel's Office.

Table of Contents

Chapter 1

Formation of a Corporation

¶ 101 Introduction

Although there are several statutory requirements to be met and various exceptions to the rules, generally speaking the formation of a corporation is something of a non-event for tax purposes. For the most part, the code works to defer taxation for all parties involved, to leave all the assets involved with all of the same tax attributes that they had prior to the transaction, and generally to do whatever can be done to leave everyone and everything alone as far as taxes are concerned.

Since formation and capitalization of a corporation results in the creation of a new taxpayer (the corporation) which owns assets previously owned by others (the new shareholders) the transaction cannot actually be ignored for tax purposes. Nonetheless, keeping in mind the idea that Congress has attempted to come as close as possible to eliminating any tax consequences of an incorporation transaction will generally lead one in the right direction when trying to determine the actual tax results of the formation of a corporation.

Typical of the Internal Revenue Code (IRC), it takes numerous statutory provisions to bring about the basic tax "non-event" of incorporation. At the shareholder level, Code Sec. 351 provides a way for the contributing shareholders to avoid the recognition of any gain or loss,[1] and Code Sec. 358 provides that each shareholder's basis in her newly issued corporate stock will be the same as her basis was in the assets transferred in, so that whatever gain or loss she does not recognize on the incorporation transaction will be built into her newly received shares of stock.[2] At the corporate level, Code Sec. 1032 provides that a corporation will not recognize any gain or loss on the issuance or other disposition of its own stock, and Code Sec. 362 provides that the corporation will take the same basis in the assets received as the shareholder had in those assets.[3]

---

[1] As discussed below, Code Sec. 351 applies to give nonrecognition whenever its requirements are met, whether or not the transaction is an incorporation or simply transfers to an existing corporation.

[2] These and other tax consequences are discussed in detail at Chapter 8.

[3] Details and additional tax consequences are discussed at ¶ 103.01(c) & (d).

These special rules are essential to make incorporation tax free to the shareholders and to the newly formed corporation because without them, the shareholders and the corporation would both be subject to the fundamental rules of Code Sec. 1001. Those rules provide generally that whenever a taxpayer sells, exchanges, or otherwise disposes of property, she realizes a gain (or loss) equal to the excess of her amount realized (the amount of money plus the value of any property or services received for the property) over her adjusted basis in the property disposed of. Code Sec. 1001(c) then provides that any such gain realized shall be recognized (taxed) except as otherwise provided. Code Secs. 351 and 1032 are the sections that "provide otherwise" for incorporation transactions.

> **Example:** A transfers land used in business, with a basis of $10,000 and a value of $100,000 to newly formed X Corp in exchange for all 100 shares of the outstanding shares of X Corp. A is the sole shareholder of X Corp., and the land is X Corp.'s sole asset. Code Sec. 351 applies.[4] A realizes a gain of $90,000 on the exchange (because her amount realized[5] (stock worth $100,000) exceeds her basis in the land ($10,000) by $90,000. Nonetheless, A recognizes no gain on the exchange, under Code Sec. 351. A's basis in the X stock is $10,000, the same as her basis was in the property transferred, under Code Sec. 358. X Corp. recognizes no gain as a result of the application of Code Sec. 1032. X Corp's basis in the land is $10,000, the same as A's basis was immediately prior to the exchange.

¶ 102 Qualifying for Code Sec. 351 Treatment

.01 Code Sec. 351(a)

Code Sec. 351 provides that "No gain or loss shall be recognized if property is transferred to a corporation by one or more persons solely in exchange for stock in such corporation and immediately after the exchange such person or persons are in control (as defined in Code Sec. 368(c)) of the corporation." Broken down to its essentials, the nonrecognition rule of Code Sec. 351 applies if: (1) one or more persons transfer(s) property for stock, and (2) immediately after that transaction, the group of persons who transferred property for stock in that transaction are in control of the corporation.[6] Code Sec. 351's grant of nonrecognition does not require that the transaction actually be the formation of a new corporation. So long as its specific requirements (which say nothing about whether the corporation is new or has already been in existence) are met, the section applies.

These requirements of Code Sec. 351, though, are not as simple as they may seem. As explained below, many of the terms have specific definitions particular to Code Sec. 351 transactions. Terms demanding attention include "property," "stock,"[7] "control," "group of persons who transferred property for stock," "transac-

---

[4] See requirements for application of Code Sec. 351 at ¶ 102.01.

[5] Code Sec. 1001.

[6] Code Sec. 368(c) defines "control" as ownership of at least 80% of the total combined voting power and 80% of all other classes of stock. *See* ¶ 102.01(e).

[7] In some cases, even the term "transfer" may require some scrutiny. Code Sec. 351 has no application to the mere assignment of income to a corporation by a shareholder.

tion," and "immediately after." In other words, every part of each requirement of Code Sec. 351 needs further elaboration.

(a) Property

For purposes of Code Sec. 351, property includes cash,[8] all tangible assets,[9] and intangible assets as well. Intangible assets that are generally considered property for purposes of Section 351 include not only assets such as stock, patents, and licenses,[10] but also such items as "industrial know-how"[11] and accounts receivable for items sold or for services rendered to third parties.[12]

The transfer of the mere right to use property, rather than property itself, does not qualify for nonrecognition under Code Sec. 351. Any other rule would allow individuals to convert what would otherwise be rental income into a nontaxable receipt. Instead, while property can be construed fairly broadly for purposes of Code Sec. 351, it is necessary to transfer, rather than to simply rent or lease that property, to receive tax free treatment.

The treatment of accounts receivable for the sale of goods or the performance of services to third parties as (nontaxable) *property* for purposes of Code Sec. 351 has occasionally encouraged taxpayers to take advantage of the ability to avoid taxation on earned income. Specifically, a cash method taxpayer in a high tax bracket who has accrued accounts receivable for services might form a corporation and transfer to that corporation existing accounts receivable for services already provided. The taxpayer's goal would be to avoid being taxed when the receivables are collected, and to ensure instead that those receivables, when collected, will be taxed to the corporation at the corporation's lower rate.[13]

The IRS has made it clear that if it believes that accounts receivable for services provided have been transferred to a corporation in a Code Sec. 351 exchange for *tax avoidance* purposes, it will feel free to respond accordingly. In such cases it may either apply the assignment of income doctrine to tax the service provider on her earned income despite the existence of Code Sec. 351, or it may apply Code Sec. 482 to allocate income and deductions between the transferor and the corporation as necessary in order to clearly reflect income.[14] The IRS has suggested that it might find such a prohibited tax avoidance purpose in cases where the corporate transferee does not actually conduct any ongoing business or where the service-performer transfers to the corporation accounts receivable but does not transfer the accounts payable from the same business.[15]

---

[8] Rev. Rul. 69-357, 1969-1 C.B. 101.

[9] Including capital assets and non-capital assets.

[10] *E.I. Dupont de Nemours & Co. v. US*, 471 F 2d 1211 (Ct. Cl. 1973).

[11] Rev. Rul. 64-56, 1964-1 C.B. 133.

[12] Rev. Rul. 80-198, 1980-2 C.B. 113.

[13] For corporate tax rates, see Code Sec. 11.

[14] Rev. Rul. 80-198, 1980 C.B. 113.

[15] *Id.* It is also possible for a transferor in a lower tax bracket to attempt to avoid taxes by retaining accounts payable while having the high-bracket corporation assume the (deductible) accounts payable. Not surprisingly, the IRS has reserved the right to apply Code Sec. 482 to such actions as well. In addition, Code Sec. 357(b) may also be applied.

(b) Services Rendered or to be Rendered to the Corporation are not Property

In order to prevent employees or other service providers to the corporation from being able to receive their compensation tax free by taking it in the form of stock, the past or future performance of services to or on behalf of the *transferee corporation* is specifically excluded from Code Sec. 351's definition of property by Code Sec. 351(d)(1). As a result, a person who receives stock in exchange for the performance of past or future services to the transferee corporation has not received that stock in exchange for "property" for Code Sec. 351 purposes, and the recipient will be taxed on the full value of the stock received at the time of receipt per Code Secs. 83 and 61.[16] The corporation that issues stock as compensation for services will be entitled to a deduction subject to the same terms and conditions as a corporation that pays cash compensation, although it is worth noting that, pursuant to Code Sec. 1032[17] the corporation that pays for services with its own stock will not recognize any gain or loss on the stock so used.

The treatment of "know-how" as "property" for Code Sec. 351 purposes has occasionally led taxpayers to attempt to characterize stock issued in exchange for the performance of future services (taxable) as instead being issued for the transfer of "know how" (tax free). Not surprisingly, the IRS looks askance at such attempts, and will look past the taxpayer's asserted classification to characterize such shares as being issued for services rather than for know-how to the extent that such characterization better reflects the realities of the situation.

Examples: (1) In a transaction that otherwise would qualify for Code Sec. 351 treatment, E receives 200 shares of X Corp stock in exchange for (a) 100 worth of services already performed for X Corp and (b) 100 worth of services to be performed for X Corp in the future. E's stock is not received in exchange for property under Code Sec. 351. E is immediately taxed on the full value of the shares received, since they are received in exchange for services rather than for property.

(2) A, who has been operating a business as a sole proprietor using the cash method of accounting, decides to incorporate the business. The business has operating assets with a basis and value of $1,000,000, Accounts Receivable of $75,000, and Accounts Payable of $80,000. A transfers all the assets and the receivables to the new corporation in exchange for all of the corporation's outstanding stock and the corporation's assumption of liability for the accounts payable. The accounts receivable are treated as "property" for purposes of Code Sec. 351.

(3) As in (2) above, A, who has been operating a business as a sole proprietor using the cash method of accounting, decides to incorporate the business. The business has operating assets with a basis and value of $1,000,000, Accounts Receivable of $75,000, and Accounts Payable of $80,000. A transfers to the new corporation the operating assets and the receivables, but the corporation does not assume liability on the accounts payable. Instead,

---

[16] See also discussion on interest at ¶ 102.01(c).   [17] Code Sec. 1032 is discussed at ¶ 103.02, *infra*.

A will remain liable on the payables so that he can use the deduction to lower his individual tax liability. The IRS will likely either rely on the assignment of income doctrine to tax A on the receivables when they are collected by the corporation, or will invoke Code Sec. 482 to ensure that the taxpayer who is taxed on the receivables is the same taxpayer who deducts the payables, whether that be A or the corporation.[18]

(c) Interest

In order to prevent taxpayers from being able to exchange existing rights to receive interest from the corporation or existing rights to receive payment for goods already sold to the corporation into a receipt of tax-free stock, Code Sec. 351(d) also excludes from the definition of "property," for purposes of Code Sec. 351, indebtedness of the corporation not evidenced by a security and any interest accrued on a corporate obligation during the transferor's holding period for the debt. As a result, the taxpayer who receives stock in exchange for either accrued interest on corporate debt or as payment of any corporate debt not evidenced by a security will be taxed.

(d) Stock

The "stock" that must be received by the transferors of property under Code Sec. 351 may be either common or preferred, and either voting or nonvoting. There are, though, some limits on what qualifies as "stock" for purposes of Code Sec. 351.

(i) Nonqualified Preferred Stock

As clever tax advisors figured out, one could, at least prior to the enactment of Code Sec. 351(g), use the workings of Code Sec. 351 to avoid, or at least defer and recharacterize (as capital gain or dividends rather than as ordinary income) income in situations that actually bore remarkably little resemblance to the exchange of property for stock in a corporation. To see how taxpayers were able to use Code Sec. 351, assume that A transferred to Publicly Traded Corp property with a basis of $100,000 and a value of $1,000,000 in exchange for Publicly Traded Corp's readily tradable bond for $1,000,000. Since a person who receives a readily tradable bond cannot report gain on the installment method,[19] A would be taxed on his $900,000 gain immediately on receipt of the bond. In addition, A would likely be taxed each year on his accrued interest income.[20] Instead, A might, as part of a 351 exchange, transfer the property to X in exchange for stock. Since A actually does not desire to invest in Publicly Traded Corp., but wants only to receive payment of $1,000,000 plus accrued interest, the parties might arrange to have the "stock" be nonvoting and preferred as to dividends, and might further arrange to ensure that the "stock" will be "redeemed" by the corporation, so that the corporation and A can rest assured that A will be cashed out in the not-too-distant future. Additionally or

---

[18] See discussion at ¶ 102.01(f).

[19] Code Sec. 453(f)(4). Another example where Code Sec. 351(g) would reverse current taxation at ordinary rates would be if A transferred in depreciated property subject to Code Sec. 1245 recapture. If such property were sold, installment sale treatment would be unavailable, but if such property were transferred to the corpora-

tion in exchange for something that qualified as stock that was not "nonqualified preferred stock, A could defer all gain until he received cash, and then could report gain as capital gain from the sale or exchange of the redeemed "stock."

[20] Code Sec. 1272.

alternatively, the parties might arrange to have the preferred stock pay "dividends" that actually depend not upon corporate earnings, but upon interest rates.

In order to assure that taxpayers could not turn sales of property into nontaxable Code Sec. 351 exchanges by merely labeling their rights to future payments as "stock" rather than as notes, Code Sec. 351(g) excludes from Code Sec. 351's definition of stock "Nonqualified Preferred Stock." Generally speaking, Nonqualified Preferred Stock (NQPS) is defined so as to include only instruments that are likely to be cashed out at an essentially fixed return within 20 years. More specifically, NQPS is defined as including only stock which is, as is typical of "preferred stock," "limited and preferred as to dividends and which does not participate in corporate growth to any significant extent."[21] Such preferred stock is "Nonqualified" (1) if the corporate issuer is or can be (by the holder) required to redeem or purchase the stock within 20 years from the issue date,[22] or (2) if the issuer has the right and is more likely than not to exercise the right to repurchase the stock within 20 years from the issue date,[23] or (3) if the dividend rate on the stock varies "in whole or in part (directly or indirectly) with reference to interest rates, commodity prices, or other similar indices."[24]

In this context, the application of Code Sec. 351(g) means that A would be taxed currently on her gain, and imputed interest would be taxed as such. While Code Sec. 351(g) can impact Code Sec. 351 transactions, the debt/equity issues that the section deals with arise in numerous other instances, and the impact of Code Sec. 351(g)'s treatment of "nonqualified preferred stock" may be as significant outside of the Code Sec. 351 arena as it is within corporate formations.

(ii) *Warrants and Contingent Stock Rights*

"Stock" for purposes of Code Sec. 351 does not include stock warrants[25] or marketable contingent rights to stock.[26] If the corporation and transferor cannot determine the exact number of shares due to the shareholder/transferor at the time of the exchange, however, the transferor may be issued nonassignable, nonmarketable contingent rights to receive additional shares based upon the company's performance.[27]

(e) Control

Code Sec. 351(a) incorporates the definition of "control" provided in Code Sec. 368(c). In turn, Code Sec. 368(c) defines control as the ownership of "stock possessing at least 80 percent of the total combined voting power of all classes of stock entitled to vote and at least 80 percent of the total number of shares of all other classes of stock of the corporation."

While there is little direct authority on exactly what is meant by "stock possessing at least 80 percent of the total combined voting power of all classes of stock entitled to vote," rulings in other, related, areas suggest that one must first

---

[21] Code Sec. 351(g)(3)(A).

[22] Code Sec. 351(g)(2)(A)(i), (ii).

[23] Code Sec. 351(g)(2)(A)(iii).

[24] Code Sec. 351(g)(2)(A)(iv).

[25] Treas. Reg. § 1.351(a)(1)(ii).

[26] *Ibid.*

[27] Rev. Rul. 66-112, 1966-1C.B. 68, *See also Hamrick v. CIR*, 43 TC 21 (1964).

understand that "voting power" resides in any class of stock that confers on its owners the right to significant participation in the management of the corporation, regardless of the label attached to the stock. Thus, "preferred" stock that has the right to select some directors or that has a meaningful vote in other matters is likely to be classified as "voting stock" for purposes of Code Sec. 368(c).[28]

While the IRS groups together all shares of stock that have "voting power" and then to determine whether the group of transferors in a Code Sec. 351 exchange have, as a group, at least 80 percent of that total voting power, it takes a very different approach to the other prong of the "control" test. Code Sec. 368(c) requires ownership of "at least 80 percent of the total number of shares of all other classes of stock." The IRS interprets Code Sec. 368(c) to require the transferor group to own at least 80 percent of *each* separate class of nonvoting stock that has been issued.[29]

(f) Group of Persons Who Transferred Property for Stock

Code Sec. 351 requires, for its application, that the "control" defined by Code Sec. 368(c) must reside in the relevant "transferor group" immediately after the exchange. In other words, the group of persons who transferred property for stock in the exchange (the "transferor" group") must be in control immediately after the exchange for that section's nonrecognition to apply.

While it is often relatively easy to determine who transfers property and receives stock in an exchange, there are a few aspects of this requirement that require some elaboration. Significantly, the transferor group does not necessarily include all taxpayers who participate in an exchange, but only those who both transfer property and receive stock as part of that exchange. Assume, for example, that Shareholders 1-10 all transfer property to X Corp in a single exchange, and that pursuant to that exchange Shareholders 1-8 receive common voting stock of X Corp while Shareholders 9 and 10 receive only cash. Shareholders 9 and 10 are not part of the transferor group because while they transferred property to X Corp, they did not receive stock in the exchange. The same is true if they receive only warrants or nonqualified preferred stock in the exchange.

Similarly, persons who do receive stock in an exchange are not part of the transferor group if they did not transfer property to the corporation as part of that exchange. As a result, if Shareholders 1-7 transfer property to X Corp in exchange for stock, and as part of the same transaction Shareholders 8, 9 and 10 receive X Corp stock in exchange for the (past, present or future) performance of services for X Corp, Shareholders 8-10 are not members of the transferor group because services performed for the transferee corporation are not property for purposes of Code Sec. 351, so they have not transferred "property" for stock as part of the exchange.

For the most part, the transferor group includes all persons who transfer some property and receive some stock in the transaction. To be a part of the group, a

---

[28] *e.g.*, Rev. Rul. 63-24, 1963-2 C.B. 148; Rev. Rul. 69-126, 1969-1CB 218 (interpreting "control" for purposes of Code Sec. 1504 rather than for Code Sec. 368(c)).

[29] Rev. Rul. 59-259, 1959-2 C.B. 115.

person need not transfer *only* property, and need not receive *only* stock in exchange. In most cases, one is part of the transferor group so long as, in the transaction, she transfers some property and receives some stock in exchange for some of the property. For example, if T transfers property worth $200 and provides services worth $100 in exchange for $300 of stock, T is part of the transferor group because she has transferred $100 of property, and she has received stock in the transaction. Indeed, if T transfers property worth $200 and provides services worth $100, and in exchange T receives stock worth $150 and $150 cash, she is still a member of the transferor group. Again, she has transferred some property and has received stock. That is generally enough to qualify her as part of the transferor group.

(g) The Transferor Group and "Control"

As noted above, Code Sec. 351 most typically applies to the formation of a corporation, but it can also apply to transfers of property to pre-existing corporations. So long as the "transferor group" is in control immediately after the exchange, the benefits of Code Sec. 351 are available regardless of the corporation's prior history. In such cases, it is important to note that Code Sec. 351 does not require that the transferor group actually acquire control in a particular transaction, or that only the stock acquired in the transaction at issue, or even only stock acquired in exchange for property counts towards the requisite control. Instead, if a person is a member of the transferor group, then any and all stock owned by that person counts towards the control requirement, regardless of how and when that stock was acquired.

To see the import of how the control requirement applies to the transferor group, assume that T purchased all of the stock of X Corp., worth $10,000,000, several years ago. T now transfers to X Corp appreciated property worth $100,000 for $100,000 worth of additional stock. Although T has acquired relatively little stock in this particular exchange, T has transferred property for stock, and T is in control of X Corp immediately after the exchange. As a result, Code Sec. 351 applies.

To take this example a step further, assume that at a later time W transfers property worth $2,000,000 for $2,000,000 worth of X stock, and that as part of the same transaction T transfers another $2,000,000 for an equal amount of additional X stock. The transferor group includes both W and T, because both have transferred property and received stock in the transaction. That group is in control immediately after the transaction, because together, including all of T's stock, they own 100% of the outstanding shares.

(h) All Stock Owned by Group Members Counts Towards Control, Regardless of When and How Acquired

Finally, any stock owned by a member of the transferor group counts for purposes of determining control regardless of how that stock is acquired. For example, if T receives in a single transaction $1,000,000 worth of stock in exchange for property and another $1,000,000 of stock in exchange for the performance of services, T is a member of the transferor group (because she has transferred some

¶102.01(g)

property for some stock in this transaction). As a result, all $2,000,000 worth of her stock counts towards the transferor group's control.

(i) Accommodation Transferors

It should not be surprising that some clever tax advisors figured out ways to use the above rules to make a relatively easy end-run around the Code Sec. 351 control requirements. To see how they did so, assume that a group of persons who planned to contribute property and receive stock in a single transaction would *not* be in control of the corporation immediately afterwards. This might be the case either because the transferor group was going to receive a less than controlling interest in a pre-existing corporation, or because the transferor group was receiving stock in a new corporation, but they would nonetheless receive less than a controlling interest because more than 20% of the newly-issued stock was going to be issued to a shareholder exclusively in exchange for services (so that the service-provider would not be a member of the transferor group because she received no stock in exchange for "property" in the exchange). In order to ensure the application of Code Sec. 351, the advisors simply asked one or more shareholders who would otherwise *not* have been members of the transferor group to accommodate those seeking Code Sec. 351 treatment by contributing a de minimus amount of property for stock in the planned transaction. Either the pre-existing shareholder or the service provider might join the current transferor group by contributing $1 cash for an additional fractional share as part of the same exchange in order to become a part of that transferor group (that is the group of persons who transfer at least some property for some stock as part of the same exchange). Once they were a part of that group, *all* of their stock, whenever and however acquired, would count for purposes of determining whether that transferor group was in control as required by Code Sec 351.

To see how this could work, assume that T owns 100 percent of the stock of X corp., worth $100,000, and that W seeks to transfer to X corp. appreciated property worth $25,000 for a 20% stock interest (25/125). On her own, W would not be entitled to Section 351 treatment. If T simply transferred in $1 for another $1 worth of stock, though, W could argue that the "transferor group" included both W and T, and that as such, the group was clearly in control of X and W should not be taxed.

In the services area, one might assume that T and W planned to form X Corp, and that T was to receive 50% of the shares in return for the performance of services and W was to receive the other 50% of the shares in exchange for appreciated property. Without more, W would be taxed in full, because she would be the only member of the transferor group and would own only 50% of the shares of X Corp. If T simply transferred in an additional $1 for a fraction of an additional share, T would then have transferred some property for some stock and would be part of the "transferor group," thus assuring that W paid no tax on the exchange.

In order to prevent these kinds of "accommodation" transfers, the Regulations provide that "stock... issued for property which is of relatively small value in comparison to the value of the stock...already owned (or to be received for services) by the person who transferred such property shall *not* be treated as

¶102.01(i)

having been issued in return for property if the primary purpose of the transfer is to qualify under this section the exchanges of property by other persons...."[30] The IRS expanded on this regulation in Rev. Proc. 77-37,[31] where it stated that if the accommodation transferor transfers property equal to or greater than 10% of the value of the stock already owned or received for services, the transferor *will* be treated as a member of the transferor group.

Examples: (1) X Corp is worth $10,000. X Corp has only one class of stock outstanding (class A voting common), and that is 100% owned by F (10,000 shares, worth $1 each), who founded the corporation many years ago. A and B each transfer property to X Corp worth $45,000. In exchange, A and B each receive 45,000 shares of class A voting common. Code Sec. 351 applies because A and B are transferors of property, and immediately after the exchange, they are in control of X because they own 90% of the sole outstanding class of stock.

(2) As in (1), X Corp is worth $10,000. X Corp has only one class of stock outstanding (class A voting common), and that is 100% owned by F (10,000 shares, worth $1 each), who founded the corporation many years ago. A and B each transfer property to X Corp worth $45,000. In exchange, A and B each receive 10,000 shares of class A voting common and 35,000 shares of newly issued class B stock. Code Sec. 351 does not apply because A and B are the transferors of property, but immediately after the exchange, they do not own at least 80% of the class A common stock. They own only 20,000 of the 30,000 shares of class A stock then outstanding.

(3) As in (1) and (2), X Corp is worth $10,000. X Corp has only one class of stock outstanding (class A voting common), and that is 100% owned by F (10,000 shares, worth $1 each), who founded the corporation many years ago. A and B each transfer property to X Corp worth $45,000. In exchange, A and B each receive 10,000 shares of class A voting common and $35,000 shares of newly issued class B stock. In addition, F also participates in the exchange by transferring to X $3,000 for an additional 3,000 shares of stock (either class A or class B—it doesn't matter for purposes of this example). Code Sec. 351 applies because A and B and F are all transferors of property, and immediately after the exchange they own 100% of all classes of stock of X Corp.

(4) As in (3), X Corp is worth $10,000. X Corp has only one class of stock outstanding (class A voting common), and that is 100% owned by F (10,000 shares, worth $1 each), who founded the corporation many years ago. A and B each transfer property to X Corp worth $45,000. In exchange, A and B each receive 10,000 shares of class A voting common and $35,000 shares of newly issued class B stock. In addition, F also participates in the exchange by transferring to X $300 for an additional 300 shares of stock (either class A or class B—it doesn't matter for purposes of this example). Code Sec. 351 does not apply. The IRS will not treat F as a transferor in this case because F has not contributed property worth an amount equal to or more than 10% of the total

---

[30] Treas. Reg. § 1.351-1(a)(ii). [31] 1977-2 C.B. 568.

¶102.01(i)

value of the stock F owns (including the newly received stock). Thus, according to the IRS, A and B are the only transferors of property, but immediately after the exchange they do not own at least 80% of the class A common stock.

(5) A, B and C join together to form ABC Corp. A and B each transfers property worth $100,000 in exchange for 100 shares of stock. C will receive 100 shares of stock in exchange for services already performed for ABC and services to be performed for ABC. Because C is receiving stock for services, A and B are the only transferors of property. Immediately after the exchange they do not own at least 80% of the class A common stock. As a result, Code Sec. 351 does not apply.

(6) As in (5), A, B and C join together to form ABC Corp. A and B each transfers property worth $100,000 in exchange for 100 shares of stock. C will receive 100 shares of stock in exchange for services already performed for ABC and services to be performed for ABC. Because C is receiving stock for services, A and B are the only transferors of property. Immediately after the exchange they do not own at least 80% of the class A common stock. As a result, Code Sec. 351 does not apply.

(7) As in (6), A, B and C join together to form ABC Corp. A and B each transfers property worth $100,000 in exchange for 100 shares of stock. C will receive 50 shares of stock in exchange for services (some already performed for ABC and others to be performed for ABC) and C will also transfer property or cash worth $50,000 for an additional 50 shares. Because C has transferred property worth more than 10% of the total value of the stock he will own, C is considered to be a transferor of property for purposes of Code Sec. 351. Immediately after the exchange, A, B and C together own 100% of the outstanding stock. As a result, Code Sec. 351 applies. Nonetheless, C will be taxed currently on the value of any stock received in exchange for the performance of services.[32]

(j) Immediately After the Exchange

In order to qualify under Code Sec. 351, the transferor group must be in control of the corporation "immediately after the exchange." As with every other term referred to in Code Sec. 351, this term can also be problematic.

Problems can arise either because taxpayers seek the benefits of nonrecognition in situations where the IRS believes that they should be taxed, or because taxpayers seek to avoid Code Sec. 351 treatment (usually to lock in capital gains) in situations where the IRS believes that such treatment is appropriate.

A typical situation in which a taxpayer may seek, and the IRS seek to deny, Code Sec. 351 treatment is one in which A has property (for example, a patent or trademark) which she seeks to sell to Publicly Traded Corp. (PT) (and which PT seeks to purchase) in exchange for $10,000,000 worth of PT stock. A direct sale would result in A's recognition of all of her realized gain. On the other hand, A might first form Temporary Corp. (Temp), transfer her property into Temp, and

---

[32] See discussion and examples at ¶ 102.01(b).

then immediately trade her Temp stock to PT in exchange for the PT stock. A could claim that rather than a single, fully-taxed, sale to PT, she engaged in a (tax-free) Code Sec. 351 exchange, followed by a (tax-free) stock for stock reorganization under Code Sec. 368(a)(1)(B).[33] If that argument were successful, all of A's gain would go untaxed until she sold her PT stock.

Another example where A might seek to have Code Sec. 351 apply and the IRS might disagree could occur if A owns property that would generate ordinary income on sale. Rather than selling the property directly, she might wish to incorporate, transfer the property for stock, and then sell the stock instead of selling the property, to generate capital gains[34] as opposed to ordinary income.

On the other hand, assume that A owns appreciated investment land, and wants to lock in that appreciation as capital gains prior to developing and selling the land (because a post-development sale would mean that all the recognized gain would be ordinary income[35]). If A developed the land and sold it, the sale would generate ordinary income. If A transferred the land to newly formed Landco in exchange for the Landco stock in a Code Sec. 351 exchange, no gain would be recognized on the exchange, so that if Landco developed and sold the land, all gain (pre and post development) would be ordinary. But if A transferred the land to newly formed Landco in an exchange to which Code Sec. 351 did not apply, A could recognize all of the pre-exchange gain as capital gain, and only the remaining gain would be taxed as ordinary income. In these cases, A might sell or give away 21% of the Landco stock immediately after incorporation of Landco, and then argue that Code Sec. 351 did not apply because A did not have 80% control "immediately after" the exchange.[36]

In addition, the question might also arise by a simple, innocent, mistake. Assume, for example, that A and B transfer equal amounts of appreciated property to new AB Corp, and each receives 50 percent of the AB Corp stock. Assume that A immediately sells one half of his stock to C for cash. If "immediately after the exchange" means right after A and B form AB Corp, then Code Sec. 351 applies. If "immediately after the exchange" means right after A sells to C, though, then Code Sec. 351 does not apply, because only A and B transferred property to AB Corp in exchange for stock, but A and B between them own only 75 percent of the AB stock "immediately after the exchange." As a result, the formation of AB Corp would be fully taxable to both A and B, even though B had nothing to do with A's sale and even if B knew nothing about the sale by A.

Because events not even known to one party to a purported Code Sec. 351 exchange can end up taking that exchange outside of Code Sec 351, any person planning a Code Sec. 351 exchange would be well advised to have assurances that

---

[33] *See* ¶ 102.01(d).

[34] As discussed *infra*, the capital gains would likely be short–term, but even short–erm capital gains can prove far superior (tax-wise) to ordinary income for some taxpayers.

[35] *See* 103.01.

[36] Alternatively, A might form Landco by transferring in something other than the appreciated land, and then "sell" the land to Landco in a separate transaction order to recognize capital gain. In that case, the issue would not be whether A was in control of Landco immediately after the exchange. Instead, the question would be whether the substance, as opposed to the form, of the transaction, was a sale or a Code Sec. 351 exchange.

others involved in the exchange have no current plans or obligations to dispose of the stock to be received in that exchange.

In all of these cases, the exact moment that is treated as "immediately after the exchange" can have significant consequences. There are several cases that have addressed this issue; and as a result there are a few clear answers. Unfortunately, more likely than not the answer to the question of exactly when is "immediately after the exchange?" is: "it depends." There are, though, a few rules of thumb that may generally be counted on:

(1) Code Sec. 351(c)(1) provides that in determining whether the transferor group is in "control" of the transferee corporation, the fact that any corporate shareholder/transferor distributes some or all of the stock it receives to its shareholders shall not be taken into account.

(2) A taxpayer who transfers property for stock as part of a Code Sec. 351 exchange and who is, at the time he receives the stock, under a binding commitment to sell or otherwise transfer that stock, will not be treated as owning the stock "immediately after the exchange." Instead, the transferred shares will be treated as owned by the purchaser "immediately after the exchange." The result is the same if the taxpayer is not under a binding commitment to transfer the stock received, but if the IRS can show that a participant's subsequent exchange of the shares received in a Code Sec. 351 exchange was "so interdependent that the legal relations created by one transaction would have been fruitless without a completion of the series."[37]

(3) A taxpayer who transfers property for shares in a Code Sec. 351 exchange and immediately sells the shares received will nonetheless be treated as having received those shares and as owning them "immediately after the exchange" so long as she was not under a binding commitment to make that sale at the time of the exchange and so long as the two exchanges were not "interdependent."[38]

(4) A taxpayer's "form" will generally be held against him. If T structures a transaction in a way that appears to qualify for Code Sec. 351 treatment and later argues that the transaction ought instead to be treated as a taxable exchange (or if he structures a transaction so that it appears taxable and later seeks to have it be governed by Code Sec. 351), his claim is likely to be rejected by the IRS and by courts. This does not mean that the taxpayer's form will be respected in other cases, where he seeks to have the form respected. It means only that since the taxpayer is the one who initially structures the transaction, the original form will not necessarily help him, but it may well hurt him.

---

[37] *Manhattan Bldg. Co.*, 27 TC 1032, 1042 (1957) (acq.). It is difficult to be certain of exactly what this phrase means, but a shareholder who transfers property for publicly traded stock in a Code Sec. 351 will be counted as a transferor of property even if she intends to and does sell the stock immediately.

[38] *Id.*

¶102.01(j)

(5) A Code Sec. 351 exchanged followed by a *donative* transfer of some or all of the stock received will not defeat the application of Code Sec. 351 to the initial exchange.[39]

(6) If the IRS is convinced that the taxpayer was not motivated by tax considerations, it *may* look more kindly at the taxpayer's actions.

Examples: (1) R and S each transfers property worth $100,000 to newly formed RS Corp in exchange for 50 shares of RS. Neither is under a binding commitment to sell the shares received, and the formation of RS Corp is not "interdependent" with any other transaction. One week later, R sells all of his RS Corp stock to G, and unrelated third party. Code Sec. 351 applies.

(2) As in (1), R and S each transfers property worth $100,000 to newly formed RS Corp in exchange for 50 shares of RS. At the time of the formation of RS, R is under a binding commitment to sell 25 of the 50 shares he receives to Y, an unrelated third party. Code Sec. 351 does not apply. Since R was under a binding commitment to sell shares of RS, that sale is treated as part of the purported Code Sec. 351 transaction. In that transaction, the only ones to transfer property to RS in exchange for stock are R and S. Immediately after the transaction, though, R and S own only 75% of the outstanding shares of RS. The other 25% are owned by Y, who was not a transferor of property in the Code Sec. 351 exchange.

(3) R and S each transfers property worth $100,000 to newly formed RS Corp in exchange for 50 shares of RS. R has already promised to give his 50 shares to his daughter D as a gift. The corporation issues 50 shares to S and the other 50 shares to R's daughter, D. The transaction qualifies for Code Sec. 351, because the transfer of 50 shares to D was donative.[40]

(4) X transfers property to Newsubco in exchange for all of the stock of Newsubco. X immediately distributes half the stock of Newsubco to its shareholders. Code Sec. 351 applies regardless of the distribution, because Code Sec. 351(c)(1) specifically provides that "In determining control for purposes of this section, the fact that any corporate transferor distributes part or all of the stock in the corporation which it receives in the exchange to its shareholders shall not be taken into account."

(5) X Corp, unrelated to R, has owned all 100 shares of SubX Corp. (worth $100,000) for many years. R and X Corp. are in similar businesses, and they enter into a binding contract to combine the two businesses. Pursuant to this binding agreement, the parties take the following steps: (1) R transfers property worth $100,000 to newly formed R Corp in exchange for 100 shares of R Corp.; and (2) Immediately upon formation of R Corp, and pursuant to a binding commitment with X Corp., R transfers all 100 shares of R Corp to SubX Corp., and X transfers an additional $100,000 to SubX Corp in exchange for an additional 100 shares of SubX Corp.[41]

---

[39] *e.g., Wilgard Realty Co. v. CIR*, 127 F2d 514 (2d cir., *cert denied* 317 US 655 (1942); *D'Angelo Associates, Inc.* 70 TC 121 (1978) (acq. in result).

[40] *Id.*

[41] This example is based on Rev. Rul. 2003-51, 2003-1 C.B. 938.

2003-51

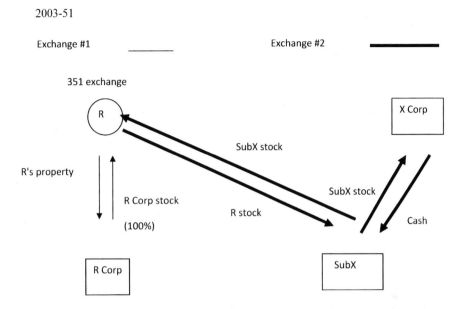

Exchange #1: R transfers R's property for 100% of RCorp stock. This would be a 351 exchange if it were a separate transaction.

Exchange #2: R transfers RCorp stock to SubX for SubX stock. At the same time, X Corp transfers cash (more than de minimus in amount) to SubX in exchange for additional SubX stock. Immediately after, R and X own all the outstanding stock of SubX. This would also be a Code Sec. 351 exchange if it were a separate transaction.

The potential problem with this series of exchanges is that immediately after Exchange #1, which would qualify as a Code Sec. 351 exchanged if viewed in isolation, R disposed of the RCorp stock received in that exchange (by immediately transferring that stock to SubX in exchange for SubX). As a result, the IRS might have determined that R was not in control of RCorp immediately after the exchange (because SubX owned the RCorp stock immediately after the second exchange). If that were the case, the first exchange would fail the "control immediately after the exchange" requirement of Code Sec. 351.

In Rev. Rul. 2003-51, however, the IRS treated the first exchange as one that was governed by Code Sec. 351. Note that R might have simply skipped the first exchange, and directly transferred the land to SubX in a qualified Code Sec. 351 exchange. SubX could then have transferred the land to its newly-formed and wholly owned subsidiary, RCorp, in a tax-free Code Sec. 351 exchange. In other words, it was clear that R was not engaging in this series of exchanges in an attempt to get tax treatment that R could not have otherwise obtained, and that R was engaging in this series of exchanges rather than in a single Code Sec. 351 exchange for nontax reasons. Had that direct alternative to tax free treatment not been available, it is doubtful that the IRS would have

¶102.01(j)

granted tax free treatment to this series of exchanges. In other words, in this particular ruling, it was important that the subsequent exchange (exchange #2) was also a tax free exchange, but it was more important that the shareholder (R) was not engaging in two "separate" transactions to achieve tax treatment that would not have been available had the shareholder engaged in a single, more direct, transaction. To attempt to generalize from this ruling, if the shareholder could have simply engaged in a single tax-free exchange to get to where it ends up, but instead engages in two purportedly "separate" (but really part of the same plan) tax-free exchanges to get to the same place, the IRS may be reluctant to assert that the first of the two exchanges was taxable (because it failed the "control immediately after" requirement of Coe Sec. 351).[42]

¶ 103 The Operative Provisions

.01 *The Shareholder*

(a) Code Section 351(a): No Gain Recognized

As explained above, if shareholders transfer property solely for stock in a transaction that meets the requirements of Code Sec. 351, the result is nonrecognition of any realized gain or loss for those shareholders under Code Sec. 351(a). This nonrecognition supersedes not only the general statement of Code Sec. 1001 that any realized gain is recognized unless otherwise provided, but, like other nonrecognition provisions, it also supersedes more specific recognition provisions. As a result, transfers by the shareholders of property otherwise subject to depreciation recapture, and transfers of installment notes, while made taxable by specific provisions aside from Code Sec. 1001,[43] nonetheless do not result in recognition of gain if done as part of a transaction subject to Code Sec. 351.[44]

(b) Code Section 351(b) Transferor's Gain Recognized

(i) *Boot*

It is not unusual for transferors in a Code Sec. 351 exchange to receive money, debt, nonqualified preferred stock,[45] or other property (any or all of which are often referred to as "boot") in addition to stock. In such cases, the requirement of Code Sec. 351(a) that the transferors receive "solely" stock in the transferee corporation is not met. Instead, a transaction that otherwise meets all of the requirements of Code Sec. 351(a) will be governed by Code Sec. 351(b). That subsection provides that if a shareholder receives boot in an exchange otherwise qualifying for Code Sec. 351 treatment, "(1) gain (if any) to such recipient shall be recognized, but not in excess of—(A) the amount of money received, plus (B) the fair market value of

---

[42] *See* Rev. Rul. 2003-51, 2003-1 C.B. 938.

[43] With respect to depreciation recapture, see Code Sec. 1245(a) "Such gain shall be recognized not withstanding any other provision of this subtitle." With respect to disposition of an installment note, see Code Sec. 453B(a) "If an installment obligation is...disposed of, gain or loss shall result..."

[44] Code Sec. 1245(b)(3) excludes Code Sec. 351 exchanges as well as other nonrecognition provisions from the recognition otherwise required on the disposition of property subject to recapture. Treas. Reg. §1.453-9(c) similarly excludes nonrecognition exchanges, including those subject to Code Sec. 351, from the general rule of recognition on the disposition of an installment obligation.

[45] See discussion at ¶ 103.01(c)(ii).

such other property received; and (2) no loss to such recipient shall be recognized."

Code Sec. 351(b) is most easily applied by seeing it as a two step process. If the basic Code Sec. 351 requirements are met, the first step in determining the tax consequences for the shareholder who receives both stock and boot is to determine the shareholder's *realized* gain—that is, the gain inherent in the transferred asset, which would be recognized if the asset were sold for its fair market value in a fully taxable transaction. That amount represents the maximum amount of gain that the transferor/shareholder can recognize, regardless of the amount of boot received. If the boot received exceeds the amount of realized gain in the asset, all of the realized gain is recognized. If the boot received is less than the total realized gain on the asset, gain is recognized (taxed) to the extent of the boot received. In no event can a shareholder recognize gain in excess of the lesser of the amount of boot received or the gain realized on the asset.

(ii) *Character of Gain Recognized*

If a shareholder recognizes gain in a Code Sec. 351 exchange, the character of that gain depends on the particular assets transferred in. The shareholder's gain is of the same character that she would recognize on a sale of that asset for cash.[46]

> **Examples:** (1) In a Code Sec. 351 exchange, T transfers land (AB=30, FMV=75) held long term as a capital asset to X Corp in exchange for X stock worth 50 and $25 cash. T realizes a gain of 45 (total amount realized= 75; T's AB in land =30. T's gain realized=45). T's 45 gain realized is recognized only to the extent of the cash and value of any other boot T receives (25). T thus recognizes a long term capital gain of 25.

> (2) In a Code Sec. 351 exchange, T transfers land (AB=30, FMV=75) (held long term as a capital asset) to X Corp in exchange for X stock worth 20 and $55 cash. T realizes a gain of 45 (total amount realized= 75; T's AB in land =30. T's gain realized=45). T's 45 gain realized is recognized to the extent of the cash and value of any other boot T receives (55). T thus recognizes his full realized gain of 45 as a long term capital gain.

(c) **Shareholder's Basis**

(i) *Stock Basis (and Holding Period) if No Boot*

In a transaction governed by Code Sec. 351(a) (that is, a transaction in which the shareholder receives solely stock and no boot), the shareholder who transfers property for stock of the corporation recognizes no gain at the time of the exchange. But Code Sec. 351 does not make gain disappear. Instead, it only defers gain, so as not to discourage taxpayers from incorporating by imposing tax on the incorporation transaction. In order to ensure that gain not recognized on the Code Sec. 351 exchange will be recognized at some later time, Code Sec. 358 sets forth the general rule that the shareholder's basis in the stock received will be the same as that of the property exchanged (referred to as an "exchange basis"[47]). As a

---

[46] See. e.g., Rev. Rul. 68-55, 1968-1 C.B. 140.   [47] Code Sec. 7701(44).

result, if, in an exchange governed by Code Sec. 351, T exchanges property with a basis of $100 and a value of $10,000 for $10,000 worth of stock of X Corp., T's basis in the stock received will be $100. The $9,900 of built-in gain on the land that went untaxed at the incorporation (increased by any later appreciation or decreased by any later depreciation in the stock value) will be recognized whenever T sells the X Corp stock.

If the shareholder/transferor receives more than a single class of stock in a Code Sec. 351 exchange, the shareholder's total stock basis is allocated among the various classes of stock received (and among the particular shares of stock received) by relative fair market values.[48]

Holding period: Not only does Code Sec. 358 ensure that the shareholder will be taxed on the right *amount* of gain on a subsequent sale of the stock, but Code Sec. 1223 helps the shareholder/transferor by also ensuring that the incorporation transaction will not adversely affect the character of her gain if she otherwise could have received long term capital gain on a taxable sale or exchange of the property transferred into the corporation. Code Sec. 1223(1) preserves long term treatment for the shareholder who transfers a capital asset to the corporation in a Code Sec. 351 exchange by providing that "[i]n determining the period for which the taxpayer has held property received in an exchange [in this case, the X stock], there shall be included the period for which he held the property exchanged if...the property has...the same basis...in his hands as the property exchanged and if the property exchanged was..." a capital asset or Code Sec. 1231 property.[49]

If the shareholder/transferor transfers in property other than a capital asset or a Code Sec. 1231 asset,[50] the shareholder can reap the benefits of escaping ordinary income on the transfer of that property, and will instead be taxed only on capital gains on the subsequent sale of the corporate stock. In such cases, though, the shareholder must at least hold the stock for an entire year to obtain long term capital gains treatment, since the holding period for stock received for other than a capital or Code Sec. 1231 asset in a Code Sec. 351 exchange begins on the date the stock is received.[51]

(ii) *Basis When Boot is Received*

Boot: If the shareholder/transferor receives boot in addition to stock in a Section 351 exchange, the boot always takes a tax basis equal to its fair market value.[52] Since the receipt of boot is not entitled to any nonrecognition or deferral of gain, there is no reason to build into the basis of that boot any deferred gain, or to ensure that any gain not recognized currently will be recognized later. To the extent the shareholder receives boot, any realized gain is recognized currently, so the boot takes a cost (fair market value) basis, just as it would in any other taxable purchase.

---

[48] Code Sec. 358(b); Treas. Reg. 1.358-2(a).

[49] Code Sec. 1231 property is depreciable and real property held for productive use in a trade or business.

[50] Code Sec. 1231 applies to real and depreciable property used in a trade or business, other than to the extent

that sale of the property would result in Code Sec. 1245 recapture.

[51] The shareholder's holding period if more than a single asset is transferred is discussed at ¶ 103.02.

[52] Code Sec. 358(a)(2).

Stock: If the shareholder/transferor receives boot in a Code Sec. 351 exchange, his basis in the stock (as opposed to the boot) received will very likely be the same as it would have been had no boot been received—that is, the same basis he had in the property transferred. This may not always be the case, however, and the possibility of a different result requires a closer examination of the Code, which, unfortunately, is more complicated than is the typical end result.

Code Sec. 358 provides that the shareholder's basis in stock received shall be the same as the basis of the property transferred,[53] decreased by the amount of boot received[54] and increased by the shareholder's gain recognized on the exchange.[55] Since any gain realized by the transferor will be recognized to extent of the boot received, the net result of Section 358 is typically that the transferor's stock basis is the same as that of the property transferred, first *decreased* by the boot received, and then *increased* by the boot received (because any gain realized is recognized to the extent of the boot received, and the transferor's stock basis is increased by the amount of that gain recognized), leaving the transferor's basis back where it started.

> *Example:* In a Code Sec. 351 exchange, T transfers land (AB=30, FMV=75) to X Corp in exchange for X stock worth 50 and $25 cash.

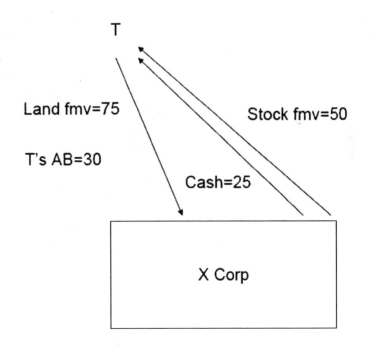

---

[53] Code Sec. 358(a)(1).
[54] Code Sec. 358(a)(1)(A)(i), (ii).
[55] Code Sec. 358(a)(1)(B)(ii).

T realizes a gain of 45. T's 45 gain realized is recognized to the extent of the cash boot T receives (25). T recognizes a gain of 25. T's basis in the X Corp stock is:

T's basis in the property transferred to X Corp:	30
Increased by T's gain recognized:	+25
Decreased by T's boot received:	-25
Total basis	=30

Note that T had a gain of 45 built into the land prior to her transfer of the land to X Corp. (the land was worth 75 and T's basis in the land was 30). Of that 45 built in (and realized) gain, T has just recognized 25 in the Code Sec. 351 exchange. The remaining 20 of realized (and not yet recognized) gain ought to be, and is, built into the X Corp stock, so that T will recognize that deferred gain of 20 when she sells the stock. T now has X Corp stock worth 50, and her basis in that stock is 30. On a sale of the stock for its current value, T will recognize the 20 gain that went unrecognized in the Code Sec. 351 exchange.

If, in this case, T received cash of 30 and stock worth 45, she would recognize gain of 30 rather than only 25. Her basis in the stock would then be 30 (her basis in the land) increased by 30 (gain recognized) and then decreased by 30 (boot received), leaving her, once again, with a stock basis (30) equal to her original adjusted basis in the land (30). Again, the remaining realized (and not yet recognized) gain ought to be, and is, built into the X Corp stock, so that T will recognize that gain when she sells the stock. T now has X Corp stock worth 45, and her basis in that stock is 30. On a sale of the stock for its current value, T will recognize the 15 gain that went unrecognized in the Code Sec. 351 exchange.

In sum, T's basis in the X Corp stock she receives will usually be the same as was her adjusted basis in the property T transferred into the corporation (because that basis will generally be increased and then immediately decreased by the amount of boot received). Generally, as the amount of boot T receives increases, so does the amount of gain T currently recognizes. In addition, as the amount of boot increases, the value of the *stock* T receives *decreases* (because the combined value of the boot and stock received must equal the value of the property T transfers into the corporation). As a result, as T receives more boot and recognizes more gain currently, she retains her same basis (in this case, 30) in *less* stock. Thus, the more gain T recognizes on the Code Sec. 351 exchange, the less gain will be built into the stock T receives (because she retains the same basis, but in stock worth less).

Example: In a Code Sec. 351 exchange, T transfers land (AB=30, FMV=75) to X Corp in exchange for X stock worth 35 and a truck worth $40. T realizes a gain of 45 (total amount realized= 75; T's AB in land =30.). T's 45 gain realized is recognized to the extent of the value of the boot T receives (35). T recognizes a long term capital gain of 35. T's basis in the X Corp stock is:

T's basis in the property transferred to X Corp:	30
Increased by T's gain recognized:	+35
Decreased by the fmv of T's boot received:	-35
Total basis	=30

T's basis in the boot (the truck) is its fair market value of 25.

If the shareholder realizes gain and receives boot in *excess* of his realized gain, however, the results change. In that case, Code Sec. 358 determines the shareholder's stock basis pursuant to the same formula as above (exchange basis, increased by shareholder's gain recognized, and decreased by the amount of boot received), but the result will no longer be equivalent to a pure exchange basis in the stock, because the gain recognized by the shareholder (which increases basis) will no longer equal the amount of boot received (which decreases basis). The shareholder who receives boot in *excess* of her realized gain will, obviously, recognize all of her realized gain (because she has received even more boot than her realized gain), but since her realized (and recognized) gain are in this case less than the boot received, the increase in her stock basis (by gain recognized) will necessarily be less than the decrease in that basis (by the boot received). In cases where the shareholder receives boot in excess of her realized gain, the fact that she will, as an initial matter, recognize all of her realized gain means that she will have *no* realized but unrecognized gain to be built into her stock basis (because she will have recognized all of her realized gain). Her basis in the stock received will instead be a fair market value, or cost, basis rather than the same basis she had in the property transferred.

Example: In a Code Sec. 351 exchange, T transfers land (AB=30, FMV=75) to X Corp in exchange for X stock worth 20 and $55 cash. T realizes a gain of 45 (total amount realized= 75; T's AB in land =30. T's gain realized=45). T recognizes all of that 45 realized gain.[56] T's basis in the X Corp stock is:

T's basis in the property transferred to X Corp:	30
Increased by T's gain recognized:	+45
Decreased by the fmv of T's boot received:	-55
Total basis	=20

Note that in this case, simply applying the formula enunciated in Section 358 results in a cost, or fair market value, stock basis. T's exchange basis (30) in the stock she receives is initially increased by her recognized gain (45). If, as here, all of T's realized gain is recognized (because the boot received exceeds her realized gain), T's basis as increased by her recognized gain *must* be equal to the full fair market value of the property she transfers into the

---

[56] In no event can T recognize more gain than she realizes, even in a fully taxable cash sale. But see discussion of Code Sec., at ¶ 103.01(b).

corporation ([initial exchange AB + Gain realized (and recognized)]= [AB + [AR (fmv) −AB]]= AB+fmv-AB=fmv). That, in turn, must also be equal to the full fair market value of all of the property she receives back from the corporation (the 55 cash boot plus the 20 stock). Of that, the boot takes a basis equal to its fair market value, the remaining basis is equal to the fair market value of the stock. All of T's gain is currently recognized, and no gain is built into the stock received.

Finally, if the shareholder realizes a *loss* in a Code Sec. 351 exchange and receives no boot, her basis in the stock received will be the same as her basis was in the property transferred,[57] thus ensuring that her realized but unrecognized loss will be built into the stock she receives. If some of the consideration the "loss" shareholder receives is boot, that means that less of the consideration she receives will be stock. In order to ensure that the same amount of loss that went unrealized on the transfer of the initial asset is built into a lesser amount (by value) of stock she receives, Code Sec. 358 provides, once again, that her basis in the stock received is reduced by the fair market value of the cash and any other boot received.

(d) Deferred Payment of Boot: Installment Sales Treatment

(i) *Timing of Recognition of Gain*

If a shareholder receives boot in the form of an installment obligation (that is, the taxpayer receives boot where at least one payment is to be received after the close of the taxable year),[58] she may be eligible to report any recognized gain using the installment method. Any *loss* realized by the shareholder in a Code Sec. 351 exchange will not be recognized at all, of course, pursuant to Code Sec. 351(a), so that the additional fact that the installment method is inapplicable to losses in its own right[59] is irrelevant.

Eligibility for the installment method to report Code Sec. 351 gain is by no means certain, however. It can depend on the property transferred by the shareholder,[60] the type of obligation received by the shareholder,[61] and the relationship between the shareholder and the corporation.[62]

If a shareholder in a Code Sec. 351 exchange realizes a gain and receives boot eligible for installment treatment under Code Sec. 453, however, she can defer taxation on some or all of that gain until actual receipt of payment. Persons eligible for installment sales treatment outside of Code Sec. 351 or other nonrecognition provisions typically determine the total amount of gain to be recognized from the exchange, divide that by the total payments to be received, and thereby determine

---

[57] Unless Code Sec. 362(e)(2) applies. See discussion at ¶ 103.02(b), infra.

[58] Code Sec. 453.

[59] Code Sec. 453(a).

[60] Installment sale treatment is not available for non-bulk sales of inventory, Code Sec. 453(b)(2). It is also unavailable to the extent that the shareholder/transferor would have recapture on a sale of the property, Code Sec. 453(i).

[61] Installment sale treatment is not available if the shareholder receives evidence of indebtedness that is either readily tradable or payable on demand. Code Sec. 453(f)(4).

[62] Installment sales treatment is not available for transfers of depreciable property between related parties, unless the taxpayer can establish the absence of a tax avoidance purpose, Code Sec. 453(g). *See also* Code Sec. 1239.

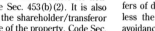

¶103.01(d)

the percentage of each payment that represents taxable gain rather than return of capital.[63] When installment sales treatment is combined with nonrecognition, as is the case with Code Sec. 351, the basic principles of installment sales treatment remain the same, but the math changes just a little. Since the shareholder will recognize gain only on receipt of payments of actual boot and will not recognize gain on receipt of stock governed by Code Sec. 351, installment sales treatment works in these cases by (1) determining the total gain that the shareholder will recognize (the lesser of the total gain realized or the total boot received, including the principal amount of the installment obligation), and then (2) dividing that total gain by the total amount of boot the shareholder will receive (that is, the total amount of cash and property other than X stock, including all principal payments on the installment note. That is the proportion of each payment of boot that represents gain rather than return of capital.[64]

Examples: (1) In a Code Sec. 351 exchange, T transfers land (AB=30, FMV=75) to X Corp in exchange for X stock worth 50, and $10 cash, and an installment note for $15 payable at the end of three years.[65] T realizes a gain of 45 (total amount realized= 75; T's AB in land =30. T's gain realized=45). T's 45 gain realized will be recognized to the extent of the cash (10) and note (15) T receives (for a total of 25). T thus will recognize a total gain of 25. Since T will recognize total gain of 25 and T receives total boot payments of 25, T will be taxed on 25/25 of each payment she receives when she receives it. T will report taxable gain of 10 in year one (when she receives 10 cash) and 20 in year three, when she receives the 20 payment on the note.

(2) In a Code Sec. 351 exchange, T transfers land (AB=30, FMV=75) to X Corp in exchange for X stock worth 25, $10 cash and an installment note of 40, with 20 payable at the end of two years and the other 20 payable at the end of four years. T realizes a gain of 45 (total amount realized= 75 (25 X stock, 10 cash, and 40 note); T's AB in land =30; T's gain realized=45). T's 45 gain realized will be recognized to the extent of the 10 cash and value of the other boot T receives (the 40 note). T will thus recognize his full realized gain of 45. Since T will recognize total gain of 45 and T will receive total boot payments of 50 (10 cash and 40 note), T will include as income 45/50 of every dollar of boot received, when she receives actual payments (not, of course, on mere receipt of the installment note that promises those future payments). Thus, in year one, T will report gain of 45/50 of the $10 cash received. In year three, when T receives 20 cash payment on the note, she will report gain of 45/50 of the 20 cash received. In year five, she will receive another 20 cash payment, and she will report as income 45/50 of that payment.

(ii) *Shareholder's Basis*

Stock received: As any shareholder in a Code Sec. 351 exchange, the shareholder who includes gain recognized on the installment method will have a

---

[63] All of this presumes that interest has otherwise been properly accounted for. This accounting for interest, stated and unstated, is a fascinating topic but not one suitable for discussion herein.

[64] Treas. Reg. § 1.453-1(f)(3).

[65] Assume that interest is otherwise properly paid and accounted for.

basis in the stock she receives that has built into it any gain or loss not recognized on the initial exchange. This basis will, as in other cases, be equal to the shareholder's exchange basis (her basis in the property transferred into the corporation) increased by any gain recognized on the Code Sec. 351 exchange, and decreased by the total value of the boot received. Because the shareholder who uses the installment method to report her gain does not recognize all of that gain immediately, there might be some question as to when the shareholder gets to increase her basis in the stock received by the gain that will be, but has not yet been recognized with respect to the note received. In order to eliminate any question with regard to the shareholder's stock basis, the regulations provide that if a shareholder is permitted to recognize gain on the installment basis in a Code Sec. 351 exchange, that shareholder's basis in the stock received is nonetheless treated as if the shareholder did *not* receive installment sale treatment.[66] In other words, the shareholder's basis in the stock received is *immediately* increased both by the gain that is currently recognized and also by the gain that the shareholder will only recognize later, when she receives actual payments on the note (that stock basis is also, of course, immediately decreased by the total amount of boot to be received, including the value of the note that will be paid only in the future).

> *Installment Note:* Code Sec. 358(b) states the general proposition that the shareholder's basis in boot received is equal to the fair market value of the boot received. This is because when, and to the extent that, the shareholder receives boot, she recognizes any realized gain on the receipt of that boot. Any realized gain (or loss) not recognized on the Code Sec. 351 exchange will be built into the stock (the nonrecognition property) the shareholder receives, and no gain or loss is generally built into the boot.

Of course, if the shareholder receives, in a Code Sec. 351 exchange, a note which allows her to report recognized gain on the installment method, T is not immediately taxed on any gain (indeed, that deferral of recognition is the whole purpose of installment sale treatment); instead, she will be taxed only as she receives actual payments of cash (or other property in the rare case that the note is payable in property other than cash). In other words, if T is permitted to defer recognition of gain by using the installment method, it is only *because* that gain will be recognized on her receipt of payments that T is allowed to avoid *current* recognition of that gain. To give T a fair market value basis in the installment note itself (as opposed to giving a fair market value basis to what T receives as payment of the note) would be to ensure that the "deferred" gain would actually *never* be taxed at all. At a minimum, it would allow T to escape the recognition of any gain by selling her installment note rather than waiting to receive the (taxable) payments due on the note.

In order to ensure that T's basis in an installment note received as boot will result in proper recognition of gain when T receives payments, T's basis in the note itself would have to be equal to the value of the note, decreased by any gain deferred by application of Code Sec 453. The regulations accomplish this by taking

---

[66] Prop. Reg. § 1.453-1(f)(3)(ii).

T's exchange basis (that is, her basis in the property transferred into the corporation in the exchange) and by allocating that basis first to the *stock* T receives up to the full value of that stock.[67] If T's total basis in the property she transferred to the corporation exceeds the value of the stock received, only that excess basis is allocated to the installment note. The result is that if the value of all of what T receives (stock and boot) exceeds her total basis in the properties and cash T transfers to X, so that T will recognize some gain, that gain is built into the installment note (because the basis goes to the stock rather than the note). Gain will be built into the stock only if and to the extent that T's total gain realized exceeds the value of the total boot received, including the installment note).

> *Examples:* (1) In a Code Sec. 351 exchange, T transfers land (AB=30, FMV=75) to X Corp in exchange for X stock worth 50, $10 cash, and an installment note for $15 payable at the end of three years.[68] As above, T's 45 gain realized will (eventually) be recognized to the extent of the total boot received—(cash (10) and note (15) for a total of 25). T thus will recognize a total gain of 25. Since T will recognize total gain of 25 and T receives total boot payments of 25, T will be taxed on 25/25 (100%) of each payment she receives when she receives it.
>
> T's initial exchange basis in the stock received, under Code Sec. 358, is 30 (her basis in the land). That basis is allocated entirely to the stock (since it does not exceed the stock's fair market value). Note that there is, as a result, 20 of gain built into the X Corp stock. This simply represents the gain that will not be recognized (either currently or under the installment method) pursuant to the Code Sec. 351 exchange.
>
> Since every dollar received as payment of the note should be taxable, T's basis in the installment note should be (and will be) 0. The regulations accomplish this by allocating all of T's 30 total basis to the stock (worth 50). No basis is allocated to the installment note. As a result, T's basis in the note is 0, and all of the payments T receives on the note will be taxable.
>
> (2) In a Code Sec. 351 exchange, T transfers land (AB=30, FMV=75) to X Corp in exchange for X stock worth 25, $10 cash and an installment note of 40, with 20 payable at the end of two years and the other 20 payable at the end of four years. T's 45 gain realized will be recognized to the extent of the 10 cash and the value of the other boot T receives (the 40 note). T will thus recognize his full realized gain of 45. Since T will recognize total gain of 45 and T will receive total boot payments of 50 (10 cash and 40 note), T will include as income 45/50 of every dollar of boot received, when she receives actual payments.

---

[67] Since the installment method is not applicable to losses in any event, the fact that the installment method applies guarantees that there is no realized loss in the exchange; since there can be no realized loss, it could never be the case that a loss would be built into the stock T receives. As a result, it would be impossible for T's stock basis to exceed its fair market value (which would result in a loss being built into the stock) in any case in which the installment applied.

[68] Assume that interest is otherwise properly paid and accounted for.

¶103.01(d)(ii)

T's initial exchange basis is 30, her basis in the property transferred into the corporation. Pursuant to the regulations, that basis is allocated to the stock to the extent of the stock's value (25) (no loss should be built into the stock, so its basis cannot exceed its value). The remaining 5 of basis is allocated to the installment boot, leaving T with an initial (before taking into account any payments made or to be made) basis in the installment method boot of 5. This is entirely consistent with the principle that T will report as gain only 45/50 of each payment received. The remaining 5/50 of each payment represents a return of that 5 basis.

(e) Receipt of Boot When the Shareholder Transfers More Than One Asset

Assume that as part of a Code Sec. 351 exchange, T transfers to X Corp. Loss Asset, with a basis of $23,000 and a value of $15,000, and Gain Asset, which has a basis of $2,000 and a value of $10,000. T realizes a gain of $8,000 on Gain Asset, and a corresponding $8,000 loss on Loss Asset. If T receives no boot, she will recognize neither the gain nor the loss. Instead, the gain and loss will net out, and T will receive stock with a total value of $25,000 ($15,000 value of Loss Asset and $10,000 value of Gain Asset) and a total basis of $25,000 ($23,000 basis from Loss Asset and $2,000 basis from Gain Asset).

If T does receive boot, though, Code Sec. 351(b) requires that she recognize her realized *gain*, but does not permit her to recognize any of her realized loss. In implementing these requirements the IRS has been a bit more generous than it might have been, given the statutory language. For example, if T receives stock worth $15,000 and cash of $10,000 in exchange for both assets in a 351 exchange, the IRS does *not* require that T recognize her entire $8,000 gain on Gain Asset while building all of her deferred loss into the stock received (basis of $23,000 in stock worth $15,000).

Instead, the IRS requires that prior to determining the amount of gain recognized, the transferor/shareholder allocate to each asset she transfers into the corporation a proportionate share (determined by each asset's relative fair market value) of the stock and the boot received in the exchange. In this exchange, for example, T transfers two assets, one (Loss) worth $15,000 and the other (Gain) worth $10,000. Since Loss Asset is worth 60% of the total value of the assets transferred by T, T must allocate to Loss Asset 60% of the stock and 60% of the boot received. Thus, T receives stock worth 60% × $15,000 ($9,000) and 60% of the cash (60% x $10,000=$6,000) for Loss Asset, and 40% of the stock (40% × $15,000=$6,000) and 40% of the boot (40% × $10,000=$4,000) for Gain Asset. Only after allocating an appropriate portion of the stock and boot to each asset does T then determine her recognized gain, stock basis, etc. with respect to each asset. The entire transaction is illustrated below:

Asset	AB	FMV	% of Total fmv	Boot Alloc'd to asset	Gain Real'd on asset	Gain Rec'd on asset	Stock Alloc'd to asset	AB of Stock Alloc'd to Asset
Gain Asset	2,000	10,000	10/25 =40%	40% × $10,000 = $4,000	$10,000 - $2,000 = $8,000	$4,000 (am't of boot rec'ved on asset	40% × $15,000 = $6,000	2,000 + $4,000 (gn rec'd) - $4,000 (boot rec'ved) = $2,000
Loss Asset	23,000	15,000	15/25 =60%	60% × $10,000 = $6,000	0	0	60% × $15,000 = $9,000	23,000 + 0 (gn rec'd) - $6,000 (boot rec'ved) = $17,000

Immediately after this, T has recognized $4,000 of gain on Gain Asset. T also has total cash of $10,000, stock received for Gain Asset with a basis of $4,000 and a value of $6,000, and stock received for Loss Asset with a basis of $17,000 and a value of $9,000. T may not, though, continue to treat the two batches of stock as separate. To permit that would enable T to sell the stock received for the Loss Asset, recognize her loss, and continue to defer at least some of her realized gain. Instead, T is required to "unify" the two batches of stock. As a result, T will have a single batch of stock worth $15,000, with a total basis of $21,000. Each individual share will have a basis equal to 21/15 of its value. In addition, each share will have a holding period that is determined 60% by reference to the holding period of Loss Asset and 40% by reference to the holding period of Gain Asset.

(f) Debt Relief

(i) *In General*

For most tax purposes, a person who transfers property subject to nonrecourse debt or whose recourse liability is assumed by another is treated as if she received cash in an amount equal to the nonrecourse debt relieved or the recourse debt assumed.[69] If that general rule held true with respect to Code Sec. 351 exchanges, it would mean that any taxpayer who transferred appreciated property subject to a liability to a newly formed corporation might face substantial tax liability. Assume, for example, that T owns a building with a basis of $100,000, a value of $300,000, and that the building is subject to a $40,000 nonrecourse liability. If T transferred this building subject to the debt to her new corporation in exchange for all of the stock, worth $260,000 (T's net equity in the building), and if the usual tax rules with respect to debt relief applied, T would be treated as receiving cash

---

[69] *See* Joshua D. Rosenberg and Dominic Daher, RO-
SENBERG AND DAHER'S THE LAW OF FEDERAL INCOME TAXA-
TION, 2007.

boot of $40,000, and would recognize $40,000 gain on the incorporation. Since so much real property is subject to liabilities, such tax consequences might be enough to deter the incorporation of most activities involving real estate.

In order to allow tax free incorporation of property subject to debt and of businesses which carry debt, Code Sec. 357(a) provides generally that if a corporation, as part of a Code Sec. 351 exchange, either assumes the debt of a shareholder/transferor or takes property from the shareholder/transferor subject to nonrecourse debt, the amount of debt relieved, assumed, or taken subject to shall not be treated as boot.[70] As a result, in the above exchange, the $40,000 of debt to which T's building was subject does not result in any current recognition of gain.

Although Congress was content to allow T to avoid current recognition of gain, it should come as no surprise that Congress was not interested in permitting permanent avoidance of realized gain. It noted that for taxpayers in T's position, the assumption of T's debt by the corporation inevitably leads to T's receipt of less stock than would have been the case were there no debt assumed. In T's case, although the building had a gross value of $300,000 (so that T would have received stock worth $300,000 had no debt been involved), T received stock worth only $260,000—the $300,000 gross value of the property transferred, reduced by the $40,000 debt to which the property was subject. In order to assure that the $200,000 of gain previously built into the building worth $300,000 is now built into stock worth only $260,000, Code Sec. 358 requires that T's initial $100,000 exchange basis in the stock received be reduced by the $40,000 of debt taken on by the corporation. T's new basis of $60,000 in the stock worth $260,000 assures that all of the gain realized but not recognized currently will remain built into the stock T now owns.

Code Sec. 358 does not act quite as directly as the above example might indicate, however. We have already seen that Code Sec. 358 provides generally that a transferor/shareholder's stock basis equals her basis in the asset(s) transferred into the corporation, increased by gain recognized on the exchange, and decreased by the amount of boot received. When dealing with debt relief, Code Sec. 358(d)(1) merely states that for purposes of Code Sec. 358 (that is, for purposes of determining the shareholder/transferor's stock basis) the corporation's assumption of shareholder debt shall be treated as boot received by the shareholder. Since the shareholder's basis is decreased by the amount of any boot received, the classification of debt relief as boot received means only that the shareholder's basis is decreased by the amount of debt relieved.

A potential problem with this arrangement arises whenever a shareholder transfers property subject to debt in *excess* of the shareholder/transferor's initial exchange basis. Assume, for example, that T transfers a building with a basis of $100,000, a value of $300,000, subject to a nonrecourse debt of $120,000, to X Corp in exchange for X Corp stock worth $180,000. The principals of Code Secs. 357 and 358 would suggest that the debt relief not be treated as boot for purposes of immediate gain recognition, but that T's initial exchange basis of $100,000 in the stock (worth $180,000) be reduced by the $120,000 of debt assumed by the

---

[70] Code Sec. 357(a).

corporation. Of course, T's initial basis of $100,000 cannot be reduced by $120,000 any more than the population of a room with 100 people in it can be reduced by 120 people. "Negative numbers," though perfectly acceptable to math teachers, have no place in the calculation of tax basis.

Since the amount of gain that can be deferred by reducing T's stock basis is limited to her initial exchange basis, to the extent that the corporation assumes debt in excess of T's initial exchange basis, any such excess debt relief results in current recognition of gain for T.[71] As a result, if, as above, T transfers to X Corp property with a basis of $100,000, a value of $300,000, subject to a nonrecourse debt of $120,000, the first $100,000 of debt relief simply reduces T's stock basis from $100,000 to 0. The remaining $20,000 of debt relief (in excess of basis) requires T to recognize $20,000 of gain. The character of that gain recognized depends on the character of the asset(s) transferred by T. If T transfers more than a single asset, any gain recognized due to an excess of debt relief over basis is, according to the regulations, allocated to each asset transferred in by T according to its relative value.[72]

Not surprisingly, T in the example is not likely to want to recognize gain currently. There are several ways for T to avoid gain in such circumstances. Perhaps the theoretically simplest (but often practically most difficult) way to avoid any current recognition would be for T to transfer to the corporation, in the same exchange, either cash or other property sufficient to increase her initial exchange basis to an amount equal to or in excess of the amount of debt assumed by the corporation.

If T has no other property to transfer into the corporation, she might choose to remain primarily liable on any debt in excess of her initial exchange basis. If, and to the extent, that T remains primarily (*not* secondarily or conditionally) liable on debt, that debt will not be treated as assumed by the corporation, so will not either reduce T's stock basis or result in gain recognition due to debt relief in excess of basis.

Finally, if the debt assumed by the corporation would otherwise exceed T's exchange basis in the stock received, T might increase her stock basis (and thereby decrease or eliminate the extent to which debt relief exceeded that basis) by transferring to the corporation her own promise to pay money to the corporation. If T's obligation is treated by the IRS and/or court as a real obligation on T's part to pay money to the corporation in the future,[73] T's exchange basis will be

---

[71] Code Sec. 357(e).

[72] Treas. Reg. § 1.357-2(b) ex 1. A more sensible approach might be to allocate the gain recognized among the assets transferred in according to the relative amount of appreciation in the assets transferred into the corporation. To see the difference, assume that T transfers property #1 with a basis of $50,000 and a value of $290,000 subject to a nonrecourse debt of $120,000 and property #2, with a basis of $50,000 and a value of $10,000, in exchange for stock worth $180,000 and $120,000 of debt relief. As in the example in the text, the $120,000 debt relief exceeds total asset basis ($100,000) by $20,000, so

T will recognize $20,000 gain. Under the regulations, because 29/30 of the total value of the assets transferred in lies in asset #1, 29/30 of T's gain recognized will be treated as recognized on asset #1. Correspondingly, because 1/30 of the total value of the assets transferred into the corporation by T resides in asset #2, 1/30 of T's total recognized gain will be treated as recognized on asset #2. Since asset #2 has only a loss, and no gain at all, built into it, it seems strange to suggest that some of T's gain is recognized on that asset, but such is the directive of the regulations.

[73] *Perachi v. CIR*, 143 F3d 487 (9th Cir. 1998).

increased by the amount of that obligation.[74] As a result, if the note equals or exceeds the gain T would otherwise recognize as a result of debt relief in excess of basis, that current recognition will be eliminated.

(ii) *Code Sec. 357(b)*

Left unchecked, the treatment of debt relief as something other than boot would allow clever transferors to avoid almost any gain recognition while nonetheless ending up with significant amounts of cash on an incorporation transaction. To see how this could be done, assume that T owns and is about to incorporate a business with assets having a total basis of $100,000 and a total value of $200,000, and that T would like to end up with $75,000 cash and stock worth $125,000. If T receives the cash from the corporation (the corporation might borrow the cash or the cash may have been contributed by a different shareholder), T will recognize $75,000 of gain. Instead, T might borrow $75,000, pledging the business assets as security, immediately prior to the incorporation. Then as part of the incorporation, the new corporation could assume (or take the assets subject to, as the case may be) that $75,000 liability, leaving T with $75,000 cash and stock worth $125,000, but this time with no recognized gain.

To prevent the use of debt relief to circumscribe the rules applicable to boot, Code Sec. 357(b) provides that if the principal purpose for the assumption of debt by the corporation in a Code Sec. 351 exchange was tax avoidance or was anything other than a bona fide business purpose, then *any and all* of that transferor's debt assumed by the corporation in the transaction (even entirely separate and pre-existing debt that was assumed for entirely legitimate business purposes) shall be treated as cash boot. Generally speaking, transferor's can avoid the penalty of Code Sec. 357(b) so long as they can show that the debt arose in the ordinary course of business (for example, accounts payable for an accrual method taxpayer) or, in the case of debt such as bank loans, that the loan proceeds either were used in the business or will accompany the other business assets into the new corporation. On the other hand, Code Sec. 357(b) will likely be applied if it appears that the shareholder used the occasion of incorporation either to get cash into her own hands or to have her personal, rather than business, debts relieved.[75]

(g) Debt Relief and Boot

If a shareholder transfers assets and receives (in addition to stock) both cash and debt relief, the actual boot is taken into account (resulting in potential gain recognition and basis adjustment for the transferring shareholder), prior to the debt relief. After taking into account the effects of the boot, the shareholder's stock basis is then adjusted to take into account the debt relief.

---

[74] Some have suggested that T has no "exchange" basis in her own note. Of course, this is as true as the assertion that T has no exchange basis in cash she transfers to the corporation, since $1 does not technically have a "basis." Nonetheless, to suggest that T's basis in stock acquired for a $100 note is anything less than $100 would be silly. It would mean that if T pays 100 to the corporation to pay off the note, T will still recognize gain of $100 when she sells the stock. It would also seem to require that the Corporation take a basis of 0 in T's note, and that as a result when T pays off the note, the corporation has $100 of gain. Such is simply not the case.

[75] Treas. Reg. § 1.357-1, -3, Boris I. Bittker and James S. Eustice, Federal Income Taxation of Corporations and Shareholders, ¶ 3.06[3] (7th ed. 2006).

Liabilities that would give rise to a deduction when paid: Put simply, if, as part of a Code Sec. 351 exchange, a corporation assumes or takes property subject to debt and the debt is one which would be deductible when paid, the debt is completely disregarded. Not only is the debt not treated as cash, it also has no impact on the shareholder's stock basis and does not result in the recognition of any gain regardless of the circumstances.

The reason that debt relief must generally be accounted for in Code Sec. 351 exchanges is that the relief of T's debt is the economic equivalent of T's receipt of cash in an amount equal to the debt relieved (followed by T's immediate use of that cash to pay off the debt). The deemed receipt of the cash is generally income, but in Code Sec. 351 transactions the income is deferred and T instead takes a reduced stock basis. Where the liability assumed is one that would be deductible when paid, the economic equivalent of the corporation's assumption of T's debt is the corporation's payment of cash to T, followed immediately by T's use of that cash to pay a deductible expense. While the deemed receipt of cash would typically result in income that needs to be accounted for either currently or later (that is, by was of T's reduced stock basis), the deemed use of that cash to pay a deductible expense would typically give rise to a deduction of an amount exactly equal to the income generated by the deemed cash receipt. Rather than separately taking into account the deemed income and the deemed deduction, the code simply concludes that since the two would cancel each other out, the entire assumption of the debt in such cases should simply be ignored. To that end, Code Sec. 357(c)(3) provides that the amount of any deductible liability is ignored for purposes of determining whether the shareholder recognizes any current gain, and Code Sec. 358(d)(2) provides that any deductible liability shall also be ignored for purposes of determining the shareholder's stock basis.

.02 Consequences to the Corporation

(a) Code Sec. 1032: Nonrecognition

Code Sec. 1032 provides that a corporation shall recognize no gain or loss whenever it sells, exchanges or otherwise issues its own stock. As a result, incorporations are generally tax free to the corporation. If, however, a corporation transfers property other than its own stock for property (or services), the corporation will recognize any gain or loss[76] inherent in that other property regardless of whether the exchange takes place in the context of a Code Sec. 351 exchange.

(b) Corporation's Basis in Transferred Assets

(i) General Rule

Code Sec. 362 ensures that any gain (or loss)[77] built into assets transferred to the corporation pursuant to a Code Sec. 351 exchange and not recognized at the time of the exchange will remain built into the transferred asset. It does so by providing that the corporation's basis in each transferred asset is the same as the

---

[76] Loss limitations may apply if the exchange is between the corporation and a more than 50% shareholder. *See* Code Sec. 267.

[77] *See* ¶ 103.02(b)(ii), for discussion of limitations on built in losses.

transferor's basis was, increased by any gain recognized by the transferor on the transfer to the corporation. As a result, if the shareholder recognizes no gain under Code Sec. 351, the corporation takes each asset with the same basis that the shareholder/transferor had in that asset. If the transferor recognizes some gain on a particular asset, the corporation's basis in that asset is equal to the shareholder's original asset basis increased by the gain recognized by the shareholder during the Code Sec. exchange on that particular asset.

Example: To see how Code Sec. 362 applies on an asset by asset basis, let us return to the example set forth at ¶ 103.01(e) , and again below, in which T transferred Gain Asset (ab=$2,000, fmv=$10,000) and Loss Asset (ab=$23,000, fmv=$15,000) in exchange for $15,000 worth of stock and $10,000 cash.

Asset	AB	FMV	% of Total fmv	Boot Alloc'd to asset	Gain Real'd on asset	Gain Rec'd on asset	Stock Alloc'd to asset	AB of Stock Alloc'd to Asset
Gain Asset	2,000	10,000	10/25 =40%	40% × $10,000 = $4,000	$10,000 - $2,000 = $8,000	$4,000 (am't of boot rec'ved on asset)	40% × $15,000 = $6,000	2,000 + $4,000 (gn rec'd) - $4,000 (boot rec'ved) = $2,000
Loss Asset	23,000	15,000	15/25 =60%	60% × $10,000 = $6,000	0	0	60% × $15,000 = $9,000	23,000 + 0 (gn rec'd) - $6,000 (boot rec'ved) = $17,000

Because T recognized gain of $4,000 on Gain Asset, the corporation takes that asset with a basis of $6,000: T's original asset basis of $2,000, increased by the $4,000 of gain recognized by T on that asset during the exchange. Since T recognized no gain (or loss) on Loss Asset, the corporation takes that asset with the same $23,000 basis that it had in T's hands.

As discussed later, if the shareholder recognizes gain because of debt relief in excess of basis instead of, or in addition to, the receipt of cash, the corporation will also increase its basis in any assets on which such gain is recognized.[78]

(ii) *Limitation on Built in Losses*

Since the transferor/shareholder takes as her stock basis the same total basis she had in the assets transferred into the corporation, she will recognize any net gain in those assets when she sells her stock. Since the corporation takes as its

---

[78] *See note* ¶ 103.01, *supra.*

¶103.02(b)(ii)

asset basis the same basis the shareholder had in each asset (increased by any gain recognized by the transferor on that asset in the Code Sec. 351 exchange), the corporation will also recognize any gain or loss in those assets when it sells them. The inevitable result is that any gain built into those transferred assets will be recognized twice, once at the shareholder level and again at the corporate level. While the doubling of taxable gain caused no concern to the IRS, taxpayers' ability to double deductible losses was another story.

The legislative response to inevitable taxpayer attempts to double losses by transferring loss assets to a corporation in a Code Sec. 351 exchange was Code Sec. 362(e)(2). That section limits the corporation's total basis in all the assets transferred by a single shareholder in a Code Sec. 351 exchange to the total fair market value of those assets. Any basis decrease is to be allocated among the transferred assets in proportion to their inherent built in losses in the shareholder's hands immediately prior to the exchange.[79] If the shareholder and corporation both elect, the basis limitation will be applied to the shareholder's stock basis rather than to the corporation's total asset basis.[80]

> **Example:** Assume that T transfers to X Co. a single asset (basis=$100,000, fmv=$40,000) in exchange for all of the stock of X Co.. Prior to the enactment of Code Sec. 362(e)(2), T's stock basis would be $100,000, and X's asset basis would also be $100,000. Code Sec. 362(e)(2) provides that absent an election, X's asset basis will be reduced to $40,000. If T and X both elect, X will take the asset with a basis of $100,000, but T's stock basis will be reduced to $40,000.
>
> If T also transferred in a second asset with a basis of $40,000 and a value of $100,000, Code Sec. 362(e)(2) would be inapplicable, because the corporation's total asset basis ($140,000) would not be in excess of the total value of the assets transferred by T ($140,000). Finally, if T transferred in the asset with a basis of $100,000 and a value of $40,000 together with an asset with a basis of $70,000 and a value of $100,000, the corporation's initial (before the application of Code Sec. 362(e)(2) total asset basis of $170,000 would exceed the total asset value ($140,000) by $30,000, so the corporation's asset basis will be reduced by that $30,000 net built in loss. Because the entire built in loss exists only in the first asset, it is that asset whose basis is reduced by $30,000 (from $100,000 to $70,000).

(iii) *Increased Basis Due to Installment Boot*

You may recall that if the shareholder receives boot in the form of an installment note which qualifies for installment sale treatment under Code Sec. 453, the shareholder is entitled to report her recognized gain using the installment method rather than including all recognized gain in the year of the exchange. In such cases, the transferee corporation cannot increase its asset basis (by gain recognized by the shareholder/transferor) until the shareholder actually recognizes that gain as the note is paid by the corporation.[81]

---

[79] Code Sec. 362(e)(2)(B).
[80] Code Sec. 362(e)(2)(C).

[81] Treas. Reg. § 1.453-1(f)(3)(iii) example (1).

The fact that the corporation cannot increase its asset basis until the transferor/shareholder actually recognizes gain on the transferred asset can lead to some interesting results. The regulations provide that if the corporation sells the transferred property prior to being able to increase its basis in that asset, then when it later makes payments on the note that result in the shareholder's recognition of gain, the corporation, since unable to increase its asset basis by the gain recognized by the shareholder (because it no longer has the asset) can instead take as a current loss (treated as a loss on the sale or exchange of the asset) the amount that it would otherwise have been able to add to its asset basis.

If the asset transferred in and for which recognized gain is to be accounted for on the installment method is depreciable, then the corporation will initially take depreciation on the asset at its transferred basis.[82] If in a subsequent year the corporation pays part of the note and the transferee recognizes some gain, then at that point the corporation will have additional asset basis, which it will be required to treat as essentially a new asset subject to depreciation. If payments are made and gain is recognized on the asset for several years, each year's gain recognized will result in additional corporate asset basis and must be treated as a new asset. A single asset may be required to be depreciated using several different accounts because each basis addition is necessarily treated as a new asset.

(c) Holding Period

Any time the corporation takes the shareholder/transferor's basis in an asset (even if that basis is increased as a result of gain recognized by the transferor or reduced as a result of Code Sec. 362(e)(2)), the corporation is also treated as having held the asset for the same period of time that the shareholder held the asset prior to the transfer.[83] As a result, if the corporation holds the transferred asset as a capital asset, it will be entitled to long term rather than short term capital gain at the moment that its own holding period combined with the period for which the shareholder held the asset prior to transfer totals one year. This is true regardless of whether or not the asset was a capital asset in the hands of the shareholder/transferor.

(d) Depreciation and Depreciation Recapture

If the shareholder transfers depreciable property to the corporation in a Code Sec. 351 exchange, the corporation steps into the transferor's shoes not only with respect to basis and holding period, but also with respect to depreciation and depreciation recapture. Code Sec. 168(i)(7) provides that with respect to the basis transferred from the shareholder to the corporation, the corporation shall be treated as the transferor for purposes of computing depreciation. To the extent that the corporation's basis is higher than the transferor's basis (because the corporation's basis is equal to the shareholder's asset basis increased by any gain recognized by the shareholder on that asset pursuant to the Code Sec. 351 exchange),

---

[82] Keep in mind, though, that to the extent the transferred asset is subject to depreciation recapture, the installment method of reporting would not be available in any event, under Code Sec. 1245. In addition, if the transferor is a more than 50% shareholder, installment treatment is not available with respect to property which would be depreciable in the hands of the corporation. Code Sec. 1239.

[83] Code Sec. 1223(2).

the property is treated as a new asset purchased by the transferee corporation, so that the corporation will have two separate depreciation accounts for the two separate components of its total asset basis.

In line with Code Sec. 168(i)(7), Code Sec. 1245 also assures that the corporation will step into the shareholder's shoes with respect to depreciation recapture. The depreciation taken by the shareholder reduced her basis in the depreciated property under Code Sec. 1016. That basis reduction is in turn reflected in the corporate/transferee's adjusted basis. Code Sec. 1245 defines the corporation's "recomputed basis" as its adjusted basis increased by any depreciation taken by the corporation or by any other person (that is, the shareholder/transferor), to the extent that the basis adjustments that accompanied the depreciation are reflected in the corporation's basis. The result is that the corporation has the same adjusted basis and the same recomputed basis as did the shareholder, and it is those two terms that determine the amount of recapture. Thus, the corporation effectively inherits any depreciation recapture that would otherwise have been recognized by the shareholder.

¶ 104 Contributions to Capital

.01 Shareholder Contributions to Capital

If the existing shareholders of any corporation make pro rata contributions to that corporation in exchange for additional stock, Code Sec. 351 would apply to make the exchange tax free to the shareholders, Code Sec. 358 would give the shareholders an exchange basis in their new stock, Code Sec. 1032 would guarantee tax free treatment to the corporation, and Code Sec. 362 would give the corporation a transferred basis in the assets received.

Often, if the shareholders do make such contributions, proportionate to their existing interests in the corporation, there is no need for, or utility to, having the corporation issue new shares. Since the new shares would be issued in proportion to current ownership percentage, they would make no change in that ownership percentage. For tax purposes, it matters not whether or not new shares are issued in these circumstances. If no shares are issued, the amount contributed is simply treated as an additional amount paid for the shares already owned.[84] No shareholder recognizes gain or loss, each shareholder's stock basis is increased by the basis in the property contributed,[85] the corporation recognizes no gain, and the corporation's basis in the contributed property is the same as it would be had the transaction been a Code Sec. 351 exchange.[86]

The same principals apply if the shareholder contributions, although not pro rata, are nonetheless made by shareholders in their capacity as shareholders, that is, if the contributions are made for the purpose of increasing the value of the corporation and not as compensation for past property or services received from the corporation or in expectation of future services or property.[87] This is the case even if the property contributed is stock of the corporation itself. Thus, for example,

---

[84] Treas. Reg. § 1.118-1.

[85] The additional basis is allocated among the outstanding shares on a pro-rata basis.

[86] Ibid, *CIR v. Fink*, 483 US 89 (1987).

[87] *CIR v. Fink*, 483 US 89 (1987).

assume that A is the 75% shareholder (75 of 100 shares outstanding) of X and has a basis in her X stock of $2 per share (total basis of $150). If A transfers (for no consideration, merely as a contribution to capital) to X 25 shares of X stock (in which A has a basis of $150), A will recognize no gain or loss, her basis in the 25 shares she has transferred will be added on to her basis in the X shares retained (so that she will now have a basis of $150 in 50 shares rather than in 75 shares), and X will recognize no gain or loss.[88]

.02 Nonshareholder Contributions to Capital

It is possible for a person to make a contribution to the capital of a corporation even if that person is not a shareholder, or for a shareholder to make a contribution to capital other than in her capacity as a shareholder. Any payment made to a corporation by a person other than a shareholder making a contribution in her capacity as such is not a contribution to capital if it is made as compensation for past property or services received from the corporation or in expectation of future services or property. Instead, such payments would simply be income to the corporate recipient.

Non-shareholder contributions to capital (including contributions by a shareholder other than in her capacity as a shareholder), as opposed to income earned by the corporation, will most likely take the form of contributions of land or other property by governments or civic groups to induce the corporation to locate in a particular area.[89] These payments are excluded from the corporation's current income under Section 118, but not without some cost. In return for the exclusion from income of non-shareholder contributions to capital, the corporation takes any such property with a basis of 0,[90] so that any gain not recognized by the corporation on receipt of that property will be taxed whenever the corporation disposes of that contributed property. If the contributed property is money, the money contributed cannot have its basis reduced, but Congress has achieved the same effect by requiring that the basis of any property acquired with that money within the year following its contribution takes a basis of 0, and if the contributed cash is not spent within the year, the basis of other property already owned by the corporation will reduced by the amount of cash contributed and unspent within the year.[91]

---

[88] X's basis in the shares contributed would be the same $2 basis per share that A had, but this would be irrelevant since X can never recognize gain or loss on the sale or exchange of its own shares under Code Sec. 1032.

[89] Treas. Reg. § 1.118-1.

[90] Code Sec. 362(c).

[91] Code Sec. 362(b)(2). The allocation of basis reduction for unspent cash contributed is to be made pursuant to as yet unenacted regulations.

Chapter 2

Application of the Federal Income Tax to Corporations

A C Corporation computes its federal income tax liability in the following fashion. Based on its methods of tax accounting, the corporation, for each tax year, computes its gross income, then subtracts its available deductions to determine its taxable income.[1] The corporation multiplies its taxable income by the applicable tax rates, then subtracts allowable credits to determine its regular income tax liability. The corporation adds its alternative minimum tax ("AMT") liability to its regular income tax liability to ascertain its total income tax liability for the tax year.

This chapter analyzes each of the above concepts and elements. Many of them are identical or similar to those used in computing the federal income tax liability of individual taxpayers. This chapter emphasizes the points of difference, the respects unique to how corporations compute their federal income tax liabilities.

Major changes to many important provisions were effected by the Small Business Jobs Act of 2010.[2] However, these changes typically are for only a few tax years, and their extension to other tax years is far from certain. Accordingly, most parts of this chapter discuss the tax laws as they stood before enactment in late 2010 of the Small Business Jobs Act and the Tax Relief, Unemployment Insurance Reauthorization and Jobs Creation Act. The final part of this chapter describes those Acts and the opportunities created by them for corporate taxpayers.

¶ 201 Accounting Methods

In general, C corporations use the accrual methods of accounting. This stems from three causes. First, taxpayers typically are on the same method of accounting for tax purposes as they use for financial purposes,[3] and corporations typically use the accrual method for financial purposes. Second, various special rules may

---

[1] Code Sec. 63(a).
[2] Pub. L. No. 111-240, 124 Stat. 2504 (Sept. 27, 2010).

[3] Code Sec. 446(a).

require use of the accrual method, either generally or for specific items.[4] Third, Code Sec. 448 makes use of the accrual method mandatory for many C corporations.[5]

Some exceptions exist, for either relief or anti-abuse purposes. Here are some of the more prominent exceptions:

- Code Sec. 448 excepts three types of corporations from mandatory accrual treatment: certain small farming businesses,[6] qualified personal service corporations,[7] and certain small corporations.[8] Tax shelters do not qualify for these exceptions.[9]

- Various sections take taxpayers off their usual accounting methods with respect to some specific types of transactions.[10]

- The IRS has general authority to take taxpayers off their usual accounting methods when those methods do not clearly reflect income.[11]

Practice Tip: Code Sec. 446(b) provides that if the taxpayer's usual accounting method does not clearly reflect income, the IRS may put the taxpayer on a different method which "in the opinion of the Secretary, does clearly reflect income." Scores of other Code sections also use the "in the opinion of the Secretary" language. The courts have held that the presence of this language in a section alters the standard of proof. Although there are dozens of exceptions, taxpayers typically bear the burden of proof in civil tax litigation and the standard of proof is "preponderance of the evidence."[12] The cases hold, however, that "in the opinion of the Secretary" language in a section raises the quantum of proof a taxpayer must establish to an "abuse of discretion" standard, which is a higher standard than the usual "preponderance of the evidence" standard.[13]

Practice Tip: Litigation outcomes under this authority have been somewhat mixed.

Example 1: An agreement settling litigation obligated Burnham Corporation, an accrual method taxpayer, to make monthly payments to an individual for the rest of her life. Burnham estimated the sum of these payments based on actuarial tables, and it deducted this amount in the year the agreement was entered into. The IRS disallowed the deduction, but the court upheld the deduction.[14] In this case, the IRS conceded that Code Sec. 446(b) did not

---

[4] *e.g.*, Code Sec. 447 (requiring that certain large-scale farming corporations use the accrual method); Treas. Reg. §1.446-1(c)(2)(i) (requiring businesses with inventories to use the accrual method).

[5] Code Sec. 448(a).

[6] Code Sec. 448(b)(1).

[7] Code Sec. 448(b)(2). Such entities are corporations substantially all of whose activities entail rendering services in health, law, engineering, accounting, architecture, actuarial services, performing arts, or consulting. Moreover, substantially all of the corporation's stock must be held by current or retired employees, their estates, or their heirs (for up to two years after death). Code Sec. 448(d)(2).

[8] Code Sec. 448(b)(3). Such corporations are those whose average annual gross receipts for the three years before the tax year in question are not over $3 million.

[9] Tax shelters are defined by reference to Code Secs. 461(i)(3) and 6662(d)(2)(C)(i).

[10] *e.g.*, Code Secs. 453-460.

[11] Code Sec. 446(b).

[12] *See* Steve R. Johnson, *The Dangers of Symbolic Legislation: Perceptions and Realities of the New Burden-of-Proof Rules*, 84 Iowa L. Rev. 413 (1999).

[13] *e.g.*, *RECO Inds. v. Comm'r*, 83 T.C. 912, 920 (1984).

[14] *Burnham Corp. v. Comm'r*, 90 T.C. 953 (1988), *aff'd*, 878 F.2d 86 (2d Cir. 1989).

"require accrual basis taxpayers to discount current deductions of long-term liabilities.[15]

However, in some other cases, the IRS has successfully asserted Code Sec. 446(b) and related sections to prevent accrual method corporations from currently deducting liabilities that will be paid only far in the future.

Example 2: A corporation manufactured and sold aircraft. It issued with each plane sold a bond setting out an unconditional promise that the corporation would pay $1,000 to the bearer of the bond when the plane was permanently retired from service. The corporation attempted to currently deduct the amounts of the bonds despite the fact that the payments would not likely be made for 15, 20, or 30 years. The IRS disallowed the deduction, and the courts held for the IRS. Under Code Sec. 446(b) and other sections, the amounts could be deducted only in the year the corresponding planes were permanently retired from service.[16]

- Several Code sections set out matching rules. For instance, under Code Sec. 267, personal service corporations are effectively put on the cash method as to payments to their cash method employee-shareholders (regardless of the level of their stock ownership).[17] This defers the corporation's deduction for the payment until the employee-shareholder takes the receipt into income. Similarly, a matching rule exists as to certain compensation plan items under Code Sec. 404.[18]

Example: Before 1982, Albertson's, Inc. entered into a nonqualified deferred compensation agreement with top executives. The parties agreed that the deferred compensation would include annual basic amounts plus additional amounts pursuant to a formula. The participants were eligible to receive the total amounts on termination of employment. They also had the option of further deferring payment for up to 15 more years. During the deferral period, the additional amounts would continue to accrue. Albertson's deducted the additional amounts that had accrued even though they had not been paid to the plan participants. The IRS disallowed the claimed deductions. The courts upheld the disallowance. The appellate court held that the matching principle of Code Sec. 404 applied and that the corporation could not deduct the amounts in question until they were received and included into income by the participants.[19]

¶ 202 Tax Year

A new corporation generally may adopt either a calendar year or any fiscal year for federal income tax purposes – as long as it uses the same period in keeping its financial books.[20] However, personal service corporations usually use the calendar year. A qualified personal service corporation is any corporation (1) substantially all

---

[15] 90 T.C. at 960.

[16] *Mooney Aircraft, Inc. v. United States,* 420 F.2d 400 (5th Cir. 1969); *see also Ford Motor Co. v. Comm'r,* 71 F.3d 209 (6th Cir. 1995) (similar result with respect to deductions for liabilities under structured settlements of tort suits against the manufacturer).

[17] Code Sec. 267(a)(2).

[18] Code Sec. 404(a)(5) & (d).

[19] *Albertson's, Inc. v. Comm'r,* 42 F.3d 537 (9th Cir. 1994), *cert. denied,* 516 U.S. 807 (1995).

[20] Code Sec. 441(c); Treas. Reg. § 1.441-1T(b)(2).

the activities of which involve services in health, law, engineering, architecture, accounting, actuarial science, performing arts, or consulting and (2) substantially all the stock of which (by value) meets certain employee-ownership requirements.[21]

> *Example:* Wee Friends is a domestic C corporation. Its employees spend all their time performing veterinary services. These services include diagnostic and recuperative services, as well as activities incident to performing these services, such as boarding and grooming animals. Wee Friends meets the ownership requirements of Code Secs. 441 and 448.

The regulations define health services to include the provision of medical services by physicians, nurses, dentists, and other similar health-care professionals,[22] and the IRS has ruled that veterinarians are "similar health-care professionals" within the meaning of the regulations. Therefore, Wee Friends meets the activities test. It is a qualified personal service corporation under Code Sec. 448 and a personal service corporation under Code Sec. 441(i). Wee Friends must use the calendar year unless one of the exceptions discussed below applies.

There are exceptions to this exception, that is, situations in which a personal service corporation may use a fiscal year. First, the corporation may attempt to establish to the satisfaction of the IRS that a business purpose (other than deferral of tax at the shareholder level) warrants use of a fiscal year.[23] Second, the corporation may adopt a fiscal year ending on September 30, October 31, or November 30 if it makes minimum distributions to shareholders to eliminate the benefit of tax deferral.[24]

Already established corporations usually must continue to use the tax year previously adopted. However, they can alter their tax years if they procure the consent of the IRS.[25]

¶ 203 Gross Income

.01 Generally

For corporations, as for individuals, determining gross income is a two-step operation. First, the taxpayer ascertains whether its receipts fall within the ambit of income taxability as defined by Code Sec. 61.[26] This step is rarely challenging. Given the section's broad reach,[27] virtually everything of economic value received by a corporation will be income in a Code Sec. 61 sense. Second, the taxpayer

---

[21] Code Sec. 448(d)(2); *see also* Code Sec. 441(i) (defining "personal service corporation" for Code Sec. 441 purposes).

[22] Rev. Rul. 91-30, 1991-1 C.B. 61; *see also* Rev. Rul. 92-65, 1992-2 C.B. 94 (limiting Rev. Rul. 91-30 to tax years starting after May 13, 1991).

[23] Code Sec. 441(i)(1); Treas. Reg. § 1.441-4T(c)

[24] Code Secs. 444 & 280H.

[25] Code Sec. 442. Procedures for seeking such approval from the IRS are set out in Rev. Proc. 92-13, 1992-1 C.B. 665.

[26] A receipt is taxable under Code Sec. 61 if it falls within any of fifteen specifically enumerated categories. However, the enumeration is non-exhaustive, so a non-enumerated type of receipt is still taxable if it fits within the broad introductory language of Code Sec. 61(a): "all income from whatever source derived." Items are within this introductory language if they are accessions wealth, have been realized, and are within the taxpayer's dominion. *Comm'r v. Glenshaw Glass Co.*, 348 U.S. 426 (1955).

[27] *See, e.g., id.* at 429 (stating that the language of § 61 evinces Congress's intention to exert its full constitutional authority to tax).

determines whether any exclusion section applies. Receipts within an exclusion are non-taxable regardless of Code Sec. 61.[28]

In general, Code Sec. 61 and the various exclusions apply equally to both corporate and individual taxpayers, but there are differences. Some aspects of Code Sec. 61 are irrelevant to corporations, such as, of course, the income inclusion for alimony received. Some exclusions also are irrelevant to corporations. Yet other exclusions are available only to corporations, such as the Code Sec. 118 exclusion for contributions to capital.[29]

> **Example:** Alpha Corporation manufactures pharmaceuticals. A business rival spreads false information that Alpha's products have led to serious adverse side effects, including death. Alpha sues the rival for defamation. Alpha prevails (whether at trial or via settlement), and it recovers substantial damages. Under former law, it was not clearly settled whether Alpha could exclude the recovery from income under Code Sec. 104(a)(2).[30] However, that section was amended in 1996. The exclusion now applies only to damages received "on account of personal physical injuries or physical sickness." A corporation cannot have such injuries. Thus, under current law, Alpha could not exclude the recovery from its gross income.

.02 Code Sec. 243 and Related Sections

Throughout most of the tenure of the modern federal income tax, dividends have been taxable. Without a relief provision, this fact could produce multiple taxation. For example, assume Corporation A is wholly owned by Corporation B, which is wholly owned by Corporation C. Assume further that A earns $100 in profits. A distributes as a dividend to B all of what remains after tax of the profit. Then B distributes as a dividend to C all of what remains after tax. The same income is taxed multiple times as it makes its way through the chain of ownership. In actuality, the problem could be much worse because chains of partial and complete ownership often are much longer than the A-B-C chain in our simple example.

Congress responded to these concerns by enacting Code Sec. 243 and several other more limited sections. Although called "deduction" sections, they actually operate as exclusions. Below, we discuss Code Sec. 243, then the related, more limited sections, then anti-abuse rules applicable to the exclusion sections.

(a) Code Sec. 243: Dividends Received by Corporations

Code Sec. 243(a) provides that a corporation "shall be allowed as a deduction an amount equal to [specified] percentages of the amount received as dividends from a domestic corporation which is subject to [federal income] taxation." Although this is phrased as a deduction, Code Sec. 243 effectively operates as an exclusion, excluding from the taxable income of the recipient corporation some or all of the dividends paid to it by a domestic corporation.

---

[28] Counts frequently state, however, that exclusions are construed narrowly. *e.g.*, *Comm'r v. Schleier*, 515 U.S. 323, 328 (1995).

[29] Code Sec. 118 is discussed in ¶ 203.01.

[30] *See, e.g.*, *Boyett Coffee Co. v. United States*, 775 F. Supp. 1001, 1003-04 (W.D. Tex. 1991).

The extent of the exclusion depends upon the degree to which the corporate shareholder owns the corporation paying the dividends. There are three tiers or levels of the Code Sec. 243 exclusion. First, if the corporate shareholder and corporations related to it[31] own 80% or more (by value or voting power) of the corporation paying the dividend, the dividend typically is 100% excludible.[32] Second, if the corporate shareholder owns at least 20% of the stock of the payor corporation, an 80% exclusion applies.[33] Third, if the corporate shareholder owns less than 20% of the stock of the payor, 70% of the dividends are excludible.[34]

> **Practice Tip:** At these levels, the Code Sec. 243 exclusion is extremely valuable. As a result, corporations may choose to use available amounts to acquire dividend-paying stock of domestic corporations rather than use the amounts to make other investments or to fund distributions to their own shareholders.

> **Example:** Aragon Corporation owns 5% of the stock of Peerless Corporation. Aragon is in the 35% bracket under Code Sec. 11(b). Assuming that none of the anti-abuse rules described below operates, the 70% exclusion will apply. Thus, Aragon will have an effective tax rate of only 10.5% (35% x 30%) on dividends it receives from Peerless.

> The 35% bracket starts at $15 million of taxable income. In lower brackets, the 70% exclusion can produce effective rates of taxation ranging from 4.5% (30% × the 15% rate) to 10.2% (30% × the 34% rate).[35]

In keeping with the purpose of Code Sec. 243 (mitigating multiple taxation), Code Sec. 243(d) excepts from the exclusion, or otherwise limits, dividends from certain tax-exempt or pass-through entities.[36] Similarly, no deduction under Code Sec. 243 should be available unless the dividend is, apart from Code Sec. 243, includible in gross income. Thus, for example, Code Sec. 243 should produce no deduction as to stock dividends that are excluded from taxation under Code Sec. 305.[37]

Given the stakes, rules are needed to determine what transfers constitute dividends and which persons qualify as shareholders. Code Secs. 301 and 316 define "dividend" for general corporate tax purposes and they control for Code Sec. 243 purposes as well.[38] The dividend recipient is the person who owns the stock on the dividend record date even if another person owns the stock on the subsequent ex-dividend date.[39]

> **Example 1:** Roberts Corporation owns 10% of the stock of Piper Corporation. Piper makes a distribution to shareholders at a time when it has no

---

[31] Relationship is defined by reference to the affiliated group rules in Code Sec. 1504, with some modifications. Code Sec. 243(b)(2). These rules are discussed in chapter 10.

[32] Code Sec. 2439(a).

[33] Code Sec. 243(c).

[34] Code Sec. 243(a)(1).

[35] *See* Boris I. Bittker & James S. Eustice, FEDERAL INCOME TAXATION OF CORPORATIONS AND SHAREHOLDERS ¶ 5.05 (7th ed. 2006).

[36] Such as dividends from mutual savings banks, domestic building and loan associations, real estate investment trusts, and regulated investment companies. Code Sec. 243(d)(1)-(3).

[37] Code Sec. 305 is discussed in Chapter 5.

[38] Code Secs. 301 and 316 are discussed in detail in Chapter 5.

[39] Rev. Rul. 82-11, 1982-1 C.B. 51.

current and no accumulated earnings and profits. Under Code Secs. 301(c)(1) and 316(a), this distribution is not a dividend. Accordingly, Roberts may not exclude/deduct its portion of the distribution under Code Sec. 243

Example 2: Under Code Sec. 243, a corporation sought to exclude/deduct an amount received from another corporation. However, the court determined that the amount constituted refund of insurance premiums previously paid, not dividends. Accordingly, Code Sec. 243 treatment was denied.[40]

Example 3: A corporation receives a payment from another corporation with respect to a financial instrument that is denominated as stock. Pursuant to Code Sec. 385, however, the instrument is recharacterized as debt for tax purposes. Since dividends can be paid only on account of stock, this recharacterization will prevent Code Sec. 243 from applying to the distribution.[41]

The existence of Code Sec. 243 and the differences in capital gain rules combine to create disparate objectives and incentives for corporations as opposed to individual taxpayers. For individuals, long-term capital gains are often taxed at less than half the rate of ordinary income, and for most of our income tax history dividends have been treated as ordinary income. Thus, individuals prefer capital gains to dividends and look for opportunities to convert dividends into capital gains. In contrast, corporations have no preferential rate on capital gains, and Code Sec. 243 can render dividends largely untaxed. Thus, especially if they do not have substantial capital loss carryovers that will soon expire, corporations typically prefer dividends to capital gains and will seek to convert capital gains into dividends.[42]

Practice Tip: One common strategy to effect such conversion involves corporate shareholders that intend to sell their stock in controlled corporations. Before selling, they may cause the controlled corporations to make dividends to them. The dividends will lower the value of the stock. Thus, the corporate shareholder will have converted what would have been capital gain into excludible dividends – if the scheme is respected by the IRS and the courts. A similar play would involve receiving a dividend before the liquidation of a subsidiary.

Such stratagems often succeed, particularly if the taxpayers carefully structure the transactions. For instance, the taxpayer should cause the dividend to be declared and paid before the sale is consummated (or even substantially negotiated), should separate in time the dividend and the sale as long as possible, and should articulate some plausible business purpose for the transactions as structured.

Example 1: Waterman Steamship Corporation wholly owned two subsidiaries. It received an offer to buy the stock of those subsidiaries for $3,500,000. Waterman rejected that offer but countered with an offer to sell the subsidiaries for $700,000 after they paid Waterman dividends of $2,800,000. The transactions occurred with some modifications. Dividends were paid in the form of

---

[40] *Liston Zander Credit Co. v. United States*, 276 U.S. 417 (5th Cir. 1960).

[41] Code Sec. 385 is discussed in Chapter 7.

[42] This situation is discussed in ¶ 205.02.

¶203.02(a)

promissory notes, which then were paid off with funds provided by the purchaser. All of the transactions – dividends, sale, and payment of the notes – occurred within a 90-minute period on one day. The Tax Court held that the distribution to Waterman was a dividend, but the circuit court reversed, concluding that the "dividend" and sale were both part of one transaction.[43]

Example 2: Litton Industries owned all the stock of Stouffer Corporation. In July 1972, Litton's board of directions discussed selling the Stouffer stock. On August 23, 1972, Stouffer declared a dividend to Litton, which it paid in the form of a $30 million negotiable promissory note. On September 7, Litton publicly announced its interest in disposing of Stouffer. After several alternatives were considered and abandoned, Litton sold the Stouffer stock to Nestle for nearly $75 million in cash and $30 million in cash for the promissory note. Litton asserted several (questionable) business purposes for the dividend. The Tax Court held that these facts were readily distinguishable from those of Waterman. It upheld dividend treatment for the $30 million payment and held Code Sec. 243 to be applicable.[44]

(b) Other Exclusion Sections

Although Code Sec. 243 is the principal section in this area, several other sections also operate. First, a special regime applies with respect to public utility corporations. Code Sec. 247 allows such corporations to deduct part of the dividends paid by them on preferred stock issued before October 1, 1942 (or issued after that date to replace such stock). This benefit is countered by Code Sec. 244. Code Sec. 244 supplants Code Sec. 243 as to public utility corporations and allows them a lesser exclusion with respect to dividends received.

A second special regime applies with respect to dividends from foreign corporations. Code Sec. 243(a) applies only to dividends received from domestic corporations. Code Sec. 245 sets up a parallel scheme for dividends received from certain foreign corporations. The Code Sec. 245(a) exclusion is in an amount equal to the Code Sec. 243 percentage. This permits the 70% and 80% exclusions, but not the 100% exclusion.[45] However, Code Sec. 245(b) provides for – in lieu of the Code Sec. 245(a) exclusion – a 100% exclusion in the case of dividends from wholly owned foreign subsidiaries.

Several restrictions somewhat dull the luster of the Code Sec. 245 exclusion. For the exclusion to apply, the recipient corporation must own at least 10% of the stock (by value or voting power) of the payor corporation,[46] and the payor corporation may not be a passive foreign investment company.[47] Moreover, the exclusion percentage applies only to "the U.S.-source portion of [the] dividends."[48] The U.S.-source portion "is an amount which bears the same ratio to [the] dividend as (A)

---

[43] *Waterman Steamship Corp. v. Comm'r*, 50 T.C. 650 (1968), *rev'd*, 430 F.2d 1185 (5th Cir. 1970), *cert. denied*, 401 U.S. 939 (1971).

[44] *Litton Inds., Inc. v. Comm'r*, 89 T.C. 1086 (1987).

[45] The 100% exclusion in Code Sec. 243 is available only with respect to members "of the same affiliated group as the corporation distributing [the] dividend."

Code Sec. 243(b)(1)(A) & (2). But foreign corporations cannot be members of affiliated groups. Code Sec. 1504(b)(3).

[46] Code Sec. 245(a)(1) & (2).

[47] Code Sec. 245(a)(2).

[48] Code Sec. 245(a)(1).

the post-1986 undistributed U.S. earnings, bears to (B) the total post-1986 undistributed earnings."[49] In most instances, the result of this limitation is that the dividends from the foreign corporation will be excludible to the extent they reflect income of the foreign corporation that has been amenable to taxation by the United States.

(c) Anti-Abuse Rules

The exclusions under Code Secs. 243, 245, and to a lesser extent 244 are valuable. In such situations, Congress always is concerned about taxpayers "pushing the envelope" to try to secure even greater benefits than Congress intended. To prevent abuse in this area, Congress limited the exclusions through four Code Secs: 246, 246A, 1059, and 301(e).

Code Sec. 246: This section contains three different limitations. First, the objective of the exclusions is to mitigate multiple taxation. Thus, Code Sec. 246(a) provides that dividends from corporations exempt from tax under Code Sec. 501 (charitable and similar organizations) or Code Sec. 521 (farmers' cooperative associations) do not qualify for exclusion/deduction by recipient corporations.

Second, Code Sec. 246(b) imposes a limit on the aggregate exclusions/deductions allowed under Code Secs. 243, 244, and 245. The limitation is calculated first with respect to the 80% exclusion, then with respect to the 70% exclusion.[50] The limit does not apply for any year for which there was a net operating loss under Code Sec. 172.[51]

Third, a once common ploy was for a corporation to buy stock shortly before a dividend was declared and then to sell that stock right after the dividend was paid. These transactions, of course, reflected no genuine investment intent but only a desire to take advantage of the dividends received exclusion/deduction. This practice is now blocked by Code Sec. 246(c), which conditions the exclusion upon the recipient corporation holding for over 45 days the stock on which the dividend is paid.[52]

Code Sec. 246A: In many instances throughout the Code, Congress has acted to bar double tax benefits from a single transaction or related transactions.[53] Code Sec. 246A is one of these provisions. It is designed to prevent a corporation from borrowing in order to buy stock, then deducting interest paid on the debt and excluding (under Code Secs. 243, 244, or 245) a large part of the dividends received on account of the stock. Code Sec. 246A seeks to do this by increasing the portion of the dividend subject to tax by the percentage of the purchase price attributable to borrowed funds.[54]

Example: Randolph Corporation buys under 20% of the stock of Pregerson Corporation. Half of the funds financing the purchase comes from Ran-

---

[49] Code Sec. 245(a)(3). These terms are further defined by Code Sec. 245(a)(4) & (5).

[50] Code Sec. 246(b)(3).

[51] Code Sec. 246(b)(2).

[52] Code Sec. 246(c)(1)(A). A similar abuse involving having simultaneous long and short positions in the stock is blocked by Code Sec. 246(c)(1)(B).

[53] *e.g.*, Code Secs. 104(a), 213(e), 264(a) & 265.

[54] Code Sec. 246A(a). However, this increase does not occur if the taxpayer qualifies for the 100% (as opposed to the 70% or 80%) exclusion, Code Sec. 246A(c), or if the recipient corporation owns at least 50% of the payor corporation, Code Sec. 246A(a) & (c)(2).

dolph's own funds; the remaining half is borrowed. Randolph receives a $100 dividend from Pregerson. Randolph will be able to exclude $35 of the dividend ($100 × .70 × .50) and will have to include remaining $65 in income.

> *Practice Tip:* The Code Sec. 246A limitation can prove difficult for the IRS to enforce. The limitation relates to the percentage of the purchase financed via "portfolio indebtedness,"[55] which is "any indebtedness *directly* attributable to investment in the . . . stock."[56] A court has held that this language requires that the consideration paid for the stock be directly traceable to a borrowing and that pro rata allocations or accounting conventions do not satisfy the "directly attributable" statutory language.[57] If the recipient corporation's financial affairs are at all complex, the IRS could have difficulty directly tracing the funds. The outcome in such cases may depend upon which party bears the burden of proof.[58]

Code Sec. 1059: Code Sec. 1059 is aimed at another potential abuse involving double tax benefits. When a dividend is paid, the value of the stock of the payor corporation normally drops by an amount approximating the amount of the dividend. Moreover, dividends are viewed as distributions of earnings and profits, not return of capital, so receipt of a dividend does not normally decrease the basis of the recipient corporation in its stock in the payor corporation.

As a result, without a special rule, the following strategy would be viable. The corporation receiving the dividend would exclude a substantial portion of it from income under Code Secs. 243, 244, or 245. Thereafter, the recipient corporation would sell its stock – perhaps at a tax loss under Code Sec. 1001 because the dividend decreased the value of the payor corporation (and so the amount realized on sale by the recipient corporation) but not the recipient's basis in its stock in the payor. The recipient corporation would deduct this loss under Code Sec. 165. The recipient would not have suffered an economic loss because the dividend compensated for the loss on sale. Nonetheless, the recipient would have garnered two tax benefits: exclusion of much of the dividend and deduction of the loss on sale.

Code Sec. 1059 clamps down on this strategem although only with respect to large dividends. Code Sec.1059 does not alter the dividends received exclusion. Instead, it requires the recipient corporation to reduce its basis in its stock in the payor corporation to the extent of the untaxed part of an "extraordinary dividend" on stock it has held for under two years.[59] Moreover, if the untaxed part of the extraordinary dividend exceeds the recipient corporation's basis in the stock, the excess is "treated as gain from the sale or exchange of [the] stock for the taxable year in which the extraordinary dividend is received."[60] In general, an extraordinary

---

[55] Code Sec. 246A(a) & (c)(1).

[56] Code Sec. 246A(d)(3)(A) (emphasis added).

[57] *OBH, Inc. v. United States*, 397 F. Supp. 2d 1148 (D. Neb. 2005).

[58] Taxpayers usually bear the burden in civil tax cases, but there are exceptions. *See* Code Sec. 7491.

[59] Code Sec. 1059(a)(1).

[60] Code Sec. 1059(a)(2). Code Sec. 1059 operates when the payor and recipient corporations are not members of the same affiliated group. Comparable rules as to affiliated corporations are discussed in Chapter 9.

dividend is a dividend that equals or exceeds 10% of the taxpayer's basis in the stock.[61]

Example: In year 1, Radnor Corporation acquired an under-20% stock interest in Paragon Corporation. Its basis in that stock is $1000. In year 2, Radnor received a $200 dividend from Paragon. In year 3, Radnor sold the stock for $900. Assuming none of the Code Sec. 1059 exceptions applies, these would be the tax consequences. First, $140 ($200 × .70) of the dividend would be excludible. Thus, $60 of the dividend would be includible in Radnor's income in year 2. Second, Radnor's adjusted basis in the stock would decrease to $860 ($1,000 - $140). Third, since the untaxed portion of the dividend did not exceed Radnor's basis in the stock, no gain would be recognized in year 2. Fourth, in year 3, Radnor would have $40 ($900 amount realized minus adjusted basis of $860) of taxable long-term capital gain.

Practice Tip: A company wishing to avoid application of Code Sec. 1059 might consider splintering a large dividend (one large enough to meet definition of "extraordinary") into a number of smaller dividends (each falling beneath the threshold). However, Congress has limited the viability of such an approach through aggregation rules in Code Sec. 1059(c)(3). One such rule aggregates all dividends received by a corporation (and in some cases related persons engaged in substitution transactions) within an 85-day period. Another aggregates all dividends with ex-dividend dates during a 365-day period if their sum exceeds 20% of the recipient's adjusted stock basis.

Subsections (c) through (f) of Code Sec. 1059 contain numerous special rules and exceptions. For example, Code Sec. 1059 usually does not apply as to stock which the recipient held for the whole time of the payor's existence,[62] to qualifying dividends eligible for the 100% exclusion,[63] or to certain preferred stock held for over five years.[64]

On the other side, some types of distributions are declared categorically to be extraordinary dividends regardless of the recipient corporation's stock holding period. These include amounts received in certain redemptions, including partial liquidations,[65] and self-liquidating preferred stock.[66] These categorical rules control over the various exceptions to Code Sec. 1059 treatment.[67]

Code Sec. 301(e): Code Sec. 316 defines "dividend' by reference to "earnings and profits," the rules for which are set out in Code Sec. 312. A number of tax benefit items are not taken into account in calculating earnings and profits for most purposes.[68] This exacts a tax cost for individual taxpayers. However, higher earnings and profits, leading to higher dividends, is beneficial to corporations because of the exclusion/deduction in Code Secs. 243, 244, and 245.

---

[61] Code Sec. 1059(c)(1), (2)(B). The percentage is reduced to 5% in the case of preferred stock. Code Sec. 1059(c)(2)(A).

[62] Code Sec. 1059(d)(6).

[63] Code Sec. 1059(e)(2).

[64] Code Sec. 1059(e)(3).

[65] Code Sec. 1059(e)(1).

[66] Code Sec. 1059(f). This term covers stock with a diminishing dividend rate or a redemption price below its issue price, or stock with rights structured to achieve similar ends.

[67] Treas. Reg. § 1.1059(e)-1(a).

[68] These rules are discussed in Chapter 5.

To correct this unintended consequence, Code Sec. 301(e) cancels for corporate taxpayers some of the Code Sec. 312-mandated increases in earnings and profits.[69] The provision applies to dividends received by corporate shareholders owning at least 20% (by value or voting power) of the stock of the payor corporation.[70]

> *Practice Tip:* As described in Chapter 2, corporations confront important choices as to whether to capitalize the corporation via equity or debt. Many factors bear on these choices. The fact that interest is deductible, but dividends are not, creates a powerful incentive to prefer debt. However, despite the above described limitations, the exclusions under Code Sec. 243 and related sections are significant and may influence the capitalization choice.

¶ 204 Deductions

.01 Deductions Generally

In the main, income tax deductions available to corporations are like deductions available to individual taxpayers. There are, however, numerous differences in detail. In some instances, the deduction scheme is more favorable to corporations; in other instances, less so. Some of the major differences are set out below.

Above-the-line/below-the-line distinction: For individual taxpayers, some deductions are above-the-line (that is, are subtracted from gross income to compute adjusted gross income) while others are below-the-line (that is, are subtracted from adjusted gross income to determine taxable income).[71] For several reasons, including the fact that they are subject to special limitations,[72] below-the-line deductions often are less valuable to individual taxpayers than are above-the-line deductions. The above-the-line/below-the-line distinction does not exist for corporate taxpayers. Corporations go straight from gross income to taxable income, without the intermediate notion of adjusted gross income.

Standard deduction and personal exemptions: These deductions are available only to individuals, not to corporations.

Charitable contributions: There are income caps on charitable deductions for both corporations and individuals, but the caps differ in both percentage and base. The total deductions a corporation can take for any year on account of charitable contributions is limited to 10% of its taxable income for the year.[73] Amounts in excess of this cap may be carried over for up to five succeeding years.[74]

> *Practice Tip:* A corporation may seek to circumvent the percentage limitation by asserting that the excess is deductible as an ordinary and necessary business expense. This strategy is blocked, however, by Code Sec. 162(b).

---

[69] Specifically, the provision directs that earnings and profits be computed for corporate shareholders without regard to subsections (k) and (n) of Code Sec. 312, Code Sec. 301(e)(1), except for subsection 312(n)(7), Code Sec. 301(e)(3).

[70] Code Sec. 301(e)(1) & (2).

[71] *See* Code Secs. 62 & 63.

[72] e.g., Code Secs. 67 & 68.

[73] Code Sec. 170(b)(2)(A). An exception exists for qualified conservation contributions by certain corporate farmers and ranchers. Code Sec. 170(b)(2)(B).

[74] Code Sec. 170(d)(2).

Example: In year 1, Acme Corporation has $1000 of taxable income. In that year, it donates $150 to the local Philharmonic Orchestra. Acme's contribution is recognized in an acknowledgment printed in the programs distributed to the audiences at performances of the Orchestra. Acme gains valuable good will as a result.

If it has no other charitable contributions for the year, Acme can deduct in year 1 $100 under Code Sec. 170. The remaining $50 can be carried over for up to the next five tax years. Despite the fact that there are business benefits to Acme from having made the contribution, the $50 Year 1 excess cannot be deducted under section 162.

Practice Tip: In general, to be deductible, charitable contributions must be paid within the tax year. However, accrual method taxpayers have some flexibility. They may elect to treat a contribution as having been made during the tax year if it (1) is authorized by the corporation's board of directors during the year and (2) is actually paid during the first two and a half months of the succeeding year.[75]

Compensation: A publicly held corporation may not deduct over $1 million each year with respect to compensation paid to its chief executive officer or its other four highest paid officers.[76]

Practice Tip: This limitation is subject to a number of exceptions, which made the rule fairly easy to circumvent. For example, performance-based compensation is outside the limitation.[77] Thus, highly paid officers may have fairly modest base salaries but with generous performance bonuses (set at performance levels likely to be attained). Accordingly, this limitation is more symbolic than substantive in many cases.

Similarly, deduction of compensation is limited for employers participating in the Troubled Assets Relief Program ("TARP"),[78] and "golden parachute" payments made to executives incident to change of ownership of the corporation may not be fully deductible.[79] For smaller corporations, particularly closely held companies, the concern is the unreasonable compensation doctrine, which stands as a barrier to deduction of compensation exceeding market-based comparable benchmarks.[80] The concern of the IRS is that excessive compensation masks what really are dividends, the incentive being that corporations can deduct salary but cannot deduct dividends. The concern about such mischaracterization arises when the person being paid is both a shareholder and an employee of the corporation.

Practice Tip: There is considerable confusion in the case law about the standards by which to measure the reasonableness of compensation. The IRS has had only mixed success in litigating this issue in recent years.

Example: Exacto Spring Corporation, a closely held company, paid its cofounder, chief executive, and principal owner salary of $1.3 million in 1993

---

[75] Code Sec. 170(a)(2).
[76] Code Sec. 162(m)(1)-(3).
[77] Code Sec. 162(m)(4).

[78] Code Sec. 162(m)(5).
[79] Code Sec. 280G.
[80] *See* Code Sec. 162(a)(2); Treas. Reg. § 1.162-7.

and $1 million in 1994. The IRS disallowed the section 162 deductions claimed by the corporation on account of such salary to the extent they exceeded $381,000 and $400,000, respectively. The Tax Court essentially "split the baby," permitting deductions of $900,000 and $700,000.[81]

The Tax Court applied a seven-factor test, with no specified weighting of the factors: (1) the type and extent of services rendered, (2) the scarcity of qualified employees, (3) the qualifications and prior earning capacity of the employee, (4) the employee's contributions to the business, (5) the corporation's net earnings, (6) the prevailing compensation paid to employees with comparable jobs, and (7) the peculiar characteristics of the corporation's business.

On appeal, the Seventh Circuit acknowledged that this test had been used by many courts, but it heavily criticized it.[82] Instead, the circuit court noted, and joined, a trend by the appellate courts to apply "a much simpler and more purposive test, the 'independent investor' test,"[83] which it described as follows:

> When, notwithstanding the CEO's "exorbitant" salary (as it might appear to a judge or other modestly paid official), the investors in his company are obtaining a far higher return than they had any reason to expect, his salary is presumptively reasonable. We say "presumptively" because we can imagine cases in which the return, though very high, is not due to the CEO's exertions."[84]

The circuit court added: "The fact that Heitz's salary was approved by the other owners of the corporation, who had no incentive to disguise a dividend as salary, goes far to rebut any inference of bad faith here."[85] The circuit court upheld the full amounts of the deductions claimed by Exacto.

Anti-abuse rules: Congress has enacted numerous anti-abuse rules, aimed at tax shelters and other perceived abuses. Many of these rules apply to individuals or S corporations but apply to C corporations either not at all or only in limited contexts.[86] Others apply uniquely or with particular force to C corporations.[87]

Interest deductions: The situation also is mixed with respect to interest deductions. On the one hand, corporations do not confront the Code Sec. 163(d) investment interest limitation[88] or the Code Sec. 163(h) personal interest limitation.[89] On the other hand, several provisions limiting interest deductions apply uniquely or mainly to corporations. They include Code Sec. 163(j) (nondeductibility of very substantial interest payments by U.S. subsidiaries of foreign corporations not taxable on interest from U.S. sources),[90] Code Sec. 163(l) (nondeductibility of

---

[81] *Exacto Spring Corp. v. Comm'r,* 196 F.3d 833 (7th Cir. 1999), *rev'g Heitz v. Comm'r,* T.C. Memo. 1998-220.

[82] The circuit court found the test, "like many other multi-factor tests, redundant, incomplete, and unclear." 196 F.3d at 835 (quotations marks and citation omitted). It also complained: "the seven-factor test invites the Tax Court to set itself up as a superpersonnel department for closely held corporations, a role unsuitable for courts." *Id.*

[83] *Id.* at 838.

[84] *Id.* at 839.

[85] *Id.*

[86] *e.g.,* Code Secs. 183(a) (hobby losses), 280A(a) (vacation homes), 464(c) (farming syndicates), 465(a)(1)(B) (at-risk rules applicable to C corporations only if over 50% of the stock is owned by five or fewer persons) & 469(a)(2)(B) (passive activity loss rules applicable to C corporations only if closely held).

[87] *e.g.,* Code Sec. 269 (acquisitions to avoid tax).

[88] Code Sec. 163(d)(1).

[89] Code Sec. 163(h)(1).

[90] Code Sec. 163(j)(1).

interest payable in, or measured by, stock of the issuer or a related corporation,[91] and Code Sec. 279 (nondeductibility of interest on junk bonds issued to acquire stock or assets of another corporation).[92]

> ***Practice Tip:*** Not all of these rules have genuine "bite." Code Sec. 279 is an example. For that section to apply, the bonds in question must be subordinated to other debt, be convertible into stock, and entail a debt-to-equity ratio exceeding 2-to-1.[93] Even then, what is disallowed each year is only interest exceeding $5 million (with some modifications).[94] Because of the laxity of these rules, section 279 has limited significance in actual practice.

Code Sec. 199 deduction: Code Sec. 199 is more historical accident than a core portion of the effort to define the income tax base. It is ironic that governments that strive to prevent taxpayers from circumventing their laws, themselves often attempt to circumvent laws (treaties) to which they have subjected themselves. Specifically, various international agreements prohibit contracting countries from employing certain devices to stimulate exports, but the United States and other governments keep trying to fashion incentives to accomplish this end while satisfying the literal terms of the agreements.

In 1972, the United States established the domestic international sales corporation ("DISC") regime to stimulate exports. Major trading partners complained that this regime violated the General Agreement on Tariffs and Trade, so the U.S. largely abandoned the DISC device in 1984,[95] replacing it with a new device: the foreign sales corporation ("FSC").[96] However, in response to fresh complaints, the World Trade Organization held the FSC regime to constitute an illegal exports subsidy. Undaunted, in 2000, Congress tried yet another device: an exclusion of certain export income, dubbed extraterritorial income ("ETI"), but ETI too was invalidated by the World Trade Organization.

Code Sec. 199 was enacted in 2004 to make up for the loss of ETI. It should end the above drama because it does not confer tax benefit selectively on income from exports. Unlike the previous deferral and exclusion regimes, Code Sec. 199 is styled as a deduction. Specifically, it allows a deduction "equal to 9 percent of the lesser of – (A) the qualified production activities of the taxpayer for the taxable year, or (B) taxable income (determined without regard to [section 199] for the taxable year."[97]

Code Sec. 199 is a peculiar section. As its wording indicates, Code Sec. 199 does not depend directly upon the taxpayer having made an expenditure, so it looks more like an exclusion than a deduction. However, there is an expenditure-based

---

[91] Code Sec. 163(l)(1) & (2).

[92] Code Sec. 279(a).

[93] Code Sec. 279(b).

[94] Code Sec. 279(a)(1) & (2).

[95] The DISC regime survives now only in weak form. When it applies, the regime allows deferral of federal income tax. However, there is a $10 million ceiling with

respect to individual shareholders and sixteen seventeenths of that amount for corporate shareholders, and there is an interest charge (based on the Treasury bill rates) on the deferral. *See* Code Secs. 991-997.

[96] Code Secs. 921-927.

[97] Code Sec. 199(a)(1). There was a phase-in period from 2004 to 2010 during which the deduction was allowable in lesser amounts.

limitation on the deduction: it may not exceed 50% of the wages paid by the taxpayer for the year.[98]

The deduction is available to taxpayers of all types – corporations, individuals, and pass-through entities. For a corporation in the 35% bracket, a 9% deduction translates into a reduction in the tax rate of slightly over 3%. If the taxpayer is in a loss of posture, however, Code Sec. 199 provides no benefit.

> *Practice Tip:* When multiple companies are involved in producing a product, it may be unclear which of them qualifies for the deduction as to income from the product.[99] When one of the involved companies is in a much higher bracket than the other, an incentive is created for the companies to structure their contractual relationship such that the Code Sec. 199 deduction will flow to the more profitable company – in return, of course, for the less profitable company receiving something of value elsewhere in the contract to compensate it for this accommodation.

"Qualified production activities income" is the excess of the taxpayer's "domestic production gross receipts" for the year over the total of its cost of goods sold allocable to those receipts plus its other expenses, losses, and deductions allocable to those receipts.[100] Thus, the corporation first allocates its gross receipts between qualified and non-qualified activities. Then it must allocate its costs (including general overhead) between qualified and non-qualified activities and subtract in order to calculate qualified income.[101]

"Domestic gross receipts" are the corporation's gross receipts from leasing, licensing, selling, exchanging, or otherwise disposing of tangible personal property, computer software, and certain sound recordings that are "manufactured, produced grown, or extracted by the taxpayer in whole or in significant part within the United States."[102] Subject to several exceptions, special rules also define as domestic gross receipts certain income from sale or lease of motion pictures, from construction within the United States, from engineering and architectural services as to construction of real property in the United States, and from sale of electricity, natural gas, or potable water produced in the United States.[103]

Net Operating Losses: A corporation may deduct against its income for a given tax year net operating losses carried forward from prior years and carried back from subsequent years. In general, net operating losses may be carried back two years then, until exhausted, carried forward twenty years.[104]

> *Practice Tip:* A taxpayer may elect to waive the carryback period, thus applying the net operating loss only to future years.[105] Normally, the election is not made because generating an immediate refund is typically better than

[98] Code Sec. 199(b).

[99] *See, e.g.*, Notice 2005-14, 2005-1 C.B. 498 (addressing whether the Code Sec. 199 deduction is allowable to the principal or to the physical manufacturer when two firms contract as to the processing of inventory).

[100] Code Sec. 199(c)(1).

[101] Allocation and expense rules are set out in Code Sec. 199(c)(2) & (3). Other special rules are set out in

Code Sec. 199(d). Regulations adopted in 2006 provide extensive guidance and implementational rules. T.D. 9263, 2006-2 C.B. 1063, accompanying Treas. Reg. §§1.999-1 to 1.999-9.

[102] Code Sec. 199(c)(4)(A) & (5).

[103] Code Sec. 199(c)(4)(A)-(D).

[104] Code Sec. 172(b)(1)(A).

[105] Code Sec. 172(b)(3).

waiting for a future refund. However, there are times when the election should be made.

Example: Luckner Corporation sustained a loss in 2010. In 2008 and 2009, Luckner had modest profits, so was in a low bracket. As a result of a major transaction that Luckner expects soon to consummate, Luckner anticipates it will be in a high bracket in 2011 or 2012. The bracket differential could exceed the time-value of money effect. Thus, Luckner might well come out ahead by waiving the carryback period and applying to the future years the net operating loss arising in 2010.

A net operating loss is the excess of deductions allowed by chapter 1 of the Code over gross income, with the computation affected by a number of special rules.[106] The net operating loss deduction is available to other types of taxpayers as well as to corporations.[107] The computational modifications tend to hit corporations less significantly than they hit other types of taxpayers. Individual taxpayers have to exclude nonbusiness deductions and certain other items from their net operating losses. It is usually presumed that everything a corporation does is related to trade or business, so these exclusions do not apply to corporations. However, a corporation's net operating loss deduction may not take into account any deduction it has under Code Sec. 199.[108]

A corporation with large unused net operating losses could be a tempting target for acquisition by a profitable corporation that wishes to use those losses. Congress frowns upon such trafficking in losses, however, so has limited it via Code Secs. 269 and 382.[109]

.02 Limitations on Deductions Generally

(a) Code Section 291

Congress enacted what has become the alternative minimum tax because of concerns that certain features of the regular income tax were being excessively or abusively used by taxpayers. Motivated by similar concerns, in 1982 Congress enacted a more limited response within the regular income tax. That response is Code Sec. 291.

The approach taken by Code Sec. 291 is to impose limitations on certain deductions and other designated preference items. The affected items include real property subject to depreciation under Code Sec. 1250; interest costs connected to financial institutions' tax exempt income from state and local bonds; percentage depletion allowances as to iron ore, coal, and lignite under Code Sec. 613; amortization of costs as to pollution control facilities under Code Sec. 169; and intangible drilling costs and costs of mineral exploration and development under Code Secs. 263, 616, 617, and related sections. The extent of the limitations imposed by Code Sec. 291 varies among the various categories of preference items.

---

[106] Code Sec. 172(c) & (d).

[107] *See* Code Sec. 172(d)(1)-(4).

[108] Code Sec. 172(d)(7). Similarly, there are special rules coordinating the net operating loss deduction with the rules as to the dividends received exclusions/deductions under Code Secs. 243 to 247. Code Sec. 172(d)(5).

[109] Code Secs. 269 and 382 are discussed in Chapter 9.

(b) Capitalization Doctrine

For corporations as well as for other types of taxpayers, the capitalization doctrine constitutes a major barrier to deductibility. The doctrine requires that costs must be added to the basis of an asset, rather than being immediately fully deducted, when the expenditure produces a long-term or continuing benefit.

The regulations set out the one-year rule under which costs must be capitalized, in whole or in part, "[if the] expenditure results in the creation of an asset having a useful life which extends substantially beyond the close of the taxable year."[110] A number of cases have interpreted this to mean that a cost need not be capitalized if the benefit it produces does not last over one calendar year even if it spills over from the tax year in question into the next tax year.[111]

The capitalization doctrine is reflected in several Code sections, including 263, 263A, 446(b), and 461.[112] It is rooted in the financial accounting idea that costs should be matched to the income they produce – although, as the law has developed, matching for tax purposes is far from congruent with what would match economically.

If costs have to be capitalized, they may not be expensed (fully deducted in the year the item is paid or incurred). Instead, they will be recoverable in installments over a number of years if one or another Code section allows depreciation or amortization of the item. If no section does so, the cost will be recoverable only terminally, when the taxpayer disposes of the asset into whose basis the cost has been capitalized.

> *Practice Tip:* Usually, of course, corporations prefer to expense costs rather than to capitalize them and recover them through depreciation or upon disposition. Normally, therefore, corporations try to expense costs whenever there is a plausible legal basis for doing so.

However, there are circumstances when capitalization is preferable to expensing. For instance, a corporation may have anticipated that, either because of projected enhanced profitability or expected tax rate hikes, it will be in a much higher bracket in future years than it is now. In that event, delaying the deduction – which is what capitalizing does – may produce the greater tax saving.

Code Sec. 263(a)(1) requires capitalization of amounts "paid out for new buildings or for permanent improvements or betterments made to increase the value of any property or estate." It would be wrong to infer that this language pertains only to the costs of tangible assets – "any property or estate" includes intangibles as well as tangibles.

---

[110] Treas. Reg. § 1.461-1(a)(1).

[111] *e.g., Zaninovich v. Comm'r*, 616 F.2d 429 (9th Cir. 1980), *rev'g* 69 T.C. 605 (1978); *see also* Treas. Reg. § 1.263(a)-4(f)(1) (providing that, in general, "a taxpayer is not required to capitalize . . . amounts paid to create . . . any right or benefit for the taxpayer that does not extend beyond the earlier of – (i) 12 months after the first date

on which the taxpayer realizes the right or benefit; or (ii) the end of the taxable year following the taxable year in which the payment is made").

[112] A number of statutory exceptions exist, however, which allow expensing in particular situations. *e.g.*, Code Secs. 179 & 263(a)(1).

Example: Unilever United States, Inc. gained control of one of its suppliers, National Starch and Chemical Corporation (later renamed INDOPCO), in a friendly takeover. As part of the process, National Starch incurred and paid substantial lawyers' fees and investment bankers' fees. National Starch maintained that these fees were deductible because they did not create or enhance any separate and distinct asset. The IRS and the courts disagreed. The Supreme Court noted that National Starch (now a subsidiary of Unilever) would benefit greatly from access to Unilever's vast resources and from synergies between the two corporations' activities. These benefits would last more than a year. Accordingly, the Court held that the expenses could not be deducted, but instead had to be capitalized.[113] The Court did not discuss when these capitalized costs could be recovered, but the likely answer is "not until National Starch ceases to exist as a corporation."

INDOPCO was a poorly written opinion that provided no obvious test for separating expensible items from capital expenditures. This led to over a decade of uncertainty. The situation has been considerably improved, however, by the promulgation of new regulations. This process began with the issuance in 2004 of Reg. § 1.263(a)-4 (amounts paid to acquire or create intangibles) and Reg. § 1.263(a)-5 (amounts paid to facilitate acquisition of a trade or business or to change the capital structure of a business). In March 2008, the process continued with the issuance of proposed regulation sections 1.263(a)-1 through 1.263(a)-3 (amounts paid or incurred to acquire, produce, or improve tangible property).

Things to watch for: In the *INDOPCO* decision, the Supreme Court stated that "deductions are exceptions to the norm of capitalization."[114] However, expensing has made significant inroads since that decision and may continue to do so. As examples, (1) the post-*INDOPCO* regulations were widely viewed as pro-taxpayer, (2) the IRS, by administrative discretion, has allowed expensing, in certain situations, of small expenses that theoretically should be capitalized,[115] (3) Congress has enacted "bonus" depreciation[116] and repeatedly (and substantially) raised the dollar ceiling on section 179 expensing of otherwise depreciable property, and (4) recent legislation temporarily extends several other expensing rules.[117] Some of these measures were inspired by unusually bad economic times. It remains to be seen whether the "expensing train" will continue its momentum in the years to come.

Practice Tip: The "expense versus capitalize" issue has been controversial for decades. A corporation considering litigating this issue against the IRS should carefully research the precedents of the various courts in which trial may occur. The fact that the taxpayer chooses the trial forum is an important advantage.

Example: The Court of Federal Claims has recognized (or created) an exception to capitalization for certain items that recur frequently when the tax

---

[113] *INDOPCO, Inc. v. Comm'r*, 503 U.S. 79 (1992).

[114] *Id.* at 84.

[115] Rev. Proc. 2002-12, 2002-1 C.B. 374 (permitting expensing of so called "smallwares" by restaurants).

[116] Code Sec. 168(k).

[117] Tax Relief, Unemployment Insurance Reauthorization, and Job Creation Act of 2010, Code Secs. 743-745.

difference between expensing and capitalizing is not great.[118] The Tax Court has expressly rejected this exception.[119] A corporation that could fit within this exception obviously would prefer to be in the Court of Federal Claims. Thus, when the IRS issues a notice of deficiency containing this adjustment, the corporation would not file a Tax Court petition. Instead, it would pay the deficiency determined by the IRS, file a refund claim, then (after the IRS denies or ignores that claim) file a complaint with the Court of Federal Claims commencing a refund suit.

> ***Practice Tip:*** A corporation that wants to change from capitalizing a cost to deducting similar costs must seek the approval of the IRS by submitting a Form 3115. The IRS recently modified procedures for obtaining such approval[120] and issued a new Audit Technique Guide to assist revenue agents examining "repairs versus improvements" issues.

.03 Deductions as to Organic Corporate Changes

Organic changes include the organization of the business and reorganizations and liquidations of it. Special deduction rules operate in each of these contexts.

(a) Organization

Expenses incurred to organize a corporation produce a benefit lasting over a year. Thus, absent a special rule, such expenses would have to be capitalized and, absent an applicable depreciation section, could be recovered for tax purposes only at the end of the enterprise.

In 1954, however, Congress enacted Code Sec. 248, which allows corporations to elect to expense some organizational expenses and to amortize the remainder.[121] Specifically, the corporation may currently deduct up to $5,000 of such expenses (reduced to the extent such expenses exceed $50,000) and may deduct the rest ratably over 180 months.[122]

> ***Practice Tip:*** Careful attention should be paid to the start of the amortization period. It begins, not with the date of incorporation, but with the date on which the corporation "starts the business operation for which it was organized."[123]

Organizational expenditures include any expenditure incident to creation of the corporation, chargeable to a capital account, and "of a character which, if expended incident to the creation of a corporation having a limited life, would be amortizable over such life."[124]

> ***Example:*** The regulations list the following as examples of qualifying organizational expenditures:

---

[118] *Cincinnati, New Orleans & Texas Pacific Railway Co. v. United States,* 424 F.2d 563 (Ct. Cl. 1970).

[119] *Alacare Home Health Service, Inc. v. Comm'r,* 81 T.C.M. 1794 (2001).

[120] Rev. Proc. 2009-39, 2009-2 C.B. 371, *modifying* Rev. Proc. 2008-52, 2008-2 C.B. 587.

[121] The election cannot be made later than the due date (including extensions) of the corporation's return for the year. Code Sec. 248 (c).

[122] Code Sec. 248(a).

[123] Treas. Reg. § 1.248-1(a)(3).

[124] Code Sec. 248(b).

legal services incident to the organization of the corporation, such as drafting the corporate charter, bylaws, minutes of organizational meetings, terms of original stock certificates, and the like; necessary accounting services; expenses of temporary directors and of organizational meetings of directors or stockholders; and fees paid to the State of incorporation.[125]

The regulations also illustrate expenses that do not qualify, including costs of issuing or selling stock (such as underwriting commissions, professional fees, and printing costs) and expenses related to transfer of assets to the corporation.[126] Expenditures incurred after the corporation's business has begun typically are not subject to deduction/amortization under Code Sec. 248. However, the line of demarcation is sometimes wavy, and some of the authorities are in tension.[127]

Practice Tip: The Code Sec. 248 election is expressly made available to "a corporation." Thus, it would seem that if organizational expenses of a new corporation were paid, not by the corporation itself, but instead an individual who is a shareholder of the corporation, those expenses could not be treated under Code Sec. 248. However, it might be successfully argued that the shareholder made the payment as a contribution to the capital of the corporation, such that the corporation could deduct the expenditures after all. The viability of such an argument would be strengthened by contemporaneous documentation (such as in the corporation's minutes) acknowledging such a relationship.

What happens to expenditures subject to the Code Sec. 248 election if the corporation is liquidated before the end of the Code Sec. 248 amortization period? Since the asset into which the costs had been capitalized has ceased to exist, the as yet unrecovered costs should then be deductible as a loss under Code Sec. 165. Similarly, expenditures not qualifying for Code Sec. 248 may be capitalized into assets other than the corporate shell. They would then be recoverable over the life of, or at the termination of, such other assets.

Practice Tip: In some such cases, cost recovery might be faster than the amortization period under Code Sec. 248. In that event, the corporation would benefit from the expenditure in question falling outside the ambit of the Code Sec. 248 election.

Example: Newco has just been formed. It incurs and pays a variety of costs qualifying under the Code Sec. 248 regulations. In addition, Newco is capitalized in part by debt payable in four years. Any costs Newco paid in connection with the borrowing would not qualify under Code Sec. 248, but – outside of Code Sec. 248 – these costs could be amortized over the term of the loan. And that would be an improved tax outcome for Newco since the four-year loan term is shorter than the Code Sec. 248 amortization period.

---

[125] Treas. Reg. § 1.248-1(b)(2).

[126] *Id.* Treas. Reg. § 1.248-1(b)(3).

[127] Compare *United States v. General Bancshares Corp.*, 388 F.2d 184 (8th Cir. 1968) (treating expenses of chang-

ing a corporation's name as nondeductible capital expenditures) to Rev. Rul. 63-259, 1963-2 C.B. 95 (treating costs of renewing a corporation's charter as subject to amortization under Code Sec. 248).

¶204.03(a)

(b) Reorganizations

The benefits conferred by a corporate reorganization presumably last over one year. Thus, the expenses of effecting the reorganization typically may not be deducted but must be capitalized. Moreover, these expenses may not be amortized.[128] Although there are occasional situations allowing more rapid cost recovery,[129] the general rule of nondeductibility applies whether the corporation paying the expenses is the acquiror[130] or the target;[131] whether the nature of the reorganization is acquisitive,[132] divisive,[133] or other;[134] and whether the transactions are taxable or tax-free.

> **Practice Tip:** Capitalization of expenses is premised on the expenditure producing a long-term or continuing benefit. Thus, a principal basis on which a taxpayer may attempt to justify deduction is that the benefits of the expenditure in question lacked long-term effect.[135]

The current controlling authority as to whether capitalization of reorganization costs is required are the post-INDOPCO intangibles capitalization regulations discussed above.[136] In addition, even if a cost must initially be capitalized, subsequent events may permit deduction. For example, costs associated with a particular plan or strategy as to a possible sale or reorganization often become deductible when the plan or strategy is abandoned.[137]

(c) Liquidations

Capitalization entails adding a cost to the taxpayer's basis in an asset. Liquidation eliminates the corporation. Typically, therefore, there is no asset into which to capitalize any costs. Thus, expenses incident to liquidation usually are deductible.

However, the result may be different when the liquidation effectively contributes to another asset, for example, when a liquidation occurs as part of a tax-free reorganization. In addition, costs attributable to disposition of assets as part of the liquidation should be considered as part of the Code Sec. 1001 computation of gain or loss as to such disposition rather than being separately deductible.[138]

---

[128] *See* Code Sec. 197(e)(7) (excluding from Code Sec. 197 intangibles fees for professional services and transaction costs incurred with respect to transactions as to which gain or loss is not recognized as a result of Code Secs. 351 to 368).

[129] For example, some expenses of creating a new corporation via a reorganization may qualify for Code Sec. 248 treatment. *e.g.*, Rev. Rul. 70-241, 1970-1 C.B. 84 (organizational expenditures paid in creating a corporation via an F reorganization qualify for Code Sec. 248 treatment).

[130] *e.g.*, *Berry Petroleum Corp. v. Comm'r*, 104 T.C. 584, 617-22 (1995), *aff'd per curiam*, 142 F.3d 442 (9th Cir. 1998).

[131] *e.g.*, *Victory Markets, Inc. v. Comm'r*, 99 T.C. 648 (1992).

[132] *e.g.*, *United States v. Hilton Hotels Corp.*, 397 U.S. 580 (1970).

[133] *e.g.*, *E.I. duPont & Co. v. United States*, 432 F.2d 1052 (3d Cir. 1970).

[134] *e.g.*, Rev. Rul. 77-204, 1977-1 C.B. 40 (bankruptcy reorganization).

[135] *e.g.*, *A.E. Staley Manufacturing Co. v. Comm'r*, 119 F.3d 482 (7th Cir. 1997); *In re Federated Department Stores, Inc.*, 171 B.R. 603 (S.D. Ohio 1994).

[136] Treas. Reg. §1.263(a)-4 & 5. However, the numerous cases decided before finalization of these regulations retain significance to the extent they are not inconsistent with the regulations.

[137] *e.g.*, *Liquidation Co. v. Comm'r*, 33 B.T.A. 1173 (1936) (loss of franchise).

[138] *e.g.*, Rev Rul. 77-204, 1977-1 C.B. 40 (Situation 2).

.04 Deductions as to Corporation-Shareholder Transactions

(b) General Rules

Unless the consolidated return regime applies,[139] Corporations and their shareholders are separate taxpayers. Accordingly, in general, the actions of the corporation cannot be attributed to the shareholder for federal income tax purposes nor can the actions of the shareholder be attributed to the corporation.

One consequence is that a corporation usually cannot claim a deduction when it pays expenses of a shareholder. The transaction typically is treated as a constructive dividend to the shareholder–includible in the shareholder's income to the extent directed by Code Sec. 301[140] and nondeductible by the corporation.[141]

> ***Practice Tip:*** There are a number of avenues by which corporations can argue for deduction despite the foregoing general rule. The viability of these approaches depends on the applicable facts. One approach is to demonstrate that the expenditure did not just benefit the shareholder but also, in whole or in part, served corporate purposes.

> ***Example:*** If a shareholder flies on a corporate airplane purely for pleasure, the value of the use may constitute a constructive dividend. To the extent the travel was for company business, however, there should be no constructive dividend and the cost of operating the airplane should be deductible by the corporation.[142]

A second approach often is argued in the alternative to the first. That is, the corporation argues that the expenditure had a corporate business purpose but, if it didn't, the payment should be viewed as additional compensation, not as a dividend. Compensation, of course, is usually deductible by the corporation under Code Sec. 162 while dividends are not deductible. The solvency of such as an argument often is undercut by the absence of formal indicia of compensation, but the argument sometimes has value for settlement purposes.

Third, special rules sometimes apply to particular contexts. For instance, Code Sec. 164(e) provides that when a corporation pays a state tax imposed on a shareholder on his interest as a shareholder, and is not reimbursed, the deduction for the tax under Code Sec. 164(a) belongs to the corporation, not the shareholder.

What about the converse, that is, situations in which the shareholder pays expenses of the corporation? This typically is treated as a contribution by the shareholder to the capital of the corporation.[143] The corporation gets the deduction; the shareholder does not.[144] The shareholder does get increased basis in his, her, or its stock in the corporation on account of the contribution, but this often is viewed by the shareholder as less than complete comfort.

---

[139] This regime is discussed in Chapter 9.

[140] Code Sec. 301 is discussed in Chapter 5.

[141] *e.g., Haverhill Shoe Novelty Co. v. Comm'r,* 15 T.C. 517 (1950).

[142] *Gibson Products Co. v. Comm'r,* 8 T.C. 654 (1947).

[143] Alternatively, particularly when the corporate minutes support this characterization, the payment may be viewed a loan by the shareholder to the corporation.

[144] *e.g., Deputy v. duPont,* 308 U.S. 488 (1940).

Practice Tip: Especially in the context of closely held businesses, it is common for shareholders to pay corporate expenses out of their own funds. One of the tasks of the tax advisor is to get clients to take seriously the tax law's separation of the entity from the individual.

Practice Tip: However, the shareholder will be able to deduct the payment if he can show that he made the payment in order to further the shareholder's own trade or business.

Example 1: Sharon is a shareholder and also an officer of Denethor Corporation. Denethor's main supplier is threatening to sell no more materials to Denethor unless Denethor pays arrearages for past materials. Were this to happen, Denethor would be put out of business. Denethor doesn't have ready sums, so Sharon pays the arrearages.

Whether Sharon can deduct the payment depends on the principal purpose motivating Sharon. If Sharon can show that she acted principally to protect her job with Denethor (rather than the value of her Denethor stock), the payment would be deemed an expense of her trade or business of being an employee. She could then deduct the payment under Code Sec. 162.[145] However, this would be a below-the-line deduction potentially subject to limitation under Code Sec. 67 and 68.[146]

Example 2: Simpson Corporations is a subsidiary of Harold Corporation. Money that Harold spends monitoring its investment in Simpson will be deductible by Harold since that activitiy is part of its trade or business. However, money that Harold spends directing the quotidian activities of Simpson will not be deductible but will instead be a capital contribution, increasing Harold's basis in its Simpson stock.[147]

(b) Transactions Between Corporations and Shareholders

Transactions between related parties are scrutinized closely because of the potential for abuse. Congress has written a number of sections into the Code to prevent abuse when corporations deal with their shareholders. These sections include the following:

Code Sec. 162(k): Dealings of a corporation in its own stock are capital transactions. When a corporation issues or reissues stock, any expenses it incurs are nondeductible and non-amortizable.[148] The same is true as to expenses of redeeming stock. A few cases, however, seemed to create exceptions to that rule in particular circumstances.[149]

In 1986, Congress closed such doors by enacting Code Sec. 162(k), which prohibits deduction of "any amount paid or incurred by a corporation in connection with the redemption of its stock."[150] Excepted from this prohibition, however, are

---

[145] *Cf. United States v. Generes*, 405 U.S. 93 (1972) (similar analysis under section 166 as to whether a bad debt was business or non-business in nature).

[146] *See* Code Sec. 62(a)(1).

[147] *e.g., Columbian Rope Co. v. Comm'r*, 42 T.C. 800 (1964).

[148] *e.g.,* Treas. Reg. § .248-1(b)(3).

[149] *e.g., Five Star Manufacturing Co. v. Comm'r*, 355 F2d 724 (5th Cir. 1966) (allowing deduction of the cost of redeeming the shares of a particularly vexatious shareholder).

[150] Code Sec. 162(k)(1).

¶204.04(b)

interest deductions allowable under Code Sec. 163, deductions "for amounts which are properly allocated to indebtedness and amortized over the term of such indebtedness," and deduction for dividends paid under Code Sec. 561.[151]

Example: Media Space, Inc. issued preferred stock to investors. The investors had the right to require Media Space to redeem the preferred stock. After several years, the investors wished to have their stock redeemed. Media Space, however, lacked the funds to effect the redemption. The investors and Media Space entered into an agreement. The investors agreed to forgo their right to redemption. In return, Media Space agreed to pay, and did pay, the investors amounts denominated as interest.

Media Space deducted the payments. The IRS disallowed the deductions. The Tax Court rejected Media Space's argument under Code Sec. 163 because the court concluded that there was no actual indebtedness.

Alternatively, Media Space argued for deduction under Code Sec. 162, and it presented persuasive evidence that forbearance payments like those at issue are common in business. One of the IRS's counters was Code Sec. 162(k). The IRS argued that Media Space, in substance, exchanged the forbearance payments and new preferred stock with deferred redemption rights for old preferred stock with nondeferred redemption rights.

The court rejected the IRS's Code Sec. 162(k) argument. It concluded that neither in form nor substance was there a reacquisition of stock. Thus, Code Sec. 162(k) did not apply, and the court upheld deduction of some of the payments.[152]

Code Sec. 267(a): Absent a special rule, the sale of property at a loss to a closely related person could trigger a tax deduction without genuine change of control. Accordingly, Congress decreed in Code Sec. 267(a)(1) that sale of property at a loss is a nonrecognition event if the buyer and the seller are within designated categories of relationship. These categories include (1) family members; (2) an individual and a corporation over 50% of whose stock he owns, directly or indirectly; (3) corporations that are members of the same controlled group; (4) grantors and fiduciaries of the same or related trusts; and (5) various taxable and non-taxable entities under stated levels of ownership.[153]

Example 1: Sanjay Gupta owns 100% of the stock of a corporation. He sells property to the corporation at a loss. Sanjay cannot deduct the loss.[154]

Example 2: To circumvent Code Sec. 267, Sanjay transfers 50% of his stock to his wife before selling the property to the corporation. The loss is still nondeductible. Under constructive ownership rules, an individual is treated as owning stock owned by his family, and a spouse is part of the family.[155] Thus, Sanjay still owns 100% of the corporation – 50% actually and 50% by attribution.

---

[151] Code Sec. 162(k)(2)(A). Code Sec. 561 is discussed in Chapter 3.

[152] *Media Space, Inc. v. Comm'r*, 135 T.C. No. 21 (2010).

[153] Code Sec. 267(b).

[154] Code Sec. 267(a), (b)(2).

[155] Code Sec. 267(b)(1), (c)(2) & (4).

Example 3: Sanjay transfers 50% of his stock, not to his wife, but to his wife's mother before selling the property to the corporation. The loss is deductible. Sanjay owns only 50% (not "over 50%" as required by Code Sec. 267(b)(2)) of the stock of the corporation; his mother-in-law's stock is not attributed to him. "The family of an individual shall include only his brothers and sisters . . . , spouse, ancestors, and lineal descendants."[156] Mothers-in-law aren't included. Presumably, Congress reasoned that most taxpayers will not give half their companies to their mothers-in-law simply to circumvent Code Sec. 267.

Code Sec. 267(a)(2) addresses a different possible abuse. Consider related parties (related under the same categories as above) who are on different methods of accounting. By strategic timing of payments, deductions could be produced before the corresponding income would be taxable. This mismatch would operate to the disadvantage of the federal fisc in a time-value of money sense. Code Sec. 267(a)(2) blocks this abuse by delaying the deduction until the income inclusion.

Example: Rostor Corporation owns 55% of the stock of Ankara Corporation. Rostor is on the accrual method; Ankara is on the cash method; both use the calendar year. Ankara performs services for Rostor in Year 1, entitling it to a $10,000 payment from Rostor in Year 2 and it receives that payment in Year 2. Under their normal accounting methods, Rostor would have a $10,000 deduction in Year 1[157] and Ankara would have a $10,000 inclusion into income in Year 2. However, section 267(a)(2) defers Rostor's deduction until Year 2.

Code Sec. 267(a)(3) grants the Treasury authority to extend the Code Sec. 267(a)(2) matching principle to "cases in which the person to whom the payment is to be made is not a United States person."[158]

Code Sec. 311(a): In general, a corporation does not recognize loss as a result of its distributing to its shareholders depreciated property, that is, property whose basis exceeds its fair market value.[159]

Practice Tip: Sometimes it is important that the shareholder receive the particular property. If that is not important, there is an alternative to distributing the depreciated property. The corporation can sell the property, then distribute the proceeds to the shareholder(s). By doing so, the corporation can deduct the loss.

Other provisions that seek to prevent abuse through transactions between related parties operate on tax benefits other than deductions. For instance, Code Sec. 453(g) denies installment sale treatment with respect to sales of depreciable property between related taxpayers; Code Sec. 1239 denies capital gain treatment with respect to sale of depreciable property between related taxpayers; and Code Sec. 482 allows the IRS to reallocate income, credit, and deduction items with respect to transactions among commonly controlled taxpayers.[160]

---

[156] Code Sec. 267(c)(4).

[157] Code Sec. 461(a) & (h)(2)(A)(i).

[158] *See* Treas. Reg. § 1.267(a)-3.

[159] For further discussion of Code Sec. 311, see Chapter 5. *See also* Code Sec. 336(d) (denying recognition of loss on certain distributions incident to liquidation). Code Sec. 336 in discussed in Chapter 7.

[160] For discussion of Code Sec. 482, see Chapter 9.

.05 Judicial Anti-Abuse Doctrines

Every legal system must confront the question of the level of formalism it will embrace or tolerate. Reflecting traditional American pragmatism, our legal system is not heavily formal. However, this is a tendency, not a constant. Formalism has reared its head in many tax decisions.

In the federal income tax, there are two dimensions of the formalism question: one factual and the other legal. The factual dimension is usually called the "form versus substance" issue. Form involves the labels that may be put upon transactions or relationships by contracts or state law. Substance adverts to the economic realities of rights and duties, benefits and burdens. Usually, but far from always, substance controls over form in federal income taxation. Thus, the parties to a contract may have designated their transaction as a sale, but the IRS and the courts may recharacterize the transaction as not a sale if the benefits and burdens as to the property have not shifted from the putative seller to the putative purchaser.[161]

The legal dimension involves literal versus non-literal interpretation of the provisions of the Internal Revenue Code. Should such provisions be applied strictly according to the literal, dictionary or term-of-art meanings of the words of the statute, or should considerations such as policy or legislative purpose be allowed to modify or even supplant literal textual meaning? Although non-literal interpretation probably is the more common style, many important tax decisions taste of a literal flavor and textual approaches appear to have gained some strength in recent years.[162]

The anti-formal tendency of the courts has been distilled into a number of judicial doctrines. Courts have applied these doctrines to prevent taxpayers, whether corporations or individuals, from obtaining tax benefits viewed as excessive or inappropriate under the circumstances of the case. The courts have confused themselves (as well as taxpayers and the IRS) through sloppy reasoning or wording, so the various doctrines have become muddled. The following discussion, therefore, paints with a broad brush.

Judicial anti-abuse rules in tax originated with cases rejecting mere shams. Although there is no crisp historical derivation, this core intuition was refined and expanded over the years into "rules" with names like business purpose, step transaction, and substance over form. Currently, much of the anti-abuse attention of the tax system is focused on the economic substance doctrine, which sometimes subsumes other anti-abuse rules, and sometimes operates parallel to them.[163]

(a) Sham Transaction Doctrine

Favorable tax consequences depend upon satisfaction of predicates specified by Congress in the applicable Code section. Quite appropriately, the IRS and the

---

[161] e.g., *Lucas v. North Texas Lumber Co.*, 281 U.S. 11, 13-14 (1930).

[162] e.g., *Gitlitz v. Comm'r*, 531 U.S. 206, 219-20 (2001) ("Because the Code's plain text permits the taxpayers here to receive these benefits, we need not address [the] policy concern [raised by the Government].").

[163] See, e.g., *Schering-Plough Corp. v. United States*, 651 F. Supp. 2d 219 (D.N.J. 2009) (applying several non-literal approaches conjunctively). For additional discussion of the various doctrines, see Joshua D. Rosenberg, Tax Avoidance and Income Measurement, 87 Mich. L. Rev. 365 (1988).

courts demand that those events actually happened and do not accept contrivances rigged to allow taxpayers to claim the requisite events transpired when in reality they did not.

> *Example:* Telsor Corporation is profitable and is looking to shift income between tax years. Ace Advertising Company is unprofitable, so has a zero effective tax rate. Both are calendar year, cash method taxpayers.
>
> Near the end of Year 1, Telsor pays Ace $10,000. Ostensibly, this is to pay for an advertising campaign, but neither Telsor nor Ace actually intends such a campaign to occur. Early in Year 2, Ace pays the $10,000 back to Telsor. Telsor claims a $10,000 section 162 deduction in Year 1, then takes the $10,000 back into income in Year 2. If this scheme is respected, Telsor will have gained a time-value of money advantage by shifting tax into a later year.
>
> The scheme will not be respected. The arrangement is simply a circular money flow with no genuine, tax-independent significance. The arrangement is a sham, and the section 162 deductions claimed by Telsor in Year 1 should be disallowed.[164]

Strictly speaking, one might say that the sham rule is not a distinct judicial anti-abuse rule at all. Instead, it can be viewed as simply an exercise of fact-finding by the courts, a finding that – since the arrangement was purely fictitious – the circumstance required by the statute as predicate to the tax benefit, did not exist.

(b) Other Doctrines

Some courts began to use the term "sham" expansively, to include both transactions that never, in essence, occurred at all and transactions that actually occurred and actually altered legal rights and responsibilities but that had no purpose apart from tax minimization. Reflecting this expanded usage, some courts described two kinds of shams: "shams in fact" (the alleged transactions never actually happened) and "shams in substance" (the transactions actually occurred but they did not alter legal rights and duties or they had no purpose other than reducing tax).[165]

> *Example:* In the famous *Goldstein* case, Mrs. Goldstein won the Irish Sweepstakes. As a self-help income averaging scheme, she implemented a scheme devised by her accountant son. The scheme involved borrowing money (used to buy Treasury bonds), then prepaying the interest on the borrowing, to create big interest deductions to offset the Sweepstakes winnings. The Tax Court held against the taxpayer, on the theory that the borrowing/purchase of Treasury bonds/prepayment of interest constituted a sham.

---

[164] It will then be up to Telsor to file a refund claim for Year 2 for the $10,000 it included in income then. Code Sec. 6511(a) prescribes that refund claims must generally be filed "within 3 years from the time the return was filed or 2 years from the time the tax was paid, whichever of such periods expires the later." On rare occasions, the limitations period can be mitigated under Code Secs. 1311 to 1314 or one of several judicial doctrines, but it would be unwise for a taxpayer to depend on the availability of such relief.

[165] *e.g., American Electric Power Co., Inc. v. United States,* 326 F.3d 737, 740-41 (6th Cir. 2003); *In re CM Holdings, Inc.,* 301 F.3d 96, 101 (3d Cir. 2002).

The Second Circuit affirmed the result but disagreed as to rationale. The Second Circuit stated that the transactions had actually occurred, so were not shams. However, the Second Circuit read Code Sec. 163 purposively, not literally. It held that the claimed interest deductions were not allowable because there was no economic purpose, no tax-independent purpose for the transactions.[166]

Three judicial anti-abuse rules – the business purpose doctrine, the substance over form doctrine, and the step transaction doctrine – emanated from, or developed along side of, the sham doctrines. These are described below.

Business purpose doctrine: Predicates for tax benefits usually are objective conditions. Congress, however, has sometimes made benefits depend upon subjective conditions as well, such as the taxpayer having a profit purpose[167] or not having a tax-avoidance purpose.[168] Even when a statute is silent as to motivation, courts sometimes interpret the statute non-literally, discovering (or creating) a purpose requirement.

Example: Although there are earlier cases in the line,[169] the business purpose requirement is often thought to stem from *Gregory v. Helvering*.[170] The statute, then as now, accorded nonrecognition treatment to corporate reorganization. The corporation in question underwent what was in form a reorganization. However, there was no business reason for the transaction; its sole purpose was to reduce taxes for the shareholder. The courts held that, given the lack of business purpose, no genuine reorganization occurred. Thus, nonrecognition treatment was denied.

Gregory is an ambiguous precedent. Judge Learned Hand's opinion for the Second Circuit and Justice Sutherland's opinion for the Supreme Court have split personalities. Although holding against this taxpayer, both opinions stated – fortunately for us! – that tax planning is legitimate.[171]

Moreover, the reach of *Gregory* is debatable. The Supreme Court's opinion held that a business purpose is inherent to the concept of "reorganization" within the meaning of the statute.[172] Taken on its own terms, that holding is narrow, applying business purpose in the particular realm of reorganizations rather than to all transactions of whatever type. Nonetheless, many courts give *Gregory* a much broader reading, applying it outside the reorganization context.

Substance over Form Doctrine: The preponderance of substance over form is not limited to tax. It is a tendency of American law generally. But the rule is not absolute. First, some areas of the law are form driven, whether by statutory language or judicial construction. For instance, gain and loss usually are not taken

---

[166] *Goldstein v. Comm'r*, 44 T.C. 284 (1965), *aff'd on other grounds*, 364 F.2d 734 (2d Cir. 1966), *cert. denied*, 385 U.S. 1005 (1967).

[167] *e.g.*, Code Sec. 165(c)(1) & (2), 183(a).

[168] *e.g.*, Code Sec. 269(a).

[169] *e.g.*, *Cortland Specialty Co. v. Comm'r*, 60 F.2d 937, 940 (2d Cir. 1932); *Pinellas Ice & Cold Storage Co. v. Comm'r*, 57 F.2d 188, 189 (5th Cir. 1932).

[170] 293 U.S. 465 (1935), *aff'g* 69 F.2d 809 (2d Cir. 1934).

[171] As Learned Hand famously wrote, "[a]ny one may so arrange his affairs that his taxes shall be as low as possible; he is not bound to choose that pattern which will best pay the Treasury; there is not even a patriotic duty to increase one's taxes." 69 F.2d at 810.

[172] 293 U.S. at 469.

¶204.05(b)

into account for tax purposes until they have been realized. Realization consists of change in the form in which a taxpayer holds its wealth, even if the amount of such wealth is not changed.

Example: The taxpayer in the *Cottage Savings* case was a financial institution. It owned a pool of mortgages that had declined in value. It exchanged that pool for a group of mortgages held by a different financial institution in similar straits.

The taxpayer suffered no economic loss as a result of the exchange because the two pools of mortgages were of equal value. However, it sustained a tax loss under section 1001 because its aggregate bases in the mortgages it gave up in the exchange exceeded the value of the mortgages it received in the exchange.

The taxpayer deducted this tax loss. The IRS disallowed the deduction, and the circuit court agreed with the IRS. The IRS argued that there was no realization: the two pools of mortgages did not materially differ because they were of equal value. The Supreme Court reversed and held for the taxpayer. The Court concluded that the fact the mortgages had different legal entitlements controlled over the fact they had equal values.[173]

Second, even when substance is primary, the degrees of substance required to support the taxpayer's chosen form vary from context to context. In some areas, a small degree of substance will suffice.

Example: If the formalities of incorporation have occurred, it is difficult to argue that the corporation's existence should be disregarded. "[T]he corporate form may be disregarded where it is a sham or unreal . . . [, if] the form is a bald and mischievous fiction."[174] However, the conduct of virtually any real business through the corporation, even if in very small degree, usually is enough substance to confirm the chosen form for tax purposes.[175]

Practice Tip: The skillful tax advisor knows that not all sections of the Code are interpreted in the same way by the courts and the IRS. There are traditions of interpretation in areas and sub-areas, and knowing those traditions can be as valuable as knowing the "black letter" law. For instance, as indicated above, the degree of required substance is lower in some areas, such as whether to respect the corporation's existence, than in some other areas. Awareness of the interpretive tradition in the particular area will help the client steer clear of peril without being excessively conservative.

Step Transaction Doctrine: Applying the judicial anti-abuse rules can be challenging enough when there is only one pertinent event or transaction. In corporate affairs, however, there often are multiple transactions that are arguably related. In

---

[173] *Cottage Savings Ass'n v. Comm'r*, 499 U.S. 554, 562 (1991).

[174] *Moline Properties v. Comm'r*, 319 U.S. 436, 439 (1943) (citing *Gregory and Higgins v. Smith*, 308 U.S. 473, 477-78 (1940)).

[175] *e.g., Ogiony v. Comm'r*, 617 F.2d 14, 16 (2d Cir.), *cert. denied*, 449 U.S. 900 (1980). This issue is discussed in greater detail in Chapter 2.

¶204.05(b)

such cases, where should the focus be? Should transactions be treated and tested as separate, or should they be collapsed?

The step transaction doctrine allows the IRS, under some circumstances, to treat a series of ostensibly distinct transactions as one integrated transaction for purposes of determining income tax effects. The problem is, however, that there is no single, settled standard under which to judge whether transactions should be separately respected or should be combined and integrated. Different courts (and sometimes the same court in different cases) have employed at least three versions of the step transaction doctrine.

(1) The version least hospitable to application of the doctrine is the binding commitment test. Under this test, transactions will be aggregated only if, at the time the first transaction is entered into, the taxpayer is under a binding obligation (such as via a contract) to take a subsequent step.[176] Obviously, such rule is easily circumvented, so has little anti-abuse "punch."

(2) Somewhat more potent is the interdependence test. It requires that transactions be integrated if they are so interdependent that the rights and obligations established by one transaction would have been pointless without consummation of the other transaction or transactions.[177]

(3) The first and second of the tests are objective; the third test is subjective. It is known as the intent test or the end result test. It integrates transactions that are taken as part of a plan to advance and achieve a particular ultimate outcome.[178] This is the most expansive version of the doctrine.

Practice Tip: The choice of which version of the step transaction doctrine to apply sometimes is the decisive choice in a case. Thus, in any case in which the doctrine may be applied, the tax advisor should carefully research the law of the judicial circuit in which the taxpayer is located and of the various trial courts in which the taxpayer may choose to litigate. Although the Tax Court is a court of nationwide jurisdiction, it typically will apply the law of the circuit to which appeal of the case would lie.[179]

Practice Tip: In most cases, it is the IRS that asserts the step transaction doctrine. However, in appropriate cases, the taxpayer may assert it.

Example: King Enterprises, Inc. was one of the shareholders of Tenco, Inc. King and the other shareholders sold their Tenco stock to Minute Maid Corporation, receiving cash, promissory notes, and Minute Maid stock. Later, Tenco was merged into Minute Maid. King did not include the value of the Minute Maid stock in its income, on the ground that the transactions should be aggregated and viewed as a reorganization under section 368(a)(1)(A), thus qualifying for nonrecognition treatment.[180] The IRS countered that the transfer

---

[176] *e.g., Comm'r v. Gordon*, 391 U.S. 83 (1968).

[177] *e.g., Reef Corp. v. Comm'r*, 368 F.2d 125, 134-36 (5th Cir. 1966), *cert. denied*, 386 U.S. 1018 (1967).

[178] *e.g., Kimbell-Diamond Mining Co. v. Comm'r*, 14 T.C. 74 (1950), *aff'd per curiam*, 187 F.2d 718 (5th Cir.), *cert. denied*, 342 U.S. 827 (1951).

[179] *See Golsen v. Comm'r*, 54 T.C. 742 (1970), *aff'd*, 445 F.2d 985 (10th Cir. 1971).

[180] King also asserted the Code Sec. 243 exclusion/deduction (discussed earlier in this chapter) with respect to the cash and notes.

of the Tenco stock to Minute Maid was a completed sale independent of the subsequent merger of Tenco into Minute Maid, thus was taxable.

The court held for King. The IRS argued that the step transaction doctrine did not apply because there was no binding commitment for the merger of Tenco into Minute Maid to follow Minute Maid's acquisition of the Tenco stock from King and the other former shareholders. The court, however, chose to apply the end result test. Concluding that the facts justified an inference that the merger was the intended result from the outset, the court held the step transaction doctrine applicable and held that nonrecognition treatment was appropriate for this Type A reorganization.[181]

(c) Economic Substance Doctrine

There have been two great waves of tax shelters in our recent tax history. The first was from the 1960s to the mid-1980s, consisting of "tax-advantaged investments" marketed to upper-income (but usually not mega-rich) individuals. This wave was stopped by 1986 legislation, principally the "passive activity loss" rules of Code Sec. 469.

The second wave came to prominence in the 1990s and, despite occasional reports of its demise, continues today. It consists of more exotic schemes marketed to corporations or very wealthy individuals, usually those who recently sold their companies and are seeking to avoid capital gains tax on tens or hundreds of millions of gain. These arrangements are structured to avoid Code Sec. 469 and, arguably, other statutory abuse rules.

The IRS has attacked shelters on many theories. The economic substance doctrine ("ESD") has emerged as the IRS's preferred weapon. Originally of judicial origin, the ESD is a "meta rule," that is, it is imposed on top other tax rules. Under the doctrine, the claimed tax benefits from an arrangement can be denied – even if the arrangement complies with the literal terms of the Internal Revenue Code – if the arrangement does not have economic substance. There have been scores of ESD cases over the decades, many of them involving corporate taxpayers.

There are two aspects of the ESD: (1) the subjective component – whether the taxpayer had a bona fide tax-independent purpose for engaging in the transactions and (2) the objective component – whether the transactions had tax-independent economic effect.

Unfortunately, the multiplication of ESD cases over the years led to less, not more, clarity in the rule. First, although lower federal courts in recent years have accepted the validity of the doctrine essentially without question,[182] there have been numerous other decisions – typically unacknowledged by the ESD cases – that have held that literal compliance with the applicable Code section is sufficient for a taxpayer to prevail.[183]

---

[181] *King Enterprises, Inc. v. United States*, 418 F.2d 511 (Ct. Cl. 1969) (per curiam). For additional discussion of acquisitive reorganizations, *see* Chapter 8.

[182] One trial court held the judicial ESD to be unconstitutional on separation of powers grounds, that decision was reversed on appeal. *Coltec Ind., Inc. v United States*, 62 Fed. Cl. 716 (2004), *vacated & remanded*, 454 F.3d 1340 (Fed. Cir. 2006), *cert. denied*, 549 U.S. 1206 (2007).

[183] The theory of these cases is that, if the section was defectively drafted, correction is up to Congress, not the

Second, the courts following the ESD disagreed on the relationship between the two components. Some courts followed the disjunctive test, meaning that the taxpayer would prevail if it carried either the subjective or objective component.[184] Some other courts followed the conjunctive test, under which the taxpayer had to carry both components in order to win.[185] Yet other courts saw the two components not as separate prongs but as parts of a single integrated inquiry.[186]

Third, the courts disagreed on the requisite quanta of non-tax purpose and effect. Would it suffice if any degree (no matter how small) of non-tax purpose or effect existed? Or would that degree have to be more than *de minimis*? Or would it have to be substantial? Or would it have to be the predominant purpose, that is, larger than the tax purpose or tax saving? Dicta or holdings from various cases supported each of the views.[187]

Fourth, the cases were not fully consistent as the stage(s) of a chain of transactions to which the ESD will be applied. Is the proper focus to collapse stages under the step transaction doctrine, to apply the ESD to the whole of the transactions, or to apply it only to the particular stage(s) most crucial to generating the claimed tax benefits?[188]

Fifth, the courts disagreed as to the standard of review. Should appellate courts review trial court conclusions as to the two components deferentially or non-differentially?[189]

As a result of these ambiguities, decisions under the judicial ESD were often hard to predict and hard to reconcile.

> **Example:** UPS derived substantial profits from selling excess value insurance to customers. After some years, UPS created a Bermuda captive insurance subsidiary to cover the excess value insurance, then distributed its stock to shareholders, making UPS and the Bermuda company sisters. An unrelated domestic corporation was interposed, but it had little real function. UPS continued to administer the insurance and process the claims as it had before, but the income was treated as income of the Bermuda company not taxable by the United States.
>
> Applying the economic substance doctrine, the Tax Court held that the income was taxable to UPS and upheld imposition of penalties. On appeal, a two-to-one decision by the Eleventh Circuit reversed, concluding that the restructuring of the excess value insurance had both real economic effects and

---

(Footnote Continued)

courts. *e.g., Gitlitz v. Comm'r*, 531 U.S. 206, 219-20 (2001); *United States v. Consumer Life Ins. Co.*, 430 U.S. 725, 751 (1977); *The Limited v. Comm'r*, 286 F.3d 324, 332, 336 (6th Cir. 2002); *Pugh v. Comm'r*, 213 F.3d 1324, 1330-32 (11th Cir. 2000); *Brown Group, Inc. v. Comm'r*, 77 F.3d 217, 222 (8th Cir. 1996).

[184] *e.g., Rice's Toyota World, Inc. v. Comm'r*, 752 F.2d 89 (4th Cir. 1985).

[185] *e.g., Pasternak v. Comm'r*, 990 F.2d 893, 898 (6th Cir. 1993).

[186] *e.g., ACM Partnership v. Comm'r*, 157 F.3d 231, 247 (3d Cir. 1998), *cert. denied*, 526 U.S. 1017 (1999).

[187] *Compare Frank Lyon Co. v. United States*, 435 U.S. 561, 583-84 (1978) ("not shaped solely by tax avoidance features") (emphasis added), *to Knetsch v. United States*, 364 U.S. 361, 366 (1960) ("did not appreciably affect [the taxpayer's]beneficial interest except to reduce his taxes") (emphasis added).

[188] *See, e.g., Coltec, supra*, 454 F.3d at 1356 ("the transaction to be analyzed is the one that gave rise to the alleged tax benefit").

[189] *See* Christopher Pietruszkiewicz, *Economic Substance and the Standard of Review*, 60 Ala. L. Rev. 339 (2009).

¶204.05(c)

non-tax business purpose. When a trial court finds a scheme so deficient that penalties are warranted and the appellate court finds the scheme successful for tax purposes, the economic substance doctrine is less than predictable as a rule of law.

Because the judicial ESD was seen as unreliable, proposals to codify the ESD were offered for about a decade. These efforts succeeded in the Reconciliation Act amendments to the Patient Protection and Affordable Health Care Act. The Act added Code Sec. 7701(o) to the Code, effective March 30, 2010. Code Sec. 7701(o) has these key features:

- The new section recognizes that the ESD does not apply in all situations. It requires the court to make a preliminary determination whether the ESD applies to the situation at hand.[190]

- The new section adopts the conjunctive test and high thresholds of significance. If the ESD applies to the case, the taxpayer must establish both that the transaction changed the taxpayer's economic position in a "meaningful" way apart from federal income tax affects *and* that the taxpayer had a "substantial" non-tax purpose.[191]

- The new section is accompanied by a strict liability penalty. Tax understatements caused by failing the ESD trigger a 40% penalty absent adequate disclosure of the transaction on the return, or a 20% penalty if the transaction is adequately disclosed. There is no reasonable cause exception.[192]

Things to watch for: The principal targets of Code Sec. 7701(o) are tax shelters and other allegedly abusive tax reduction arrangements. Major shelter cases often take many years from audit through trial and appeal. Thus, many cases arising before the effective date of Code Sec. 7701(o) remain pending. The shelter cases decided in the last nine months of 2010 – that is, cases arising before the new provision's effective date but decided after that date – did not cite Code Sec. 7701(o).[193] Thus, they do not appear to have been influenced by the codification.

The other major question is whether Code Sec. 7701(o) will, in the cases to which it is applicable, produce different results from the pre-codification judicial ESD. Some have predicted that there will be little change in actual case outcomes, but it is too early to know.

Code Sec. 7701(o) clarifies some matters, such as the conjunctive relationship of the subjective and objective components. However, other old questions – such as the precise stage(s) of the transaction to be scrutinized and the appropriate standard of appellate review – remain unsettled. In addition, Code Sec. 7701(o) raises new questions. For example, it is unclear what specific meanings should be

---

[190] Code Sec. 7701(o)(1).

[191] Code Sec. 7701(o)(1)(A) & (B).

[192] Code Secs. 6662(b)(6) & (i), 6664(c)(2) & (d)(2).

[193] *e.g., Sala v. United States*, 613 F.3d 1249 (10th Cir. 2010); *Stobie Creek Investments LLC v. United States*, 608 F.3d 1366 (Fed. Cir. 2010); *Bemont Investments LLC v.*

United States, 2010-2 USTC ¶ 50,551 (E.D. Tex. 2010); Fidelity Int'l Currency Advisor A Fund LLC v. United States, 2010-1 USTC ¶ 50,418 (D. Mass.), *amended & superseded* by 2010 WL 4116469 (D. Mass. 2010); *Nevada Partners Fund LLC v. United States*, 2010-1 USTC ¶ 50,379 (S.D. Miss. 2010).

ascribed to the statutory terms "meaningful" and "substantial." In addition, major ambiguities exist as to the types of transactions to which Code Sec. 7701(o) will and will not apply.

> **Practice Tip:** The legislative history does provide some limited guidance. Code Sec. 7701(o) is not intended to affect taxpayer choice among certain economic alternatives, for instance, a corporation's choice between debt versus equity as ways to capitalize the company, or a taxpayer's use of a foreign corporation versus a domestic corporation for engaging in crossborder transactions. In addition, Code Sec. 7701(o) will not apply to tax benefits that Congress intended to confer regardless of economic reality.[194]

However, some distrust legislative history, especially reports of the Joint Committee, rather than the House Ways and Means Committee or the Senate Finance Committee,[195] and the legislative history addresses only a few of the possible questions. Thus, practitioners have repeatedly asked Treasury and the IRS to provide detailed guidance as to how they intend to apply Code Sec. 7701(o) and the strict liability penalty, including creation of an "angel list" of types of transactions the agencies view as falling outside the scope of the codified ESD. Thus far, these requests have not been satisfied. Some guidance has been published, but it is general in nature and Treasury and the IRS have refused to provide an angel list.[196]

Government officials justify this limited guidance on the ground of not intruding upon the prerogatives of Congress and the courts. However, the true reason probably is that Treasury and the IRS prefer matters to remain murky. Their reasoning may be that a moving target is harder to hit than a fixed target, *i.e.*, that taxpayers can plan more effectively to blunt or circumvent a clear rule than a fluid standard. If this is in fact the motivation of Treasury and the IRS, serious "rule of law" questions are raised about the agencies' behavior.

> **Practice Tip:** Private letter ruling requests often are an important means by which taxpayers can achieve greater certainty as to tax consequences of planned transactions. However, the IRS has announced that it will not issue private letter rulings on the ESD. Nonetheless, some measure of comfort comes from the IRS's announcement that revenue agents will not be free to assert the ESD and the associated penalty on their own but will have to obtain higher-level approval from the Large Business and International Division.

¶ 205 Tax Rates

.01 Rates on Ordinary Income

Code Sec. 11(a) imposes income tax on corporations. Code Sec. 11(b) establishes a progressive rate structure. Tax liability for the year is the sum of 15% of the corporation's taxable income up to $50,000 plus 25% of taxable income between

---

[194] Joint Comm. on Tax'n, Technical Explanation of the Revenue Provisions of the Reconciliation Act of 2010, at 152 n. 344 (JCX-18-10 Mar. 21, 2010).

[195] *See, e.g.*, Michael Livingston, *What's Blue and White and Not Quite as Good as a Committee Report: General Explanations and the Role of "Subsequent" Tax Legislative History*, 11 Am. J. Tax Pol'y 91 (1994).

[196] Notice 2010-62, 2010-40 I.R.B. 411 (interim guidance on Code Sec. 7701(o)).

$50,001 and $75,000 plus 34% of taxable income between $75,001 and $10,000,000 plus 35% of taxable income over $10,000,000.

However, there are three important modifications of these rates. One relates to eligibility. The second requires related corporations to share the lower rates. The third phases out the lower rates for very high-income corporations.

First, personal service corporations are not eligible to use the rate ladder. Instead, their taxable incomes are taxed at a flat 35%.[197] Such corporations are those substantially all of whose activities involve rendition of services in enumerated professional fields and substantially all of the stock of which is held by employees, former employees, or their estates or estates' beneficiaries.[198]

Second, Code Secs. 1551 and 1561 apply when corporations are members of a controlled group of corporations. The sections require the whole group to share the tranches of income qualifying for each of the lower Code Sec. 11(b) rates.[199]

The third modification of the general corporate rate table appears in Code Sec. 11(b)(1) itself. The rates below 34% are phased out for corporations with taxable incomes over $100,000, and the 34% rate is phased out for corporations with taxable incomes over $15,000,000.[200]

These phase-outs produce a "double bubble." Marginal rates rise and fall twice. Specifically,[201]

Taxable Income	Rate
Up to $50,000	15%
Over $50,000 but not over $75,000	25%
Over $75,000 but not over $100,000	34%
Over $100,000 but not over $335,000	39%
Over $335,000 but not over $10,000,000	34%
Over $10,000,000 but not over $15,000,000	35%
Over $15,000,000 but not over $18,333,333	38%
Over $18,333,333	35%

Practice Tip: Normally, taxpayers attempt to defer income, if possible, into later tax years and to accelerate deductions into earlier tax years. Deferral of tax is valuable because of the time-value of money. However, the existence of bubbles in the corporate tax rates can reverse the usual incentive.

Example: Paragon Plastics, Inc. expects to have $92,000 of taxable income for 2010 and projects having $150,000 of taxable income for 2011.

---

[197] Code Sec. 11(b)(2). The Code Sec. 11(b) rates also do not apply to mutual savings banks conducting life insurance business, insurance companies, regulated investment companies, and real estate investment trusts. Code Sec. 11(c). These entities are subject to special tax regimes under sections 594, 801 et seq., and 851 et seq., respectively.

[198] Code Sec. 11(b)(2) & 448(d)(2).

[199] Code Sec. 1551 and 1561 are discussed in greater detail in Chapter 10.

[200] In the former of these phase-outs, the corporation's tax is increased by the lesser of 5% of the excess of taxable income over $100,000 or $11,750. In the latter of the phase-outs, the corporation's tax is increased by the lesser of 3% of the excess of taxable income over $15,000,000 or $100,000. Code Sec. 11(b)(1).

[201] These figures were computed by Boris I. Bittker & James S. Eustice, FEDERAL INCOME TAXATION OF CORPORATIONS AND SHAREHOLDERS ¶ 5.01[1] (7th ed. 2006).

Because of when it bills, Paragon has some flexibility as to timing of income. Moving $8,000 of income from 2011 to 2010 will save Paragon tax. The $8,000 would be taxed at 34% in 2010 (because the 34% rate extends up to $100,000), but it would be taxed at 39% in 2011 (because the 39% rate applies between $100,000 and $335,000). This would save Paragon $400 ($8,000 × the 5% rate differential). Paragon would be paying tax earlier, paying $2,720 ($8,000 × .34) extra in 2010 taxes. However, Paragon would earn an attractive 14.71% rate of return ($400 ÷ $2,720).

The feasibility of such a strategy, of course, depends on two conditions: the corporation's being able to fairly accurately predict its income for at least two years and its being able to legally shift income between the years. Among the many devices used by corporations to accelerate taxation of income are obtaining prepayments for services or sales,[202] assigning rights to future income, and accelerating cancellation-of-indebtedness income or gain on installment sales.

.02 Rates on Capital Gains and Treatment of Capital Losses

Code Sec. 1(h) grants individual taxpayers a preferential rate of taxation on long-term capital gains. Before 1987, corporations had a similar preference. The landmark Tax Reform Act of 1986 eliminated the preferential rate for corporations. Current Code Sec. 11 contains no provision comparable to Code Sec. 1(h).

The ghost of a preferential rate exists in Code Sec. 1201(a). This section provides that if the normal rate under Code Sec. 11 ever exceeds 35%, then a corporation's rate of tax on net capital gains may not exceed 35%.[203] This provision has little practical significance, however. First, Code Sec. 1201(a) marks to the Code Sec. 11 rate "determined without regard to the last 2 sentences of section 11(b)(1)." Those last two sentences set out the increased rates for taxable incomes over $100,000. Since Code Sec. 1201(a) disregards those increased rates, the current Code Sec. 11 rate does not exceed 35% for Code Sec. 1201 purposes, thus the Code Sec. 1201(a) 35% cap does not now come into play. Second, should the Code Sec. 11 rate (as determined for Code Sec. 1201 purposes) ever rise above 35% in some future year, Congress could avail itself of the expedient of amending or repealing Code Sec. 1201(a) to abolish the cap.

Practice Tip: The fact that corporations do not enjoy a preferential rate as to capital gains diminishes the incentive of corporations to attempt to shift income from ordinary to capital status, as individual taxpayers often try to do. Although diminished, however, an incentive does remain in some instances. This is because, as described in greater detail below, corporations can use capital losses only to offset capital gains and because capital losses not so used expire relatively quickly. Thus, a corporation having soon-expiring capital losses may be tempted to classify some of its ordinary income as capital gain. If

---

[202] Although the line is not always easy to draw, prepayments should be distinguished from mere deposits. The receipt of prepayments is taxable; the receipt of mere deposits is not. *e.g., Comm'r v. Indianapolis Power & Light Co.*, 493 U.S. 203 (1990).

[203] Code Sec. 1201(a) also applies if the rates under Code Sec. 511 (taxation of banks) and 831(a) and (b) (taxation of insurance companies) exceed 35%.

it does so successfully, it will offset the gain by the losses, in effect sheltering the gain from tax.

Example: In the famous *Corn Products* case,[204] the taxpayer entered into futures contracts in order to assure itself of sufficient corn for its processing operations. In the tax year at issue, it did not need additional corn, so it disposed of its futures contracts, realizing a gain. The corporation reported this as capital gain. The IRS, and ultimately the Supreme Court, disagreed. The Court held that the futures contracts were integral to the corporation's business operations and thus were ordinary, not capital, in nature.[205]

In the tax years at issue in *Corn Products*, corporations did enjoy a preferential capital gain rate. However, the *Corn Products* scenario could also arise today. If the corporation in Corn Products' position had otherwise unusable (and soon to expire) capital losses, it would be tempted still to seek capital treatment for the gain – in order to offset the capital losses against the gain, which it could not do if the gain was treated as ordinary income.

The foregoing planning considerations implicate the tax treatment of corporate capital losses. Code Sec. 1211(a) provides that a corporation can use losses from sales or exchanges of capital assets only to offset capital gains. What if a corporation has more capital losses than capital gains for a particular tax year? Code Sec. 1212(a)(1) provides that the excess losses may be carried back to the three preceding years, then (if any excess remains) carried forward to the five succeeding years.

Corporations may find themselves with excess capital losses because of unfortunate investments. In addition, features of the tax code may have an effect. For instance, what might otherwise be capital gain upon the sale of certain kinds of property may be converted into ordinary income by depreciation recapture provisions such as Code Secs. 1245 or 1250.[206] However excess capital losses are generated, their relatively short usable duration[207] means that corporations need to think strategically about how they will use the losses before they expire, whether by producing more capital gains or by "refreshing" capital losses.

Practice Tip: Capital losses can be refreshed by transactions that both yield capital gains now (producing something the soon-to-expire capital losses can be applied against) and built in capital losses that will accrue and therefore expire later. The net effect is to shift the capital loss to later years, thus avoiding their imminent expiration.

Example: One means by which such refreshing may sometimes be accomplished is by entering into a partnership in which the corporation with the soon-to-expire capital losses is allocated early on a disproportionately large

---

[204] *Corn Products Refining Co. v. Comm'r*, 350 U.S. 46 (1955).

[205] 350 U.S. at 50-53; *see also Arkansas Best Corp. v. Comm'r*, 485 U.S. 212, 219-23 (1988) (holding that *Corn Products* is not a general exception to Code Sec. 1221 but only an application of Code Sec. 1221(a)(1)).

[206] On the other hand, there are countervailing features, such as Code Sec. 1231, which can convert ordinary income into capital gain and capital loss into ordinary loss.

[207] As described in ¶ 204 above, the period during which net operating losses may be used substantially exceeds the period during which excess capital losses may be used.

share of the partnership's capital gains, to be balanced later by being allocated a disproportionately large share of the partnership's capital losses. Such an arrangement would have to be crafted to comply with the "substantial economic effect" and other anti-abuse rules.[208] In particular, because the arrangement would be tax motivated, the corporation would do well to scrupulously observe all formalities (that is, to make sure that actual behavior is consistent with how the deal is "papered") and to imbue it with genuine substance.

¶ 206 Credits

A number of income tax credits matter principally to corporate taxpayers. Here, we note four of them: (1) the foreign tax credit, (2) the general business credit and (3) the credit for prior year minimum tax liability.

.01 Foreign Tax Credit

Code Sec. 27(a) allows a credit against U.S. income tax for taxes imposed by foreign countries and U.S. possessions. The credit is extremely important to corporations that transact substantial amounts of business overseas. The credit occasions an enormous amount of planning, the success of which has caused Congress to enact statutes, and the Treasury to promulgate regulations, to curb perceived abuse.

Full exploration of the foreign tax credit is beyond the scope of this book.[209] In brief, the direct foreign tax credit allows U.S. citizens, domestic corporations, and in some cases foreign persons to credit foreign income taxes paid against U.S. income tax liability.[210] In some cases, foreign taxes paid in lieu of an income tax are creditable.[211] A so called indirect credit also is available. It deems foreign income taxes paid by certain subsidiaries of U.S. parent corporations as having been paid by the parent under certain circumstances.[212] Congress has tried a variety of mechanisms to curb perceived abuses of the credit, including (at various times) overall, per-country, and basket (various types of income) limitations.[213]

.02 General Business Credit

Code Secs. 38 through 45Q set out business related tax credits. Code Sec. 38, the general business credit, provides the framework for many of the other sections. Specifically, Code Sec. 38(a) allows a credit equal to the sum of (1) the business credit carryforwards carried to the tax year, (2) the current year business credit, and (3) the business credit carrybacks applied to the tax year.

Code Sec. 39 provides the rules governing carrybacks and carryforwards of unused business credits. Code Sec. 38(b) defines the current year business credit

---

[208] As to "substantial economic effect," see Code Sec. 704(b)(2); Treas. Reg. § 1.704-1; William G. Cavanagh, Targeted Allocations Hit the Spot, Tax Notes, Oct. 4, 2010, p. 89. Other anti-abuse rules are discussed elsewhere in this book including Part IV of this chapter.

[209] For detailed discussion, see Charles H. Gustafson, Robert H. Peroni & Richard Crawford Pugh, TAXATION OF INTERNATIONAL TRANSACTIONS, Chapters 5 & 7 (3d ed 2006).

[210] Code Secs. 901 & 906. A foreign levy is an "income tax" for this purpose if it is a "tax" and if its "predominant character" is that of an income tax in the sense of subtitle A of the Internal Revenue Code. Treas. Reg. § 1.901-2.

[211] Code Sec. 903; Treas. Reg. § 1.901-2.

[212] Code Sec. 902.

[213] Code Sec. 904. For additional discussion, see Paul R. McDaniel, Hugh J. Ault & James R. Repetti, INTRODUCTION TO UNITED STATES INTERNATIONAL TAXATION Ch. 6 (2005).

as the sum of 35 particular credits. The following provides a roadmap to these particular credits.

Investment credit: The general business credit includes the investment credit under Code Sec. 46.[214] The investment credit has expanded and contracted frequently over the decades, reflecting the tug between the desire to encourage economic growth and the need to protect the fisc. The current version of the investment credit is less robust than some prior versions. The current version is the sum of (1) a credit under Code Sec. 47 for expenditures to rehabilitate certain historic buildings and structures, (2) a credit under Code Sec. 48 with respect to certain kinds of energy credit, (3) a credit under Code Sec. 48A as to investments in qualifying advanced coal projects, and (4) a credit under Code Sec. 48B for investments in qualifying gasification projects. At-risk and other special rules as to the investment credit are set out in Code Secs. 49 and 50.

Work opportunity credit: The general business credit includes the work opportunity credit under Code Sec. 51. A related welfare-to-work credit is provided by Code Sec. 51A. Code Sec. 52 sets out special rules governing Code Secs 51 and 51A, including a rule treating "all employees of all corporations which are members of the same controlled group of corporations . . . as employed by a single employer" and allocating the credits among such corporations.[215]

> ***Things to watch for:*** The work opportunity credit was enacted in 1996. It is supposed to give employers incentive to hire disadvantaged individuals. Employers claim the credit by having job applicants complete Form 8850. The employer submits the form, within 28 days of the employee's start of work, to its state Department of Labor State Workforce Agency ("SWA"). The SWA checks the information and issues a certification of eligibility, which the employer needs to claim the credit.
>
> Many employers automated their job application processes, expecting that SWAs would allow 8850 forms to be submitted electronically. Most SWAs, however, do not accept the forms electronically, and those that do so typically require employers to keep original, signed hard-copy forms. This imposes substantial burdens on employers and undercuts their ability to take full advantage of the credit. The IRS Advisory Council has recommended that the IRS encourage the Department of Labor to mandate that SWAs treat hard copies of electronically signed 8850 forms as equivalent to original, signed hard-copy forms.[216]

Other employment credits: The general business credit includes a variety of other employment-related credits. They include: the empowerment zone employment credit under Code Sec. 1396, the Indian employment credit under Code Sec. 45A, the employer social security credit under Code Sec. 45B, the small employer pension plan startup cost credit under Code Sec. 45E, the employer-provided child

---

[214] Code Sec. 38(b)(1).

[215] Code Sec. 52(a).

[216] Internal Revenue Service Advisory Council 2010 Public Report, at 8-12. For IRS reaction to proposals of the

Advisory Council, see Nicole Duarte, *IRS Rejects Many Suggestions from Advisory Council*, Tax Notes, Nov. 22, 2010, p. 882.

care credit under Code Sec. 45F, the employee retention credit under Code Sec. 1400R with respect to Hurricanes Katrina, Rita, and Wilma, the mine rescue team training credit under Code Sec. 45N, and the differential wage payment credit under Code Sec. 45P.

Things to watch for: The Affordable Care Act[217] enacted in March 2010 created a new small business health care tax credit in Code Sec. 45R. The credit is designed to encourage small businesses to offer medical insurance coverage to their employees for the first time or to maintain coverage they already offer.

In December 2010, the IRS released guidance as to how to claim the credit for tax year 2010. The guidance consisted of new Form 8941 "Credit for Small Employer Health Insurance Premiums," instructions to the form, and a detailed Notice.[218]

Small businesses can claim the credit for 2010 through 2013 and for any two years thereafter. For 2010 through 2013, the maximum credit for eligible small businesses is 35% of premiums paid. Starting in 2014, the maximum credit grows to 50% of premiums paid.

The maximum credit goes to employers with ten or fewer full-time equivalent (FTE) employees and which pay average wages of $25,000 or less each year. The credit is entirely phased out for employers having 25 or more FTEs or paying average wages of $50,000 or more each year.

Fuel, energy, and conservation credits: The general business credit includes many such credits. They include the alcohol fuels credit under Code Sec. 40, the enhanced oil recovery credit under Code Sec. 43, the renewable electricity production credit under Code Sec. 40A, the low sulfur diesel fuel production credit under Code Sec. 45H, the marginal oil and gas well production credit under Code Sec. 45I, the advanced nuclear power facility production credit under Code Sec. 45J, the nonconventional source production credit under Code Sec. 45K, the new energy efficient home credit under Code Sec 45L, the energy efficient appliance credit under Code Sec. 45M, the portion of the alternative fuel vehicle refueling property credit to which Code Sec. 30C(d)(1) applies, the carbon dioxide sequestration credit under Code Sec. 45Q, and the portion of the new qualified plug-in electric drive motor vehicle credit to which Code Sec. 30D(d)(1) applies.

Other credits: The general business credit also includes the following additional credits: the research credit under Code Sec. 41, the low-income housing credit under Code Sec. 42, the disabled access credit under Code Sec. 44, the orphan drug credit under Code Sec. 44C, the new markets credit under Code Sec. 45D, the distilled spirits credit under Code Sec. 5011, the railroad track maintenance credit under Code Sec. 45G, the Hurricane Katrina housing credit under Code Sec. 1400P, and the agricultural chemical security credit under Code Sec. 45O.

---

[217] Patient Protection and Affordable Care Act, Pub. L. No. 111-148, 124 Stat. 119 (Mar. 23, 2010).

[218] Notice 2010-82, 2010 WL 4914634 (Dec. 4, 2010), modifying Notice 2010-44, 2010-22 I.R.B. 717.

Many of the above credits are small in amount and are hedged in by numerous conditions, restrictions, and limitations. Also, they have a variety of effective dates. Not all apply to each tax year.[219]

.03 Credit for Prior Year Minimum Tax Liability

Part VII of this chapter discusses the corporate alternative minimum tax ("AMT"). In brief, the AMT is a parallel tax to the regular income tax. It broadens the tax base by limiting various tax preference items and so can result in tax liability even when no liability would exist under the regular income tax.

Included among the AMT preference items are timing differences. Some income items that are taken into account later for regular tax purposes are accelerated for AMT purposes,[220] while some deductions taken into account earlier for regular purposes are deferred for AMT purposes.[221] These timing differences raise the specter of double taxation.

Code Sec. 53 guards against this possibility. It allows corporations to credit AMT liability paid in prior years and attributable to timing differences against later years' regular income tax liability. The credit cannot exceed the excess of regular tax liability (reduced for certain other tax credits) for the year over AMT liability for the year.[222] The credit can be carried forward indefinitely but cannot be carried back.[223]

¶ 207 AMT

.01 Generally

Congress became concerned about reports of taxpayers with high levels of economic income who, by virtue of strategic utilization of favorable statutory provisions, wound up paying little or nothing in federal income tax. To curb this, Congress enacted in 1969 a minimum tax on the tax preference items of individuals and corporations. The general idea was to return to the tax base tax-favored items that the taxpayer was using to excess.

The regime has undergone major modifications. The current version, the alternative minimum tax ("AMT"), took form in the 1980s but continues to be the subject of experimentation and refinement. In science fiction tales, one reads of alternative universes and dimensions. The AMT has something of that nature in relation to the regular income tax. The AMT is a virtually complete tax regime, having its own tax base, tax rates, carryovers, and credits. As a result, a corporation must in effect keep two sets of tax books, one for regular income purposes and one for the AMT. The principal steps in calculating the AMT liability of a corporate taxpayer are as follow:

---

[219] To further complicate the picture, some credits cease to exist and then return. For instance, the R&D credit lapsed after 2009, but is widely expected to be retroactively reinstated.

[220] Such as gain on installment sales. Code Sec. 56(g)(4)(D)(iv).

[221] Such as the excess of accelerated depreciation over straight-line depreciation. Code Sec. 56(a)(1).

[222] Code Sec. 53(c)-(f).

[223] Code Sec. 53(b).

(1) The corporation computes its regular taxable income and its regular tax liability in the usual fashion, using the normal exclusions, deductions, credits, and rates.

(2) The corporation then determines its alternative minimum taxable income ("AMTI"), which is designed to reflect the corporation's actual economic income better than the regular taxable income does. The starting point in calculating AMTI is regular taxable income; to that are added tax preference items under section 57 and the adjustments under sections 56 and 58.[224]

(3) An exemption amount is then subtracted from the AMTI. The basic annual exemption for corporations is $40,000. However, the exemption is subject to a phase-out. The exemption is reduced by 25% of the excess of AMTI over $150,000. The exemption disappears entirely once a corporation's AMTI exceeds $310,000.[225]

(4) The amount that remains after this subtraction constitutes the tax base for the AMT. That base is multiplied by the applicable tax rate, which is a flat 20% for corporations.[226]

(5) The liability thus calculated is reduced by any applicable AMT credits. These may include the AMT foreign tax credit and the general business credit.[227]

(6) If the tentative minimum tax (as calculated above) for the tax year exceeds the regular income tax for the year, the excess is added to the regular liability to determine the total tax liability for the year.[228]

Things to watch for: The AMT has added greatly to the complexity of the tax system; it can produce economic distortions; and it sets traps for the unwary. As a result, the AMT has never been popular. Both taxpayer groups and government panels have called for its abolition.[229]   Thus far, the huge revenue consequences of repeal have stymied such proposals, but additional such proposals are highly likely to be advanced in the future and may eventually succeed.

.02 AMTI

As noted above, the key to determining AMTI lies in the Code Sec. 57 preference items and the Code Sec. 56 and 58 adjustments. There are dozens of such preferences and adjustments, not all of which will be rehearsed here.[230] By

---

[224] Code Sec. 55(b)(2).

[225] Code Sec. 55(d)(2) & (3). A controlled group of corporations must share a single exemption. Code Sec. 1561(a)(3).

[226] Code Sec. 55(b)(1)(B)(i).

[227] Code Secs. 38(c), 55(b)(1)(B)(ii) & 59(a).

[228] Code Sec. 55(a). For this purpose, the regular income tax is "the regular tax liability for the taxable year (as defined in section 26(b)) reduced by the foreign tax credit under section 27(c), the section 936 credit allowa-ble under section 27(b), and the Puerto Rico economic activity credit under section 30A." It does not include increase of tax as a result of Code Secs. 45(e)(11)(c), 49(b), 50(a), or 42(j) or (k).

[229] *e.g.,* President's Advisory Panel on Federal Tax Reform, Simple, Fair & Pro-Growth: Proposals to Fix America's Tax System 85-87 (Nov. 2005).

[230] The IRS form on which AMT liability is computed (Form 4626) and the instructions to that form conveniently collect these items and adjustments.

way of illustration, some of the items of principal significance to corporations include the following:

- *Accelerated depreciation:* Depreciation is allowable for both regular and AMT purposes, but depreciation deductions typically are available in lesser amounts under the AMT than under the regular tax as to the early years an asset is held and used in business.[231] Often, this means reduction of the rate of depreciation for tangible personal property from 200% to 150%. When the asset is sold, the adjusted basis used for computing gain for AMT purposes reflects the AMT depreciation rate.[232]

- *Net operating losses:* In lieu of the Code Sec. 172 net operation loss deductions available for regular tax purposes, an alternative tax net operating loss deduction is allowed. In general, it is limited to 90% of AMTI (determined without regard to the deduction itself).[233]

- *Tax-exempt interest:* Corporations are required to include in their AMTI the interest they receive on certain otherwise tax-exempt bonds, so called private activity bonds (also known as industrial development or industrial revenue bonds) that are issued by states and localities but the proceeds of which are used by companies. The amounts required to be included are reduced by expenses as to the arrangements that would be deductible except for the fact that they produce normally tax-exempt income.[234]

- *ACE adjustment:* This is the most significant AMT adjustment for many corporations. The adjusted current earnings ("ACE") adjustment increases AMTI by 75% of the amount by which the corporation's ACE exceeds its AMTI determined without regard to the ACE and net operating loss adjustments. This adjustment is directed at large corporations that record big earnings for financial accounting purposes (causing share prices and perhaps incentive compensations to rise) but report little or no regular income tax.[235]

The preferences and adjustments used in calculating AMTI are computed after taking into account the percentage reductions reflected by Code Sec. 291 in calculating the regular income tax.[236] As a result of the way AMTI is computed, many corporations that have little or no regular tax liability do have AMT liability.

.03 Exemption for Small Corporations

Congress realized that the revenue potential of the corporate AMT involves principally large companies and that the AMT can impose excessive burdens on small businesses. Thus, in 1997, Congress exempted small businesses from the reach of the AMT. A corporation qualifies as "small" for this purpose if its average gross receipts were $5,000,000 or less for the three-year period ending with its first post-1996 tax year.[237] Thereafter, a corporation that initially met the test will

---

[231] Code Sec. 56(a)(1)(A).
[232] Code Sec. 56(a)(6).
[233] Code Sec. 56(a)(4) & (d).
[234] Code Sec. 57(a)(5).

[235] Code Sec. 56(g).
[236] Code Sec. 59(f).
[237] Code Sec. 55(e)(1)(B).

continue to be exempt from the AMT as long as its average gross receipts for the previous three years do not exceed $7,500,000.[238]

Should the corporation later have too large average gross receipts, it will lose its exemption and become liable for the AMT. However, certain preferences and adjustments will reflect only activities entered into after the corporation lost its exemption.[239] As noted in ¶ 207.03, corporations subject to the AMT may have an AMT credit under Code Sec. 53. That credit is limited for corporations that formerly were exempt from the AMT but later lost that exemption.[240]

¶ 208 Recent Legislation

Part of the response of the federal government to the economic woes of recent years has been enacting tax relief and stimulus measures. As of the time of the writing of this book, the latest of these measures are the Small Business Jobs Act of 2010 (hereafter the "Jobs Act"), signed by the President on September 27, 2010, and the Tax Relief, Unemployment Insurance Reauthorization, and Job Creation Act of 2010 (hereafter the "Tax Relief Act") signed by the President on December 17, 2010. Major provisions of those Acts are sketched below.

.01 Jobs Act

The title of the Jobs Act is somewhat misleading – important provisions of the Act affect large and medium-sized businesses, not just small businesses. The Act is estimated to provide $12 billion in tax incentives. The bulk of the provisions of the Jobs Act are favorable to taxpayers, but some revenue offsets are provided.

(a) Taxpayer-Friendly Provisions

The Jobs Act makes changes affecting individuals, C corporations, and pass-through entities. The focus below is on provisions that directly or indirectly affect corporations.[241]

- A prior stimulus measure, Code Sec. 168(k), created 50% bonus first-year depreciation. That measure had expired on December 31, 2009. The Jobs Act retroactively revived that provision and extended it through the end of 2010. The Jobs Act also extended (through 2011), the extra year of bonus depreciation for property with a recovery period of at least ten years and for tangible property used to transport property or people. Qualifying equipment must have been purchased and placed in service not later than December 31, 2010. The Act also created a new long-term contract accounting rule, permitting contractors to benefit from bonus depreciation even when contracts are not completed within the same year.

- To simplify asset accounting and for economic stimulus, Code Sec. 179 has long allowed taxpayers to expense (rather than to capitalize and depreciate)

---

[238] Code Sec. 55(e)(1)(A).

[239] Code Sec. 55(e)(2) & (3).

[240] Code Sec. 55(e)(5).

[241] The following are among the significant changes made by the Jobs Act that have principal significance for non-corporate taxpayers: (1) increased exclusion (100% exclusion) of gain from disposition of qualified small

business stock under Code Sec. 1202; (2) allowing retirement plan distributions to be rolled over to a designated Roth account; (3) allowing deduction of medical insurance costs in computing self-employment tax; (4) partial annuitization of non-qualified annuities; and (5) reduction (from seven years to five years) of the section 1374 S corporation built-in gain period.

the cost of acquiring certain assets. Congress has repeatedly tinkered with the expensing cap. Before the Jobs Act, for 2011, the expensing limit had been scheduled to drop to $25,000, reduced by the amount by which the cost of qualifying property placed in service during the year exceeds $200,000.

The Jobs Act liberalizes Code Sec. 179 in two ways for 2010 and 2011. First, it increases the expensing cap to $500,000 and the investment limit to $2,000,000. Second, the Act expands the types of property that qualify for Code Sec. 179 expensing. Such types now include qualified real property, that is, qualified leasehold improvement property, qualified restaurant property, and qualified retail improvement property. Expensing of qualified real property is capped at $250,000.

- Code Sec. 280F limits depreciation of certain kinds of property and imposes strict substantiation requirements. The Jobs Act eases the Code Sec. 280F limits as to passenger automobiles, and it removes cell phones and similar personal communication devices from the reach of Code Sec. 280F.

- Before the Jobs Act, Code Sec. 195 allowed taxpayers to elect to deduct qualified trade or business start-up expenses (as defined in Code Sec. 195(c)(1)) up to $5,000, reduced by the taxpayer's start-up expenses in excess of $50,000. For 2010, the Jobs Act raises the deduction cap to $10,000 and the phase-out threshold to $60,000.

- The Jobs Act extends to five years the carryback period for eligible small business credits, the sum of general business credits for the year as to eligible small businesses. This extended period applies to credits for a taxpayer's first tax year beginning after 2010. Eligible entities include corporations whose stock is not publicly traded and whose average annual gross receipts for the preceding three-year period did not exceed $50 million.

- Before the Jobs Act, Code Sec. 38(c) limited use of the general business credits to the amount by which the company's regular income tax liability exceeded its tentative minimum tax liability. As a result, small and medium-sized businesses often did not utilize the general business credit. The Jobs Act effectively allows small businesses (again defined by the $50 million average gross receipts standard[242]) to use business credits determined in years beginning in 2010 to offset AMT liability and, to a degree, regular tax liability.[243]

- Code Sec. 6707A imposes penalties on taxpayers that fail to disclose their participation in certain tax shelters.[244] The penalty was sometimes harsh to small businesses in that the penalty amounts could be disproportionate to the tax benefits claimed through the participation. The Jobs Act restructured the Code Sec. 6707A penalty amounts to alleviate this possibility.

---

[242] In applying this standard, the Code Sec. 448(c)(2) and (3) aggregation rules are applied.

[243] For detailed discussion of this change, see Dean Zerbe, Shane T. Frank, Dhaval R. Jadav & Benjamin E.

Yaker, *Small Business Jobs Act: Big Benefits for Small Businesses*, Tax Notes, Nov. 15, 2010, p. 827.

[244] Code Sec. 6707A is further discussed in Chapter 11.

Practice Tip: The restructuring is effective for Code Sec. 6707A penalties assessed after December 31, 2006. In anticipation of possible legislative correction, the IRS temporarily ceased collection Code Sec. 6707A penalties between June 2009 and June 2010. For penalties collected outside this time frame, the retroactive effective date of the Jobs Act change creates opportunity to file refund claims.

(b) Other Provisions

Although the Jobs Act is taxpayer-friendly on balance, the Act contains some provisions that taxpayers will greet with less enthusiasm. These provisions were inspired in part by the desire to find offsets for the revenue losses from the taxpayer-friendly changes and in part by general compliance concerns. The major changes include the following:

- Code Sec. 6271 and other sections impose penalties for failure to file accurate information returns with the IRS and failure to furnish statements to payees. The Jobs Act substantially increases the penalty amounts for such failures. The increases apply to both large and small filers (although in different amounts) and to both intentional and negligent failures. The strengthened penalties apply to information returns required to be filed after 2010.

- One of the major changes in the IRS Restructuring and Reform Act of 1998 was creation of the collection due process ("CDP") rules of Code Secs. 6320 and 6330. The CDP rules have proved highly controversial. Some think that the disadvantages (impeded tax collection) posed by the CDP rules exceed their advantages (greater fairness). The Jobs Act modifies the CDP regime in a limited respect. The IRS will now be permitted to proceed with levies against certain federal contractors before a CDP hearing is granted. This provision applies to levies made after September 27, 2010.

- The Code Sec. 861 sourcing rules are an important part of how the United States taxes international transactions. In the *Container Corp.* case,[245] the Tax Court applied the sourcing rules to hold that a foreign parent was not taxable by the U.S. on guarantee fees paid by a U.S. corporation. The Jobs Act prospectively overturns *Container Corp.* It amends Code Sec. 861 to treat amounts received for guarantees of indebtedness as U.S.-source income when it is paid by a U.S. person or by a foreign person with effective connection to a U.S. trade or business.

- Three times in 2010, Congress has raised the estimated tax payments required from corporations with assets of over $1 billion. The first increase was in the Hiring Incentive to Restore Employment ("HIRE") Act in March. The second was in House Joint Resolution 83, signed by the President in July. The Jobs Act is the third.[246]

---

[245] *Container Corp. v. Comm'r*, 134 T.C. No. 5 (2010).

[246] Another significant compliance provision in the Jobs Act is of principal significance to individuals. With stated exceptions, the Act requires certain persons who receive rental income from real property to file information returns with the IRS reporting payment of $600 or more to service providers for rental property expenses.

¶208.01(b)

Things to watch for: In the short-term, the Jobs Act on net benefits taxpayers. In the long term, however, the adverse provisions may prove more enduring. The major pro-taxpayer provisions are temporary, and whether – and for how long – they may be extended will depend on economic conditions. The anti-abuse and compliance provisions, however, typically are not temporary and are likely to remain in the Code for a long time to come.

.02 Tax Relief Act

Two of the major pieces of tax legislation of the George W. Bush Administration were the Economic Growth and Tax Relief Reconciliation Act of 2001 and the Jobs and Growth Tax Relief Reconciliation Act of 2003. Important pro-taxpayer provisions of those Acts were scheduled to expire on December 31, 2010. It was widely perceived that allowing expiration of all those provisions would have been both politically and economically calamitous.

A lame duck session following the November 2010 election considered compromise legislation agreed to by the President and congressional Republican leaders. Despite a filibuster and vociferous opposition from both the political Left and Right, that legislation was enacted in December 2010.

The most important provisions of the Tax Relief Act temporarily (for two years) extend major tax benefits for individual taxpayers.[247] However, the Act also contains provisions significant to corporate taxpayers, including the following:

- The Jobs Act extended bonus depreciation through 2010. The Tax Relief Act provided for 100% bonus depreciation for property placed in service from September 9, 2010 to December 31, 2011, and for 50% bonus depreciation for property placed in service in 2012. It also allows taxpayers to elect to accelerate some AMT credits in lieu of bonus depreciation.

- The Jobs Act increased the Code Sec. 179 maximum amount and phase-out threshold for tax years beginning in 2010 and 2011. The Tax Relief Act returns these amounts to the 2007 levels for tax years beginning in 2012.

- The Tax Relief Act extends numerous energy-related credits and other benefits.

- The Tax Relief Act extends various business credits, including the R & D credit, Indian employment credit, New Markets credit, and work opportunity credit.

- The Tax Relief Act extends a number of expensing rules, including for mine safety equipment, U.S. film and television productions, and environmental remediation costs.

---

[247] These include temporarily extending (1) the 2010 individual brackets, (2) repeal of the personal exemption phase-out and the itemized deduction limitation, (3) current capital gains and dividends treatment, (4) various personal credits, and (5) various educational incentives. The Act also provides AMT relief, limits the revived estate tax, and temporarily reduces employee-paid payroll taxes.

Chapter 3

Corporate Penalty Taxes[1]

¶ 301   **Accumulated Earnings Tax**
¶ 302   **Personal Holding Tax**

¶ 301 Accumulated Earnings Tax

.01 Corporations Subject to the Accumulated Earnings Tax

Code Sec. 532(a) of the Internal Revenue Code states that all corporations may be subject to the accumulated earnings tax unless specifically exempted in Code Sec. 535(b).[2] If a corporation can be formed or availed of by the shareholders to avoid personal income tax on corporate dividends, it may be subject to the tax.[3] This includes public and private corporations, subsidiaries, and foreign corporations. Those corporations whose shareholders are not subject to the U.S. federal income tax cannot be used to avoid that income tax, so they are exempt from the tax. Likewise, those companies not capable of accumulating earnings and profits are exempt from the tax.[4]

(a) Public Corporations

At least one corporation has argued that public corporations with widely dispersed shareholders should not be subject to the tax.[5] In *Technalysis*, the corporation argued that it could not have the required tax-avoidance intent because of its large and disparate shareholder population.[6] The court rejected this argument by relying on Code Sec. 532(c), which states that the number of shareholders does not determine whether accumulated earnings tax can apply to a given corporation.[7] The court further said that it was not even necessary for the officers and directors who make the decisions about the accumulation of earnings be shareholders.[8]

(b) Subsidiaries

Subsidiaries are also subject to the tax. If a subsidiary is found to have accumulated earnings and profits beyond its reasonable business needs, it will be taxed accordingly. A corporation cannot avoid the accumulated earnings tax by accumulating earnings and profits in a subsidiary. However, a subsidiary may accumulate earnings and profits for the reasonable business needs of its parent

---

[1] The authors wish to sincerely thank Ms. Rachel Jardine (University of San Francisco School of Law May 2012 Juris Doctor degree candidate) for her invaluable research and assistance with this chapter.

[2] Code Sec. 532(a).

[3] *Id.*

[4] *Id.*

[5] *Technalysis Corp. v. Comm'r*, 101 T. C. 397 (1993).

[6] *Id.* at 403.

[7] *Id.* at 404-405.

[8] *Id.*

company, and the parent company may accumulate earnings and profits for the reasonable needs of its subsidiary.[9]

(c) Certain Foreign Corporations

If a foreign corporation has shareholders that pay U.S federal income tax, it may be subject to the accumulated earnings tax.[10] Only those earnings derived from U.S. sources would be taxed.

Shareholders of a foreign corporation could pay tax on dividends from that corporation in one of two ways: (1) the shareholder is a citizen or resident of the U.S.; (2) the shareholder is a nonresident alien but pays U.S. income tax on corporate distributions because Code Sec. 871 of the Internal Revenue Code applies to the shareholder.[11] Code Sec. 871 governs when and how a nonresident alien pays taxes on income derived from the United States.

(d) Corporations Exempt from Accumulated Earnings Tax

Code Sec. 532(b) of the Internal Revenue Code lists those corporations that are exempt from the accumulated earnings tax. The language in the Code is straightforward. Three types of corporations are listed specifically, and there are two other types of corporations that are exempt through other tax authorities.

Personal holding companies are not subject to the accumulated earnings tax because their undistributed dividends are taxed under the Code Sec. 541 personal holdings company tax. Perhaps another way of looking at the personal holdings company exemption is to consider that the accumulated earnings tax places a tax on those earnings that are accumulated beyond the reasonable needs of the business. A personal holding company does not have business needs in the ordinary sense, so it would be very difficult to assess the accumulated earnings tax for personal holdings companies using the same rules applied to other corporations.

Companies that are exempt from tax under Subchapter F (Code Sec. 501 and following) of the Internal Revenue Code are not subject to the accumulated earnings tax. This subchapter exempts certain organizations from tax obligations because they are not profit-seeking.

Passive foreign investment companies are exempt from the accumulated earnings tax. According to Code Sec. 1297 of the Code a foreign corporation qualifies as a passive foreign investment corporation if 75% or more of its gross income for the taxable year comes from passive income, and if the average percentage of assets held for the production of that passive income is at least 50%.

Though not specifically mentioned in Code Sec. 532(b), companies whose shareholders are not subject to the U.S. federal income tax for corporate distributions may be exempt from the accumulated earnings tax.[12] The reasoning is that if the shareholders do not pay tax on the corporate distribution, the corporation

---

[9] *Id.*

[10] A foreign corporation is also subject to the tax if it has any owners of a beneficial interest that pay U.S. federal income tax.

[11] Treas. Reg. § 1.532-1.

[12] PLR 9422028 (Mar. 2, 1994).

cannot have the intent to avoid shareholder taxes on its distribution. This rule comes from a private letter ruling, so a determination that none of the shareholders is subject to the federal income tax must be very fact specific.

Finally, S corporations are not subject to the accumulated earnings tax; S corporations cannot accumulate income, and so there can be no excess accumulated earnings and profits to tax under the accumulated earnings tax.[13]

.02 Computing Accumulated Taxable Income

(a) In General

Code Sec. 535(a) of the Code gives the general formula for computing a corporation's accumulated taxable income. This accumulated taxable income is what is taxed under the accumulated earnings tax. The general formula for the accumulated taxable income (ATI) is as follows:

ATI = (Code Sec. 63 Taxable Income) – (Code Sec. 535(b) adjustments) – (Code Sec. 561 dividends paid deduction) – (Cpde Sec. 535(c) accumulated earnings credit)

The final computation of ATI should reflect the earnings and profits that the corporation could have distributed to shareholders, but did not.

(b) Taxable Income

The definition of taxable income for the purposes of the accumulated earnings tax is basically the same as the definition provided in Code Sec. 63 of the Code, but there are a couple of differences. The tax benefit rule and the rules for a short taxable year have special considerations for the accumulated earnings tax.

The tax benefit rule as generally applied requires that where a company deducts an expense that reduces its tax burden, and that expense is later recovered, the company must include the amount of its reduced taxes in income. However, if the expense did not change the amount of taxes the company would have paid, the recovery of the expense does not have to be included in taxable income. Sometimes a corporation may have taken a deduction in a previous year that did not reduce its income tax, but it may have reduced its accumulated earnings tax. With regard to the accumulated earnings tax, however, recovery of that expense does not have to be recorded as accumulated taxable income despite the fact that the company realized a tax benefit from the deduction.

However, sometimes a corporation takes a deduction that affects the amount of accumulated earnings tax paid but is not applicable to regular income tax (as opposed to simply not changing the amount of income tax). If that deducted expense is later recovered, then it must be counted as accumulated taxable income.

Generally when a corporation has a short taxable year, it annualizes its income under Code Sec. 443(b). However, under Code Sec. 536, accumulated taxable income is not annualized when a corporation has a short taxable year. Instead, the

---

[13] A corporation cannot avoid the accumulated earnings tax by making an S election; thereafter it cannot accumulate income during the S election years.

accumulated taxable income is computed based on the taxable income acquired during the short year. Code Sec. 535(b) adjustments are made as usual.

(c) Code Sec. 535(b) Adjustments to Taxable Income

Code Sec. 535(b) lists several deductions that reduce taxable income to an amount that more accurately reflects the corporation's excess accumulated earnings and profits. For the most part, these deductions are straightforward, and the Code clearly defines them. Occasionally the deductions are more complicated.

(i) *Code Sec. 535(b)(1) Taxes*

Under Code Sec. 535(b), corporations may deduct the following taxes that accrue during the taxable year: the federal income tax, war profits, and excess profits taxes of foreign countries and U.S. possessions. These taxes are deductible when they are accrued, regardless of the accounting system the corporation follows.[14] If a corporation contests a tax, that tax is not considered accrued, and so cannot be deducted. The personal holding company tax, excess profits tax,[15] and the accumulated earnings tax itself are not deductible.

(ii) *Code Sec. 535(b)(2) Charitable Contributions*

A corporation may deduct the value of all charitable contributions when calculating accumulated taxable income. The 10% limit imposed by Code Sec. 170(b)(2) does not apply to accumulated taxable income.[16]

(iii) *Code Sec. 535(b)(3) Special Deductions*

With the exception of Code Sec. 248, the deduction allowed under Part VIII (Code Secs.241-248) of the Internal Revenue Code are not deductible for purposes of calculating accumulated taxable income.[17]

(iv) *Code Sec. 535(b)(4) Net Operating Loss*

A corporation cannot deduct net operating losses from previous years, nor can it defer a loss to a future year, when calculating accumulated taxable income; this allows accumulated taxable income to more accurately reflect current dividend-paying power.

(v) *Code Sec. 535(b)(5) Net Capital Losses*

Corporations may deduct net losses from the sale or exchange of capital assets, regardless of the limit imposed by Code Sec. 1211(a). However, only those losses that occurred during the taxable year are allowable; no carryover losses can be deducted.[18] The capital loss deduction is further reduced by one of two ways. It may be reduced by the amount of the accumulated earnings and profits of the corporation as of the close of the preceding taxable year, or it may be reduced by the nonrecaptured capital gains deductions.[19]

---

[14] Treas. Reg. § 1.535-2.

[15] Treatment of the excess profits tax in this section is rather complicated. *See* Treas. Reg. § 1.535-2 for more details.

[16] Code Sec. 535(b)(2).

[17] Code Sec. 535(b)(3).

[18] Code Sec. 535(b)(7) does not apply to this subsection.

[19] Treas. Reg. § 1.535-2.

Net Capital Loss Deduction = (Net Capital Loss) – (accumulated taxable income at the close of the previous year)

Net Capital Loss Deduction = (Net Capital Loss) – (nonrecaptured capital gains deduction)

The deduction is reduced by whichever amount is smaller (thus allowing for a larger deduction). The nonrecaptured capital gains deduction is equal to the Code Sec. 535(b)(6) deductions of previous years minus the capital losses of previous years that were disallowed under Code Sec. 1211.[20]

Nonrecaptured Capital Gains = (Code Sec. 535(b)(6) deductions of previous years) – (Code Sec. 1211 disallowed capital losses of previous years)

Net Capital Loss Deduction = (Net Capital Loss) – (Code Sec. 535(b)(6) deductions of previous years) + (Code Sec. 1211 disallowed capital losses of previous years)

(vi) *Code Sec. 535(b)(6) Net Capital Gains*

A corporation may deduct net capital gains reduced by the taxes paid on those gains. For purposes of accumulated taxable income, net capital gains is the difference between capital gains for the taxable year minus the short-term capital losses for the taxable year. Under Code Sec. 535(b)(7), net capital losses of the previous year count as short-term capital losses in the current year.[21]

Net Capital Gains = (capital gains for the taxable year) – (short-term capital losses for the taxable year + net capital losses of the previous year)

The deduction is reduced by the amount of taxes the corporation paid on capital gains that year.[22] The calculation of capital gains on which taxes were paid is different from the calculation of capital gains for purposes of accumulated taxable income, but that does not matter.

Net Capital Gains Deduction = (Code Sec. 535(b)(6) net capital gains) – (capital gains taxes for the taxable year)

(vii) *Code Sec. 535(b)(7) Capital Loss Carryovers*

Like net operating losses, capital losses cannot be carried over or back for purposes of accumulated taxable income. However, a net capital loss for a taxable year is counted as a short-term capital loss in the next taxable year.[23] Remember that this rule does not apply to the calculation of the net capital loss deduction under Code Sec. 535(b)(5).

(viii) *Code Sec. 535(b)(8) Special Rules for Mere Holding or Investment Company*

Code Sec. 535(b)(8) contains special provisions for calculating the accumulated earnings of a holding or investment company. Mere holding or investment companies bear an increased risk of having to pay the accumulated earnings tax because they are assumed to have a tax avoidance purpose.[24] These companies should carefully note these special provisions.

---

[20] *Id.*
[21] Code Sec. 535(b)(7).
[22] Treas. Reg. § 1.535-2.

[23] *Id.*
[24] Code Sec. 533(b).

Capital losses are treated differently for holding and investment companies. Normally, companies may deduct the net capital losses in the taxable year when calculating their accumulated earnings.[25] However, holding and investment companies may not deduct net capital losses. Nor may they deduct the net capital loss from the previous taxable year.[26]

However, there is some good news for holding and investment companies. They may deduct the short-term capital gains for the taxable year. However, the amount of this deduction cannot exceed the amount of the capital loss carryover of that year. Code Sec. 1212 defines the capital loss carryover.[27] So, the greater the amount of capital loss carryovers, the greater the amount of short-term capital gains that can be deducted.

(ix) *Code Sec. 535(b)(9) Special Rule for Foreign Corporations*

Foreign corporations that file a U.S. federal income tax return generally calculate their accumulated earnings by the same method as U.S. corporations.[28] However, foreign corporations treat gains and losses slightly differently. Under Code Sec. 535(b)(6), only gains and losses that are connected with the conduct of a trade or business in the United States (and are not exempt from tax under a treaty) may be deducted. This makes sense; otherwise, a foreign corporation could shelter all of its U.S. derived income with foreign gains and losses.

(x) *Code Sec. 535(b)(10) Special Rule for Controlled Foreign Corporations*

When a foreign corporation is a controlled foreign corporation, it is allowed an additional deduction. The corporation may deduct the portion of its income that is included in the gross income of a U.S. shareholder. The definition of a U.S. shareholder for this section is found in Code Sec. 951(b).

(d) Code Sec. 535(c) Accumulated Earnings Credit

Another element in the calculation of accumulated taxable income is the accumulated earnings credit. This credit really functions as a deduction, as accumulated taxable income is reduced by the amount of the credit.[29] The purpose of this reduction of accumulated taxable income is to avoid penalizing a corporation for retaining the earnings and profits that are necessary for business.

The accumulated earnings credit is calculated by subtracting the capital gains deduction from the reasonably retained earnings and profits of the taxable year.[30]

Accumulated Earnings Credit = (reasonably retained earnings and profits of the taxable year) – (Code Sec. 535(b)(6) net capital gains deduction of the taxable year)

Retained earnings and profits equal earnings and profits for the taxable year minus the Code Sec. 561 dividends paid deduction.[31]

---

[25] This adjustment was discussed above, and is defined in Code Sec. 535(b)(5).

[26] This is permitted for other corporations under Code Sec. 535(b)(7)(A).

[27] Usually Code Sec. 1212 does not apply when determining capital loss carryovers for purposes of the accumulated earnings tax, but in this case it does.

[28] Foreign corporations only calculate those accumulated earnings that are derived from U.S. sources.

[29] Code Sec. 535(a).

[30] Code Sec. 535(c).

[31] *Id.*

Retained Earnings and Profits = (Earnings and profits for the taxable year) – (Code Sec. 561 dividends paid deduction)

The retained earnings and profits of previous years are instructive in determining whether the current year's retained earnings are for the reasonable needs of the business.[32]

The Code provides for a minimum credit in case the above calculation should be insufficient. The minimum credit equals $250,000 (or $150,000 in the case of certain personal service corporations) minus accumulated earnings and profits at the close of the previous taxable year.[33]

Minimum Accumulated Earnings Credit = ($250,000) – (previous year's accumulated earnings and profits)

The minimum credit is rarely helpful since most corporations have more than $250,000 in accumulated earnings and profits.

Personal service corporations calculate the accumulated earnings credit as outlined above, but if the minimum credit is used, $150,000 is the starting point rather than $250,000. A corporation may be a personal service corporation if it mainly provides services in the fields of health, law, engineering, architecture, accounting, actuarial science, performing arts, or consulting.[34]

Holding companies may only take advantage of the minimum credit; they may not use the deduction defined in Code Sec. 535(c)(1).[35] When calculating their deduction, holding companies use $250,000 as the starting point.[36] Courts have strictly construed the language of the Code when determining whether a corporation is a holding company.[37] A corporation must be "merely" or only a holding company.[38] Any side businesses disqualify it as a "mere" holding company.[39]

(e) Code Sec. 561 Dividends Paid Deduction

(i) *In General*

After the Code Sec. 535(b) adjustments are made and the accumulated earnings tax is calculated, the next step in computing accumulated taxable income is to subtract the dividends paid. Code Sec. 561 of the Code governs the types of dividends that are to be subtracted. For companies subject to the accumulated earnings tax, two kinds of dividends may be subtracted, dividends paid during the taxable year and consent dividends for the taxable year.[40] Code Secs. 562 and 563 of the Code further define what qualifies as a paid dividend for purposes of accumulated taxable income.

(ii) *Dividends Paid or Deemed Paid*

Code Sec. 562 determines which dividends paid during the taxable year qualify for the dividends paid deduction. Under Code Sec. 562, only those dividends

---

[32] Treas. Reg. § 1.535-3.
[33] Code Sec. 535(c)(2).
[34] Treas. Reg. § 1.535-3.
[35] Code Sec. 535(c)(3).
[36] *Id.*

[37] *See Dahlem Foundation v. Comm'r*, 54 T.C. No. 1566, 54 T.C. 151 (July 30, 1970).
[38] *Id.*
[39] *Id.*
[40] Code Sec. 561.

described in Code Sec. 316 qualify for the deduction. In order to qualify for the deduction, a dividend must meet two conditions: it must be paid out of the earnings and profits, either accumulated or current, and it must be proportional to the share ownership (in other words, preferential dividends are excluded from the deduction). Distributions made when a corporation is liquidated may also qualify for the deduction, but only if the distributions can be traced to the earnings and profits of the corporation. If a dividend is paid in property other than cash, the general rule is that the value of the property is the distributor's adjusted basis in the property.[41]

Some dividends may qualify for the dividends paid deduction even if they are paid after the close of the taxable year. Code Sec. 563 determines which dividends paid after the end of the taxable year qualify for the deduction. The dividend must be paid within two months and fifteen days of the close of the taxable year. This rule is quite liberal; it applies even if the shareholder who receives the dividend became a shareholder after the close of the taxable year. It applies even if the corporation is acquired by another corporation,[42] if the corporation becomes an S-corporation,[43] or if the corporation becomes a personal holding corporation during that two-and-a-half-month period.[44]

(iii) *Consent Dividends*

Consent dividends, defined in Code Sec. 565, allow the corporation to retain the amount of the dividend while treating it as a distribution. The shareholder must consent to this treatment of dividends, hence the term consent dividend. The shareholder treats the dividend as income, but the corporation retains it. The corporation treats the amount as a contribution to capital paid to the corporation. Under Code Sec. 561(a)(2), these consent dividends are deducted from the earnings and profits of a corporation.

(f) Other Considerations

The discussion of the requirements of Code Sec. 535 for the computation of accumulated taxable income is now complete. However, two other sections of the Code bear on what counts and what does not count as accumulated taxable income.

(i) *Code Sec. 936(a) Possession Income*

Code Sec. 535 makes no mention of possession income (defined in Code Sec. 936). However, Code Sec. 936(g) prevents possession income from being counted as accumulated taxable income. Therefore, accumulated taxable income does not include income that can be protected by the possession tax credit, nor can the possession tax credit be used to protect accumulated taxable income. The two are kept separate.

(ii) *Code Sec. 482 Bargain Income*

Under Code Sec. 482, the IRS may impute income to a corporation that received goods or services at a discounted price. Code Sec. 482 makes no mention

---

[41] The IRS ruled in a private letter ruling PLR 9335030 (June 4, 1993) that if the property is appreciated, the value is the fair market value at the time of distribution.

[42] *See* Rev. Rul. 72-345.
[43] *See* Rev. Rul. 72-152.
[44] *Id.*

of accumulated taxable income specifically, but a revenue ruling ruled that income allocated to a corporation under Code Sec. 482 should be included in accumulated taxable income.[45] This falls within the spirit of Code Sec. 482 since the purpose of that section is to prevent tax evasion.

(g) Filing a Return as a Foreign Corporation

(i) *Defining Accumulated Taxable Income*

A foreign corporation follows the same basic rules for calculating accumulated taxable income outlined above. The one major difference is that foreign corporations start with taxable income that comes from U.S. sources.[46] Foreign corporations are subject to the tax regardless of whether they have filed a U.S. federal income tax return.[47]

If a foreign corporation files a U.S. income tax return, calculate their accumulated taxable income by reducing their U.S. income by allowable adjustments, the dividends paid deduction, and the accumulated earnings credit. This calculation is very similar to the calculation of any other U.S. corporation.

However, if a foreign corporation does not file a U.S. income tax return, the corporation is not allowed to reduce their U.S. income by the Code Sec. 535(b) adjustments, the dividends paid deduction, or the accumulated earnings credit.[48] Foreign corporations therefore have a strong incentive to file a U.S. tax return if they are in any danger of the accumulated earnings tax.

(h) Filing a Consolidated Return

Filing a consolidated return does not change a corporation's exposure to the accumulated earnings tax. Accumulated taxable income is simply calculated on a consolidated basis.

(i) *Consolidated Dividends*

If a corporation is filing a consolidated return, the rules for the dividends paid deduction are generally the same. The most important exception deals with consent dividends. If a consent dividend is paid out to a member of the group filing a consolidated return, that dividend is not counted for purposes of the deduction. Only those consent dividends paid to non-members may be subtracted in the calculation of accumulated taxable income.[49]

.03 Determining the Corporation's Tax Avoidance Purposes

Before the accumulated earnings tax can be levied against a corporation, the IRS must find that the corporation had the intention of retaining its earnings so that its shareholders could avoid paying personal income tax on distributions received from the corporation. To understand the application of the accumulated earnings tax, one must therefore understand the scope of the tax avoidance that the accumulated earnings tax is meant to prevent as well as the means by which the IRS determines whether a corporation possesses this tax avoidance purpose.

---

[45] Rev. Rul. 78-430.
[46] Treas. Reg. § 1.535-1(b).
[47] Treas. Reg. § 1.532-1(c).

[48] Treas. Reg. § 1.535-1(b).
[49] Treas. Reg. § 1.1502-43(c)(1).

(a) Scope of Tax Avoidance Purpose

There are two main aspects to the scope of the tax avoidance purpose that a corporation must have to be subject to the accumulated earnings tax. First, tax avoidance only has to be one of the purposes for which a corporation retains earnings. Second, if the corporation intends for even one shareholder to avoid taxes, it may be subject to the accumulated earnings tax.

(i) *Tax Avoidance Need Only Be One of the Purposes*

A corporation may have many reasons for retaining earnings. However, if the tax benefit to shareholders is one of the contributing factors to the decision to accumulate earnings, the corporation will be subject to the accumulated earnings tax.[50] Tax avoidance does not even have to be the main purpose for retaining earnings. This position is tempered somewhat by the fact that mere knowledge that shareholders will receive a tax benefit from retained earnings is not enough to trigger the accumulated earnings tax.[51] If a corporation wants to avoid the accumulated earnings tax, it must show that knowledge of the tax benefit to shareholders did not contribute to the decision to accumulate earnings.

(ii) *Tax Avoidance Need Only Apply to One Shareholder*

Sometimes a powerful shareholder may act to block the distribution of dividends in order to avoid the personal income tax.[52] If the corporation permits even a single shareholder to retain earnings for that tax avoidance purpose, it will be penalized under the accumulated earnings tax. In the case of a subsidiary owned by a parent corporation, a subsidiary may be penalized if the shareholders of the parent company receive the tax benefit of the subsidiary's retained earnings. In this case, the subsidiary would be penalized for retaining earnings for the tax benefit of its parent corporation's shareholders, not the subsidiary's shareholders.

(b) Factors Indicating Tax Avoidance Purpose

Whether a corporation intends for shareholders to avoid income taxes by retaining earnings is a question of subjective intent. However, the IRS must analyze objective data to determine this subjective intent. The IRS presumes that unless there is a business purpose for the accumulated earnings, they are being retained for tax avoidance purposes. Factors indicating a tax avoidance purpose therefore focus on whether or not a corporation has a legitimate business need for the retained earnings, or if the retained earnings have been used for a legitimate business need.

(i) *Reasonableness of Accumulations*

The most important factor in determining whether a corporation accumulated its earnings for tax avoidance purposes is if the corporation has accumulated capital beyond its reasonable business needs.[53] Section .04(b) infra discusses what constitutes reasonable business needs. If a corporation has accumulated more earnings

---

[50] *Trico Products Corp. v. Comm'r*, 46 B.T.A. 346, 373 (1942).

[51] *U.S. v. Donruss Co.*, 393 U.S. 297, 309 (1969).

[52] *Atlantic Properties, Inc. v. Comm'r*, 519 F. 2d 1233 (1975).

[53] Code Sec. 533(a).

than it needs for business purposes, this is *prima facie* evidence that the corporation retained earnings for tax avoidance purposes.

(ii) *Holding or Investment Company Status*

If a corporation is merely a holding or investment company with no business activities, the IRS assumes any accumulated earnings must have been retained for tax avoidance purposes.[54]

(iii) *Failure to Pay Dividends*

A corporation's failure to pay dividends will count against them in an accumulated earnings tax analysis. If the corporation has accumulated earnings beyond its reasonable business needs, the lack of a dividend payment will strengthen the presumption that the corporation had a tax avoidance purpose.

A corporation can justify its lack of dividend payments by showing that it was unable to make a dividend payment (e.g. the corporation operates close to the margin). Corporations should consider issuing consent dividends if liquidity is an issue.

If a corporation accumulates a significant amount of earnings, it may use its history of good dividend payments to rebut the presumption of tax avoidance.

(iv) *Loans to Shareholders*

The fact that a corporation makes a loan to a shareholder unrelated to its business suggests that it has earnings in excess of its business needs. The corporation could have distributed the earnings as dividends, but chose instead to make a loan unrelated to the business. Loans to shareholders may indicate an intent to avoid taxes in two ways. First, a loan to a shareholder or a corporate expenditure for the personal benefit of a shareholder is not a reasonable business need. That money therefore represents earnings that were retained for non-business purposes, thus indicating a tax avoidance purpose.[55] Second, loans to shareholders may represent a tax-free substitute for dividends, further indicating a tax avoidance purpose.[56] Corporations may justify loans to shareholders if they can show a legitimate business purpose for the loans.[57]

(v) *Tax Rate of Shareholders*

The marginal tax rate of shareholders used to be another indicator of tax avoidance purpose. The theory was that the higher the marginal tax rate of the shareholders, the greater the incentive to avoid income taxes on dividends. However, now that qualified dividends are taxed at a lower rate, the shareholder tax rate is less useful. If tax rates change, the shareholder tax rate may become a more important indicator.

---

[54] Code Sec. 533(b).

[55] *Cummins Diesel Sales of Oregon v. Comm'r*, 321 F. 2d 503 (1963).

[56] Former Code Sec. 531 Audit Guidelines.

[57] *Peterson Bros. Steel Erection Co. v. Comm'r*, T.C. Memo 1988-381 (1988).

¶301.03(b)(v)

(vi) *Low Compensations to Shareholder-employees*

In the past, courts have held that low compensation to shareholder-employees suggests a tax avoidance motive.[58] The reasoning was that shareholders want to avoid taxes by receiving lower compensation. In the cited case, the lower compensation was accompanied by personal loans to the shareholder-employee. Certainly this scheme would allow the shareholder-employee to lower his tax burden. However, low compensation could also indicate that the corporation does not have the funds to pay a higher salary. This would suggest that the corporation has not improperly accumulated earnings.

(vii) *Unrelated Investments*

Like personal loans to shareholders, the fact that a corporation makes investments unrelated to its business may indicate that it has accumulated earnings in excess of its business needs; however, there may be many legitimate reasons for making investments. Investments may be made to improve the balance sheet of a company that has issued debt, and so investments should be considered in conjunction with long-term debt.

(viii) *Additional Factors*

Courts take a broad look at companies that contest the accumulated earnings tax. Many other various factors may be considered when determining the purpose for accumulating earnings. These factors are not considered independently; they are often seen as corroborating evidence for other factors that indicate a tax avoidance purpose. Such additional factors include a corporation's need to diversify or enter unrelated fields, documentation indicating business needs, whether a corporation is public or closely held, whether subsidiaries are controlled, and the ratio of a corporation's assets to its liabilities. The main lesson to be learned from this non-exhaustive list of additional factors is that courts examine companies holistically to determine a corporation's motivations for accumulating earnings and its ability to pay a dividend.

.04 Contesting the Accumulated Earnings Tax: Defining Reasonable Needs in More Detail

(a) Burden of Proof

In order to present a *prima facie* case, the IRS simply needs to show that a corporation has accumulated earnings and profits beyond reasonable business needs.[59] The corporation must bear the burden of proof to the contrary in court. The corporation can do this by proving by a preponderance of the evidence that the earnings were accumulated for reasonable business needs and not for the purpose of avoiding taxes.[60] Code Sec. 534 of the IRC lays out clearly the particulars of how the burden of proof shifts between the taxpayer corporation and the IRS.

Bear in mind that a mere holding company has a very difficult time meeting its burden of proof with regard to reasonable business needs because of the presump-

---

[58] *Herzog Miniature Lampworks v. Comm'r*, 481 F. 2d 857 (2d Cir. 1973).

[59] Code Sec. 533(a).

[60] Code Sec. 533(a).

tion that it has no business activities. In order to avoid this, a corporation should try to characterize itself as something more than a holding company.[61]

(b) Reasonable Needs of a Business

Though the accumulated earnings tax is meant to address the intent of the corporation, the factual inquiry centers on what constitutes the reasonable business needs of the corporation.[62] Whoever prevails on that question will prevail in court.

Code Sec. 537 of the IRC broadly defines the reasonable needs of a business. This broad definition lays out three categories of business needs: (1) reasonably anticipated needs, (2) Code Sec. 303 stock redemptions, and (3) excess business holdings stock redemptions. The reasonably anticipated needs of a business is the category most open to interpretation; Code Sec. 303 stock redemptions is a statutory category, and the excess business holdings stock redemptions category is a relic of the past. When it comes to establishing its reasonably anticipated needs, the corporation needs to provide objective evidence that the accumulated earnings are going to be used for legitimate business purposes. This evidence should be in the form of specific, definite, and feasible plans for the accumulated earnings.[63]

The regulations on Code Sec. 537 and the former Code Sec. 531 audit guide are very useful tools for determining what is a reasonable business need. These should be consulted for a more detailed discussion of reasonable business needs.

(c) Reasonably Anticipated Business Needs

(i) *Working Capital*

Working capital is the most significant component of reasonably anticipated business needs. A good grasp of accounting principles helps to understand the full nuances of working capital. The American Institute for Certified Public Accountants is helpful in providing technical definitions for the terms used in this section. This chapter simply provides a broad overview of the conceptual basis of working capital. Other sources should be consulted for a more technical description of how to calculate working capital.

Working capital is the amount of capital a corporation needs to operate during one operation cycle. Working capital may also include the amount needed to cover the regular and ordinary expenses that occur during the year but beyond the operating cycle. This capital is usually fairly liquid so it can be used quickly to meet obligations it incurs while producing the goods or services provided by the corporation. A corporation's actual net working capital can be calculated by subtracting current liabilities from current assets. However, when determining a corporation's reasonable business needs, working capital is calculated according to what the corporation needs, not what it has. If a corporation has a lot more working capital than it actually needs, this suggests that the corporation is inappropriately accumulating earnings, although the final determination depends on the other business needs of the corporation in addition to working capital.

---

[61] *See* 4 West's Legal Forms, Business Organizations Div. VII § 42.43 (3d ed. 2011).

[62] *See* Code Secs. 533 and 534.
[63] Treas. Reg. § 1.537-1.

The most common formula that courts use to calculate working capital is the Bardahl formula, so named for the case *Bardahl Manufacturing Co. v. Com'r*.[64] The formula is designed to calculate the reasonable costs of operating a business when its cash needs are the highest.

Reasonable working capital = (operating cycle expressed as a fraction of the year) (operating costs for the whole year)

The operating cycle is the length of time during which a business converts cash to raw materials, raw materials to inventory, inventory to sales and accounts, and sales and accounts to cash. It is calculated according to the following formula:

Operating cycle = inventory cycle + accounts receivable cycle – credit cycle

The inventory cycle consists of the period of time when expenditures are made but no cash is coming in. The accounts cycle is the period of time when the corporation makes a sale or receives an account and then collects the money due on that sale or account. The credit cycle is the average time that a corporation's accounts payable for the purchase of inventory remains unpaid, in other words, the length of time it takes for the corporation to pay up on the accounts related to inventory. The credit cycle is not always relevant to the final calculation of the Bardahl formula.[65] The final operating cycle should be expressed as a decimal of the length of the year (e.g. three months is expressed as 0.25).

When determining the operating cycle, the peak cycle approach (as opposed to the average cycle approach) is generally used, especially for seasonal businesses. This means that the length of the operating cycle is determined using numbers from the months during which the corporation is operating at peak levels. This approach ensures that the corporation will have enough capital on hand to cover the corporation's busiest period of operation. Some courts have been hesitant to use the peak cycle approach and instead prefer the average cycle approach, so it is important to verify the approach used in a given jurisdiction.[66]

After calculating the operating cycle of a business, the next step to calculating working capital is to determine the operating costs of a business during the whole year.

Costs of operation = cost of goods sold + operating expenses other than depreciation and amortization

Depreciation and amortization costs are not included in the working capital calculation, but they are included in the analysis of reasonable business needs when considering the costs of acquiring or replacing property.

The Bardahal formula has several limitations. First of all, the formula is only a guideline that exists for administrative convenience. *Suwannee Lumber Mfg. Co. v. Com'r*, T.C. Memo 1979-447. It should not be used for auditing purposes, and in the

---

[64] *Bardahl Manufacturing Co. v. Comm'r*, 24 TCM 1030 (July 23, 1965).

[65] *See Central Motor Co. v. U.S.*, 583 F. 2d 470 (10th Cir. 1978).

[66] *See W. L. Mead, Inc. v. Comm'r*, T.C. Memo 1975-215 (1975).

¶301.04(c)(i)

4th circuit, it cannot even be used as evidence, it is simply an argument based on evidence.[67]

Secondly, the Bardahl formula does not always take into account anomalies in a corporation's business operations. The working capital of the audited year may be unusually high or unusually low, but the formula is attempting to estimate the working capital needs of the following year, not the audited year. If there are any unusual circumstances relating to working capital in the audited year, perhaps numbers from a different year should be used.[68]

Thirdly, the Bardahl formula does not take into account the increased capital needs because of inflation or expansion.

Finally, the Bardahl formula is not easily adaptable to different types of businesses. It works reasonably well for businesses that produce goods of some kind, but it is much harder to apply to service businesses. Sometimes operating cycles can be estimated by looking at how long a company must pay out expenses before billing clients. The Former Code Sec. 531 Guidelines suggest that the formula be altered to "consider the average length of time required to perform on a contract rather than use the operating inventory turnover concept."[69]

Though the Bardahl formula is the most prevalent formula used to calculate working capital, other methods of calculating working capital exist. The First Circuit uses the Apollo formula.[70] In the past, rules of thumb were used. One rule of thumb was to allow working capital equal to one year of operating expenses.[71] Another rule of thumb determined working capital needs by allowing a ratio of current assets to current liabilities of 2.5:1.[72]

(ii) *Acquisition or Replacement Property, Plant, Equipment*

Acquisitions that represent an expansion or improvement of a business are reasonably anticipated business expenses. As always in the case of anticipated business expenses, there must be specific, definite, and feasible plans to acquire or replace property.

The amount of money reserved for acquisition or replacement property has no fixed formula, but it should be less than the depreciation of the assets to be replaced.[73] It seems that some courts are concerned with a double deduction of depreciation, and thus want to exclude it from other calculations of business expenses.[74]

(iii) *Acquisition or Expansion into Other Business*

A corporation may reserve money for an acquisition of or expansion into another business, but it must have real plans for doing so during the taxable year.

---

[67] *Bahan Textile Machinery Co., Inc. v. U.S.*, 453 F. 2d 1100 (4th Cir. 1972).

[68] *Materials Co. v. Comm'r*, 57 T.C. at 597, n. 9 (1972).

[69] Former Code Sec. 531 Guidelines at ¶ 638.2(3).

[70] *Appollo Industries, Inc. v. Comm'r*, 358 F. 2d 867 (1st Cir. 1966).

[71] *J. L. Goodman Furniture Co. v. Comm'r*. 11 T.C. 530 (1948).

[72] *Cadillac Textiles, Inc. v. Comm'r*, T.C. Memo 1975-46; *Bremerton Sun Publishing Co. v. Comm'r*, 44 T.C. 566, 586 (1965).

[73] Rev. Rul. 67-64.

[74] *See Battlestein Inv. Co. v. U.S.*, 442 F. 2d 87 (5th Cir. 1971).

The acquisition or expansion must be more than a passive investment, but should represent an actual increase in business activity. If the plans for acquisition or expansion are abandoned, the money reserved for those plans should be distributed to shareholders. Corporations can strengthen the argument that they need money for acquisition or expansion if they have a history of expansion or if they have an acquisition policy.

(iv) *Business Contingencies*

A corporation may reserve some money for unanticipated stresses on the business. However, corporations cannot reserve funds for extremely unlikely or unrealistic hazards. This category of reasonably anticipated business needs is not very well defined, but there are some guidelines. Code Sec. 537(b)(4) of the Code expressly allows businesses to self-insure for product liability loss.[75] The Secretary of the Treasury gives guidelines for what constitutes appropriate reserves for product liability loss insurance.[76] The Former Code Sec. 531 Audit Guidelines also provide a non-exhaustive list of approved contingencies for which corporations can reserve funds. This list includes: an actual or potential lawsuit and other legal liabilities, a possible business reversal resulting from the loss of a customer, accumulations to guard against competition, retirement plans for employees, and self-insurance plans (including key man life insurance and common types of risk insurance).[77]

Corporations may also accumulate funds to deal with realistic business contingencies such as an unsettled industry, particular industry dangers, or the threat of a strike. In the case of these contingencies, a corporation would do well to have evidence supporting the significant probability of these contingencies. It is less certain whether a corporation could accumulate funds to guard against more general economic ills such as adverse market conditions or a recession, though recent history suggests that it would be prudent to do so.[78]

(v) *Taxes*

Taxes and interest on taxes that a corporation knows will fall due (for example the accumulated earnings tax for a prior year) are considered reasonable business expenses. Taxes that are paid on a current basis are sometimes considered in the Bardahl formula for working capital under operating costs.[79]

(vi) *Long-term Debt*

Relieving a corporation of long-term debt is a reasonable business expense if the debt was taken on to begin with for legitimate business purposes. A corporation may therefore accumulate funds to lighten its debt load if the debt is linked to the corporation's trade or business.[80] Approved long-term debt includes repayment to bond holders if the repayment is made under contract obligations. In addition, the Former Code Sec. 531 Audit Guidelines suggest that a corporation should not have

---

[75] Code Sec. 537(b)(4).

[76] *Id.*

[77] Former Code Sec. 531 Guidelines at ¶ 637.4.

[78] BNA Portfolio 796-3rd § VII(B)(4) (2008).

[79] *Empire Steel Castings, Inc. v. Comm'r*, T.C Memo 1974-34 (1974).

[80] Treas. Reg. § 1.537-2.

¶301.04(c)(iv)

to go into debt for planned expansions or for the operations of the business. Therefore, the corporation can accumulate capital to meet those needs without penalty.[81]

Some cases have muddled the application of the principle that business-related long-term debt is a reasonable expense.[82] However, regulations and other authorities make it clear that such long-term debt obligations are reasonable business expenses.

(vii) *Stock Redemptions*

Like long-term debts, in order for stock redemptions to be considered a reasonable business expense, they must be for a legitimate business purpose as well. Usually the business purpose of stock redemptions is to maintain smooth business management. The corporation may redeem the stock of a troublemaking shareholder and thereby allow the continuing unimpeded functioning of the corporation. The Former § 531 Audit Guidelines suggest that redeeming the stock of a minority shareholder is acceptable, but redeeming the stock of a majority shareholder is not acceptable for business purposes, probably because a majority shareholder cannot interfere with business functions since the majority interests are also the interests of the corporation. In the case of publicly held corporations, stock redemption plans that are made for the sake of maintaining a good investor pool are a legitimate business need.[83] Another acceptable business need related to stock redemptions is insurance premiums to protect buy-sell agreements between the corporation and the shareholder.

As always, any business expenses related to future stock redemptions must be supported by specific, definite, and feasible plans in order to be considered a reasonable business need.

(d) Code Sec. 303 Redemption Needs

Code Sec. 537(a)(2) of the Code allows the corporation to retain funds to make stock redemptions under Code Sec. 303. Code Sec. 303 governs how a corporation redeems the stock of a shareholder who has died. The corporation may reserve the full amount that would be due under a Code Sec. 303 redemption, including all shares and any allocable death taxes and funeral expenses.

(e) Excess Business Holdings Redemptions

The excess business holdings redemption component of reasonable business needs is mostly a relic of the past. Under Code Sec. 537(a)(3), corporations that redeem stock from private foundations that held the stock on May 26, 1969 are allowed to count the that stock redemption as a reasonable business need. The reason for this is that private foundations who held stock at that time were sometimes forced to liquidate their stock if it was considered an excess business holding. Corporations would then have to redeem the stock from the private foundations so the foundations could liquidate their stock. The excess business

---

[81] Former Code Sec. 531 Audit Guidelines ¶ 637.5.

[82] *See, e.g., Smoot Sand & Gravel Corp. v. Comm'r,* 274 F. 2d 495 (4th Cir. 1960).

[83] *Technalysis Corp. v. Comm'r,* 101 T.C. 397 (1993).

holdings redemption provision in Code Sec. 537 simply ensures that a corporation will not be penalized for this forced redemption under the accumulated earnings tax.

.05 Conclusion

The accumulated income tax exists so that corporations cannot intentionally allow shareholders to avoid income taxes. Corporations may effectuate this tax avoidance purpose by retaining earnings rather than distributing them to shareholders.

When a corporation accumulates earnings beyond its reasonable business needs, this is evidence of a corporation's intent to allow shareholders to avoid taxes. In order to show that accumulated earnings are going to be used for reasonable business expenses, the corporation must have specific, definite, and feasible plans for the funds, and those plans must be legitimately related to the business.

If a corporation did accumulate earnings in order to allow shareholders to avoid income taxes, the corporation will be taxed at 15% on the accumulated taxable income. The accumulated taxable income represents the earnings that the corporation could have paid out in dividends, but did not. It is calculated by reducing taxable income by various deductions, by the accumulated earnings credit, and by the dividends paid deduction.

Most corporations are subject to the accumulated earnings tax with the specific exceptions of those corporations listed in Code Sec. 532(b), as well as corporations whose shareholders do not pay income tax and S corporations. Foreign corporations are only exposed to the tax with regard to income that comes from U.S. sources.

Holding companies are especially vulnerable to the accumulated earnings tax because they have very few business expenses. Corporations that provide services may have difficulty in calculating reasonable business needs because it is more difficult to determine their working capital.

The best way to avoid the accumulated earnings tax is to have well-documented plans that are related to the business for all of the retained income.

¶ 302 Personal Holding Tax

.01 Introduction

(a) Purpose

Code Secs. 541 through 547 of the Internal Revenue Code define the personal holdings tax. The personal holdings tax is a penalty tax imposed on personal holding companies that have not distributed enough of their income to shareholders. The purpose of the tax is to prevent people from accumulating income at a lower taxable rate by keeping it in a corporation. Individual taxpayers would have an incentive to do this as long as the corporate income tax rate is lower than the individual income tax rate. The personal holdings tax is structured so there is no advantage to letting dividends accumulate in the corporation rather than distributing it. The personal holdings tax adds a third level of taxation in addition to the corporate level and the individual level.

(b) Scope

The scope of the personal holdings tax base is potentially very broad; it applies to any corporation that meets the definition of a personal holding company, and there is no intent requirement. A corporation or its shareholders do not need to intend to avoid taxes in order to be subject to the tax. Only the corporations specifically excluded in the Code are exempt from the personal holdings tax.

The tax itself taxes the undistributed personal holding company income ("PHCI") at 15%, though this rate is only guaranteed until 2013.

.02 Defining a Personal Holding Company

The most important question in a personal holdings tax analysis is whether a corporation is a personal holding company. If a corporation is a personal holding company according to the Code Sec. 543 definition, it is subject to the tax.

The Code outlines two tests to determine whether a corporation is a personal holding company, the income test and the stock ownership test. The income test analyzes a corporation's sources of income to determine whether the income is passive. The stock ownership test determines whether a corporation is closely held enough to be considered a personal holding company. The income test is the most important test because most closely held corporations meet the stock ownership test.

(a) The Income Test

The income test is found in Code Sec. 542(a)(1) of the Code. Simply stated, if a corporation's ratio of PHCI to adjusted ordinary gross income is 60% or more, the corporation is a personal holding company under the income test. What is less simple is defining PHCI and adjusted ordinary gross income.

Code Sec. 543(a) defines PHCI. This section identifies certain kinds of passive income that may qualify a corporation as a personal holding company. Code Sec. 543(b) defines adjusted ordinary gross income.

(i) Determining Adjusted Ordinary Gross Income Code Sec. 543(b)(2)

There are three steps to determining adjusted ordinary gross income. The first step is to determine gross income under Code Sec. 61. The second step is to adjust gross income to get ordinary gross income by subtracting certain capital gains. The third step is to adjust certain categories of ordinary gross income that may also qualify as PHCI.

Gross Income Under Code Sec. 61

Generally the rules for calculating gross income are straightforward; Gross income is calculated under Code Sec. 61. However, some businesses have more complicated gross income calculations. Some of those complications may affect a corporation's personal holding company status.

Because a company's personal holding company status is determined by the ratio of personal holding company income to adjusted ordinary gross income, a company will want to make the adjusted ordinary gross income amount be as large as possible, and made the personal holding company amount as small as possible. So, when calculating adjusted ordinary gross income, corporations will want to count as many things as possible as income, and have as few deductions as possible. The tragedy is that in maximizing gross income in order to avoid the PHC tax, a corporation is of course increasing its regular income tax burden.

Service companies sometimes inadvertently lower their gross income for purposes of the PHC tax if they do not have a profit motive when they enter into a transaction.[84] In other words, if they are simply providing services at cost with no aim for profit, the receipts from that transaction will not count as income. Methods of accounting should be examined carefully to make sure that there are no adverse consequences for the personal holding tax.

Finally, insurance companies other than life insurance companies must follow special rules for determining gross income for the PHC tax. Insurance companies should follow Code Sec. 543(c). This section is rather straightforward, and references Code Sec. 832(b) of the Code.

Definition of "Ordinary Gross Income"

Once gross income has been calculated, the next step is to subtract capital gains and Code Sec. 1231 gains to arrive at ordinary gross income.[85] Though this step is fairly simple, two details bear highlighting. The first is that Code Sec. 1231 gains are always subtracted, even if they are not treated as capital gains. The second is that Code Sec. 1245 recapture is not subtracted, since it is not a gain. In other words, Code Sec. 1245 recapture is included in ordinary gross income.[86]

Definition of "Adjusted Ordinary Gross Income"

Code Sec. 543(b)(2) defines adjusted ordinary gross income. Adjusted ordinary gross income makes adjustments to certain categories of gross income that may qualify as PHCI. These categories include: rental income, mineral, oil, and gas income, and interest income

The first step to calculating adjusted income is to define the category of ordinary gross income to be adjusted. The second step is to reduce that income according to Code Sec. 543(b).

Adjustments to Rental Income

Rental income is rather broadly defined in Code Sec. 543(b)(3). According to that section, there are two components to rental income, compensation that a corporation receives for allowing another party to use property, and interest paid to the corporation on the sale of real property that the corporation held for sale to customers in the ordinary course of business. This broad definition is limited by five statutory exceptions to rental income, listed in Code Sec. 543(b)(3). They are:

---

[84] *Comm'r v. Kresge Dept. Stores, Inc.*, 44 B.T.A. 1210 (1941).

[85] Code Sec. 543(b)(1).

[86] Ways and Means Committee Report, H.R. Rep. No. 479, 88th Cong., 1st Sess. A-99–A-100 (1963); PLR 9611003.

¶302.02(a)(i)

PHCI as defined in Code Sec. 543(a)(6) (relating to the rental of tangible property to a 25% shareholder), copyright royalties, produced film rents, compensation for the rental of tangible property that is produced by the corporation if production of that kind of property is a substantial part of business operations, and active business computer software royalties. None of these categories is part of the rental income that will be adjusted.

Once gross income from rentals has been properly defined, it is reduced under Code Sec. 543(b)(2)(A) by four deductions. They are: (1) depreciation and amortization (this deduction only applies if the rental property is usually rented out for at least three years at a time), (2) property taxes, (3) interest on a mortgage, and (4) rent. Only those portions of deductions that are allocable to the source of the rental income should be deducted. It is possible for the rental deductions to exceed the gross rental income. In this case, rental income falls to zero; it never falls below zero.

Adjustments to Mineral, Oil, and Gas Income

Adjusting gross income from mineral, oil, and gas royalties under Code Sec. 543(b)(2)(B) is the next step in calculating adjusted ordinary gross income. Gross income from mineral, oil, and gas royalties includes income from working interests in oil and gas wells as well as royalties.

The gross income is reduced by the following four deductions: (1) depreciation, amortization, and depletion, (2) property and severance taxes, (3) interests, and (4) rents. Again, only those portions of deductions that are allocable to the sources of mineral, oil, and gas income may be deducted.

Like rental income, mineral, oil, and gas income cannot be reduced below zero. However, income from royalties and income from working interests in wells are treated separately for this purpose. The following example illustrates this:

A taxpayer corporation has $60,000 of income from royalties, and $40,000 of income from working interests. The taxpayer allocates $50,000 of deductions to each kind of income. Working interest income is reduced to zero, but royalty income is $10,000.

Exclusion of Certain Interest Income

Under Code Sec. 543(b)(2)(C), two categories of interest income are excluded from adjusted ordinary gross income. Because PHCI is a subset of adjusted ordinary gross income, these categories of interest income are also excluded from PHCI.

The first category is very narrow. The parsed language of Code Sec. 543(b)(2)(C) shows that there are five conditions to meet in order to exclude this kind of income:

(1) Interest received on a direct obligation of the United States;

(2) held for sale to customers;

(3) in the ordinary course of trade or business;

(4) by a regular dealer who is making a;

(5) primary market in such obligations.

¶302.02(a)(i)

The second category of excluded income is interest on a condemnation award, a judgment, or a tax refund; this exception protects corporations from unexpected swings in income.

(ii) *Determining Personal Holding Company Income Code Sec. 543(a)*

Personal holding company income is a portion of adjusted ordinary gross income. PHCI should represent income from passive activities. Much of the minutiae of the Code in this section are intended to distinguish passive activities from more substantial business activities. Because PHCI is a subset of adjusted ordinary gross income, if a certain kind of income is excluded from adjusted ordinary gross income, it is excluded from personal holding company income.

The Code language in Code Sec. 543(a) lists all the categories of adjusted ordinary gross income that constitute PHCI in separate subsections. Each subsection then continues to describe conditions that, if met, will exclude that income category from PHCI.

Dividends, Interests, Royalties, and Annuities

Code Sec. 543(a)(1) describes all the dividends, interests, royalties (with some exceptions), and annuities that are included in PHCI.

Dividends

Dividend income consists of Code Sec. 316 dividend income and Code Sec. 551 dividend income (relating to foreign PHCI taxed to US shareholders).[87] The regulations under Code Sec. 551 provide more detail for those corporations who have Code Sec. 551 income.

Corporations should bear in mind that no dividends received deduction is allowed when calculating the amount of PHCI for purposes of determining PHC status. However, the dividends received deduction is available for calculating the undistributed PHCI that will be taxed.

Interest

For purposes of calculating PHCI, interest is defined as any amount received for the use of money loaned if such amounts are included in gross income.[88]

Despite this straightforward definition, there are some idiosyncrasies to the definition of income when calculating PHCI. Some of those idiosyncrasies have already been discussed. It bears repeating, however, that interest that is excluded from adjusted gross income is also excluded from PHCI.[89] It also bears repeating that interest received on debts arising from the sale of real estate held primarily for sale to customers in the ordinary course of business is also not treated as interest. This is considered rental income under Code Sec. 543(b)(3).[90]

---

[87] Treas. Reg. § 1.543-1(b)(1).
[88] Treas. Reg. § 1.543-1(b)(2).

[89] See the discussion of adjusted ordinary gross income, supra, for the definitions of the excluded interest.

[90] See discussion of rent under adjusted ordinary gross income, *supra*.

¶302.02(a)(ii)

Second, the IRS may treat some amounts as interest even though they are not labeled as such in the contract. For example, small loan companies sometimes charge "investigation fees," and these fees may be counted as interest.[91] These sums are generally incidental fees or charges associated with a larger transaction.[92] Lastly, Code Sec. 61 imputed interest is also counted as interest for Code Sec. 543(a)(1).

Royalties

Income from royalties is generally counted as PHCI. However, some kinds of royalties get separate treatment in Code Sec. 543(a). Those are: copyright royalties, mineral, oil, and gas royalties, produced film royalties, and active business computer software royalties.

Like interest, sometimes income may be counted as royalty income even if the parties do not designate it as such. For example, sometimes a corporation will sell some property in exchange for a percentage of revenue from that property. Depending on the circumstances, this may be counted as royalty income or as gains from the sale of a capital asset.[93] Likewise, a court may decide that a transaction that was described as a joint venture actually creates royalty income.[94]

Distinguishing between royalties and rent can be very difficult. Generally, income from the right to use intangible property (as opposed to tangible property) is considered royalty income.

Royalties from certain qualified computer software companies may be excluded from PHCI. In order to qualify for the exception, a corporation must meet all the requirements listed in Code Sec. 543(d). Various private letter rulings have been issued clarifying what kind of income is "attributable to computer software," and thus excluded from PHCI.[95]

Determining the appropriate category for income from selling the use of property can make a great difference to the calculation of PHCI. This is because some categories of income may be excluded from PHCI all together if certain conditions are met. Excluding that income may end up determining a corporation's PHC status. That is why there is so much dispute about the nature of royalty income and what category it really belongs to.

Annuities

Annuities are included in PHCI.[96] However, they are only included in PHCI to the extent that they are included in gross income.[97] Code Sec. 72 governs the inclusion of annuities in gross income.

---

[91] *Seaboard Loan & Sav. Ass'n, Inc. v. Comm'r*, 45 B.T.A. 510 (1941).

[92] BNA portfolio 797-3rd § IV(E)(1)(b)(3) (2011).

[93] *See Reddler Conveyor Co. v. C.I.R.*, 303 F. 2d 567 (1962); *Dairy Queen of Oklahoma, Inc. v. C.I.R.*, 250 F. 2d 503 (1957).

[94] *See Wm. J. Lemp Brewing Co. v. C.I.R.*, 18 T.C. 586 (1952).

[95] *See* Code Sec. 543(d)(2)(B).

[96] Code Sec. 543(a)(1).

[97] Treas. Reg. § 1.543-1(b)(4).

¶302.02(a)(ii)

Rents

The adjusted income from rents as defined in Code Sec. 543(b)(3) is included in PHCI.[98] However, some corporations may exclude rental income from PHCI if they meet certain conditions.

Figuring out what is rent income and whether that income falls under PHCI can be a thorny problem. This is because some rent income is the result of substantial business activity, which Congress does not want to penalize under the personal holding company surtax, but other rental income is the result of passive activity, which is the kind of income that the personal holding company surtax is meant to regulate.[99] The mere use of the terms "lease" and "rent" do not determine whether a transaction is rental or otherwise.[100]

The rent that is defined in Code Sec. 543(b)(3) is the rent that is included in PHCI. This definition is fairly complicated. If a corporation has a particular question about the characterization of its rental activities, it should examine the case law and other tax authorities.

Sometimes a corporation may exclude its rental income. Code Sec. 543(a)(2) outlines a two-prong test to determine whether a corporation's rental income can be excluded from PHCI. First, adjusted rental income must be 50% or more of the corporation's adjusted ordinary gross income. Second, the corporation can only retain a portion of personal holding company income that equals 10% or less of ordinary gross income (rental income excluded). This ensures that most of the PHCI has been distributed in dividends.

The 10% prong bears more explanation. Here is the formula for the 10% rule:

(Sum of dividends) >(PHCI–rental income) - 10% of ordinary gross income

In this formula, PHCI is calculated without taking into account rental income (including rental income from a 25% shareholder). The sum of dividends includes dividends paid, dividends deemed paid at the end of the taxable year, and consent dividends.

If a corporation has not made enough disbursements to qualify for the rental income exclusion, it may issue a dividend (or a consent dividend) within 2.5 months after the close of the taxable year, in order to qualify for the rental income exclusion.

Mineral, Oil, and Gas Royalties

Mineral, oil, and gas royalties are part of PHCI. As with rental income, there are two questions to be answered in the analysis of mineral, oil, and gas royalty income.

First, what is the definition of mineral, oil, and gas royalty income? Second, how can a corporation exclude such income from PHCI?

---

[98] See above for a Code Sec. 543(b)(3) discussion of the definition of rent.

[99] See Sen. Rep. No. 1707, 89th Cong., 2d Sess. At 63 (1966).

[100] See, e.g., *White's Ferry, Inc. v. Comm'r*, T.C. Memo 1993-639.

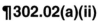

¶302.02(a)(ii)

The definition of mineral, oil, and gas income is fairly simple. Overriding royalties and production payments, in addition to other royalties, are also considered mineral, oil, and gas royalty income.

A corporation can avoid including these royalties by meeting three conditions: First, adjusted mineral, oil, and gas royalties is at least 50% of adjusted ordinary gross income (analogous the 50% test for rentals); second, the non-mineral, oil, and gas royalties PHCI equals no more than 10% of ordinary gross income; and third, the Code Sec. 162 deductions associated with the royalties (excluding the deductions for compensation of shareholders rendering personal service, and excluding deductions that are specifically listed in other sections), are at least 15% of adjusted ordinary gross income. The formulae for the 10% and 15% tests are as follows:

(PHCI–mineral, oil, and gas royalties) ≤ 10% of ordinary gross income

Note that total PHCI is used in this test, not the PHCI remaining after dispersals. 15% test:

(Code Sec. 162 deductions) – (Code Sec. 162 deduction of compensation for shareholders that provide personal service) – (Code Sec. 162 deductions that are also specifically listed in other sections) ≥ 15% of adjusted ordinary gross income

Copyright Royalties

Copyright royalties are included in PHCI. Copyright royalties consist of the right to use U.S. copyrights, and interest in U.S. copyrighted works. Code Sec. 543(a)(4) gives a good definition of copyright royalties.

A corporation may exclude copyright royalties from PHCI if it meets three tests, similar to the three tests for mineral, oil, and gas royalties. Under the 50% test, copyright royalties, except for copyright royalties on works created by any shareholder of the corporation, must equal at least 50% of ordinary gross income (note ordinary gross income, not adjusted ordinary gross income. This is because copyright royalties are not adjusted under Code Sec. 543(b)).

The 10% rule for copyright royalties is a little more complicated than previous rules. Non-copyright royalties PHCI must equal 10% or less of ordinary gross income. Though most income from copyright royalties is excluded from PHCI for purposes of this test, income from copyright royalties on works created by any shareholder that owns 10% or more of the corporation's stock is counted in PHCI. Like the 10% under mineral, oil, and gas royalties, dispersed dividends are not excluded from PHCI in this calculation. There is an added twist to this 10% rule, though; dividends are not included in PHCI if they are received from a corporation in which the taxpayer corporation owns at least 50% of the voting power and value.[101] The corporation paying the dividend must also meet the 50% rule and the 25% rule under this section.[102]

PHCI – (copyright royalties) + (copyright royalties from works created by any 10% or more shareholder) – (dividends from qualifying corporations) ≤ 10% ordinary gross income

---

[101] Code Sec. 543(a)(4)(B).   [102] *Id.*

Finally, in order to exclude copyright royalty income from PHCI, a corporation's Code Sec. 162 deductions must be at least 25% of ordinary gross income reduced by royalties paid or accrued and Code Sec. 167 deductions. The Code Sec. 162 deductions are calculated by excluding deductions for compensation to shareholders for personal services, deductions for royalties paid or accrued, and deductions specifically included in other sections.

(Code Sec. 162 deductions) – (deductions for compensation to shareholders for personal services) – (deductions for royalties paid or accrued) – (deductions specifically allowable under other sections) ≥ 25% of (ordinary gross income–royalties paid or accrued–Code Sec. 167 deductions)

Produced Film Rents

Produced film rents are a part of PHCI, unless certain conditions are met. The rules governing when income is excluded from PHCI are more lax for produced film rents than for other rental income.

The definition of produced film rents is in Code Sec. 543(a)(5)(B). It consists of income from interests that were acquired before the film was substantially created. The income that producers receive from the profits of the film is also considered produced film rental income, but only to the extent that the producer actively participated in the creation of the film.

There is only one test for a corporation to meet in order to exclude produced film rent from PHCI. Produced film rents must be at least 50% of ordinary gross income.

Rents from 25% Shareholders

Rents from 25% shareholders are PHCI, and under Code Sec. 543(a)(6), this rent is treated differently from the rental income described in Code Sec. 543(a)(2). Code Sec. 543(a)(6) defines rent from a 25% shareholder, and describes when that rent can be excluded from PHCI. The definition for rent from a 25% shareholder describes a very narrow category of income. It is compensation received for the use of, or right to use, the corporation's tangible property where the person who is entitled to use the property owns either directly or indirectly 25% or more of the stock value at any time during the taxable year. Broken into components, the definition looks like this:

(1) Compensation received for

(2) the use of, or right to use,

(3) the corporation's tangible property

(4) when the person who is entitled to use the property

(5) owns either directly or indirectly

(6) 25% or more of the stock value at any time during the taxable year.

Some components of the definition need more explanation. Stock ownership is determined according to Code Sec. 544 rules. The right to use corporate property may come directly from the corporation, or it may come from a subleasing arrangement.

¶302.02(a)(ii)

A corporation may exclude 25% shareholder rental income from PHCI if its PHCI is 10% or less of its ordinary gross income. Corporations need to make two changes to PHCI when calculating PHCI to determine its percentage of ordinary gross income. Firstly, 25% shareholder rental income is excluded as well as Code Sec. 543(a)(2) rental income from PHCI. Secondly, rental income from intangible property is also excluded from PHCI as long as: (1) that intangible property is used in connection with tangible property that is substantially owned by the corporation, and (2) the property is being used in an active business enterprise.

Personal Service Contracts

Income from a contract under which the corporation must perform personal services is included in PHCI. Only the income from a particular kind of personal service contract is only included in PHCI. Code Sec. 543(a)(7) defines that contract. The person who performs the services of the contract must be designated by someone other than the corporation, or designated in the contract. The contract may be written or oral.[103] Any income from the sale or disposition of the personal service contract also counts as PHCI. Personal service contract income is only included in PHCI if at some time during the taxable year, the person who is designated to perform the contract owns at least 25% of the stock value. Stock ownership is determined under Code Sec. 544. Another condition is that the designated person must complete the services of the contract without "important and essential" services from other people not designated in the contract.[104] It must be possible for the designated person to complete the contract without substantial help.

One purpose of this paragraph in the Code seems to be to prevent individuals who provide personal services from escaping taxation by keeping all the income from their services in a corporation of which they are the sole owner.[105] Those individual service providers who are incorporated should therefore take note that all of their income from service contracts likely qualifies as PHCI.

Estates and Trusts

Any gross income that a corporation receives under the rules of estates and trusts counts as PHCI.[106]

(iii) *The Sixty Percent Trust*

Once PHCI has been calculated, and adjusted ordinary gross income has been calculated, a corporation can determine whether it meets the first condition of a personal holding company: PHCI must be at least 60% of adjusted ordinary gross income. Even if PHCI is 59.999% of adjusted gross income, the corporation will not meet the 60% test. In close cases, corporations may take measures to adjust the numerator or denominator (legally, of course) to bring the ratio of PHCI to adjusted ordinary gross income below 60%.

---

[103] Rev. Rul. 69-299.
[104] Treas. Reg. § 1.543-1(b)(8)(ii).

[105] *See Gerald D. Roberts Consultants, Inc. v. Comm'r*, 62 T.C.M. 890 (1991).
[106] Code Sec. 543(a)(8).

This test is very objective. If PHCI is 60% or more of adjusted ordinary gross income, the corporation may be a personal holding company if it meets the stock ownership test as well. It is not necessary that the corporation intend to be a personal holding company. Corporations should therefore be careful not to accidentally fall into the definition of a personal holding company if they do not want to be exposed to the personal holding company tax.

(b) Meeting the Stock Ownership Requirements of the Personal Holding Company Tax

If a corporation meets the income test, meaning that its PHCI is at least 60% of its adjusted ordinary gross income, it must also pass the stock ownership test to be subject to the personal holding company tax. The stock ownership test is outlined in Code Sec. 542(a)(2). It states simply that more than 50% of the value of outstanding stock must be owned directly or indirectly by five or fewer people. Stock ownership is governed by Code Sec. 544. Stock ownership rules are important not only for determining whether a corporation meets the stock ownership test, but also for accurately calculating PHCI. Sometimes stock ownership affects whether a certain category of income counts as PHCI. This was discussed in the sections addressing the calculation of PHCI. By way of review, there are three categories of income that must satisfy a stock ownership test in order to be PHCI: income from personal services contracts, income from rental to a 25% shareholder, and income from copyright royalties. See the previous sections for a discussion of how stock ownership affects PHCI.

Determining stock ownership requires carefully considering three questions: How is the value of stock determined? How is the quantity of outstanding stock determined? How is stock ownership determined?

(i) *Valuation of stock*

What matters for purposes of the stock ownership test is not the percentage of shares that a shareholder owns, but the percentage of the value of the corporation that a shareholder owns. Share ownership and value ownership are related, of course, because when shareholders purchase shares, they are purchasing ownership of the corporation. Calculating what portion of company ownership is represented by each share of stock is therefore an important part of the stock ownership test. This is stock valuation.

Stock valuation depends on a few factors. One factor is the number of classes of stock that have been issued. The shares in different classes of stock may have different values. If only one class of stock is outstanding, the percentage of value ownership is the same as the percentage of share ownership. If there are more classes, the relative value of each class must be calculated. Preferential dividend rules, voting power, and priority rules may all affect the valuation of shares when there is more than one class of shares outstanding.

Another factor in the valuation of stock is whether and how to value options and warrants. Options and warrants give the holder the right to own shares in the

¶302.02(b)

future. Under some circumstances, the IRS may choose to treat options and warrants as stocks.[107]

Whether a corporation is public or private is another factor that greatly affects stock valuation. Valuing the stock of a closely held corporation will probably be difficult simply because the information necessary for valuing the corporation is not readily available. The Treasury Regulations give some guidelines about how to value stock.[108] The stock should be valued in light of all the circumstances according to factors such as: corporation's net worth, earning and dividend-paying capacity, appreciation of assets, and other factors.[109]

Fair market value of shares may often be helpful in determining stock value, but is not always the same as the book value of shares. If there is ever a large difference between the two (especially if this results in the corporation's book value saying it is not a PHC, but the fair market value would), the corporation must explain it.[110]

(ii) *Amount of Stock Outstanding*

The general rule for calculating the amount of outstanding stock is to tally the shares subscribed and paid for. It is not necessary to have issued certificates for all the outstanding shares.[111] Apart from the number of outstanding shares, there are a few special circumstances that might change the amount of outstanding stock.

Nominal indebtedness may be considered equity (and thus part of the outstanding stock) in some circumstances.[112] This may change how easy or hard it is to meet the stock ownership test. The rules for when indebtedness may be considered equity should be analyzed so a corporation does not inadvertently fall into PHC status.

Consistent with the notion that it is not share ownership that matters but value ownership, even if a corporation does not issue stock, if the value of its profits flow to one or more individuals, the corporation may be considered a PHC.[113]

(iii) *Ownership by Individuals*

After answering the questions of how much outstanding stock is there and how much that stock is valued, the final question is determining who owns it. Code Sec. 542 states that stock must be owned by individuals, but it may be owned directly or indirectly. Code Sec. 542 has no time factor to the ownership requirement; if at **any time** during the taxable year the ownership requirement is met, the corporation may be considered a PHC.

Code Sec. 542 sheds some light on who is considered an individual. Those corporations listed under Code Secs. 401(a), 51(c)(17), 509(a), or a trust organized under Code Sec. 642(c), are considered individuals. However, if a Code Sec. 501(c)(3) corporation is not private, it will not be considered an individual. This may be because Congress wanted to avoid penalizing public non-profits.

---

[107] Code Sec. 1504.

[108] Treas. Reg. § 1.542-3(c).

[109] *Id.*

[110] *Id.*

[111] Treas. Reg. § 1.542-3(b).

[112] Code Sec. 385.

[113] *Steven Bros. Found., Inc. v. Comm'r,* 324 F. 2d 633 (8th Cir. 1963).

¶302.02(b)(iii)

Code Sec. 544 lays out the rules for figuring out who owns stock in cases where ownership is ambiguous or not direct. These are the only codified attribution rules that determine stock ownership for personal holding tax purposes. The following subsection is devoted to an analysis of the attribution rules.

(c) Determining the Effective Ownership of Stock Under Code Sec. 544

The stock attribution rules of Code Sec. 544 are very important to the application of the personal holding company tax.[114] The rules determine whether a corporation is a PHC under the stock ownership test, the second requirement of the personal holding company definition.[115] Additionally, the rules affect the amount of a corporation's PHCI. These rules are therefore an important component of the personal holding company analysis. The attribution rules define which individuals own a corporation's stock in two different situations. The first situation is when a business entity and not an individual person owns stock. The second situation is when shareholders are related to each other somehow, either through family relationships or business relationships. In both of these situations, individuals may constructively own shares of a PHC.

An individual can constructively own shares of a PHC in one of five ways: (1) the individual has an interest in a corporation, partnership, estate, or trust that owns stock in the PHC, (2) the individual is partners with another shareholder, (3) the individual is related to another shareholder of the PHC, (4) the individual has an option to buy stock in the PHC, and (5) the individual owns convertible securities.

(i) *Constructive Ownership through a Corporation, Partnership, Estate, or Trust*

When a business organization such as a corporation, partnership, estate, or trust owns shares in a corporation, ownership is assigned to individuals according to their interest in the organization that owns the shares. Code Sec. 544(a)(1) provides the rules for attributing shares to the appropriate individuals.

A special note about trusts: if several trusts own the stock of a PHC, the trusts must have separate trustees in order for the beneficiaries of the trusts to be considered separately (look at the rules more carefully if this is a particular issue). Also, if a trust has a lifetime beneficiary and a remainderman, both will be considered to have an interest in the trust, and therefore both will be considered individual shareholders of any stock the trust might own.

This attribution rule always applies to corporations, even if it does not change a corporation's PHC status or the amount of PHCI.

(ii) *Constructive Ownership through Family*

Under Code Sec. 544(a)(2), an individual constructively owns all the stock of the shareholders who are related to him or her. This rule applies even if the family members constructively own the shares under Code Secs. 544(a)(1) or 544(a)(3) (those sections cover constructive ownership through corporation, partnership,

---

[114] See Code Secs. 542(a)(2), 543(a)(4), and 543(a)(6)-(7).   [115] Code Sec. 542(a)(2).

estate, trust, or options).[116] A family equals brothers and sisters (including half siblings), spouse, lineal ancestors (parents, grandparents, great-grandparents, etc.), and lineal descendants (children, grandchildren, great-grandchildren, etc.). Note the difference in the definition of a family from Code Sec. 318.

Family members only constructively own the stock of other family members if doing so would cause the corporation to become a PHC under Code Sec. 542(a)(2), or to have PHCI under Code Secs. 543(a)(4), (6), or (7).

(iii) *Constructive Ownership through Partnership*

Under Code Sec. 544(a)(2), each partner is the actual or constructive owner of all stock held by all other partners. For a definition of partnership, see Code Sec. 7701(a)(2). It is a broad definition that covers many types of organizations.

This rule applies to partners who only have minor interests, or who are limited partners.[117] It also applies when the shares are constructively owned by the partners under Code Secs. 544(a)(1) and 544(a)(3) (those sections cover constructive ownership through corporations, partnerships, estates, trusts, or options).[118]

Partners only constructively own stock of other partners if doing so would cause the corporation to become a PHC under Code Sec. 542(a)(2), or to have PHCI under Code Secs. 543(a)(4), (6), or (7).

Because of this partnership rule, the companies owned by private equity funds generally meet the stock ownership requirement of the PHC definition; accordingly these companies should be especially vigilant in their efforts to avoid the application of the PHC tax.

(iv) *Constructive Ownership through Options*

If an individual has the option to buy shares, he constructively owns those shares for personal holding company tax purposes. Options are only counted as stock if doing so would cause the corporation to become a PHC under Code Sec. 542(a)(2), or to have PHCI under Code Secs. 543(a)(4), (6), or (7).

(v) *Convertible Securities*

Code Sec. 544(b) states that convertible securities are treated as stock for PHC tax purposes. Similar to options, outstanding securities that can be converted into stock will be counted as stock, even if the securities cannot be converted during the taxable year. The owners of convertible securities will therefore be counted as shareholders. Sometimes different classes of convertible securities have different conversion dates. Those securities with a later conversion date do not have to be considered stock. Convertible securities will only be considered stock if doing so would cause the corporation to be a PHC under Code Sec. 542(a)(2), or to have PHCI under Code Secs. 543(a)(4), (6), or (7).

---

[116] Code Sec. 544(a)(5).

[117] *See American Valve Co. v. U.S.*, 137 F. Supp. 249 (S.D.N.Y. 1956).

[118] Code Sec. 544(a)(5).

.03 Computing Undistributed Personal Holding Company Income

Only the undistributed portion of PHCI is taxed.[119] A corporation may be a PHC, but may not have to pay any PHC tax because all of its PHCI was distributed. The rate is 15% of the UPHCI (until 2013).

(a) Taxable income

Code Sec. 545(a) outlines how to calculate undistributed PHCI. This calculation begins with taxable income, not PHCI. There will be some elements of UPHCI that are not in PHCI.[120] The next step is to make adjustments listed in Code Sec. 545(b), (c), and (d). Under certain conditions, foreign companies only have to pay taxes on the percentage of undistributed PHCI that is attributable to the U.S. shareholders' interests. Those conditions are: Less than 10% of the foreign corporation is owned by U.S. shareholders, during the last half of the taxable year. The highest percentage of shares owned by the U.S. shareholders at any point during the last half of the year is used to determine the percentage of undistributed PHCI that is taxed.

(b) Code Sec. 545(b) Adjustments to Taxable Income

(i) *Taxes*

To avoid a double tax on all taxable income, reduce taxable income by the federal income tax and by the excess profits tax (if any) accrued in the taxable year. For purposes of this deduction, the income tax is determined according to the accrual method, even if the corporation generally uses a different method of accounting.[121]

No deduction is allowed for contested taxes that are unpaid.[122] They may be deducted if the corporation pays the tax and then sues for a refund.[123] There is no deduction for accumulated earnings tax or for the PHC tax itself.

Foreign taxes and possessions taxes are also deductible.[124] If a corporation elects to take a foreign tax or a possessions tax as a credit, those taxes may not be deducted.

(ii) *Charitable Contributions*

Usually, corporations are only allowed to deduct charitable contributions up to 10% of their taxable income (known as the contribution base for purposes of deducting charitable contributions) each year, and any contributions beyond that limit can only be carried over a few years. Individual taxpayers are allowed to deduct a lot more each year, and the carryover period may be more generous as well. When determining the undistributed PHCI, corporations may deduct the same proportion of charitable deductions as individual taxpayers, but they must use the corporate carryover rules. In addition to the differences in the amount that may be deducted, the contribution base for the charitable contribution deduction is also

---

[119] Code Sec. 545 defines undistributed PHCI.

[120] Active business income is not included in PHCI, but it may be included in undistributed PHCI. Code Sec. 543(b)(1) provides that Code Sec. 1231 gains are subtracted.

[121] Treas. Reg. § 1.545-2(a)(1)(i).

[122] *Id.*

[123] *LX Cattle Co. v. U.S.*, 629 F. 2d 1096 (5th Cir. 1980).

[124] Code Sec. 545(a)(1).

¶302.03

different. Start with the contribution base that corporations usually use,[125] but only deduct a limited amount of expenses and depreciation of property.[126]

(iii) *Dividends Received Deduction*

PHCs are not allowed to take the dividends received deductions described in Code Secs. 241-249. However, the deductions listed under Code Sec. 248 still apply.[127] This means that while normally corporations do not have to pay taxes on dividends received, if a corporation is a PHC, it may have to pay taxes on those dividends if it does not distribute them to shareholders.

(iv) *Net Operating Loss*

Under Code Sec. 172 of the Code, a regular corporation is allowed to carry back or carry forward the deductions for net operating losses. However, when a PHC is calculating undistributed PHCI, the net operating loss deduction carryover rules as defined in Code Sec. 172 do not apply. Instead, a PHC may only carry forward the net operating losses of the previous taxable year.

The net operating loss of the previous taxable year is calculated without the advantage of the dividends received deductions. For a regular corporation, the cost of operations is weighed against its income reduced by the dividends received deductions.[128] The income of a PHC is not reduced by the dividends received deductions, so its net operating loss is less than that of a regular corporation's.[129]

(v) *Net Capital Gain*

Code Sec. 545(b)(5) allows net capital gain to be deducted.

Net capital gain – regular income tax from gain = deduction

Tax is deducted in other deductions, so it is excluded from the net capital gain deduction. Congress certainly does not want a double deduction for taxes. This deduction does not apply to any capital gains from coal or domestic iron ore.[130] For foreign corporations, the deduction must be connected to a trade or business within the United States. This prevents corporations from using foreign capital gains as a shield for undistributed PHCI.

(vi) *Certain Expenses and Depreciation*

The deduction for certain expenses and depreciation under Code Sec. 545(c)(6) is for corporations that own property that produces a tax loss. In other words, the property produces more deductions than profit.

The general rule is that a PHC may only take expense or depreciation deductions (Code Sec. 162 or Code Sec. 167, respectively) on that property to the extent that the PHC realizes income from that property. However, a PHC may deduct the full value of the losses if it meets certain requirements set by the IRS.

---

[125] Code Sec. 170(b)(2).

[126] The limit on the expense and depreciation deduction is described in Code Sec. 545(b)(6).

[127] Code Sec. 248 deals with the deduction of organizational expenditures.

[128] Code Sec. 172(d).

[129] The net operating loss of the previous year is calculated according to Code Sec. 172(c) minus the dividends paid deduction.

[130] Code Sec. 631(c).

This prevents corporations from creating a tax shelter within its operations by holding a piece of property that may be used for personal purposes.

Three conditions to allow complete deduction of expense and depreciation that must all be met: (1) income received from property was the highest possible, (2) the business in which the property was used was a bona fide profit-seeking business, and (3) reasonable expectation of profit from the property, or the use of the property was necessary for the business.

The burden of proof is on taxpayer; the court may only overrule IRS if the IRS' refusal to allow the deduction was arbitrary and an abuse of power.

(c) Code Sec. 545(c) Adjustments

This section outlines how to calculate undistributed PHCI from foreign corporations that are wholly owned by non-resident aliens for the last half of the taxable year. Undistributed PHCI for foreign companies is the income from personal service contracts, defined in Code Sec. 543(a)(7). This income is reduced only by those deductions that are attributable to the income, and is further adjusted by the requirements of Code Sec. 545(b)

(d) Dividends Paid Deduction

After Code Sec. 545(b) adjustments are made to undistributed PHCI, it is further reduced by the dividends paid deduction. This deduction is described in Code Sec. 561 and following, with some additional rules from Code Sec. 316.

Applying the deduction is rather straightforward. Figuring out what goes into the deduction can prove difficult. The following subsections describe what kind of distributions may be deducted under the dividends paid deduction.

(i) *In General*

There are three components to the dividends paid deduction: dividends paid during the taxable year, consent dividends, and carryover dividends.

Dividends are considered paid when the shareholders receive them.[131] Corporations should therefore distribute shareholder dividends in plenty of time for the shareholders to receive them before the close of the taxable year.

(ii) *Definition of Dividend*

Code Sec. 316 provides the general definition of a dividend. Simply put, a dividend is a distribution that a corporation makes to its shareholders out of its earnings and profits. These distributions can include stock redemptions as well as the more straightforward dividend payment.

Usually, the total amount of dividends that a corporation pays does not exceed its earnings and profits. However, a PHC may have undistributed PHCI that exceeds its earnings and profits. If this happens, a corporation may issue a distribution out of its undistributed PHCI, and this will count as a dividend.[132] This

---

[131] Treas. Reg. § 1.561-2(a). This applies to corporations that use the accrual method of accounting as well.

[132] Code Sec. 316(b)(2).

¶302.03(c)

allows a PHC to take advantage of the dividends paid deduction even when its distribution does not come out of its earnings and profits.

Code Secs. 316(b)(2)(B) and 562(b) of the Code also allow a PHC undergoing liquidation to count the distributions it makes pursuant to the liquidation as dividends, as long as it meets the following requirements:

(1) Must be a complete liquidation, not a partial one.

(2) Must occur within 24 months of the decision to liquidate.

(3) If a corporate shareholder is receiving the distribution, the whole distribution may be counted for the dividends paid deduction as long as the distribution is proportional to the shareholder's interest in the PHC[133] (a corporation cannot mask a preferential dividend in liquidation proceedings –preferential dividends do not count for the dividends paid deduction).

(4) If a non-corporate shareholder receives the distribution, the distribution counts for the dividends paid deduction as long as the PHC tells the shareholder that the distribution is being treated as a dividend, and as long as the distribution is proportional to the shareholder's interest in the PHC.[134]

(iii) *Preferential Dividends*

No preferential dividends may be included in the dividends paid deduction.[135] What is a preferential dividend? A dividend may be preferential in three ways: (1) certain members of a shareholder class get a bigger dividend than others, (2) certain classes of shareholders get bigger dividends than they are entitled to, or (3) certain shareholders receive their distributions earlier than others, even though the total distributions at the close of the year may be proportional.

The dividends of the preferred shareholder and the deprived shareholder are withheld from the dividends paid deduction.[136]

Originally enacted to prevent the manipulation of dividend distribution according to income tax brackets of the shareholders, no tax avoidance intent is necessary in order to exclude preferential dividends from the deduction.

(iv) *Distributions by Member of an Affiliated Group*

Code Sec. 562(d) states that if a PHC is part of an affiliated group and makes a distribution to one of its affiliates, that distribution may count for the dividends received deduction. In order to count for the deduction, the distribution must be considered a dividend even if the recipient was not affiliated with the PHC.

Bear in mind that if the recipient of the distribution is also a PHC, there will be tax consequences for receiving a distribution that is designated as a dividend. That dividend will be part of its PHCI.

---

[133] Code Sec. 562(b).
[134] Code Sec. 316(b)(2)(B).
[135] Code Sec. 562(c).
[136] Treas. Reg. § 1.562-2(a).

¶302.03(d)(iv)

(v) *Dividends Paid after Close of Taxable Year*

If a corporation finds itself in a tight spot and has too much undistributed PHCI on its books, it can make a distribution within two and a half months after the close of the taxable year. However, the corporation is limited in the amount it can distribute. It can only make distributions up to the amount of the remaining undistributed PHCI (after other dividends paid have been deducted), or up to 20% of the sum of the dividends actually paid during the taxable year, whichever is less. So if a corporation has made very few distributions during the taxable year, it would not be helped very much by this provision.

(vi) *Dividend Carryover*

Sometimes a corporation pays out more in dividends than it has in undistributed PHCI. When this happens, can a corporation carry forward the excess dividends to offset undistributed PHCI in a different year? The answer is yes. Code Sec. 564 lays out how this can be accomplished.

Excess dividends may be carried forward for two years. So, if a PHC still has undistributed PHCI after deducting the current year's paid dividends, it may look back to the previous two years and deduct any excess dividends that were paid during that period. This is a bit repetitive, but in the interest of clarity, the excess dividends paid during those two previous years must be the result of dividends actually paid that year, not dividends carried over from earlier years.

The PHC that is taking advantage of the dividend carryover rule in the current year need not have been a PHC in the previous two years. The excess dividends will be calculated as if it had been a PHC, even if it did not meet the definition for those years.

(vii) *Consent Dividends*

Sometimes corporations, for whatever reason, are illiquid and are not able to actually pay dividends to their shareholders. Congress does not want to put corporations in the position of having to borrow funds to pay dividends or pay the PHC tax, so it provided for the payment of consent dividends in Code Sec. 565. A consent dividend is an agreement between the company and its shareholders that the dividends will be reinvested into the company. Shareholders pay taxes as if they had received the dividend, and the company avoids taxes as if it had actually distributed the dividend. Consent dividends may be deducted under the dividends paid deduction.

Consent dividends may not violate the rules against preferential dividends. Another limitation on consent dividends is in Code Sec. 565(b)(2), which states that a consent dividend must qualify as a dividend under Code Sec. 316 if the full amount of the consent dividend were actually distributed on the last day of the taxable year. In order to be counted as a dividend for the dividends paid deduction, the distribution cannot exceed accumulated earnings and profits, or, in the alternative, a company's undistributed PHCI. This is to prevent shareholders from having to pay more in income tax than necessary.

¶302.03(d)(v)

(viii) *Deficiency Dividends*

Deficiency dividends distributed according to the rules of Code Sec. 547 may be deducted from undistributed PHCI. This is not technically a dividends paid deduction since it is permitted under Code Sec. 547 and not Code Sec. 561, but it serves more or less the same purpose. A PHC may only take advantage of this last-chance option if there was a good-faith failure on its part to plan for the PHC tax.[137]

Deficiency dividend may only be issued in response to a determination that it is a PHC; a forward-thinking company cannot anticipate PHC liability and distribute a deficiency dividend "just in case."

The deficiency dividend has two time limits: it must be issued within 90 days of the court determination of PHC status, and it must be issued before a claim is filed under Code Sec. 547(e).[138]

A deficiency dividend must be actually distributed, it may not be issued as a consent dividend.[139] The dividend must also conform to the restrictions on preferential dividends listed under the dividends paid deduction.

Though a deficiency dividend can eliminate the undistributed PHCI on which the corporation would otherwise be taxed, it cannot eliminate the interest that the corporation owes on the tax. See other tax authorities for the specific details of deficiency dividends.

.04 Considerations When Filing Returns for a Personal Holding Company

(a) Consolidated Returns

If a group of affiliated corporations file a consolidated return under Code Sec. 1501, they are treated as one corporation for purposes of the PHC tax. This could be for the benefit or detriment of an individual corporation, so choose your affiliates wisely. If a group as a whole fails the income test, all the individuals will have failed the income test, as well. However, there are some exceptions where the members of a consolidated group may be considered separately. Affiliated groups will be considered separately under two circumstances. The first situation is if one member of an affiliated group meets the "80% of 10%" income test. The second situation is if any member of the group is excluded from PHC status under Code Sec. 542(c).

The income test for ineligible groups, called the "80% or 10% test," is two-pronged. Firstly, any member of the group derives 10% or more of its adjusted ordinary gross income from sources outside the group. Secondly, at least 80% of that outside income is PHCI. Sometimes whether a certain sum counts as PHCI depends on the amount relative to the rest of adjusted ordinary gross income. When analyzing how much of outside income is PHCI, the outside income is kept separate from the rest of the income.

Identifying outside income therefore becomes very important to deciding whether an affiliated group can be considered on a consolidated basis. Dividends

---

[137] *See* Code Sec. 547(g).

[138] Deadline for the Code Sec. 547(e) filing is 120 days after the PHC determination.

[139] Treas. Reg. § 1.547-2(a)(3).

received by a parent corporation get special treatment under this test, so check tax authorities on Code Sec. 542(b)(4) to get a more detailed analysis.

If a group is eligible for consolidated treatment, it undergoes the income test to determine PHC status on a consolidated basis. Treasury Regs. §§ 1.1502-1 through 100 outline the methods for determining consolidated PHCI. Code Sec. 542(b) also contains requirements for consolidated filing. One thing to note on the treatment of dividends is that inter-group dividends are excluded from income calculations for PHC tax purposes. There are several revenue rulings on the topic of dividends issued within affiliated groups.[140] These rulings and other authorities should be consulted for a more detailed understanding of the consolidated treatment of dividends.

Many small details and changes can change the PHC profile of an affiliated group. If corporations are planning to file a consolidated return, they should plan and carefully scrutinize the tax situation of each affiliate to make sure there are no adverse tax consequences.

(b) The PHC Return

Filing a separate PHC tax return is not required. However, corporations need to provide certain information to the IRS with their income tax returns. They should include the items comprising adjusted ordinary gross income, and the names and addresses of all individuals meeting the stock ownership requirement. Corporations may include this information on a Schedule PH with Form 1120. Leaving out this information in a tax return may result in extending the statute of limitations on the PHC tax assessment.[141]

.05 Corporations Excepted from Personal Holding Company Status

The reach of the personal holding company tax is very broad because all that is necessary for it to apply is for the corporation to meet the definition of a personal holding company. There are some exceptions to this broad reach, however. Eight types of corporations are specifically exempt from the penalty tax, even if they otherwise meet the definition of a personal holding company. Code Sec. 542(c) identifies the exceptions to the personal holding company tax.

(a) Tax Exempt Corporations

Corporations that are exempt from taxes under subchapter F (Code Secs. 501-530) are also exempt from the personal holding company tax. Even if these companies are taxed under Code Secs. 511 and 514 because they have business or debt-financed income unrelated to their tax exempt purpose, they do not lose tax exempt status for purposes of PHC tax.[142]

(b) Banks

Banks as well as domestic building and loan associations are not subject to the PHC tax. Banks must have a legitimate business purpose in order to qualify for the

---

[140] *See, e.g.*, Rev. Rul. 71-531; Rev. Rul. 74-131; Rev. Rul. 79-60.

[141] *See, e.g., West Coast Ice Co. v. Comm'r*, 49 T.C. 345 (1968).

[142] Code Sec. 501(b).

exception.[143] Banks are defined in Code Sec. 581, and domestic building and loan associations are defined in Code Sec. 7701(a)(19). Banks are exempt from the PHC tax because a bank's business purpose requires that it have large stores of cash available.

(c) Life Insurance Companies

Life insurance companies are excluded from the PHC tax. In order to be exempt from the tax, the life insurance company must meet the Code Sec. 816(a) definition. This definition states that at least half the business must be dedicated to life insurance business. Like banks, the accumulated reserves of life insurance companies are essential to the company's ability to meet its fiduciary duty to its clients

(d) Surety Companies

The not well defined, surety companies are nevertheless excluded from the PHC tax. A company probably cannot escape the PHC tax by having a minor surety business on the side[144] or by merely being authorized to be a surety company.[145]

(e) Foreign corporations

Foreign corporations cannot be personal holding companies, so they are excluded from the PHC tax.[146]

(f) Lending or Finance Companies

A lending or finance company as defined by Code Sec. 542(d) is exempt from the PHC tax. In order to be exempt from the tax, the company must meet four conditions. These conditions are the 60% test, the 20% test, the business expense test, and the loans to shareholders limitation.

Code Sec. 542(d)(1)(A) 60% test: To meet this test, 60% of a corporation's ordinary gross income must be derived directly from active and regular conduct of a lending or finance business.

A lending or finance business consists of the following activities: making loans; purchasing or discounting accounts receivable, notes, or installment obligations; rendering services or making facilities available in connection with above activities; rendering services or making facilities available to another corporation involved in lending and finance as long as the two corporations are affiliates.

There are many caveats about what is or is not a lending or finance business. Case law and other tax law authorities should be consulted if this exemption may apply to a corporation.

Code Sec. 542(c)(6)(B) 20% test: Personal holding company income that is unrelated to its lending activities cannot be more than 20% of ordinary gross income. Code Sec. 542(c)(6)(B) provides guidance on what kind of lending activi-

---

[143] *Palm Beach Trust Co. v. C. I. R.*, 9 T.C. 1060, 1066 (1947). The bank in this case was organized to manage family members' mortgages.

[144] See Private Letter Ruling 9052036.

[145] *Mun. Secs. Co. v. Com'r*, 4 T.C.M. 120 (1945).

[146] Code Sec. 542(c)(5).

ties are not sources of PHCI. Code Sec. 542(d)(3) addresses how affiliates of lending and finance companies are treated.

Business-expense test: The business expense test gives requirements for the amount of deductions a lending or finance company must take. The test requires the sum of deductions listed in Code Sec. 542(d)(2) ("business deductions") that flow from the lending or finance business must be at least 15% of the first $500,000 of ordinary gross income from the finance and lending business and 5% of all the rest of that income. The following example illustrates the application of this test:

$600,000 of ordinary gross income comes from lending and finance activities. Business deductions must be at least $80,000: 15% ($75,000) of the first $500,000, and 5% ($5,000) of the remaining $100,000.

It is important to note that a corporation must meet the business expense test to qualify for the personal holding company tax exception as a lending and finance company.[147] If it meets all the other tests yet does not meet the business expense test, it is not exempt from PHC status.

Loans-to-shareholder limitation: A corporation cannot loan more than $5,000 at any one time during the taxable year to a shareholder who owns at least 10% of the corporation's outstanding shares.[148] Some corporations may try to characterize such activities as banking activities rather than lending or financing activities. However, such activities also do not qualify a corporation for an exception as a bank under Code Sec. 542(c)(2).[149]

(g) Small business investment companies[150]

In order for small business investment companies to qualify for PHC exemption, it must meet three conditions. It must: (1) be licensed under the Small Business Administration; (2) actively provide funds to small businesses under the Small Business Investment Act; and (3) ensure that no shareholder of the small business investment company has a 5% or more interest in a small business that receives funds from the investment company.

(h) Corporations in Title 11[151]

A company is exempt from the PHC tax if it is in Chapter 11 bankruptcy or if is involved in receivership, foreclosure, or other similar proceedings in a federal or state court. However, a company cannot avoid the PHC tax if its main purpose for getting involved in such a case is to avoid the PHC tax.

(i) S Corporations

Because S corporations are exempt from all taxes in Chapter 1 of the internal revenue code, it is also exempt from the PHC tax. This is true even if an S corporation might otherwise qualify as a personal holding company.

---

[147] Rev. Rul. 70-612.
[148] Code Sec. 542(c)(6)(D).
[149] Rev. Rul. 79-156.

[150] Code Sec. 542(c)(7).
[151] Code Sec. 542(c)(8).

Chapter 4

Nonliquidating Distributions

¶ 401 Introduction

The general idea that underlies taxation of nonliquidating distributions is that distributions of corporate profits are taxable as dividends, but distributions that are more akin to a return of capital are not. Although dividends are taxed to the recipient shareholder and are tax-neutral to the distributing corporation,[1] administrative convenience, if not an accurate measurement of shareholder income, is enhanced by looking at *corporate* earnings, rather than individual *shareholder* profit, to determine whether distributions represent profit and are dividends. Thus, Code Sec. 316 defines as a dividend any distribution made by a corporation to its shareholders "out of its earnings and profits accumulated after February 28, 1913."

If Code Sec. 316 limited dividends only to distributions made from accumulated earnings and profits, however, any inactive corporation that had deficits in earnings and profits because of historic losses might be used by shareholders of new, profitable, businesses to prevent distributions from being treated as dividends, because the corporation's accumulated earnings and profits deficits could cancel out the current year's earnings. As a result, Code Sec. 316 also defines as a dividend any distribution out of earnings and profits for the *current* year (or out of a combination of accumulated and current earnings and profits together). Nor can a corporation that has earnings and profits escape dividend treatment for its shareholders by announcing that any distribution is not "out of" those earnings and profits, since Code Sec. 316(a) states that "except as otherwise provided in this title, every distribution is made out of earnings and profits to the extent thereof."

Distributions that exceed corporate earnings and profits are treated as a return of capital, reducing the shareholder's stock basis under Code Sec. 301(c)(2), and

---

[1] With the exception that the distributing corporation recognizes gain on the distribution of appreciated property, Code Sec. 311(b).

nondividend distributions in excess of the shareholder's stock basis result in shareholder capital gain, under Code Sec. 301(c)(3).

¶ 402 Earnings and Profits: the General Concept

Since a distribution is a dividend only to the extent that it is made from the corporation's earnings and profits, a useful starting place in determining whether or not a distribution is a dividend is to understand the concept of earnings and profits. Basically, earnings and profits represent the corporation's real net economic profits that have not yet been distributed as dividends: if, and to the extent, that the corporation's actual net worth (excluding unrealized appreciation of corporate assets) exceeds the amounts with which the corporation was capitalized, it is likely that the excess value represents earnings and profits. Thus, earnings and profits are in many respects similar to the idea of retained earnings or earned surplus, with the primary difference being that earnings and profits cannot be reduced by corporate action that does not involve either the actual spending of money[2] or the making of an actual dividend distribution to its shareholders.[3]

Although the corporation is required to use the same accounting method for earnings and profits as it does for tax purposes,[4] to determine earnings and profits the corporation is required to make adjustments to its taxable income, because taxable income itself is in many respects not an accurate measurement of real economic profit. In most situations (other than unrealized or unrecognized appreciation or decline in value of corporate assets) where taxable income differs from real economic profit, taxable income must be adjusted, in determining earnings and profits, to bring it in line with economic reality.

.01 Areas Where Taxable Income Understates Actual Profits

Since earnings and profits are simply a measurement of the corporation's economic earnings and do not take into account any tax-based incentives, preferences, or remedial or redistributive provisions, corporations must include in determining earnings and profits items that are clear accessions to wealth that are specifically exempted or excluded from taxable income by the Code. Tax exempt interest income, nontaxable life insurance proceeds (to the extent the proceeds exceed the amount paid for the insurance), and nontaxable recoveries excluded under the tax benefit rule are the most obvious examples.[5]

In addition to including in earnings and profits real economic profits that may be excluded from tax, corporations cannot subtract from earnings and profits certain tax deductions that do not represent actual economic loss. As discussed later, corporations that receive dividends can deduct some or all of the dividend received for purposes of determining income tax liability,[6] but since those dividends received do enrich the corporation, they also increase earnings and profits by the

---

[2] In other words, the corporation cannot reduce earnings and profits by simply designating some amount as reserves, even though it may be able to reduce its retained earnings simply by making such a designation.

[3] The corporation's retained earnings, but not its earnings and profits, may be reduced by making a nontaxable stock distribution. See discussion in Chapter 5.

[4] Treas. Reg. § 1.312-6(a).

[5] *Ibid.*

[6] Code Sec. 243.

entire amount received.[7] As a result, the dividends received deduction cannot be taken into account in determining earnings and profits.

In addition, depreciation is limited to straight line for purposes of determining earnings and profits,[8] and depletion is limited to actual cost.[9] Neither net operating loss carryforwards or carrybacks nor capital loss carryovers are available for determining earnings and profits,[10] but this is only because all actual losses are fully accounted for in the year actually incurred for purposes of earnings and profits.[11]

.02 Areas Where Taxable Income Overstates Actual Profits

On the other hand, some expenses that do represent a real decrease in the corporation's economic profit are *not* deductible for tax. If outlays do represent a real expense, such outlays and losses will decrease earnings and profits regardless of their possible nonimpact on taxable income. For example, a corporation cannot deduct from its taxable income the federal income tax it pays, but since these payments leave the corporation with that much less of its actual profit, the corporation can decrease its earnings and profits by federal income taxes paid or incurred.[12] Other nondeductible expenses that do reduce economic profits and thus earnings and profits are travel expenses made nondeductible by Code Sec. 162 or by Code Sec. 274, expenses of producing tax exempt income, and nondeductible costs of certain term life insurance policies.

.03 Timing Differences between accounting for Tax Income and Earnings and Profits

As mentioned, a corporation is required to use the same accounting method for determining earnings and profits that it uses for determining taxable income, but the IRS mandates several timing changes from taxable income in order to more accurately reflect actual corporate profits. Among these are straight line, rather than accelerated depreciation of tangibles under Code Sec. 168,[13] capitalization and amortization, rather than immediate deduction, of Code Sec. 179 expenses,[14] certain adjustments to LIFO inventory accounting,[15] immediate inclusion of gain on installment sales, even if payments are not to be received until later,[16] and immediate reduction of earnings and profits for capital losses in excess of capital gains and for operating losses that generate NOL carryovers for income tax purposes.

¶ 403 Consequences of Distributions

.01 Corporate Level Consequences

(a) Gain on Distributions of Appreciated Property

Aside from impacting earnings and profits, which in turn relate to shareholder rather than corporate tax consequences (that is, whether a distribution is a dividend, a return of capital, or capital gain to the shareholder), the only significant

---

[7] Treas. Reg. § 1.312-6.

[8] Code Sec. 312(k).

[9] Code Sec. 312(n)(2).

[10] Treas. Reg. § 1.312-6(d).

[11] *See* ¶ 402.03 *infra.*

[12] Rev. Rul. 70-609, 1970-2 CB 78.

[13] Code Sec. 312(k).

[14] Code Sec. 312(k)(3)(B).

[15] Code Sec. 312(n)(4).

[16] Code Sec. 312(n)(5).

effect of a distribution to the distributing corporation occurs when the corporation distributes property other than, or in addition to, cash. A corporation that distributes appreciated property recognizes gain on the distribution as if it had sold the property to the distributee at its fair market value.[17] Significantly, a corporation that distributes property with a basis in excess of value does not recognize any loss on that distribution,[18] so that distributions of loss property are quite unpopular.

(b) Effect of Distributions on Current Earnings and Profits

Code Sec. 316 states that any distribution is a dividend to the extent that it is out of the current year's earnings and profits (1) computed as of the close of the taxable year, (2) without diminution by reason of any distributions made during the taxable year, and (3) without regard to the amount of current earnings and profits at the time the distribution was made. As a result, any transaction the corporation enters into during the taxable year, including a Code Sec. 301 distribution of property, can increase its earnings and profits for the current year, and thus increase the earnings and profits from which that distribution can be made. Code Sec. 312(b)(1) states that if a corporation distributes property with a fair market value in excess of its adjusted basis,[19] its current earnings and profits are increased by such excess. On the other hand, if the corporation distributes property with a basis in excess of its value (loss property), the distribution has no effect on the current year's earnings and profits, since such earnings and profits are determined "without diminution by reason of any distributions made during the taxable year."[20]

Thus, if X has no accumulated earnings and profits, current earnings and profits from operations (determined as of the close of the taxable year, and not taking into account the distribution) of $50,000, and distributes to its sole shareholder land with a basis of $20,000 and a value of $65,000. The distribution itself generates current earnings and profits of $45,000 (the excess of the value of the property over its adjusted basis) under Code Sec. 312(b)(1), so that earnings and profits determined as of the end of the year and without diminution by reason of any distributions is $95,000. Since current earnings and profits exceed the amount distributed,[21] the entire $65,000 distribution is a dividend.

---

[17] Code Sec. 311(b)(1). If the distributed property is subject to a liability, the value of the property is treated as not less than the liability it secures, Code Secs. 311(b)(2), 336(b).

[18] Code Sec. 311(a). It appears that Code Sec. 311(a) sets forth the general rule that the distributing corporation recognizes no gain or loss, and that Code Sec. 311(b) is merely an exception to that rule, when in fact, the more generally applicable rule is that enunciated by Code Sec. 311(b) (especially since corporations are deterred from actually distributing loss property). The reason for this apparently awkward statutory construction is not simply to mimic similar construction in Code Sec. 351, but because at one time Code Sec. 311(a) was the general rule, and distributing corporations recognized no loss or gain on distributions of property. Rather than simply eliminate the word "not" from Code Sec. 311(a), congress decided that it would be prudent both to add a new provision and

to leave the old rule in place when it came to allowing potential deductions for distributing corporations.

[19] Note that the property's adjusted basis for purposes of determining earnings and profits may be different from its adjusted basis for purposes of determining taxable income. This is especially likely to be the case if the property is being depreciated by the corporation. Since depreciation for earnings and profits purposes is slower than tax depreciation under Code Sec. 312(k), and the property's basis is decreased by any depreciation taken on the property, the depreciable property's basis will be decreased more slowly for purposes of earnings and profits, so its adjusted basis for earnings and profits will likely be somewhat higher.

[20] Code Sec. 316.

[21] If property is distributed, the amount of the distribution is the cash plus the fair market value of any other property distributed. Code Sec. 301(b)(1).

.02 Characterization of Distributions at the Shareholder Level

(a) The Amount Distributed

Not surprisingly, Code Sec. 301(b) defines the amount of any distribution as the amount of cash distributed and the fair market value (as of the date of distribution) of any other property distributed. If distributed property is subject to a liability, or if the shareholder assumes a liability in connection with the distribution, the amount of the distribution is, not surprisingly, the net value of all of the property distributed.[22]

(b) Shareholder's Basis in Distributed Property

If a corporation distributes property to a shareholder, the shareholder takes that property with a fair market value basis, regardless of what the corporation's basis had been in the property and regardless of whether the corporation recognized a gain (because the property had been appreciated) or whether the corporation was not able to recognize a loss in the property (under Code Sec. 311(b)).

(c) Allocation of Earnings and Profits Among Several Distributions

If current earnings and profits equal or exceed the amount distributed by the corporation during the year, then all such distributions are dividends. If there are earnings and profits for the current year but they are less than the total amount distributed during the year, then those current earnings and profits are allocated among any distributions made during the year according to the relative amount distributed and without regard to *when* the distributions were made.[23] Whether or not the rest of the distributions are also dividends depends on whether the corporation has *accumulated* earnings and profits. If accumulated earnings and profits equal or exceed the distributions not out of current earnings and profits, then all of the distributions are dividends. If there are some accumulated earnings and profits, but in an amount less than the amount distributed in excess of current earnings and profits, then those accumulated earnings and profits that do exist are allocated among the distributions made during the year in accordance with their chronological order, and the later distributions will be classified as other than dividends to the extent they exceed the current and accumulated earnings and profits available to be allocated to them.

To see this rule in context, assume that X Corp has no accumulated earnings, current earnings and profits of $120,000, and that it makes cash distributions of $90,000 in January, $60,000 in November, and $30,000 in December. Because current earnings and profits of $120,000 (determined as of the end of the year) are less than the total amount distributed ($180,000), they will be allocated among the

---

[22] Code Sec. 301(b) provides that the amount of any distribution shall be its value reduced by any liabilities assumed or taken subject to by the distributee, but that in no event shall the amount be reduced below zero. The net value of property distributed could be reduced to below zero only if the distributee assumed a recourse obligation of the corporation, since nonrecourse liabilities in excess of the property's value need not be paid. If a shareholder receives property but assumes a recourse obligation in an amount in excess of the total value received by the shareholder, the entire transaction would not be treated as a 301 distribution in any event. Rather than receiving something from the corporation, the shareholder is making a net contribution to the corporation. It would be treated as either a Code Sec. 351 exchange, or a contribution to capital from the shareholder to the corporation.

[23] Rev. Rul. 74-164, 1974 CB 74.

distributions by relative amount. Since 90/180 of the total is distributed in January, 90/180's (1/2) of the $120,000 (1/2 of $120,000=$60,000) total current earnings and profits are allocated to that distribution, so that 6/9 (2/3) of each dollar distributed in January is a dividend, and the other third of each dollar distributed is either a reduction of basis or capital gain, depending on the shareholder's initial stock basis. Similarly, since 60/180's, or 1/3, of the total is distributed in November, 1/3 of the total current earnings and profits ($40,000) are allocated to that distribution, so that 40/60 (once again, 2/3) of each dollar distributed in November is a dividend and the other third is either return of capital or capital gain. Finally, 30/180's, or 1/6, of the total $120,000 current earnings and profits is allocated to the December distribution so that, again, 2/3 of each dollar distributed in December is a dividend and the remainder is either return of capital or capital gain.

If the distributing corporation has no current earnings and profits but instead has a deficit in earnings and profits for the current year, any distributions made will nonetheless be dividends if and to the extent that there are accumulated earnings and profits available at the time of the distribution. Although current earnings and profits, if there are any, are determined "without regard to the time the distribution was made," if there is a current earnings and profits *deficit* and only *accumulated* earnings and profits, the timing of the distribution becomes more significant. The regulations provide that the current year's deficit is deemed to accrue ratably throughout the year, and that as it accrues, it eliminates accumulated earnings that were available at the beginning of the year.[24] Thus, for example, assume that X Corp has $100,000 accumulated earnings and profits and a $100,000 earnings and profits deficit for the current year. If X distributed $100,000 on January 1, the entire distribution would be a dividend, because none of the current year's deficit would have yet been accrued. If, instead, X distributed $100,000 at the end of the day on December 31, none of the distribution would be a dividend, because the entire current year's deficit would have been accrued, and the accumulated earnings and profits that were there on January 1 would have been entirely offset by the accrued current deficit. If, instead, X had distributed the $100,000 exactly half way through the year, $50,000 of that distribution would have been a dividend, since half of the accumulated earnings and profits would have been eliminated by the current deficit that would have accrued by that time.

.03 Final Corporate Level Consequences: Effect of Distributions on Following Year's Accumulated Earnings and Profits

While corporate distributions made during the year do not diminish the current year's earnings and profits available to turn those distributions into dividends, they do reduce the amount of accumulated earnings and profits as of the beginning of the following year. Generally speaking, earnings and profits as of the beginning of the year following a distribution equal (1) the total earnings and profits (current plus accumulated) available to be distributed, (2) reduced (but not below 0) by any dividends distributed during the year, and then (3) reduced by (a) any carried over accumulated deficit in earnings and profits (if the dividend was

---

[24] Treas. Reg. § 1.316-(2)(b).

entirely the result of current earnings and profits) or (b) any current deficit accrued after the distribution, if there is a deficit in earnings and profits for the current year. Basically, since dividends are distributions of earnings and profits, any dividend distributed reduces earnings and profits by the amount of that dividend. Any distribution that is not a dividend is by definition not a distribution of earnings and profits, and thus does not reduce earnings and profits. Thus, no distribution by a corporation can create or increase a deficit in earnings and profits. Accumulated earnings and profits deficits can exist because of operating deficits in prior years, and earnings and profits deficits can be increased by the current year's operating deficits.

The impact of distributions on reducing the earnings and profits that will be carried forward to the following year, while relatively easy to set forth, is not nearly as easy to deduce from the Code. Code Sec. 312(a) states that earnings and profits shall be decreased (but not below zero) by the amount of cash, the principal amount of any obligations of such corporation,[25] and the adjusted basis of any other property distributed. It is important to remember, though, that this section that *reduces* earnings and profits cannot be applied until calculating the following year's accumulated earnings and profits, because *current* earnings and profits are to be determined *without regard* to any diminution by reason of any distributions made during the year.

In addition, Code Sec. 312(a)(3), which suggests that earnings and profits are to be reduced by the adjusted basis of any property distributed, is immediately reversed in most situations by Code Sec. 312(b)(2), which requires that earnings and profits be reduced by the "fair market value" of distributed property rather than the property's adjusted basis for any property that had a built-in gain at the time of distribution. This makes sense because any appreciation in the distributed property was accounted for by increasing current earnings and profits under Code Sec. 312(b)(1) by the amount of gain inherent in the distributed property. Later decreasing earnings and profits by the value of the property means that the net result is that the corporation has added to its earnings and profits any economic profit in the distributed property, and then subsequently reduced its earnings and profits by the amount of the dividend distributed when it distributed the property.

To see how the increases and decreases in earnings and profits work together, assume that X Corp has accumulated earnings and profits of $100,000, earnings and profits for the current year of $50,000 (not taking into account the distribution) and in March distributes land with a basis (for both taxable gain and earnings and profits) of $40,000 and a value of $200,000. The distribution results in taxable gain and current earnings and profits for X of $160,000 (the excess of the property's value over its adjusted basis, giving X total current earnings and profits of $210,000. The entire distribution of $200,000 is a dividend (and the shareholder takes a $200,000 fair market value basis in the distributed property under Code Sec. 301(d)). X's earnings and profits carried over as accumulated to next year are $210,000 (total current earnings and profits) plus $100,000 (accumulated earnings

---

[25] Or the issue price of any obligations that have original issue discount.

and profits carried into the year) minus the $200,000 distributed, leaving it with accumulated earnings and profits of $110,000 as of the beginning of the next year.

The only exception to the notion that (next year's accumulated) earnings and profits are always reduced by the amount of dividends distributed during the year arises if a corporation distributes property with a basis (for earnings and profits purposes) in *excess* of its value. The accrued loss in that distributed property will never be recognized for income tax purposes,[26] but it is taken into account for earnings and profits purposes. This accounting for built in loss in distributed property is accomplished by decreasing the corporation's subsequent year's accumulated earnings and profits (but not below 0) by the basis of the distributed loss property. The net result is that earnings and profits for the following year will be decreased not just by the amount of dividends paid out, but also by the loss inherent in the distributed property. Since this loss represents a real economic loss, albeit one that cannot be used in calculating taxable income, it is appropriate that it reduce earnings and profits.

Again, an example may be helpful. Assume that X corp again has $100,000 accumulated earnings and profits, and $50,000 current earnings and profits, not taking into account the distribution. X distributes to its sole shareholder property with a basis of $140,000 and a value of $30,000. The property has built in loss, but that loss is not recognized under Code Sec. 311(a).[27] Total earnings and profits available for the distribution are $150,000 ($100,000 accumulated plus $50,000 current, not diminished by reason of the distribution) so that the entire $30,000 distribution is all a dividend. The corporation's accumulated earnings and profits as of the beginning of the next year are $10,000 ($150,000 available reduced by the $140,000 basis of the distributed property under Code Sec. 312(a).

If a corporation distributes property subject to a liability, both the amount distributed and the decrease in the following year's accumulated earnings and profits are equal to the net fair market value of the property distributed. Thus, assume that X has $120,000 current earnings and profits and distributes land with a basis of $100,000 and a value of $180,000, subject to a nonrecourse liability of $90,000. X first recognizes gain of $80,000 (the excess of the basis over the gross value of the distributed property) under Code Sec. 311(b), and increases its current earnings and profits by that same amount under Code Sec. 312(b), leaving X with total current earnings and profits of $200,000. Since the shareholder receives property with a net worth of $90,000 ($180,000 gross value less the $90,000 liability), the shareholder has a $90,000 dividend (because there is more than enough current earnings and profits), and takes the property with a gross fair market value basis of $180,000. X's ending earnings and profits are decreased by the dividend distributed, or $90,000; but the Code and regulations take a somewhat indirect path to this outcome. Code Sec. 312(c) states that in making the adjustments to earnings and profits required by Code Secs. 312(a) and (b), "proper adjustment" shall be made for any liabilities to which the distributed property is

---

[26] See discussion of 311, *infra*.

[27] Because the loss on the distributed property goes permanently unrecognized, the distribution of loss prop-

erty is rarely a good idea regardless of its effect on earnings and profits.

subject, or any corporate liabilities assumed by the distributee shareholder. The regulations in turn explain that this proper adjustment requires that the reduction in earnings and profits (for purposes of determining the subsequent year's accumulated earnings and profits) must be reduced by the amount of any liability to which the distributed property was subject (or which was assumed by the shareholder in the distribution). Since that reduction in the corporation's earnings and profits would otherwise equal the gross value of the property, the reduction in earnings and profits for next year is instead the *net* value of the distributed property, which is also the same as the amount distributed[28] and the amount of the dividend, assuming sufficient earnings and profits.[29]

¶ 404 Constructive Dividends

Dividends are taxed in full to noncorporate shareholders, and provide no deduction to the corporation that issues the dividend. As a result, it behooves the corporation that wants to get cash or property into the hands of its noncorporate shareholder to make that transfer by way of almost anything other than a dividend. Of course one way to avoid characterization of payments as dividends is to avoid characterizing the interest in the corporation as equity. Classification of interests in corporations as either debt or equity is discussed at length elsewhere.[30] But characterization of an interest as debt is by no means the only way for corporate payers to avoid characterization of payments as dividends. Corporations and their shareholders have sought many ways to make payments from the corporations to their shareholders either deductible to the paying corporation, nontaxable to the recipient shareholder, or both.

Payments from corporations to shareholders are deductible to the paying corporation (although includable as ordinary income to the recipient shareholder) if they are compensation, and corporations in the past have attempted to so characterize what would otherwise be Code Sec. 301 distributions. Code Sec. 301 provides that it governs payments made by a corporation to a shareholder with respect to its stock, and any payment made by a corporation to a shareholder which is made because of the payee's stock ownership will be treated under Code Sec. 301 regardless of whether it is explicitly designated as such. As a result, if a corporation makes pro rata payments to its shareholders equal to 10% of the value of each share, but designates the payment to one or two of the shareholders as "compensation," the IRS is quite likely to replace that compensation label with one that reads dividend.[31] The problem for the IRS is that it not always simple to determine if, and to what extent, any payment made to a shareholder is in fact compensation rather

---

[28] Code Sec. 301(b)(2).

[29] Treas. Reg. §1.312-3. If the corporation distributes property that has declined in value, the proper charge to earnings and profits would be the excess of the distributed property's basis over the liability. Treas. Reg. §1.312-3 also seems to require that the charge to earnings and profits be "increased by the amount of gain recognized to the corporation under Section 311(b)." That part of the regulation is in fact inoperative, because it has been superseded by Code Sec. 312(b)(2), which works the appropriate result without reference to the regulation.

[30] *See* ¶ 405.02(c).

[31] In fact, the IRS need not actually characterize the payment as a dividend rather than as compensation if it can instead show that the "compensation," albeit not a 301 distribution, is "unreasonable," and for that reason not deductible under Code Sec. 162. In some cases it might be easier for the IRS to show merely that compensation is unreasonable; in others, such as the above example, it might be easier to show that the payment is not compensation at all, but is instead a dividend.

than a distribution of profits. In most cases where the issue arises, the payments are not pro rata and are not quite so easily seen as dividends. Often there is a payment to a single owner-employee. In other cases payments may benefit the owner indirectly, such as by way of "compensation" to the owner's children. In cases where payments initially characterized as compensation are recharacterized by the IRS as nondeductible dividends, the courts have used numerous factors to determine the ultimate tax treatment of the payments.[32]

Corporations under the control of a single shareholder-employee may also attempt to go a step beyond characterizing payments for the benefit of the shareholder as compensation, to characterizing them as payment of shareholder-employee business expenses. If successful in so doing, the result is not only a deduction at the corporate level, but also exclusion at the shareholder-recipient level. Examples may include meal, transportation, entertainment, housing or other expenses that are personal rather than business expenses and that would not in fact be deductible under Code Sec. 162 or excludable under Code Sec. 132 as working condition fringes.[33]

Since deductible payments to or on behalf of shareholders also include rental payments for property used by the corporation, corporations may attempt to characterize payments to shareholders as such rental. While there is no problem generally with a corporation renting property from its shareholders, when the IRS determines that the "rental" payments exceed the actual fair rental value of the leased property, it may seek to recharacterize those payments as Code Sec. 301 distributions.

In addition to characterizing payments as deductible rent, corporations and their shareholders may instead seek to characterize a payment as a one-time payment to purchase property, thus resulting in return of capital, capital loss, or capital gain for the selling shareholder. Once again, though, if the amount paid exceeds the actual value of the property "sold," the payment may well be recharacterized as a Code Sec. 301 distribution.

Finally, corporations may simply characterize payments as loans rather than as distributions to shareholders. If so characterized, Code Sec. 7872 requires the imputation of interest if little or no interest is actually paid. If neither interest nor the loan is intended to be paid, however, the entire transaction may well be characterized as a Code Sec. 301 distribution.

---

[32] In *Mayson Mfg. Co. v. CIR*, 178 F2d 115, 119 (6th Cir. 1949), the court stated that among the factors used to determine whether a payment is reasonable compensation are "the employee's qualifications; the nature, extent and scope of the employee's work; the size and complexities of the business; a comparison of salaries paid with the gross income and the net income; the prevailing general economic conditions; comparison of salaries with distributions to stockholders; the prevailing rates of compensation for comparable positions in comparable concerns; the salary policy of the taxpayer as to all employees; and in the case of small corporations with a limited number of officers the amount of compensation paid to the particular employee in previous years." Recently, in *Menard, Inc. v. CIR*, 560 F3d 620 (7th Cir. 2009), the Seventh Circuit found that perhaps the most significant factor, though, is the judgment of the very board that sets the compensation or determines the amount of the bonus, making it quite difficult for the IRS to successfully recharacterize amounts initially characterized by the corporation as compensation.

[33] It is worth noting that even to the extent that such expenses are properly deductible under Code Sec. 162, that deduction can be substantially restricted by Code Sec. 274.

Corporations may also attempt to surreptitiously get value into the hands of shareholders without dividend treatment by renting or selling property to shareholders (as opposed to renting or purchasing from shareholders). Again, to the extent that the shareholder receives value in excess of the amount she pays the corporation, that excess may be recharacterized as a Code Sec. 301 distribution.

It is important to keep in mind that corporations may make payments in any of the above ways *on behalf* of their shareholders in addition to, or instead of, making them directly *to* the shareholders. The most obvious of these, noted above, is "compensation" paid to a family member that bears no relationship to services actually performed, but such payments can easily take the form of rents, payments to purchase property, or below value rentals to the shareholder's family.

It is equally important to keep in mind that in addition to indirectly benefitting a shareholder by making a transfer to a family member, a corporation might also indirectly benefit a shareholder by enriching a different corporation controlled by that shareholder. Thus, sales, exchanges, and other payments made by corporations owned by a common (noncorporate) parent in which one corporation clearly benefits to the others detriment may be recharacterized by the IRS as a distribution from the corporation suffering the detriment to the common parent, followed in turn by a Code Sec. 351 exchange or contribution to capital from that common parent to the benefited corporation.[34]

¶ 405 Corporate Shareholders: Dividends Received Deduction and Anti-Abuse Restrictions

.01 Dividends Received Deduction

Without some limitations, the double tax regime of Subchapter C could easily turn into a triple, quadruple, or greater tax on corporate income. Corporate earnings taxed to one corporation would be taxed again when distributed to a corporate shareholder, taxed again when distributed to a corporate shareholder of the second corporation, and taxed again and again as each distributee corporation in turn distributed its earnings to its own corporate shareholders. To prevent this, Code Sec. 243 allows corporate shareholders a deduction equal in amount to some or all of the dividends it receives. If the distributee is a less than 20% shareholder, it can deduct 70% of any dividends received, leaving it to pay tax on 30% of such dividends.[35] If the shareholder-distributee corporation is a member of the same affiliated group as the distributing corporation, it is entitled to a 100% dividends received deduction under Code Sec. 243(a)(3) and (b), thus effectively exempting the dividend received from tax.[36]

---

[34] Such transactions may also be subject to recharacterization under Code Sec. 482. See discussion at Chapter 9.

[35] Under Code Sec. 246(b), the total dividends received deductions allowed for any distributee corporation are generally limited to 80% of the corporations taxable income (not taking into account the dividends received deduction) in the case of the 80% deduction or 70% of the corporation's taxable income in the case of the dividends received deduction. Basically, this means simply that if

the corporation receives dividends the remaining 20% or 30% of the dividends received will be taxed and cannot be offset by other deductions in excess of the corporation's other income. The dividends received deduction can, though, create or increase corporate NOLs.

[36] The same 100% dividends received deduction is also available to a small business investment company operating under the Small Business Investment Act of 1958, Code Sec. 243(a)(2). In many cases where the distributee and the distributing corporation are members of an affili-

If the distributee corporation owns at least 20% (by vote and value) of the stock of the distributing corporation it is entitled to a deduction equal to 80% of the dividends received, but this 80% dividends received deduction comes with certain built-in restrictions on the definition of a dividend for purposes of its application. Recall that for purposes of determining earnings and profits, certain tax accounting actions that under-represent actual income are disregarded, so that a corporation's earnings and profits may significantly exceed its taxable income.[37] For example, for earnings and profits purposes, gains from installment sale are accounted for at the time of the sale rather than only when payments are received,[38] depreciation deductions are limited to straight line for earnings and profits purposes,[39] and Code Sec. 179 deductions are required to be capitalized and amortized rather than being immediately deducted in full.[40]

Code Sec. 301(e) provides that solely for purposes of determining the taxable income (and adjusted stock basis) of a distribution to any 20% shareholding corporation, the distributing corporation's earnings and profits shall be determined without reference to any of these timing adjustments that appear in Code Secs. 312(k) and 312(n).[41] The result is that the amount of the distributing corporation's earnings and profits will likely be lower for purposes of determining what part of a distribution to a 20% shareholding corporation is a dividend, so that the dividend to the 20% shareholding corporation may be less than it would be to any other shareholder (and the amount of the distribution characterized as a return of capital may be greater). Since less of the distribution may be characterized as a dividend, the 80% dividends received deduction will apply to less of that distribution than might otherwise be the case.

.02 Anti-abuse Restrictions on the Code Sec. 243 Deduction

(a) Code Sec. 246(c) Holding Period Requirement

Corporations quickly realized that they could take advantage of the ability to receive dividends at greatly reduced tax costs. Essentially, the dividends received deduction gave corporations the ability to recover some of their capital investment in stock without either paying tax or reducing their basis. To see the benefits for corporate distributees, assume that X Corp was about to pay a 10% dividend. Y Corp might purchase $1,000,000 worth of X stock for $1,000,000, receive a $100,000 dividend, and pay tax on only 30% of that dividend. Since $100,000 of Y's $1,000,000 investment has just been returned by way of the (mostly untaxed) dividend, the X stock Y just purchased for $1,000,000 and from which Y just extracted $100,000 is now worth only $900,000. Y can sell the X stock, ex-dividend, for its ex-dividend value of $900,000, giving it a $100,000 capital loss which it can use to offset $100,000

(Footnote Continued)

ated group, the group likely files a consolidated return. In that case, the consolidated return rules apply to the distribution. The distribution would be untaxed under those rules, with appropriate adjustments to the distributee's stock basis. *See* Chapter 9, *infra*.

[37] Code Secs. 312(k), 312(n).

[38] Code Sec. 312(n)(5).

[39] Code Sec. 312(k).

[40] Code Sec. 312(k)(3)(B).

[41] Code Sec. 301(e) does not change the impact of Code Sec. 312(n)(7) on the distributing corporation's earnings and profits. Code Sec. 312(n)(7) is not one of these timing adjustments, however. It relates only to the impact on earnings and profits of a redemption taxed as a distribution.

of capital gains that would otherwise be taxed at the 35% rate.[42] Basically, Y has been able to take out $100,000 of its $1,000,000 investment in X without reducing its basis and while paying tax on only 30% of what it receives. It can then sell what is left at a $100,000 tax loss (it has no economic loss, because although it receives only $900,000 for the X stock, it also has the $100,000 dividend it just received from X) which is 100% deductible. Y has thus included only $30,000 in income, while deducting $100,000 from income, all by way of a simple, quick, and economically risk-free and neutral transaction.

Congress has not prevented corporations like Y from taking advantage of the dividends received deduction, but it has prevented corporations from doing so in the economically risk-free way described above. Corporate risk is ensured in two ways. First, Code Sec. 246(c)(1)(B) disallows the dividends received deduction if, at the time of the dividend, the corporate shareholder is under an obligation to make related payments with respect to positions in substantially similar or related property (that is, if the shareholder's market risks and benefits from owning the stock are effectively eliminated).

In addition, Code Sec. 246(c) provides that in order for a distributee corporation to be entitled to the dividends received deduction, it must hold the stock of the distributing corporation for 45 consecutive days, including the day on which the dividend is effective. It does not matter, under Code Sec. 246(c), whether the distributee corporation acquires the stock 45 days prior to the dividend, or holds it 45 days after the dividend, or acquires it some days before and holds onto it for some more days after the dividend, so long as its holding period is at least 45 days.[43] What does matter, though, is that during that entire 45 day period, the stock must be held subject to real market risk. Code Sec. 246(c)(4) does not count as part of the required 45 day holding period any time during which the corporate shareholder has the ability to sell (through option, contractual obligation, or already made short sale) the stock in a way that would effectively eliminate market risk, or during which the shareholder has protected itself against market risk by having sold an option to buy the stock, or during which the shareholder has otherwise effectively protected itself against market risk by holding other positions with respect to substantially similar or related property.[44]

(b) Code Sec. 1059 Basis Reduction for Extraordinary Dividends

(i) *The Problem*

If Code Sec. 246(c) were the only restriction on the dividends received deduction, the clever corporation could easily guarantee after-tax benefits far in excess of any potential market risk by simply ensuring itself a large enough dividend. For example, assume that Y purchases $1,000,000 of X stock, and X immediately declares an 80% dividend payable to current shareholders. Y immediately recovers $800,000 of its outlay while being taxed at its 35% rate on only 30%

---

[42] Code Sec. 1201(a) limits to 35% the tax rate on corporate capital gains. Corporations do not benefit from lower rates on capital gains available to other taxpayers.

[43] The requisite holding period is 90 days rather than 45 days if the dividends are preferred dividends attributable to a period in excess of one year, Code Sec. 246(c)(2).

[44] *See* Treas. Reg. § 1.246-3.

($240,000) of the $800,000 dividend received (Y's total tax liability of .35 × $240,000=$84,000). Assuming that the market is indeed risky and that Y sells the X stock for $0 after 45 days, Y will have a tax loss of $1,000,000, deductible (against capital gains) in full, providing Y with a $350,000 tax benefit. This amount exceeds, by $64,000, Y's total outlays, consisting of its $200,000 economic loss and its $84,000 tax payment on the taxed part of the dividend received.

Tax avoidance transactions such as those attempted by Y have been put to rest by Code Sec. 1059. Y's ability to maximize its tax benefit while still avoiding any real risk despite holding the stock for more than 45 days was enabled by its simply extracting a large dividend rather than a more modest one, thus maximizing the leverage of the dividends received deduction. Code Sec. 1059, in turn, prevents Y from utilizing the dividends received deduction to extract cash without reducing its basis in the distributing corporation stock in the case of large, or "extraordinary" dividends. Code Sec. 1059 does not interfere with the dividends received deduction, which is available regardless of the size of the dividend so long as the requirements of Code Sec. 246 have been met. Instead, Code Sec. 1059 restricts the corporation's ability to deduct a noneconomic tax loss on its subsequent sale of the Y stock.

(ii) *How Code Sec. 1059 Works*

Recall that in the above example, Y paid $1,000,000 for the X stock but immediately recovered $800,000 of that amount by way of the dividend. When Y sold the X stock for $0, its economic loss on the sale was only $200,000, but its tax loss was $1,000,000. When it applies, Code Sec. 1059 takes the unwarranted tax loss away by requiring that Y reduce its basis in the X stock by the nontaxed portion of any dividend received from X. Thus, if Y is taxed on only $240,000 of the $800,000 dividend received, then, without the application of Code Sec. 1059, the other $560,000 of the dividend received reduced the value, but not the basis, of Y's X stock without tax. Code Sec. 1059, when it applies, prevents this by requiring that Y must reduce its basis in the X stock by the nontaxed portion of the dividend received.[45] On these facts, then, when Y receives the $800,000 dividend, $560,000 of which is exempted from tax because of the dividends received deduction, Y must reduce its basis in the X stock by that same $560,000, leaving it with a basis in the X stock of $440,000. When Y subsequently sells the X stock for $0, its tax loss will be $440,000 rather than $1,000,000. This in turn represents its $200,000 economic loss on the X stock, plus the $240,000 (30% of the $800,000 dividend received) on which it actually paid tax. Y now suffers an economic loss of $200,000. It has already paid tax on $240,000 and now deducts a $440,000 loss. The tax consequences follow the actual economics of Y's transactions.

(iii) *When 1059 Applies*

There are some significant limits on the application of Code Sec. 1059. Code Sec. 1059 applies only to distributions made by corporations not members of the distributee's affiliated group (so that any distributee entitled to a 100% dividends

---

[45] Code Sec. 1059(a)(1). In the rare case that the nontaxed portion of the dividend received actually exceeds the distributee's stock basis, the distributee is required to recognize capital gain in an amount equal to such excess, Code Sec. 1059(a)(2).

received deduction will also be unaffected by Code Sec. 1059),[46] only in the case of one or more extraordinary dividends, and only if such dividends are announced before the distributee has held the stock of the issuing corporation for more than two years.[47] The corporation that waits more than two years is not subject to basis reduction.[48]

An extraordinary dividend is any dividend on common stock that exceeds 10% of the distributee corporation's basis (or fair market value),[49] if the distributee establishes such value (to the secretary's satisfaction) of the stock.[50] If the stock is preferred stock that does not pay fixed dividends at least annually, dividends are extraordinary if they exceed more than 5% of the stock's basis (or value).[51] If the stock is preferred stock that does pay fixed dividends at least annually, such dividends are much less subject to manipulation, so that (a) Code Sec. 1059 does not apply at all if the distributee holds the stock for at least 5 years (before and or after the distribution) and (b) even if the distributee does not hold the stock for a total of 5 years, such fixed annual dividends are generally extraordinary only if and to the extent that they exceed 15% (instead of only 5%) of basis or value.[52]

In order to prevent corporations such as Y from extracting large amounts as dividends unhampered by Code Sec 1059, Code Sec. 1059(c) aggregates ostensibly separate distributions from the same corporation. All dividends that have ex-dividend dates within any 85 day period are aggregated and treated as a single dividend for purposes of determining whether they are extraordinary. In addition, if the total dividends with ex-dividend dates within a single 365 day period exceed 20% of the stock's basis or value, all such dividends are aggregated and treated as extraordinary. In order to prevent a corporation such as Y from escaping the aggregation rules by simply transferring the stock of the distributing corporation to one or several subsidiaries, each of which receives a "separate" distribution, Code Sec. 1059 also applies the dividend aggregation rules if the shares are owned by different taxpayers (for example, subsidiaries) who nonetheless have a transferred basis in the X shares (for example, as a result of a Code Sec. 351 exchange or a contribution to capital by Y).[53]

(c) Debt Financed Portfolio Stock

In addition to extracting funds by way of an essentially tax-free dividend and then taking a tax deductible loss on a later sale, corporations also used the dividends received deduction to extract funds by way of an essentially tax free

---

[46] Code Sec. 1059(e)(2). The Code Sec. 1059 restriction will apply, though to an affiliated corporation to the extent that the distribution was earned (that is, the dividend was accrued) by the distributee or to the extent that the distribution represents gain on property of the distributing corporation that was accrued prior to the time the corporations were members of the affiliated group, Code Sec. 1059(e)(2)(B).

[47] The two year period does not include any time during which the distributee corporation is protected from market risk, Code Sec. 1059(d)(3). On the other hand, if the distributee corporation has owned the stock during the entire life of the distributing corporation, the two year restriction is waived, Code Sec. 1059(d)(6).

[48] A non pro rata redemption of stock from a corporation that is treated as a dividend under Code Sec. 302 is also subject to Code Sec. 1059 regardless of the two year holding period, as are certain Code Sec. 304 transactions treated as dividends and partial liquidations.

[49] Code Sec. 1059(c)(4).

[50] Code Sec. 1059(c)(1), (2).

[51] Code Sec. 1059(c)(2)(A).

[52] Code Sec. 1059(e)(3). There may be a basis reduction though, to the extent that a dividend on such stock does not exceed 15% but was accrued prior to the distributees acquisition of the stock.

[53] Code Sec. 1059(c)(3)(C).

dividend while using tax deductible interest payments to finance the stock purchase. In a type of interest arbitrage transaction familiar to tax lawyers and accountants, Y might borrow $1,000,000 to purchase $1,000,000 of X Corp stock. Assume that Y pays 5% interest on its $1,000,000 debt, and that the X stock pays annual 5% dividends. The transaction is economically neutral, can potentially be virtually risk free, but is highly advantageous from an after-tax perspective. Although Y is taxed on only 30% of the $50,000 dividends it receives annually, it is entitled to deduct 100% of the interest paid annually to finance the stock purchase. With no actual economic cost, Y gets for itself an annual net tax deduction of 70% of $50,000, or $35,000.

This situation is addressed, albeit without too much force, by Code Sec. 246A. The idea behind Code Sec. 246A is that to the extent that portfolio stock[54] is debt financed, the distributee corporation, which is deducting the interest it pays (on the debt used to finance the stock), cannot at the same time take advantage of the dividends received deduction with respect to dividends it receives on that stock. Instead, if and to the extent that the distributee's outgoing interest payment is deductible, the dividends it receives from the debt-financed shares are taxable. Thus, since Y in the above example is deducting all $50,000 of the interest it pays to finance the X stock, Y will be entitled to no dividends received deduction with respect to the dividends received from X. If, instead, Y had paid $500,000 cash and the X stock was only 50% debt-financed, 50% of Y's dividends received deduction would be disallowed, because the X stock was only 50% debt-financed. In no case will the dollar amount of the reduction in the dividends received deduction exceed the deductible interest actually paid or incurred allocable to the dividend, however.[55] The extent to which any shares are debt-financed can vary, so the percentage of stock that is debt-financed is determined under Code Sec. 246 by determining the average indebtedness percentage during the period for which the dividend accrued.[56]

The most significant problem with the application of Code Sec. 246A lies in the determination of the extent to which any portfolio stock is actually "debt-financed." Shares are debt financed under Code Sec. 246A only if, when, and to the extent that there is "indebtedness directly attributable to the investment in the portfolio stock."[57] In other words, Code Sec. 246A applies only when indebtedness is directly traceable to the dividend-paying stock. Unless funds were clearly borrowed to purchase the stock in issue, or unless that stock is pledged as security for a particular debt, such direct tracing is difficult, if not impossible. As a result, Code Sec. 246A provides little hindrance for the reasonably well advised corporation.[58]

¶ 406 Bootstrap Sales

In the right circumstances, the dividend received deduction can also be quite useful for a corporation wishing to sell a subsidiary. To see how this might work,

---

[54] Basically, any stock if the distributee corporation owns less than 50% of the distributing corporation's outstanding shares by vote and value, Code Sec. 246A(c)(2).

[55] Code Sec. 246A(e).

[56] Code Sec. 246A(d).

[57] Code Sec. 246A(d)(3)(A).

[58] *OBH, Inc. v. US*, 397 F. Supp. 2d 1148, 1164 (D. Neb. 2005).

assume that P Corp owns 100% of the stock of S Corp (but that P and S do not file a consolidated return[59]), that P has a basis in its S stock of $2,000,000, and that Y Corp is interested in purchasing the S stock for its value of $5,000,000. Rather than selling the S stock for cash and being taxed on a $3,000,000 gain, P might choose to have S distribute a $3,000,000 dividend, thereby reducing its value to only $2,000,000 (coincidentally the same amount as P's basis in the S stock), and then selling what is left of S to Y for that $2,000,000. Because P is the parent of S Corp, it will be entitled to a 100% dividends received deduction, so will pay no tax on the $3,000,000 dividend from S. Nor will it have any taxable gain if it sells S stock with a basis of $2,000,000 for an amount realized of $2,000,000. P will have its $5,000,000 with no apparent taxable gain at all.

This transaction has significant potential to reduce P's taxes, but there are also limits to its availability and utility. First, a $3,000,000 dividend in this case, and almost any dividend large enough to make a substantial impact on the sales price of the S stock, is likely to be an "extraordinary dividend" as defined by Code Sec. 1059.[60] So long as P and S are members of an affiliated group (which is clearly the case if P owns 100% of S), Code Sec. 1059 will not reduce P's basis in the S stock,[61] but if P owned less than 80% of the S stock, so that they were not members of an affiliated group and the dividend was not entitled to the 100% dividends received deduction, Code Sec. 1059 would apply to reduce P's stock basis and impose capital gains on P unless P held the S stock for at least two years prior to the distribution.[62]

Assuming, though, that Code Sec. 1059 presents no problems, there may be some practical problems with this transaction. First of all, of course, it is not likely that S has $3,000,000 cash on hand to pay a dividend, or that S is in a position to sell assets to raise that cash, since such an asset sale would likely result in significant gain, and would also significantly interfere with S's business operations. If, instead, S were to distribute assets in kind to P, S would still recognize gain as if the assets were sold for their fair market value (assuming that S is not completely liquidated under Code Sec. 332).[63]

The simplest way for S to pay the $3,000,000 might be to either borrow the money to pay the dividend or to pay the dividend in the form of a promissory note to P. Immediately after paying out the dividend note, S is worth only $2,000,000. If Y Corp so chooses, after it purchases the S stock for its current value of $2,000,000, it might then take the other $3,000,000 it had planned to use to purchase the S stock and simply contribute that to the capital of S so that S could then use that amount to pay off the dividend-note. The net cost to Y is $5,000,000 ($2,000,000 for the S stock

---

[59] If P and S filed a consolidated return, any dividend distribution would necessarily result in a basis adjustment to P's stock which would prevent P from taking advantage of the dividends received deduction.

[60] Greater than 10% of basis or value, in the case of common stock. *See* discussion at ¶ 405.02, *supra.*

[61] To be technically accurate, Code Sec. 1059 might still apply to the extent that the dividend was paid out of earnings and profits accrued prior to the time that P and S were members of an affiliated group or to the extent that the profits were due to appreciation in property that accrued before P and S became members of an affiliated

group. Code Sec. 1059(e)(2). *See* discussion at ¶ 405, *supra.*

[62] P's basis in the S stock will be reduced by the nontaxed portion of the dividend received, or in this case, by 100% of the dividend received. Since P's basis in the S stock ($1,000,000) was less than the nontaxed portion of the dividend received ($4,000,000), the excess of the nontaxed portion of the dividend received ($4,000,000) over P's basis in the S stock ($4,000,000 – $1,000,000 = $3,000,000) would be treated as capital gain under Code Sec. 1059(a)(2), leaving P without any tax benefit at all.

[63] *See* ¶ 405.02.

¶406

and a $3,000,000 contribution to capital to pay the debt), the net benefit to P is $5,000,000 ($3,000,000 dividend and $2,000,000 sales price, the net tax to P, if this works, is $0.

Not surprisingly, the IRS will likely have some problems with this transaction, which it will then attempt to turn into problems for the taxpayers involved. There is no doubt that if S in fact pays a dividend to P prior to and separate from the sale to Y, P will be entitled to the dividends received deduction, and will recognize gain on a subsequent sale to Y only if and to the extent that P's amount realized exceeds its basis in the S stock. Nor is there any doubt that if Y purchases S for $5,000,000 cash without any pre-sale dividend, P will be taxed on a $3,000,000 gain. The sole issue in this case is whether the "dividend" from S to P will be respected and treated as a transaction separate from the sale of the S stock, or whether the entire series of events will be recharacterized as being in substance a single sale from P to Y, with the purported "dividend" from S to P being in reality only a vehicle for the transfer of part of the purchase price from Y to P that will be disregarded for tax purposes.

The case law, while providing useful guidance, is not perfectly clear on the result. What is clear is that if the dividend and sale are negotiated together between the buyer and seller (or if the stock sale is negotiated prior to the dividend), if they happen at essentially the same time, and if there is no possible justification for the dividend other than to facilitate the sale with reduced tax to the seller, the transaction will be treated as a single sale, the dividend will be disregarded, and the transaction will be treated as a sale of the S stock for a price equal to the actual amount paid plus the amount of the recharacterized "dividend."[64] On the other hand, if the dividend substantially predates any negotiation of a sale and the identification of any particular purchaser, and if there is some business purpose served by the sale other than just facilitating the sale at a reduced price and taking advantage of the dividends received deduction, the form of the dividend as a separate transaction will be respected.[65] Between these two clear situations lay a good many murkier ones. The result in these cases is unclear.[66]

---

[64] *Waterman S.S. Corp. v. CIR*, 430 F2d 1185 (5th Cir. 1970), *cert. denied*, 401 US 939 (1971).

[65] *Litton Industries, Inc. v. Commissioner of Internal Revenue Litton Indus.*, 89 TC 1086 (1987) (acq. in result);

TSN Liquidating Corp. v. US, 624 F2d 1328 (5th Cir. 1980).

[66] *See* discussion in Boris I. Bittker and James S. Eustice, FEDERAL INCOME TAXATION OF CORPORATIONS AND SHAREHOLDERS, ¶ 8.07 (7th ed. 2006).

Chapter 5

Redemptions

¶ 501 Introduction

When a corporation redeems, or buys back, its own shares, the selling shareholder may well be in exactly the same position she would have been had she sold those shares to any other person. For example, if T, who owns 500 of 5,000,000 outstanding shares of X Corp, sells those shares for $5,000, it matters not at all to her whether she sells the shares to a third party or to X Corp itself. Either way, she has cashed out.

On the other hand, at other times a redemption may look much more like a dividend than like any kind of sale or exchange. For example, assume that A and B each own 50% (5,000 out of a total of 10,000 outstanding shares) of the stock of X Corp., that X Corp is worth a total of $100,000 ($10 per share), and that X purchases 100 shares from each shareholder for their value of $1,000. Afterwards, A and B each own 4,900 of 9,800 outstanding shares of X Corp. As they were immediately prior to the redemptions, A and B are still each 50% shareholders of X Corp. They each retain 50% of the voting power and 50% of the economic rights of X Corp. The only change in circumstance for A and B brought about by the redemptions is that each shareholder has received $1,000 cash from X Corp. The nontax consequences of the redemptions are exactly the same as those of a nonliquidating (Code Sec. 301) distribution of $1,000 to each shareholder. Unlike a sale or exchange, each shareholder retains the same 50% interest in X Corp that it had prior to the redemption; exactly like a Code Sec. 301 distribution, each shareholder has received cash from X Corp without any diminution in its retained interest in X Corp.

The basic idea of Code Sec. 302 is that if a redemption more closely resembles a Code Sec. 301 distribution to the shareholders than it does a sale or exchange to a third party, the redemption will be taxed as a Code Sec. 301 distribution. On the other hand, if a redemption more closely resembles a sale or exchange than it does a Code Sec. 301 distribution to the shareholders, it will be taxed as a sale or exchange. This general rule is set forth in Code Sec. 302(b)(1), which states simply that a redemption will be taxed as a sale or exchange rather than a dividend if it is not "essentially equivalent to a dividend." In turn, a redemption looks more like a sale or exchange if the shareholder receives money or other property in *exchange* for some or all of her interests (voting control and or economic interests) in the corporation; and it looks more like a dividend if the shareholder receives property from the corporation while basically *retaining* her continuing interests in the corporation. The benefits of this general rule lie in its simplicity. The problems with this rule lie in the fact that it is so much more easily set forth than it is applied. It calls for a conclusion that cannot always be easily reached, because while some redemptions may obviously look like dividends and others may equally obviously look like sales or exchanges, many redemptions have some aspects of each.

In order to provide greater certainty for shareholders and their corporations planning redemptions, Congress set forth more definite, objective criteria to supplement the general rule of Code Sec. 302(b)(1) for determining the tax consequences of a redemption to the shareholders. These more objective criteria appear in Code Secs. 302(b)(2) and 302(b)(3).

¶ 502 Attribution

.01 Introduction

All of the tests for determining whether a redeeming shareholder gets sale or exchange treatment or dividend treatment ultimately depend on whether that shareholder has received payment from the corporation in exchange for some or all of her interest in the corporation, or whether she has received property while essentially retaining her corporate interests. As a result, it would appear that a logical starting place for determining the tax treatment of a redemption is to determine what the shareholder's interests in the corporation are immediately prior to the redemption and to determine what her interests are immediately after the redemption. To that end, it is important to note that for purposes of Code Sec. 302, the shareholder's interests in a redeeming corporation may extend well beyond any shares she actually owns in that corporation. This is because Code Sec. 302(c)(1) states that with certain limited exceptions discussed later, stock ownership for purposes of Code Sec. 302 is determined by taking into account the stock attribution rules of Code Sec. 318. Code Sec. 318, when made applicable, such as by Code Sec. 302(c)(1), has the sole function of *treating* taxpayers as being the owners of shares that they do not own in fact.

The general idea behind the attribution rules of Code Sec. 318 is that, in situations where Code Sec. 318 is directly invoked, taxpayers are treated as owning shares that they do not actually own but that are likely subject to some significant influence by the taxpayer. To that end, individuals are treated as owning shares actually owned by close family members; entities are treated as owning shares actually owned by their owners or beneficiaries; owners and beneficiaries are treated as owning shares actually owned by the entities they own; and anyone owning an option to acquire shares is treated as owning the shares subject to that option.

.02 Sequential Attribution

Unless otherwise provided in Code Sec. 318, the attribution rules have at least the theoretical potential to become almost boundless. This is because under Code Sec. 318(a)(5)(A), stock constructively owned by a taxpayer by reason of the application of Code Sec. 318 is treated as actually owned by that taxpayer for purposes of being re-attributed to some other taxpayer by a second (third, fourth, etc.) application of the same or a different attribution rule of Code Sec. 318. For example, if Taxpayer B is treated as owning shares because of B's relationship with Taxpayer A, then if Taxpayer C has an identified relationship with Taxpayer B, C will be treated as owning the shares that are actually owned by A but attributed to B, despite the fact that C may have no direct relationship at all with A, the actual owner of those shares.[1]

Because the same shares may be treated as owned by any number of persons, the application of Code Sec. 318 can sometimes be confusing. Fortunately, unless a shareholder is redeeming shares, its application is irrelevant, because the section only applies when specifically invoked by another section, such as Code Sec. 302.

.03 Specifics

(a) Family Attribution

Code Sec. 318(a)(1)(A) provides that an individual shall be treated as owning the stock owned directly or indirectly by his spouse,[2] children, grandchildren and parents.[3] Thus, assume that Grandfather (GR) is the father of Mom (M), who is in turn the mother of Child (C). GR is treated as owning any stock actually owned by M or C, and is also treated as owning any stock not actually owned by M or C but treated as owned by M or C under some other part of Code Sec. 318. M is similarly treated as owning any stock owned directly by her father GR or her child C, whether that stock is actually owned by GR or C or whether the stock is only treated as owned by GR or C under some other provision of Code Sec. 318. Since a grandchild is not treated as owning shares owned by a grandparent, C is treated as owning any shares owned (directly or by attribution under some other part of Code Sec. 318) by M, but there is no attribution from GR to C.

Although a grandchild is not treated as owning shares owned by a grandparent, one might suggest that, as a result of potential sequential attribution pursuant to Code Sec. 318(a)(5)(A), discussed briefly above, any stock owned (directly or by attribution) by GR would be treated as owned by M, and any stock owned (directly or indirectly) by M is treated as owned by C, so that any stock owned by GR actually will be treated as owned by C, at least indirectly. Such is not the case. Indeed, if family attribution did work that way, then every individual might be treated as owning every share of stock owned by every other individual, since we could all trace our ancestry (and thus stock attribution) back to Adam and Eve[4] and

---

[1] Code Sec. 318(a)(5)(A).

[2] Other than a spouse who is legally separated under a decree of divorce or separate maintenance.

[3] Code Sec. 318(a)(1)(B) provides that legally adopted children are treated as children by blood.

[4] For those unsure about Adam and Eve, we might use DNA to trace our ancestry back enough generations to be related at least to others of the same race or geographic origins.

then back down again to any other human descended from them. In order to prevent anything like this from happening, Code Sec. 318(a)(5)(b) provides that any stock treated as owned by a person because of family attribution (Code Sec. 318(a)(1)) cannot then be treated as owned by any other person because of family attribution (that is, by a second application of Code Sec. 318(a)(1)). As a result, while GR's stock may be attributed to M by way of family attribution, that stock cannot then be treated as owned by C by way of a second application of family attribution.

In order to ensure that individuals do not use the restriction on sequential family attribution to disclaim other forms of attribution, Code Sec. 318(a)(5)(D) provides that if shares could be attributed from one person to another either by way of family attribution or by way of option attribution, they shall be considered as owned by reason of option attribution. The sole result of this rule is that if one family member (M) has an option to acquire shares from another family member (G) from whom the same shares could be attributed by way of family attribution, those shares will be treated as owned (by M) by way of the option attribution so that they can then be reattributed to another family member (C).

(b) Attribution from Entities to Owners or Beneficiaries

Code Sec. 318(a)(2) provides that any stock owned by a partnership, estate or trust is treated as owned by the partners or beneficiaries in accordance with their percentage interest in the entity that actually owns the stock. Thus if Partnership owns 21 shares of X Corp, and A, who is a 1/3 partner in Partnership, redeems some stock of X Corp, then for purposes of determining whether A gets sale or exchange treatment on the redemption, A is treated as owning (both before and after the redemption) seven of the 21 shares actually owned by Partnership. Similarly, if it was not A who was redeeming shares of X Corp, but instead was A's son Sonny who was redeeming shares of X Corp, then it would be Sonny who would be treated as owning seven of the 21 shares of X Corp actually owned by Partnership. This is because the seven shares attributed from Partnership to A are treated as actually owned by A for purposes of reattributing those shares from A to any other person with a close enough relationship (that is, a relationship specified in Code Sec. 318) to A.

Attribution from C corporations to their shareholders is significantly more limited than attribution from partnerships to their partners or from trusts to their beneficiaries. Indeed, there is no attribution at all from a C corporation to a shareholder unless the shareholder owns at least 50% (by value) of the corporation's outstanding stock.[5] In determining whether any shareholder owns 50% of Corporation X's stock (for purposes of treating the shareholder as owning shares of Corporation Y that are actually owned by Corporation X), the section takes into account not only the shares of Corporation X actually owned by the shareholder, but also the shares of Corporation X constructively owned by the shareholder by reason of the application of Code Sec. 318. If a shareholder does own (directly or indirectly) at least 50% of the stock of any corporation, that shareholder is treated as

---

[5] Code Sec. 318(a)(2)(C).

owning a proportion of the stock actually or constructively owned by that corporation in proportion to the percentage of stock of that corporation owned by the shareholder. For example, assume that T redeems some shares of Y Corporation, that Corporation X owns 100 shares of Y Corp, and that T also owns 51% of the outstanding shares of Corporation X. T will be treated as owning (both before and after the redemption of her Y Corp stock) 51 of the 100 shares of Y Corp actually owned by Corporation X. On the other hand, if T owned only 49.9% of the outstanding shares of Corporation X, there would be no attribution at all from Corporation X to T.

(c) Attribution from Owners or Beneficiaries to Entities

Just as owners and beneficiaries are treated as owning stock actually owned by the entities they own (or in which they have a beneficial interest), entities are treated as owning shares actually owned by their owners or beneficiaries. Attribution *from* entities to owners or beneficiaries under Code Sec. 318(a)(3) differs from attribution *into* entities under Code Sec, 318(a)(3) in an important respect, however: attribution into entities is not proportionate. Instead, a partnership is deemed to own 100% of all shares owned by any of its partners, and a trust or estate is deemed to own 100% of all shares owned (directly or indirectly) by it beneficiaries. Thus, for example, a partnership is treated as owning 100% of the shares owned by even a 1% partner.

As with attribution from corporations to shareholders under Code Sec. 318(a)(2), attribution from shareholders into their corporations does not exist at all unless the shareholder is at least a 50% shareholder of the corporation in question.

(d) Limitations on Entity Attribution

The combination of attribution into an entity *from* its owners or beneficiaries with attribution out of that same entity to *other* owners or beneficiaries could, if unchecked, lead to situations where attribution was entirely unwarranted. For example, Partner A, who owns a 10% interest in Investment Partnership, might be deemed to own shares actually owned by Partner Z, who does not know and has never met Partner A, just because Partner Z owns a 5% interest in the same Investment Partnership. Without some limit, Investment Partnership would be treated as owning all of the shares owned by any of its partners, including Z, and A, as a partner of Investment Partnership, would be treated as owning at least a portion of any shares owned directly or indirectly by the partnership. Similarly, if A and Z were unrelated and had never met but were both beneficiaries of the same trust or estate, they would each be treated as owning at least a portion of the stock owned by the other. In order to prevent such attribution among unrelated parties who simply share interests in a single entity, Code Sec. 318(a)(5)(C) provides that any shares attributed *into* an entity (under Code Sec. 318(a)(3)) because they are owned by an owner or beneficiary of that entity shall not be reattributed out of that entity (under Code Sec. 318(a)(2)) to a different owner or beneficiary.

¶502.03(d)

(e) Option Attribution

Under Code Sec. 318(a)(4), a person is treated as owning any shares that she has an option to acquire (or for which she has an option to acquire an option to acquire, etc.). Option attribution exists regardless of the option price.

Examples:

X has 100 shares outstanding, owned as follows:	Y has 100 shares outstanding, owned as follows:	P is owned as follows:
Child (C): 50	X: 80	M: 33%
Mom (M): 5	GR: 5	S1: 33%
Grandfather (GR): 5	M: 5	S2: 33%
Partnership (P): 30	S1: 5	
Stranger 1 (S1): 5	S2: 5	
Stranger 2 (S2): 5		

This ownership is represented below. Thin lines represent 5% ownership. Thicker lines represent greater than 5% ownership, as marked.

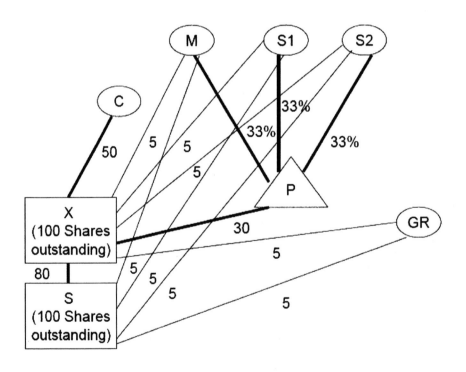

If M redeems 3 of the 5 shares of X that she owns, her ownership both prior to and after the redemption will include not only the shares that she actually owns, but also: 5 shares owned by her father GR, by way of family attribution (Code Sec. 318(a)(1)); 50 shares owned by C by way of family

¶502.03(e)

attribution; and 10 of the 30 shares owned by P, by way of attribution from P to M under Code Sec. 318(a)(2). Note that although P is deemed to own the 10 shares of X owned by S1 and S2 by way of attribution under Code Sec. 318(a)(3), those shares cannot be reattributed to M under Code Sec. 318(a)(2) because of Code Sec. 318(a)(5)(C). M's redemption would thus bring her ownership from a total of 70/100 (70%) to 67/97 (69%).

If C redeems 10 of the 50 shares of X that he owns, his ownership of X includes not only the shares he owns directly, but also, by family attribution from M, the 5 shares of X owned directly by M and the 10 shares of X owned by P and attributed to M under Code Sec. 318(a)(2). C's redemption would thus bring his ownership from 65/100 (65%) to 55/95 (58%). Not that there is no attribution from GR to C, and no double family attribution (from GR to M and then from M to C).

Assume in the above example that M had an option to purchase the 5 shares of X owned by GR. While there is no family attribution from GR to C, and no double family attribution (from GR to M to C), M's option to purchase the shares owned by GR would result in those shares being attributed to her, and shares attributed by way of option attribution under Code Sec. 318(a)(4) can be again attributed, this time by family attribution, to C. Code Sec. 318(a)(5)(D) states that option attribution takes precedence over family attribution just so that C could not avoid the attribution in cases like this. As a result, in this case, C's ownership would go from 70/100 to 60/95.

If P redeems 10 shares of X, its ownership of X includes not only the shares of X that P owns directly, but also all of the X shares owned by its partners, under Code Sec. 318(a)(3). This means that P is treated as owning the 5 shares owned by S1, the 5 owned by S2, and the 5 owned directly by M. In addition, though, the 50 X shares owned by C are attributed to M by way of family attribution, as are the 5 shares owned by GR. Those 55 shares are treated as owned by M for purposes of then attributing ownership to P, under 318(a)(3). As a result, P's ownership of X goes from [30 (directly owned) +5 (from S1) +5 (from S2) + 60 (from M)=] 100/100 (100%) to 90/90 (100%).

In addition, note that if P redeemed all 30 of the X shares it owned, its ownership will go from 100/100 to 70/70, leaving it with no diminishment in its interest at all after taking into account attribution.

If GR redeems 3 shares of S, his ownership of S includes not only the shares he owns directly, but also the 5 owned directly by M (by way of family attribution) and the 5 shares owned directly by C (by way of family attribution—there is family attribution from grandchild to grandparent even though there is no family attribution from grandparent to grandchild). In addition, because C owns at least 50% of X, any shares owned by X are attributed to C in proportion to C's ownership of X, under Code Sec. 318(a)(2)(C). Thus, C is treated as owning 1/2 of the 80 shares of S actually owned by X. In turn, since GR is treated as owning any shares owned by C, GR is treated as owning the 40 shares of S that C owns by attribution from X, under Code Sec. 318(a)(1). As a

¶502.03(e)

result, GR's ownership of S goes from 55/100 (55%) before the redemption to 52/97 (94%) after the redemption.

It is worth noting (but does not change the actual result) that P owns 30% of X. Because there is no attribution from a corporation to a shareholder except with a 50% or greater shareholder, P's ownership of X does not bring with it any attribution of the S stock actually owned by X. In addition, P is treated as owning the 10 S shares owned by S1 and S2 because of Code Sec. 318(a)(3). Those shares are not reattributed to M (and to GR) because such reattribution is prevented by Code Sec. 318(a)(5)(B).

Note that if GR redeemed all of his 5 shares in S, his interest would be reduced from 55% to 45/90 (50%). In this case, however, GR might be able to take advantage of Code Sec. 302(c)(2), discussed in the next section.

.04 Cutting Off Family Attribution

While Code Sec. 318's attribution rules are generally made applicable to redemptions by their incorporation in Code Sec. 302(c)(1), Code Sec. 302(c)(2) provides an exception to the application of family attribution in certain circumstances. Code Sec. 302(c)(2) is the result of requests for help from owners of family businesses who wanted to cash out, retire and pass the business on to the next generation. Typically, they would want to have the corporation redeem all of their shares for cash and notes, leaving their children to own and run the company. In the days when tax rates were higher and family attribution applied, these retirees would likely be treated as owning the shares owned by the next generation, thereby essentially guaranteeing dividend treatment and a 70% tax rate on whatever they received, regardless of their stock basis. Congress enacted Code Sec. 302(c)(2) just for such people.

Code Sec. 302(c)(2) allows individuals to cut off family attribution if a number of conditions are met. Most importantly, the redeeming shareholder must completely divest herself of all interests in the corporation (other than any debt obligations, which she likely will receive in the redemption). She can own no stock (other than what would be attributed from other family members) directly or indirectly (that is, through any other kinds of attribution), and she cannot have any other interest in the corporation (including as an officer, director, or employee), other than as a creditor. As a result, a redeeming shareholder who continues as an employee cannot cut off family attribution, and the IRS has also attacked (as such continuing interests in the corporation), although not always successfully, virtually any other type of relationship that might indicate any sort of continuing financial interest in the corporation, no matter how attenuated.

In order to make this severance of the shareholder from the corporation meaningful, Code Sec. 302(c)(2)(A)(ii) prevents the redeeming shareholder from acquiring any prohibited interest (other than by bequest or inheritance) for 10 years following the redemption distribution. And in order to make this 10 year requirement meaningful, Code Sec. 302(c)(2)(A) also requires both that the distributee notify the Secretary of any acquisition of a prohibited interest in the corporation during that 10 year period and that the distributee agree to extend the statute of limitations for the year of the redemption until a year after she notifies the Secretary of any such acquisition during that period.

Congress allowed taxpayers to cut off family attribution so that they could retire, cash out, and avoid the high rate then applicable to dividends. If left entirely unchecked, though, the ability to cut off family attribution might allow taxpayers to defeat its somewhat restrictive spirit. For example, if A owns all of the shares of X Co. and wants to withdraw cash in a transaction taxed as a sale or exchange, he might simply give some shares to his wife W. W could immediately redeem those shares and cut off family attribution, entitling herself to sale or exchange treatment. Alternatively, A might give to W all of the shares *except* those he wanted to redeem, redeem the rest, and cut off family attribution (from W).

In order to prevent abuse of the ability to cut off family attribution, Code Sec. 302(c)(B) provides that if the redeemed shares were either given to or received from a related person (as defined by Code Sec. 318(a) within the 10 years prior to the redemption, family attribution cannot be cut off unless the stock transfer to the related party did not have as one of its principal purposes the avoidance of federal income tax. This prohibited tax avoidance purpose will not likely be found, however, unless the stock transfer and redemption are part of a plan to allow the related parties to essentially get cash out of the corporation without working any real change in control of the company, so that the typical retirement redemption preceded by a gift of some stock to the next generation will not cause a problem.

.05 Entities Cutting Off Family Attribution

If only redemptions by family members themselves could benefit from cutting off family attribution, some significant traps could arise for family owned and oriented entities. For example, assume that Father and Daughter each own 50% of X Corp., and the family plans for Father's shares to be redeemed and for Daughter to assume 100% ownership and management of the corporation. If Father's shares are redeemed for cash and notes, Daughter's shares would, absent a cutting off of family attribution, be attributed to Father, leaving him with 100% ownership even after the redemption and denying him sale or exchange treatment. Fortunately, Father can cut off family attribution (from Daughter) and receive sale or exchange treatment. If, instead, Father dies and Mother inherits Father's shares, Mother can also redeem those shares, cut off family attribution (from Daughter), and receive sale or exchange treatment. If Father dies and Father's *estate* redeems the shares that belonged to Father, though, the result could be drastically different. The situation is represented below.

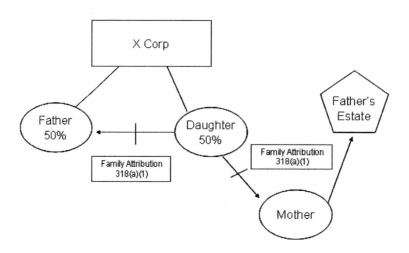

Father can cut off family (318(a)(1)) attribution if he redeems
Mother can cut off family (318(a)(1)) attribution if she redeems
Attribution from Mom to Estate is under 318(a)(3). But estate can cut off
family attribution (from Daughter to Mom) if it redeems

If the estate could not cut off family attribution, then Mother would be treated as owning the shares actually owned by Daughter (by way of family attribution under Code Sec. 318(a)(1)), Father's estate would be treated as owning all of the shares owned, directly or indirectly, by its beneficiary, Mother (by way of attribution under Code Sec. 318(a)(3)), and as a result Father's estate would be treated as owning all of the shares actually owned by Daughter. The result of the redemption would be that the estate will have gone from owning (including by attribution) 100 of 100 shares outstanding to owning (including by attribution) 50 of 50 shares outstanding. There would have been no reduction at all in its proportionate ownership, and dividend treatment would apply.

In this case, the only attribution to Father's estate would be under Code Sec. 318(a)(3) (attribution from a beneficiary to the estate), and attribution into (or out of) an entity can never be cut off. The only type of attribution that can ever be cut off is family attribution, and there could never be family attribution directly to the estate, or to any other entity, simply because an estate (or a corporation or trust or partnership), being a nonphysical entity, can have no parents, children or grandchildren. What is significant in the above situation is that Mother, the actual beneficiary of Father's estate, and the only person whose stock ownership is attributed directly to the estate, actually owns no shares of X Corp. It is not family attribution from Mother to the estate, but family attribution from Daughter to Mother, that gets in the way of sale or exchange treatment for the estate. Code Sec. 302(c)(2)(C) provides help for the estate in this situation.

Code Sec. 302(c)(2)(C) allows family attribution to or from beneficiaries of an estate or trust or owners of a partnership or corporation to be cut off if the beneficiaries or owners themselves own no shares in the corporation directly or indirectly (other than through family attribution) and if the entity and each beneficiary or owner files the requisite promise to notify the Secretary of any acquisition of a prohibited interest and accompanying waiver of the statute of limitations.

¶ 503 Treatment of Redemptions: Sale or Exchange or Dividend

To return to the fundamental issue in redemptions, if a redemption more closely resembles a Code Sec. 301 distribution to the shareholders than it does a sale or exchange of stock by the shareholder to a third party, the redemption will essentially be taxed as a Code Sec. 301 distribution (that is, the entire amount distributed by the corporation will be taxed as a dividend to the shareholder to the extent of available earnings and profits). On the other hand, if a redemption more closely resembles a sale or exchange than it does a Code Sec. 301 distribution to the shareholders, it will be taxed as a sale or exchange (that is, the shareholder will be taxed only on the excess of her amount realized over her basis in the redeemed shares, and that amount will be taxed as capital gains). This general rule is set forth in Code Sec. 302(b)(1), which states simply that a redemption will be taxed as a sale or exchange rather than a dividend if it is not "essentially equivalent to a dividend." In turn, a redemption looks more like a sale or exchange if the shareholder receives money or other property in *exchange* for some or all of her interests (voting control and or economic interests) in the corporation; and it looks more essentially equivalent to a dividend" if the shareholder receives property from the corporation while basically *retaining* her continuing interests in the corporation. We discuss these differences more in a bit, but for now it is enough to simply realize that the distinction is not always easy to make. It is for that reason that other parts of Code Sec. 302(b) provide a more exact, bright-line, test.

.01 Complete Termination of Interest: Code Sec. 302(b)(3)

Perhaps the brightest line in Code Sec. 302 is in Code Sec. 302(b)(3), which grants sale or exchange treatment if the distribution is "in complete redemption of all of the stock of the corporation owned by the shareholder. The most important attribute of this apparently bright line, however, is that it is not quite as obvious as it might first appear. The shareholder who sells all of her shares back to the corporation may still own some shares by attribution from family members, entities, or owners or beneficiaries, and a distribution is in complete termination of interest only if the shareholder owns no shares either directly or indirectly by attribution immediately after the redemption. The sole, and significant, exception to this rule is that the shareholder who retains no interest in the corporation other than as a creditor can cut off any family attribution that would otherwise exist. Indeed, the only real significance of Code Sec. 302(b)(3) is its relevance to cutting off family attribution. Likely, any other redemption that would qualify as a complete termination of interest under Code Sec. 302(b)(3) would qualify under Code Sec. 302(b)(1) or 302(b)(2) in any event.

.02 Substantially Disproportionate Distribution: Code Sec. 302(b)(2)

Code Sec. 302(b) provides a fairly straightforward safe harbor that, if met, guarantees the redeeming shareholder sale or exchange treatment. To qualify, the shareholder must redeem a sufficient amount of voting stock so that immediately after the redemption, the shareholder owns (1) less than 50% of the total combined voting power of all classes of stock entitled to vote, and (2) less than 80% of the percentage of voting stock than she owned immediately prior to the redemption.[6] If these tests are met, the redeeming shareholder will also receive sale or exchange treatment on any nonvoting shares redeemed as part of the same transaction.[7]

To see how this test works, assume that R owns 60 shares of X Co., and is a 25% partner in the RA partnership, which owns the other 40 outstanding shares of X. R owns 70% of the X shares, including 10% by attribution from the partnership. If 30 of R's shares are redeemed, then R will own 30 shares directly and 10 by attribution, leaving her with 40 out of a total of 70 shares still outstanding (57%). The redemption will not receive sale or exchange treatment under Code Sec. 302(b)(2) because neither of the two tests have been met. R still owns more than 50% of the common stock outstanding, and her current percentage ownership (57%) is not less than 80% of her previous ownership percentage (70%—57% is approximately 81% of 70%). If, instead, 40 of R's shares are redeemed, then R will own 20 shares directly and 10 by attribution, leaving her with 30 of 60 shares still outstanding (50%). Because she has not reduced her ownership to less than 50% of the voting stock, she still fails to qualify under Code Sec. 302(b)(2). If, instead, 50 of R's shares are redeemed, R will own 10 shares directly and 10 by attribution, leaving her with 20 out of 50 shares still outstanding, and satisfying both the Code Sec. 302(b)(2) tests.

As is the case throughout corporate tax, the step transaction doctrine applies, so that if the redemption is part of a planned series of redemptions, the IRS will look at the series rather than any individual part of that series before allowing sale or exchange treatment under Code Sec. 302(b)(2).[8]

.03 Not Essentially Equivalent to a Dividend

Code Sec. 302(b)(1) states simply that a redemption will be taxed as a sale or exchange rather than a dividend if it is not "essentially equivalent to a dividend." A dividend or its equivalent is a shareholder getting money or property from her corporation while basically retaining her interest in the corporation, as opposed to a shareholder getting money or property in *exchange* for some or all of her interest in that corporation. Fortunately, case law and rulings provide some, but not all, of the specifics left out of the statute.

First of all, for any redemption to not be essentially equivalent to a dividend, there must be some reduction in the shareholder's proportionate interest in the corporation, so that any strictly proportionate redemption will not qualify. In at least

---

[6] The 80% test must also be met with respect to common stock by value, if there is any nonvoting common stock outstanding, Code Sec. 302(b)(2)(C) flush language.

[7] Treas. Reg. § 1.302-3(a).

[8] Code Sec. 302(b)(2)(D).

one well-known case, the application of the 318 attribution rules made application of this apparently straightforward concept a bit more significant than might at first appear. In *US v. Davis*[9] the taxpayer, his wife, and their two children each owned 25% of the corporation's outstanding shares. When the corporation redeemed its outstanding preferred shares, all of which had been owned by the taxpayer, the Court determined that because of family attribution (which the taxpayer could not cut off because he still owned directly 25% of the common stock), the taxpayer owned (either directly or indirectly, through Code Sec. 318(a)(1)) 100% of all of the corporation's outstanding shares both before and after the redemption. As a result, his proportionate interest in the corporation was unchanged and the redemption was taxed as a dividend.

In addition to proportionate redemptions, dividend equivalence will also be found, and sale or exchange treatment will typically be denied, if even a disproportionate redemption still leaves a shareholder with effective control of the redeeming corporation. Thus, a shareholder who goes from 57% ownership of common voting stock to 51% ownership will not get sale or exchange treatment for that redemption.[10] One exception to this general rule that retained control is incompatible with a redemption being not essentially equivalent to a dividend is that the shareholder whose redemption may leave her with majority control but brings her below a supermajority (although the IRS seems to take this view only in the face of imminent corporate action that would require a supermajority).[11]

Generally, if after a redemption (1) the shareholder's proportionate interest in the corporation has decreased and (2) the shareholder does not control the corporation after the redemption,[12] the shareholder can expect to qualify the redemption as not essentially equivalent to a dividend. The IRS has taken issue with this approach only in cases where (1) the shareholder owned both voting and nonvoting stock, (2) only nonvoting stock was redeemed, and (3) while not personally owning (directly or through attribution) a majority of the voting stock, the redeeming shareholder owned a sufficient amount of voting stock so that, as a practical matter, she could control corporate action as an important part of a two or three shareholder coalition.[13]

.04 Redemptions Combined with Stock Sales

Code Secs. 302(b)(1), (2), and (3) all condition sale or exchange treatment on a significant reduction in the shareholder's stock ownership. They differ only in how they determine the significance of a reduction. Regardless of which subsection

---

[9] 397 U.S. 301 (1970).

[10] Rev. Rul. 75-502, 1975-2 C.B. 111.

[11] Compare *Wright v. US*, 482 F. 2d 600 (8th Cir. 1973) (reduction to below 2/3 majority needed for extraordinary corporate action made reduction not essentially equivalent to a dividend, even in the apparent absence of any forthcoming action that would require a 2/3 vote), with Rev. Rul. 78-401, 1978-2 CB 127 (reduction to less than supermajority that still leaves shareholder with more than 50% control does not result in sale or exchange treatment if corporate action requiring supermajority is not imminent).

[12] There is some authority, with which the IRS disagrees, that since the Code Sec. 302(b)(1) test is based on "facts and circumstances", so long as there is any reduction at all in the shareholder's proportionate interest taking into account attribution, the application of attribution rules in determining corporate control is one of several facts that may, or may not, be taken into account depending on the actual circumstance of the relationship between the redeeming shareholder and the person whose shares would be attributable to the shareholder under Code Sec. 318. *Cerone v. CIR* 87 TC 1 (1986).

[13] Rev. Rul. 85-106, 1985-2 C.B. 116.

is being applied, a shareholder can reduce her stock interest in the redeeming corporation by combining the redemption with an actual sale or exchange of stock to a third party. After initially balking at the idea,[14] the IRS now agrees that if a redemption and a stock sale by the same shareholder are part of a single integrated plan, the results of the actual sale should be taken into account in determining the reduction in the shareholders interest in the corporation, regardless of the order in which the redemption and sale actually take place.[15]

In other words, assume that A owns all 100 of the outstanding shares of X corp., and that pursuant to an integrated plan A redeems 50 shares in January and then sells the remaining 50 shares to B (an unrelated party) in February. The IRS will treat the January redemption as part of what is ultimately a complete termination of interest and A will receive sale or exchange treatment. Treating the component transactions separately would instead have left A with dividend treatment, as she would have gone from owning 100/100 to 50/50 of the outstanding X shares. Of course, in these situations it is still incumbent on the taxpayer to establish that the redemption and sale are part of a single integrated planned transaction.[16]

¶ 504 Tax Consequences of Redemptions

.01 Sales or Exchanges

(a) Shareholder

The shareholder who receives sale or exchange treatment on the redemption of stock is treated no differently than the shareholder who simply sells stock to a third party. She recognizes gain or loss equal to the difference between her amount realized (the amount of cash plus the value of any property received) and her basis in the stock redeemed. The gain is either short or long term capital gain depending on how long she has held the shares redeemed.

(b) Redeeming Corporation

The corporation that buys back shares in a transaction treated as a sale or exchange under Code Sec. 302(b) will recognize gain or loss (assuming that Code Sec. 267 does not apply to disallow a loss if the redemption is from a person who remains a majority shareholder even after the redemption) on any property exchanged for the shares. The redeeming corporation recognizes no gain or loss (and gets no deduction under Code Sec. 162(k)) on the cash purchase of its stock; and it is unconcerned about its basis in the redeemed share because Code Sec. 1032 prevents it from recognizing gain or loss on its own stock in any event.

The only other tax consequence to the redeeming corporation has to do with its adjustment to earnings and profits. If the corporation sells or exchanges

---

[14] *See Zenz v. Quinlivan*, 213 F. 2d 914 (6th Cir. 1954).

[15] Rev. Rul. 75-447 (1975-2 CB 113).

[16] In *Neidermeyer v. CIR*, 62 TC 280, *aff'd per curiam* 535 F. 2d 500 (9th Cir. 1976), *cert denied* 429 US 1000 (1976) the taxpayers transferred some shares in September and the rest of their shares in December. Their assertion that the two transactions were part of a single plan that resulted in a complete termination of interest were rejected. The court cited as important, but not always determinative, factors, the lack of a written plan, the lack of any binding obligation, and the fact that no such plan was ever communicated to anyone else at the time of the initial transfer.

property for the stock, its current year's earnings and profits will be adjusted, along with its current year's tax liability, by any gain or loss recognized by the redeeming corporation.[17] In addition, however, the redeeming corporation will reduce its earnings and profits by the lesser of (1) the amount it distributes in payment for the stock or (2) the ratable share of earnings and profits attributable to the redeemed stock. For example, if the corporation redeems 20% of its outstanding stock, earnings and profits will be reduced by the lesser of the amount paid by the corporation or 20% of the corporation's earnings and profits, taking into account all other distributions during the year.[18]

.02 Redemptions Treated as Dividends

(a) Shareholders Generally

The shareholder whose stock redemption is treated as a distribution governed by Code Sec. 301 is taxed as she would be on receipt of any other distribution. The distribution is a dividend to the extent of the shares' allocable share of corporate earnings and profits.[19] As any other distribution, amounts in excess of allocable earnings and profits are treated first as a return of capital and then as capital gain to the extent the amount distributed exceeds the shareholder's stock basis.

(b) Corporate Shareholders

If the redeeming shareholder is itself a corporation, dividend treatment is typically good news, because it brings into play the dividends received deduction of Code Sec. 243. For purposes of determining whether the corporate shareholder owns enough shares to qualify for the 100% or 80% dividends received deduction, as opposed to the typical 70% deduction, the IRS will look at the percentage of stock owned immediately after the redemption.[20]

One potential limitation on the benefits of the dividends received deduction in redemptions treated as dividends is that if the redemption is not entirely pro-rata, the corporation that receives the dividends received deduction is required by Code Sec. 1059(e)(1)(A) to reduce its basis in the stock it retains by the amount of the dividends received deduction, and is required to recognize gain immediately if the amount of the dividends received deduction exceeds its basis in its remaining shares.

(c) Shareholder's Basis in Redeemed Stock

Regardless of whether the shareholder whose stock redeemed is an individual or a corporation, the entire amount realized by the redeeming shareholder is treated as a distribution. Unlike any other Code Sec. 301 distribution, the shareholder has actually transferred property (the redeemed shares) in which it had a basis, and has not been able to take that basis into account in the transaction. Instead, the shareholder gets to otherwise take into account her basis in the redeemed stock.[21] The general rule is that the shareholder simply retains that

---

[17] This assumes that the property has the same adjusted basis for earnings and profits purposes as it does for gain or loss purposes. See discussion in Chapter 4.

[18] Code Sec. 312(n)(7).

[19] Code Secs. 301 and 316.

[20] Code Sec. 243(b)(1)(A).

[21] Subject to Code Sec. 1059, as discussed above, if the shareholder is a corporation.

unused basis by adding it to the basis of the shares she still has, on a pro-rata basis.[22]

Complications can arise where the redeeming shareholder redeems all of the shares that she actually owns, but nonetheless receives dividend rather than sale or exchange treatment because of attribution. For example, assume that A owns 50% of X (with a total basis of $50), A is a 60% partner in the AB partnership, which owns the other 50% of the outstanding X stock, and all of A's X shares are redeemed for $50 cash. Taking into account attribution, A's ownership goes from 50% (owned directly by A) + 60% × 50% (by attribution from the partnership), or a total of 80%, to 0 shares owned directly but 60% of the X stock by attribution from the partnership (there are now only 50 shares of X outstanding, all of which are owned by the partnership, and A is a 60% partner treated as owning 60% of all shares actually owned by the partnership). If, as is likely, A does not receive sale or exchange treatment, A will be taxed on a $50 distribution, and A will have no stock to which he might attach his $50 unused basis in the redeemed shares. The current regulations suggest that since A cannot use this basis because she has no more X stock, this $50 basis from A can be added to the basis of the X stock owned by the related party whose stock ownership (and attribution to A) prevented A from getting sale or exchange treatment on the redemption. In other words, the partnership can increase its basis in the X stock by the $50 of basis that went unused by A.[23]

Unfortunately, this ability to switch basis (and, as a result, gain or loss) between taxpayers led to some abuse. If the redeeming shareholder would not have been taxed on the dividend in any event and the related shareholder could take advantage of the extra basis by selling its X stock (with the added basis) at a loss, the two parties could, and did, work together to redeem shares for the purpose of extracting tax advantage by shifting stock basis. In response, the IRS proposed, revoked, and then re-proposed regulations that would prevent this basis shifting between taxpayers. Instead, these regulations leave the unused basis with the redeeming shareholder, but suspend the shareholder's use of that basis (that is, to generate a capital loss in the amount of the unused basis) until such time as the related shareholder (in this case, the AB partnership) whose attributed stock caused the dividend treatment disposes of its stock of X.[24]

(d) The Distributing Corporation

The corporation that makes a redeeming distribution treated as a Code Sec. 301 distribution to the shareholder is treated just like any other corporation making a Code Sec. 301 distribution, and simply ignores, for tax purposes, the reacquisition of the redeemed shares.

.03 *Common Uses of Redemptions to Get Cash from Corporations*

Shareholders and their corporations have often used redemptions to attempt to extract cash or property from corporations at reduced rates, or with no taxable

---

[22] Treas. Reg. § 1.302-2(c).
[23] Treas. Reg. § 1.302-2(c), ex. 1.

[24] Prop. Treas. Reg. § 1.302-5(a)(3), (d), (e), 79 Fed. Reg. 3509, 3514-15 (Jan. 21, 2009) ex. 4.

income at all. Some of these attempts have been successful. Others have not. What follows is a description of a few of the more well known attempts.

(a) Redemptions to Satisfy Shareholder Obligations to Purchase Stock

Assume, as has been the case in some shareholder buy-sell agreements, that A and B are equal (50%) shareholders of AB Corp., and that they have agreed that when either shareholder dies or becomes disabled, the remaining shareholder is unconditionally obligated to purchase the shares owned by the newly deceased (or newly disabled) shareholder for an amount determined by a previously agreed upon formula. Assume further that A dies and B becomes obligated to purchase the shares previously owned by A for $2,000,000. If B has no cash but the corporation does, it should not be surprising if B looks to the corporation for that cash. She might, of course, simply have the corporation distribute $2,000,000 to her and (assuming adequate earnings and profits) pay tax on a $2,000,000 dividend, or she might redeem stock. Unfortunately, since B will continue to be the 100% shareholder of the corporation, any redemption by her would be taxed as a dividend. Instead of doing either of these, past taxpayers in B's situation have instead simply had the corporation redeem A's shares directly from A's estate. Since the estate was terminating its interest in the corporation, it would receive sale or exchange treatment on the redemption and was taxed at only capital gains rates (and had a stepped up basis in any event). Since B ended up having nothing at all to do with the transaction, B reported nothing for tax purposes.

Unfortunately for B, the IRS sees this transaction somewhat differently than B would like. If a taxpayer has a "primary and unconditional obligation" to perform a contract, assigns that contract to her corporation, and the corporation performs in the shareholder's place, the IRS treats the assignment to the corporation of the contractual obligation as a constructive distribution to the assigning shareholder.[25] In B's case, the IRS would treat the redemption of A's shares as a constructive distribution by the corporation of $2,000,000 to B, followed by B's purchase of A's shares for that $2,000,000. Rather than avoiding tax, B would be taxed on a $2,000,000 dividend (assuming sufficient earnings and profits).

This result is by no means limited to Buy-Sell agreements. According to the IRS, any time that a shareholder has a primary and unconditional obligation to make a payment or purchase and that payment or purchase is instead made by the corporation, the transaction will be recharacterized as a distribution to the shareholder followed by the shareholder's payment to the obligee. The result might well be that B will be taxed on a $2,000,000 dividend even if A's shares are acquired for their real fair market value. For example, if the corporation was worth $4,000,000 prior to redeeming A's shares and only $2,000,000 after the redemption, B has gone from owning a 50% interest in $4,000,000 to owning a 100% interest in $2,000,000. In other words, B can be taxed on the $2,000,000 dividend even though she actually receives no value from the corporation. B's basis in her corporate stock will be

---

[25] *Sullivan v. US*, 244 F. Supp. 605 (1965), *aff'd*, 363 F. 2d 724 (1966), *cert denied*, 387 US 905 (1967), *rehearing* *denied*, 388 US 924 (1967); Rev. Rul. 69-608, 1969-2 C.B. 42.

¶504.03(a)

increased by the $2,000,000 treated as distributed to her and then used to purchase the shares from A, but that will likely provide little consolation.

B can avoid this recharacterization relatively easily. All that she needs to do is to ensure that the corporation does not assume a contractual obligation for which she is unconditionally and primarily liable. Any agreement either originally drafted to make the corporation, rather than the shareholder, primarily liable to purchase the redeemed shares will result in no tax liability imposed on B if the corporation carries out the purchase, and any agreement originally drafted to make B primarily liable can be amended to impose that liability on the corporation so long as the amendment is agreed to prior to the time that B becomes primarily and unconditionally liable to make the purchase.

(b) Redemptions Incident to Divorce

The general principles described above may also result in constructive dividend treatment when one spouse has a primary and unconditional obligation to purchase the shares owned by her former (or soon to be former) spouse. For example, if H and W each own "½ the shares of X Corp, W is (primarily and unconditionally) required to buy all of the X shares owned by H, and instead W has X Corp redeem H's shares for cash or other property, the general principles described above would treat the transaction as a constructive dividend to W followed by W's purchase of the X stock from H. The only difference between this case and one not relating to divorce would appear to be that Code Sec. 1041 applies to transfer between the spouses so that the second part of the recharacterized transaction, that is, W's purchase from H using the proceeds of the constructive dividend, would be tax free to both H and W, and W would take a transferred basis rather than a cost basis in the shares previously owned by H.

Prior to 2003, some courts had a bit of trouble with these kinds of exchanges, and the IRS was quite unhappy with some unexpected results. In response, treasury enacted regulations under Code Sec. 1041 that change the expected results described above only by giving taxpayers substantial leeway to determine the outcome. Taxpayers can, of course, initially structure property settlements involving stock either as requiring W to redeem some of her own shares and use the proceeds to acquire H's shares (an actual redemption by W), or as making W primarily and unconditionally obligated to purchase H's shares (a constructive distribution to W if the corporation, rather than W herself, actually redeems H's shares), or as requiring the corporation to redeem H's shares (an actual redemption by H, tax-free to W). Under the Code Sec. 1041 regulations, the taxpayers' chosen structure will be respected by the IRS unless the taxpayers themselves file a request to treat the transaction as if it were structured one of the other ways.[26] In other words, regardless of how the transaction is legally structured under state law, the divorcing taxpayers can choose to have the transaction taxed either as a constructive distribution to W followed by a tax-free 1041 exchange by W of the distributed cash for H's stock, or as a direct redemption of stock by H.

---

[26] Treas. Reg. § 1.1041-2.

¶504.03(b)

(c) Redemption Following Charitable Contributions of Stock

It is not only shareholders who have a legal obligation to make a payment that may want to have the cash come from their corporation in the form of a redemption. In addition to using corporate cash to satisfy an existing obligation, shareholders have also used (indirectly) corporate cash to finance a charitable contribution. For example, assume that A, the sole shareholder of X Corp, who has most of his cash inside X, wants to make a deductible charitable contribution. If she gets cash from her corporation and transfers it to the charity, the tax benefit of the charitable contribution deduction will be offset by the likely dividend consequences of her cash withdrawal (whether framed as a redemption or as a straightforward dividend). If A instead simply gives to the charity of her choice some stock of X corp, she will be entitled to a charitable contribution deduction, but the charity will likely be left owning some stock of X Corporation, which A might well like to avoid, and which the charity itself will likely find unmarketable and less than useful.

A can get her charitable contribution deduction, and the recipient can rid itself of the shares of A's closely held corporation, by having X simply redeem the donated shares any time after the contribution. The IRS initially attempted to recharacterize charitable donations of stock followed by redemptions of the donated stock as constructive distributions to or redemptions by the donor/shareholder, followed by a charitable contribution of the distributed cash or property, leaving the shareholder/donor with dividend income equal to the charitable contribution deduction. Now, however, the IRS accepts stock donations followed by redemption of the donated shares as separate transactions (leaving the donor with a charitable contribution deduction without any corresponding income, and leaving the tax exempt entity to redeem the stock), so long as at the time of the transfer of the shares, the charitable donee is not under a legal obligation to redeem the shares and so long as it cannot be put under such an obligation by the corporation without its subsequent consent.[27]

(d) Redemption to Pay Death Taxes

In cases where stock makes up a significant portion of a decedent's estate (35% in the case of stock of a single corporation, or stock of two separate corporations, if each interest is worth at least 20% of the value of the net estate),[28] Code Sec. 303 allows redemptions to be treated as sales or exchanges even though they might otherwise be taxed as distributions. Although the section is concerned with redemptions used to pay death taxes, it makes no effort to actually trace the use of the redemption proceeds. Instead, it makes sale or exchange treatment available only if and to the extent that the redeeming shareholder is actually liable for inheritance taxes,[29] and only to the extent that the redemption distributions are made within 90 days from the expiration of the statute of limitations for the assessment of such taxes.[30]

---

[27] Rev. Rul. 78-197, 1978-1 CB 83.

[28] For this purpose, the gross estate minus deductible (under Code Sec. 2053) funeral and administrative expenses, Code Sec. 303(a)(2).

[29] Code Sec. 303(a), (b)(3).

[30] Code Sec. 303(b)(1)(A).

¶ 505 Stock Sales to Affiliated Corporations: Code Sec. 304

.01 Introduction

A noncorporate shareholder anxious to get cash out of a corporation while avoiding dividend taxation (by avoiding a redemption taxed as a dividend) might be tempted to arrange to do so by establishing and conducting business through two corporations rather than one. To see how this might work, assume that A owns all of Corporation X and Corporation Y, both of which are successful, have earnings and profits, and have cash on hand that A would like to receive while being taxed only on her gain rather than on her entire amount realized, and being taxed only at capital gains rates. Rather than simply having the corporations issue dividends or redeem some of her shares (which redemptions would be taxed as dividends because of A's continuing control), A might get cash from X by selling to X some shares of Y, and she might get cash from Y by selling to Y some shares of X. In either case, A retains control of both corporations, but would appear to be able to get cash out of either without much tax. Another way to apparently accomplish the same tax goal would be for A to own only one corporation (P Corp), but have that corporation in turn set up a subsidiary (S Corp). Whenever A wanted cash without much tax, rather than redeem P stock she could simply sell some P stock to S, which she would continue to control through her ownership interest in P.

Code Sec. 304 was designed to prevent exactly these tactics. Code Sec. 304 provides generally that (1) if one or more persons controls (50% or more of the stock by voting power or value) two or more (brother-sister) corporations and sells stock of one of those corporations to the other, or (2) if the shareholder of a parent corporation sells that stock to the parent's subsidiary, the transaction will be treated as a Code Sec. 301 distribution rather than as a sale or exchange unless the shareholder's reduction in interest in the corporation whose stock is sold is sufficient to receive sale or exchange treatment under Code Sec. 302(b).

.02 Brother-Sister Specifics: When Code Sec. 304 Applies

As mentioned above, Code Sec. 304 applies when one or more persons controls two or more corporations and sells shares of one to the other, or when a person sells stock of a parent to its subsidiary. While wholly owned Brother-Sister corporations or a wholly owned Parent corporation present the most obvious applications of Code Sec. 304, Code Sec. 304 also applies to numerous other situations. Assume, for example, that A owns 70 of 100 outstanding shares of X Co. and 60 of 100 outstanding shares of Y Co., and that A sells 30 shares of X to Y. Because A has at least 50% control of both corporations, Code Sec. 304 applies, so that the transaction will not receive sale or exchange treatment unless the decrease in A's ownership of X stock would be sufficient to provide sale or exchange treatment under Code Sec. 302(b). In this case, A's direct ownership of X goes from 70/100 (70%) to 40/100 (notice that unlike in a real redemption, the number of outstanding shares of X does not change. Only the ownership of those shares changes). In addition, though, immediately after the transaction, A is still the 60% owner of Y, and Y now owns 30 shares of X. As a result, A continues to own 18 shares of X by attribution (under Code Sec. 318(a)(2)). A's ownership of X goes from 70% to 58%, likely not enough to provide A with sale or exchange treatment.[31]

In addition, Code Sec. 304 can apply even when no single shareholder controls either of the corporations, but where co-owners act in concert. Assume, for example, that A, B, C and D each own 25 of the 100 total outstanding shares of both X Corp. and Y Corp., and that each sells five shares of X to Y. Because Code Sec. 304 applies if one or more shareholders control each of two corporations, it applies in this case. A, B, C, and D each goes from owning 25 of 100 shares of X directly to owning only 20 shares of X directly, but each continues to own 25% of Y, which now owns 20 shares of X, so that, taking into account attribution, no shareholder has reduced her ownership interest in X and no one gets sale or exchange treatment.

Without some additional limitations, though, these shareholders could, with little effort, avoid Code Sec. 304 entirely. Assume that A, B, C, and D each owns 25% of X Corp., and 25% of Y Corp., that Y Corp in turn owns 60% of Z Corp, and that the remaining shares of Z are owned by numerous unrelated and uninvolved persons, as pictured below.

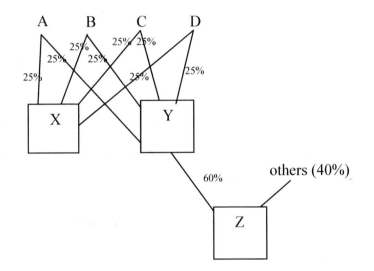

A, B, C, and D could still act together to sell an equal number of their shares, say 6 shares per person, of X stock to Z. Once again, their actual interests in X will remain unchanged, because the X stock they do not own directly is now owned by Z, which is in turn effectively controlled by Y, which is in turn controlled by A, B, C, and D.

Absent some special rules, Code Sec. 304 would have no application to this transaction. While A, B, C and D obviously control X, they do not seem to be in 50%

---

[31] A redemption that brings A's ownership below the amount needed to control extraordinary corporate actions (for example, from 70% to 58%, if a two thirds majority is required) might qualify for sale or exchange treatment under Code Sec. 302(b)(1) as not essentially equivalent to a dividend if, at least in the eyes of the IRS, such ex-traordinary corporate action was imminent. In this case, however, since A owns 60% of Y, A can still effectively control all 20 of X shares now owned by Y, so A still controls the same 70 shares of X that he did prior to the transaction. As a result, sale or exchange treatment would be highly unlikely.

¶505.02

or greater control of Z, the purchasing corporation. Y has 60% control of Z, but there is typically no attribution from Y to the selling shareholders, because none of them is a greater than 50% shareholder of Y. Special rules that make Code Sec. 304 applicable to this transaction appear in Code Sec. 304(c)(1). That subsection provides that for purposes of determining whether there exists the 50% or more control required for the application of Code Sec. 304, if one or more persons (A, B, C and D) are in control of one corporation (Y) that in turn owns at least 50% of another corporation (Z), then those persons owning the first corporation (A, B, C, and D) shall be treated as in control of that second corporation (Z). As a result, if A, B, C, and D each sell six shares of X to Z, Code Sec. 304 will apply to the transaction.[32]

Of course the fact that Code Sec. 304 applies to a transaction does not automatically change the tax consequences. It only requires that the transaction be run through the Code Sec. 302(b) tests to determine the actual outcome. Even though Code Sec. 304(c)(1) treats A, B, C, and D as being "in control" of Z, making Code Sec. 304 applicable, it would appear that none of the X stock now owned by Z will be attributed to the individual Y shareholders, because none of the individuals is a 50% or greater shareholder of Y.[33] In this case, each shareholder would appear to go from owning 25% of X immediately prior to the transaction to owning 19% of the X stock immediately afterwards. Thus it would appear that the distributions qualify as substantially disproportionate and the shareholders receive sale or exchange treatment.

In order to make it more likely that Code Sec. 304 will change the ultimate result so that the individual shareholders in cases such as this receive Code Sec. 301 distribution treatment rather than sale or exchange treatment, Code Sec. 304(b)(1) provides that for purposes of determining whether the shareholders have sufficiently reduced their interest in the corporation whose stock they sell, the corporate attribution rules shall apply between corporations and shareholders without regard to whether or not the shareholder owns at least 50% of the corporation's stock. Since Y is treated as owning 60% of the shares owned by Z, and A, B, C, and D, because they are each 25% shareholders of Y, are now treated as owning 25% of the shares attributed to Y from Z. Each shareholder's interest in X has, thus, been reduced, pro rata, from 25% to 22.6%, likely resulting in across the board dividend treatment.[34]

---

[32] In addition, Code Sec. 304(c)(3) provides that for purposes of determining control under Code Sec. 304, there is attribution into and/or out of a corporation to any shareholder that owns at least 5% of the corporation's stock, rather than the 50% ownership usually required for any corporate-shareholder attribution under Code Sec. 318. In this case, that would mean that A, B, C, and D would each be treated as owning 25% of any shares actually or constructively owned by Z. Note, however, that in this case Z owns no shares of X prior to the transaction, so attribution from Y to the individuals would be meaningless. Obviously, Z owns some shares of X after the transaction, and attribution rules particular to

Code Sec. 304 will apply to that situation as well. *See* ¶ 505.03, *infra*.

[33] Note that Code Sec. 304(c)(3) provides that attribution between corporations and their shareholders exists so long as the shareholder owns at least 5%, rather than 50%, of the corporation's outstanding shares. What is important in this case is that Code Sec. 302(c) applies only for purposes of determining whether Code Sec. 304 applies to require that a transaction be run through the redemption tests. Only the regular attribution rules apply for purposes of determining whether any of the Code Sec. 302 tests have actually been met by the selling shareholder.

[34] See discussion at ¶ 505.03(b)(i).

.03 How Code Sec. 304 Changes the Outcome

(a) Sale or Exchange Treatment Under Code Sec. 302(b)

Not surprisingly, transactions under Code Sec. 304 that receive sale or exchange treatment are essentially treated as the actual sales or exchanges that they are. The selling shareholder recognizes gain or loss equal to the difference between her basis in the stock sold and her amount realized, and the purchasing corporation takes a cost basis in the shares it acquires.

(b) Code Sec. 304 Transactions that are Recharacterized

(i) *In General*

The idea underlying Code Sec. 304 is that a transaction in which the shareholder's interest in the corporation whose stock is sold (the "issuing corporation") is not sufficiently reduced will result in dividend treatment rather than sale or exchange treatment for the selling shareholder, but the statute does a bit more than simply characterize the payment from the purchasing corporation to the shareholder. In addition to accounting for (generally, as a dividend) the cash (or property) coming out of the purchasing corporation into the hands of the shareholder, the Code must also account for the fact that stock of the issuing corporation goes from the shareholder into the purchasing corporation. Code Sec. 304 accomplishes all of this by treating the stock sale as two separate transactions: (1) a Code Sec. 351 transfer of the sold stock by the shareholder to the purchasing corporation in exchange for an amount of stock of the purchasing corporation equal in value to the stock actually sold, followed by (2) a redemption by the purchasing corporation of the stock issued in the Code Sec. 351 exchange.

The statue, thankfully, is a bit easier to make sense of when applied to the facts of a specific transaction. To do so, assume that A owns 80 of 100 outstanding shares of X Corp. (with a basis and value of $1 per share) and 80 of 100 outstanding shares of Y Corp. (with a basis and value of $1 per share), and that A sells 40 shares (total basis $40) of X to Y for their value of $40. Because A is in control of both X and Y, Code Sec. 304 applies. Immediately after the sale, A owns 40 shares of X directly, and another 32 shares by attribution from Y, so that A does not receive sale or exchange treatment. Code Sec. 304 treats this as two transactions. In the first, A transfers 40 shares of X to Y in exchange for 40 shares of Y in a Code Sec. 351 exchange. In the second, Y redeems those same newly issued 40 shares for $40. The diagram below indicates both parts of the transaction.

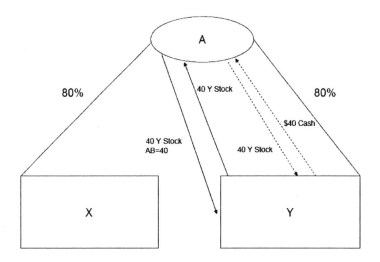

As a result of part (1) of this transaction, the Code Sec. 351 exchange in which A transfers property (the X stock) to Y in exchange for Y stock, A recognizes no gain, under Code Sec. 351, and A's basis in the 40 shares of the Y stock he is deemed to receive is the same ($40) as was his basis in the property he transfers to Y (the X shares, with a value and basis of $40), under Code Sec. 358.

In part (2) of this transaction, the deemed redemption of the newly issued Y stock, the first fact to note is that this redemption is one that will never be treated as a sale or exchange, and there is no need to run this deemed redemption through any of Code Sec. 302(b)'s tests for sale or exchange treatment. The stock being "redeemed" is the same stock that was just "issued" in the same transaction, so the net result is necessarily no real change in A's ownership of Y stock. As a result, the $40 received in exchange for the Y stock is treated as a distribution from Y to A. In order to make dividend treatment more likely, Code Sec. 304(b)(2) provides that this distribution from Y to A is a dividend to extent of Y's earnings and profits and that if Y has insufficient earnings and profits to make the entire distribution a dividend it will also be a dividend to extent of X's earnings and profits, reducing Y's, and then X's, earnings and profits in turn as they are used to ensure dividend treatment.

Since this deemed redemption of the (deemed) newly issued Y stock is treated as a Code Sec. 301 distribution, A's basis in the redeemed shares will be transferred to the other Y shares that A holds. Since A's basis in the deemed (newly issued and) redeemed Y shares is an exchange basis from his basis in the X shares actually transferred to Y, the net result is that A's basis in his Y stock will be increased by whatever his basis was in the X shares actually transferred to Y.

The net results of steps (1) and (2) are, then, that (1) the amount paid to A is treated as a dividend to the extent of the earnings and profits of Y, and, if necessary, of X as well, (2) A's basis in her Y shares is increased by whatever her basis was in

¶505.03(b)(i)

the X shares transferred to Y[35] (in this case, since A transferred to Y X stock with a basis of $40, A's total stock basis in Y will be increased from $80 by $40 to $120), and (3) Y's basis in the shares it gets from A is the same as A's basis was in those shares ($1 per share, for a total basis of $40 in the block of 40 shares).

(ii) *The Intersection of 351 and 304*

Not surprisingly, corporations and shareholders quickly attempted to avoid the dividend treatment that often resulted from the application of Code Sec. 304. One way to do so that was at least somewhat successful for some period of time was change the structure of the transaction just a little bit in a way that seemed to implicate Code Sec. 351. To see how this worked, assume the same facts as in the example above: A owns 80 of 100 outstanding shares of X Corp. (with a basis and value of $1 per share) and 80 of 100 outstanding shares of Y Corp. (with a basis and value of $1 per share), and A again transfers 40 shares (total basis $40) of X to Y. This time, though, assume that instead of receiving $40 cash from Y, A receives only $30 cash and also receives 10 shares of Y stock, worth $10. Because A is in control of both X and Y, Code Sec. 304 would again seem to apply. Immediately after the sale, A again owns 40 shares of X directly, and another 32 (or so) shares by attribution from Y, so that A does not receive sale or exchange treatment. Indeed, the only difference from the above hypothetical is that now A owns 90 rather than 80 shares of Y, so there is a bit more of the X stock owned by Y that is attributed to A. As above, it would appear that A is taxed on a dividend of at least $30 (the cash received). The transaction is pictured below.

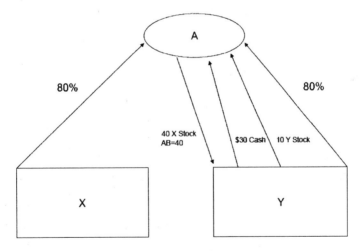

The issuance of the single share of Y stock together with the cash used to be (but is no longer) potentially quite significant to the characterization of this

[35] If A actually owns no shares of Y but was treated as owning Y stock because of attribution rules, then A may actually increase her basis in the X shares she owns by the amount that would have otherwise gone to increase her basis in Y. In other words, although she would at that point own fewer shares of X than she did initially, her basis in the X shares she retains would remain the same as her basis was in all of the X stock she owned immediately prior to the Code Sec. 304 transaction.

transaction. One might now also describe this transaction by saying that A has transferred property (the X stock) to Y in exchange for 10 shares of Y stock and $30 cash. Since A owns (a bit more than) 80% (90/100 shares) of the Y stock outstanding, A is in control of Y immediately after this exchange. As a result, this entire transaction qualifies as a Code Sec. 351 exchange (A has transferred to Y property for stock plus boot, and A is in control of Y immediately after the exchange).[36] Since A has received boot, any gain realized by A will be recognized to the extent of the boot received.[37] In this hypothetical, however, A has transferred property (the X stock) with both a basis and value of $40. A realizes, and thus recognizes, no gain at all. If this transaction is treated as a Code Sec. 351 exchange, A thus avoids Code Sec. 304 and its accompanying dividend treatment entirely.

Not surprisingly, this attempt to convert Code Sec. 304 transactions into Code Sec. 351 transactions has been addressed in the Code and no longer works to help A. Instead, Code Sec. 304(b)(3) provides that Code Sec. 304(a), and not Code Sec. 351, shall apply to any property received in a distribution described in paragraph 304(a) (that is, any transaction to which Code Sec. 304 applies). Since property is defined as excluding any stock of the corporation making the distribution,[38] the Y stock that Y distributes is governed by Code Sec. 351 in our example, but nothing else is affected by Code Sec. 351. The net result is that A is taxed on a $30 dividend (the cash received from Y). A is also treated as having engaged in a Code Sec. 351 exchange in which she transferred 10 shares of X for 10 shares of Y. This exchange is not taxed to either A (under Code Sec. 351) or Y (under Code Sec. 1032). A's basis in these 10 Y shares is the same as her basis was in the 10X shares transferred in exchange (in this case, $10); and Y's basis in the 10 X shares received in the Code Sec. 351 exchange is the same as A's basis was in those shares, the same result for Y that Code Sec. 304 treatment would have required, simply determined directly, rather than indirectly, under Code Sec. 362.

.04 Parent-Subsidiary Transactions

As mentioned above, Code Sec. 304 also applies if the shareholder of a corporation sells some of that corporation's stock to another corporation controlled by the issuing corporation (the corporation whose stock is sold). Control for this purpose is defined not as the typical 80 percent ownership, but, consistently with the rest of Code Sec. 304, as ownership of at least 50% by vote or value. Thus, for example, assume that A is an 80% shareholder of P (owning 80 of 100 outstanding shares, with a basis and value of $1 per share), and sells 1/4 (20 shares) of her P stock to S for $20. Further assume that S is 50% owned by P. Since control for purposes of Code Sec. 304 is defined as ownership of at least 50% of a corporation's outstanding shares, P is in control of S for purposes of Code Sec. 304. Code Sec. 304 applies, and the transaction is treated as a redemption by P of 20 shares previously owned by A. Immediately after this exchange, A owns 60 shares of P directly, and also owns, by way of attribution from P, 60% of whatever outstanding P shares that P itself owns by attribution from S. Since P owns 50% of the S stock, P

---

[36] *See generally* Chapter 1.

[37] Code Sec. 351(b).

[38] Code Sec. 317(a).

will be treated as owning 50% of the 20 shares owned by S, or 10 shares. A in turn is treated as owning 6 (60%) of those shares. A's reduction in ownership of P from 80% to 66% will not result in sale or exchange treatment under Code Sec. 302(b).[39]

As a result of the above, the deemed redemption by P of 20 shares will be treated as a Code Sec. 301 distribution from P to A. The distribution will be a dividend to the extent of P's earnings and profits and, if P has insufficient earnings and profits, to the extent of S's earnings and profits in addition (with a subsequent reduction in the earnings and profits of whichever corporations earnings and profits the distribution comes from). Since the entire $20 received by A is treated as a dividend, A's total basis in her P stock remains unchanged (at $80), even though she now only owns 60 shares instead of 80. In other words, the basis of the redeemed shares is added on to the basis of A's other shares in P.[40] Unlike in a brother-sister 304 transaction, in a parent-subsidiary transaction governed by Code Sec. 304, the purchasing subsidiary simply takes a cost basis in its newly purchased P stock.[41]

As is the case with Brother-Sister transactions governed by Code Sec. 304, not every sale or exchange that comes within the purview of Code Sec. 304(a)(2) will eventually receive dividend treatment. For example, assume that A is a 20% shareholder of P (owning 20 of 100 outstanding shares), and sells 1/4 (five shares) of her P stock to S, a corporation 50% owned by P. Again, Code Sec. 304 applies because A is selling stock of a corporation (P) to another corporation (S) of which the issuer is in 50% control. Immediately after this exchange, A owns only 15 shares of P directly, but because Code Sec. 304 brings into play the corporate attribution rules without regard to Code Sec. 318's 50% shareholder requirement, A will also own, by way of attribution, a portion of the P shares owned by S. P will be treated as owning 50% of the 5 P shares owned by S (for a total of 2.5 shares), and A is treated as owning 15% of whatever shares are owned, directly or indirectly, by P (15% of 2.5=.375 shares). Although Code Sec. 304 applies to this transaction, A's reduction in ownership of P from 20% to 15.375% will nonetheless result in sale or exchange treatment under Code Sec. 302(b), so that the actual sale or exchange from A to S will simply be treated as the sale or exchange that it is, and no person's tax consequences will be impacted by the application of Code Sec. 304.

.05 Concurrent Brother-Sister, Parent-Subsidiary Transactions under Code Sec. 304

Code Sec. 304's broad definition of control (50%) and broadened application of corporate-shareholder attribution rules (no 50% shareholder restriction) make for some potentially interesting situations. With just a little imagination, one can turn virtually any Brother-Sister relationship into a parent-subsidiary relationship or virtually any parent-subsidiary relationship into a brother-sister relationship.[42] Code

---

[39] Under Code Sec. 302(b)(1), a reduction from 80% to 66% might receive sale or exchange treatment (at least where extraordinary corporate action is imminent) because the shareholder's interest may be reduced from that of one who can control even extraordinary corporate action requiring a 2/3 vote to one who can control only action requiring majority control. In this case, however,

A's continued control over P (and thus over P's interest in S) will likely result in dividend treatment.

[40] Treas. Reg. § 1.304-3(a).

[41] Rev. Rul. 80-89, 1980-2 C.B. 106.

[42] We hope you will take our word on this, since the impact is nil.

Sec. 304(a)(1) seems to state that a transaction will be treated as a brother-sister purchase only if it is not a parent-subsidiary purchase, which, if applied technically could mean that no transaction would be treated under the brother-sister rules because every brother-sister relationship could be potentially characterized as a parent-subsidiary relationship with just a bit of effort. The regulations suggest, however, that if two corporations have a brother-sister relationship under Code Sec. 304 without attribution, that relationship will not be recharacterized as a parent-subsidiary relationship by technical application of the attribution rules.[43]

---

[43] Prop. Reg. § 1.304-2(a)(5), 1.304-2(c), Ex. 1.

¶505.05

Chapter 6

Liquidations and Partial Liquidations

¶ 601 Introduction

Put simply, for tax purposes there are two types of liquidations: taxable and tax-free. With some exceptions, tax-free status is given only to the liquidation of a subsidiary by its parent corporation. All other corporate liquidations are taxable.

In a taxable liquidation, the liquidating corporation generally recognizes any gain or loss on assets sold or distributed to shareholders, and the shareholders recognize gain or loss on their shares equal to the difference between their amount realized (the amount of cash and the fair market value of any assets received) and their basis in the shares they held. In a tax-free liquidation, the general rule is that neither the liquidating subsidiary nor the parent corporation recognizes any gain or loss, and the parent steps into the shoes of its former subsidiary with respect to virtually all tax-relevant attributes, including asset basis, holding period, depreciation, recapture, and earnings and profits.

Of course, the big picture is never the entire picture, but for the most part the rest of this chapter merely fills in details and sets forth some limits and restrictions on these general rules.

¶ 602 What is a "Liquidation" for Tax Purposes

Obviously, a formal dissolution of a corporation under applicable state law means that the corporation has been liquidated for tax purposes, as well as for any other purposes. But it is important to note that it is possible for a corporation to liquidate for tax purposes either before such formal dissolution or even in the absence of any such dissolution. Liquidation (for tax purposes) can occur *prior* to dissolution if the corporation ceases to be a going concern, so that its activities are merely for the purpose of winding up its affairs, paying its debts, and distributing any remaining balance to its shareholders.[1] Liquidation can occur in the *absence* of

---

[1] Treas. Reg. § 1.332-2(c) states that: "A status of liquidation exists when the corporation ceases to be a going concern and its activities are merely for the purpose of winding up its affairs, paying its debts, and distributing any remaining balance to its shareholders. A liquidation may be completed prior to the actual dissolution of the liquidating corporation....".

any formal dissolution if the corporation winds up all its affairs but, rather than dissolving, retains a nominal amount of assets solely to preserve its legal existence.[2]

In addition to knowing when a liquidation is *completed* for tax purposes, it is also vital to know exactly when a liquidation is *begun*. The tax consequences of nonliquidating distributions may be quite different from those of liquidating distributions, so it is imperative to know whether any distribution that takes place prior to the final one is part of the liquidation or is a separate transaction that would be characterized as either a redemption or a Code Sec. 301 distribution that occurred sometime prior to the tax liquidation.

The general answer is given by Code Sec. 346(a), which states that "...a distribution shall be treated as in complete liquidation of a corporation if the distribution is one of a series of distributions in redemption of all of the stock of the corporation pursuant to a plan. If the liquidating corporation adopts a formal written plan of liquidation prior to the first of a series of liquidating distributions, those and subsequent distributions will be treated as liquidating distributions,[3] so long as the distributions are made pursuant to the plan of liquidation and are concluded in a timely manner. As to what is timely, the IRS has sanctioned periods of up to three years.[4] It is by no means clear that distributions pursuant to plans carried out in excess of three years will *not* be treated as part of the liquidation,[5] but their result is at least uncertain.

If the liquidating corporation fails to adopt a formal written plan prior to making one or more distributions, those distributions may still be treated as liquidating distributions, but only if the corporation can establish that all the distributions were clearly intended to be part of a plan of liquidation.

¶ 603 Taxable Liquidations

.01 Shareholders

(a) The General Rule: Code Sec. 331(a)

Code Sec. 331 states that amounts received by a shareholder in a complete liquidation of a corporation shall be treated as in full payment in exchange for the stock. Any shareholder simply recognizes capital[6] gain or loss equal to the difference between her stock basis and the value of the cash and other property received (net of any corporate liabilities assumed or taken subject to by the shareholder, of course). Unlike other transactions, this is true even for losses recognized by a related (owner of more than 50% of the corporation's stock) shareholder. Code Sec. 267(a)(1), which disallows any deduction of losses on all other sales or exchanges between corporations and their related persons, specifically exempts from its application liquidating distributions.

---

[2] "Nor will the mere retention of a nominal amount of assets for the sole purpose of preserving the corporation's legal existence disqualify the transaction [as a liquidation]." Treas. Reg. § 1.332-2(c).

[3] See discussion at ¶ 604.01.

[4] Rev. Proc. 99-3, 1999-1 IRB 103. But note that Treas. Reg. § 1.331-1(d) requires special reporting by shareholders if the plan both contemplates and successfully concludes the liquidation within one year.

[5] In *Estate of Charles Fearon*, 16 TC 385 (1951) (acq.), a liquidation was found to have occurred over a 23 year period, *but* that case did predate the current Code and Regulations.

[6] Assuming the shareholder is not a registered securities dealer.

Not surprisingly, since the liquidation is fully taxable to all parties, Code Sec. 334(a) provides that the former shareholders take a fair market value basis in any noncash assets received in the liquidation. Since there is no deferred gain or loss for the former shareholders, there is no reason they should have any gain or loss built into the property they receive.

(b) Shares Acquired at Different Times

If a shareholder has acquired shares at different times, so that different shares have different bases or holding periods, the amount received by the shareholder must be allocated to each separate block of shares according to their relative fair market value, and then the gain or loss on each block must be calculated separately. If all of the shares are held long term, and if all of the liquidating distributions are made within the same taxable year, this leads to exactly the same result as would simply determining the difference between the shareholder's total stock basis and the shareholder's total amount realized.

(c) Liquidating Distributions Made Over Time

If it is the liquidating *distributions*, rather than the initial stock acquisitions, that occur over time, the IRS has been significantly more generous on the timing of gain than it has been on the timing of loss. Rather than requiring installment sale treatment (where a portion of the shareholder's total gain would be taxed on each distribution) the IRS allows the shareholder who will receive an amount in excess of her stock basis to report no gain at all until the total amount distributed to her exceeds entire stock basis.[7] In other words, If T owns shares with a basis of $150,000 and a value of $300,000, and she receives liquidating distributions of $100,000 per year for three years, she will report no gain at all in year one, only $50,000 in year two and $100,000 gain in year three, thus allowing her maximum deferral.

On the other hand, if the shareholder receiving payments over time has a loss rather than a gain, none of that loss can be recognized until the final payment has been received.[8] As a result, if T's stock basis had been $600,000 and she was to receive, in liquidation, $100,000 per year for three years, only at the end of year three could she deduct her $300,000 loss.

(d) Shares Acquire Over Time and Liquidating Distributions Made Over Time

If shares have been acquired at different times and liquidating distributions are also extended over more than a single calendar year, the combination of allocating the payments made among the different blocks of shares, and the deferral of shareholder gain and loss can get a bit more interesting.

Example: Assume that T purchased 100,000 shares of X Corp for $10,000 ten years ago (Old Block) and purchased another 100,000 shares for $290,000

---

[7] Rev. Rul. 85-48, 1985-1 CB 126. The generosity of this approach is made apparent by the IRS's disregard of Code Sec. 453 and Treas. Reg. §1.453-111(d), both of which suggest that the IRS would be justified in requiring gain to be recognized on the installment method rather than allowing shareholder's to wait until all basis has been recovered prior to imposing any tax at all.

[8] Rev. Rul. 69-334, 1969-1 CB 98.

¶603.01(d)

five years ago (New Block). X is liquidating, and T will receive three annual payments of $100,000 each in liquidation. T's total stock basis is $300,000 ($10,000 for the first block and $290,000 for the second block). T's total amount realized will be $300,000. But although his total amount realized will exactly equal his total adjusted basis, T does not simply go about recognizing no gain or loss.

Instead, T must first allocate his payments to the different blocks of stock in proportion to their fair market value, so that T will be treated as receiving $150,000 of his liquidating distributions in exchange for the Old Block of 100,000 shares and $150,000 for the New 100,000 shares. With respect to the Old Block, then, T's total amount realized will be $150,000 and his total basis is $10,000. When T receives his first $50,000 payment, he will recognize gain of $40,000 (the excess of his amount realized aver his stock basis). In years two and three each $50,000 payment will be taxed in full. With respect to New Block, T will ultimately recognize a loss of $140,000 to offset the total $140,000 gain on Old Block, but T can recognize none of that loss until year three, when he receives his final payment.

(e) Liquidating Distributions of Recently Acquired Installment Obligations

As described above, liquidating distributions may consist of property as well as cash. Often, though, a liquidating corporation and its shareholders might find it easier for the corporation to sell its assets to a third party rather than distribute them to its shareholders.

As discussed below, the corporation will generally recognize any gain or loss inherent in the asset whichever way it proceeds, and each shareholder will recognize gain or loss equal to the difference between her stock basis and the value of whatever she receives in liquidation.

Nonetheless, there is one way in which the shareholder can at least postpone some or all of her gain recognition. Code Sec. 453(h)(1) provides that if the liquidation is completed within 12 months after the plan of liquidation is adopted by the corporation, and if, during that 12 month period, the corporation sells any property to a third party on the installment method and then distributes that installment contract to a shareholder in a liquidating distribution, the shareholder may choose to *not* treat the receipt of the installment obligation as a current distribution of property. Instead, the shareholder may elect to treat the actual payments made by the third party on the installment obligation as the actual liquidating distribution.

To see how Code Sec. 453(h)(1) works, assume that X Corp has a single asset (basis $100,000, fmv $500,000) and a single shareholder named S (basis $100,000, fmv $500,000). If X Corp either sells the asset and distributes the cash received, or simply distributes the asset in kind, S will recognize gain of $400,000[9] on receipt of the cash or property (and X Corp will also be taxed on $400,000 gain).[10] However, if

---

[9] Of course, the actual amount S receives would actually be decreased by any tax X pays. See discussion of taxation of liquidating corporation at ¶ 603.02, *infra*.

[10] See discussion at ¶ 603.02, *infra*.

X Corp sells the property to an unrelated third party (Y) for five annual payments of $100,000 beginning in year one, and then distributes to S the installment obligation it received from Y, S may report that in year one she has received only $100,000 (the payment received from Y) as a liquidating distribution, and she may treat the four remaining annual payments of $100,000 as the remaining liquidating distributions from X Corp.

Keep in mind that if a shareholder receives liquidating distributions over more than a single taxable year, it may generally report no gain at all until it has received distributions in excess of its entire stock basis, so that it would at first appear that S may report no gain in year one (because she is treated as having received a liquidating distribution of $100,000 and her stock basis is $100,000) and she can report her $400,000 gain only as she receives payments from Y whose total is in excess of her basis in the Y stock. Code Sec. 453(h)(2), though, requires that if Code Sec. 453(h)(1) is brought into play, then shareholder must report any gain recognized on the installment method rather than treating payments first as a return of capital and only as gain after the entire stock basis has been recovered. Code Sec. 453(h)(1) is subject to restrictions similar to the rest of Code Sec. 453 when it comes to sales to related parties and sales of inventory.

(f) Liquidating Distributions not Subject to Current Valuation

Occasionally a taxpayer might argue that while she has received all of her liquidating distributions, at least some of what she has received is made up of assets that cannot be valued (for example, contingent rights such as royalties or mineral rights), so that gain or loss cannot be determined (or taxed) until the value is finally established at some time in the future. This argument is very rarely successful. The IRS has made it clear that virtually any asset can (and must) be appraised and valued accurately at the time of distribution, and the shareholder is taxed on his or her gain based on that accurate valuation. Only in "rare and extraordinary circumstances" might the IRS allow taxpayers to delay current taxation by establishing that some asset is truly impossible to value.[11] The IRS's strong position against what is generally referred to as "open transaction" reporting is no different in the corporate liquidation context than it is in any other context where a taxpayer attempts to defer tax by claiming an inability to value property received.

.02 The Liquidating Corporation

(a) The General Rule: Gain and Loss Recognized

A liquidating corporation that distributes only cash will obviously recognize no gain or loss on the distribution. The general rule for the liquidating corporation that distributes property other than (or in addition to) cash is set forth in Code Sec. 336: " . . . gain or loss shall be recognized to a liquidating corporation on the distribution of property in complete liquidation as if such property were sold to the distributee at its fair market value." In some important ways, though, the liquidating corpora-

---

[11] Rev. Rul. 58-402, 1958-2 CB 15.

tion is treated even better (and in other ways a bit worse) than it would be on actual sales to the distributee shareholder.

(b) Limits on Losses: Code Sec. 336(d)

(i) *Code Sec. 336(d) (1)*

The most important distinction between a liquidating distribution and an actual sale to the distributee shareholder arises on distributions to greater than 50% shareholders. Corporations and their greater than 50% shareholders are "related parties" under Code Sec. 267(b), and Code Sec. 267(a)(1) disallows any losses on sales between such related parties. Significantly, though, Code Sec. 267(a)(1) by its own terms does not apply to liquidating distributions by a corporation, so that losses on liquidating distributions to such shareholders may be allowed.

Nonetheless, while Code Sec. 267 does not apply to liquidating distributions, Code Sec. 336 does contain some restrictions on the deductibility of losses on certain distributions to such related parties. Code Sec. 336(d)(1)(A)(i) provides that if any property (other than cash) is distributed by the liquidating corporation and the related shareholder does not receive her exact pro-rata share of any particular asset, the distributing corporation can recognize no loss on that particular property distributed to that related shareholder.

To see how Code Sec. 336(d)(1)(A)(i) works, assume that X Corp is owned 60% by shareholder A and 40% by shareholder B. X Corp in turn owns Loss asset (basis $100,000, fmv $40,000), Gain asset (basis $10,000, fmv $40,000) and cash of $20,000. X Corp will recognize the $30,000 gain in Gain asset no matter whether it sells the asset prior to liquidation, distributes the asset all to A, or all to B, or some to A and the rest to B. With respect to Loss asset, X will recognize the entire $60,000 loss in that asset if it distributes the asset pro rata to A and B (that is, in proportion to each shareholders stock ownership—here 60% to A and 40% to B), or if it distributes the loss asset entirely to B (the less than 50% shareholder). But if X Corp distributes some amount other than 60% of the Loss asset in kind to A (the related shareholder), then any loss on that part of the asset distributed to A will be disallowed. If X Corp distributes the entire Loss asset to A, it will recognize none of the $60,000 loss. If it distributes half of the Loss asset to A and half to B, it will recognize the $30,000 loss on the half distributed to B, but none of the $30,000 loss on the half distributed to related shareholder A; and if it distributes the Loss asset 75% to A and 25% to B, it will recognize the $15,000 loss on the 25% distributed to B but none of the loss on the 25% distributed to A.

Even if a related shareholder receives exactly her pro rata share of loss property, Code Sec. 336(d)(1)(A)(ii) provides that the liquidating corporation will not be able to recognize its loss on any part of the asset distributed to the related shareholder if that loss asset has been acquired by the corporation in either a 351 exchange or as a contribution to capital within five years prior to its distribution in liquidation. As with Code Sec. 336(d)(1)(A)(i), the corporation can avoid the restriction on deducting its loss to the extent it distributes the loss asset to an unrelated shareholder, but the loss is disallowed on any part of the asset distributed to the related shareholder, regardless of who actually contributed the property to

¶603.02(b)

the corporation and regardless of whether the loss was built into the asset at the time of its contribution within the last five years or whether it was all incurred after the asset was received by the liquidating corporation.

(ii) *Code Sec. 336(d)(2)*

The only other restriction on losses by a liquidating corporation in a taxable liquidation is prescribed by Code Sec. 336(d)(2). Under that section, if, within two years prior to the corporation's adoption of a plan of liquidation,[12] the corporation has acquired property with a built in loss in either a 351 exchange or a contribution to capital, that built-in loss will be disallowed, regardless of what shareholder the property is distributed to, unless the corporation can show that the recently contributed built-in loss asset had a "clear and substantial" relationship to the corporation's current or future business.[13] The greater the amount of built-in loss in the property, the more closely the IRS is likely to scrutinize the actual relationship of the asset to the corporation's business needs.[14]

Code Sec. 336(d)(2) acts differently from Code Sec. 336(d)(1) in two ways: (1) the loss limitation applies regardless of which shareholder receives the tainted property, and (2) the loss disallowed is not necessarily the entire loss in the property at the time of *distribution*, but only any of that loss that was built into the property at the time of *contribution*. The statute disallows only the built- in loss by reducing the corporation's basis (but not below 0) in the built-in loss asset by the amount of loss built into the asset at the time of the contribution.[15]

To see how this works, assume that shareholders A, B, C, and D each own 25% of the stock of X Corp. In 2011 in a 351 transaction in which all shareholders contribute property of equal value, A contributes Loss property (basis $100,000, fmv $60,000), and Loss property has no clear and substantial relationship to X Corp's business. Within two years, X Corp adopts a plan of liquidation. Pursuant to that plan, among cash and other assets distributed, it distributes Loss property to Shareholder C. At the time of the distribution, Loss property is worth only $35,000. For purposes of determining X Corp's realized loss on this distribution, X Corp's basis in Loss property is reduced by the built-in loss (at the time of contribution) of $40,000 (the excess of Loss property's basis ($100,000) over its value ($60,000) at the time of contribution). Thus, under Code Sec. 336(d)(2), X is treated as having distributed a property with a basis of $60,000 and a value of $35,000 (its actual value at the time of distribution). The $25,000 loss that accrued after the property was already in the corporation's hands (where the property decreased in actual value from $60,000 to only $35,000) is allowed.

---

[12] Code Sec. 336(d)(2)(B)(I)(ii) actually refers to property contributed in a 351 exchange or contribution "as part of a plan" to enable the soon to be liquidating corporation to recognize the built-in loss in the property. But Code Sec. 336(d)(2)(B)(2) then states that any property contributed within the two years prior to the adoption of the plan of liquidation is adopted "shall, except as provided in the regulations, be treated as part" of such a plan. The legislative history of the provision suggests that any contribution made prior to the two year period could be treated as part of such a plan "only in the most rare and unusual cases." H.R. Rep. No.99-841, 99th Cong., 2d Sess. II-200 (1986).

[13] This language appears not in the statute itself, but in the legislative history. H. R. Rep. No. 99-841, 99th Cong., 2d Sess. II-201 (1986).

[14] H.R. Rep. No.99-841, 99th Cong., 2d Sess. II-200 (1986).

[15] Code Sec. 336(d)(2)(A).

¶603.02(b)(ii)

To take this example a step further, assume that by the time of the liquidating distribution (of the built-in Loss property) to shareholder C, shareholder C was no longer a 25% shareholder but owned more than 50% of the stock of X Corp. In that case, Code Sec. 336(d)(2) might still apply to reduce X Corp's basis and realized loss on the distribution to C, but more importantly, the distribution would now be a distribution to a related shareholder. As a result, Code Sec. 336(d)(1) would disallow any and all losses on any property contributed within the five years prior to the liquidation and distributed to the related shareholder. Thus, a $15,000 loss might still be *realized* by X Corp on the distribution of Loss asset to C even after the application of Code Sec. 332(d)(2), but no loss at all could be *recognized*, or taken into account for tax purposes because of the application of Code Sec. 336(d)(1)(B).

¶ 604 Tax Free Liquidations

.01 Qualification

When a corporation liquidates its 80% owned subsidiary corporation, that liquidation is likely to be tax free to the parent under Code Sec. 332 and tax free to the liquidated subsidiary under Code Sec. 337. In addition, the parent will step into the subsidiary's shoes with respect to basis, holding period, depreciation, recapture, earnings and profits, and almost all other tax attributes under Code Sec. 381. If there are any minority shareholders (that is, if the parent owns at least 80% of the subsidiary's stock but less than 100%) any liquidating distributions to the minority shareholders are governed by Code Sec. 331 at the shareholder level and Code Sec. 336 at the liquidating corporation level.

(a) Stock Ownership

To be more technically precise, Code Sec. 332 imposes both stock ownership requirements and time requirements in order for a liquidation to qualify as tax free. The ownership requirements are that at every moment from the time the plan of liquidation is adopted until it receives its final distribution, the parent must own stock sufficient to meet the requirements of Code Sec. 1504(a)(2). Code Sec. 1504(a)(2)[16] in turn requires that the parent corporation own at least 80% of the voting power and 80% of the value of the outstanding stock of the subsidiary. For purposes of determining both the value of all outstanding stock and the parent's share of ownership of that stock, nonvoting, nonconvertible preferred stock that does not participate in corporate growth is ignored.[17]

(b) Timing

The time requirement can be met in either of two ways. It is met if all of the liquidating distributions occur within a single taxable year of the distributing corporation.[18] Alternatively, the time requirements will be met if (1) the liquidating corporation adopts a formal plan of liquidation, (2) that plan provides that all liquidating distributions shall be completed within three years following the taxable

---

[16] Code Sec. 1504(a)(2) is also discussed at Chapter 9, ¶ 904, *infra*, in conjunction with affiliated corporations.

[17] Code Sec. 1504(a)(4). If nonvoting preferred stock does participate in corporate growth, either because its redemption or liquidation rights exceed the issue price plus a reasonable redemption premium or in any other reason, however, it is not disregarded. Code Sec. 1504(a)(4).

[18] Code Sec. 332(b)(2).

year in which the plan is adopted, and (3) all such distributions actually are completed within that time.[19]

A liquidating subsidiary that adopts a three year plan of liquidation to which it assumes that Code Sec. 332 will apply, may end up failing to meet the three year distribution requirement. If it ultimately fails that requirement, then Code Sec. 332 would not apply to the liquidation and all of the liquidating distributions, including those made prior to year four, are ultimately taxable. In order to ensure that the IRS can collect appropriate taxes if what had seemed to be a Code Sec. 332 liquidation ends up failing to meet the requirements and becomes taxable under Code Secs. 336 and 337, the parent corporation may be required by the IRS to post a bond, waive the statute of limitations, or do both if the distributions are not completed within the subsidiary's taxable year in which the plan is adopted.[20]

(c) Planning

Code Sec. 332 is not by its terms elective. Either its requirements are met and the section applies or the requirements are not met and the liquidation is taxable. Nonetheless, as with practically everything in corporate tax, the determination of whether the IRS and courts will determine that the terms of Code Sec. 332 are met depends on facts and circumstances and may be subject to some taxpayer discretion. In some cases, taxpayers may attempt to qualify for Code Sec. 332's nonrecognition by taking potentially questionable actions to meet either the ownership or the time requirements, and at other times corporations with losses might attempt to disqualify liquidations from nonrecognition, by taking actions specifically designed to prevent the liquidation from meeting either the ownership or the time requirements of Code Sec. 332.

To see how these situations might come about, assume that X Corp owns 75% of the outstanding stock of Y Corp. X Corp is considering liquidating Y Corp, but would prefer that the liquidation be tax-free. In order to obtain tax-free status for the liquidation, X might first acquire 80% ownership of X Corp (by acquiring some stock either from other shareholders or from the corporation itself, or by having Y Corp redeem some of the stock held by the other shareholders to reduce the total stock outstanding, thereby increasing X's percentage ownership) and then adopt a formal plan of liquidation immediately thereafter. Because the parent corporation must own at least 80% of the outstanding stock of the liquidating corporation at all times from the time the plan of liquidation is adopted until the final distribution is made, whether or not the liquidation qualifies for Code Sec. 332 treatment depends on whether the "plan of liquidation" is actually adopted after X Corp already has 80% control or whether the plan is found to have been adopted at sometime prior to X's acquisition of that 80% control. If X Corp acquires the requisite 80% control by purchasing shares from the other shareholders and Y Corp adopts the formal plan of liquidation after that purchase, the form of the transaction will likely be respected by the IRS.[21]

---

[19] As is the case with taxable liquidations, the fact that the liquidating corporation maintains its legal existence does not prevent the liquidation from being established, so long as only nominal assets are retained and those assets are neither intended to be nor are used for any business purpose.

[20] Code Sec. 332(b) (second sentence); Reg. § 1.332-4.

[21] Rev. Rul. 75-521, 1975-2 CB 120.

On the other hand, if X does not acquire control by purchasing the shares from the other shareholders, but instead X achieves the requisite 80% control because Y Corp redeems shares from the other shareholders, the IRS will take note of the fact that essentially all that happened was a series of distributions by Y (the liquidating) Corp. The first distribution is made by Y in exchange for some or all of the shares owned by the minority shareholders, and the remaining distributions are made in exchange for the shares held by X Corp (the parent). In this case, even if the formal written plan of liquidation is adopted only after X Corp is in control of Y (that is, after the redemption of the minority shareholders), the IRS may conclude that in substance the payments by Y Corp to the minority shareholders in redemption of their stock followed shortly by payments to the majority shareholder in redemption of its stock were part of a single transaction, and that the actual (if not the formal) plan to liquidate Y Corp was adopted *prior* to the redemption of the minority shareholders.[22] If that indeed were the case, then the plan of liquidation would have been adopted prior to the time that X Corp became the 80% shareholder. Since Code Sec. 332 requires that the parent must be the 80% shareholder from the time the plan of liquidation until the liquidation is completed, a finding that the plan was adopted before X Corp was the 80% shareholder would make Code Sec. 332 inapplicable. While it is true that the IRS is more likely to ignore the later adoption of a formal plan of liquidation where X Corp acquires control of Y Corp through redemption rather than by purchase from minority shareholders, even in these cases the IRS and the courts might still respect the later adoption of the plan of liquidation if they find that no plan of liquidation actually existed prior to the redemption of the minority shareholders.[23]

To see how corporations might attempt to *avoid* Code Sec. 332 rather than to *qualify* for Code Sec. 332, for example if there are losses that either the parent or the subsidiary or both might want to recognize, assume that P starts out owning 100% of the stock of S but wants to liquidate S in a taxable liquidation. It is fairly well (but not completely) established that P can avoid the application of Code Sec. 332 by ensuring that at some time after the adoption of the plan of liquidation and prior to completion of that plan it reduces its ownership to below the 80% required by Code Sec. 332.[24]

P might also attempt to avoid the application of Code Sec. 332 by intentionally failing to meet the time requirements imposed by that section. One of those requirements is that if there is no plan of liquidation adopted prior to the initial liquidating distribution, the liquidation must be completed within S's taxable year during which the initial distribution was made. As a result, S might attempt to avoid Code Sec. 332 by failing to adopt a plan of liquidation and then taking more than a single taxable year to complete that "unplanned" liquidation. In this situation S ought not be surprised to find the IRS asserting that its actions clearly indicate the

---

[22] Rev. Rul. 70-106, 1970-1 C.B. 70.

[23] *George L. Riggs, Inc.*, 64 TC 474, 488–489 (1975) (acq.).

[24] *CIR v. Day & Zimmerman, Inc.*, 151 F 2d 517 (3d Cir. 1945), *Granite Trust Co. v. US*, 238 F 2d 670 (1st Cir.

1956), *Avco Mfg. Corp.*, 25 TC 975 (1956) (nonacq.). We mention that the proposition may not be completely established only because we not that the IRS's last published word on the subject, albeit about 55 years ago, was a nonacquiescence in Avco.

presence of a plan of liquidation, so that even in the absence of a formal written plan the liquidation will be found to be covered by Code Sec. 332.[25]

Since the alternative time requirement for Code Sec. 332 is that S adopt a plan of liquidation that contemplates completing the liquidation within three years following the year in which the plan is adopted, and that the liquidation actually be completed within that time, P and S might also attempt to avoid Code Sec. 332 by either adopting a plan to liquidate over more than three years following the current taxable year, or by simply extending the liquidation over more than the permitted three years after the year in which the plan of liquidation is adopted. If they adopt a "plan" to liquidate over more than the permitted three years but actually complete the liquidation within that three year period, the IRS might well argue that the initial plan actually contemplated a timely (for Code Sec. 332 purposes) liquidation from the start, even if that plan was reflected only in substance but not in form. If the actual distribution is prolonged over more than the allowable three year period, the IRS might attack the form and apply Code Sec. 332 to leave losses (as well as any gains) unrecognized if there is no business purpose but only a tax avoidance purpose for extending the distribution period.[26]

.02 Consequences to the Parent Distributee

The most obvious consequence of the application of Code Sec. 332 to a liquidation is that the parent recognizes no gain or loss on any of the liquidating distributions. There is more, though. The parent generally takes a transferred (from the liquidated subsidiary) basis in each asset it receives, under Code Sec. 334. If there is a net loss built into all of the assets received by the parent in the liquidation (if the total basis of all of the assets received from the subsidiary exceeds the total value of such assets), however, the parent's total asset basis is limited by Code Sec. 334(b)(1)(B). The basis reduction in such a case would be calculated the same way it is when a shareholder transfers assets with a net built-in loss in a Code Sec. 351 exchange (that is, the total basis reduction is equal to the total net built in loss, and then the basis of each asset is reduced in proportion to the amount of the total net built in loss attributable to that asset.[27]

As is the case virtually any time a taxpayer takes a transferred asset basis, the parent also takes a tacked holding period in each asset received, under Code Sec. 1223(2). The parent also steps into the subsidiary's shoes with respect to recapture[28] and depreciation method and timing.[29] In addition, under Code Sec. 381, the parent steps into the subsidiary's shoes with respect to virtually every other tax-significant attribute (including Net Operating Losses, capital loss carryovers, earnings and profits, and accounting methods (including inventories and installment sales).[30]

---

[25] *Burnside Veneer Co. v. CIR*, 167 F 2d 214 (6th Cir. 1948). *International Inv. Co. v. CIR*, 11 TC 678, 685 (1948), *aff'd per curiam*, 175 F2d 772 (3d Cir. 1949). Of course if it is the taxpayer rather than the IRS that argues that the substance rather than the form of the transaction should prevail, neither the IRS nor the courts are likely to be too receptive, since the taxpayer's adopted form is usually held against it. Tax Avoidance and Income Measurement, Mich. L. Rev.

[26] Again, if the Taxpayer seeks Code Sec. 332 treatment despite failing to meet even a technical requirement of the statute, its form is likely to be held against it.

[27] See discussion at ¶ 603.02, *supra*.

[28] Code Sec. 1245(a)(2)(A).

[29] Code Sec. 168(i)(7).

[30] Code Section 381 is discussed at length in Chapter 8, reorganizations.

.03 Consequences to the Liquidating Corporation: Code Sec. 337

If a liquidation qualifies as tax free to the parent under Code Sec. 332, any liquidating distributions made to that parent are tax free to the liquidating subsidiary under Code Sec. 337. Were that all there was to Code Sec. 337, the liquidating subsidiary might recognize no gain by distributing all of its gain assets to its parent tax free under Code Sec. 337, but contrive to nonetheless recognize its *losses* by transferring its loss assets to its corporate parent in payment of any *debt* it might have to the parent, rather than as liquidating distributions. To preclude this, Code Sec. 337(b)(1) provides that in a Code Sec. 332 liquidation, any transfer of property from the subsidiary to the parent in payment of debt shall, for purposes of Code Sec. 337, be treated as a liquidating distribution (meaning, of course, that no gain or loss will be recognized on the transfer by the liquidating subsidiary).

.04 Consequences on Distributions to Minority Shareholders in the Context of a Code Sec. 332 Liquidation

While liquidating distributions from the subsidiary to the parent are tax-free to both parties, if there are minority shareholders, any liquidating distributions to those shareholders are taxed to both the liquidating subsidiary and the minority shareholders. Any gain or loss that the shareholders have is taxed under Code Sec. 331, since Code Sec. 332 has no application at all to those shareholders. Additionally, any gain in the assets distributed to the minority shareholders is taxed to the liquidating corporation under Code Sec. 336, since Code Sec. 337 by its terms also applies only to distributions made to the parent corporation.

In order to prevent the liquidating subsidiary from deferring its gains by distributing its gain assets to the parent while recognizing its losses by distributing any loss assets to minority shareholders, Code Sec. 336(d)(3) provides that no loss shall be recognized by the liquidating subsidiary on any property distributed in any liquidation to which Code Sec 332 applies. Since Code Sec. 332 applies to the *liquidation,* even if not to the specific *distribution* to the minority shareholders, the liquidating subsidiary cannot recognize any loss on any distributions even to minority shareholders.

Since a subsidiary liquidating under Code Secs. 332 and 337 cannot recognize any loss on distributed assets, whether the distribution is to the parent corporation or to the minority shareholder, the liquidating subsidiary may attempt to recognize any losses it has by transferring those losses outside of the liquidation, for example by selling those assets to third parties.

> ***Example:*** To see how these sections apply, assume that S is owned 80% (voting and value) by P Corp (160 shares, basis $50,000) and 20% by M (40 shares, basis $50,000). S has Depreciable property (which it is depreciating over five years on a straight line basis and on which it has so far taken depreciation deductions of $40,000) with a basis of $10,000 and a value of $30,000. S also has Loss asset (basis $100,000, value $20,000), Gain asset (basis $15,000, value $40,000), and cash of $210,000. S adopts a plan of liquidation, pursuant to which it intends to distribute all of its assets in years 1 (the year in which the plan is adopted) and 2. In accordance with that plan, in year 1, S

¶604.03

distributes to M Gain asset (basis $15,000, value $40,000) in exchange for all of M's stock and distributes $10,000 of the cash to P in exchange for 10 of P's 160 shares. In year two, S distributes to P the Depreciable property (basis $10,000, value of $30,000), Loss asset (basis $100,000, value $20,000), and the $210,000 cash in exchange for the remaining 150 of P's shares.

The liquidation is planned to be and is in fact completed within three years. P owns 80% of the S stock at the time the plan is adopted, and after the year one distributions P owns 100% (all 150 of the shares still outstanding). Code Secs. 332 and 337 thus apply to all liquidating distributions from S to P.

The year one distribution to M is, of course, taxable to M under Code Sec. 331. Because M's stock basis of $50,000 exceeds her amount realized ($40,000, the value of Gain asset), M realizes and recognizes a (capital) loss of $10,000 in year one. In addition, under Code Sec. 336, S recognizes a gain of $25,000 on the distribution of that asset to M, as if it has sold the asset for its fair market value. Finally, M takes a $40,000 fair market value basis in Gain asset, under Code Sec. 334(a).

Had S distributed to M Loss Asset rather than Gain Asset, the results to M would not have changed. M would still realize and recognize a loss equal to the excess of her stock basis over the value of the property received, and would still take a fair market basis in the property received. However, although S recognized its *gain* when it distributed the Gain asset to M, S would not recognize its *loss* were it to distribute the Loss asset to M, because Code Sec. 336(d)(3) prevents S from recognizing any loss on any distribution in any liquidation in which Code Secs. 332 and 337 apply (to the distribution(s) to the parent corporation).

The distributions from S to P are, obviously, governed by Code Secs. 332 and 337. The year one distribution of $10,000 cash, and the year two distribution of Loss Asset, Depreciable property and the remaining cash are tax free both to P, under Code Sec. 332, and to S, under Code Sec. 337.[31] P takes the same basis that S had in each of the assets received from S, under Code Sec. 334(b)(1) and the same holding period that S had, under Code Sec. 1223(2). P will be subject to the same recapture to which S would have been subject on the sale of Depreciable property, under Code Sec. 1245(a)(2)(A), and P will continue to depreciate the asset the same way that S would have depreciated it had it not liquidated, under Code Sec. 168(i)(7). Finally, P will accede to S's other tax attributes under Code Sec. 381.

¶ 605 Partial Liquidations

The treatment of partial liquidations is set forth in Code Sec. 302, which also governs the treatment of stock redemptions. Generally speaking, a partial liquidation results in capital gain for noncorporate shareholders. Corporate shareholders receiving partial liquidation distributions are treated as if they received dividends

---

[31] Since the liquidation is not completed within year one, P may be required to post a bond or to waive the statute of limitations in year one to protect the IRS against the possibility that the liquidation might ultimately fail the requirements of Code Sec. 332.

unless the transaction generates sale or exchange treatment under one of the other tests in Code Sec. 302(b).[32] Although partial liquidations are defined and ruled by Code Sec. 302, and although partial liquidations are in some ways treated as redemptions for noncorporate shareholders, the concept of partial liquidation comes, historically, from distributions that were, as the name implies, more like (partial) liquidations than they were like stock redemptions. The concept was most notably applied in Joseph W. Imler,[33] when a corporation that had conducted two businesses suffered a fire that ultimately made it essentially impossible to continue conducting one of those businesses. As a result, the company distributed fire insurance proceeds in redemption of some of the shareholders' stock. Since the redemption was pro-rata, the IRS argued that each shareholder should be taxed on a dividend. The shareholders argued, and the court agreed, that the corporate contraction that took place as a result of the fire was more like a liquidation of part of the corporation than it was like a dividend. As a result, it was "not equivalent to a dividend" and should not be taxed as such.[34]

Partial liquidations are defined in Code Sec. 302(e), and that definition includes, but is not limited to, distributions if the requirements of Code Sec. 302(e)(2) are met; and the requirements of Code Sec. 302(e)(2) closely resemble the idea behind *Imler*. In order to qualify as a partial liquidation under Code Sec. 302(e)(2), the distributions must be pursuant to a plan and occur within the taxable year in which the plan is adopted or in the immediately succeeding taxable year. Aside from the time requirement, and like *Imler*, the distributions must consist of all of the assets of a qualified business or be attributable to the corporation's ceasing to conduct a qualified business, and immediately after the distribution the corporation must still be actively engaged in the conduct of a qualified business.

Code Sec. 302(e)(3) defines a "qualified trade or business as one that has been conducted for at least five years and that was not acquired within the past five years in a transaction in which gain or loss was recognized in whole or in part.[35] These requirements are essentially identical to the requirements for a qualified business under Code Sec. 355, and are discussed in more detail in conjunction with Code Sec. 355.[36] The purpose of these requirements is to prevent corporations with earnings and profits and distributable cash or liquid assets from using those assets to either start or purchase a business which the controlling shareholders want to acquire in any event, distribute the business itself rather than distribute the cash, and allow the shareholders to report capital gains (assuming their amount realized exceeds their basis) rather than dividend income.

One might think that in order to meet the clear requirement that the distributing corporation must both *retain* an active business and *distribute all of the assets* of

---

[32] The sole impact on corporate distributees of a distribution that qualifies as a partial liquidation is that any part of the distribution it receives that is taxed as a dividend may be subjected to the basis reduction rules of Code Sec. 1059 regardless of the generally applicable two year holding period requirement. Code Sec. 1059(e)(1).

[33] 11 TC 836, 840 (1948) (acq.).

[34] *Joseph W. Imler*, 11 TC 836, 840 (1948) (acq.).

[35] The business may have been acquired in a nontaxable reorganization or liquidation within the last five years, however, for a qualified trade or business this shall be determined without regard to whether the redemption is pro rata with respect to all shareholders of the corporation. Code Sec. 302(e)(4).

[36] *See* Chapter 7.

¶605

an active business, the corporation must begin with at least two qualified active businesses, but this is not necessarily the case. The regulations that governed partial liquidations[37] suggest that the definition of the active conduct of a trade or business for purposes of partial liquidations be guided by the meaning given that term for purposes of Code Sec. 355 transactions, and Code Sec. 355 now permits a corporation that has only a single business to essentially divide that in two and have two qualified businesses. Whether the same can now be said for purposes of partial liquidations is unclear.

If a distribution does not meet the specific requirements of Code Sec. 302(e)(2) it may nonetheless qualify as a partial liquidation if it is otherwise "not essentially equivalent to a dividend (determined at the corporate level rather than at the shareholder level)."[38] While this standard is less than clear, it generally refers to situations where a corporation either ceases to conduct one of two or more entire businesses (that is, situations similar to those described in Code Sec. 302(e)(2)), or where unanticipated events (such as a fire) cause the corporation to restructure and cut back significantly on its business and distribute either the insurance or other proceeds from the damage or restructuring.[39]

If a distribution qualifies as a partial liquidation for noncorporate shareholders (the only effect of such treatment for corporate shareholders is to invoke the basis reduction rules of Code Sec. 1059 on any corporate dividend received in the same distribution), the shareholders are taxed (capital gain or loss) on the difference between their amount realized and their basis in the stock exchanged. If the distribution is proportionate, it may well be simply a pro rata distribution to the shareholders without the surrender of any shares. In that case, the shareholders who receive partial liquidation treatment allocate a portion of the overall stock basis to the exchange (thus limiting the amount of gain, or, if the basis is sufficient, resulting in capital loss) despite the fact that they surrender no actual stock. The portion of their total stock basis allocated to the exchange is equal to the portion of the total value of their stock that is accounted for by the distribution (in other words, if a shareholder receives 50% of the pre-distribution value of her stock in a partial liquidation, she allocates 50% of her total stock basis to the partial liquidation).

As noted, the requirements to qualify as a partial liquidation are quite similar to those to qualify as a Code Sec. 355 distribution.[40] There are significant tax differences between partial liquidations and Code Sec. 355 transactions, however. At the corporate level, if Code Sec. 355 applies, the distributing corporation recognizes no gain on the distribution of appreciated property,[41] while a distribution in partial liquidation results in the full taxation of any gain, but the nonrecognition (and disappearance, because the distributee takes a fair market value basis) of any loss

---

[37] Treas. Reg. §1.346-1. These regulations were enacted at the time that partial liquidations were treated under Code Sec. 346 rather than Code Sec. 302. While Code Sec. 346 has been repealed, the regulations have not been. Thus, they may refer to nonexistent statutes, but their general instructions likely still will be respected.

[38] Code Sec. 302(e)(1).

[39] See Boris I. Bittker and James S. Eustice, FEDERAL INCOME TAXATION OF CORPORATIONS AND SHAREHOLDER, ¶9.07.

[40] See Chapter 7.

[41] Code Sec. 355(c), 361.

built into that property.[42] At the shareholder level, the recipient of a distribution in partial liquidation recognizes gain or loss equal to the difference between her allocable stock basis and her amount realized, while the recipient of a Code Sec. 355 distribution recognizes no gain or loss at all.[43] Thus, unless the distributee has a loss built into her stock whose tax value exceeds the tax cost of any gain that would be recognized by the distributing corporation on the distribution, Code Sec. 355 is preferable from a tax standpoint.[44]

In the vast majority of cases, corporations and their shareholders will attempt to have distributions treated as Code Sec. 355 distributions rather than as partial liquidations. The basic difference between the two is that Code Sec. 355 requires the distribution of the stock of a subsidiary conducting an active business, while Code Sec. 302(e) requires the distribution of the assets or proceeds of an active business outside of corporate solution. Most transactions can be structured either way. The corporation that has no subsidiary can simply create one[45] and then distribute the stock of that new subsidiary rather than the assets, and thus qualify for Code Sec. 355. The corporation that already has a subsidiary but wishes to qualify for partial liquidation treatment can simply liquidate the subsidiary and distribute only its former assets.

About the only time that a corporation cannot convert a partial liquidation into a Code Sec. 355 transaction is when one of the businesses is sold or destroyed so that only the proceeds, and no active business, remains. On the other hand, about the only time that a corporation cannot convert a Code Sec. 355 distribution into a partial liquidation is when the subsidiary cannot be liquidated under Code Sec. 332 but must remain separately incorporated.[46]

---

[42] Code Sec. 311 determines the gain recognition, while the shareholder's cost basis is determined by Code Sec. 1012.

[43] Code Sec. 355(a).

[44] An additional tax cost of a partial liquidation comes into play if any of the shareholders of the distributing corporation is itself a corporation. The corporation will be treated as receiving a dividend that may well be at least partially taxable even after the application of Code Sec. 243. In addition, Code Sec. 1059 will apply to require the corporate shareholder to reduce its stock basis by the amount of the untaxed dividend received.

[45] Under Code Sec. 351 or Code Sec. 368(a)(1)(D).

[46] Rev. Rul. 79-184, 1979-1 C.B. 143.

Chapter 7

Corporate Divisions

Reorganizations can be used to divide or to acquire businesses. Divisive reorganizations are addressed in this chapter.[1] Acquisitive reorganizations are discussed in chapter 9.

In many contexts – such as Code Sec. 1031 like-kind exchanges and Code Sec. 351 exchanges whereby sole proprietorships become corporations – the Code accords nonrecognition treatment when there has been a mere change of form. That approach applies to divisive reorganizations as well. When done correctly, corporate divisions are nonrecognition events. Code Sec. 355 is the principal section directing how nonrecognition is achieved. Code Sec. 355 sets out the requirements for nonrecognition treatment that must be satisfied in every situation in which the shareholders' investment in one corporation is to be split between or among two or more corporations.

As always, Congress is concerned that taxpayers may push the envelope, that nonrecognition treatment may be abused. Specifically, Congress does not want what really are dividends to go tax-free by being disguised as nontaxable corporate divisions, or ordinary income to be transmuted into capital gain. Many of the requirements – and consequently much of the complexity – of Code Sec. 355 reflect Congress's attempt to draw lines of demarcation between dividends and genuine corporate divisions.

> **Example:** Asgard Corporation has assets which it wants to put into the hands of its shareholders. If (without liquidating) Asgard distributes the assets direct to its shareholders, the shareholders may be treated as having received dividends, depending upon the extent of Asgard's earnings and profits compared to the amounts distributed.[2] For most of our nation's tax history, dividends have been taxed as ordinary income.[3]

---

[1] In the parlance of the tax profession, the word "reorganization" typically is not used to denote corporate divisions. The word is so used here, however, to capture the conceptual relationships that exist between divisive and acquisitive transactions.

[2] *See* Code Secs. 301(c)(1) & 316(a). These sections are discussed in Chapter 5.

[3] 2003 legislation made most dividends taxable as net capital gains, thus taxable at a 15% rate for most individual shareholders. Code Sec. 1(h)(1) & (11). That provision was due to expire on January 1, 2011. However, the

Alternatively, Asgard could transfer the assets into a subsidiary, then distribute the stock in the subsidiary to Asgard's shareholders. If the requirements of Code Sec. 355 are met, the transfer would be a nonrecognition event. Later, the shareholders might sell their stock in the distributed subsidiary, realizing capital gain, which (especially if long term) is taxed considerably less heavily for individual shareholders in the top bracket than is ordinary income.[4]

Code Sec. 355 has taken on greater significance as a result of the repeal by Congress of the *General Utilities* doctrine. Before such repeal, corporations could distribute appreciated property – in operating or liquidating distributions – to their shareholders without recognition of gain at the corporate level.[5] Since Congress closed those doors in 1986,[6] Code Sec. 355 corporate divisions have been among the few avenues by which corporations can distribute appreciated property without recognition of gain at the corporate level.

¶ 701 of this chapter describes the three types of corporate divisions. ¶ 702 and ¶ 703 examine the requirements for valid Code Sec. 355 transactions, considering respectively requirements in the statute and requirements in the regulations. ¶ 704 discusses recognition and nonrecognition of gain in Code Sec. 355 transactions. ¶ 705 considers procedural aspects.

¶ 701 Types of Corporate Divisions

Corporate divisions come in three varieties: spin-offs, split-offs, and split-ups.

.01 Spin-Offs

This is the most frequently encountered form of corporate division. It involves a corporation that owns a subsidiary, either a subsidiary that has been in existence for some time or a subsidiary newly created in order to effectuate the division. The corporation owning the subsidiary distributes the stock of the subsidiary pro rata to the corporation's shareholders. As a result, the corporation and the former subsidiary become brother-sister corporations, owned in the same proportions by the shareholders of the distributing corporation.

.02 Split-Offs

In a spin-off, the shareholders receive stock in the subsidiary without surrendering any of their stock in the distributing corporation. In contrast, in a split-off, one or more of the shareholders of the distributing corporations give up some or all of their stock in the distributing corporation in return for receiving stock in the distributed subsidiary. Moreover, unlike in a spin-off, the distribution does not have to be pro rata.

(Footnote Continued)

Tax Relief Act of 2010 extended the provision for two more years: 2011 and 2012. Tax Relief, Unemployment Insurance Reauthorization and Job Creation Act of 2010, § 102, Pub. L. 111-312, 124 Stat. 3296. Absent further legislation, dividends will again be taxed as ordinary income beginning in 2013.

[4] See Code Sec. 1(h).

[5] *General Utilities & Operating Co. v. Helvering*, 296 U.S. 200 (1935).

[6] *See* Code Secs. 311(b) (operating distributions) & 336(a) (liquidating distributions). These sections are discussed in Chapters 5 and 7, respectively.

.03 Split-Ups

This type of corporate separation entails a parent corporation distributing to its shareholders the stock of two or more subsidiaries as part of the complete liquidation of the parent corporation. The distribution may be pro rata or non-pro rata.

.04 Examples

Example 1: For ten years, Albacron Corporation has owned all the stock of Afton Corporation. Albacron distributes the stock of Afton to Albacore's shareholders pro rata, and all the Albacron shareholders retain all of their Albacron stock. This is a spin-off.

Example 2: Beshire Corporation owns a shop that sells bait, lures, gear, and sundries to fishermen. It also owns boats and employs fishing guides. Beshire's customers are fishermen who rent the boats owned by Beshire and pay for the services of the guides employed by Beshire. The owners of Beshire desire to separate the activities.

Thus, a new corporation, Berwick Corporation, is formed. Beshire transfers the shop and the shop's inventory to Berwick in return to all of Berwick's stock. Beshire retains the boats and the guides' contracts. Thereafter, Beshire distributes its Berwick stock to Beshire's shareholders.

If the distribution is pro rata and no Beshire shareholder surrenders any Beshire stock, this is a spin-off. If, however, one or more Beshire shareholders exchange Beshire stock for Berwick stock, this is a split-off.

Example 3: Cambrai Corporation owns and operates two apartment buildings with rental housing units. The shareholders desire to separate the two buildings into different corporations. There are a number of options. Cambrai could exchange one of the buildings for all of the stock of a newly formed subsidiary, then spin-off or split-off the subsidiary.

Alternatively, Cambrai could exchange one of the buildings for all of the stock of newly formed subsidiary C1 Corporation, and exchange the other building for all of the stock of newly formed subsidiary C2 Corporation. Cambrai would then have as assets only the C1 and C2 stock. Then Cambrai could be liquidated, distributing the C1 stock and the C2 stock to Cambria's shareholders. This alternative would be a split-up. In the split-up, all Cambrai shareholders could receive some C1 stock and some C2 stock, or some of the shareholders could receive only C1 stock and the other shareholders could receive only C2 stock.

.05 Purposes of Corporate Divisions

The three kinds of divisions can serve a variety of business purposes. These purposes include the following:

- Resolving disagreements among shareholders. This motivation is particularly significant as to split-ups. Different shareholders or blocs of shareholders may have different visions of where to take the company. Or, personal

¶701.05

animosities may develop between or among shareholders that spills over into the business, threatening friction or deadlock. A split-up allows the shareholders to go their separate economic ways.

- Separate stable from speculative business activities or safe from hazardous activities. It may be that one line of business is likely to do well. The other activity is risky, holding promise for big returns but posing the chance of major loss. The shareholders may not want to take the chance that the risky activity may drag the stable activity down with it. Any of the three types of corporate divisions can guard against such an eventuality by cloaking each of the two activities in its own mantle of limited liability.

- Meet regulatory requirements. Federal or state law may make it necessary or expedient for regulatory reasons to separate the two business activities. For instance, an antitrust decree may compel a corporation to divest itself of some aspect(s) of the business it had carried on. Any of the types of corporate divisions may accomplish such ends.

Example: Oil companies owned by John D. Rockefeller were subject to regulation by different federal agencies. The FTC regulated sales while the ICC regulated pipelines through which the oil was transported. The agencies sometimes took different views that, as a practical matter, put the companies in a regulatory cross-fire. To alleviate this situation, and to minimize state taxation, the companies put the transportation assets and activities into subsidiaries and then spun them off.

These events occurred long before the enactment of current Code Sec. 355, at a time when spin-offs were recognition events. Accordingly, these spin-offs were held to be taxable dividends.[7] Under current law, these spin-offs would be nontaxable events, assuming satisfaction of applicable statutory and regulatory requirements.

¶ 702 Statutory Requirements

A valid Code Sec. 355 transaction must meet requirements set out in the statute itself, meet requirements set out in the regulations, and avoid a number of disqualification rules. This part addresses the statutory requirements. The other rules are addressed in ¶ 703 below.

Practice Tip: Because separations can entail complex transactions and because the statutory and regulatory requirements discussed below are complicated, taxpayers request private letter rulings on separations more often than they do on many other types of reorganizations. The IRS has committed itself to attempt to issue Code Sec. 355 letter rulings within ten weeks of its receiving the request,[8] and the IRS often comes respectably close to achieving that goal.[9]

---

[7] *Rockefeller v. United States*, 257 U.S. 176 (1921).

[8] Rev. Proc. 2005-68, 2005-2 C.B. 694.

[9] One commentator estimates that the IRS issues such rulings within 17 weeks overall and within 14 weeks when taxpayers request expedited treatment. J. William Dantzler Jr., *Spinoffs: Still Remarkably Tax Friendly*, Tax Notes, Nov. 8, 2010, p. 683, at 684

To receive such expedited handling, the taxpayer must (1) state on the first page of the ruling request "Expedited Handling Is Requested," (2) provide a copy of the request letter along with the formal request, (3) furnish a draft ruling providing all required information, and (4) meet any further requirements set out in any relevant revenue procedure.

Diminishing the utility of this option is the fact that the IRS refuses to rule on certain aspects of Code Sec. 355 transactions, including (1) whether the transaction constitutes a prohibited device, (2) whether there is an adequate business purpose, and (3) whether the division and a related acquisition are part of a prohibited plan under Code Sec. 355(e).[10]

Code Sec. 355(a) sets out the following requirements for nonrecognition treatment:

- A corporation, called the "distributing corporation," must make a distribution. The distribution must be either (i) a distribution "to a shareholder, with respect to its stock" or (ii) a distribution "to a security holder," in exchange for its securities.[11]

- The distribution must be solely of stock or securities of a corporation, called the "controlled corporation," which the distributing corporation "controls immediately before the distribution."[12]

- The distribution "was not used principally as a device for the distribution of the earnings and profits of" either the distributing or the controlled corporation.[13]

- Both the distributing and the controlled corporations must be involved in the active conduct of a trade or business for requisite durations.[14]

- The distributing corporation must distribute "all of the stock or securities in the controlled corporation held by it immediately before the distribution," or it must distribute stock constituting control of the controlled corporation and establish to the IRS's satisfaction that the retention of some stock "was not in pursuance of a plan having as one of its principal purposes the avoidance of Federal tax."[15]

- The transaction may not be of a nonqualified nature.[16]

If these threshold requirements and others to be described later are satisfied, it is irrelevant whether or not the distribution is pro rata, whether or not any shareholder surrenders stock in the distributing corporation, and whether or not the distribution is pursuant to a plan of reorganization.[17] Several of the above requirements merit additional discussion. They are addressed in the following subsections.

---

[10] *See* Rev. Proc. 2011-3, §§ 3.01(39), 4.01(28)-(29) & 4.02(2), 2011-1 I.R.B. 111; Rev. Proc. 2003-48, 2003-2 C.B. 86.

[11] Code Sec. 355(a)(1)(A).

[12] *Id.*

[13] Code Sec. 355(a)(1)(B).

[14] Code Sec. 355(a)(1)(C) & (b).

[15] Code Sec. 355(a)(1)(D).

[16] Code Sec. 355(d)-(g).

[17] Code Sec. 355(a)(2).

.01 Distribution

Previously, we described the three forms of distributions: spin-offs, split-offs, and split-ups. As an alternative, in unusual cases, taxpayers have argued that making a bargain purchase of controlled corporation stock from the controlling corporation constituted a distribution for Code Sec. 355 purposes. In this rarely litigated area, the cases are divided.[18]

.02 Stock or Securities

Does distribution of, not stock itself, but rights to buy stock qualify (assuming satisfaction of other elements)? The cases noted immediately above as to the distribution element also considered this issue.[19] So again, the situation has rarely arisen, and, when it has, the cases have been divided. Issues involving nonqualified types of stock and securities are discussed below in subpart ¶ 704.

.03 Control

Code Sec. 355 defines "control" by reference to Code Sec. 368(c).[20] Under Code Sec. 368(c), to be in control, the distributing corporation must have owned "stock possessing at least 80 percent of the total combined voting power of all classes of stock entitled to vote and at least 80 percent of the total number of shares of all other classes of stock of the [controlled] corporation."

.04 Device

A recurring question in law is whether to rely upon a precise rule or a general standard. A rule provides greater clarity, which is good because it promotes certainty and predictability but is bad because it usually yields more readily to creative circumvention. A standard affords greater flexibility, which is good for anti-abuse purposes but bad for responsible planning.

This tension is on display with respect to the device requirement of Code Sec. 355. The "not a device to distribute E&P" aspect of the statute is a standard, and it has both the virtues and vices of a standard. The device element has substantial anti-abuse power; indeed, in recent years the IRS has been placing more reliance on this element than others (such as the active business element) when attacking arrangements of which the IRS disapproves. But this utility comes at the cost of considerable unpredictability. It is far from easy to know when the IRS will assert, and the courts will find, that a corporate separation should be denied nonrecognition treatment because it is a device to distribute earnings and profits.

The term "device" appears in *Gregory v. Helvering*,[21] one of the most famous (if often misunderstood) cases in American tax jurisprudence. Gregory illustrates the concern that animates Code Sec. 355: preventing taxpayers from gaining nonrecognition or capital gain treatment for what actually is an earnings and profits bail-out, *i.e.*, a dividend.

---

[18] *See Redding v. Comm'r*, 71 T.C. 597, rev'd, 630 F.2d 1169 (7th Cir. 1980); *Baan v. Comm'r*, 45 T.C. 71 (1965), *aff'd sub nom. Comm'r v. Gordon*, 382 F .2d 499 (2d Cir. 1967), *but rev'd as to another taxpayer*, 382 F.2d 485 (9th Cir. 1967). The Supreme Court reversed the Second Cir-

cuit and affirmed the Ninth Circuit but on other grounds. 391 U.S. 83 (1968).

[19] *Redding, Baan & Gordon supra*, note 18.
[20] Code Sec. 355(a)(1)(D)(ii).
[21] 293 U.S. 465 (1935).

Example: Ms. Gregory owned all the stock of United Mortgage Corporation, which owned 1000 highly appreciated shares in Monitor Securities Corporation. Ms. Gregory wanted the Monitor shares, but she wished to avoid the ordinary income treatment that would have obtained had United simply distributed the Monitor shares to her as a dividend.

So, Ms. Gregory caused Averill Corporation to be organized. Three days later, United transferred the Monitor stock to Averill, for which all of the Averill shares were issued to Ms. Gregory. Averill had no other assets. Averill never transacted any business, nor was it intended that Averill would transact business. Later, Averill was liquidated, with Ms. Gregory receiving the Monitor stock in return for her Averill stock. If this scheme had succeeded, Ms. Gregory would have obtained the desired stock but paid tax at capital gain, not ordinary income, rates.

The Supreme Court held the scheme to be invalid. It observed:

> [F]ixing the character of the proceeding by what actually occurred, what do we find? Simply an operation having no business or corporate purpose – a mere device which put on the form of a corporate reorganization as a disguise for concealing its real character, and the sole object and accomplishment of which was the consummation of a preconceived plan, not to reorganize a business or any part of a business, but to transfer a parcel of shares to [Ms. Gregory].

> [T]he rule which excludes from consideration the motive of tax avoidance is not pertinent to the situation, because the transaction upon its face lies outside the plain intent of the statute. To hold otherwise would be to exalt artifice reality.[22]

After having earlier excluded spin-offs entirely from nonrecognition treatment, Congress in 1951 permitted nonrecognition treatment subject to conditions, including the device prohibition. Code Sec. 355 does not define "device."

The regulations take up – with a vengeance – the slack left by the statute. The regulations define "device" at length. Specifically, the regulations set out three factors indicative of "device," three factors indicative of "not a device," and three circumstances which usually are not devices. This approach is a general "facts and circumstances" inquiry in which no one consideration is decisive.[23] Unfortunately, this elaboration adds to, rather than diminishes, the uncertainty noted earlier.[24]

(a) *Device Factors*

Under the regulations, the presence of any of the following may indicate that the arrangements constitute a device contrary to the statute: (1) the distribution is pro rata, (2) after the distribution, the distributee-shareholder(s) sold or exchanged the distributed stock or securities, or (3) the nature and use of the assets of the corporations involved suggest a device.[25] These factors are examined in greater detail below.

---

[22] *Id.* at 469-70.

[23] *See* Treas. Reg. § 1.355-2(d)(1).

[24] In this respect, the device regulations resemble the nine factors in the hobby loss regulations under Code Sec. 183, the five factors as to "debt versus equity" classi-fication under Code Sec. 385(c) (plus the even larger number of factors in the Code Sec. 385 case law), and the over 20 factors relevant to the "employee versus independent contractor" categorization. Having too many factors can be as bad as having too few factors.

[25] Treas. Reg.. § 1.355-2(d)(2).

Pro rata distribution: A distribution that is exactly or nearly pro rata among the shareholders looks more like a dividend than does a disproportionate distribution.[26] Although there obviously is some force to this, the regulations exist in uneasy relationship to the statute, which states that Code Sec. 355's rule of nonrecognition "shall be applied without regard to . . . whether or not the distribution is pro rata."[27] The reasoning of the Treasury and the IRS presumably is that, under the regulations, "pro rata" distribution receives only some weight and is not necessarily dispositive. Despite this reasoning (or rationalization), the regulation remains in tension with the statute.

Subsequent Sale or Exchange: This portion of the regulation also is in tension with the statute – but in two ways, one seemingly favorable to taxpayers and the other seemingly adverse to them. The statute provides:

> the mere fact that subsequent to the distribution stock or securities in one or more of [the] corporations are sold or exchanged by all or some of the distributees (other than pursuant to an arrangement negotiated or agreed upon prior to such distribution) shall not be construed to mean that the transaction was used principally as such a device.[28]

The "other than" parenthetical could be read as per se disallowing nonrecognition treatment when there was a prearranged post-distribution sale or exchange. But the regulations do not go that far; they treat such pre-arrangement as "substantial," but not conclusive, evidence.[29]

On the other hand, the non-parenthetical language of the statute could be read to mean that sales that have not been prearranged should not constitute evidence of a prohibited device. The regulations, however, treat them as evidence (though they do not treat such sales as "substantial" evidence as prearranged sales are).[30] "Generally, the greater the percentage of the stock sold or exchanged after the distribution, the stronger the evidence of device. In addition, the shorter the period of time between the distribution and the sale or exchange, the stronger the evidence of device."[31]

The regulations amplify the "subsequent sale or exchange" factor in three additional respects. First, the regulations provide that a sale or exchange is "always" prearranged "if enforceable rights to buy or sell existed before the distribution."[32] Second, the sale or exchange will "ordinarily" be seen as prearranged "[i]f a sale or exchange was discussed by the buyer and the seller before the distribution and was reasonably to be anticipated by both parties."[33] Third, "if stock is exchanged for stock in pursuance of a plan of reorganization, and either no gain or loss or only an insubstantial amount of gain is recognized on the exchange, then the exchange is not treated as a subsequent sale or exchange."[34]

---

[26] Treas. Reg. § 1.335-2(d)(2)(ii) ("A distribution that is pro rata or substantially pro rata among the shareholders of the distributing corporation presents the greatest potential for the avoidance of the dividend provisions of the Code and, in contrast to other types of distributions, is more likely to be used principally as a device.").

[27] Code Sec. 355(a)(2)(A).

[28] Code Sec. 355(a)(1)(B).

[29] Treas. Reg. § 1.355-2(d)(2)(iii)(B).

[30] Treas. Reg. § 1.355-2(d)(2)(iii)(C).

[31] Treas. Reg. § 1.355-2(d)(2)(iii)(A).

[32] Treas. Reg. § 1.355-2(d)(2)(iii)(D).

[33] *Id.*

[34] Treas. Reg. § 1.355-2(d)(2)(iii)(E).

Nature and Use of Assets: The regulations provide that "the nature, kind, amount, and use of the assets of the distributing and the controlled corporations" are relevant to the determination of whether the arrangement was used principally as a prohibited device.[35]

Another of the elements of Code Sec. 355, discussed later, is the active trade or business requirement. The regulations state that the existence of assets not used in an active trade or business – such as cash and other liquid assets not related to a business's reasonable needs – is evidence of device.[36]

The mere existence of some such assets is not dispositive. "The strength of the evidence of a device depends on all the facts and circumstances."[37] The presence of a valid business purpose helps rebut a finding of device.[38]

Continued economic integration of the two businesses after the separation is also evidence of a device. This is particularly so if the integration or relationship continues for a long time after the division and if the secondary business could be sold without serious business disruption.[39]

> **Example 1:** For the last six years, Murphree Corporation has processed and sold meat products, and it derived income from no other source. Murphree transfers its assets related to its sales function to a new subsidiary. Murphree then distributes the stock in the subsidiary to Murphree's shareholders. Thereafter, the former subsidiary buys the meat products produced by Murphree and resells them. This scenario is suggestive of a device.[40]

> **Example 2:** For the last eight years, Nautilus Corporation has manufactured and sold steel and steel products. Nautilus owns all of the stock of a subsidiary, which, for the past six years, has owned and operated a coal mine used solely to supply Nautilus's needs in making steel. Nautilus then distributes the stock in the subsidiary to Nautilus's shareholders. Thereafter, the former subsidiary continues to provide coal to Nautilus. This scenario is suggestive of a device.[41]

(b) *Nondevice Factors*

The regulations identify three factors which, if present, tend to indicate that the transactions do not constitute a prohibited device: (1) the existence of a corporate business purpose, (2) the fact that stock in the distributing corporation is publicly traded and widely held, and (3) distribution to domestic corporate shareholders.[42] These factors are elaborated below.

Corporate Business Purpose: As discussed below, the existence of a corporate business purpose is an independent requirement for nonrecognition treatment under Code Sec. 355. In addition, it figures into the device element. When this (or any other nondevice) factor is present, whether it is strong enough to defeat any

---

[35] *Id.* § 1.355-2(d)(2)(iv)(A).

[36] *e.g.,* Rev. Rul. 86-4, 1986-1 C.B. 174 (holding that transfer of even a small portion of investment assets not related to the transferred business may indicate a device).

[37] Treas. Reg. § 1.355-2(d)(2)(iv)(B).

[38] *e.g.,* Rev. Rul. 83-114, 183-2 C.B. 66.

[39] Treas. Reg. § 1.355-2(d)(2)(iv)(C).

[40] *Id.* § 1.355-3(c) Example (10).

[41] *Id.* § 1.355-3(c) Example (11).

[42] *Id.* § 1.355-2(d)(3).

¶702.04(b)

present device factor will depend upon all the facts and circumstances.[43] These facts and circumstances include, but are not limited to, the following:

    (A) the importance of achieving the purpose to the success of the business;

    (B) the extent to which the transaction is prompted by a person not having a proprietary interest in either corporation, or by other outside factors beyond the control of the distributing corporation; and

    (C) the immediacy of the conditions prompting the transaction.[44]

Publicly Traded and Widely Held: "The fact that the distributing corporation is publicly traded and has no shareholder who is directly or indirectly the beneficial owner of more than five percent of any class of stock is evidence of nondevice."[45] Some corporations are owned over 5% by investment funds which have various clients. It is unresolved whether, in such cases, the fund is considered the shareholder (in which case there would be an over-5% shareholder) or the clients of the fund are considered, beneficially, to be the owners (in which case, assuming a sufficient number of clients, there would not be an over-5% shareholder).

Distribution to Domestic Corporate Shareholders: Code Sec. 243 provides a deduction (in effect, an exclusion) for dividends received by a corporation. The amount of the exclusion ranges from 70% to 80% to 100%, depending on the extent of the recipient's stock ownership of the payor.[46] The exclusion is available only to domestic corporations.

The device element of Code Sec. 355 is an anti-abuse rule. If, because of Code Sec. 243, a dividend would be entirely or substantially nontaxable, there is little abuse to be averted. Accordingly, the regulations identify as a nondevice factor the fact that the stock of the controlled corporation is distributed to one or more corporations that would qualify for the 80% or the 100% exclusion were Code Sec. 355 not to apply.[47]

    Practice Tip: The regulations do not specifically identify as a nondevice factor the fact that the distribution is to a corporation that would qualify for the 70% exclusion. However, that fact, if present, should not be irrelevant. It should receive some weight in the "all of the facts and circumstances" analysis that the device element commands.

(c) *Transactions Usually Not Considered Devices*

The restrictions in Code Sec. 355 stand sentinel against transmuting ordinary income into capital gain. When capital gain treatment would be available in any event, there is no need to foreclose Code Sec. 355 treatment. Recognizing this, the regulations prescribe three situations which "ordinarily" are not considered to involve prohibited devices even if one or more of the indicative factors are present.[48] These situations are: (1) the absence of earnings and profits, (2) Code Sec. 303(a) transactions, and (3) Code Sec. 302(a) transactions.

---

[43] *Id.* § 1.355-2(d)(3)(i) & (ii).
[44] *Id.* § 1.355-2(d)(3)(ii).
[45] *Id.* § 1.355-2(d)(3)(iii).

[46] Code Sec. 243 is discussed in detail in Chapter 3.
[47] Treas. Reg. § 1.355-2(d)(3)(iv).
[48] Treas. Reg. § 1.355-2(d)(5)(i).

Absence of Earnings and Profits: A distribution is a dividend only to the extent that the distributing corporation has current or accumulated earnings and profits.[49] Thus, the regulations provide that a distribution ordinarily is not a device if the distributing and controlled corporations have no accumulated E&P at the start of the year and no current E&P at the date of the distribution and if no distribution of property by the distributing corporation immediately before the division would generate gain producing E&P.[50]

Code Sec. 303(a) Transactions: When the stock of a closely held company constitutes a large part of a decedent's gross estate, the estate may have to dispose of some of the stock in order to pay federal or state death taxes or funeral and administration expenses. As a result of the Code Sec. 1014 stepped-up basis provision, if the disposition is accorded sale or exchange treatment, there typically will be little or no gain for income tax purposes. However, because of attribution rules, the normal operation of Code Sec. 302 could result in denial of sale or exchange treatment, causing the estate to suffer ordinary income taxation.[51] Under the circumstances, this would seem like adding insult to injury.

Accordingly, Congress enacted Code Sec. 303. If certain conditions are satisfied, that section affords sale or exchange treatment in the above situation.[52] The Code Sec. 355 regulations provide that a distribution that satisfies Code Sec. 303 is not ordinarily considered a device.[53]

Code Sec. 302(a) Transactions: A redemption of stock within the meaning of Code Sec. 302(a) is treated as a sale or exchange of the stock, qualifying for capital gain (or loss) treatment. The Code Sec. 355 regulations provide that a distribution which constitutes a redemption under Code Sec. 302(a) is not ordinarily considered a device. For this purpose, the ten-year reacquisition rule of Code Sec. 302(c)(2)(A)(ii) and (iii) is disregarded.[54]

Example: *Rafferty v. Commissioner*[55] was decided before the regulations assumed their current form. Nonetheless, the case remains influential as to the device requirement (as well as the active business requirement discussed in subpart ¶ 702.05 below). The Raffertys owned all the outstanding shares of Rafferty Brown Steel Co., Inc. ("RBS"), a steel manufacturer. At the suggestion of their accountant, they organized Teragram Realty Co., Inc. RBS transferred realty it owned to Teragram in exchange for all of Teragram's outstanding stock. The realty was then leased back to RBS for ten years. Two years later, the Raffertys organized another corporation, RBS Connecticut, which acquired warehouse assets.

Mr. Rafferty consulted his accountant about estate planning, especially the orderly disposition of RBS. He wanted his sons to join him at RBS. He wanted to exclude his daughters (and possible future sons-in-law) from active manage-

---

[49] Code Secs. 301(c)(1) & 316(a).
[50] Treas. Reg. § 1.355-2(d)(5)(ii).
[51] The Code Sec. 302 rules are discussed in Chapter 6.
[52] Code Sec. 303 is discussed in Chapter 6.

[53] Treas. Reg. § 1.355-2(d)(5)(iii).
[54] *Id.* § 1.355-2(d)(5)(iv).
[55] 55 T.C. 490, *aff'd*, 452 F.2d 767 (1st Cir. 1971), *cert. denied*, 408 U.S. 922 (1972).

¶702.04(c)

ment of the business, but he wanted to provide them property that would produce steady income.

The accountant recommended forming Teragram, distributing its stock, and eventually using this stock as future gifts to the daughters. The Raffertys acted on this advice, and they accepted the accountant's opinion that the distribution of the Teragram stock would satisfy Code Sec. 355. The IRS concluded that Code Sec. 355 was not satisfied, in part on the ground that the distribution was primarily a device for distributing the E&P of RBS, Teragram, or both.

The Tax Court, although it ultimately held for the IRS, found that there was no device because an adequate business purpose existed for separating and distributing the Teragram stock, namely to facilitate the Raffertys' desire to make bequests to the children under the estate plan.

The appellate court was less receptive to this contention. It first noted that an estate planning purpose was personal to the Raffertys, instead of being a corporate purpose. The Raffertys attempted to spin the personal purpose as a corporate purpose by stressing the desirability of avoiding possible interference with the steel business by possible future sons-in-law. The court, however, distinguished a prior case relied on by the taxpayers,[56] noting that a substantial falling-out had already actually occurred in the prior case but there was "only an envisaged possibility of future debilitating nepotism" in *Rafferty.*[57]

The circuit court did acknowledge that "a purpose of a shareholder, qua shareholder, may in some cases save a transaction from condemnation as a device,"[58] and it rejected the view "that a taxpayer's personal motives cannot be considered." However, the appellate court maintained that "a distribution which has considerable potential for use as a device for distributing earnings and profits should not qualify for tax-free treatment on the basis of personal motives unless those motives are germane to the continuance of the corporate business."[59]

In assessing whether such "considerable potential" existed, the court considered two factors. The first was "how easily the taxpayer would be able, were he so to choose, to liquidate or sell the spun-off corporation. Even if both corporations are actively engaged in their respective trades, if one of them is a business based principally on highly liquid investment-type, passive assets, the potential for a bail-out is real."[60] The court noted that it would have been easy to arrange sale of Teragram's real property, in part because the buildings were usable for multiple purposes.

The court then considered a second factor. "If the taxpayers could not effect a bail-out without thereby impairing their control over the on-going business, the fact that a bail-out is theoretically possible should not be enough to demonstrate a device because the likelihood of it ever being so used is

---

[56] *Coady v. Comm'r,* 33 T.C. 771 (1960), *aff'd per curiam,* 289 F.2d 490 (6th Cir. 1961), acq. 1965-2 C.B. 3.

[57] 452 F.2d at 770.

[58] *Id.*

[59] *Id.*

[60] *Id.* at 771.

¶702.04(c)

slight."[61] The court concluded that, in Rafferty, "the land and buildings at which RBS carried on its steel operations were [not] so distinctive that sale of Teragram stock would impair the continued operation of RBS, or that the sale of those buildings would in any other way impair Rafferty's control or other equity interests in RBS."[62]

Practice Tip: The case law is not fully consistent as to the extent to which a personal (albeit legitimate) motive of shareholders, as opposed to a business motive of their corporation, should immunize the transactions from classification as a device. *Rafferty* gave it some weight; some other decisions give it even more weight.[63]

On the other hand, the regulations – albeit the regulations under the independent business purpose requirement, not the regulations specific to the device requirement – take a less favorable view of the effect of a shareholder's personal motive. These regulations are addressed below as part of the discussion of the business purpose requirement.

Things to watch for: For about a decade, the significance of the device element has been somewhat undercut by the fact that most dividends have been taxed as capital gains, not (as has usually been the case) ordinary income. The 2010 Tax Relief Act extended that treatment but only temporarily – for two years.[64] Its fate thereafter will depend heavily on the outcome of 2012 elections. If dividends revert to ordinary income status, the importance of the device element will grow.

.05 Active Business

Code Sec. 355 does not apply unless either of two conditions is satisfied. The conditions are:

(A) the distributing corporation, and the controlled corporation . . ., [are] engaged immediately after the distribution in the active conduct of a trade or business, or

(B) immediately before the distribution, the distributing corporation had no assets other than stock or securities in the controlled corporations and each of the controlled corporations is engaged immediately after the distribution in the active conduct of a trade or business.[65]

The first of these conditions is the more common and will be the focus of our discussion. By way of definition, the statute adds the following requirements:

• The corporation must have actively conducted the trade or business "throughout the 5-year period ending on the date of the distribution."[66]

---

[61] Id.

[62] Id.

[63] e.g., Estate of Parshelsky v. Comm'r, 303 F.2d 14, 19 (2d Cir. 1962).

[64] Tax Relief, Unemployment Insurance Reauthorization and Job Creation Act of 2010, § 101, Pub. L. 111-312, 124 Stat. 3296.

[65] Code Sec. 355(1). For this purpose, a de minimis amount of assets held by the distributing corporation is disregarded. Treas. Reg. § 1.355-3(a)(1)(ii).

[66] Code Sec. 355(b)(2)(B).

- The corporation did not acquire the trade or business within that five-year period "in a transaction in which gain or loss was recognized in whole or part."[67]

- Control of the corporation conducting the trade or business either (i) was not acquired by the distributing corporation or any distributee corporation, directly or indirectly, during the five-year period or (ii) was so acquired but was acquired "only by reason of transactions in which gain or loss was not recognized in whole or in part, or only by reason of such transactions combined with acquisitions before the beginning of the [five-year] period."[68]

Special rules are provided with respect to corporations that are members of affiliated groups, as generally defined in Code Sec. 1504. In general, members of the same affiliated group are treated as one corporation for purposes of this requirement.[69]

> **Example 1:** Andalusia Corporation owns all the stock in Cordoba Corporation. Both Andalusia and Cordoba actively conduct business for the requisite time period. Andalusia distributes all the Cordoba stock to Andalusia's shareholders, and both Andalusia and Cordoba continue to actively conduct business thereafter. The active business requirement is met.[70]

> **Example 2:** The same fact as Example 1, except that Andalusia transfers all its assets other than the Cordoba stock to a new corporation in exchange for all the new corporation's stock. Andalusia then distributes the stock of both Cordoba and the new corporation to Andalusia's shareholders. The active business requirement is met.[71]

(a) *Trade or Business*

The government originally took the position that Code Sec. 355 does not apply to the division of a single business, that there had to be at least two businesses that were being separated. After losing a number of cases,[72] the government abandoned that position. The current regulations accept that Code Sec. 355 applies to single-business divisions.

> **Example 1:** For over five years, Bullfinch Corporation conducted a single business of constructing sewage disposal plants and other facilities. Bullfinch transferred half of its assets to a new subsidiary. These assets include a contract to build a sewage disposal plant, construction equipment, cash, and other assets. Bullfinch keeps other such contracts and other equipment, cash, and assets. Then Bullfinch distributed the stock in the subsidiary to one of Bullfinch's shareholders in exchange for all of that shareholder's Bullfinch stock. The "active conduct of business" requirement is satisfied as to both Bullfinch and the subsidiary.[73]

---

[67] Code Sec. 355(b)(2)(C).

[68] Code Sec. 355(b)(2)(D).

[69] Code Sec. 355(b)(2) & (b)(3).

[70] Treas. Reg. § 1.355-3(a)(2) Example (1).

[71] *Id.* Example (2)

[72] *Rafferty v. Comm'r*, 452 F.2d 767 (1st Cir. 1971), *cert. denied*, 408 U.S. 922 (1972); *United States v. Marett*, 325 F.2d 28 (5th Cir. 1963); *Coady v. Comm'r*, 289 F.2d 490 (6th Cir. 1961). The IRS accepted these decisions in Rev. Rul. 75-160, 1975-1 C.B. 112.

[73] Treas. Reg. § 1.355-3(c) Example (4). These are the facts of *Coady.*

¶702.05(a)

Example 2: For six years, Cyclops Corporation has owned and operated two factories that produce edible pork skins. The whole output of one factory and part of the output of the second factory are sold to unrelated Polyphemus Corporation. The remainder of the output of the second factory is sold to other customers. To eliminate packaging errors, Cyclops opens a new factory. Orders from Polyphemus are handled at the two original factories, and orders from other customers are handled at the new factory. Eight months later, Cyclops transfers the new factory and related assets to a new subsidiary, then distributes the stock of the new subsidiary to Cyclops' shareholders. The "active conduct of business" requirement is satisfied as to both Cyclops and the subsidiary.[74]

The current regulations provide that a corporation is

> treated as engaged in a trade or business immediately after the distribution if a specific group of activities are being carried on by the corporation for the purpose of earning income or profit, and the activities included in such group include every operation that forms a part of, or a step in, the process of earning income or profit. Such groups of activities must include the collection of income and the payment of expenses.[75]

There are, however, two activities that do not constitute trades or business for purposes of the "active conduct of business" requirement of Code Sec. 355: investment and use of property without significant services.

Investment: Investing, even active investing, does not constitute a trade or business for Code Sec. 162 purposes.[76] This distinction is made for Code Sec. 355 purposes as well – in keeping with the section's purpose to prevent tax-advantaged bail-outs of corporate profits by separating saleable assets not required in order to conduct the business.

Thus, the regulations provide: "The active conduct of a trade or business does not include . . . [t]he holding for investment purposes of stock, securities, land, or other property."[77] This is so even if the corporation has a substantial budget and staff "to analyze and review the [investment] portfolio, research and investigate corporate situations, purchase and sell, pick up and deliver securities, and maintain books of account."[78]

Example: Enkidu Corporation manufactures and sells soap and detergents; it also owns investment securities. Enkidu transfers the securities to a new subsidiary and distributes the stock in the subsidiary to Enkidu's shareholders. Enkidu satisfies the "active conduct of business" requirement (assuming other aspects are met), but the subsidiary does not. Holding investment securities does not qualify. Accordingly, Code Sec. 355 does not apply to the separation.[79]

Practice Tip: Give the above, the IRS has been suspicious of attempts to extend Code Sec. 355 treatment when a finance business is separated from the

---

[74] *Id.* Example (5). These are the facts of *Marett.*

[75] Treas. Reg. § 1.355-3(b)(ii).

[76] *e.g., Comm'r v. Higgins*, 312 U.S. 212, 217-18 (1941).

[77] Treas. Reg. § 1.355-3(b)(3).

[78] Rev. Rul. 66-204, 1966-2 C.B. 113.

[79] *Id.* § 1.355-3(c) Example (1).

associated retail sales business.[80] The IRS has lost some of the cases.[81] However, a taxpayer hoping to succeed in such a case would face difficult challenges under the "active conduct of business" test. Moreover, even if the taxpayer were to prevail at that level, the other Code Sec. 355 requirements, particularly the device requirement discussed above in subpart ¶ 702.04, would stand as further barriers.

Use of Property: In several contexts, the Internal Revenue Code distinguishes between what might loosely be called passive and active use of property.[82] Section 355 is one of those contexts. The regulations provide: "The active conduct of a trade or business does not include . . . [t]he ownership and operation (including leasing) of real or personal property used in a trade or business, unless the owner performs significant services with respect to the operation and management of the property.[83]

> *Example:* Patna Corporation leases vacant land to an unrelated parking lot operator. Patna provides no services to the operator. Patna is not engaged in the active conduct of a trade or business for Code Sec. 355 purposes.[84]

> *Practice Tip:* It can be important, but not always easy to determine, whether the owner renders "significant services" as to property. A taxpayer to whom this issue is important may wish to consult rulings in which the IRS has approved the activities as being significant. In one such ruling, the owner sought, acquired, and developed new properties; advertised for and investigated prospective tenants; negotiated leases; serviced mortgages and paid insurance, taxes, and utilities costs; periodically renovated and restored the properties; and provided maintenance and repairs, including trash collection, ground maintenance, janitorial services, pest control, and maintenance of HVAC and plumbing systems.[85]

(b) *Active Conduct of the Business*

When is an economic activity engaged in with sufficient energy that it constitutes the active conduct of a trade or business? This involves a facts and circumstances inquiry, but the regulations provide general guidance.

> Generally, the corporation is required itself to perform active and substantial management and operational functions. Generally, activities performed by the corporation itself do not include activities performed by persons outside the corporation, including independent contractors. A corporation may satisfy the requirements . . . through the activities that it performs itself, even though some of its activities are performed by others.[86]

> *Example:* A and B are the officers and shareholders of P corporation. A and B are both farmers; they also farm individually owned farms not owned by

---

[80] *See, e.g., Id.* § 1.355-3(b)(iii).

[81] *Hanson v. United States*, 338 F. Supp. 602 (D. Mont. 1971); *Wilson v. Comm'r*, 42 T.C. 914 (1964), *rev'd & remanded on other grounds*, 353 F.2d 184 (9th Cir. 1965).

[82] For example, the mere co-ownership of property that is maintained, kept in repair, and rented or leased does not constitute a partnership, even if customary services are furnished in connection with the maintenance and repair. The furnishing of additional services by the co-owners (directly or through agents) will cause the activity to rise to the level of a partnership. *e.g.*, Treas. Reg. § 301.7701-1(a)(2); Rev. Rul. 75-374, 1975-2 C.B. 261.

[83] Treas. Reg. § 1.355-3(b)(2)(iv)(B).

[84] Rev. Rul. 68-284, 1968-1 C.B. 143.

[85] Rev. Rul. 79-394, 1979-2 C.B. 141, *amplified by* Rev. Rul. 80-181, 1980-2 C.B. 121.

[86] Treas. Reg. § 1.355-3(b)(iii).

P. Each tract of land held by P is leased for a year at a time to tenant farmers, who share with P the income and the expenses of the tracts. The tenant farmers plant, raise, and harvest the crops. They also supply the equipment used, and they maintain and repair the equipment, irrigation systems, fences, and other fixtures on the properties. After consulting with A and B, the tenant farmers buy the pesticides, herbicides, and fertilizers, and similarly sell the crops.

A and B spend substantial time on their individual interests. On behalf of P, they occasionally inspect the crops and the improvements on the tracks. The tenants make necessary corrections in the ways they see fit. A and B decide each year what portions of the tracts to lease. They also review each tenant farmer's accounting of operations and sales.

P transfers half of all its property to a newly formed subsidiary, then distributes all stock in the subsidiary to B in exchange for all of B's stock in P. Thereafter, P and the subsidiary conduct operations in the same manner as before the separation. Because of the absence of active and substantial operational and managerial activities, the active business requirement is not met. Code Sec. 355 does not apply.[87]

(c) *Five-Year Period*

The active business requirement could be easily circumvented if it contained no time element. Congress enacted the five-year requirement to prevent taxpayers from avoiding dividend treatment by distributing assets that had been used for little or no time in an active trade or business.[88] It would be a mistake to think, however, that the requirement constitutes a particularly bright line. A number of implementational issues blur the clarity of the requirement. These issues are described below.

Quantum of assets: Does the active trade or business have to constitute a particular portion of the assets of the corporation prior to the separation? Probably not. The IRS has approved nontaxability of separations when the active business represented the minority of the asset value of the corporation.[89] The IRS usually will not give a favorable ruling if the assets are under 5% of the pre-separation business's total gross assets.[90] However, that is a ruling position, not a rule of law. An under-5% situation likely would be sustained as long as the businesses are active for long enough and Code Sec. 355's other requirements are met.

Duration of the period: Five years means five complete calendar years, beginning with the date of the distribution. Actively conducting a business during parts of five tax years, during five full tax years involving some short and some regular years, or during five other types of accounting periods would not suffice.[91]

Start of the period: The five-year period starts when the corporation begins conducting the business. The IRS formerly took the position that this happened only when all elements of the business had commenced and income was being

---

[87] Rev. Rul. 86-126, 1986-2 C.B. 58.

[88] S. Rep. No. 1622, 83d Cong. 2d Sess. 50-51 (1954).

[89] *e.g.*, Rev. Rul. 74-79, 1974-1 C.B. 81 (under one-third); Rev. Rul. 73-44, 1973-1 C.B. 182 (under one-half).

[90] Rev. Proc. 99-3, § 4.01, 1999-1 C.B. 103.

[91] *Elliott v. Comm'r*, 32 T.C. 283, 291-92 (1959).

produced.[92] That position was rejected by the courts, however,[93] and the IRS appears no longer to be asserting that position. If the corporation acquired the active business by getting the stock of the corporation conducting it, the period starts when the acquisition closes rather than when the contract for acquisition was entered into.[94]

Temporary cessation of the business: Assume that, after the five-year period has started but before five years have passed, the business declines to the point of dormancy or is otherwise interrupted. Would that prevent satisfaction of the requirement? Usually not, especially if the interruption is beyond the corporation's control and if the conduct of the business has resumed by the time the division is effected.[95]

> **Example 1:** A corporation manufactured equipment. Its sole customer (an unrelated party) unexpectedly went bankrupt. This caused the corporation to close its plant and significantly curtail its workforce during one of the five years. However, the corporation continued to employ workers to maintain its equipment, to redesign its products, and to search for new customers. The five-year active business requirement was satisfied.[96]

> **Example 2:** Property of a corporation was put out of operation as a result of fire. The corporation attempted, both before and after the division, to return the property to operation, but these efforts were unsuccessful. The five-year active business requirement was not satisfied.[97]

Redirection of the business: The corporation need not preserve the character of the business unchanged throughout the entire five-year period. The requirement will be satisfied as long as the changes are not so extensive as to produce a new or different business.[98]

> **Example 1:** For the past nine years, Atherton Corporation has owned and operated a department store in the downtown area of a city. Three years ago, it acquired land in the city's suburb and built a new department store on it. Atherton transfers the suburban store and related assets to a new subsidiary and distributes stock in the subsidiary to Atherton's shareholders. After the distribution, each store has its own manager and is operated independently of the other. The five-year active business requirement is met as to both Atherton and its former subsidiary.[99]

> **Example 2:** For the past six years, Bokara Corporation has owned and operated hardware stores in several states. Two years ago, Bokara bought all the assets of a hardware store in Colorado, where Bokara had not previously operated. Bokara transfers the Colorado store and related assets to a new subsidiary and distributes the stock of the subsidiary to Bokara's shareholders. After the distribution, the Colorado store and Bokara's stores each have their

---

[92] *e.g.*, Rev. Rul. 57-492, 1957-2 C.B. 247.

[93] *e.g., King v. United States*, 458 F.2d 245 (6th Cir. 1972).

[94] *Russell v. Comm'r*, 40 T.C. 810 (1963), *aff'd per curiam*, 345 F.2d 534 (5th Cir. 1965).

[95] *e.g.*, Rev. Rul. 57-126, 1957-1 C.B. 123.

[96] Rev. Rul. 82-219, 1982-2 C.B. 82.

[97] *Spheeris v. Comm'r*, 54 T.C. 1353 (1970), *aff'd*, 461 F.2d 271 (7th Cir. 1972).

[98] Treas. Reg. § 1.355-3(b)(3)(ii).

[99] Treas. Reg. § 1.355-3(c) Example (7).

own managers and the stores operate independently. The five-year active business requirement is met as to both Bokara and its former subsidiary.[100]

Practice Tip: In both of the immediately prior examples (Atherton and Bokara) drawn from the regulations, Treasury included the statement that the distributing corporation and the new corporation were independently managed. At the time the regulations were written (and indeed for many years), it was thought that, in general, Code Sec. 355 required complete separation of the companies. Thus, absent unusual circumstances (and then only for a limited time), continuing common management of the separated companies or overlap on their boards of directors was viewed as problematic. This concern may have been overstated, however, and such features may not necessarily be fatal to nonrecognition treatment.[101]

One context in which the "redirection" question can arise is when the corporation that ultimately will make the distribution acquires another company. If the acquired entity is in the same business, the acquisition will not compromise a subsequent corporate division. The outer limits of "sameness" cannot, of course, be limited sharply. There is an "eye of the beholder" quality to when the threshold separating sameness and difference is crossed. Close attention to the facts of favorable rulings may help define whatever comfort zone may exist.

Example 1: Firenza Corporation had been a dealer in Brand X automobiles for over five years. It acquired a franchise to sell Brand Y automobiles and bought the assets of a former Brand Y dealer. After operating the new Brand Y dealership for three years (while also continuing to operate the original Brand X dealership), Firenza transferred the Brand X assets to a subsidiary and distributed the stock in the subsidiary to Firenza's shareholders. The IRS ruled that the five-year active business requirement was satisfied. The Brand Y dealership was not a new business but only an expansion of Firenza's existing business. The Brand X and Brand Y products were similar, and conducting the dealerships entailed highly similar operations and expertise.[102]

Example 2: Li Corporation had for many years operated a store where it sold shoes. To exploit a new mercantile medium, it later began selling shoes through a web site. Less than five years after it began doing so, the corporation divided, and nonrecognition treatment was claimed under Code Sec. 355. The IRS approved such treatment. The inauguration of the web-based selling was merely an expansion of Li's business. The same product was sold through the store and the web; the same corporate name was used; sales through the two channels involved some (though not all) of the same expertise; and the web business benefited significantly from the goodwill created through the store.[103]

---

[100] *Id.* Example (8).

[101] For a detailed argument to this effect, see J. William Dantzler Jr., *Spinoffs: Still Remarkably Tax Friendly*, Tax Notes, Nov. 8, 2010, p. 683, at 693-99.

[102] Rev. Rul. 2003-18, 2003-1 C.B. 467.

[103] Rev. Rul. 2003-38, 2003-1 C.B. 811.

¶ 703 Regulatory Requirements

The regulations add to the statutory requirements – or, to mollify those who believe that Treasury cannot legitimately add to the statutes –embellish or elaborate on ideas implicit in Code Sec. 355. There are three principal regulatory requirements: business purpose, continuity of interest, and continuity of enterprise. These are described below.

.01 Business Purpose

The business purpose requirement originally entered Code Sec. 355 analysis as a result of case law, such as the *Gregory* case discussed previously in this chapter. Congress has not written a business purpose requirement into the statute, but Treasury added such a requirement to the Code Sec. 355 regulations in 1989. "The principal purpose for this business purpose requirement is to provide nonrecognition to readjustments of corporate structures required by business exigencies and that effect only readjustments of continuing interests in property under modified corporate forms."[104]

We earlier explored business purpose in the context of the device element, where the existence of such a purpose is one factor suggestive that the transactions are not a device principally for distributing earnings and profits. Although there is conceptual interrelationship, the business purpose element is independent of the device requirement and other Code Sec. 355 requirements.[105] The presence of a business purpose satisfies the business purpose requirement, but it does not guarantee nonrecognition treatment. For instance, the device element may not be satisfied because the business purpose nondevice indicator may be trumped by more powerful device indicators. Conversely, the "not a device" element may be satisfied but nonrecognition treatment still fail because the business purpose element is not met.

> **Example:** The taxpayer separated his retail furniture business and the consumer financing function related to the furniture business. The courts held that the separation was not a device. Nonetheless, nonrecognition treatment was denied because the taxpayer failed to establish that there was a business purpose for the transactions.[106]

Below, we consider first purposes that are valid, then those that are not valid.

(a) Valid Purpose

"A corporate business purpose is a real and substantial non-Federal tax purpose germane to the business of the distributing corporation, the controlled corporation, or the affiliated group . . . to which the distributing corporation belongs."[107] The regulations do not exhaustively enumerate valid business purposes. Indeed, it would be futile to attempt to encapsulate the nearly infinite diversity of such purposes.

---

[104] Treas. Reg. § 1.355-2(b).
[105] *Id.*

[106] *Comm'r v. Wilson*, 353 F.2d 184 (9th Cir. 1965).
[107] Treas. Reg. § 1.355-2(b)(2). "Affiliated group" is defined for this purpose in Treas. Reg. 1.355-3(b)(4)(iv).

The regulations do, however, set out examples which are helpful by way of illustration. They include: (1) complying with an antitrust divestiture order, (2) allowing shareholders to divide the business in order to go their separate ways, (3) protecting one line of business from the risks and vicissitudes of another line of business, (4) improving the company's posture for rate-making in a regulated industry, and (5) allowing a key employee, who otherwise might leave the company, to acquire an ownership stake in the business.[108]

Practice Tip: A normal procedure for taxpayers unsure whether the IRS will accept a particular objective as an adequate business purpose would be to submit a private letter ruling request. The IRS's willingness to rule in this area, however, has fluctuated. Concerned that too much of its staff resources would be consumed in dealing with such requests, the IRS has sometimes suspended ruling on Code Sec. 355 business purpose or has issued general guidance designed to reduce the need for taxpayers to submit ruling requests.

Example 1: In 1996 guidance, the IRS identified the following as among the generally acceptable business purposes for distributions incident to corporate separations: retaining key personnel, facilitating stock offerings or borrowing, effecting cost savings, helping in effectuation of acquisitions of or by the distributing corporation or the controlled corporation(s), enhancing the "fit and focus" of the enterprise, improving competitive strength, and reducing risks.[109]

Example 2: In 2004 guidance, the IRS considered the following situation. D is a corporation whose stock is publicly traded and widely held. D owns subsidiaries, some of which engage only in Business 1 and others of which engage only in Business 2.

The two businesses attract different investors; some investors do not wish to invest in D because of one or the other of the two Businesses. For that reason, D believes that the stock of the companies would be more highly valued were the businesses to be separated.

Accordingly, D transferred the companies engaged in Business 2 to new subsidiary C, in exchange for all of the stock in C. Then, D distributed the C stock to D's shareholders pro rata. D continued to own the companies conducting Business 1.

The increase of share price would benefit the shareholders. In addition, two benefits to the corporations were asserted. First, D had used equity-based incentives to compensate many employees. The stock value increase anticipated as a result of the separation would allow continued use of such incentives without excessive cost or dilution of existing stockholders' interests.

Second, as part of its overall strategic planning, D expanded both Business 1 and Business 2 through acquiring assets and stock of other corporations. D sometimes uses its own stock as compensation in such acquisitions. The stock value increase anticipated as a result of the separation would

---

[108] Treas. Reg. § 1.355-2(b)(5) Examples 1-5 & 8.   [109] Rev. Proc. 96-30, 1996-1 C.B. 378.

¶703.01(a)

facilitate such acquisitions while preserving capital and minimizing dilution of the interests of existing stockholders.

The IRS ruled that both of these asserted corporate benefits constituted valid business purposes.[110]

Practice Tip: As noted in Example 1 above, improved "focus and fit" can be an acceptable business purpose.[111] However, this justification has a "mushy" and thus malleable quality to it, so it can be asserted pretextually to attempt to cloak what really is a bailout of earnings and profits. Accordingly, the IRS may subject such a rationale to particularly close scrutiny, especially when the distributing and controlled corporations are closely held.[112]

When does the business purpose have to exist? The IRS has ruled that the business purpose requirement is satisfied if a valid corporate purpose existed at the time of distribution of the controlled corporations(s), even if unexpected conditions subsequently prevent the realization of that purpose.[113]

(b) *Invalid Purpose*

Reducing Federal Taxes: Unsurprisingly, reducing federal taxes does not qualify as an acceptable business purpose.[114]

Example: Pascow Corporation owns all of the stock of Jasmine Corporation. It would be desirable for Jasmine to be an S corporation, but a corporation with a corporate shareholder is ineligible to elect S status.[115] Thus, Pascow distributes all of the Jasmine stock to Pascow's five shareholders, all of whom are individuals who are U.S. citizens or U.S. resident aliens. Jasmine is now eligible to file an S election.[116] This distribution is a recognition event. Enabling the filing of an S election is not an acceptable corporate business purpose.[117]

Reducing State, Local, or Foreign Taxes: Reducing a corporation's liability for taxes to a sovereign other than the federal government is considered a valid business purpose in a variety of income tax contexts. The Code Sec. 355 regulations, however, add the proviso that reducing non-federal taxes is an unacceptable purpose "if (i) the transaction will effect a reduction in both Federal and non Federal taxes because of similarities between Federal law and the tax law of the other jurisdiction and (ii) the reduction of Federal taxes is greater than or substantially coextensive with the reduction of non-Federal taxes."[118]

Example: The facts are the same as in the immediately preceding Pascow/Jasmine example, except that the corporations operate in a state that imposes a state income tax but has S corporation rules substantially similar to

---

[110] Rev. Rul. 2004-23, 2004-1 C.B. 585.

[111] *See also* Rev. Rul. 2003-110, 2003-2 C.B. 1083 (approving this business purpose with respect to separating a pesticide manufacturing business from a baby food manufacturing business in order to improve consumer perception of the latter).

[112] *See* Rev. Rul. 2003-74, 2003-2 C.B. 77 (approving a "fit and focus" purpose in part on the ground that the distributing corporation was publicly held).

[113] Rev. Rul. 2003-55, 2003-1 C.B. 961.

[114] Treas. Reg. § 1.355-2(b)(1).

[115] Code Sec. 1361(b)(1)(B).

[116] Code Sec. 1361(b)(1)(A) & (C).

[117] Treas. Reg. § 1.355-2(b)(5) Example (6)(i).

[118] Treas. Reg. § 1.355-2(b)(2); *see, e.g., Virginia Historic Tax Credit Fund 2001 LP v. Comm'r*, 98 T.C.M. 630 (2009), *rev'd on other grounds*, 2011 WL 1127056 (4th Cir. Mar. 29, 2011).

those of the Internal Revenue Code. Making the S election would substantially decrease the state tax burden on Jasmine and its shareholders. However, there would be no business purpose acceptable under Code Sec. 355 if, as likely is the case, the reduction in federal income taxes would equal or exceed the reduction in state income taxes.[119]

Alternative Means of Accomplishing the Business Purpose: Often, there are several different avenues by which desired ends can be accomplished. A corporate division may further certain otherwise acceptable results. However, "[i]f a corporate business purpose can be achieved though a nontaxable transaction that does not involve the distribution of stock of a controlled corporation and which is neither impractical nor unduly expensive, then . . . the separation is not carried out for that corporate business purpose."[120]

> **Example:** Rimini Corporation manufactures and sells toys; it also manufactures and sells candy. Historically, the toy business has been more volatile economically and has higher product liability tort exposure. The shareholders of Rimini wish to protect the candy business from the risks and vicissitudes of the toy business. Rimini transfers the toy business to a new subsidiary and distributes the stock of that subsidiary to Rimini's shareholders.

> Although reducing business risks and vicissitudes is generally a valid corporate business purpose, nonrecognition treatment will not be accorded to this corporate separation. The transfer of the toy business to the new subsidiary would be tax-free under Code Sec. 351.[121] Moreover, that transfer would be enough, under state corporate law, to achieve risk-and-vicissitude reduction. The creation of the subsidiary and the transfer of the assets suffice to achieve limited liability, protecting the candy business that remains in Rimini. The distribution of the subsidiary's stock to the shareholders adds little or nothing to advancing the business purpose.[122]

Personal, Not Corporate, Motives: Earlier, when discussing the business purpose nondevice factor in the device element, we noted that the authorities have not been consistent as to how much, if at all, a personal, nontax motive can help a taxpayer secure nonrecognition treatment under Code Sec. 355. Some cases accord great weight to such a motive; other cases accord it less weight.

The IRS takes a stricter view, maintaining that, in general, a corporate purpose is required and a shareholder purpose will not suffice.[123] There is an important caveat, though. The regulations repeat that "[a] shareholder purpose (for example, the personal planning purposes of a shareholder) is not a corporate business purpose," but then add:

> Depending upon the facts of a particular case, however, a shareholder purpose may be so nearly coextensive with a corporate business purpose as to preclude any distinction between them. In such a case, the transaction is carried out for one or more corporate business purposes.[124]

---

[119] Treas. Reg. § 1.355-2(b)(5) Example (7).
[120] Treas. Reg. § 1.355-2(b)(3).
[121] Code Sec. 351 is discussed in Chapter 2.
[122] Treas. Reg. § 1.355-2(b)(5) Example (3).
[123] *e.g.*, Rev. Rul. 69-460, 1969-2 C.B. 51.
[124] Treas. Reg. § 1.355-2(b)(2).

Example: Goeke Corporation operated both an automobile dealership and an automobile rental business. It split off the rental business. This served the estate planning purposes of the corporation's 70-year-old majority owner – a personal, noncorporate motive. However, the separation also was used to remove inactive shareholders, ensuring that, after the majority shareholder's eventual demise, only persons who were active in Goeke's business would continue as shareholders. This was important because of a requirement in the franchise policy of the automobile manufacturer. The IRS ruled that the personal and corporate purposes were coextensive and inseparate. Thus, the corporate business purpose requirement was satisfied.[125]

.02 Continuity of Interest

An adequate degree of continuity of ownership or proprietary interest is a requirement for a tax-free reorganization under Code Sec. 368.[126] Although the Code Sec. 368 continuity of interest regulations do not directly apply to Code Sec. 355,[127] the Code Sec. 355 regulations create a similar, if not necessarily congruent, requirement. Specifically, and in addition to the other requirements,

> section 355 requires that one or more persons who, directly or indirectly, were the owners of the enterprise prior to the distribution or exchange own, in the aggregate, an amount of stock establishing a continuity of interest in each of the modified corporate forms in which the enterprise is conducted after the separation.[128]

The IRS typically wants to see at least 50% continuity.[129] Courts, however, may be willing to accept a somewhat lower percentage.[130]

Example 1: Darius Corporation engages in one business directly and a second business indirectly through its wholly owned subsidiary Xerxes Corporation. The two lines of business are of equal value. Unrelated individuals A and B each own 50% of the Darius stock. Darius distributes all of the Xerxes stock to B in exchange for all of B's Darius stock. Thus, after the transaction, A owns 100% of the Darius stock and B owns 100% of the Xerxes stock. The continuity of interest requirement is met because one or more persons who owned Darius before the distribution own, in the aggregate, an amount of stock establishing continuity of ownership in each of Darius and Xerxes after the distribution.[131]

Example 2: The same facts as in Example 1 except that (1) under a plan to acquire an interest in Darius without acquiring an interest in Xerxes, individual C bought half of A's Darius stock and (2) immediately thereafter, Darius distributed all the Xerxes stock to B in exchange for all B's Darius stock. Thus, after the transactions, A owns 50% of the Darius stock and B owns 100% of the Xerxes stock. The continuity of interest requirement is met

---

[125] Rev. Rul. 75-337, 1975-2 C.B. 124. For additional examples, see Rev. Rul. 2003-52, 2003-1 C.B. 960; Ltr. Rul. 200422040 (May 28, 2004); Ltr. Rul. 200339007 (Sept. 26, 2003).

[126] *See* Chapter 9.

[127] T.D. 8760, 1998-1 C.B. 803, 805.

[128] Treas. Reg. § 1.355-2(c)(1).

[129] *See, e.g.,* Rev. Proc. 96-30, §4.06, 1996-1 C.B. 696, *amplified & modified,* Rev. Proc. 2003-48, 2003-2 C.B. 86.

[130] *e.g., Nelson v. Helvering,* 296 U.S. 374 (1935).

[131] Treas. Reg. § 1.355-2(c)(2) Example (1).

because one or more of the persons who owned Darius before the distribution own, in the aggregate, an amount of stock establishing continuity of ownership in each of Darius and Xerxes after the distribution.[132]

Example 3: The same facts as in Example 1 except that C, pursuant to the plan, bought all of A's Darius stock. Thus, after the transactions, neither A nor B owns any Darius stock and B owns 100% of the Xerxes stock.

The continuity of interest requirement is not met. The owners of Darius before the distribution do not, in the aggregate, own an amount of stock establishing continuity of ownership in both of Darius and Xerxes. A and B, taken together, do retain 50% of the original, pre-distribution business, but they have failed to have a sufficient interest in Darius.[133]

Example 4: The same facts as in Example 1, except that C, pursuant to the plan, bought 80% of A's Darius stock. Thus, after the transactions, A owns 20% of the Darius stock and B owns 100% of the Xerxes stock.

The continuity of interest requirement is not met. The owners of Darius before the distribution do not, in the aggregate, own an amount of stock establishing continuity of ownership in both Darius and Xerxes. Taken together, A and B own all of Xerxes and, unlike in Example 3, do have some ownership of Xerxes. However, that Xerxes ownership interest is only 20%, which is insufficient.[134]

.03 Continuity of Enterprise

The Code Sec. 355 regulations do not address continuity of business enterprise with the same specificity with which they address continuity of proprietary interest. Nonetheless, the regulations do state: "Section 355 contemplates the continued operation of the business or businesses existing prior to the separation."[135] The IRS has deemed this a strong enough hook by which to drag into Code Sec. 355 a continuity of enterprise requirement which at least resembles that requirement under Code Sec. 368. The precise degree of similarity or divergence has not been settled by either case law or administrative authority.

Practice Tip: Although the continuity of interest and continuity of enterprise requirements are independent of each other and of the other Code Sec. 355 requirements, the facts that affect one of the requirements may affect others as well.

Example 1: Penrod is a shareholder of the distributing corporation. Immediately after the distribution to him of stock in the controlled corporation, Penrod disposes of that stock. Depending on the circumstances, the IRS may contend that the continuity of interest requirement is not met and/or that the device or control requirements are not met.

Example 2: Before the separation, Rennard Corporation conducted Business 1 and Business 2. It puts Business 2 into a subsidiary, then distributes the

---

[132] *Id.* Example (2)
[133] *Id.* Example (3).

[134] *Id.* Example (4).
[135] Treas. Reg. § 1.355-1(b).

subsidiary stock to Rennard's shareholders. Shortly thereafter, Business 2 is discontinued. The IRS may contend that the continuity of enterprise requirement is not met and/or that the active business requirement is not met. The greater degree to which the active business requirement has been developed and the frequent overlap of the active business and continuity of enterprise requirements partly explain why the continuity of enterprise requirement has not been developed in detail in the Code Sec. 355 context.

¶ 704 Recognition and Nonrecognition of Gain

In general, if a separation satisfies all of the statutory and regulatory requirements of Code Sec. 355, the transactions are tax-free to the distributing corporation, the controlled corporation, and the distributee shareholders. However, a variety of anti-abuse rules mandate at least partial recognition of gain in certain circumstances. A failed Code Sec. 355 separation – one which (intentionally or unintentionally) does not meet all of the statutory and regulatory requirements – does result in recognition of gain.

.01 Treatment of Distributee Shareholders

Code Sec. 355(a)(1) sets out the general rule that, if the various elements are satisfied, distributees do not recognize gain or loss as a result of receiving stock or securities. This applies whether or not the distribution is pro rata, the shareholder surrenders stock in the distributing corporation, or the distribution is pursuant to a plan of reorganization.[136]

However, Code Sec. 355(a)(3) imposes four limits on this general rule. First, recognition occurs if either the distributees receive a greater principal amount of securities in the controlled corporation than they surrender or the distributees receive securities in the controlled corporation and no securities are surrendered.[137]

Second, as described below, distributees are taxable with respect to boot they receive. For this purpose, stock of a controlled corporation is treated as boot if acquired by the distributing corporation in a recognition event within five years before the separation.[138]

> **Practice Tip:** Although such stock is boot, it appears from the language of Code Sec. 368(c) that it is counted in determining whether the control requirement discussed above is satisfied.

Third, recognition occurs to the extent distributees receive stock, securities, or other property that is attributable to interest accrued on securities since the start of the holder's holding period.[139] This includes nonqualified preferred stock for purposes of Code Sec. 351(g)(2).[140]

Fourth, nonqualified preferred stock is treated as boot if it is received in a distribution with respect to stock other than nonqualified preferred stock.[141] Again, nonqualified preferred stock is defined by reference to Code Sec. 351(g)(2).

---

[136] Code Sec. 355(a)(2).
[137] Code Secs. 355(a)(3)(A) & 356(d)(2)(C).
[138] Code Sec. 355(a)(3)(B).

[139] Code Sec. 355(a)(3)(C).
[140] Code Sec. 351(g) is discussed in Chapter 2.
[141] Code Sec. 355(a)(3)(D).

As is true with respect to nonrecognition provisions in the Code generally, gain is recognized when boot is distributed. The key section here is Code Sec. 356, which is made applicable to corporate divisions by Code Sec. 355(a)(4). Different rules apply to situations in which the distributee surrenders stock (split-offs and split-ups) than to situations in which no stock is surrendered (spin-offs). When stock is not surrendered but boot is received, the sum of money received and the fair market value of the non-cash boot received is treated as a distribution to which Code Sec. 301 applies.[142]

Example 1: Aragorn and Arwen each own 50 of the 100 outstanding shares of the stock of Osgiliath Corporation, which has only one class of stock. Osgiliath has a wholly owned subsidiary. Osgiliath distributes to each of Aragorn and Arwen half of the shares of the subsidiary plus $100 in cash. Neither Aragorn nor Arwen surrender any of their stock in Osgiliath. The $100 in cash received by each of Aragorn and Arwen is a distribution subject to Code Sec. 301.[143]

Example 2: The same facts as in Example 1, except that Osgiliath distributes to Aragorn 50 shares of the subsidiary's stock (but no cash); it distributes to Arwen 30 shares of the subsidiary's stock plus $100 in cash; and it retains the remaining 20 shares of stock in the subsidiary. Aragorn has received no boot. Arwen's $100 in cash is a distribution to which Code Sec. 301 applies.[144]

Practice Tip: The tax effects when Code Sec. 301 applies depends upon into which of the tranches of Code Sec. 301(c) the distribution falls. The first tranch is that the distribution is a dividend up to the amount of the corporation's current and accumulated earnings and profits. In *Example 2* above, the $100 received by Arwen would be a dividend to the full extent of Osgiliath's earnings and profits, not just Arwen's share of Osgiliath's earnings and profits.

Arwen could minimize this hit by surrendering Osgiliath stock equal in value to the subsidiary stock and the cash she received. This results from two things. First, Arwen's recognized gain cannot exceed her realized gain, which would be zero were Arwen to proceed as noted. Second, because she surrendered some stock, any recognized gain would be a dividend only to the extent of Arwen's share of Osgiliath's earnings and profits, not the totality of Osgiliath's earnings and profits.

Different outcomes ensue when the distributee shareholder surrenders stock in the distributing corporation. When stock is surrendered and boot is received, gain is recognized up to the sum of the cash and the fair market value of the non-cash boot received.[145] Such gain is treated as a dividend if the distribution "has the effect of the distribution of a dividend. . . . The remainder, if any, of the gain recognized [is] treated as gain from the exchange of property."[146] Determining whether receipt of the boot has the effect of a dividend is done under the principles

---

[142] Code Sec. 355(b). Code Sec. 301 is described in Chapter 5.

[143] Treas. Reg. § 1.356-2(b) Example (1).

[144] *Id.* Example (2).

[145] Code Sec. 356(a)(1).

[146] Code Sec. 356(a)(2).

of Code Sec. 302.[147] If the terms of the exchange fail to specify the boot that is received for particular stock or securities surrendered, "a pro rata share of the [boot]received [is] treated as received in exchange for each share of stock or security surrendered, based on the fair market value of such surrendered share of stock or security."[148]

> **Example 1:** Rakoff Corporation has 1000 shares of a single class of stock outstanding. Each share has a fair market value of $1. There are five unrelated shareholders. One of them, Shanna, owns 400 of the 1000 shares. Rakoff owns all of the stock of a subsidiary, the fair market value of which is $200. Rakoff distributes all of the subsidiary stock plus $200 in cash to Shanna in exchange for all of her Rakoff stock. The exchange satisfies the requirements of Code Sec. 355.

> The subsidiary stock Shanna received represents a continuing interest in part of Rakoff's assets that formerly were held by Shanna indirectly. The boot reduced Shanna's proportionate interest in the overall enterprise of Rakoff and the subsidiary. Accordingly, under Code Sec. 302 principles, the boot is treated as received in redemption of Shanna's Rakoff stock, and Shanna's interest in Rakoff immediately before the exchange is compared to the interest she would have retained had Shanna surrendered only the Rakoff shares equal in value to the $200 of boot.[149]

> **Example 2:** The same facts as in Example 1, except Shanna surrendered only the 200 shares for which she had received the cash boot. Before the exchange, Shanna owned 40% (400 out of 1000) of the outstanding shares in Rakoff. After the exchange, she owns 25% (200 out of 800) of such shares. Her post-exchange interest is 62.5% (25% divided by 40%) of her pre-exchange interest. This would still be treated as an exchange of property since it would constitute a substantially disproportionate redemption under Code Sec. 302(b)(2).[150]

The Code Sec. 356 rules as to separations include the following additional rules:

- *Losses*: What if the distributee realized a loss, not a gain, as a result of transactions involving boot? The loss is not recognized.[151]

- *Securities as boot*: Securities are "other property" boot,[152] subject to two exceptions. First, securities are not "other property" if they would be allowed to be received without recognition of gain.[153] Second, if the principal amount of the received securities in the controlled corporation exceeds that of the surrendered securities in the distributing corporation, "other property" includes only the fair market value of the excess.[154]

---

[147] *Comm'r v. Clark,* 489 U.S. 726 (1989).

[148] Treas. Reg. § 1.356-1(b).

[149] Rev. Rul. 93-62, 193-2 C.B. 118.

[150] *Id.*

[151] Code Sec. 356(c).

[152] Code Sec. 356(d)(1).

[153] Code Sec. 356(d)(2)(A).

[154] Code Sec. 356(d)(2)(C).

- *Nonqualified preferred stock*: Nonqualified preferred stock – as defined in Code Sec. 351(g)(2) – is "other property" except to the extent it could be received without recognition of gain.[155]

- *Code Sec. 306 stock*: To the extent any money or property is received in exchange for Code Sec. 306 stock, the fair market value of the property is treated as a distribution to which Code Sec. 301 applies.[156]

- *Recharacterization*: The principle that substance controls over form applies no less vigorously in this area than in most other areas of tax law. Thus, transactions formally within Code Secs. 355 and 356 may, if warranted by the underlying realities, be treated as transactions of a different sort. As examples, if the stockholder or security holder received more stock or securities than would be commanded by his or her interest in the corporation, the transactions may be recharacterized in part as gifts from the other interest holders,[157] compensation for goods or services rendered,[158] or rent.[159]

- *Cash for fractions of shares*: Sometimes an interest holder's stake in the enterprise would entitle him or her to receive a number of shares plus some fraction of an additional share. Commonly, to avoid fractional shares, an amount of cash equal to the value of the fraction is distributed instead. The IRS takes the view that such receipt of cash is a separate transaction consummated after receipt of the shares and so is not boot.[160]

.02 Treatment of Distributing Corporation

(a) Generally

In general, the distributing corporation recognizes no gain or loss on a distribution which is within Code Sec. 355 and is not pursuant to a plan of reorganization.[161] This is an exception to the repeal of the *General Utilities* doctrine.[162] Neither Code Sec. 311(b) nor Code Sec. 336(a) applies to a transaction within Code Sec. 355.[163]

However, the general rule of nonrecognition as to a distributing corporation applies only as to distribution of "qualifying property." If nonqualifying property is distributed and its fair market value exceeds its adjusted basis in the hands of the distributing corporation, gain is recognized to the distributing corporation as if the property had been sold to the distributee shareholder at fair market value.[164]

In general, qualified property includes any stock or securities in the controlled corporation.[165] If the transaction qualifies as a D reorganization as well as under

---

[155] Code Sec. 356(e).

[156] Code Sec. 356(f).

[157] Code Sec. 356(g)(1); Treas. Reg. § 1.356-5(a).

[158] Code Sec. 356(g)(2); Treas. Reg. § 1.356-5(b).

[159] *e.g.* Rev. Rul. 77-20, 1977-1 C.B. 91.

[160] *e.g.*, Treas. Reg. § 355-6(b)(iv).

[161] Code Sec. 355(c)(1).

[162] *General Utilities & Operating Co. v. Helvering*, 296 U.S. 200 (1935) (repealed by Code Secs. 311(b) and 336(a)). For discussion of these provisions, see chapters 5 and 7, respectively.

[163] Code Sec. 355(c)(3).

[164] Code Sec. 355(c)(2)(A). For this purpose, property subject to a liability or as to which the shareholder assumes a liability of the distributing corporation, has a fair market value of not less than the liability. Code Sec. 355(c)(2)(B).

[165] Code Sec. 355(c)(2)(B).

Code Sec 355, qualified property includes stock, securities, and debt obligations of the controlled corporation.[166]

(b) Divisions Related to D Reorganizations

A corporate separation can be achieved by distributing the stock of an existing subsidiary without transferring any additional assets. However, it sometimes is desirable for sound business reasons for the controlling corporation to transfer additional assets to the controlled corporation as part of the transactions. When this is done, nonrecognition treatment will be preserved only if the transactions satisfy both Code Secs. 355 and 368(a)(1)(D). A D reorganization entails transfer, pursuant to a qualified plan of reorganization, by one corporation of some or all of its assets to another corporation, which it or its shareholders control immediately after the transfer.[167]

In general, a corporation that is a party to a reorganization does not recognize gain or loss when it distributes property to its shareholders pursuant to a plan of reorganization.[168] This is so even if the property is appreciated as long as it is qualified property, as defined above.[169]

What if, in the D reorganization, the distributing corporation gets cash or other property from the controlled corporation as well as stock in the controlled corporation? Generally, this does not cause recognition as long as the money or other property is distributed to the shareholders[170] or to creditors of the corporation.[171] However, in the latter case – distribution to creditors – nonrecognition occurs only up to the aggregate basis of the assets that had been contributed to the controlled corporation.[172]

(c) Disqualified Distributions

As noted previously, Code Sec. 355 is among the few exceptions to the repeal of the *General Utilities* rule. This inspired some taxpayers to push the envelope, by trying to transfer ownership of a subsidiary while avoiding tax on the parent selling the subsidiary.

> **Example:** The party interested in acquiring the subsidiary might buy stock in the parent of the subsidiary. Later – after a time sufficient to satisfy the continuity of shareholder interest requirement described previously – the parent might distribute the stock of the subsidiary to the acquiring party in exchange for the acquiror's stock in the parent in a fashion sufficient to satisfy the requirements of Code Sec. 355. Without a special rule blocking this maneuver and variations on it, such a scheme could convert what would be a taxable sale of a subsidiary into a nontaxable acquisition.

In 1990, Congress sought to foreclose such strategies by enacting Code Secs. 355(c)(2) and 355(d). Code Sec. 355(d)(1) provides that, upon a disqualified distribution, any stock or securities in the controlled corporation are not treated as

---

[166] Code Sec. 361(c)(2)(B).

[167] See Chapter 9 for detailed discussion of D reorganizaitons.

[168] Code Sec. 361(c)(1).

[169] Code Sec. 361(c)(2).

[170] Code Sec. 361(b)(1)(A).

[171] Code Sec. 361(b)(3).

[172] *Id.*

qualifying property for purposes of Code Secs. 361 and 355(c)(2). As a consequence, the distribution would be stripped of the cloak of nonrecognition.

Practice Tip: When Code Sec. 355(d) operates, it requires recognition of gain by the distributing corporation. However, this has no effect on the distributee shareholders. The transaction remains tax free to the shareholders.

A distribution is disqualified if, immediately after it, either "any person holds disqualified stock in the distributing corporation which constitutes a 50 percent or greater interest in [it]" or "any person holds disqualified stock in the controlled corporation . . . which constitutes a 50 percent or greater interest in [it]."[173]

Stock is disqualified for these purposes if (1) it was acquired by purchase during the five-year period ending on the distribution date or (2) it was received in the distribution to the extent attributable to distributions on stock described in (1) or to distributions on securities acquired by purchase during the five-year period.[174] "Purchase" has a broad meaning for this purpose. It means an acquisition of any type as long as the acquiror's basis in the property is not carryover basis and the property is not acquired in an exchange to which Code Sec. 355 (or Code Secs. 351, 354, or 356) applies.[175]

Elaborate special rules implement these general rules. In the main, these special rules are anti-abuse in nature, broadening the reach of Code Sec. 355(d).

- *Suspension of the five-year period:* Code Sec. 355(d)'s potency diminishes if the purchaser can wait until the five-year period expires, causing stock to cease to be disqualified and thus the distribution not to be disqualified. Extension of the five-year period, therefore, contributes to the anti-abuse "sting" of the subsection.

  Code Sec. 355(d)(6) provides that the running of the five-year period is suspended during any period during which the holder's risk of loss as to stock or securities is "substantially diminished" as a result of options, short sales, any special class of stock, or "any other devise or transaction."

- *Aggregation and attribution rules:* An obvious way for taxpayers to attempt to circumvent numerical thresholds (like the 50% rule above) is by fractioning activities between or among two or more persons, either related or otherwise acting in concert. Congress understands that and wrote rules to foreclose such circumvention.

  For Code Sec. 355(d) purposes, a person and all related persons are treated as one person,[176] so are persons acting pursuant to a plan or arrangement as to acquiring stock or securities in the distributing corporation or the controlled corporation.[177] In addition, the entity attribution rules of Code Sec. 318(a)(2) are applied to determine stock ownership.[178] These rules provide

---

[173] Code Sec. 355(d)(2). The 50% test is met by possession of that quantum of either the value or the voting power of all classes of stock. Code Sec. 355(d)(4).

[174] Code Sec. 355(d)(3).

[175] Code Sec. 355(d)(5)(A).

[176] Code Sec. 355(d)(7)(A). Whether persons are related is determined under the rules of Code Secs. 367(b) and 707(b)(1).

[177] Code Sec. 355(d)(7)(B).

[178] *See* Code Sec. 355(d)(8)(A). The Code Sec. 318 rule is modified so that attribution from corporations occurs

for attribution from partnerships, estates, trusts, and corporations. If a party is treated as holding stock or securities under these rules, the stock or securities are treated as having been acquired by purchase on the later of the date the interest in the entity was purchased or the date the securities are acquired by purchase by the entity.[179]

- *Regulatory relief:* Code Sec. 355(d)(9) grants Treasury the authority to promulgate regulations to carry out the purposes of the subsection. In part, Treasury has used that power to mitigate some of the possible harshness of the provision. Specifically, the regulations state that "a distribution is not a disqualified distribution if the distribution does not violate the purposes of section 355(d)." Those purposes are not violated if the distribution neither increases ownership in the distributing corporation or controlled corporation by a disqualified person nor provides a disqualified person with a purchase price basis in the stock of a controlled corporation.[180] A disqualified person is one who directly or indirectly holds, immediately after the distribution, disqualified stock in the distributing corporation or the controlled corporation.[181]

Example: Doric Corporation owns all the stock of subsidiary Eudora Corporation, and Eudora owns all the stock of Fandall Corporation. Xander buys 60% of the Doric stock for cash. Within five years thereafter, Eudora distributes the Fandall stock to Doric. Under the attribution rules, Xander is treated as having bought 60% of the stock of both Eudora and Fandall on the date it bought the Doric stock. The Fandall stock Doric received is attributable to a distribution on purchased Eudora stock. Accordingly, the Eudora stock and Fandall stock are both disqualified stock, and Xander is a disqualified person.

However, there is no violation of the purposes of Code Sec. 355. Xander did not increase direct or indirect ownership in Eudora or Fandall. Moreover, Doric's basis in the Fandall stock is not a purchased basis because both the Eudora stock and the Fandall stock are treated as acquired by purchase solely under the attribution rules. Thus, Eudora's distribution of the Fandall stock to Doric is not a disqualified distribution.[182]

(d) Prohibited Stock Acquisitions

In general, Code Sec. 355(e) provides that, if there is a distribution to which the provision applies, any stock or securities in a controlled corporation is not qualified property for purposes of Code Secs. 355 and 361. As a result, the distributing corporation recognizes gain as if it sold the stock or securities at their fair market value as of the date of the distribution.[183] This recognition of gain does not lead to adjustment of the basis of the assets or stock of either the distributing or

---

(Footnote Continued)

when a person owns as little as 10% of the stock of the corporation.

[179] Code Sec. 355(d)(8)(B).

[180] Treas. Reg. § 1.355-6(b)(3)(i).

[181] Treas. Reg. § 1.355-6(b)(3)(ii).

[182] Treas. Reg. § 1.355-6(b)(3)(iv) Example 1. The regulation sets out many additional examples.

[183] Code Sec. 355(c)(2) & (e)(1). However, Code Sec. 355(e) does not apply to any distributions to which Code Sec. 355(d) applies. Code Sec. 355(e)(2)(D).

the controlled corporation. This rule applies to distributions which are parts of plans or series of transactions under which one or more persons acquire (directly or indirectly) stock constituting an at least 50% interest in the distributing corporation or any controlled corporation.[184]

Such a plan is rebuttably presumed to exist if one or more persons acquire such an interest in the distributing or controlled corporation during a four-year period starting on the date that is two years before the distribution date.[185] However, the plan or series is disregarded if, immediately after completion of the transactions, the distributing corporation and all controlled corporations are members of the same affiliated group.[186]

Congress enacted Code Sec. 355(e) in 1997, in part to overthrow *Morris Trust*[187] and similar authorities.

> **Example:** In *Morris Trust*, American was a bank that also had an insurance business. Security National, an unrelated bank, wished to acquire American but could not, under applicable law, operate an insurance business. To facilitate the acquisition, American transferred the insurance business to a wholly owned subsidiary, then spun off the subsidiary to American's shareholders. American then merged into Security National.
>
> The IRS maintained that the transactions did not satisfy Code Sec. 355 because it is intrinsically incompatible to engage essentially simultaneously in a corporate separation and an amalgamating corporate reorganization. The circuit court rejected the IRS's contention and held for the taxpayer. It found nowhere in the Code itself or the relevant legislative history any prohibition on such division-and-acquisition.[188]

(e) Code Sec. 355(g)

In a number of contexts, the Code imposes limitations on investment companies that are not imposed on companies engaged in other kinds of economic activities.[189] Code Sec. 355 is one of those contexts. Congress intends to confer the benefits of Code Sec. 355 on active operating concerns, not on investment companies or "incorporated pocketbooks." To effectuate this intention, Congress enacted Code Sec. 355(g) in 2005, with transitional rules and effective dates applying to transactions in and after 2006 and 2007. The current version of the subsection is described below.

Code Sec. 355 does not apply if (i) "either the distributing corporation or controlled corporation is, immediately after the transaction, a disqualified investment corporation" and (ii) any person owns a 50% or greater interest in any disqualified investment corporation immediately after the separation, "but only if

---

[184] Code Sec. 355(e)(2)(A).

[185] Code Sec. 355(e)(2)(B).

[186] Code Sec. 355(e)(2)(C). Affiliated group has the same meaning as in Code Sec. 1504 without regard to the Code Sec. 1504(b) exceptions.

[187] *Comm'r v. Morris Trust*, 367 F.2d 794 (4th Cir. 1966).

[188] *Id.* at 799. The court also rejected the IRS's alternative argument that Code Sec. 355(e)'s active business requirement was not satisfied because American's banking business had not been continued in unaltered corporate form.

[189] *e.g.*, Code Secs. 351(e)(1), 541 & 1375.

such person did not hold such an interest in such corporation immediately before the transaction.[190]

A distributing corporation or a controlled corporation is a disqualified investment corporation if the fair market value of its investment assets is at least two-thirds of the fair market value of all its assets.[191] In general, investment assets are cash, stock or securities, partnership interests, debt instruments, "any option, forward or futures contract, notional principal contract, or derivative," foreign currency, or "any similar asset."[192] However, Congress provided the following exceptions from investment asset status:

- assets held for use in active and regular conduct of lending, finance, banking, and regulated insurance businesses;[193]
- securities held by dealers and which are marked-to-market under Code Sec. 475;[194]
- interests in or issued by "a corporation which is a 20-percent controlled entity with respect to the distributing or controlled corporation";[195]
- interests in or issued by partnerships one or more of whose trades or business are taken into account in determining whether the distributing or controlled corporation meets Code Sec. 355(b)'s active trade or business requirement.[196]

Look-through rules are provided as to the last two of these exceptions. That is, the distributing or controlled corporation is treated as owning its ratable share of the assets of the 20% controlled entity and its ratable share of the assets of the partnership.[197]

¶ 705 Procedural Aspects

Given the complexity of Code Sec. 355 and related sections, the IRS needs information early on, before much of the statute of limitations period has already run,[198] in order to decide whether and how to audit for possible separation – related issues. The Code has authorized Treasury to require information reporting.[199] Treasury has used that authority to promulgate regulations requiring Code Sec. 355 reporting from both distributing corporations and significant distributees. The current regulations, described below, were simplified in 2006 and 2007 to ease reporting burdens and facilitate e-filing.

.01 Distributing Corporations

Every corporation which distributes stock or securities of a controlled corporation under Code Sec. 355 must attach a statement to its income tax return for the year. The statement should list the names and employer identification numbers of

---

[190] Code Sec. 355(g)(1) & (3). Attribution rules apply under Code Sec. 355(g)(3)(B). "Transaction" includes "a series of transactions." Code Sec. 355(g)(4).

[191] Code Sec. 355(g)(2)(A)(i).

[192] Code Sec. 355(g)(2)(B)(i).

[193] Code Sec. 355(g)(2)(B)(ii).

[194] Code Sec. 355(g)(2)(B)(iii).

[195] Code Sec. 355(g)(2)(B)(iv)(I).

[196] Code Sec. 355(g)(2)(B)(v)(I). The active trade or business requirement is discussed in subpart ¶ 702.05 above.

[197] Code Sec. 355(g)(2)(B)(iv)(II) & (v)(II).

[198] See Code Sec. 6501(a) (establishing, as a general rule, a three-year limitations period for assessment of additional tax liabilities).

[199] Code Sec. 6001.

the controlled corporation(s) and all of the significant distributees, the date of the distribution, and the fair market values and bases of distributed property. In addition, if the IRS issued a private letter ruling as to the transactions, the date and number of the ruling should be given.[200]

Additional information must be reported in some circumstances. If a transfer of assets under Code Secs. 351 or 368 occurs before the separation, the distributing corporation must file a statement setting out the information required by the regulations under those sections.[201] Similarly, if the corporations or shareholders involved in the transactions are foreign persons, additional information reporting may be required.[202]

.02 Significant Distributees

A distributee is significant for information reporting purposes if that person received controlled corporation stock in the Code Sec. 355 transaction and, immediately before the distribution or exchange, that person owned at least 5% of the total outstanding stock of the distributing corporation (if publicly traded) or 1% (if not publicly traded). Alternatively, if the distributee is a security holder, not a stockholder, the person is significant if that person received stock or securities in the transaction and, immediately before, owned securities in the distributing corporation that had a basis of at least $1 million.[203]

Each significant distributee must attach an information statement to its income tax return for the year in which the distribution is received. The statement should include the names and employer identification numbers of the controlled and distributing corporations, the distribution date, the bases (immediately before the transactions) of the stock or securities transferred by the distributees, and the fair market values (again, immediately before the transactions) of stock or other assets received by the distributees.[204]

> **Practice Tip:** The parties also are required to keep records that support the reported information.[205] However, appraisals are not necessarily required. The IRS typically will accept taxpayers' good faith estimates of fair market values and bases.[206]

---

[200] Treas. Reg. § 1.355-5(a)(1).

[201] Treas. Reg. §§ 1.351-3 & 1.368-3.

[202] e.g., id. § 1.355-5(a)(2) (requiring each 10% U.S. shareholders of a controlled foreign corporation to file required statements with their returns).

[203] Treas. Reg.. § 1.355-5(c)(1).

[204] Treas. Reg. § 1.355-5(b).

[205] Treas. Reg. § 1.355-5(d).

[206] T.D. 9264, 2006-1 C.B. 1150.

Chapter 8

Acquisitive Corporate Reorganizations

¶ 801   Introduction
¶ 802   Acquisitive Reorganizations Involving Only Two Entities
¶ 803   Triangular Reorganizations
¶ 804   Additional Corporate Actions in Conjunction with Reorganizations
¶ 805   Acquisitive D Reorganizations

¶ 801 Introduction

Tax free reorganizations include many distinct kinds of transactions. They may take very different forms and serve very different purposes, and the tax *consequences* of the various "tax free" reorganizations can also vary significantly. [1] There are basically three different kinds of corporate transactions that can qualify as reorganizations: 1) acquisitive reorganizations, in which one corporation basically acquires another, 2) divisive reorganizations, in which what was one corporation essentially becomes two separate (non-parent-subsidiary) corporations; and (3) corporate restructuring in which one corporation changes its capital structure, its name or location, or its financial status (by way of bankruptcy). All of these reorganizations are defined in Code Sec. 368, which is entirely a definitional section. If a transaction is one that is defined as a reorganization under Code Sec. 368, the actual tax consequences are determined by the application of other sections whose application is triggered by the transaction's definition as a reorganization. As discussed later, a full understanding of the tax consequences of a reorganization can require a knowledge of almost all the rest of corporate tax, since many other provisions are either directly involved in the determination of the tax consequences, or the actual provisions applied, while different in name from those applicable to other kinds of transactions, are quite similar in effect.

Because Code Sec. 368 began as a fairly simple and lean provision, it has been supplemented by some significant case law. Because corporate transactions have since become quite complex, though, so has Code Sec. 368. As a result, for almost any reorganization, there are both statutory and common law requirements. For the most part, the more detailed the statutory requirements, the less significant is the case law. Most of the common law of reorganizations are theoretically applicable to

---

[1] Just as tax free incorporations governed by Code Sec. 351, not all tax free reorganizations are actually tax free, although they certainly can be completely tax free and do almost always result in tax reduction, if not in tax elimination for all parties involved.

all types of reorganizations, but as a practical matter are usually significant only in the type of reorganization in which it first arose. In setting forth the relevant common law doctrines, we will do so in the context in which each doctrine has the most significance, and refer to it in the other areas in which it may have potential application as well.

¶ 802 Acquisitive Reorganizations Involving Only Two Entities

.01 Mergers

An "A" reorganization[2] has the simplest statutory definition of any reorganization: "a statutory merger or consolidation." It is likely for this reason that it carries with it the target of most of the common law surrounding reorganizations.

(a) Continuity of Interest

(i) *In General: Amount, Type and Time of Continuity Required*

The theoretical basis for granting nonrecognition to reorganizations is that they do not represent any real significant change in what the selling shareholder owns. In the context of an A reorganization, the theory was that the former T shareholders would exchange their T stock for A stock, T would disappear, and everything that was in T would now be part of A. The former T shareholders would now be shareholders of A, so that they would simply be following their investment across corporations.

Even in theory this notion is somewhat of a stretch, because if T is a small corporation and its former shareholders become minority shareholders in a much larger A, they are hardly simply following their investment. Their investment has significantly changed. Nonetheless, this "theoretical" problem paled in comparison to the factual problems that stemmed from the liberalization of state merger laws that came about after the enactment of Code Sec. 368(a)(1)(A), and it was these practical problems with state merger laws that gave rise to some of the most significant common law surrounding reorganizations.

While state merger laws originally contemplated, and required, that the T shareholders exchange their T stock for A stock,[3] these laws over time came to include acquisitions of T by A for consideration that is primarily, if not exclusively, cash and notes rather than A stock. While T shareholders that received cash or notes would have been taxed in any event,[4] any T shareholders that did receive A stock could defer gain if this was a "reorganization," and T might well be able to avoid gain on what was essentially a cash sale. As a result, neither the IRS nor courts were willing to call such transactions reorganizations.

To assure that at least some significant percentage of the T stock was exchanged for A stock, the IRS and courts have required that in order to qualify as a reorganization, there must be "continuity of shareholder interest." The exact

---

[2] Because almost all reorganizations are defined in Code Sec. 368(a)(1), many of these are referred to by their subparagraph in Code Sec. 368(a)(1), so that an A refers to a reorganization described in Code Sec. 368(a)(1)(A), a B refers to a reorganization described in Code Sec. 368(a)(1)(B), etc.

[3] Or, if A already owned the T stock, that A exchange its T shares directly for the T assets.

[4] *See* ¶ 802.01(a)(ii).

amount and form of such continuity necessary to qualify as a reorganization[5] long went unspecified, and over the years has been subject to change and to litigation. As a result of the litigation and the Treasury's reaction and regulations, most, but not all, of the issues surrounding what is required to establish continuity of interest have been resolved.

Probably the most important part of the continuity of interest doctrine is that, generally speaking, at least a certain percentage of the T stock must be exchanged by the T shareholders for A stock.[6] The A stock can be either common or preferred,[7] and it matters not, for continuity of interest purposes, whether or not the A stock is given to the former T shareholders on a pro rata basis and, if not, which T shareholders receive the A stock and which receive other consideration.

Although continuity of interest is generally represented by the exchange of T stock for A stock, it may well be the case that A itself already owns some of the T stock prior to embarking on the plan of reorganization. If so, and if T merges into A, A will be exchanging its own T stock not for A stock, but for a direct interest in the former T assets that become part of A in the merger. It is difficult to imagine a more clear and direct continuing of shareholder interest than for A to acquire some or all of the T assets in exchange for the T stock which it already owns, so that any T stock that A owned prior to the merger and surrenders in the merger also counts for purposes of determining continuity of interest.[8] As a result, if A owns 50% of the T stock prior to the merger, and then transfers 25 A stock and $25 cash to the remaining T shareholders and T merges into A, 75% of the T stock has been transferred for a continuing interest in T (25% for A stock and 50% for T itself by A in the merger).

The biggest issue still not completely resolved, however, is exactly *how much* of the T stock must be exchanged for that A stock (or for the T assets, if A is already a T shareholder). The Supreme Court has held that when 38% of the T stock was exchanged for A stock in a merger under state law, that was enough to establish continuity.[9] The IRS long ago announced that 50% continuity of interest is sufficient for ruling purposes.[10] More recently the IRS provided an example in the regulations in which 40% continuity of shareholder interest was sufficient.[11] For those not willing or able to meet the 40% continuity of interest level, there is some authority that allows still lesser amounts.[12]

Issues surrounding the *time* when continuity of interest is to be measured have been resolved, thereby simplifying some of the more complex dilemmas that arose. At one time, the IRS required that once the T shareholders received the requisite

---

[5] The requirement of continuity of shareholder interest applies to all reorganizations, but is rarely an issue outside of A reorganizations because in other areas the statute specifies the specific consideration required.

[6] Treas. Regs. § § 368-1(e)(1), 1.368-1(e)(2) (1998).

[7] In fact, at least until additional regulations are issued and effective, the A stock can even include nonqualified preferred stock. Interests in A that are labeled debt but that are determined by the IRS and/or courts to be equity may also count as stock for continuity of interest purposes, but if the corporate issuer labels the instruments poses, but if the corporate issuer labels the instruments

as debt and the IRS believes it will be better served by holding the issuer to that characterization, the issuer and the T shareholders will likely be bound by their chosen form for the transaction.

[8] Treas. Reg. § 1.368-1(e)(1)(i).

[9] *John A. Nelson Co. v. Helvering*, 296 US 374 (1935).

[10] Rev. Proc. 77-37, 1977-2 CB 568.

[11] Treas Regs. § 1.368-1(e)(v), Exs. 1 and 2.

[12] *See* Boris I. Bittker and James S. Eustice, FEDERAL INCOME TAXATION OF CORPORATIONS AND SHAREHOLDERS, ¶ 12.21.

¶802.01(a)(i)

amount of A stock, they have some intention to hold onto that stock (post-reorganization continuity of interest), so that even if the T shareholders received only A stock in exchange for their T stock there was no continuity of interest if shareholders holding enough of the A stock planned to sell that stock in the near future. On the other side, the IRS also raised issues if the T shareholders who traded their T stock for the A stock had only recently acquired their T stock (pre-reorganization continuity of interest). The regulations now address these issues.

The regulations set as the time for determining continuity of interest the date on which the contract between A and T becomes binding.[13] As a general rule, if at that time at least 40% of the T stock is to be exchanged for A stock (and assuming that the contract is not later modified), the IRS will find continuity of interest.

(ii) *Direct and Indirect Transfers of Other Property by A to the T Shareholders in Connection With the Reorganization*

In determining continuity of interest, the IRS will take into account transactions prior to or subsequent to the merger (or, indeed, transactions at the same time as the reorganization) if A uses those transactions to directly or indirectly transfer cash or other property to the T shareholders. To see how this can occur, assume that T (worth $100) merges into A, and the T shareholder (ST) receives $100 worth of A stock. Continuity of interest would appear to be met, because all of the T stock is traded for A stock. Assume, though, that shortly after the merger, and in connection with the apparent reorganization, A redeems for cash $80 of the A stock recently issued to ST. The net result is the transfer by A to ST of $80 cash and only 20 A stock, and the IRS will not find continuity of interest.[14]

Similar kinds of events can occur prior to, rather than after, an attempted merger. For example, assume that A intends to acquire T in a merger, but that some of the T shareholders, owning 40% of the T stock, desire to cash out prior to the merger. A might make a cash purchase of that T stock, and then, after it already owns 40% of T, it might proceed with the merger. If the earlier cash purchase is unrelated to the reorganization, then both the A stock used in the merger and the T stock already owned by A will count towards continuity of interest. On the other hand, if the cash purchase is made in connection with the merger, the IRS will view the consideration for the merger to include the $40 cash used to purchase the T shares, rather than the shares themselves.

Alternatively, T might redeem the stock of those dissenting shareholders for cash prior to the merger, so that at the time of the merger T is worth only $60 rather than $100. For purposes of determining continuity of interest, the redemption will generally be disregarded, even if part of a plan, so that continuity requirements will be satisfied so long as at least 40% of the 60 T stock ($24 worth of the T stock) still outstanding at the time of the reorganization is exchanged for A stock. So long as the property used to redeem the T shareholders comes from T itself, and does not come, directly or indirectly, from A, this transaction is fine.

---

[13] And the date for valuing the stock of A and T is the close of business on the previous day. Treas. Reg. § 1.368-1(e)(2)(ii).

[14] Treas Reg. § 1.368-1(e)(8) ex. 4.

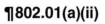

On the other hand, the regulations clearly indicate that if the cash used to redeem the T stock prior to the reorganization comes, directly or indirectly, from A, then that cash will be treated as part of the consideration transferred from A to the T shareholders for purposes of determining continuity of interest. As a result, the transaction will be viewed as if A paid 40 cash for the 40 shares redeemed by T. Thus, at least 40 of the remaining 60 of consideration coming from A must be A stock to satisfy 40% continuity of interest.[15]

Of course, a clever A might figure out numerous more indirect ways to transfer the cash to T in the above example, or to ST in the previous example, including purchases of the newly issued A stock from ST by A's subsidiary, or other closely related entities, shortly before or after the merger of T into A. Not surprisingly, all such acquisitions will be taken into account for purposes of determining whether the former T shareholders actually received enough A stock to satisfy continuity of interest requirements. The regulations provide generally that if, in connection with a reorganization (which might be before, during, or after the reorganization), a person related to the acquiring corporation acquires T stock for property (other than A stock), then for purposes of determining continuity of interest, that T stock so acquired will not count toward continuity of interest (in other words it will be treated as if acquired by A for property other than A stock).[16] A related party, for these purposes, includes a member of the same affiliated group or a corporation, which would be treated as under common control for purposes of Code Sec. 304.[17]

The issue left open by the regulations in this, and many other cases, is when is an acquisition of T stock for property, by A or by a person related to A, made "in connection" with the purported reorganization, and when is that acquisition a separate, unrelated or unconnected, transaction. The regulations state that "all facts and circumstances" must be considered. As in most of corporate tax, this means that the answer is never completely clear. If the parties can establish that a subsequent acquisition for cash of T stock by SA or a related party was not even under consideration at the time of the merger, they will certainly be safe. Alternatively, if the cash acquisition preceded the merger, the parties will be safe if they can establish that a subsequent merger was not even under consideration at the time of the cash acquisition. As discussed elsewhere, outside of either of these cases, however, there is always some room for argument.[18]

(b) Continuity of Business Enterprise

Since the original notion behind tax free reorganizations was that the T shareholders would follow their interests into A, the IRS sought not only some assurance that the T shareholders were taking on an interest in A, but also that A maintained some continuing interest in what had been in T. For example, no one sought to provide tax free treatment if A acquired T simply to strip off and sell all of T's assets and put T out of business. It was out of these concerns that the continuity of business enterprise (COBE) doctrine arose. The regulations now require that A

---

[15] Treas. Reg. § 1.368-1(e)(8) ex. 9.

[16] Treas. Reg. § 1.368-1(e)(3).

[17] Treas. Reg. § 1.368-1(e)(4). The parties are related for this purpose if the relationship exists at the time of, immediately before, or immediately after the reorganization.

[18] See discussion of step transaction doctrine and substance versus form at ¶ 804.03.

¶802.01(b)

(or members of the qualified group of which A is the parent)[19] either (1) continue a significant line of business in which T engaged, or (2) continue to use a significant portion of T's historic business assets.[20] The IRS will take into account all facts and circumstances in determining whether one of several business in which T was engaged is significant and in determining whether a particular portion of T's assets is significant.[21] If A is a member of a qualified group of corporations,[22] continuity of business enterprise can become significantly easier to establish. The regulations provide that for purposes of evaluating continuity of business enterprise, A is treated as owning all of the assets and operating all of the business owned or operated by any and all of the other members of its group.[23]

In addition to preventing A from getting tax free treatment for selling off all of the T assets and business, the regulations also seek to prevent T from itself going out of business and selling off its business assets and then using a reorganization to avoid any tax to its shareholders. Generally a corporation that goes out of business and sells its assets might either liquidate, resulting in taxable gain to its shareholders, or remain as a corporation dedicated to investments, which will result in potential double taxation of those investments and potential penalty taxes.[24] The corporation might seek to avoid this result by selling off its assets and then merging into a mutual fund or regulated investment company. The T shareholders would end up with investment assets instead of T stock, and they would have avoided any tax on that transaction. The COBE regulations clearly prevent this from qualifying as a reorganization.[25]

The regulations do not suggest that a corporation cannot merge into another corporation if at any time in the past it has sold its assets and become dedicated to investments, nor do they suggest that an acquiring corporation can never sell the assets or dispose of the business it acquired in the reorganization. The unresolved issue under the regulations is exactly when the disposition of assets and/or the business will be viewed as part of the plan of reorganization. The examples in the regulations make it clear that the plan of reorganization can exist at least three years before the reorganization is culminated, where T sold its assets for cash and invested in a diversified portfolio of stocks and securities as part of a plan to later merge into a regulated investment company.[26] Once again, though, the parties are left to simply consider all of the relevant facts and circumstances in making the determination of whether and when the plan of reorganization existed.

It is worth noting that what the regulations require is that there be continuity of the T business in order to qualify as a reorganization. They do not require continuity of business enterprise for the *acquiring* corporation. In some cases, the parties may be able to allow T to sell of its business and nonetheless engage in a tax free reorganization by simply reversing the direction of the reorganization. To see

---

[19] Treas. Reg. § 1.368-1(d)(4)(i).

[20] Treas. Reg. § 1.368-1(d).

[21] Obvious factors in determining whether a portion of assets is significant are both the relative importance of the assets to the business and the net value of those assets. Treas. Reg. § 1.368-1(d)(3)(iii).

[22] A "qualified group" for this purpose is quite similar to an affiliated group of corporations. *See* ¶ 505.

[23] Treas. Reg. § 1.368-1(d)(4)(i).

[24] See discussion at ¶ 704.02[e].

[25] Treas. Reg. § 1.368-1(d)(5) ex. 3.

[26] Treas. Reg. § 1.368-1(d)(5) ex. 3.

¶802.01(b)

how this can occur, assume that T is worth $100, that T is wholly owned by ST, and that the parties had considered having T sell its assets for cash, invest the cash in a diversified portfolio, and then merge into A, a corporation worth $1,000 and wholly owned by SA. The proposed merger of T into A will not satisfy the continuity of business enterprise requirements. Instead, though, the parties might structure the merger as one in which A merges into T for T stock. As a result T will end up with the cash from its own assets sale, and with the entire A business, which will continue. Although the continuing corporation will be T rather than A, A's former shareholder, SA, will have received $1,000 worth of T stock in the merger and will end up owning 1,000/1,100 of all the T stock outstanding, and controlling T, just as she would have controlled A had the attempted merger gone the other way.

Reversing the merger is not necessarily a cure-all, however. There may be some nontax related difficulties involved with having T rather than A be the surviving corporation. In addition, it is not guaranteed that the IRS will not go after the reversed transaction as not satisfying continuity of business requirements. The basic continuity of business requirements developed in common law and preceded the regulations. The fact that the regulations do not specifically require continuity of the business of the acquiring corporation is not a guarantee that the IRS will simply approve of the above transaction.

(c) Mergers as Acquisitive Reorganizations

Another issue raised by the liberalization of state merger laws, although a more recent development than continuity of interest or continuity of business enterprise, is the requirement that an A reorganization be an acquisitive rather than a divisive transaction. In other words a merger, at least for federal income tax purposes, cannot be used to separate T into two or more businesses or investments, only one of which is acquired by A (or A's qualified group of corporations)[27] instead, it must result in T being entirely merged into the acquiring corporation and its qualified group.

In recent years, state merger laws have included transactions that involved the separation, rather than the acquisition, of T, and those changes in merger laws have triggered both rulings and regulations in response. The regulations now require that for a transaction to qualify under Code Sec. 368(a)(1)(A), the state statute under which the transaction occurs must *require* that as a result of the merger or consolidation, and simultaneously with the effective time of the merger or consolidation: (1) all of the assets (other than those distributed in the transaction) and liabilities (other than those satisfied in the transaction) of T must be acquired by A's qualified group of corporations; and (2) T's separate legal existence must cease for all purposes.[28] Thus, any transaction in which T either retains a separate legal existence[29] or divides its assets between two or more unrelated corporate acquirers will not qualify as a merger for federal income tax purposes.

---

[27] *See* ¶ 802.02(a).

[28] Treas. Reg. § 1.368-2(b)(1)(ii).

[29] Even after T's legal existence is ended, its former officers, directors or agents may nonetheless remain liable under state law for actions previously taken. Treas. Reg. § 1.368-2(b)(2)(ii)(B).

While the regulations prevent T from *separating* into two or more corporations as a result of the merger, they do not prevent T from "shrinking" as part of the merger. So long as continuity of business enterprise requirements are met, T can either distribute assets to its shareholders or sell assets and distribute the proceeds to its shareholders in conjunction with the reorganization.[30]

(d) Mergers involving Disregarded Entities

Put quite simply, for purposes of Code Sec. 368, disregarded entities are disregarded. In other words, if a corporation is the sole shareholder of a disregarded entity, the entity is not treated as anything other than assets of the corporate shareholder. Thus, assume that A owns all of LLC and that LLC is a disregarded entity. If T merges under state law into LLC and the T shareholders receive sufficient A stock as consideration, the transaction will be treated as a merger of T into A, and the separate existence of LLC will be disregarded. If, on the other hand, LLC merges into Corporation Y under state law and A receives Y stock as consideration for LLC, the transaction will be treated as if A simply sold some assets (whatever assets were in LLC) to Y in exchange for Y stock, and no reorganization will have occurred, since no corporation, but only a disregarded entity, was actually acquired by Y.[31]

(e) Creeping Mergers

A merger under state law may well take place after a series of stock acquisitions by A. If it does, it becomes necessary to determine whether any or all of those acquisitions by A of T stock that precede the merger are treated as part of the reorganization or as entirely separate transactions. This determination potentially impacts not only continuity of interest,[32] but also tax consequences to the shareholders who sold or exchanged their stock prior to the final merger. To see how tax consequences for the T shareholders can be affected, assume that T is worth $100 and has 100 shares of stock outstanding. Assume also that in year one, A acquires 60 of the T shares in exchange for $60 worth of A stock. In year three, A transfers to the remaining T shareholders $20 cash and $20 worth of A stock and T merges into A under the applicable state law. If the two incidents are treated as part of the same transaction, which is a merger of T into A, then the T shareholders who exchanged their T stock for A stock in year one will reap the rewards of reorganization treatment and pay no tax on any gain they realized in that exchange. If the two transaction are treated as separate, the T shareholders who made the exchange with A in year one will be fully taxed.

As to the results in year three, it is quite possible that the applicable state law will treat the separate liquidation of T in year three as a merger. Nonetheless, it will not be so characterized for tax purposes.[33] Instead, it will be taxed as stock purchase by A (for cash and A stock) followed by a Code Sec. 332 liquidation of a subsidiary. Although the liquidation will still be tax free to A and T, the T shareholders who receive A stock will be taxed under Code Sec. 331, and cannot

---

[30] Treas. Reg. § 1.368-2(b)(1)(iii) ex. 8.
[31] Treas. Reg. § 1.368-2(b).

[32] *See* ¶ 802.01(b).
[33] Treas. Reg. § 1.332-2(d).

¶802.01(d)

avoid gain as they would were the transaction a Code Sec. 368(a)(1)(A) reorganization.

To see how continuity of interest can also be affected by the separation or integration of events, assume instead that A's year one acquisition of 50% of the T stock was a cash purchase, and that A subsequently transferred $25 cash and $25 worth of A stock to the remaining T shareholders in year three and T merged into A. If the events are treated as a single transaction for tax purposes, then the total consideration paid by A is $75 cash and only 25 A stock. There is likely no continuity of interest. As a result, the T shareholders who exchange their stock in year three will be taxed in full (as were the T shareholders who sold their T stock for cash in year one).[34] If, instead, the transactions are treated as separate, the exchange in year three is tax free to the T shareholders who receive A stock, because there is 74% continuity of interest. Twenty five percent of the T stock has been exchanged for A stock, and another 50% has been exchanged by A for a direct interest in the T assets.

.02 Asset Acquisitions in the Absence of a Merger: Code Sec. 368(a)(1)(c)

While some acquisitions that qualify as mergers under applicable state law do not accomplish the kind of transaction that Congress intended to make tax free under Code Sec. 368 and thus do *not* qualify as reorganizations, it is equally true that there are transactions that *do* accomplish the kind of transaction that congress intended to make tax free, but which do *not* qualify as mergers under state law. It was with these in mind that Congress enacted Code Sec. 368(a)(1)(C). That section includes as reorganizations certain asset acquisitions that are similar in effect to mergers but which, generally for some technical reason, do not qualify as such under the applicable state law.

Since C reorganizations do not rely on state law to set forth any requirements, the requirements to qualify are set forth explicitly in the statute. Basically, qualification as a C reorganization requires that: (1) A acquire substantially all of the T assets;[35] (2) the consideration used to acquire the assets be primarily A voting stock;[36] and (3) T must liquidate.[37] The first two of these basic requirements merit some explanation.

(a) "Substantially All"

When originally codified, C reorganizations did not, as they do now, require that T liquidate. The purpose of the requirement that A acquire substantially all of the target assets was to ensure that only an acquisitive, and not a divisive reorganization, could qualify. The acquisitive nature of a C reorganization is now basically guaranteed by the requirement that T liquidate, but the substantially all require-

---

[34] The merger of T into A will nonetheless qualify as a tax free liquidation to T and A, so that their tax results will remain essentially unchanged.

[35] Code Sec. 368(a)(1)(C).

[36] Code Secs. 368(a)(1)(C), 368(a)(2)(B).

[37] The IRS may (but almost never will) waive the requirement that T liquidate immediately, Code Sec. 368(a)(2)(G)(ii). If T does not liquidate immediately, T

and its shareholders will nonetheless both be taxed as if T had liquidated, and the actual liquidation will be required to take place within 12 months. In addition, the only reason that the IRS will accept for granting the waiver is that T will retain nothing at all other than its charter, and is doing so solely for the purpose of selling only that charter to an unrelated party. Rev. Proc. 89-50, 1989-2 CB 631.

ment remains, having perhaps outlived its utility but not yet having lived long enough to have become entirely clear.

Case law suggests that an acquisition by A of all of T's operating business assets will qualify as "substantially all" of T's assets, so that a distribution by T to its shareholders of cash and investment assets in connection with the plan of reorganization will not result in the denial of tax free treatment.[38] The IRS, though, set forth its basic guidelines for determining what constitutes "substantially all" of the target assets prior to the time that Congress amended Code Sec. 368 to require that T liquidate in order to qualify as a C.[39] As a result, the IRS's announced position is somewhat strict. At one time, the IRS suggested that T could retain no assets over and above those needed (and actually used) to pay off any liabilities not assumed by A.[40] Later (but still before the liquidation requirement was added by statute), the IRS stated that it would rule favorably on the issue if A acquired at least 70% of T's gross assets and 90% of T's net worth, thus leaving at least a bit more than necessary for T to pay off its liabilities.[41]

To see how this 70-90 test applies, assume that T has 100 assets, each used in its business and each with a basis and value of $1. If T has no liabilities, A must acquire at least $90 worth of the T assets, or it will have failed the 90% of net worth prong. If T has liabilities of $20, A must acquire assets with a gross value of 100 (70% of 100), but it also must acquire assets with a net value (that is, net of any liabilities assumed or taken subject to by A) of at least $72 (90% of T's net value of $80).

If T has liabilities of $40 and a net value of only $60, A must nonetheless acquire assets with a gross value of at least $70 (and a net value of at least $54). Thus, A can acquire substantially all of T's assets by acquiring all $80 worth and taking on not more than $26 of T's liabilities, or by acquiring $70 worth of T's assets and taking on not more than $16 of T's liabilities, or some other combination that meets both prongs of the test.

Perhaps the most interesting aspect of the IRS's apparent position is that in determining whether A has acquired substantially all of T's assets, it appears to take into account any property distributions by T to its shareholders that are part of the plan of reorganization.[42] In contrast, the regulations enacted to ensure that A reorganizations are acquisitive and not divisive in nature clearly allow T to distribute property *to its shareholders* in connection with the merger. This distribution to shareholders in an A can occur before or simultaneously with the merger, and will not disqualify the merger from qualification so long as there is simple con-

---

[38] *James Armour, Inc.*, 43 TC 295 (1965). *Gross v. CIR*, 88 F2d 567 (5th Cir. 1937); *CIR v. First Nat'l Bank of Altoona*, 104 F2d 865 (3d Cir. 1939), *cert. dismissed*, 309 US 691 (1940); *American Mfg. Co.*, 55 TC 204 (1970); *Ralph C. Wilson*, 46 TC 334 (1966); *Moffatt v. CIR*, 363 F2d 262 (9th Cir. 1966), *cert. denied*, 386 US 1016 (1967); *Smothers v. US*, 642 F2d 894 (5th Cir. 1981).

[39] Rev. Rul. 57-518, 1957-2 C.B. 253; Rev. Proc. 97-37, 1977-2 C.B. 568.

[40] Rev. Rul. 57-518, 1957-2 C.B. 253. The IRS did state in the ruling that the nature and purpose of the assets not acquired was important, though, so the ruling is not inconsistent with the possibility that the acquisition of all of T's operating assets is sufficient.

[41] Rev. Proc. 97-37, 1977-2 C.B. 568.

[42] "All payments to dissenters and all redemptions and distributions (except for regular, normal distributions) made by the corporation immediately preceding the transfer and which are part of the plan of reorganization will be considered as assets held by the corporation immediately prior to the transfer," Rev. Proc. 97-37, 1977-2 CB 568.

tinuity of interest and continuity of business enterprise.[43] The IRS might label a merger as divisive, and thus not qualified under Code Sec. 368(a)(1)(A), *only if T assets are retained by T itself* (if state law allows T to continue in existence subsequent to its merger into A), or if T's assets are split up between two or more acquiring corporations rather than a single acquiring corporation (if such a division would be permissible under state merger law). The statutory requirement that A acquire "substantially all" of T's assets to qualify as a C certainly would appear to allow the IRS to take into account T assets distributed to T shareholders prior to or at the time of the transaction, but *why* the IRS would treat C reorganizations so differently than it treats mergers in this respect is unclear. A purported C reorganization accompanied by a (taxable) distribution to shareholders would seem no more divisive than an A reorganization accompanied by the exact same distribution.

(b) Consideration: A Voting Stock

(i) *Debt Relief*

While Code Sec. 368(a)(1)(C) appears to describe as a reorganization A's acquisition of T "solely for all or part of its voting stock," the consideration permissible is actually somewhat broader than that. The section goes on to say that in determining whether the exchange is solely for stock, A's assumption of any T liabilities shall be disregarded. The result is that A can use any combination of A voting stock and debt assumption as consideration for acquiring the T assets, so long as the amount of A voting stock is sufficient to establish continuity of interest.[44]

(ii) *Other Property*

Code Sec. 368(a)(2)(B) also allows limited additional consideration in C reorganizations. Specifically, A can transfer to T cash or other property; but if it does so, A must acquire at least 80% of the gross value of all of T's property solely for A voting stock. If A acquires all of T's assets and assumes none of T's liabilities, this rule is fairly straightforward and allows for 20% boot.[45] If A either acquires less than all of T's assets or takes on some T liabilities as consideration, though, things become a bit more complicated. This is because the statute does not actually limit the amount of boot that A can use, but instead specifies the minimum amount of T's gross assets (80%) that A must acquire in exchange for A voting stock if any boot at all is used.

To see how this applies, assume that T is worth $100, has 100 assets each worth $1, and has liabilities of $30. If A acquires all of T's assets in exchange for 70 A voting stock and assumes $30 of T's liabilities, the requirements of a C have been met, since the consideration is solely A voting stock and debt assumption. If A instead acquires all of T's assets for 80 A voting stock and $20 cash, the requirements again have been met, since A acquires 80% of the T assets in exchange for A voting stock. On the other hand, assume that A acquires all of T's assets for $79 A

---

[43] Treas. Reg. §1.368-1(e)(1)(ii), -1(e)(8) ex. 9, -2(b)(1)(ii), -2(b)(3) ex. 8.

[44] This will always be the case unless more than 60% of the total consideration is debt relief rather than A voting stock. *See* discussion of continuity of interest at ¶ 802.01(b).

[45] According to Treas. Reg. §1.368-2(d)(1), the boot cannot consist of stock of A's parent corporation or subsidiary, however. The statutory foundation for this restriction is difficult to ascertain.

voting stock, $20 of T's liabilities that A assumes, and $1 cash boot. The transaction will fail as a C because A has paid something other than debt assumption and A voting stock, and thus will not meet the requirements unless it acquires at least 80% of T's gross asset value for A voting stock. Finally, assume that A acquires $80 worth of T's 100 assets in exchange for consideration of 79 A voting stock and $1 cash. Again, because there has been some consideration other than A voting stock and debt assumption, the transaction will not qualify as a C unless A acquires at least 80% of the gross value of T for A voting stock.

(c) Creeping C Reorganizations

As in almost every area of corporate tax, in determining whether a series of events qualify as a C reorganization, it may be necessary in the first instance to determine whether the step transaction doctrine applies—that is, to determine whether a series of events will be treated as separate transactions or whether they will be integrated and treated as a single transaction. Among the most likely series of events that may, or may not, be recharacterized are: (1) an acquisition by A of some T stock, followed by an acquisition by A of all of T's assets in exchange at least in part for A voting stock; (2) an acquisition by A of some T assets, followed by an acquisition by A of the rest (or most of the rest) of T's assets in exchange at least in part for A voting stock; and (3) the disposition by T of some assets followed by A's acquisition of most or all of the rest of T's assets at least in part for A voting stock.

The last of these three possible issues was discussed above. According to the IRS's pronouncements to date, A must acquire "substantially all" of T's assets, and T's assets for this purpose include not only assets that T owns at the moment that the contract is signed, but also assets that T owned prior to that time that T transferred to shareholders by distribution or redemption as part of the planned acquisition by A. Note this does not require that T refrain from *selling* any of its assets to unrelated third parties in connection with the reorganization, so long as the transaction (including the asset sale, if it is part of the plan of reorganization) meets the continuity of business enterprise restrictions that apply to all reorganizations.[46] All that is required under the "substantially all" test for these purposes is that the proceeds of any asset sale made by T in connection with the reorganization are considered part of T's assets, so that if T distributes a significant portion of those proceeds to its shareholders, problems will arise.[47]

If T sells some of its assets to A in connection with the reorganization, though, the result will likely turn out differently. Unless A's purchase of T assets is treated as a separate transaction, any property A transfers to T for those assets will be treated as part of the consideration exchanged in the attempted reorganization. If that consideration takes the form of anything other than A voting stock and assumption of T's debt, there will likely be a problem (unless, of course, A nonetheless acquires at least 80% of the gross value of T's assets solely for A voting stock).[48]

---

[46] See discussion at ¶ 802.01(b).
[47] Rev. Rul. 88-48, 1988-1 C.B. 117.

[48] If A used A voting stock in the related asset acquisition, it may argue that acquisition should be treated as part of the reorganization because it may increase the

More frequent than asset sales to A preliminary to an attempted C reorganization may be stock acquisitions by A. If A acquires T stock in a transaction that is separate from the C reorganization, and then later acquires substantially all of T's assets in exchange for a combination of A voting stock and the T stock already owned by A, the second transaction will qualify as a C reorganization. The T stock already owned by A and used by A in acquiring T's assets represents an unarguable continuity of interest in T on A's part, and it will be treated the same as A voting stock for the purposes of Code Sec. 368(a)(1)(C).[49] To see how this impacts the results, assume, again, that T has 100 assets (and no liabilities), each worth $1. In a separate, earlier transaction, A purchased[50] T stock now worth $40. A now acquires all of T's assets for the $40 of T stock it already has, $40 worth of A voting stock, and $20 cash (the cash and the A voting stock go to the other T shareholders), and T is liquidated. The transaction is a valid C, because A has acquired 80% of the gross value of T's assets for a combination of A voting stock and its previously owned T stock, which is treated as A voting stock for purposes of determining whether the transaction qualifies.

Similarly, the transaction would qualify as a C if T had $30 of liabilities, and in the second transaction (after A already owned $40 worth of T stock), A acquired the T assets for the 40 T stock it already owned, 30 A voting stock, and the assumption of T's $30 liabilities. The T stock is treated as A voting stock for purposes of determining whether the transaction qualifies as a C, and the only other consideration is the assumption of debt, which can be used in a C under Code Sec. 368(a)(1)(C).

If A acquires T stock in a transaction that is treated as part of the reorganization, though, things change (again). This would be the case, for example, if A acquired T stock and then liquidated T as part of a single planned asset acquisition. The consideration paid by A to acquire the T stock will be treated as part (or all, depending on whether A acquired part or all of the T stock) of the consideration paid to acquire the T assets. As a result, if A acquired the T stock for anything other than A voting stock, the transaction is threatened (and will not qualify as a C unless at least 80% of the gross value of the T assets are acquired for A voting stock). On the other hand, if A did use solely A voting stock (or at least enough A voting stock to meet the requirements of Code Sec. 368(a)(1)(C)) to acquire all of the T stock, and then (as part of the same transaction) T is liquidated and A ends up with all of the T assets, the transaction will be treated as if A directly acquired all of the T assets for A voting stock, and will qualify as a C reorganization. As a result, rather than having to meet the stricter standards of Code Sec. 368(a)(1)(B), which relate to stock acquisitions and which prohibit any boot at all, the transaction will be judged under the standards of Code Sec. 368(a)(1)(C).[51]

(Footnote Continued)

amount of T assets acquired for A voting stock. Unfortunately, if A had structured the transactions as separate it will likely find itself bound by its own form if that form is not to A's advantage.

[49] Treas. Reg. § 1.368-2(d)(1), (4)(i).

[50] Since we are assuming that the stock purchase is a separate transaction, whether A acquired the T stock for

A voting stock, cash, something else, or some combination of the above is irrelevant. All that matters is that A owns the T stock and did not acquire it in conjunction with the plan of reorganization.

[51] Rev. Rul. 67-274, 1967-2 C.B. 141. In this ruling, in which A acquired all of the T stock and then liquidated T, the consideration paid by A was all A voting stock. As a

.03 Stock Acquisitions: Code Sec. 368(a)(1)(B)

B reorganizations involve A's acquisition of the stock, rather than the assets, of the target. To qualify under Code Sec. 368(a)(1)(B), A must be in control of the target immediately after the exchange. Control is defined in Code Sec. 368(c) as ownership of at least 80% of the total voting power and 80% of the total shares of each class of nonvoting stock. Code Sec. 368(a)(1)(B) does not require that A *acquire* control of T in the exchange, but only that A have control of T immediately after the exchange. As a result, if, for example, A already owns 79% of the T stock and later, in a separate transaction, acquires another 1% solely for A voting stock, giving it a total of 80%, that subsequent transaction may qualify as a B reorganization. Similarly, if A already owns 80% of the T stock, any subsequent acquisition of T stock will qualify as a B reorganization. So long as A's stock acquisition was a transaction separate from the reorganization, it matters not how, or in exchange for what, A had acquired the T stock in the earlier, separate, transaction.

The only significant requirement, other than control, for a stock acquisition to qualify as a B is that the *only* consideration that A can use is A voting stock. No cash, or other property, or nonvoting stock may be transferred to any T shareholders for any part of their T stock in the reorganization.[52] The IRS and the courts have given no ground on their interpretation of this requirement. Voting stock does not include warrants to purchase voting stock, or any other A securities.[53] While the IRS allows for the contract to include the transfer of additional shares of A voting stock to the T shareholders contingent on future valuation, if those contingent rights are themselves either assignable or readily marketable, they will be treated as boot (that is, something other than A voting stock) and their presence will disqualify the transaction from treatment as a reorganization.[54]

On occasion, the IRS has looked hard at direct or indirect transfers of property to T shareholders that are connected with the reorganization. If the IRS believes that these transfers are properly characterized as consideration for T stock, it will treat them as such, so that treatment as a reorganization will be denied.[55] Examples of such indirect payments that can disqualify the reorganizations could include "employment contracts" or lease agreements between controlling T shareholders and A where the compensation paid is actually in exchange for T stock rather than for any services or the use of any property that might be provided, or the payment of shareholder expenses incurred in connection with the reorganization.

(Footnote Continued)

result, the acquisition would have qualified as a tax free reorganization in any event–either as a B if the acquisition and liquidation were treated as separate transaction, or as a C if they were integrated and treated as a single exchange (or as an A if the transaction was a merger under state law). If A uses any boot in the stock acquisition, so that the stock acquisition when looked at as a separate transaction would not qualify as a reorganization, the IRS might well be more inclined to hold the taxpayer's adopted form against it and treat the two transactions (the stock acquisition and the liquidation of T) as separate, with the result that the stock acquisition part would be taxable in full to the T shareholders.

[52] Solely for the sake of convenience, the IRS does allow A to pay T shareholders cash instead of having to distribute fractional shares. Rev. Rul. 66-365, 1966-2 C.B. 187.

[53] *Helvering v. Southwest Consol. Corp.*, 315 US 194, *reh'g denied*, 315 US 829, *reh'g denied*, 316 US 710 (1942).

[54] Rev. Proc. 77-37, 1977-2 C.B. 568; Rev. Proc. 84-42, 1984-1 CB 521. These rulings also limit the amount of contingent voting stock to not more than 50% of the total amount to be transferred to the T shareholders in the reorganization.

[55] Rev. Rul. 75-360, 1975-2 C.B. 110.

If some T shareholders demand cash rather than A voting stock, T can redeem those shareholders or otherwise pay out cash to its shareholders without disqualifying the reorganization, so long as the property paid out to the T shareholders by T does not come, directly or indirectly, from A or a party related to A.[56] Not surprisingly, if A, or a related party,[57] directly or indirectly, transfers property to T (either before, after, or at the time of the reorganization), and T uses that property to redeem some T stock or to pay extraordinary dividends or other amounts to its shareholders in conjunction with the reorganization, the transfer by A to T (and eventually to the T shareholders) will be treated as consideration (other than A voting stock, of course) paid by A to the T shareholders, and will disqualify the reorganization.[58]

It nonetheless appears that the IRS is a bit more generous in its treatment of payments to T itself than it is of transfers by A to T's shareholders, even though any such payments will somehow go to the benefit of T's shareholders. It has ruled that A can assume certain of T's expenses incurred in conjunction with the reorganization without that assumption being treated as a prohibited payment to the shareholders,[59] and it has also ruled that A can purchase T stock directly from T for cash, and that such cash purchase from T will be treated as separate from a transaction that otherwise qualifies as a B reorganization.[60]

Unlike in an asset acquisition, in a B reorganization T remains alive as a corporation and retains its separate identity. As a result, there is no need for A to either pay T obligations or to directly assume such obligations, or to issue A bonds in place of any T bonds outstanding. If S does any of these things, the IRS will treat them as transactions separate and independent from the B reorganization,[61] so long as they are not disguised payments of property to the T shareholders in exchange for their T stock. If, for example, T debts are held by T shareholders in proportion to their holdings of T stock and A acquires them for an amount above their value, the IRS will likely take a closer look. Similarly, if T shareholders have guaranteed T's obligations and A assumes that guarantee liability as a condition of the exchange, the value of the release given to the T shareholder will likely be treated as a transfer of some value other than A voting stock and may result in the denial of reorganization treatment.[62]

---

[56] Treas. Reg. § 1.368-1(e)(8) ex. 9.

[57] Within the meaning of Treas. Reg. § 1.368-1(e)(4). Basically this would include a member of the same affiliated group or a corporation that would be treated as related for purposes of invoking Code Sec. 304. *See* Chapter 5.

[58] Rev. Rul. 73-102, 1973-1 C.B. 186.

[59] Rev. Rul. 73-54, 1973-1 C.B. 187.

[60] Rev. Rul. 72-522, 1972-2 C.B. 215. In order to come under this ruling, A would have to engage in an acquisition of T stock solely for A voting stock, and that acquisition, treated separately from A's cash purchase of stock from T, would have to separately and independently qualify as a B.

[61] Rev. Rul. 98-10, 1998-1 C.B. 643.

[62] Rev. Rul. 79-4, 1979-1 C.B. 150; Rev. Rul. 79-89, 1979-1 C.B. 152.

.04 Tax Consequences of a Two-Entity (linear) Acquisitive Reorganization

(a) T Shareholders and Security Holders

(i) Overview

The idea of reorganizations is that they are tax free, but Code Sec. 368 does not provide that tax free treatment. It merely defines what transactions qualify as "reorganizations." Code Sec. 354(a)(1) provides that T shareholders who trade their T stock for A stock in what qualifies as an A, B, or C reorganization (as well as other reorganizations discussed later) receive nonrecognition. To be more precise, Code Sec. 354(a)(1) appears to state that the T shareholders receive tax free treatment to the extent that "stock or securities" in T are exchanged for "stock and securities" in A. Code Sec. 354(a)(2)(A) then immediately dismisses the implied possibility of tax free treatment for T shareholders who trade T stock for A securities other than or in addition to A stock. It does so by limiting nonrecognition if the principal amount of A securities received exceeds the principal amount of T securities surrendered. The net result is that the T shareholder recognizes no gain to the extent that she receives A stock[63] for T stock, and the T security holder recognizes no gain to the extent that she receives A stock or securities in exchange for T securities. If and to the extent that a T shareholder receives A securities for T stock, the A securities are treated as boot.

Code Sec. 354 applies only to the T shareholder who exchanges T stock *solely* for A stock. If a shareholder receives both A stock and boot, the exchange is governed by Code Sec. 356, which states that if Code Sec. 354 would apply but for the fact that the T shareholder receives boot in addition to the T stock, any gain realized is recognized to the extent of the boot received. To the extent that a T shareholder receives A securities in excess of the value of T securities she surrenders in the exchange, the excess A securities are treated as boot and will result in gain recognition.[64] As with a Code Sec. 351 exchange, the shareholder who receives boot in addition to A stock will not recognize a loss on the exchange, since Code Sec. 356, like Code Sec. 351(b) overrides the nonrecognition rule of Code Sec. 354 only to provide for the recognition of gain.[65]

While securities received in excess of securities exchanged are treated as boot, it is worth noting that shareholders who receive, in exchange for T stock, either contingent rights to additional A stock or A stock warrants will not be taxed upon receipt, regardless of the value of those rights or warrants. The regulations accomplish this result by treating such rights to acquire additional A stock as a "security" that has no principal amount.[66] Since only securities with a principal amount in excess of the principal amount of securities surrendered are treated as boot, rights treated as having no principal amount could never be so treated.

---

[63] Consistent with Code Sec. 351, both Code Secs. 354 and 356 treat nonqualified preferred stock as boot, unless it is received in exchange for nonqualified preferred stock of T, Code Secs. 354(a)(2)(C), 356(e).

[64] Code Sec. 356(d).

[65] Code Sec. 356(c) explicitly states that no loss in recognized.

[66] Treas. Reg. § 1.356-3(b).

¶802.04

If a T shareholder exchanges T stock *only* for cash or other boot, neither Code Sec. 354 nor Code Sec. 356 apply to that exchange.[67] Instead, the exchange will be treated as if the T shareholder simply sold the T stock back to T (a redemption), and tax consequences on that exchange will be determined by application of the redemption rules.

Allocation of Boot among Blocks or classes of T stock: If a T shareholder has more than one block of T stock or more than one class of T stock, the exchange of each separate block or class of T stock is treated as a separate exchange. The plan of reorganization can specify which consideration is being paid to the shareholder for which classes or blocks of stock, so long as the specification is economically reasonable.[68] Thus, if the shareholder holds some shares with a gain and others whose value does not exceed their basis, the terms of the reorganization exchange can specify that, to the extent it comports with the actual value of the different shares, the boot is received in exchange for the shares which have no realized gain, and can thus be taken tax free. Indeed, if the T shareholder receives boot equal in value to an entire block or class of T stock she owns that has a loss, she can allocate *only* boot to that class of stock, avoid the application of Code Secs. 354 and 356 to the exchange of that stock for boot (because she has no received no A stock in exchange for that class of T stock) and potentially recognize a *loss* on that class[69] while avoiding the recognition of any gain on her appreciated stock (by not allocating any boot to that stock).[70]

If T shareholders do own different blocks or classes, it is useful to ensure that the plan of reorganization specifies which T stock is being exchanged for which consideration. If the terms of the exchange do not specify exactly what consideration is being paid for what stock, the regulations will treat the exchange as if each kind of consideration was received for each share of stock in proportion to each share's value.[71]

(ii) *Securities Exchanged and Received*

To the extent that a taxpayer receives either A securities or A stock in exchange for T securities, she recognizes no gain on the exchange. But this does not always mean that the T security holder who receives only A stock and/or securities will avoid tax in a reorganization. To the extent that a T security holder receives any amount in any form (even in the form of A stock) attributable to interest accrued on the T securities, that amount is taxed (as ordinary income).[72] In addition, questions may arise as to whether what is exchanged and/or received is actually a "security." While a debt with a term of less than five years may be classified as something other than a security and a note with a term of more than 10

---

[67] Code Sec. 356(a)(1). Even in a qualified A or C reorganization, any particular shareholder can receive cash so long as enough of the T stock is traded for appropriate consideration. The T shareholder who receives any A stock at all, though, will not recognize any loss on the reorganization, but will have any gain or loss realized effectively built into her basis in the A stock.

[68] Treas. Reg. § 1.356-1(b); 1.356-1(d) ex. 4.

[69] After application of the redemption rules to that exchange.

[70] Prop. Treas. Reg. § 1.356-1(e) ex. 5. This particular example is only a proposed regulation and has not been finalized, but it is only this example of how the rules work, and not the rules themselves, that has not been finalized.

[71] Treas. Reg. § 1.356-1(b).

[72] Code Sec. 354(a)(2)(B).

years likely will be a security, the exact definition is somewhat vague. The IRS and courts will look at several factors, and then decide.[73]

(iii) *Character of Gain Recognized*

If a T shareholder does recognize gain as a result of the receipt of boot for T stock, it is possible, although not likely, that such gain will be characterized as a dividend[74] rather than as gain from the sale or exchange of her T stock.[75] Solely for purposes of determining whether the shareholder's gain will be taxed as a dividend, the shareholder will be treated as if she received, in the reorganization, A stock equal in value to all of her T stock. She will then be treated as if she redeemed an amount of the A stock equal in value to the boot she received. If that redemption would have resulted in a dividend, she will receive dividend treatment for her actual gain recognized in the reorganization. If she would have received sale or exchange treatment on the redemption, her gain on the reorganization will receive capital gain treatment.

To see an example of the above kind of characterization, assume that T is worth $100, and T merges into A. ST owned 20 shares of T worth $20 and in which she had a basis of $10. In the merger, ST receives A stock worth $15 and $5 cash. A realizes a gain of $10 (the excess of her amount realized of $20 over her basis in the T stock of $10). That $10 gain is recognized to the extent of the boot ($5 cash) ST receives, so that ST recognizes a gain of $5.

To determine whether that $5 gain is taxed as a dividend, assume that ST initially received $20 worth of A stock and then redeemed 5 of that A stock for cash. In order to determine whether that deemed redemption by A (of the $5 worth of A stock treated as originally issued to ST in the reorganization for the boot actually received) will receive sale or exchange treatment or dividend treatment, one must know ST's ownership interest in A (not T) immediately prior to and immediately after the deemed redemption. In other words, one must determine what percentage of the A stock ST would have owned if she had owned $20 worth of A stock, and what percentage of A she owned when she held only $15 worth of A stock, and then apply the Code Sec. 302 tests. Without delving into any more specifics, any time that A is, after the reorganization, significantly larger than T was prior to the reorganization, ST is likely to be a minority shareholder of A and is likely to receive sale or exchange treatment on any deemed redemption, even if ST was a controlling shareholder of T prior to the redemption. Only if ST was a controlling shareholder of T and T (prior to the reorganization) was either as large or larger than A is there any real possibility that the deemed redemption might result in characterizing ST's gain as a dividend.

(iv) *Timing of Gain Recognized*

If a shareholder receives boot in the form of an installment obligation, rather than reporting her gain immediately she may be permitted to report that gain using

---

[73] *See* Boris I. Bittker and James S. Eustice, Federal Income Taxation of Corporations and Shareholders ¶ 12.41.

[74] To the extent of the shareholder's ratable share of T's accumulated earnings and profits as of the date of the reorganization. It is not clear, though, exactly what earnings and profits are involved. It could be A's, it could be T's, or it could be a combination of both.

[75] Code Sec. 356(a)(2).

the installment method.[76] The installment method is not available if the shareholder's gain is characterized as a dividend,[77] but is otherwise generally available in reorganizations as it is in Code Sec. 351 exchanges. Whether or not it is available in any particular case depends only on whether the generally applicable requirements of Code Sec. 453 are met (for example the installment method is not available with respect to publicly traded securities). As with Code Sec. 351 and other nonrecognition exchanges that involve the receipt of installment boot, the shareholder would first determine her total gain to be recognized, then divide that by the total boot received, and include as gain that percentage of each payment when received.[78]

(v) *Shareholder Basis*

The T shareholder who receives boot other than cash takes a basis in the boot equal to the property's fair market value.[79] Code Sec. 358, which determines the former T shareholder's basis in her A stock, is the same section that determines the shareholder's basis in a Code Sec. 351 exchange, and all of the same principles apply.[80] The former T shareholder's basis in any stock received from A in the reorganization is an exchanged basis (the same as her basis was in the T stock she transferred) increased by any gain she recognized on the exchange (regardless of whether the gain is taxed as capital gain or as a dividend), and decreased by the amount of boot received.

If the shareholder recognizes no gain in the reorganization (because she receives no boot), her basis in the A stock is the same as her basis was in the T stock, so that any gain not recognized in the reorganization will be recognized by the shareholder when she sells the A stock. If the shareholder receives boot and recognizes gain, then the more boot she receives, the more gain she recognizes and the more her basis is adjusted upwards. Correspondingly, because her stock basis is also adjusted downwards by the boot received, the more her basis will be adjusted downwards. As a result, the upward and downward adjustments will typically balance each other out, and the shareholder's basis in the A stock will be the same as was her basis in the T stock. The only time that a former T shareholder will have a basis in her A stock that differs from what her basis was in the T stock is if the former T shareholder has no unrecognized gain in the exchange.[81]

(vi) *Holding Period*

Finally, the shareholder who acquires A stock for T stock in a reorganization will take a holding period in the A stock that will include any time during which she had held the T stock she transferred in the exchange, under Code Sec. 1223(1). That section provides for a tacked holding period whenever the taxpayer takes property (such as the A stock) with the same basis (in whole or in part) as the property exchanged (the T stock) so long as the property exchanged was a capital

---

[76] Code Sec. 453(f)(6).

[77] Prop. Treas. Reg. § 1.453-1(f)(2).

[78] See discussion of Code Sec. 453 with respect to Code Sec. 351 exchanges at Chapter 9.

[79] Code Sec. 358(a)(2).

[80] See discussion of Code Sec. 358 at ¶ 802.04.

[81] If the shareholder receives boot in excess of her realized gain so recognizes all of her gain, she will simply take a cost basis in the A stock. If the shareholder has realized but unrecognized loss in the exchange, her basis in the A stock she receives will be the same as her basis was in the T stock, less any boot received.

asset. Unless the T shareholder was a securities dealer, the T stock was a capital asset in her hands.

(vii) *Code Sec. 306*

It is possible, though not likely, that the T shareholders who receive A stock in an acquisitive reorganization may have that stock tainted by Code Sec. 306. By its terms, Code Sec. 306 taints preferred stock received in a reorganization either if it is received for Code Sec. 306 stock of T[82] or if the effect of the transaction was substantially the same as the receipt of a stock dividend. The regulations assert that if T shareholders exchange their T common stock on a pro rata basis for a combination of A common and A preferred, the A preferred will be treated as Code Sec. 306 stock.[83] In light of Clarke,[84] however, it is doubtful that the receipt of any preferred stock of A could be seen as having substantially the same effect as a stock dividend, and it is doubtful that the pre-Clarke regulation still applies.

(b) Tax Consequences to the Target

Since a B reorganization involves only the exchange of T stock, and involves no action at all by T itself, there are, quite simply, no tax consequences to T in a B reorganization. While the target might well end up with no tax liability as a result of an asset acquisition as well, the path to that result, or some other result, as the case may be, is not quite as direct.

In an asset acquisition (that is, either an A or a C reorganization), the ultimate result for T is that so long as its assets go to the acquiring corporation, and the consideration for those assets goes to the T shareholders or creditors, T will recognize no gain or loss. On the other hand, to the extent that either some of T's assets do not go to A, or that some of the consideration paid by A does not go to the T shareholders or creditors, T may well end up with some taxable gain (but not loss). For tax purposes, in an asset acquisition T is treated as engaging in two separate, but related, transactions: (1) T transfers some or all of its assets to A in exchange for A stock (and boot, if there is any); and (2) T liquidates, distributing whatever it has to its shareholders and creditors. To the extent that T merely functions as a conduit for the two step transfer of stock and other property from A to its shareholders and creditors, T will recognize no gain or loss on either of these transactions. To the extent that T does anything else, though, it risks incurring some tax liability.

The tax consequences of T's initial exchange of its assets to A are provided for in Code Sec. 361(a), which states that a corporation a party to a reorganization[85] recognizes no gain or loss if, in pursuance of the plan of reorganization, it exchanges property solely for stock or securities in another corporation (A) a party to the reorganization. Code Sec. 361(b) then provides that if T also receives money or other property in addition to A stock and/or securities, T will still recognize no gain, even on the receipt of the boot, so long as that boot is distributed (to T's shareholders or creditors[86]) in pursuance of the plan of reorganization. The basic

---

[82] Code Sec. 306(c)(1)(C).
[83] Treas. Reg. § 1.306-3(d) ex. 1.
[84] *Comm'r v. Clark*, 489 U.S. 726 (1989).

[85] Code Sec. 368(b)(2) includes T as such a party.
[86] Code Sec. 361(b)(3).

reason that T will not recognize no gain on the receipt of the boot is that the shareholders who receive the boot distributed by T will recognize any of their realized gain on that receipt. Since T is liquidated by state statute in a merger (or at least a merger that qualifies as an A reorganization) and T is required by Code Sec. 368(a)(2)(G) to distribute it's stock securities and other property in a C reorganization, it is difficult (but not impossible)[87] to imagine a situation in which it might do something with the boot other than distribute it to shareholders or creditors.

It is also possible that, as part of the reorganization, A might assume some of T's liabilities or take some of T's assets subject to debt. If that happens, then the debt relief is a part of the consideration T receives in exchange for its assets, and it is consideration that T cannot in turn distribute. Instead, to the extent that A assumes T liabilities (or takes property from T subject to nonrecourse debt), the exchange is governed by Code Sec. 357, which is the same section that governs debt relief for the shareholder in a Code Sec. 351 exchange. Under that section, any T debt assumed by A is not treated as boot paid to T. Instead, T's basis in any A stock it receives is reduced under Code Sec. 358(d) by the amount of debt assumed by A. In reality, T's basis in the A stock is essentially irrelevant for purposes of determining tax consequences for any of the parties. In addition, in a Code Sec. 351 exchange, if the amount of T's debt (excluding liabilities that would be deductible when paid, Code Sec. 357(c)(3)) assumed by a person who transfers property for stock exceeds the transferor's total basis in all of the assets transferred, the transferor will recognize gain equal to the excess of liabilities assumed over her stock basis. Code Sec. 357(c) does not apply to acquisitive reorganizations. As a result of all of this, A's assumption of T's liabilities almost never has any real impact on T's, or anyone else's, tax consequences.

The tax consequences to T of its liquidation and distribution to shareholders are determined by Code Sec. 361(c). That section provides that T will recognize no gain on the distribution to shareholders or creditors of "qualified property." Qualified property is in turn defined as the stock of any corporation that is a party to the reorganization that is received in pursuance of the plan of reorganization. In other words, T's distribution to shareholders and creditors of any A stock received in the reorganization is tax free to T. Thus, T may recognize gain on the distribution of any property other than A stock. To the extent that it distributes any boot received in the reorganization, though, T is not likely to even realize any gain, because T's basis in any boot received will be equal to the property's fair market value at the time of the receipt, under Code Sec. 358(a)(2).

As a result, the only time that T will recognize any gain[88] on its liquidating distributions to its shareholders and creditors is if and to the extent that it retains some of the assets that it had prior to the reorganization and then distributes them in pursuance of the plan of reorganization. With respect to these assets, T would

---

[87] T might use the cash it receives to buy some asset that it will then distribute, or it might sell the boot it receives and distribute the cash.

[88] T will not recognize a loss on any distribution in pursuance of a plan of reorganization, Code Sec. 361(c)(1).

recognize gain whether it had distributed them prior to the liquidation,[89] or whether it distributed them in liquidation in the absence of a reorganization.[90]

While Code Sec. 361 generally exempts T from tax on both its exchange of assets to A and on its distribution to its shareholders of what it received from A in the reorganization, it is possible for T to recognize gain or loss on an intermediate step in the reorganization. T may sell property to third parties in conjunction with the reorganization, and if it does so, those sales or exchanges will be taxed as independent transactions, and T will recognize gain or loss equal to the difference between its amount realized and its basis in assets so sold. If T sells assets it owned prior to the reorganization, its basis in those assets is determined without regard to the reorganization. If T sells boot it received in the reorganization, its basis is the fair market value of those assets at the time they are received.

If T sells to third parties some of the A stock it receives in the reorganization, T's basis in the stock sold will be a pro rata portion of its basis in all of that class of A stock that it received in the reorganization. In turn, T's total basis in the A stock received is determined under Code Sec. 358, which applies to T the same way it does to shareholders who receive stock for property in a Code Sec. 351 exchange.[91] Essentially, T's basis in all of the A stock received will be equal to T's total asset basis, reduced by any T liabilities A assumed in pursuance of the plan of reorganization. That total stock basis will then be allocated among the various classes of A stock in proportion to the relative value of each class.[92]

(c) Tax Consequences to A

(i) *Gain, Basis and Holding Period*

The tax consequences to an acquiring corporation in a reorganization are straightforward, and similar to the consequences to the acquiring corporation in a Code Sec. 351 exchange. A recognizes no gain or loss when it issues its stock for property (T stock or T assets) under Code Sec. 1032. In addition, A's basis in whatever it acquires (T stock or T assets) is a transferred basis (the same as the basis the property has in the hands of the transferor) increased by any gain recognized to the transferor on the exchange.[93] Since no boot is permissible in a B reorganization, no T shareholder can recognize gain, and A's basis in (and holding period for[94]) the T stock will be the same as it was in the hands of the transferor. Although it is theoretically possible that T may recognize gain on the exchange with A in either an A or a C reorganization, such an occurrence is highly unlikely.[95]

---

[89] Code Sec. 311(b).

[90] Code Sec. 336(a).

[91] *See* ¶ 802.04(a).

[92] In addition, T's holding period for the A stock received will include T's holding period for the assets exchanged, to the extent that those assets were capital assets in T's hands, Code Sec. 1223(1)

[93] Code Sec. 362(b).

[94] Code Sec. 1223(2).

[95] The possibility could arise if T receives boot and does not distribute the boot received to either its shareholders or creditors. This, in turn, could result only if T either uses cash boot received from A to purchase some asset from an unrelated third party, or sells some non-cash boot received from A to a third party in pursuance of the plan of reorganization. While T might also recognize some gain on its distribution of property in pursuance of a plan of reorganization under Code Sec. 361(c), A's asset basis would be increased only on any gain T recognized on the *exchange* with A, and not by any gain T might later recognize on either a sale or a distribution in conjunction with the reorganization.

As a result, A's basis in the T assets will virtually always be the same as T's basis was in those assets.

The only apparent difference between the determination of A's asset basis when it acquires property for its stock in an acquisitive reorganization and when it acquires property for its stock in a Code Sec. 351 exchange is in Code Sec. 362(e)(2), which generally limits the acquiring corporation's total asset basis in the assets received from a single transferor to an amount not in excess of the total value of the assets received from that transferor.[96] Code Sec. 362(e)(2) applies, by its own terms, only to Code Sec. 351 exchanges and not to reorganizations. Interestingly, the IRS has at least proposed regulations that ignore this restriction and would apply the Code Sec. 362(e)(2) limit to property received in a reorganization as well.[97]

(ii) *Carryover of Other Tax Attributes from T to A*

In either an A or a C reorganization, in addition to acquiring the T assets with T's same basis and holding period, A also steps into T's shoes with respect to numerous other tax attributes described in Code Sec. 381. Among these are Net Operating Losses, earnings and profits, capital loss carryovers, accounting methods, inventories, depreciation, and installment sales. All of these, in addition to operating rules and limitations on these carryovers, are described at length in Chapter 9.

¶ 803 Triangular Reorganizations

.01 *Linear Reorganizations Followed by Drop Downs*

Triangular reorganizations are those that include three, rather than only two, corporate parties to the reorganization. The three parties involved are T, A, and a subsidiary of A ("S"). The earliest type of triangular reorganization was simply a typical A, B or C acquisitive reorganization following which A would transfer to a subsidiary part or all of what it just received. In an A or a C reorganization, A transferred to its subsidiary some or all of the assets it had just acquired from T. In a B reorganization, A transferred to its subsidiary some or all of the T stock it had just acquired.

Early on, the IRS argued (successfully) that these transactions failed to qualify as reorganizations. According to the IRS and the courts, these transactions lacked the requisite continuity of interest because the former T shareholders owned stock of A, but the former T assets (or, in the case of a B reorganization, the T stock) were now owned by S rather than by A. Thus the former T shareholders lacked any interest in the corporation (S) that now owned either the T assets or the T stock.[98]

Code Sec. 368(a)(2)(C) directly addresses this now ancient problem. It simply states that an A, B, or C reorganization "shall not be disqualified by reason of the

---

[96] See discussion of Code Sec. 362(e)(2) at ¶ 803.04.

[97] Code Sec. 362(e)(2)(A)(i) applies the basis limitation to "any transaction which is described in subsection (a)" and subsection (a) of 362 describes only property received in a Code Sec. 351 exchange. Property received in a reorganization is described instead in Code Sec.

362(b). Interestingly, Prop. Treas. Reg. 1.362-4(b)(5) states that "Section 362(e)(2) can apply to a transfer regardless of whether the basis of the property would, but for Section 362(e)(2), be determined under Section 362(b)."

[98] *Helvering v. Bashford*, 302 US 454 (1938).

fact that all or part of the assets or stock which were acquired in the transaction are transferred to a corporation (S) controlled by the corporation acquiring such assets or stock." The regulations make it clear that the drop down need not stop at the subsidiary level. S can in turn drop the T stock or assets down to its own subsidiary, which can drop it down another level, etc.[99]

.02 Acquisitions Using Stock of A Parent Corporation

Often for reasons unrelated to tax, a corporate acquirer that wishes to have the stock or assets it acquires owned by a subsidiary, rather than owning them itself, would prefer to structure a transaction as one in which its subsidiary acquires the assets (or stock) directly, rather than one in which A acquires the assets in a reorganization and then transfers those assets to its subsidiary. By avoiding even temporary acquisition of the T assets, A might ensure itself against any possibility that it could be held responsible for any of T's liabilities under state law. It might also save itself a bit of paperwork on the asset transfer, and it might be able to avoid involvement of its own shareholders in the acquisition. At the same time that Congress expressly approved of acquisitive reorganizations followed by drop downs, it also qualified as reorganizations transactions in which A first transfers its own stock to its subsidiary S, and then S acquires the T stock or assets, using as consideration the A stock rather than its own stock.

(a) Bs and Cs

Both Code Sec. 368(a)(1)(B) and Code Sec 368(a)(1)(C) were amended in 1954 to permit the acquiring company (which we now refer to as S rather than A) to acquire the T assets or stock either for its own voting stock "or in exchange solely for all or a part of the voting stock of a corporation which is in control of the acquiring corporation." The IRS strictly interprets the "either or" part of these alternatives. An acquisition using *both* stock of the acquiring corporation and stock of its parent will be disqualified.[100] Thus, while a C can involve some boot so long as at least 80% of the gross target assets are acquired either for A voting stock or solely for S voting stock, none of the boot can consist of stock of the nonacquiring corporation. If S uses 99 A voting stock and 1 S voting stock, or 99 S voting stock and 1 A voting stock, the transaction will not qualify as a C. Similarly, if A uses 99 A voting stock and 1 S voting stock, C reorganization treatment will be denied.

(b) Code Sec. 368(a)(2)(D)

In addition to B and C reorganizations, As can also be accomplished by a corporation using stock of its parent. Unlike Code Sec. 368(a)(1)(B) and (C), Code Sec. 368(a)(1)(A) was not amended; instead, Congress separately enacted Code Sec. 368(a)(2)(D) to specifically endorse such mergers. That section allows S to use stock of its controlling parent to accomplish a merger under state law so long as (1) the transaction would have qualified as a merger if the controlling parent had been the acquiring corporation, (2) no stock of the acquiring corporation is used in

---

[99] Treas. Reg. § 1.368-2(k). See in depth discussion of these regulations at ¶ 802.01.

[100] Treas. Reg. § 1.368-2(c) sets forth this limitation in the case of a B. Treas. Reg. § 1.368-2(d)(1) sets forth the identical limitation with respect to a C.

the reorganization, and (3) the acquiring corporation acquires substantially all of the target assets.

The first of these three conditions does not actually require that T could have merged into A under federal or state law. Indeed, the parties may have chosen a triangular merger precisely because there were state law restrictions on the merger of T directly into A. Instead, Code Sec. 368(a)(2)(D) requires simply that the state merger law be acceptable under the regulations,[101] that the T shareholders receive enough A stock to ensure continuity of interest, and that there be continuity of business enterprise.[102]

The second limitation in Code Sec. 368(a)(2)(D), that there be no S stock used in the triangular reorganization using A stock, is similar to the limitation imposed by the regulations on triangular B and C reorganizations. The statutorily imposed restriction in Code Sec. 368(a)(2)(D) appears to be less restrictive than the limitation imposed on triangular Bs and Cs by the regulations. While the regulations prohibit the use of any combination of A stock and S stock in a B or C reorganization, Code Sec. 368(a)(2)(D) prohibits only the use of S stock in a reorganization where the primary consideration is A stock. It appears that, unlike a B or a C, an A can qualify even if there is some A stock used, so long as S uses enough of its own stock to establish continuity of interest.

The requirement that S acquire "substantially all of the properties" of the target for the transaction to qualify is consistent with the requirements of a C reorganization, if not with a linear A. Thus, while the target in a linear A can distribute cash or other property to its shareholders in conjunction with the reorganization so long as it retains and transfers to A enough assets to assure continuity of interest and continuity of business enterprise, it would appear that the target in a Code Sec. 368(a)(2)(D) reorganization, like the Target in a C reorganization, must retain "substantially all of the properties" that it had prior to the reorganization,[103] and cannot distribute more than a small amount of its pre-reorganization assets to its shareholders in connection with the reorganization.

.03 Reverse Triangular Mergers: Code Sec. 368(a)(2)(E)

In practical effect, a reverse triangular merger more closely resembles a B reorganization than anything else. The end result of a Code Sec. 368(a)(2)(E) transaction is that A owns T as at least an 80% controlled subsidiary. Unlike a B reorganization, however, a reverse triangular merger allows A to use (and the former T shareholders to receive) up to 20% boot in addition to A voting stock. Speaking nontechnically, the parties can accomplish this result simply by having A properly package (in a temporary subsidiary) all of the consideration it will pay the T shareholders (that is, the A voting stock and whatever boot it uses). The diagrams below show (hopefully) how this happens.

---

[101] That is, that the target be required to cease its separate existence and that simultaneously all of its assets (other than those distributed in the transaction or used to pay off liabilities) become the property of the acquiring corporation. Treas. Reg. § 1.368-2(b)(1)(ii).

[102] Treas. Reg. § 1.368-2(b)(2).

[103] See discussion at ¶ 802.01.

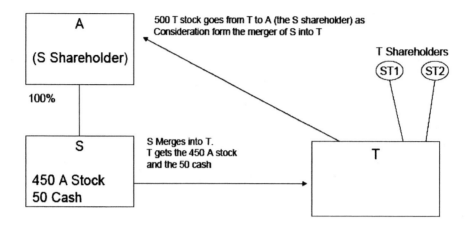

As the "merger" part of this reverse triangular merger, A's subsidiary S merges under state law into the "acquiring corporation," T. In exchange for all of the properties in S, worth a total of 500, T transfers to the S shareholder 500 T stock. Because the S shareholder (A) receives 500 T stock there is clearly continuity of shareholder interest. At least if the exchange ended at this point, there is likely also continuity of business enterprise, because T has acquired all of the assets formerly in S.[104]

It is at this point that Code Sec. 368(a)(2)(E) comes into play. That section states that this merger (of S into T) "shall not be disqualified by the fact that stock of" S's controlling parent (A) "is used in the transaction," if two requirements are met. Despite the phrasing of the section as simply ensuring that the merger of S into T will not be disqualified, it is likely that the fact that one of S's assets is A stock would likely not disqualify this merger of S into T regardless of whether any other requirements of Code Sec. 368(a)(2)(E) are met (assuming continuity of business enterprise).

The primary benefit of Code Sec. 368(a)(2)(E) is not really that it ensures that the merger of S into T will not be disqualified, but that it includes in the tax free reorganization an additional exchange. The exchange actually enabled by Code Sec. 368(a)(2)(E) is that "in the [merger] transaction, former shareholders of the surviving corporation [T] exchanged, for an amount of voting stock of the controlling corporation [A], an amount of stock in the surviving corporation which constitutes control of such corporation [T].[105]

---

[104] Possibly, whether or not there is sufficient continuity of business enterprise to qualify this reorganization may depend on whether or not S is newly formed for this purpose. If so, it may have no "historic" business or assets to be continued, but if T acquires all of S, continuity of business enterprise is quite likely.

[105] As to whether this distribution by T pursuant to the reorganization would otherwise disqualify the merger of S into T, see discussion of post reorganization exchanges at ¶ 803.04.

¶803.03

The diagram below simply adds this exchange to the merger of S into T shown above. This exchange is represented by the thicker lines.

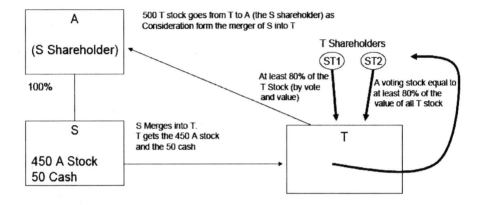

The idea is that pursuant to the merger of S into T, T acquires from S A stock equal in value to at least 80% of all T stock outstanding[106] (taking into account the T stock just issued to A in the merger). T immediately distributes this A stock to its shareholders, in exchange for (at least 80% of) their T stock. The former T shareholders thus have A stock, and A now has a controlling ownership of T. Because this is all part of a reorganization, neither the T shareholders nor T itself are taxed on the exchange of T stock for A stock.[107]

In order to qualify the entire exchange under Code Sec. 368(a)(2)(E), one additional requirement must be met. After the transaction, T must hold substantially all of its properties and substantially all of the properties owned by S, aside from any A stock and boot that A put into S to be transferred to the T shareholders as part of the reorganization.[108] Often, S is a new corporation formed for the sole purpose of carrying the A stock (and boot, if there is any) to T and its shareholders. As a result, S often has no other assets, so the requirement that T retain S's other assets has no real impact.

The IRS has been somewhat lenient in considering the effect on a reverse triangular merger of actions taken prior to and in conjunction with a Code Sec. 368(a)(2)(E) transaction that facilitate A's acquisition of a controlling interest in T. Similar to a B reorganization, If T uses some of its properties to simply pay

---

[106] More specifically, a controlling interest as defined by Code Sec. 368(c), meaning at least 80% by vote and at least 80% of the value of each class not entitled to vote).

[107] If the exchange of T stock for A stock had not been part of a reorganization, it would have been taxed as a redemption to both the T shareholders and to T itself.

[108] Code Sec. 368(a)(2)(E) seems to require that after the transaction T hold substantially all of the properties held by T and substantially all of the properties held by S other than the A stock that is distributed by T to its

shareholders in exchange for their T stock. The regulations ease this requirement, though. In determining whether T holds substantially all of the properties previously owned by S, they make it clear that for purposes of applying the substantially all test to S's property, S's property is deemed not to have included any cash or other property that A transferred into S so that S can, in turn, distribute that property to its shareholders for their T stock or use that property to pay off its liabilities or reorganization expenses. Treas. Reg. § 1.368-(2)(j)(3)(iii).

¶803.03

dividends to its shareholders or to redeem shareholders prior to the exchange, the cash or other property paid out by T will not be treated as boot paid to the shareholders that might interfere with the tax free status of the exchange, so long as the property distributed does not come, directly or indirectly, from A or S.[109] In addition, apparently unlike in a C reorganization, any property that T uses to pay or redeem its shareholders in conjunction with the reorganization will not be considered as property owned by T for purposes of determining whether T continues to own substantially all of its assets after the exchange.[110] As a result, T can redeem as much of its stock as it desires prior to and in pursuance of the plan of reorganization so long as the distributed property does not come from A[111] and so long as T retains enough of its assets to ensure continuity of interest.[112]

In addition to allowing T to redeem some of its stock in conjunction with the reorganization, the IRS also permits A or S to acquire some of the T stock for A voting stock directly from the T shareholders, rather than just from T as consideration for the acquisition of S in the merger, if done in conjunction with the Code Sec. 368(a)(2)(E) exchange. So long as the IRS is convinced that the direct stock acquisition from the T shareholders for A voting stock, the merger of S into T, and the exchange of T stock for A voting stock by most or all of the remaining T shareholders are part of a single transaction, the IRS will treat the A shares transferred directly by A or S to the T shareholders as if they were transferred by A to S, by S to T, and then distributed by T to its shareholders in exchange for their T stock. Thus, so long as at least 80% of the T stock has been exchanged for A voting stock, either directly with A or S or in an exchange with T, the IRS will treat the combined exchanges as meeting the requirement that the T shareholders exchange a controlling interest in T for A voting stock "in the exchange."

Unlike in a B reorganization, though, any T stock that A had acquired in a separate and independent transaction may result in disqualification of the Code Sec. 368(a)(2)(E) transaction. That is because unlike in a B reorganization, Code Sec. 368(a)(2)(E) clearly requires that the former T shareholders must exchange a controlling interest in T for A voting stock "in the exchange." If, for example, A had acquired 25% of the T stock in a separate transaction several years ago, so that only 75% of the T stock was owned by persons other than A, there would be no way that A could acquire a controlling interest in the exchange. Unless A could sell the T stock it already owned and bring its ownership below 80% to begin with, a Code Sec. 368(a)(2)(E) transaction would be impossible.

To see how all of this applies, assume, in the reproduced diagram below, that T has 500 assets, each worth $1, and that each of the two T shareholders (ST(1) and ST(2)) owns 250 of the total 500 shares of T outstanding.

---

[109] Treas. Reg. § 1.368-(2)(j)(3)(iii). If the money or other property that T transfers to its shareholders does come from A, directly or indirectly, it will be treated as if it came from A (along with the other S assets) in the merger of S into A, but unlike in a B reorganization, some of the T stock can be exchanged for cash or other property so long as at least 80% of the T stock is exchanged for A stock.

[110] Treas. Reg. § 1.368-(2)(j)(3)(iii).

[111] Some of the distributed property can also come from A, of course, as long as there is also enough A voting stock used so that 80% or more of the former T shares are exchanged for A voting stock.

[112] Of course, any T shareholders who receive property other than A stock will be taxed in a redemption or distribution.

¶803.03

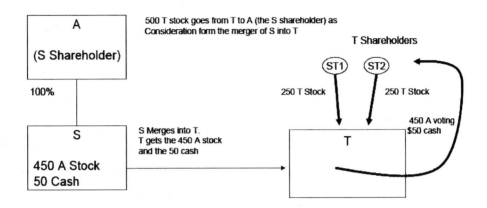

As a result of this transaction, the following occur: (1) S merges into T; (2) former T shareholders exchange a controlling interest in T (here, 450/500, or 90% of the T shares) for A voting stock; (3) T ends up owning substantially all of the assets it owned prior to the transaction; and (4) T ends up owning substantially all of the assets owned by S prior to the transaction, excluding any property put into S for the purpose of being paid out to the T shareholders for their T stock. The transaction qualifies under Code Sec. 368(a)(2)(E).

Assume instead that immediately prior to the transaction and as part of the plan of reorganization, T distributes to ST(1) 250 assets in redemption of ST(1)'s T stock. S has only $250 worth of A voting stock and no cash in it when it merges into T, and then ST(2) exchanges her 250 shares of T for the 250 A voting stock. The 250 shares redeemed prior to the merger are not considered in determining whether a controlling interest in T has been exchanged solely for A stock in the transaction, so that ST(2) has exchanged 250/250 shares of T for A voting stock. The assets distributed by T in the redemption are not taken into consideration in determining whether T retains substantially all of its assets, so that T is seen as retaining 100% of its assets. Again, the transaction qualifies under Code Sec. 368(a)(1)(E).

Assume further that in the above example, instead of containing only 250 worth of A voting stock, S's assets are 210 A voting stock and $40 cash, and the A voting stock and cash are transferred to ST(2) in exchange for her 250 T voting stock. In the exchange, 210/250 shares (84%) of T shares have been exchanged for A voting stock. Again, the transaction qualifies.

Assume instead that A acquired ST(1)'s 250 shares solely for A voting stock in a separate transaction eight years ago, so that in this transaction S has 250 A voting stock, S merges into T, and ST(2) exchanges her 250 shares for the A voting stock just acquired by T. Since only 50% of the T shares have been acquired in exchange for A voting stock in this transaction, it fails to meet the requirements of Code Sec. 368(a)(2)(E).

¶803.03

.04 Tax Consequences of Triangular Reorganizations

(a) Acquisitive Reorganizations Followed by a Drop Down

(i) T, and T Shareholders

Code Sec. 368(a)(2)(C) provides that acquisitive reorganizations will not be disqualified as reorganizations simply by reason of the fact that the property acquired by A is transferred to a subsidiary as part of the transaction. It does not, though, determine the tax consequences of that reorganization. In order to ensure that these transactions would not only qualify as reorganizations but would also be tax free to the parties involved, Congress did a bit more. As with any reorganization, the T shareholders tax consequences are determined by the application of Code Secs. 354 and 356. Those sections provide tax free treatment to persons who exchange stock of a corporation a party to a reorganization for stock of another corporation a party to a reorganization. In order to ensure that these provisions continued to apply to the T shareholders even if the T assets ended up in S rather than A, Code Sec 368 states that in an A, B, or C followed by a drop down, A, the corporation in control of the ultimate recipient of the T stock or assets, is a "party to the reorganization." As a result, the fact that T or its shareholders receive stock of A and do not receive stock of the ultimate recipient of their stock or property (S) has no impact on the tax consequences to the transferors of that stock or property.

As a result, if a transaction is structured as a linear reorganization followed by a drop down into A's subsidiary, the results to T and/or its shareholders are no different than those of a reorganization without the drop down. The T shareholders have exchanged stock of a party to the reorganization (A) for stock of another corporation a party to the reorganization, so that their gain, if any, is determined by Code Sec. 354 and 356 (if they also receive boot). Their basis is, as in any reorganization, governed by Code Sec. 358. For determining the tax results, if not the reorganization status of the transaction, A's transfer of the T stock or assets it acquired to S is taxed as a separate Code Sec. 351 exchange, and that entire exchange has no impact on T or its shareholders.

If the transaction is an asset acquisition, T, having exchanged property for stock of a party to a reorganization, is taxed (or not taxed, as is more likely the case) under Code Sec. 361 and its basis in the A stock is determined by Code Sec. 358.

(ii) S and A

The tax consequences to both A and S in any linear reorganization followed by a drop down of the T stock or assets to S are fairly straightforward. The first step is simply to determine the tax consequences of the linear reorganization for A. As discussed above,[113] A has acquired the T stock or assets for A stock (or perhaps some A stock and boot); and as is always the case, A recognizes no gain or loss on the sale or exchange of its own stock under Code Sec. 1032. If, as is rarely the case, A also transfers property other than cash in exchange for the T stock or assets, it

---

[113] *See* ¶ 803.01.

will recognize any realized gain or loss on that other property under Code Sec. 1001.

A's basis in the property it acquires (that is, the T stock or assets) is, as already explained, determined under Code Sec. 362. This basis, determined essentially the same as it is in any Code Sec. 351 exchange, is the same basis that the transferor had, increased by any gain recognized by the transferor on the exchange. The practical possibility of T or the T shareholders (in the case of B) recognizing any such gain, though, is essentially nil.[114]

The second step in determining the tax consequences for A and S is basically to treat the drop down as the Code Sec. 351 exchange that it is.[115] A recognizes no gain or loss on the receipt of S stock for property (and presumably nothing other than S stock is issued by S in this exchange). While it is possible that A can recognize gain on a Code Sec. 351 exchange not related to a reorganization under Code Sec. 357(c), if S assumes or takes property subject to liabilities[116] and the total liabilities assumed or taken subject to by S exceed the total basis of the assets transferred by A, Code Sec. 357(c) does not apply to acquisitive reorganizations. In addition, as discussed shortly, liabilities in excess of basis would not lead to any gain recognition by any of the parties if the transaction is structured as a direct triangular reorganization in which S simply uses A stock to acquire the T assets.[117] Perhaps in concession to the taxpayers available alternatives, the IRS has decided that it will not apply Code Sec. 357(c) even to those parts of an acquisitive reorganization (such as a drop down) to which Code Sec. 351 would apply.

A's basis in the S stock under Code Sec. 358 is the same as its basis was in the T stock or assets that A has just transferred to S, increased by any gain A recognizes on the exchange (presumably none), decreased by any boot received by A (of which there will likely be none) and also decreased (but not below zero) by any liabilities assumed or taken subject to by S.[118] If S is a pre-existing subsidiary of A and A receives additional stock in the drop down, A's basis in the newly issued stock does not change A's basis in the other stock A already owned. If, though, S was a pre-existing subsidiary of A and A does *not* receive any additional S stock in the dropdown, A's new additional basis is simply added to the basis of the shares of T that A already owns, and is allocated among those shares in accordance with their relative fair market value.

As is the case with any Code Sec. 351 exchange, S recognizes no gain or loss when it exchanges its own stock to A for property under Code Sec. 1032, and S's basis in the property it acquires from A (the T stock or assets) is the same as A's basis was in that property, increased by any gain recognized by A on the exchange, determined under Code Sec. 362.

---

[114] *See* ¶ 802.04(c).

[115] See discussion of Code Sec. 351 at ¶ 802.04(a).

[116] Other than liabilities that would be deductible if paid, Code Sec. 357(d). See discussion at ¶ 802.04(b).

[117] Treas. Reg. § 1.368-(c)(1)(ii).

[118] Code Sec. 358.

(b) Direct Triangular Reorganizations Using Stock of the Parent

Several thorny issues could (and used to) arise in direct triangular reorganizations, in which S used A stock to acquire the T stock or assets. Fortunately for almost everyone involved, those issues have been put to rest. The tax outcome, if not the way the IRS got there, is straightforward. In a triangular A (including a transaction qualifying under Code Sec. 368(a)(2)(D)), B, or C, all of the parties are essentially treated the same as they are in an A, B or C reorganization followed by a drop down. In other words, the tax consequences are the same whether the reorganization is done as a reorganization followed by a drop down or as a drop down followed by a reorganization.

(i) *T Shareholders*

Code Sec. 368(b) ensures the tax free status of triangular reorganizations using stock of the corporation controlling the acquiring corporation to T and to the T shareholders by including as parties to the reorganization not just the target and the acquiring corporation, but also the corporation that is in control of the acquiring corporation and whose stock is used to acquire the T assets or stock. Thus, both T (under Code Sec. 361, if it is an asset acquisition) and the T shareholders (under Code Secs. 354 and 356) treat A stock received from S the same way they would treat such stock from A if A were the acquiring corporation.

(ii) *S*

When the acquiring corporation uses its own stock to acquire T stock or assets in a reorganization, tax free status is guaranteed by Code Sec. 1032, which prevents a corporation from recognizing any gain or loss any time it transfers its own stock. When S transfers stock of A, rather than its own stock, to acquire T stock or assets, the exchange is not explicitly covered by Code Sec. 1032. It *is* explicitly covered, though, by the regulations. Treas. Reg. § 1.1032-2(b) provides that when S uses A stock in a triangular A, B or C, S's use of the A stock is treated as a disposition of shares of its own stock, thus ensuring the application of Code Sec. 1032 and tax free treatment to S.

(iii) *A*

A recognizes no gain on its transfer of A stock to S (or to anyone else, in any context) under Code Sec. 1032. The determination of A's basis in its S stock, though, is more interesting. If A transfers its own stock to S in exchange for S stock in the absence of a triangular reorganization, A's basis in its S stock would be, under Code Sec. 358, the same as A's basis was in the property S transferred to S. Since A would have no basis (or a basis of 0) in its own stock, it would take that same 0 basis in its S stock.

Treas. Reg. § 1.358-6(c) prevents this from happening whenever A's transfer of A stock to S is part of a triangular reorganization. That section provides that in a triangular C or in a triangular merger under Code Sec. 368(a)(2)(D), for purposes of determining A's basis in the S stock, A is treated as if (1) A had acquired the T assets (and assumed any T liabilities actually assumed by S) directly, and then (2) A transferred the T assets to S in a Code Sec. 351 exchange. A's basis in the T assets, determined under Code Sec. 362, would be the same as was T's basis, increased by any gain recognized by T on the exchange (there will be no such gain, however).[119]

A's basis in the S stock is thus the same basis that T had in own assets, reduced by any liabilities assumed by S in the exchange. The regulation also provides that in the event that the T liabilities assumed by S in the reorganization exceed T's basis in those assets, so that A is treated as transferring to S assets whose basis is exceeded by the liabilities assumed, A's basis in the S stock received will be 0, but A will recognize no gain under Code Sec. 357(c).[120]

In a triangular B, the same principals apply. A's basis in the S stock will be the same as was the former T shareholders basis in the T stock acquired in the reorganization, by way of a deemed transferred basis to A (from the T shareholders) under Code Sec. 362, followed by a deemed exchange basis in the S stock under Code Sec. 358.

If S is a pre-existing wholly owned subsidiary prior to the reorganization, A may transfer its own stock to S to facilitate the reorganization without actually receiving additional S stock in the exchange. In that event, A will simply increase its basis in the S stock it already owns by an amount equal to the basis it would have taken in newly issued S stock.[121]

(c) Reverse Triangular Merger

As is the case with other triangular reorganizations, the tax treatment of all of the parties to a reverse triangular merger is fairly straightforward. The T shareholders who exchange their T shares for A voting stock (and perhaps boot) have exchanged stock of a party to a reorganization for stock of another party to a reorganization, and are thus governed by Code Secs. 354 and 356.

T itself has engaged in two separate exchanges, both of which are tax free. As the acquiring corporation in the "merger," T is not taxed when it issues its own stock for the S assets, under Code Sec. 1032, and T takes as its basis in those assets whatever S's basis was in those assets. This may be significant if T retains some of those assets rather than distributing them to its shareholders.

When T immediately transfers the S assets to its shareholders in exchange for their T stock, T is exchanging property (the property it received from S, which is primarily, if not exclusively, A voting stock) for stock of a corporation a party to the reorganization (its own stock, which it acquires from its former shareholders) and is exempt from tax under both Code Sec. 354 and 361.[122]

---

[119] See ¶ 803.04(b).

[120] Code Sec. 357(c) provides that if a transferor is relieved of liabilities in excess of her asset basis in a Code Sec. 351 exchange, that excess debt relief will result in taxable gain to the transferor. Code Sec. 357(c) does not, by its terms, apply to acquisitive reorganizations. The IRS thus gives A the benefit of treating the drop down as part of the reorganization for purposes of Code Sec. 357(c) without giving A the zero basis in S stock that it might have argued for had it treated the transaction as a drop down followed by a reorganization instead of the other way around.

[121] Treas. Reg. § 1.368-6(c)(1) discusses "adjustments" to A's basis in S stock. If none was outstanding earlier, the adjustments are simply made from a starting point of 0.

[122] Code Sec. 354 would appear to apply because T is transferring A stock to its shareholders in exchange for T stock. Code Sec. 361 would appear to apply because T is distributing "qualified property" (the A stock) to its shareholders. In any event, T is not taxed.

The regulations provide that A's basis in the T stock it acquires in the reorganization is determined as if (1) T had merged into A, and then (2) A had transferred the T assets in a Code Sec. 351 exchange to T.[123] In other words, A's basis in the T stock will be the same as if the transaction had been a forward triangular merger.[124]

While the regulations provide that A's basis in T stock acquired in a reverse triangular merger is determined in a manner consistent with forward triangular reorganizations under Code Sec. 368(a)(2)(D), it is worth pointing out that a reorganization under Code Sec. 368(a)(2)(E) is actually a *stock* acquisition rather than an *asset* acquisition; but A's basis in the T stock is determined as if the transaction were an asset acquisition–that is, A's stock basis in the T stock is the same as T's basis was in its *assets* (adjusted if there were liabilities assumed), and bears no relationship to what the T shareholders' basis was in the T stock acquired by A. The regulations enable A to take a basis in its T stock determined by reference to the former T shareholders' basis in their stock rather than by reference to T's asset basis only if the transaction also qualifies as a B reorganization. In turn, a Code Sec. 368(a)(2)(E) transaction can qualify as a B reorganization only so long as the former T shareholders receive no boot.

> *Example:* In order to see all of the above rules at work, assume that T owns 100 assets, each with a basis and value of $1, and that T has $20 of liabilities. ST owns all of the T stock, worth $80 (basis $40). A forms S by transferring to S A voting stock worth $80. S acquires all of the T assets, subject to the $20 liabilities, in exchange for the 80 A voting stock, in a triangular C reorganization, and T liquidates, distributing the A voting stock to ST in exchange for ST's T stock.

> As in any acquisitive reorganization, ST is governed by Code Sec. 354 (and Code Sec. 356 if ST received boot). In this case, ST receives only stock of another corporation a party to a reorganization, so ST recognizes no gain under Code Sec. 354. ST's basis in the A stock is $40, the same as her basis was in the T stock, under Code Sec. 358. T recognizes no gain or loss on the exchange of its assets for the A stock, under Code Sec. 361(a), and recognizes no gain or loss on the distribution of the A stock to its shareholders under Code Sec. 361(c).

> A and S are both treated as if A acquired the T assets and liabilities in a C reorganization and then transferred those assets and liabilities to S in exchange for the S stock. A recognizes no gain or loss when it acquires the T assets solely for A stock, under Code Sec. 1032. A's basis in the T assets is the same as T's basis was in those assets under Code Sec. 362(b). On the deemed transfer of the T assets from A to S, A recognizes no gain or loss under Code Sec. 351. A's basis in the S stock, under Code Sec. 358, is the same as its basis was in the T assets ($100) reduced by the former T debt now assumed by S

---

[123] Treas. Reg. § 1.358-6(c)(2).

[124] If A acquires less than all of the T stock in the reorganization, A's basis will be only an equivalent percentage of what it otherwise would be. For example, If A acquires 90% of the T stock in a reverse triangular merger, A's basis in the T stock will be 90% of what it would be if A had acquired 100% of the T stock. Treas. Reg. § 1.358-(6)(c)(2)(B).

($20), leaving A with a stock basis of $80. S recognizes no gain or loss under Code Sec. 1032, and takes a basis in the T assets equal to that of A, which in turn was the same as that of T in those assets ($100), under Code Sec. 362.

If in the above example the reorganization had been a reverse triangular merger rather than a triangular C, the results would have nonetheless been the same as those of the triangular C for all parties, including A and S.

¶ 804 Additional Corporate Actions in Conjunction with Reorganizations

Virtually any triangular reorganization involves the combination of at least two exchanges. The regulations permit the corporations involved to engage in many more exchanges as part of the plan of reorganization without threatening the qualification of the reorganization itself.

.01 Full or Partial Drop Downs

First, the IRS has gone well beyond endorsing an acquisitive reorganization followed by a single drop down of the acquired property (T stock or assets) to a subsidiary. The regulations essentially allow the acquiring corporation to transfer the assets or stock acquired in a reorganization to any member of its "qualified group" without risking the qualification of the reorganization.

Treas Reg. § 1.368-1(d)(4) defines a qualified group, for purposes of reorganizations, as one or more chains of corporations so long as the issuing corporation is in control[125] of at least one subsidiary, and the issuing corporation together with one or more of its subsidiaries or group members is in control of each of the other corporations. This requirement is similar to the definition of an affiliated group.[126] The example of a qualified group used throughout many of the examples in the regulations is shown below.

---

[125] Control for this purpose is defined by Code Sec. 368(c) as 80% by vote and 80% by value of each class of nonvoting stock).

[126] Code Sec. 1504.

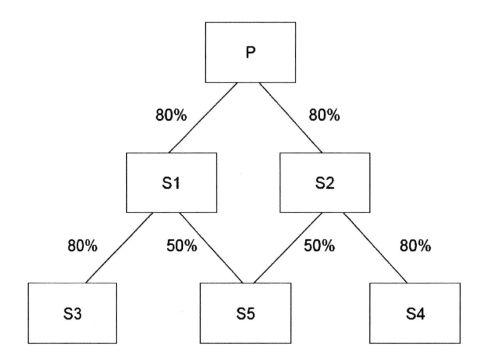

Using this example of a qualified group, the regulations make clear that if P acquires T stock or assets in what would otherwise qualify as an A, B, C, P can transfer (by way of a Code Sec. 351 transaction, contribution to capital, or a sale) some or all of the stock or assets (or both) that it acquires to any of S1 through S5, and whichever S acquires the assets or stock from P can in turn transfer some or all of that stock or assets to any other of the S's. The only limitations on any of these transfers are that (1) the acquiring corporation cannot terminate its corporate existence, and in the case of a stock acquisition, the target cannot terminate its corporate existence, and (2) the corporations involved must remain part of the qualified group.[127]

Similarly, if S acquires T stock or assets in a triangular reorganization, S can transfer some or all of what it acquires to any one or more members of the qualified group without disqualifying the reorganization. In addition, A can transfer some or all of the S stock or assets to one or more members of the qualified group. Again, the only limitations on these transfers are that A, T, and S (where S is the acquiring corporation) retain their corporate existence[128] and remain a part of the qualified group.

---

[127] Treas. Reg. § 1.368-2(k)(1)(ii).

[128] Of course, in a reverse triangular merger in which S is merged into T, S is not required to maintain its corporate existence.

¶804.01

Thus, not only can there be multiple drop downs of the acquired stock or assets, but such stock or assets can be divided among several different corporations (so long as they are members of the qualified group). The regulations also make it clear that the division of the acquired assets among several members of the qualified group will also not raise continuity of business enterprise issues. Treas. Reg. § 1.368-1(d)(4)(i) simply states that the issuing corporation (that is, the corporation whose stock is used to acquire the assets or stock) shall be treated as holding all of the assets and all of the businesses of all the members of its qualified group.

The acquiring corporation's ability to divide the targets assets is not limited only to reorganizations that are asset acquisitions. If the original reorganization was a stock acquisition, the acquiring corporation can nonetheless distribute some of the assets of that controlled corporation. All that the regulations require to ensure that the original acquisitive reorganization is not disqualified is that T not terminate its corporate existence and that whatever is left of T remain part of the qualified group of corporations.

If any of these intragroup transfers take place in conjunction with a qualified reorganization, the fact that they may be part of the plan of reorganization does not necessarily make them tax free (especially if the transfer takes place by way of sale). Instead, it simply allows them to take place without disqualifying the reorganization. Each of the transfers will be treated and taxed as transactions separate from the reorganization, usually tax free under Code Sec. 351 and its accompanying sections.

.02 Distributions of Acquired Stock or Assets

In addition to allowing a corporation to drop down the assets or stock it acquired in a reorganization, the regulations also allow the acquiring corporation to distribute up to its shareholders the stock or assets acquired in the reorganization. If the reorganization was a stock acquisition (either a B or an (a)(2)(E)), the acquiring corporation (either A in a linear reorganization or a reverse triangular merger, or S in a triangular A, B or (a)(2)(D)) can distribute to its shareholders T stock so long as T remains a member of the qualified group. Whether the original reorganization was a stock acquisition or an asset acquisition, the acquiring corporation can distribute to its shareholders some of either its own assets or assets of the acquired target, so long as the distribution does not result in the liquidation of the distributing corporation.

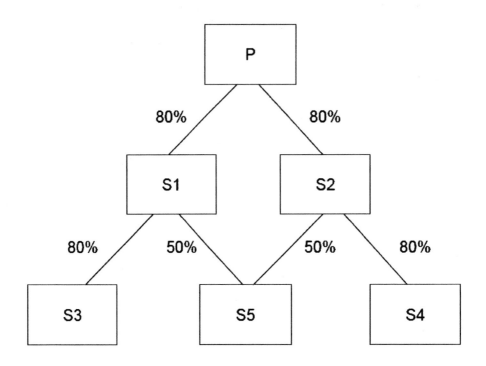

To see how this works, let us return to the qualified group of corporations used in the regulations, and again pictured, above. If P acquires the T assets in an A or a C, P can transfer those assets however it wishes among the entire qualified group. Similarly, if P acquires the T stock in a B or in an (a)(2)(E), it can transfer the T stock however it wishes among the members of the qualified group. In addition, if P acquires the T stock, it can have T distribute assets to P that P can distribute among members of the qualified group, so long as T retains enough assets to maintain its corporate existence.

If, instead, S1 acquired the T assets using T stock (or by way of a drop down from P), it can distribute those assets (as well as its own) among all members of the group (including P) in any way it sees fit, so long as S1 is not liquidated. Similarly, if S1 acquired the T stock using A voting stock in a triangular B or in a reverse triangular merger, S1 can transfer the T stock or the T assets in any way it sees fit among all members of the group, including P, so long as S is not liquidated. S1 can also have T distribute assets that S1 can then transfer to any other group members so long as T is not liquidated.

Again, none of these subsequent transfers will disqualify the initial reorganization. Instead, each will be treated as a separate transaction and will be taxed (or exempted from tax) under separate tax provisions that govern the transfer.

¶804.02

.03 Liquidating Transfers: Step Transaction Doctrine Can Apply

One limitation on these transactions is that the initial reorganization is not protected by these regulations if either T (in the case of a stock acquisition) or S (in the case of a triangular reorganization) is liquidated. If this occurs as part of the original transaction, though, it is likely that the transaction will nonetheless qualify as a reorganization, albeit not the one it initially appeared to be.

To see the impact of distributions that are part of the reorganization transaction and that terminate a corporation's existence in what would otherwise have been a qualified stock acquisition, assume that A acquires all of the T stock for A voting stock, and that A liquidates T as part of the transaction. As discussed earlier,[129] this transaction will not qualify as a B, because A ends up with all of the T assets. It will, though, qualify as a C,[130] or as an A if done under a qualifying state merger law. The result is that, unlike in a B, A can use some boot in addition to A voting stock.

Assume instead that the original exchange looked like a reverse triangular merger rather than a B reorganization. In that case, A forms S, using A voting stock. S merges into T, A receives T stock, and all of the former T shareholders exchange their T stock for the A voting stock that was acquired by T when S merged into T. Assume that as part of the same transaction, T merges into A (which had just become the owner of all of the T stock). While this exchange will not qualify as a reverse triangular merger, because T's corporate existence is not continued, it will nonetheless qualify as an A reorganization. As part of the single transaction, A has acquired the T assets by way of T's merger into A, and the T shareholders have received sufficient A stock to meet the continuity of interest requirements.[131]

¶ 805 Acquisitive D Reorganizations

As discussed later,[132] D reorganizations are typically divisive rather than acquisitive. Largely as the result of historical accident, though, a D reorganization can, in very limited circumstances, be acquisitive. This can occur only if, as part of the transaction: (1) A acquires substantially all of the assets of T;[133] (2) T then distributes all of its assets, including the consideration it just received from A, to its shareholders;[134] and (3) immediately after the exchange, the T shareholders own at least 50% (by vote and value) of the A stock.[135]

Typically, in order for the shareholders of T to be in control of A immediately *after* the exchange, either the T shareholders must have also been in control of A *before* the exchange, or T must have acquired enough stock of A in the exchange to gain control of A. Thus, there are only two scenarios in which an acquisitive D reorganization is possible.

---

[129] *See* ¶ 802.03.

[130] Rev. Rul. 67-274, 1967-2 C.B. 141.

[131] Rev. Rul. 2001-46, 2001-2 C.B. 321.

[132] *See* ¶ 903.04(d).

[133] Code Sec. 354(b)(1)(A).

[134] Code Secs. 368(a)(1)(D), 354(b)(1)(B).

[135] Code Secs. 368(a)(1)(D) and 368(a)(2)(H).

To see the first of these, assume that SH owns all of the stock of both A and T (SH must have at least 50% of the stock of each corporation, by vote and value, to qualify). A acquires substantially all of the T assets for a mixture of A stock and boot, and then T liquidates, distributing to SH the A stock and boot just received, as well as any other assets it may have. The result is that instead of owning two corporations, A and T, SH now owns a single corporation (A) that has all the assets previously in the two separate corporations.

Note that A's acquisition of substantially all of the T assets for A stock and boot might well have qualified as a Code Sec. 351 exchange (if the T shareholders have 80% control of A immediately after the exchange, as they do in this example). Because this qualifies as a reorganization and not just a Code Sec. 351 exchange, though, not only the transfer of assets to A, but also the distribution by T of the A stock[136] and the exchange by the T shareholders of their T stock for A stock[137] are also part of the tax free transaction.

In addition, note that T's transfer of assets to A for A stock and boot might have qualified as a C reorganization (because A has acquired substantially all of the T assets) if enough of the consideration from A was A voting stock. Because this transaction qualifies as a D reorganization, however, the requirement that A voting stock be used and the limitations on boot imposed in C reorganizations do not apply.

Finally, the transfer by T of substantially all its assets to A for A stock and the liquidation of T (which transfers all its assets to ST) might have qualified as a merger of T into A (if it was a merger under applicable state law and if enough (about 40%) of the consideration for the T assets was A stock to ensure continuity of shareholder interest). Because it qualifies as a D reorganization, though, the continuity of interest limitations do not apply, so that even less than 40 A stock can be used.

To see the other way that an acquisitive D reorganization might take place, assume that T is an existing corporation, that T forms a new subsidiary (A), transfers all its assets to A in exchange for A stock and boot, and then T liquidates and distributes the A stock and boot to the T shareholders. Essentially, A has become the new T. While this transaction has met all the requirements of an acquisitive D, it may also qualify as an F reorganization.[138] If so, it will be treated as an F and not as a D.[139]

---

[136] Code Sec. 361(c).
[137] Code Sec. 354.

[138] *See* ¶ 903.03.
[139] Rev. Rul. 57-276, 1957-1 C.B. 126.

Chapter 9

Related Corporations

There are various degrees of relationship between and among corporations. Broadly speaking, there are three tranches operative in the tax laws: (1) Corporation A owns some stock in Corporation B, but not over 50%, (2) Corporation A owns over 50% but less than 80% of the stock in Corporation B, and (3) Corporation A owns 80% or more of the stock of Corporation B. All three tranches trigger particular Code provisions, sometimes conferring benefits and sometimes imposing limitations. For example, the Code Sec. 243 dividends received exclusion/deduction is engaged by stock ownership under 50%.[1]

Unsurprisingly, higher levels of ownership trigger additional special rules. Thus, for example, over 50% stock ownership (along with satisfaction of some additional requirements) can trigger the Subpart F anti-deferral rules with respect to controlled foreign corporations.[2] At 80% ownership, nonrecognition sections often come into play.[3]

This chapter is concerned with the two higher tranches of control. It examines major tax rules, not addressed elsewhere, that operate when corporations are related at high levels of ownership or other control.

This chapter addresses four such sets of rules: (1) Code Secs. 1551 to 1563, requiring sharing of rate brackets and other tax characteristics among commonly owned corporations, (2) Code Sec. 482, authorizing the IRS to patrol transfer pricing among commonly controlled corporations, (3) Code Secs. 269 and 381 through 384, dealing with ownership and survival of tax attributes when corporations come under different control, and (4) Code Secs. 1501 to 1504, authorizing the filing of consolidated returns by affiliated corporations.

¶ 901 Limitations on Multiple Benefits: Code Secs. 1551 to 1563

Congress recognized that the same person(s) sometimes own multiple corporations. There can be good business reasons – such as reducing exposure of assets

---

[1] For discussion of Code Sec. 243, see Chapter 3.

[2] *See* Code Sec. 957(a). The Subpart F rules are beyond the scope of this book.

[3] *e.g.*, Code Sec. 351 (discussed in Chapter 2), Code Sec. 337 (discussed in Chapter 7) & Code Sec. 354 (discussed in Chapter 9).

to potential liabilities, facilitating estate planning, or cabining the reach of burdensome governmental regulations or contractual provisions – for fractioning business and assets among multiple corporations rather than concentrating them in a single corporation. But this same approach could lead to tax abuse: multiple runs up the Code Sec. 11(b) brackets and multiple utilizations of tax reduction opportunities available under the Code. Congress responded to the possibility of abuse by enacting Code Sec. 1551 and later Code Sec. 1561.[4]

.01 Code Sec. 1551

Code Sec. 1551 has been with us since the 1939 Code. Below, we consider first the predicates to application of the section, then the consequences of its application.

(a) Predicates

Code Sec. 1551 is a mix of objective and subjective aspects. Specifically, the section is triggered if the following elements are present:

- Property (other than cash) is transferred directly or indirectly,
- The transfer is made by a corporation or by five or fewer shareholders who are in control of the corporation,
- The transfer is made to a controlled subsidiary or to a sister corporation,
- The transferee corporation was created in order to receive the transfer or it is not actively engaged in a trade or business, and
- A major purpose of the transfer is to receive the benefits of the graduated Code Sec. 11(b) rates or to receive the credit available with respect to the accumulated earnings tax.[5]

Example 1: Tathlum Corporation owns two office buildings, renting out office space in them. Both buildings are profitable. Later, Tathlum forms a wholly owned subsidiary, Songhay Corporation, and transfers one of the two office buildings to Songhay. If the purposes elements are met, Code Sec. 1551 applies.

Example 2: Same facts as in Example 1, except that Tathlum does not transfer an office building to Songhay when Songhay is organized. Instead, Tathlum transfers cash to Songhay and Songhay uses that cash to buy one of the office buildings from Tahtlum. If the purposes elements are met, Code Sec. 1551 still applies. The section covers indirect transfers as well as direct transfers.[6]

Control for Code Sec. 1551 purposes means ownership of stock representing 80% or more of the voting power or the value of the transferee corporation.[7] When the "five or fewer shareholders" aspect applies, those shareholders must own stock possessing 80% or more of the voting power or value and possessing over 50% of the voting power or value when there is taken into account each person's stock

---

[4] Several other sections act similarly to Code Secs. 1551 and 1561 although in more limited contexts. For example, Code Sec. 179(d)(6) treats all members of a controlled group as one taxpayer for purposes of the cap on expensing under Code Sec. 179.

[5] Code Sec. 1551(a).

[6] Code Sec. 1551(a)(2); *see also* Treas. Reg. § 1.1551-1(g)(2) & (g)(4) (Example 3).

[7] Code Sec. 1551(b)(1).

ownership only to the extent the ownership is identical as to each of the corporations.[8] In determining stock ownership, the constructive ownership rules of Code Sec. 1563(e) apply.[9]

The last of the above elements has spawned the greatest degree of controversy.[10] The burden of proof is on the transferee corporation – and at a heightened standard: the section applies unless the transferee shows "by the clear preponderance of the evidence" that securing tax benefits "was not a major purpose of [the] transfer."[11] A "major purpose" is a lower standard than a "principal purpose." For example, a major purpose is present if tax avoidance is one of two approximately equal purposes.[12]

> **Practice Tip:** Taxpayers who are unsure whether Code Sec. 1551 may apply to them might consider seeking a private letter ruling from the IRS. Each year the IRS issues a revenue procedure setting out its current policy as to issuing letter rulings on whether transfers are within Code Sec. 1551.

(b) Consequences

When the predicates are satisfied and Code Sec. 1551 applies, the section gives the IRS the authority to disallow to the transferee corporation either or both of two tax benefits: (1) the Code Sec. 11(b) tax brackets lower than the highest bracket or (2) the credit for purposes of the accumulated earnings tax created by Code Sec. 535(c).[13]

.02 Code Sec. 1561

Despite the fact that taxpayers bear a substantial burden of proof as to purpose, the fact that Code Sec. 1551 contains purpose requirements has been perceived as a problem with the section, resulting in uncertainty in application. Instead of amending Code Sec. 1551, Congress left it in place and added Code Sec. 1561.

(a) Predicate

Code Sec. 1561 contains no purpose element. It applies with respect to "component members of a controlled group of corporations."[14] The key to the section is definition of this "controlled group" concept. Code Sec. 1563 sets out intricate definitional rules.

Code Sec. 1563 defines a "controlled group of corporations" to include both parent-subsidiary and brother-sister groups.[15] A parent-subsidiary group has a common parent (a corporation which owns 80% of the stock, by value or voting power, of another corporation) and includes corporations that are connected to the

---

[8] Code Sec. 1551(b)(2).

[9] Code Sec. 1551(b).

[10] Among cases testing this element, see *Massey's Auto Body Shop, Inc. v. Comm'r*, T.C. Memo. 1979-414; *Coastal Oil Storage Co. v. Comm'r*, 25 T.C. 1304 (1956), *aff'd as to this issue*, 242 F.2d 396 (3d Cir. 1957).

[11] Code Sec. 1551(a).

[12] *See* Treas. Reg. § 1.1551-1(h) (tax avoidance can be a major purpose even if a valid business purpose also exists but does not predominate).

[13] Code Sec. 1551(a).

[14] Code Sec. 1561(a).

[15] As well as combined groups partaking of both types of groups. Code Sec. 1563(a)(3).

common parent and are at least 80% owned by one or more of the other corporations in the group.[16]

A brother-sister group consists of two or more corporations when five or fewer individuals, trusts, or estates own over 50% (by value or voting power) of the stock of each corporation, "taking into account the stock ownership of each such person only to the extent such stock ownership is identical with respect to each such corporation."[17] Attribution rules (similar, but not identical, to those in Code Sec. 318) apply.[18]

(b) Consequences

Corporations that are component members of a controlled group of corporations in effect must share several tax attributes or opportunities. Specifically, such corporations are limited to:

- amounts in each Code Sec. 11(b) bracket that do not aggregate to more than the maximum in each bracket to which a single corporation would be entitled,
- a single credit pursuant to Code Sec. 535(c) for purposes of the accumulated earnings tax, and
- a single exemption for minimum tax purposes.[19]

> *Practice Tip:* For the most part, Code Secs. 1551 and 1561 overlap as to the Code Sec. 11 brackets. In such cases, the IRS tends to emphasize Code Sec. 1561, presumably because it is not clouded by purposes elements. Litigated Code Sec. 1551 cases have been rare in recent years.

> *Practice Tip:* The fact that the Code squelches multiple runs up the rate brackets removes one tax incentive for use of multiple corporations. Others remain, however. For example, having multiple corporations owning different assets and conducting different businesses may allow more precisely tailored use of the numerous elections permitted by the Code. Similarly, a single enterprise might be too large to allow stock in it to qualify for Code Sec. 1244 treatment,[20] a problem that might be solved by splintering the enterprise into multiple corporations. There can be nontax benefits as well, such as facilitating estate planning and minimizing the effects of labor unrest. Thus, numerous advantages and disadvantages must be considered in deciding how many corporations to create and use.

¶ 902 Transfer Pricing: Code Sec. 482

This part examines five topics as to Code Sec. 482: (1) the need for the section, (2) the predicates to application of the section, (3) the reach of the section, that is, what kinds of adjustments the IRS may and may not make under Code Sec. 482, (4) specific types of transactions, and (5) administrative aspects as to Code Sec. 482.

---

[16] Code Sec. 1563(a)(1).

[17] Code Sec. 1563(a)(3).

[18] Code Sec. 1563(d) & (e).

[19] Code Sec. 1561(a). Code Sec. 1561(b) provides special rules for short tax years.

[20] See Code Sec. 1244(c)(1)(A) & (3)(A) (limiting the permissible size of small business corporations). Code Sec. 1244, when it applies, allows certain losses on small business stock to be treated as ordinary, not capital, in character.

.01 Need for Code Sec. 482

When transactions occur between parties that are unrelated, are dealing at arm's length, and have adverse tax interests, the law typically assumes that the terms of the transactions will reasonably correspond to economic reality. Accordingly, such transactions usually need little scrutiny from the IRS.

No such sanguine assumption can be made when taxpayers are related. Such parties can be largely indifferent to economic allocations between themselves. In this environment, the possibility of collusive and abusive tax reduction schemes is ever present.

Example: Hiro Agaki owns all of the stock of both Corporation A and Corporation B. A is in a high bracket; B is in a low bracket. B performs services for A, the fair market value of which is $50. Were A and B unrelated and dealing at arm's length, B would charge $50. B would take the $50 into income, and A would take a $50 Code Sec. 162 deduction.

But A and B are not unrelated. Thus, in the absence of an effective tax anti-abuse rule, there would be a temptation to price the transaction differently in order to save taxes. Instead of $50, B might charge $500 (or $5,000) for the services. If this overvaluation is not corrected, the effect will be to shift $450 (or $4,950) from a high tax bracket to a low bracket. In essence, Hiro would be shifting money from his right pocket to his left pocket – but saving money in the process.

The temptation to mis-price transactions in order to reduce tax would exist if the related corporations are domestic entities which happen to be in different brackets because, for example, of different levels of profitability in the current year or because one of the corporations has substantial net operating loss carryovers. The temptation also would exist when one of the related corporations is a domestic entity and the other is a foreign entity, especially if the country in which the foreign entity operates imposes no taxes or lower-than-U.S. taxes on the type of income involved.

Example: A group of investors owns two companies, one in Brazil and the other in the United States. Between them, the companies profitably produce and sell orange juice. The Brazilian company owns orange groves in Brazil. It picks and squeezes the oranges, sells the product to the U.S. company, and ships the juice to the United States. The U.S. company markets the orange juice in the U.S.

The cost of the Brazilian activities is $1 million. The cost of the U.S. activities is $500,000, and the U.S. company sells the product for $3.5 million. Thus, there is a total of $2 million of profit from the operations taken as a whole. This $2 million should be appropriately divided between the two companies and then taxed by Brazil and the United States.

Not wanting to pay tax, however, the investors create a third company, this one sited in the Netherlands Antilles, a tax haven that imposes no tax on business profits. The Brazilian corporation sells the juice to the Netherlands Antilles corporation for $1 million. Then the Netherlands Antilles corporation

¶902.01

sells the juice to the U.S. Corporation for $3 million. If this scheme succeeds for tax purposes, all $2 million of profits has been removed from taxation.

These examples show that possible related party abuses can involve either domestic companies or foreign companies. Reflecting the growing importance of international trade and the significance of multi-national corporations and corporate groups, the IRS has made greater use of Code Sec. 482 in recent decades and that use has been more in the international context than in the purely domestic context.[21]

If it had nothing else, the IRS might attempt to attack such arrangements through "substance over form" and other judicial doctrines.[22] However, such doctrines are too uncertain in their application to be fully satisfactory. Accordingly, Congress felt it necessary to give the IRS considerable authority to re-price and otherwise recast transactions for federal tax purposes. Code Sec. 482 is the vehicle by which Congress did so.

> ***Practice Tip:*** The federal government is not the only level that needs to protect its tax base against erosion by abusive related-party transactions. The states do also. Since most state income taxes piggyback onto the federal income tax, states can get the benefit of Code Sec. 482 adjustments made by the IRS. In addition, most states, by statute, confer upon their own tax authorities broad powers to make 482-like adjustments.[23] Thus, related parties engaged in transactions between themselves need to take into account possible state-level adjustments as well as possible federal-level Code Sec. 482 adjustments.

.02 Predicates to Application of Code Sec. 482

Unlike most sections of the Code, Code Sec. 482 is reasonably short. It contains no subsections and only two sentences. The second sentence is important but narrow, establishing a valuation rule as to transfers and licenses of certain intangible property.

The first sentence is of more general significance. If three predicates are satisfied, the first sentence of Code Sec. 482 grants the IRS authority to "distribute, apportion, or allocate gross income, deductions, credits, or allowances between or among [related businesses]." The three predicates are: (1) transactions occur between or among "two or more organizations trades, or businesses," (2) these businesses are "owned or controlled directly or indirectly by the same interests," and (3) the IRS determines that the reallocation "is necessary in order to prevent evasion of taxes or clearly to reflect the incomes of [the businesses]." These predicates are developed below.

---

[21] A recent report contained case studies of six United States multinational corporations. It found that the corporations had an effective tax rate on their worldwide income of less than 25% during at least one multiyear period after 1999. Joint Comm. on Tax'n, Present Law and Background Related to Possible Income Shifting and Transfer Pricing (July 20, 2010) (JCX-37-10). Studies such as these add political weight to the imperative of effective administration of Code Sec. 482.

[22] These judicial doctrines are discussed in Chapter 3.

[23] For discussion of some of these state correspondents of Code Sec. 482, *see* Scott L. Brandman, Philip W. Carmichael, Kendall L. Houghton & Maryann H. Luongo, *Limitations on State Transfer Pricing Adjustments*, State Tax Notes, Dec. 14, 2010, p. 771; John D. Snethen & Katherine Erbeznik, *Playing "the Price Is Right" with State Transfer Pricing Studies*, State Tax Notes, Jan. 3, 2011, p. 23.

(a) Two or More Organizations

The statutory language is broad. Code Sec. 482 is most often applied to corporations, but other types of entities – such as partnerships and limited liability companies – also are within the section's ambit.[24]

Indeed, there need not even be a formally organized entity. A Schedule C sole proprietorship constitutes a "trade or business," so can be within Code Sec. 482. However, an individual conducting economic activities that do not rise to the level of a trade or business is outside Code Sec. 482.

> *Example 1:* Jane owns all of the stock of J Co. Inc. She also conducts a separate business as a Schedule C sole proprietor. Jane makes a loan to J. Co. The amount is paid by a check drawn on the bank account of the sole proprietorship, and Jane reports the interest received from J Co. on the Schedule C attached to her return. The loan bears an interest rate well above the commercially reasonable rate, which allows J Co. to claim larger interest deductions. If the loan is treated as coming from the Schedule C activity, the "two or more organizations, trades, or businesses" predicate is satisfied.

> *Example 2:* The same facts as in Example 1 except that the loan is paid from Jane's personal bank account, not from her sole proprietorship's bank account, and she reports the interest income on line 8a of her Form 1040, not on the Schedule C accompanying the Form 1040. If the loan is treated as coming from Jane personally, not from the Schedule C activity, the "two or more organizations, trades, or businesses" predicate is not satisfied. Being a shareholder is an investment function, and investment does not constitute a trade or business.[25]

(b) Common Ownership or Control

This is the predicate that has produced the greatest volume of authority. The regulations define control broadly as "any kind of control, direct or indirect, whether legally enforceable, and however exercisable or exercised . . . . It is the reality of the control that is decisive, not its form or the mode of exercise."[26]

> *Example:* Two corporations each owned exactly 50% of the stock of a third corporation. Thus, neither was in control by itself. The two shareholder corporations, however, acted in concert. The reality of this practical cooperation trumps the theoretical possibility of shareholder deadlock. Accordingly, the "common control" requirement was held to be met.[27]

"A presumption of control arises if income or deductions have been arbitrarily shifted."[28] Control is assessed as of the time the transactions are

---

[24] *See* Treas. Reg. § 1.482-1(i)(1) (Code Sec. 482 may apply whether or not the organizations are incorporated, whether or not they are members of the same affiliated group, and whether they are domestic or foreign).

[25] *e.g., Higgins v. Comm'r,* 312 U.S. 212 (1941).

[26] Treas. Reg. § 1.482-1(i)(4).

[27] *B. Forman Co. v. Comm'r,* 453 F.2d 1144 (2d Cir.), *cert. denied,* 407 U.S. 934 (1972); *see also* Treas. Reg. § 1.482-1(i)(4) (stating that control can exist when two or more unrelated taxpayers act in concert or with a common purpose).

[28] Treas. Reg. § 1.482-1(i)(4).

¶902.02(b)

planned, and the requirement can be met even if control no longer exists when, later, the transactions were actually completed.[29]

(c) Clear Reflection of Income

The third predicate is that the IRS "determines that [recasting the transaction] is necessary in order to prevent evasion of taxes or clearly to reflect the income of any of [the]organizations, trades, or businesses." Three aspects of this predicate are noteworthy:

    (1) The statutory language is in the disjunctive. Thus, the element is met if the recharacterization is needed to prevent tax evasion or if it is needed to clearly reflect income. "Evasion" probably is better understood in this context as "avoidance," which has a less pejorative connotation. The second aspect (clear reflection of income) is easier to establish than the first aspect (prevent evasion or avoidance) because the second aspect is purely objective while the first aspect includes a subjective component. Accordingly, the IRS typically argues Code Sec. 482 cases in terms of clear reflection of income. As a result, arguments by taxpayers that they were animated by business purposes, not by tax reduction objectives, are irrelevant.

    (2) The predicate is satisfied if the way the transaction was priced or structured distorts the income of even one of the organizations, trades, or businesses. It need not be shown that the taxable incomes of all of the involved organizations were distorted or even that, taking them all together, there was an "on net" distortion.

    (3) The language "if [the IRS] determines" is procedurally significant. The courts have held that the presence of such language heightens the burden of the taxpayer contesting the IRS's Code Sec. 482 adjustment. Normally, in civil tax litigation, the burden of proof is on the taxpayer and the standard of proof is "preponderance of the evidence," that is, any disturbance in the taxpayer's favor, no matter how slight, of evidentiary equipoise. The presence of the "if [the IRS] determines" language, the courts have held, raises the standard of proof to "abuse of discretion," which is a higher standard than mere preponderance.[30]

Moreover, to satisfy this heightened burden, taxpayer must do more than attack the methodology used by the IRS in making the adjustment. The taxpayer must establish a result superior to that reached by the IRS.[31]

.03 Arm's Length Standard

The goal of Code Sec. 482 is to clearly reflect income, and the arm's length standard is the mechanism by which that goal is to be accomplished. "In determining the true taxable income of a controlled taxpayer, the standard to be applied in

---

[29] *DHL Corp. v. Comm'r*, 285 F.3d 1210 (8th Cir. 2002).

[30] *e.g., American Terrazzo Strip Co. v. Comm'r*, 56 T.C. 961 (1971).

[31] *e.g., E.I. duPont de Nemours & Co. v. United States*, 608 F. 2d 445, 454-55 (Ct. Cl. 1979), *cert. denied*, 445 U.S. 962 (1980); *Perkin-Elmer Corp. v. Comm'r*, 66 T.C.M. 634 (1993).

every case is that of a taxpayer dealing at arm's length with an uncontrolled taxpayer."[32]

The Holy Grail in Code Sec. 482 analysis is the comparable, that is, an actual price charged in a similar transaction between unrelated taxpayers.[33] There are two phases of the search: finding the best method and making appropriate adjustments.

(a) Method

There are various lenses through which one can look in attempting to find a good comparable. These lenses are the various methods. Leading method described in regulations are identified in the following section.

In many situations, the former regulations prescribed ordering. That is, method A was used if feasible; if not, method B was used; if feasible; etc. That approach has yielded to a "best method" approach under the current regulations. "The arm's length result of a controlled transaction must be determined under that method that, under the facts and circumstances, provides the most reliable measure of an arm's length result. Thus, there is no strict priority of methods, and no method will invariably be considered to be more reliable than others."[34]

The principal considerations that determine which method is best are the extent to which the controlled transaction and the uncontrolled transaction are comparable, the quality of the available data, and the reliability of the assumptions used.[35] Plainly, such matters are not determinable with scientific precision. Consequently, which method to apply is often highly controversial.

(b) Adjustments

Even the best comparable will diverge, to greater or lesser degree, from the transaction under examination. Adjustments (increases or decreases of price) must be made to reflect such differences.

The regulations identify differences that may warrant adjustments and give examples of their application.[36] The identified items are:

- *Functions*: the economic activities carried out in the transaction under scrutiny and the comparable, as well as the resources applied in them.

- *Contract terms*: differences between the contracts in the two transactions, such as the type of consideration, sale levels, contract length, modification rights, nature of warranties, associated transactions, payment terms, and nature of continuing business relations.

- *Risks*: including financial risks, credit risks, collection risks, product liability risks, market risks, R&D risks, and general business risks.

---

[32] Treas. Reg. § 1.482-1(b)(1).

[33] *Id.* ("because identical transactions can rarely be located, whether a transaction produces an arm's length result generally will be determined by reference to the results of comparable transactions under comparable circumstances").

[34] Treas. Reg. § 1.482-1(c)(1).

[35] Treas. Reg. § 1.482-1(c)(2).

[36] Treas. Reg. § 1.482-1(d).

- *Economic conditions*: including size and nature of geographical markets, market shares, degree of competition, costs, economic health of the industry, and alternatives available to the parties.

- *Nature of product or services*: including the extent to which intangible property is embedded in tangible property conveyed in the transactions.

In addition to the factors calling for adjustment, the regulations identify several "special circumstances." They include market share strategy, geographic market differences, and location-based savings.[37]

> **Practice Tip:** Transfer pricing valuation is far from science; rather, it is an imprecise art. The regulations recognize that applying the above principles can yield a range of reasonable results, and they provide that no Code Sec. 482 adjustment should be made if the taxpayer's pricing falls within the range of results that could obtain in an arm's length transaction.[38]

.04 Reach of Code Sec. 482

The power created by Code Sec. 482 is broad, but not unlimited. A number of issues have been explored over the decades to define the outer limits of that power. The following are among those issues:

Creation of Income: It would be possible to read the language of Code Sec. 482 as giving the IRS power to reallocate items among taxpayers but not giving the IRS the power to create income (or other items) that did not already exist. Some early cases took that view, but that view has now been rejected. Code Sec. 482 gives the IRS power to compel a corporation to recognize income as a result of its transactions with a related organization, trade, or business – even though no amount was charged in the transaction and no income was brought into the economic family from sources outside it.[39]

> **Example:** E. Lonnie Russell had used some equipment in a mining venture. The venture had been unsuccessful, and Russell was no longer using the equipment. He leased it to Wellington Park Land Company. Wellington was wholly owned by Russell's wife and children. Russell received no rental payments from Wellington pursuant to the lease. The IRS used Code Sec. 482 to impute rental income to Russell.
>
> The trial court held for Russell, in part on the ground that Code Sec. 482 cannot be used to create income. The circuit court reversed, observing that the old view has been abrogated – Code Sec. 482 can be used to create income.[40]

Code Sec. 482 Versus Nonrecognition Rules: In an area as dizzyingly complex as the federal income tax, conflicts between rules are inevitable. Can the IRS make a Code Sec. 482 adjustment in situations to which a nonrecognition rule applies? The answer is "yes," but it is unsettled precisely how big that "yes" is. The regulations

---

[37] *Id.* § 1.482-1(d)(4).

[38] *Id.* § 1.482-1(e).

[39] A leading case to this effect is *Latham Park Manor, Inc. v. Comm'r*, 69 T.C. 199 (1977), *aff'd without published*

op., 618 F.2d 100 (4th Cir. 1980). This result is confirmed by the regulations. *e.g.*, Treas. Reg. § 1.482-1(f)(1)(ii).

[40] *Central Bank of the South v. United States*, 834 F.2d 990, 994 (11th Cir. 1987) (per curiam), *rev'g* 646 F. Supp. 639 (N.D. Ala. 1986).

take the position that Code Sec. 482 trumps nonrecognition rules.[41] Some cases, however, hold that this is true only in defined and narrow circumstances, such as certain tax-motivated property transfers and separation of income from the expenses incurred to produce that income.[42]

Choice of Business Form: How a taxpayer makes certain fundamental business choices will affect how income and other tax items are distributed among that taxpayer and related entities. However, assuming that the arrangements are otherwise legitimate and are not shams, the IRS cannot use Code Sec. 482 to challenge these fundamental decisions.

> **Example 1:** Alpha Corporation and Beta Corporation are owned by the same shareholders. The shareholders decide to engage in a new line of business. That business could be conducted through a division of Alpha, through a division of Beta, through a subsidiary of Alpha, through a subsidiary of Beta, through a partnership between Alpha and Beta, or through a new corporation owned by the shareholders directly. The choice the shareholders make among these alternatives will affect how much income and other tax items each of the various entities has. But this is an inevitable result of the fact that taxpayers are allowed to choose how to conduct their affairs. Assuming that other rules of law are observed,[43] the IRS cannot use Code Sec. 482 to challenge these choices and reallocate income or other items between or among the entities.

> **Example 2:** Artemesia owns all of the stock of Chi Corporation and Delta Corporation. Chi was organized in the United States. Delta was organized in the United Kingdom. Artemesia becomes aware of a business opportunity in Africa. That opportunity could be exploited by conducting the business through Chi or through Delta. The choice Artemesia makes between these alternatives will affect the income, tax credits, and other tax items of Chi and Delta and also will affect the revenue flowing into the federal treasury since Chi is taxable by the United States and Delta is not. Nonetheless, the IRS typically could not use Code Sec. 482 to, in effect, require that the African business be conducted through Chi rather than through Delta.

Effect of Legal Restrictions: What if non-tax law in the jurisdiction in which the transactions were conducted prohibit the taxpayer from charging a price that would fairly reflect an uncontrolled, arm's length transfer price? The IRS often has maintained that Code Sec. 482 allows it to disregard such restrictions. This reflects the IRS's suspicion that such restrictions are collusive, imposed for the tax convenience of the taxpayer, not for any legitimate reasons of the government of the jurisdiction whose laws create the restrictions. However, the IRS usually has lost in cases testing this issue.

---

[41] Treas. Reg. § 1.482-1(f)(1)(ii).

[42] *e.g., Eli Lilly & Co. v. Comm'r*, 84 T.C. 996 (1985), *aff'd as to this issue*, 856 F.2d 855 (7th Cir. 1988).

[43] Such as, if a new corporation is organized, the "business activity" requirement. *See Moline Properties v. Comm'r*, 319 U.S. 436 (1943) (discussed in Chapter 2).

Example 1: Spanish law prohibited a foreign affiliate from paying royalties for the use of patents. This restriction was held sufficient to defeat a Code Sec. 482 adjustment for failure to pay a reasonable royalty.[44]

Example 2: Saudi Arabia allowed certain corporations to buy Saudi Arabian crude oil at below market prices. Saudi Arabia also established an official selling price for Saudi Arabian crude (which price was below the market price), and it prohibited the corporations from reselling that crude at higher prices than the official selling price. The corporations honored the official selling price. The resale price restriction was held sufficient to defeat IRS adjustments for reselling the crude at below market prices.[45]

Practice Tip: This issue usually arises in the international context. However, in certain regulated industries, the restrictions may be imposed by domestic law, whether federal or state.[46]

Correlative Adjustments: Code Sec. 482 adjustments should be made globally, not selectively. That is, when the IRS uses Code Sec. 482 to increase the taxable income of corporation A, it typically also should decrease the taxable income of related corporation B, when A and B are the parties to the transaction(s) being adjusted. The regulations acknowledge the obligation of the IRS to make such adjustments correlative to the primary adjustment.[47]

Example: Rutan Corporation and Sylvan Corporation are under common ownership or control. Rutan sells goods to Sylvan, charging $50. The IRS determines that $75 would have been the sale price between unrelated parties dealing at arm's length. Accordingly, the IRS raises Rutan's income by $25. The IRS should make a correlative adjustment with respect to Sylvan. Typically, this correlative adjustment would increase Sylvan's deductions by $25.

Use of Code Sec. 482 by Taxpayers: Sometimes an arrangement that seems clever when created, proves to be unwise in light of later events. When this happens, can the taxpayer invoke Code Sec. 482, or request the IRS to invoke it, in order to undo the arrangement for tax purposes? The usual answer is "no." The statute confers authority upon the IRS, and it is within the discretion of the IRS to exercise that authority or to refrain from exercising it.

Example: Titan Corporation and Uranus Corporation are under common ownership or control. Both use the calendar year. At the beginning of the year, the common owners projected that Titan would be in a higher bracket for the year than Uranus. Accordingly, in January, Titan and Uranus engaged in a transaction, the transfer price of which was manipulated to shift income from Titan to Uranus. However, the projection proved erroneous, and Uranus turned out to be in a higher bracket than Titan for the year. In general, Titan and Uranus cannot re-price the transaction under Code Sec. 482.

---

[44] *Proctor & Gamble Co. v. Comm'r*, 961 F.2d 1255 (6th Cir. 1992).

[45] *Texaco, Inc. v. Comm'r*, 98 F.3d 825 (5th Cir. 1996), *cert. denied*, 520 U.S. 1185 (1997).

[46] *e.g., Comm'r v. First Security Bank*, 405 U.S. 394 (1972).

[47] *e.g.*, Treas. Reg. §§ 1.482-1(g)(2), 1.482-1T(e)(3).

¶902.04

Practice Tip: The regulations do provide one opportunity. They permit taxpayers to report the results of controlled transactions "based upon prices different from those actually charged" as long as doing so is "necessary to reflect an arm's length result." However, a taxpayer can take advantage of this opportunity only on a timely filed return.[48]

.05 Specific Transaction Types

The regulations prescribe special treatment for certain categories of transactions. Five categories are addressed below. Collectively, they cover most related-party transactions. Transactions not so covered are handled under the general provisions of the regulations.

(a) Services

Regulations were finalized in 2009 to address "any activity" by a member of a group of controlled taxpayers "that results in a benefit . . . to one or more members of the controlled group."[49] The regulations provide that fees for intercompany services need be charged only if the services result in benefit to another member of the controlled group.[50] No fees need be charged if the probable benefits are so indirect or remote that an unrelated recipient would not have paid for them.[51]

The regulations specify six methods for determining an arm's length price for services.[52] However, unspecified methods also may be used if they are more reliable. The six identified methods are as follows:

Comparable Uncontrolled Services Price Method: CUSP compares the price charged to that of an uncontrolled services transaction, with emphasis on the similarity of the services and on whether non-routine intangibles are present. CUSP resembles the Comparable Uncontrolled Price Method (described below) as to transfers of tangible property.

Gross Services Margin Method: This approach examines the amount charged in light of the gross profit margin in uncontrolled transactions involving similar services. It resembles the resale price method (described below) as to transfers of tangible property.

Cost-of-Services-Plus Method: This approach looks to the profit mark-up in similar uncontrolled transactions, considering a percentage of comparable transaction costs. It resembles the cost-plus method (described below) as to transfers of tangible property.

Comparable Profits Method: This method looks to objective indicators of profit level determined from financial information of uncontrolled taxpayers engaged in similar transactions.

Services Cost Method: This allows related parties to render some services at cost, with no mark-up. This is a limited exception with many qualification require-

---

[48] Treas. Reg. § 1.482-1(a)(3).
[49] Treas. Reg. § 1.482-9(l)(1).
[50] Treas. Reg. § 1.482-9(l).

[51] Treas. Reg. § 1.482-9(l)(3)(ii).
[52] Treas. Reg. § 1.482-9(b) to (g).

ments. It is designed to obviate administrative burdens for corporate groups that share back-office services.

Profit-Split Method: This method refers to the relative values of each party's contribution to the overall profit produced.

> **Practice Tip:** Courts will deviate from the methods identified by the regulations when no identified method fits the situation. However, the identified methods will be used if possible, for several reasons: the IRS has more experience and expertise in transfer pricing matters than judges do; the regulations reflect enormous intellectual effort over generations; and Code Sec. 482 cases are unpredictable enough without judges making up new methodologies.

> **Example:** U.S. Steel organized a subsidiary, Orinoco, to develop deposits of iron ore in Venezuela and another subsidiary, Navios, to transport the ore from Venezuela to the United States. Navios was organized in Liberia, a tax haven. Under Code Sec. 482, the IRS challenged the pricing of the services rendered by Navios.

> The Tax Court rejected the method used by the IRS and instead applied two methods of its own. Despite applying the deferential "clearly erroneous" standard, the circuit court reversed. It concluded that services performed for independent parties were sufficiently comparable to services performed for U.S. Steel that established methods under the regulations could be used with reasonable reliability.[53]

(b) Interest

A tempting way to shift income is for one related party to make a loan to another, with the rate of interest set artificially high or low. Code Sec. 482 can be used to foil such schemes.[54] The regulations provide that the arm's length standard generally will be met as long as the interest rate charged is not less than 100%, and not more than 130%, of the federal rate applicable to debt of comparable maturity.[55]

(c) Use of Tangible Property

Compensation for the use of tangible property is rent. The regulations provide for comparing the rent charged between related parties to rent charged between unrelated parties "under similar circumstances considering the period and location of the use, the owner's investment in the property or rent paid for the property, expenses of maintaining the property, the type of property involved, its condition, and all other relevant facts.[56]

(d) Transfer of Tangible Property

The regulations describe five methods for this category of transactions. Again, an unspecified approach may be used, but only if it is the most reliable indicator of arms length pricing.[57] The five described methods are as follows:

---

[53] *United States Steel Corp. v. Comm'r*, 36 T.C.M. 586 (1977), *rev'd*, 617 F.2d 942 (2d Cir. 1980).

[54] As can other Code sections, in appropriate circumstances. *e.g.*, Code Secs. 467, 483, 1273, 1274 & 7872.

[55] Treas. Reg. § 1.482-2(a)(2).

[56] Treas. Reg. § 1.482-2(c)(2)(i).

[57] Treas. Reg. § 1.482-3(e)(1)

Comparable Uncontrolled Price Method: The CUP method typically provides the best method by which to price sales or other transfers of tangible property – as long as comparability adjustments and special circumstances are small or manageable.[58] This method is available when the related-party seller sells not only to the related-party buyer but also sells similar property under similar circumstances to unrelated buyers. The method also is available when the related-party buyer buys not only from the related-party seller but also buys similar property under similar circumstances from unrelated sellers. The method also is available – although more adjustments may be needed – when similar transactions occur among other parties, unrelated to the controlled corporations.[59] The CUP method cannot be used when the differences between the transaction under scrutiny and the alleged comparable are substantial or when needed adjustments have not been, or cannot be, made.[60]

Practice Tip: Before one applies CUP or any other method, it first must be determined that the putative sale in question is a legitimate transaction. If, instead, it is a mere sham, the IRS need not apply Code Sec. 482; rather, it may disregard the transaction entirely for tax purposes.[61]

Resale Price Method: This method looks to the gross profit margin that obtains in similar uncontrolled transfers. It is best used when a party buys and then resells property without significantly altering the property or otherwise adding value.[62]

Cost-Plus Method: This method considers the gross profit mark-up achieved in similar uncontrolled transfers. It is used principally when the transferor produced or assembled the goods that later were sold.[63]

Comparable Profits Method: This adverts to indicators of profit level that are derived for companies engaged in uncontrolled but otherwise similar transfers. Comparability looks mainly to what resources are used and what risks are assumed, and all material adjustments must be made.[64]

Profit-Split Method: This method evaluates the relative value each of the parties contributes to the total profit produced. There are two alternatives: comparable profit split and residual profit split. The method is best used when both of the parties own non-routine intangibles or when the activities of the parties are highly interrelated.[65]

(e) Transactions as to Intangible Property

Currently, this is the hottest front in the Code Sec. 482 wars. Intangible property transactions include sale, licensing, and other transfers. The regulations define intangible property as assets of the following types that have substantial value independent of the services of any individual:

---

[58] *See id.* § 1.482-1(c)(2)(i).

[59] *See generally* Treas. Reg. § 1.482-3(a)(1) & (b).

[60] *e.g., Paccar, Inc. v. Comm'r*, 58 T.C. 754 (1985). For an extended discussion of comparability, see *Bausch & Lomb Inc. v. Comm'r*, 92 T.C. 525 (1989), *aff'd*, 933 F.2d 1084 (2d Cir. 1991).

[61] *e.g. U.S. Gypsum Co. v. United States*, 452 F.2d 445 (7th Cir. 1971) (observing: "The fact that a taxpayer may

properly arrange its affairs to minimize taxation does not give it license to create purposeless entities or to engage in transactions with subsidiaries which independent parties would not dream of concluding.").

[62] Treas. Reg. § 1.482-3(a)(2) & (c).

[63] Treas. Reg. § 1.482-3(a)(3) & (d).

[64] Treas. Reg. §§ 1.482-3(a)(4) & 1.482-5.

[65] Treas. Reg. §§ 1.482-3(a)(5) & 1.482-6.

patents, inventions, formulae, processes, designs, patterns, or know-how; copyrights and literary, musical, or artistic compositions; trademarks, trade names, or brand names; franchises, licenses, or contracts; methods, programs, systems, procedures, campaigns, surveys, studies, forecasts, estimates, customer lists, or technical data; and other similar items which derive their value from their intellectual content or other intangible properties rather than from their physical attributes.[66]

For several reasons, it is challenging to develop rules to monitor pricing of related party transfers and use of such property. First, these property types are a moving target. Intellectual property has ever increasing velocity in the Information Age. Second, the standard approach to Code Sec. 482 valuation – identification of comparables – is rendered difficult by the fact that intangibles often are unique. Third, transfers often occur early in the life of an intangible, before it is known whether the intangible will be fabulously valuable or worthless. Fourth, intangibles can be transferred easily and quickly – by executing sale or licensing documents and providing the information.

Example: WellChem Corporation is a pharmaceutical company. At any given time, it has numerous potential new drugs in research and development. Most of these candidate products eventually will be determined to be ineffective or excessively dangerous. They will be abandoned, and WellChem will "eat" the expenses that had been invested in them up to the point of abandonment. However, a few candidate products will succeed, producing enormous profits that will more than offset all costs.

WellChem's practice is to perform most research and development itself in the United States. It takes deductions or credits against U.S. income tax for the costs of such R&D. At some point before their commercial viability has been established, WellChem transfer rights to the candidate products to foreign subsidiaries in low-tax jurisdictions.

As a result of various code provisions,[67] WellChem will pay U.S. taxes as a result of these transfers. However, unless Code Sec. 482 is effective, this practice can be highly beneficial to WellChem. It will get the U.S. tax benefits of the R&D costs; the tax costs of transferring the potential products may be small because of their unproven nature; and profits from the successful products will accrue outside the reach of the federal income tax.

The regulations specify three methods with respect to evaluating intangible property transactions: the Comparable Uncontrolled Transaction Method, the Comparable Profits Method, and the Profit-Split Method. The first of these is similar to the Comparable Uncontrolled Price Method described above as to tangible property transfers, and the second and third are essentially the same as the same-named methods also described as to tangible property transfers. In addition, as usual, an unspecified method may be used if it is more reliable in the situation.[68]

---

[66] *Id.* § 1.482-4(b).

[67] *e.g.*, Code Sec. 367 (requiring recognition of gain on transfers of appreciated property by U.S. persons to foreign corporations and certain other foreign persons).

[68] Treas. Reg. § 1.482-4(c).

Because of the difficulty of this area, two other regimes exist to complement the established methods: the "super royalty" provision created by the second sentence of Code Sec. 482 and cost sharing arrangements under the regulations.

Super royalty: The WellChem example set out above illustrated one of the challenges in valuing intangibles: subsequent events – hard to predict at the time of the transfer – may cause an intangible to become far more valuable later. This is a problem as long as application of Code Sec. 482 is confined to one moment, such as the time of transfer.

Based on that realization, Congress in 1986 added a second sentence to Code Sec. 482: "In the case of any transfer (or license) of intangible property . . . , the income with respect to such transfer or license shall be commensurate with the income attributable to the intangible."

This sentence moves past the "only one valuation moment" problem. It authorizes the IRS to periodically review and adjust the compensation paid by one related party to another on account of the partial or complete transfer of an intangible.[69]

Example: Refer to the facts of the prior example involving WellChem. One of the many candidate products transferred by WellChem to a subsidiary is Product A. The development of Product A was not complete as of the time of transfer. Substantial unanswered questions existed as to the efficacy, safety, and commercial viability of Product A. As a result, the value of Product A was speculative and low when Product A was transferred from WellChem to its subsidiary.

After additional R&D by the subsidiary, many candidate products proved unsuccessful. Product A, however, proved very successful. It was approved for use by governmental authorities, was widely marketed, and generated substantial profits.

The IRS may consider the adequacy of the consideration for the transfer of Product A from WellChem to the subsidiary at the time of transfer. At this initial stage of consideration, the IRS will use whichever of the three methods described in the regulations as is best, or an unspecified method if better.

Moreover, even if the initial compensation was appropriate at the time of transfer, the super royalty provision allows the IRS to reevaluate the adequacy of the consideration later – once or more than once.

As Product A becomes successful, the subsidiary will be deemed to have paid additional consideration to WellChem, consideration reasonably related to the income generated by Product A. This consideration will be included in WellChem's income and be taxed by the United States. Reevaluation typically occurs annually. The methods set out in the regulations, or a better unspecified method, are used to determine the appropriate levels of consideration during the periodic reevaluations.

---

[69] Treas. Reg. § 1.482-4 (f) (2).

Practice Tip: Periodic reevaluation could create excessive administrative burdens for the IRS and compliance burdens for taxpayers. To mitigate these possibilities, the regulations set out a number of exceptions to preclude multiple adjustments. These exceptions involve transactions as to the same intangible, transactions involving comparable intangibles, evaluations using methods other than the Comparable Uncontrolled Transaction Method, extraordinary events, and a five-year safe harbor testing period.[70]

Cost Sharing: The regulations recognize cost sharing agreements as an alternative to royalty and similar compensation agreements. A cost sharing agreement exist when the parties have made a good faith effort to measure and to bear their respective portions of the expenses and risks as to development of an intangible, on terms that unrelated parties would have agreed to in a joint venture involving the same activity.[71] The agreement must be in writing, and it must provide for adjustments in the event of changed conditions. If these requirements are met, a Code Sec. 482 reallocation typically will not be made.

Things to watch for: The IRS has been concerned that cost sharing agreements have been abused by taxpayers. Regulations finalized in 2009 added considerably to the complexity of the cost sharing qualification rules and seem to have been animated by hostility to such agreements. The regulations have been heavily criticized, however, and the IRS has recently lost some high-profile cost sharing agreement cases.[72] It is probable that the area will remain controversial for many years to come. Indeed, the IRS has stated that cost-sharing arrangements continue to be a top priority for examination.[73]

In addition, the Administration has proposed legislation to limit income shifting via transfers of intangible property. In its tax proposals for both the Fiscal Year 2011 and Fiscal Year 2012 budgets, the Administration urged Congress to provide (or in the Administration's view to "clarify") that intangible property for Code Sec. 482 purposes and Code Sec. 367(d) purposes includes workforce in place, going concern value, and goodwill. The Administration also recommends, in the case of transfer of multiple intangibles, that the IRS be allowed to value the intangible on an aggregate basis when doing so would yield a more reliable result. Further, the Administration's proposals would allow the IRS to value intangible property taking into account the profits or prices the controlled taxpayer could have realized. If enacted, the proposals would be effective starting in 2012.[74]

---

[70] Treas. Reg. § 1.482-4(f)(2)(ii).

[71] Treas. Reg. § 1.482-7A(a) & (b).

[72] *Xilinx, Inc. v. Comm'r*, 598 F.3d 1191 (9th Cir. 2010); *Veritas Software Corp. v. Comm'r*, 133 T.C. 297 (2009), *nonacq.*, AOD-2010-05, 2010 WL 4531284 (Nov 12, 2010).

[73] See David D. Stewart, *Cost-Sharing Arrangements Still a Top Priority*, IRS Official Says, Tax Notes, Dec. 13, 2010, p. 1184.

[74] *See* U.S. Dep't of Treasury, General Explanations of the Administration's Fiscal Year 2012 Revenue Proposals 43-45 (Feb. 2011).

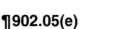

¶902.05(e)

.06 Administrative Aspects

(a) Reporting

Code Sec. 482 examinations are heavily fact-intensive. When key information is not preserved at all or is maintained only overseas, the IRS will have difficulty. Thus, Congress has enacted provisions to enhance the IRS's access to information.

Code Sec. 6038A authorizes the IRS to require U.S. corporations at least 25% foreign owned to file annual reports with the IRS, and Code Sec. 6038C authorizes the IRS to require further reporting as to foreign corporations engaged in business in the United States. Reporting corporations must maintain books and records in the United States or, if abroad, readily accessible to the IRS.

Corporations failing to honor these duties are subject to substantial penalties. However, these obligations are mitigated, in some instances, by exceptions for (1) situations in which the transactions between related corporations are de minimis in amount, (2) corporations with under $10 million in gross receipts from the United States, and (3) some corporations residing in countries with which the United States has income tax treaties.[75]

(b) Examination

Transfer pricing is an area of continued focus for the IRS. The IRS recently reorganized and rechristened the former Large and Mid-Size Business Division as the Large Business & International Division. The IRS believes that this realignment of resources will improve its policing of transfer pricing.

In late 2010 and early 2011, the IRS assembled its most experienced transfer pricing examiners and economists in its Transfer Pricing Practice headed by a Transfer Pricing Director. This unit is responsible for developing a strategic program to staff transfer pricing cases more effectively in order to improve issue development and resolve issues more expeditiously.

In 2010, the IRS conducted a Transfer Pricing Pilot program to enhance identification of cases with potentially broad impact. In addition, the IRS increasingly is pursuing joint transfer pricing audits with other countries' revenue agencies through the Forum on Tax Administration of the Organization for Economic Cooperation and Development.[76]

(c) Penalties

To enhance compliance, the Code has an imposing array of penalties.[77] Code Sec. 6662(e) is of particular relevance in the Code Sec. 482 context. The Code Sec. 6662 accuracy-related penalty applies if any of the five enumerated bases exists. One of them is Code Sec. 6662(e), which applies to large valuation misstatements or when "the net section 482 transfer price adjustment for the taxable year exceeds the lesser of $5,000,000 or 10 percent of the taxpayer's gross receipts."[78]

---

[75] Treas. Reg. § 1.6038A-1c), (h) & (i).

[76] These developments as to transfer pricing examinations are described in the Prepared Remarks of IRS Commissioner Doug Shulman before the 23rd Annual Institute on Current Issues in International Taxation. *See* IRS Information Release, IR-2010-122 (Dec. 9, 2010).

[77] Civil tax penalties are described in greater detail in Chapter 10.

[78] Code Sec. 6662(e)(1)(A)(ii).

Certain exceptions apply. The most important of them for present purposes is when the taxpayer reasonably used one of the methods approved by the Code Sec. 482 regulations.[79]

The normal penalty rate under Code Sec. 6662 is "20 percent of the portion of the underpayment to which [section 6662]applies."[80] This amount is raised to 40% if the Code Sec. 482 adjustment exceeds the lesser of $20 million or 20% of the taxpayer's gross receipts for the year.[81]

(d) Dispute Resolution

It is essential to the integrity of the system that the tax law include something like Code Sec. 482. However, no one is especially happy about the results produced under Code Sec. 482 in actual operation.

The IRS does not do particularly well in Code Sec. 482 litigation. Although, as described above, the IRS has the benefit of the taxpayer bearing a heightened standard of proof, this advantage has been more than offset by several factors, including (1) Code Sec. 482 cases are fact-intensive and taxpayers typically know far more about their industry and its conditions than does the IRS; (2) transfer pricing involves balancing many economic considerations, and courts tend to be reluctant to second-guess the business judgment of taxpayers; and (3) most importantly, in high-stakes litigation, taxpayers characteristically massively out-spend the IRS on experts and legal counsel. As a result, the IRS often loses big Code Sec. 482 cases.

> **Example 1:** The largest Code Sec. 482 case involved Exxon and Texaco. The amounts at issue, including deficiencies and interest, far exceeded $10 million. The IRS lost the whole case.[82]

> **Example 2:** In a fairly recent Code Sec. 482 case, the Tax Court held that the IRS improperly valued a nearly $1.7 billion cost sharing buy-in amount the IRS maintained Veritas should have been paid by its subsidiary in Ireland. The court approved Veritas' use of the comparable uncontrolled transaction method in determining the transfer price for pre-existing intangibles.[83] Although the Government chose not to appeal the decision, the IRS disagrees with it and will continue to litigate similar cases.[84]

Corporations are not wildly enthusiastic about Code Sec. 482 either. Taxpayers don't always win, of course. The IRS tends to do better in the non-mega-bucks cases, and it sometimes recovers a significant amount in even very large cases.[85] Even when taxpayers do prevail, victory usually comes at the cost of great expense, delay, and uncertainty.

---

[79] Code Sec. 6662(e)(3)(B).

[80] Code Sec. 6662(a).

[81] Code Sec. 6662(h)(1), (2)(A)(iii).

[82] *Exxon v. Comm'r*, 66 T.C.M. 1707 (1993), *aff'd sub nom. Texaco, Inc. v. Comm'r*, 98 F.3d 825 (5th Cir. 1996), *cert. denied*, 520 U.S. 1185 (1997).

[83] *Veritas Software Corp. v. Comm'r*, 133 T.C. 297 (2009).

[84] AOD-2010-05, 2010 WL 4531284 (Nov. 12, 2010).

[85] For example, the IRS recovered about $3.4 billion in settlement of a Code Sec. 482 controversy with pharmaceutical giant GlaxoSmithKline. *See* IRS Information Release IR-2006-142 (Sept. 11, 2006); *see also Sunstrand Corp. v. Comm'r*, 96 T.C. 226 (1991) (in which the IRS won about 40% of the dollars at issue). Similarly, a March 28, 2011 statement issued by global pharmaceutical giant AstraZeneca PLC announced it would pay the IRS $1.1 billion to settle all transfer price issues for 2000 to 2010.

¶902.06(d)

Accordingly, both the IRS and taxpayers have incentive to try to improve upon the prolix and cumbersome process of audit, administrative appeal, trial, and judicial appeal of Code Sec. 482 cases. One possible device is arbitration. The parties could submit to arbitration before litigation commences or, by consent, under Tax Court Rule 124 as a substitute for trial.

A prominent Code Sec. 482 arbitration involving Apple Computer Inc. took place in the 1990's,[86] but arbitration has not been used greatly since. This technique may receive a boost in the future from income tax treaties. A number of such treaties – including the United States treaties with Mexico, Germany, and the Netherlands – authorize (although they do not require) use of binding arbitration if the treaty partners' competent authorities cannot reach agreement as to transfer pricing issues. In addition, arbitration provisions are included in the influential model tax treaty developed by the Organization for Economic Cooperation and Development.[87]

Another device is Advance Pricing Agreements ("APAs"). The objective is to resolve Code Sec. 482 issues early and without confrontation. The taxpayer initiates the APA process by informing the IRS of the related-party transaction before the return for the year is filed. The taxpayer suggests how the transaction should be treated for tax purposes. The IRS and the taxpayer discuss the proposed tax treatment. If agreement is reached, the taxpayer files the return consistently with the agreement and the IRS accepts the treatment on audit, saving both parties time and money.

> **Practice Tip:** A corporation wishing to avail itself of the APA process will find procedures set out in detail in Revenue Procedure 2004-40.[88] Although they have accomplished some good, APAs have not entirely fulfilled the high hopes that once existed for them. The IRS reports annually on the progress of and problems with the APA program.

In its 2011 report, the IRS stated that it had completed 69 APAs in 2010, while 350 requests for APAs remain pending. As in every year of the program, the number of submissions exceeded the number of completions. Staffing of the program decreased from 39 in 2009 to 35 in 2010. One APA completed in 2010 took almost ten years to finalize. Since the APA program started in 1991, a total of 1,523 cases have been accepted and 973 APAs have been completed.[89]

¶ 903 Tax Attributes: Code Secs. 269 and 381 to 384

Through its operations, a corporation acquires many types of tax attributes. These include basis in assets, accounting methods, net operating loss ("NOL") carryovers,[90] capital loss carryovers, earnings and profits, and many other items.

---

[86] See James P. Fuller, *Apple Arbitration*, 7 Tax Notes Int'l 1046 (1993).

[87] See, e.g., Michael J. McIntyre, *Comments on the OECD Proposal for Secret and Mandatory Arbitration of International Tax Disputes*, 7 Fla. Tax Rev. 622 (2006).

[88] 2004-2 C.B. 50.

[89] IRS Announcement 2011-22 (Mar. 29, 2011).

[90] As used here, NOL carryovers include both NOL carrybacks (the application of NOLs to years preceding the year in which the NOLs arose) and NOL carryforwards (the application of NOLs to years subsequent to the year in which the NOLs arose). The term carryover also is sometimes used as a synonym of carryforward.

In general, tax attributes remain with the corporation that developed or accumulated them. The corporation typically cannot transfer the attributes to another corporation. However, one corporation may succeed to attributes of another corporation as a result of certain tax-free reorganizations. Moreover, even when attributes remain with the corporation, changes in ownership (by stock sales or otherwise) can effectively shift who benefits from future use or application of the attributes. As a result, the Internal Revenue Code contains a number of provisions to curb potentially abusive shifts and applications of tax attributes.

The rules as to basis are addressed in other chapters.[91] This part of this chapter explores the rules as to NOL carryovers and other tax attributes.

.01 NOLs Generally

An NOL is the excess of a corporation's deductions – modified in the ways specified by Code Sec. 172(d) – over its gross income for a given tax year.[92] Code Sec. 172 allows corporations (and other taxpayers engaged in a trade or business) to apply and deduct NOLs in other tax years. In general, NOLs may be carried back to each of the two preceding years and then, if not already consumed, carried forward to each of the succeeding twenty years.[93] However, taxpayers can elect to forgo the carryback period, in which case they would be able to apply the NOL only to the succeeding up-to-twenty years.[94]

> **Practice Note:** There sometimes are good reasons to waive the carryback period. For example, if the taxpayer anticipates that its tax rates will rise in the near future – either because of a legislated increase or because enhanced profitability will push the taxpayer into higher brackets – a corporation would get a "bigger bang for the NOL buck" by applying NOLs to future years than to past years.

If the corporation does want to waive the carryback period, it should be attentive to how it implements that choice. The IRS sometimes has argued that a waiver was not made with sufficient clarity and thus was ineffective.[95]

The election is effected by attaching a statement to the corporation's income tax return for the year the loss is incurred. The statement must state that election is pursuant to Code Sec. 172(b)(3) and contains additional information.[96] The election is irrevocable.[97]

The earliest predecessor of current Code Sec. 172 was added to the tax law in 1918 in order "to ameliorate the unduly drastic consequences of taxing income strictly on an annual basis. [The provisions] were designated to permit a taxpayer

---

[91] See Chapters 5, 7, 8, and 9 for the basis effects of liquidations, corporate divisions, and corporate reorganizations, respectively.

[92] Code Sec. 172(c).

[93] Code Sec. 172(b)(l)(A). From time to time, Congress enacts special NOL rules as relief for particularly economically stressed industries or for geographical areas suffering the effects of natural disasters or other unusual events. *e.g.*, Code Sec. 172(b)(l)(B)–(D).

[94] Code Sec. 172(b)(3).

[95] *e.g., Miller v. Comm'r*, 104 T.C. 330 (1995), *rev'd*, 99 F.3d 1042 (11th Cir. 1996); *Young v. Comm'r*, 83 T.C. 831 (1984).

[96] Treas. Reg. § 301.9100-12T.

[97] Code Sec. 173(b)(3).

to set off its lean years against its lush years, and to strike something like an average taxable income computed over a period longer than one year."[98]

> *Practice Tip:* "Tax year" usually means a twelve-month period, whether calendar or fiscal. However, it can mean any period for which an income tax return should be filed.[99] For instance, short periods for which returns are due often are created when a corporation is formed, reorganized, or liquidated at some time other than the first day of a normal twelve-month period. Such short periods constitute tax years for purposes of application of NOLs.

The use of NOLs is limited both by sections discussed below and by Code Sec. 172 itself. A major limitation involves corporate equity reducing transactions ("CERTs"). This limitation was enacted in 1989 by a Congress concerned with the use of the federal fisc to help finance the wave of leveraged buyouts and buybacks that occurred in the 1980s. In such transactions, acquisition of the stock of existing shareholders was financed by heavy borrowing. Interest paid on such borrowings pushed the corporations into loss postures. These losses generated NOLs which were carried back to prior years, generating tax refunds that helped pay off the borrowings.

Congress responded by enacting Code Sec. 172(b)(l)(E) and 172(h), which prevent a corporation from carrying back part of its NOLs if a million dollars or more of its interest expense is allowable to a CERT. Both "major stock acquisitions" and "excess distributions" are CERTs.

A major stock acquisition entails acquisition by a corporation under a plan for the corporation, or by a group of persons acting in concert with the corporation, to acquire stock representing 50% or more of the voting power or value of another corporation.[100] All such plans as to another corporation are treated as one plan, and all acquisitions during any 24-month period are treated as being pursuant to one plan.[101]

An excess distribution is the amount by which the total of the corporation's distributions and redemptions during the tax year on account of its stock exceeds the greater of (i) 150% of the average distributions and redemptions the corporation made during the previous three years or (ii) 10% of the corporation's fair market value at the beginning of the tax year.[102] For this purpose, preferred stock described in Code Sec. 1504(a)(4) and distributions and redemptions with respect to such stock are disregarded.[103] In addition, the excess is reduced by proceeds (other than the corporation's own stock) that a corporation obtains by issuing stock during the year.[104]

The limitation on use of the NOL occurs if the corporation is involved in a CERT in the tax year or in the succeeding two tax years. The involvement occurs –

---

[98] *Libson Shops v. Koehler*, 353 U.S. 382, 386 (1957). For an example of the harshness that motivated enactment of the NOL carryover provisions, *see Burnet v. Sanford & Brooks Co.*, 282 U.S. 359 (1931).

[99] Code Sec. 7701(a)(23).

[100] Code Sec. 172(h)(3)(B)(i). However, acquisitions pursuant to a Code Sec. 338 election are excepted from CERT status. Code Sec. 172(h)(3)(B)(ii).

[101] Code Sec. 172(h)(3)(D)(i) & (ii).

[102] Code Sec. 172(h)(3)(C).

[103] Code Sec. 172(h)(3)(E)(i).

[104] Code Sec. 172(h)(3)(E)(ii).

¶903.01

in the case of a major stock acquisition – if the corporation is the acquired entity or the acquiring entity or a successor thereto, or – in the case of an excess distribution – if the corporation is the distributing or redeeming corporation or a successor thereto.[105]

The extent to which the NOL from the year of the CERT and the two succeeding years can be carried back is limited to the smaller of (1) the corporation's interest expense for the year that is allocable to the CERT or (2) the extent to which the corporation's interest expense for the year exceeds the average of the corporation's interest expense for the three years preceding the year of the CERT.[106] Amounts that may not be carried back may be carried over to future years. Under a *de minimis* rule, no reduction occurs if the lesser of the two is under $1,000,000.[107]

The Treasury is empowered to issue regulations to carry out the purposes of the CERT rules, including how a corporation's interest expense is allocated to a CERT, application to successor corporations and to cases when a corporation joins or leaves an affiliated group filing a consolidated return, prevention of avoidance, and application when more than one corporation is involved in a CERT.[108]

.02 Code Sec. 269

(a) Pre-Code Sec. 269 Case Law

For the remainder of this part, we turn our attention to the rules outside of Code Sec. 172 that affect use of NOLs and other tax attributes. In the early years of the modern income tax, there were no such outside sections. However, some limits on use of NOLs were imposed as a result of case law. A number of cases held that carrybacks and carryforwards could be used only by the same entity as had suffered the losses.[109]

Relatedly, in *Libson Shops*, a case arising under the 1939 Code, the Supreme Court required that there be continuity of the business enterprise that incurred the NOL and held that NOL carryovers could be deducted only against income later produced by the continuing enterprise.[110] There was considerable controversy as to whether the Libson Shops doctrine survived under the 1954 Code. However, it is clear that the doctrine does not apply to transactions subject to the 1986 Code. In particular, Code Sec. 382 – discussed below – ousts *Libson Shops* from applicability.[111]

(b) Code Sec. 269(a)

Congress's first attempt, outside of Code Sec. 172, to address abuses of NOLs and other tax attributes was Code Sec. 269, enacted in 1943. Its more general portion is Code Sec. 269(a), which provides that the IRS "may disallow [a] deduction, credit, or other allowance" if (1) any person or persons acquire . . . directly or

---

[105] Code Sec. 172(b)(2)(E)(ii) & (iii).

[106] Code Sec. 172(h)(2)(C).

[107] Code Sec. 172(h)(2)(D). In addition, special rules apply "[i]f an unforeseeable extraordinary adverse event occurs during a loss limitation year but after the [CERT]." Code Sec. 172(h)(2)(E).

[108] Code Sec. 172(h)(5).

[109] *e.g.*, *New York Central R.R. Co. v. Comm'r*, 79 F.2d 247 (2d Cir. 1935), *cert. denied*, 296 U.S. 653 (1936).

[110] *Libson Shops v. Koehler*, 353 U.S. 382 (1957).

[111] H.R. Rep. No. 841, 99th Cong. 2d Sess. II-194 (1986) (Conf. Comm.).

indirectly, control of a corporation, or (2) any corporation acquires . . . directly or indirectly, property of another corporation, not controlled . . . immediately before such acquisition, by such acquiring corporation, or its shareholders, the basis of which property, in the hands of the acquiring corporation, is determined by reference to the basis in the hands of the transferor corporation.

It is a further condition for application of Code Sec. 269(a) that "the principal purpose for which such acquisition was made is evasion or avoidance of Federal income tax by securing the benefit of a deduction, credit, or other allowance which such person or corporation would not otherwise enjoy."

For these purposes,

- "Person" includes any individual, estate, trust, company, corporation, partnership, or association.[112]

- "Acquires" is understood broadly, involving both single transactions and transactions including a series of related steps.[113] Examples include: incorporating a new corporation,[114] cancelling debt in return for getting new stock,[115] obtaining stock of a parent,[116] return of stock as a return of contractual default,[117] and redemption of other shareholders' stock.[118]

- "Control" entails "ownership of stock possessing at least 50 percent of the total combined voting power of all classes of stock entitled to vote or at least 50 percent of the total value of shares of all classes of stock of the corporation."[119] There are no attribution rules within section 269, and no external attribution rules apply.[120] The language "directly or indirectly" applies to the mode of acquisition, not to the identity of the owner.

Example 1: Axton Corporation owns 45% of the voting stock of Borgen Corporation. Axton purchases another 5% of Borgen's voting stock. The previous acquisition of the 45% was not made with the prohibited purpose. The later acquisition of the 5% was made with the prohibited purpose. Code Sec. 269 applies.

Example 2: Axton Corporation owns 45% of the voting stock of Borgen Corporation. Juan Serrano owns 60% of the voting stock of Axton. Serrano buys (not from Axton) 5% of the voting stock of Borgen. Serrano is both the legal and the beneficial owner of the 5%, and there is no agreement, understanding, or course of practice whereby the 5% is made available for the use of Axton. Code Sec. 269 does not apply.

Example 3: The same facts as Example 2 except that Serrano makes the 5% purchase for the benefit of Axton. Serrano holds the legal title, but Axton is allowed to vote the stock and Serrano passes on the dividends from Borgen to

---

[112] Treas. Reg. § 1.269-1(d).

[113] *PEPI, Inc. v. Comm'r*, 448 F.2d 141 (2d Cir. 1971).

[114] *Borge v. Comm'r*, 405 F.2d 573 (2d Cir. 1968).

[115] *Jupiter Corp. v. United States*, 83-1 USTC ¶ 9168 (Cl. Ct. 1983).

[116] Rev. Rul. 80-46, 1980-1 C.B. 62.

[117] *Swiss Colony, Inc. v. Comm'r*, 428 F.2d 49 (7th Cir. 1970).

[118] *Younker Bros., Inc. v. United States*, 318 F. Supp. 202 (S.D. Iowa 1970).

[119] Code Sec. 269(a).

[120] *e.g., Thomas E. Snyder Sons Co. v. Comm'r*, 34 T.C. 400 (1960), *aff'd*, 288 F.2d 36 (7th Cir.), *cert. denied*, 368 U.S. 823 (1961).

Axton. Ownership for federal income tax purposes adverts to beneficial, not legal, ownership.[121] Thus, Axton has acquired control. Code Sec. 269 applies if the 5% purchase was made with the prohibited purpose.

Example 4: Conlon Corporation owns 40% of the stock of Dargon Corporation. As a result of redemption of the shares of a different stockholder, Conlon's ownership of Dargon rises to 50%. Conlon has indirectly acquired the requisite degree of control. Code Sec. 269 applies if the redemption was motivated by the prohibited purpose.

If Code Sec. 269(a) applied only to acquisitions of stock, it could be circumvented by acquiring assets instead of stock. Thus, Code Sec. 269(a)(2) covers acquisition of assets with carryover basis. In a sale of assets, of course, the acquiror obtains cost basis, not carryover basis, in the acquired assets. Thus, Code Sec. 269(a)(2) applies principally to tax-free corporate reorganizations. However, the provision is not triggered if the acquiring corporation and the transferor corporation were under common control before the transaction. Thus, for instance, Code Sec. 269(a) is not triggered when a profitable corporation and a loss corporation owned by the same person(s) are merged or consolidated.

(c) Tax Avoidance Purpose

Common to Code Sec. 269(a)(1) and 269(a)(2) is the prohibited motivation that "the principal purpose" of the acquisition was avoiding income tax by getting a tax benefit the acquiror would not otherwise enjoy.

Example 1: Randano Corporation is very profitable. Saldini Corporation is unprofitable and has large NOLs. Randano and Saldini are unrelated. Randano wants to acquire Saldini by merging Saldini into itself, in order to offset Randano's taxable profits by applying Saldini's NOLs against them. Since Saldini and Randano are separate and unrelated companies, Randano would not normally be able to use Saldini's NOLs. Absent a predominant non-tax motive, the prohibited purpose is present here.

Example 2: The same facts as in Example 1 except that Saldini wants to acquire Randano. Saldini's NOLs are about to expire. By merging Randano into itself, Saldini can use the NOLs to offset Randano's taxable income, thus in effect getting that income tax free. Saldini would not normally be able to use the about–to–expire NOLs since it has no taxable income of its own. Absent a predominant non-tax motive, the prohibited purpose is present here.

The statutory language is "evasion or avoidance" of income tax, which resembles the language of Code Sec. 482 ("to prevent evasion of taxes or clearly to reflect . . . income"). Avoidance is the broader term and, in practical effect, swallows evasion.[122]

For Code Sec. 269 to apply, the avoidance purpose must be the acquiror's "principal" purpose. It need not be the sole purpose, but it must "exceed in

---

[121] *e.g., Kean v. Comm'r,* 469 F.2d 1183 (9th Cir. 1972); *Ach v. Comm'r,* 358 F.2d 342 (6th Cir. 1966), *cert. denied,* 358 U.S. 899 (1966).

[122] *See* Treas. Reg. § 1.269-1(b) (stating that evasion or avoidance of tax is not limited to cases in which criminal or civil fraud penalties may be asserted).

¶903.02(c)

importance" the non-tax reduction purposes.[123] The strengths of the various motivations are measured as of the time the transaction is effected,[124] but subsequent events may shed light on the purpose that existed at that time.[125]

> **Example:** Assume that the acquiror has three purposes for acquiring the requisite stock or assets to meet section 269 thresholds. The prohibited purpose constitutes 40% of the acquiror's motivation, and two non-tax business purposes each constitute 30% of the acquiror's motivation. Although the prohibited purpose exceeds in significance each of the other two purposes, the prohibited purpose did not exceed 50% of the motivation. Code Sec. 269 does not apply.[126]

> **Practice Tip:** Non-tax business purposes accepted by the IRS or the courts have included: the refusal of the other party to the transaction to do the deal in another form; facilitating a more effective business structure or model; creating a financially stronger or more attractive entity in order to improve credit worthiness or attract outside investors; acquisition of more physical resources, intellectual capability, or service or productive capacity; and protection of markets or supplies.[127]

There are obvious difficulties in ascertaining with any reasonable degree of precision what a taxpayer's purposes are, much less quantifying them. But, whatever the difficulty, determining and weighing rental states are familiar operations in both the tax and nontax law. For Code Sec. 269, as well as for other Code sections, subjective purpose will be inferred from the objective circumstances, with all facts and circumstances being taken into consideration.[128]

Code Sec. 269 once contained a presumption of prohibited purpose based on the relation of the basis of acquired assets, purchase price, and acquired tax benefits, but that presumption was repealed in 1976. The regulations, however, identify certain transactions that ordinarily evince the prohibited purpose. They include: (1) a profitable corporation acquiring a loss corporation so as to make the loss corporation's NOLs available for use, (2) splitting off profit-making assets so as to produce NOLs in order to obtain refunds of previously paid income taxes, (3) acquisition of built-in loss property and realization of those losses, and (4) transferring profit-making assets to an unprofitable related company to allow utilization of its otherwise unusable NOLs.[129]

The burden of proof as to principal purpose typically is where it usually is in civil tax litigation – on the taxpayer.[130] In theory, Code Sec. 7491 may allow the shift of the burden of proof to the IRS. However, there are so many conditions to that

---

[123] Treas. Reg. § 1.269-3(a).

[124] *e.g., Capri, Inc. v. Comm'r*, 65 T.C. 162 (1975).

[125] *e.g., Swiss Colony, Inc. v. Comm'r*, 52 T.C. 25 (1969), *aff'd*, 428 F.2d 49 (7th Cir. 1970).

[126] *U.S. Shelter Corp. v. United States*, 87-2 USTC ¶ 9588 (Cl. Ct. 1987); VGS Corp. v. Comm'r, 68 T.C. 563 (1977), acq. 1979-1 C.B. 1.

[127] *e.g., D'Arcy-MacManus, Inc. v. Comm'r*, 63 T.C. 440 (1975); *Clarkdale Rubber Co. v. Comm'r*, 45 T.C. 234 (1965); *Naeter Bros. Pub. Co. v. Comm'r*, 42 T.C. 1 (1964), *acq*, 1964-2 C.B. 6; *Baton Rouge Supply Co. v. Comm'r*, 36 T.C. 1 (1961), *acq.* 1961-2 C.B. 4.

[128] Treas. Reg. § 1.269-3(a).

[129] Treas. Reg. § 1.269-3(a) to (c).

[130] *See generally Welch v. Helvering*, 290 U.S. 111 (1933); David M. Richardson, Jerome Borison & Steve Johnson, Civil Tax Procedure 223-24 (2d ed. 2008).

shift that it occurs rarely and is of little value when it does occur.[131] In litigation, whichever party bears the burden of proof will lose the case if it fails to present convincing proof of purpose. Usually, that is the taxpayer.[132] Sometimes it is the IRS.[133]

(d) Code Sec. 269(b)

Congress added subsection (b) to Code Sec. 269 in 1984. The subsection allows the IRS to disallow deductions, credits, and other allowances if all of four conditions are satisfied: (1) a corporation makes a qualified stock purchase with respect to another corporation, (2) no Code Sec. 338 election is made as to the purchase, (3) the acquired corporation is liquidated under a plan of liquidation adopted within two years after the acquisition, and (4) "the principal purpose for such liquidation is the evasion or avoidance of Federal income tax by securing the benefit of a deduction, credit, or other allowance which the acquiring corporation would not enjoy."[134]

"Qualified stock purchase" and "acquisition date" have the same meanings as in Code Sec 338.[135] Accordingly, the first of the four conditions entails 80% purchase of a corporation's stock within twelve months.[136] The fourth condition has the same meaning as under Code Sec. 269(a).

The IRS's power under Code Sec. 269(b) to disallow "deductions" clearly extends to NOL carryovers in existence at the time of the corporate acquisition. However, the courts are divided as to outer reaches of Code Sec. 269(b). Some courts have limited disallowance to pre-acquisition losses, that is, those which accrued economically before the acquisition.[137] Other courts allow application of Code Sec. 269(b) not just to pre-acquisition losses but also to post-acquisition losses, especially when they are related to built-in losses.[138]

> ***Practice Tip:*** Because of the circuit conflict, the IRS tends to prefer to assert Code Sec. 382 instead of Code Sec. 269 when possible. This usually is possible since Code Sec. 382 often covers the ground that Code Sec. 269 covers.[139] However, as seen below, there are some situations in which Code Sec. 269 applies but Code Sec. 338 does not.

(e) Code Sec. 269(c)

When applicable, subsections (a) and (b) of Code Sec. 269 could result in total disallowance of the item at issue. Subsection (c) gives the IRS flexibility. It provides: "In any case to which subsection (a) or (b) applies the [IRS] is author-

---

[131] *See* Steve R. Johnson, *The Danger of Symbolic Legislation: Perceptions and Realities of the New Burden–of–Proof Rules*, 84 Iowa L. Rev. 413, 427-46 (1999).

[132] *e.g., Scroll, Inc. v. Comm'r*, 447 F.2d 170 (5th Cir. 1971).

[133] *e.g., Daytona Beach Kennel Club, Inc. v. Comm'r*, 69 T.C. 1015 (1978). In this case, the IRS had the burden of proof because it raised section 269 as a new issue not set out in the notice of deficiency. For discussion of the circumstances under which the IRS bears the burden of proof, see Johnson, *supra* n. 131, at 482-88.

[134] Code Sec. 269(b)(1).

[135] Code Sec. 269(b)(2).

[136] Code Sec. 338(d)(3).

[137] *e.g., Hall Paving Co. v. United States*, 471 F.2d 261 (5th Cir. 1973); *Zanesville Inv. Co. v. Comm'r*, 335 F.2d 507 (6th Cir. 1964).

[138] *e.g., Luke v. Comm'r*, 351 F.2d 568 (7th Cir. 1965); *R.P. Collins & Co. v. United States*, 303 F.2d 142 (1st Cir. 1962).

[139] *See, e.g.,* Code Sec. 382(h) (applying to built-in losses the same rules as NOL carryovers).

¶903.02(d)

ized" to do any of three things: (1) allow the item in part if the IRS "determines that such disallowance will not result in the evasion or avoidance of Federal income tax for which the acquisition was made"; (2) "distribute, apportion, or allocate" items of income, deduction, credits, or other allowances among "the corporations, or properties, or parts thereof, involved" to the extent the IRS "determines will not result in the evasion or avoidance of Federal income tax for which the acquisition was made"; or (3) to exercise the IRS's powers in part under (1) and in part under (2).

> *Practice Tip:* Code Sec. 269(c) provides that the IRS "is authorized" to make such partial adjustments. This language appears to confer discretion on the IRS, but not to mandate action by the IRS. If the taxpayer believes that Code Sec. 269(c) should apply but the IRS agent chooses not to apply it, can the taxpayer ask a court to compel the IRS to exercise the Code Sec. 269(c) power?

In some contexts, the Code provides that the IRS's exercise or non-exercise of its discretion is judicially reviewable,[140] but there is no such provision here. In other contexts, courts sometimes have held judicial review to be available – on an abuse of discretion standard –even in the absence of a statutory provision.[141] Arguably, reviewability could be countenanced by the Administrative Procedure Act, which provides liberally for judicial review of agency actions.[142]

Whatever arguments theoretically could be marshalled, there is an absence of authority holding that the IRS's refusal to apply Code Sec. 269(c) is judicially reviewable.

(f) Current Significance of Code Sec. 269

Code Sec. 269 is not among the most prominent sections of the Code in current practice. There are three reasons for this. First, as noted, Code Sec. 269 is triggered only when tax avoidance is the over-50% motivation for the transactions. This is a high threshold, and the uncertainty associated with this subjectivity can daunt the IRS as well as taxpayers.

Second, Code Sec. 269 has been largely, though not wholly, eclipsed by other anti-abuse rules. The attentive reader will have noticed that the dates of the cases and rulings cited in this discussion of Code Sec. 269 tend to predate 1986. This is no accident. The enactment and amendment of other provisions –especially the 1986 amendments to Code Sec. 382 – have given the IRS tools that usually are more reliable then Code Sec. 269.

Third, ironically, the existence of these other sections makes more problematic the fulfillment of the "principal purpose" element of Code Sec. 269. Code Secs. 382, 383, or 384 (discussed later in this chapter) could apply to nearly every acquisition to which Code Sec. 269 also could apply. Since these other sections

---

[140] *e.g.,* Code Sec. 6404(h) (review of IRS decisions not to abate interest).

[141] *e.g., Kean v. Comm'r,* 469 F.2d 1183 (9th Cir. 1972) (late filing of shareholder consent to S election).

[142] 5 U.S.C. §§ 701(a), 702, 704 & 706. Treasury and the IRS are subject to the APA. 5 U.S.C. § 551(1). Agency action is defined to include agency failures to act. 5 U.S.C.. § 551(13).

impose tax costs on the acquisitions, it becomes harder for the IRS to maintain that the main purpose for the acquisitions is tax avoidance.[143]

Nonetheless, at least in theory, the IRS has the power to assert Code Sec. 269 even when other sections also could apply.[144] Moreover, there remain situations in which only Code Sec. 269, and not the other sections, applies. Accordingly, despite its diminished status, Code Sec. 269 cannot be ignored by the careful tax advisor.

> ***Example:*** For five years, for investment reasons, Milhouse Corporation, a profitable company, has owned 49% of the voting stock of Peyton Corporation, a loss company. Peyton has substantial NOLs that will soon expire. Milhouse wants to merge Peyton into Milhouse in order to use those NOLs to offset its income. Under the applicable state law, however, a majority of shares must vote in favor of a merger, and the non-Milhouse shareholders oppose merging Peyton into Milhouse. In order to effectuate the merger, Milhouse acquires an additional 2% of the voting stock in Peyton.

> Because there has not been an increase of over 50 percentage points in Milhouse's ownership of Peyton stock within the Code Sec. 382 testing period, Code Sec. 382 would not apply to this transaction. However, Code Sec. 269 would apply.

.03 Code Sec. 381

In general, the tax attributes developed by one corporation remain with that corporation. Two principal events that occasion a transfer of one corporation's attributes to another are: certain reorganizations under Code Sec. 368 and liquidation of an 80% subsidiary into its parent under Code Sec. 332.[145] Subject to anti-abuse rules in Code Secs. 172, 269, and 382-384, Code Sec. 381 describes when and what tax attributes may pass from one corporation to another. Below, we discuss Code Sec. 381 from three perspectives: (1) covered events, (2) covered attributes, and (3) operating rules.

(a) Covered Events

Covered events are the transactions that give rise to transfer of corporate attributes. There are three such events. Code Sec. 381(a) provides that a corporation (the acquiring corporation), which acquires the assets of another corporation (the distributor or transferor corporation) succeeds to designated tax attributes of the distributor if the acquisition occurs in either:

(1) a distribution to which Code Sec. 332 applies, that is, liquidation of an 80% subsidiary,[146]

(2) a reorganization under paragraphs A, C, or F of Code Sec. 386(a)(1), that is, a merger, consolidation, stock-for-assets acquisition, or reincorporation merger,[147] or

---

[143] *See* Treas. Reg. § 1.269-7 (noting that Code Secs. 382 and 383 may situationally overlap Code Sec. 269 and providing that the fact that deductions and credit may be limited by Code Secs. 382 and 383 is pertinent to whether tax avoidance was the purpose for the acquisition of stock or property).

[144] *See, e.g.,* H.R. Rep. No. 99-841, at II-194 (1986) (Conference Comm.).

[145] Code Secs. 368 and 332 are addressed in Chapters 9 and 7, respectively.

[146] Code Sec. 381(a)(1).

[147] Code Sec. 381(a)(2).

(3) a reorganization under paragraphs D or G of Code Sec. 368(a)(1), that is a forward subsidiary merger or a bankruptcy reorganization but only if they meet the requirements of Code Sec. 354(b)(1)(A) and (B).[148] These incorporated Code Sec. 354 requirements mandate that the acquiring corporation obtains substantially all the assets of the transferor corporation and that the transferor corporation distributes all its stock, securities, and other properties pursuant to a plan of reorganization.

Reorganizations under paragraphs B (stock-for-stock acquisitions) and E (recapitalizations) of Code Sec. 368(a)(1) are not covered events, meaning that they do not result in the passing of tax attributes. This is because these transactions shift stockholdings, but they do not entail transfer of assets to another corporation as required by Code Sec. 381(a). In addition, corporate divisions under Code Sec. 355 are outside the ambit of Code Sec. 381.[149]

Whether the covered event is a liquidation or a reorganization, only one corporation may be treated as the acquiring corporation and thus can succeed to the tax attributes of the transferor corporation. Usually, the corporation treated as the acquiring corporation is the one that, under the plan of liquidation or reorganization, ultimately obtains all the assets of the transferor corporation. If no one corporation obtains all the assets, the corporation that initially obtains the assets will be deemed the acquiring corporation, whether or not it ultimately retains any of those assets.[150]

> **Example 1:** Monhadrian Corporation acquires all the assets of Plugots Corporation in a C reorganization. Monhadrian then transfers all those assets to Monhadrian's wholly owned subsidiary. The subsidiary is treated as the acquiring corporation and succeeds to Plugots' tax attributes.[151]

> **Example 2:** Same facts as Example 1 except that Monhadrain transfers some of the assets to its wholly owned subsidiary and keeps the rest of the assets. Monhadrian is treated as the acquiring corporation.[152]

> **Example 3:** Same facts as Example 1 except that Monhadrian has two wholly owned subsidiaries and it divides the assets between them. Monhadrian is treated as the acquiring corporation.[153]

(b) Covered Attributes

When a covered transaction occurs, what tax attributes pass from the distributing to the acquiring corporation? That is the province of Code Sec. 381(c). The contents of subsection (c) have changed over the years as some items have been added to and others removed from its ambit. In current form, subsection (c) covers 22 tax attributes. They are:

- NOLs
- earnings and profits

---

[148] Code Sec. 381(a)(2) & succeeding flush language.

[149] S. Rep. No. 1622, 83d Cong., 2d Sess. 52 (1954), reprinted in 1954 U.S. Code Cong. & Ad. News 4621, 4914.

[150] Treas. Reg § 1.381(a)-1(b)(2).

[151] *Id.* § 1.381(a)-1(b)(2)(ii) Example 2.

[152] *Id.* Example 3.

[153] *Id.* Example 4.

- capital loss carryovers
- accounting methods
- inventories
- depreciation methods
- installment method
- amortization of bond discount or premium
- treatment of certain mining development and exploration expenses
- contributions to pension plans, employees' annuity plans, and stock bonus and profit-sharing plans
- recovery of tax benefit items
- involuntary conversions under Code Sec. 1033
- dividend carryover to personal holding company
- certain obligations of the distributing corporation
- deficiency dividend of personal holding company
- percentage depletion on extraction of ores or minerals from the waste or residue of prior mining
- charitable contribution carryovers
- successor insurance company
- deficiency dividend of regulated investment company or real estate investment trust
- Code Sec. 38 Credit
- Code Sec. 53 Credit
- enterprise zone provisions.[154]

Practice Tip: Is the Code Sec. 381 enumeration exhaustive? In other words, may the principles of Code Sec. 381 apply even to tax attributes that are not expressly listed in Code Sec. 381(c)? Probably so. The regulations state that no inference should be drawn as to whether an acquiring corporation succeeds to tax attributes of the distributing corporation that are not listed in subsection (c).[155] That seems to suggest that this listing is not exhaustive and that not-specifically-covered tax attributes are not necessarily outside the scope of Code Sec. 381.

Some of these items do not warrant extended treatment here, either because they are not of general significance or because their treatment is straightforward. For instance, "[t]he acquiring corporation shall be entitled to deduct, as if it were the distributor or transferor corporation, expenses deferred under Code Sec. 616 (relating to certain development expenditures) if the distributor or transferor corporation has so elected."[156] Similarly, "[t]he acquiring corporation shall be considered to be the distributor or transferor corporation for the purpose of

---

[154] Code Sec. 381(c)(1)-(26).
[155] Treas. Reg. § 1.381(a)-1(b)(3).

[156] Code Sec. 381(c)(10).

¶903.03(b)

determining the applicability of Code Sec. 613(c)(3) (relating to extraction of ores or minerals from the ground)."[157]

Other items are more significant or entail more complicated treatment. These other items are addressed below.

(i) *NOLs*

This is the attribute that has occasioned the most planning and sparked the most frequent controversy between the IRS and taxpayers. Code Sec. 381 allows acquiring corporations to use NOLs of the transferor corporation but with three limitations:

First, the transferor's NOLs may only be carried forward, and they must first be applied to the first tax year ending after the date of the transfer from the transferor corporation to the acquiring corporation.[158]

Second, the amount of that NOL taken in that first tax year is limited to the extent it is attributable to the transferor. This is determined by ratio. Use of the NOL is "limited to an amount which bears the same ratio to the taxable income (determined without regard to [an NOL] deduction) of the acquiring corporation in [the tax] year as the number of days in the . . . year after the distribution . . . bears to the total number of days in the . . . year."[159]

Third, if the transferor corporation and the acquiring corporation each have a loss in the year of acquisition, the transferor's loss year is deemed to have occurred before the acquiror's loss year. Similar rules operate when determining taxable income for a previous year.[160]

(ii) *Earnings and Profits*

In general, the acquiring corporation succeeds – as of the close of the transfer date – to the earnings and profits balance of the transferor corporation, whether that balance is a surplus or a deficit.[161] However, a deficit can be used only to offset the acquiror's earnings and profits accumulated after the transfer. In applying this limitation, earnings and profits for the year in which the transfer occurs are allocated to the post-transfer period in the ratio that the days of the year after the transfer date bear to the total days in that year.[162]

(iii) *Capital Loss Carryovers*

The acquiring corporation succeeds to capital loss carryovers of the transferor corporation subject to limitations generally paralleling the NOL limitations described above.[163]

(iv) *Accounting Method*

Unsurprisingly, if the transferor corporation and the acquiring corporation used the same method of tax accounting, that use "shall" continue after the

---

[157] Code Sec. 381(c)(18).
[158] Code Sec. 381(c)(1)(A).
[159] Code Sec. 381(c)(1)(B).
[160] Code Sec. 381(c)(1)(C).

[161] Code Sec. 381(c)(2)(A).
[162] Code Sec. 381(c)(2)(B).
[163] Code Sec. 381(c)(3).

¶903.03(b)(iv)

transfer.[164] When different methods were used before the transfer(s), the regulations set out lengthy rules as to which of the methods is to continue in use.

If the transferor and acquiring corporations' businesses will continue to operate separately, the different accounting methods may continue to be used for the businesses.[165] If the businesses will be integrated, the "principal method of accounting" must be identified and used. This method is determined by reference to which business predominates based on aggregate adjusted asset bases and gross receipts.[166]

(v) *Depreciation Methods*

For depreciation purposes, the acquiring corporation steps into the shoes of the transferor corporation to the extent of the transferor's basis in the acquired assets.[167] The acquiring corporation may depreciate any excess basis under a reasonable method, which may be the same method or a different method from that used by the transferor.[168]

(vi) *Recovery of Tax Benefit Items*

In general, under Code Sec. 111 and case law, a taxpayer must include in income recovery of an amount for which the taxpayer previously took a deduction or credit unless the deduction or credit did not reduce the taxpayer's tax liability when taken. An acquiring corporation steps into the transferor corporation's shoes for purposes of these rules.[169]

(c) Operation Rules

Subsection (b) of Code Sec. 381 establishes three additional conditions or operating rules. First, the tax year of the transferor corporation ends on the date of the distribution or transfer to the acquiring corporation.[170] As a result, the transferor must file a tax return for the tax year that closes on that date.

Second, the date of distribution or transfer is deemed to be the day on which the distribution or transfer is completed. However, if the transferor and acquiror file the statements required under the regulations,[171] the date when substantially all the properties have been distributed or transferred may be used instead if the transferor halted all operations (except liquidating activities) after that date.[172]

Third, the acquiring corporation is prohibited from carrying back an NOL or a net capital loss for a tax year ending after the transfer date to a tax year of the transferor corporation.[173]

These three operating rules do not apply when the covered event is an F reorganization.[174] When this exception applies, the acquiror is treated as the transferor would have been treated had there been no reorganization.[175] Thus, the transfer does not end the tax year, the corporation retains its tax attributes, and pre-

---

[164] Code Sec. 381(c)(4).

[165] Treas. Reg. § 1.381(c)(4)-1(b)(2).

[166] *Id.* § 1.381(c)(4)-1(b)(3) & (c)(2).

[167] Code Sec. 381(c)(6).

[168] Treas. Reg. § 1.381(c)(6)-1(b).

[169] Code Sec. 381(c)(12).

[170] Code Sec. 381(b)(1).

[171] Treas. Reg. § 1.381(b)-1(b)(3).

[172] Code Sec. 381(b)(2).

[173] Code Sec. 381(b)(3).

[174] Code Sec. 381(b).

[175] Treas. Reg. § 1.381(b)-1(a)(2).

reorganization losses can be carried back to be used against pre-organization income.

.04 Code Sec. 382[176]

(a) Introduction

If it is determined that the NOLs from one taxable year may be used to offset taxable income earned in a prior year, or to carry the losses forward to be used in a future year, Code Sec. 382 can act to impose limitations on such use following a substantial change in the ownership of the corporation.[177]

The limitation on the ability to use NOLs following an ownership change reflects a policy decision that corporations should not be allowed to offset income with losses incurred by a different corporation, and also acts to discourage corporations from trafficking in their losses. Without such limitations, a defunct corporation with no valuable business assets holding a cache of unusable losses would be an attractive target for a profitable corporation interested in generating losses to offset its taxable income. Congress long ago determined that it should discourage the acquisition of corporations with no discernible value or apparent connection to the business of the acquiring corporation other than beneficial tax attributes.

Like much of the Internal Revenue Code, the provisions of Code Sec. 382 and the regulations thereunder are complex and intricate. This chapter will not discuss all of the nuances in detail, but will attempt to provide a practical overview.

(b) Overview of Code Sec. 382

Broadly speaking, Code Sec. 382 limits a corporation's ability to use prior year losses to offset otherwise taxable income following a change of ownership. In its current form, Code Sec. 382 applies only to restrict losses in cases where there is a substantial change in the ownership of the loss corporation's stock. Code Sec. 382 does not reduce or eliminate the overall amount of available losses. Instead, Code Sec. 382 restricts the amount of losses that can be used in any particular taxable year following an ownership change.[178]

The general rule under Code Sec. 382(a) states that the amount of the taxable income of any "new loss corporation" for any "post-change year" that may be offset by "pre-change losses" shall not exceed the "section 382 limitation" for such year. The general rule reads simply enough to limit the losses available to a corporation following a change of ownership, but the difficulty lies in discerning the detail underlying each highlighted term.

(c) Loss Corporation

A loss corporation is defined as any corporation that is otherwise entitled to use a net operating loss, a net operating loss carryforward, or a net unrealized built-

---

[176] The authors wish to sincerely thank Ms. Dawn Mayer, JD, LLM in Taxation (Tax Manager, University of San Francisco Office of Internal Audit and Tax Compliance) for her invaluable research and assistance with the discussion of Code Sec. 382.

[177] Code Sec. 382 also limits the use of recognized built-in losses following an ownership change, discussed in more detail below.

[178] The restrictions under Code Sec. 172 continue to apply, so that the NOLs of a corporation subject to Code Sec. 382 may expire if not used within a specified amount of time.

in loss for the taxable year in which an ownership change occurs. An old loss corporation is a loss corporation that generated losses prior to an ownership change, while a new loss corporation is a loss corporation entitled to use the losses of an old loss corporation following an ownership change.

The same corporation may be both an old loss corporation and a new loss corporation; for example, in the case of a shift in the stock ownership of a single corporation. Alternatively, in the case of a merger or other reorganization, the old loss corporation and the new loss corporation may differ.

Although an old loss corporation may technically cease to exist as a result of a merger or reorganization, it is treated as continuing for purposes of Code Sec. 382. Stock of the acquiring corporation is treated as stock of the old loss corporation for purposes of measuring each shareholder's ownership interest, and in cases where an ownership change occurs, the acquiring corporation must separately account for the losses of the old loss corporation for purposes of applying the Code Sec. 382 limitation for up to five years.

(d) Ownership Change

A loss corporation is subject to the limitations under Code Sec. 382 only if an ownership change has occurred with respect to such corporation. Unfortunately, determining whether an ownership change has occurred is one of the most difficult aspects of Code Sec. 382.

A loss corporation must evaluate whether an ownership change has occurred immediately following the occurrence of an "owner shift" or "equity structure shift" (referred to as a "testing date").

(i) *Owner Shifts*

An owner shift occurs as a result of any change in ownership that affects the percentage of stock held by a 5% shareholder (defined in more detail below, but generally including any holder of at least a 5% interest in the corporation). Such shifts might include the sale of stock by a 5% shareholder, a redemption by a loss corporation that affects the ownership percentage of one or more 5% shareholders, or the issuance of stock by a loss corporation that affects a 5% shareholder.

(ii) *Equity Structure Shifts*

An equity structure shift includes any tax-free reorganization defined under Code Sec. 368, other than certain divisive D reorganizations, G reorganizations (involving corporations in bankruptcy), or F reorganizations (involving a mere change in corporate form). Code Sec. 368(g)(3)(B) also states that an equity structure shift includes a taxable reorganization, such as a public offering or similar transaction, to the extent provided in the regulations.[179]

Although Code Sec. 382 includes a distinction between owner shifts and equity structure shifts, the two types of changes can overlap. For example, a reorganization described in Code Sec. 368(a)(1)(A) would constitute an equity structure shift,

---

[179] The Treasury Department has thus far declined to exercise its regulatory authority to define certain taxable reorganization-type transactions as equity structure shifts.

but could also result in a change in the percentage of stock owned by a 5-percent shareholder and therefore also constitute an owner shift. As a result, there appears to be little practical significance in defining a transaction as one particular type of shift, and in fact, the preamble to the temporary regulations under Code Sec. 382 confirms as much.[180] Further, the regulations provide that any equity structure shift that is not also an owner shift will not require the corporation to determine whether an ownership change has occurred, effectively rendering the concept of an equity structure shift irrelevant.[181]

(iii) *Determining an Ownership Change*

An ownership change has occurred if, over the three-year period ending with the testing date (referred to as the "testing period"), the percentage of stock of the loss corporation owned by one or more 5% shareholders has increased by more than 50 percentage points over the lowest percentage of stock that was owned by such persons during the testing period. It is important to note that the analysis considers percentage points, not percentage change. For example, a shareholder whose interest in a corporation increases from 20% to 40% has experienced a 100% increase in his ownership, but only 20 percentage points.

The separate increases in ownership of each 5% shareholder whose ownership in the corporation increased during the testing period are added together to determine whether the 50 percentage point threshold was reached. Because the occurrence of an ownership change is measured over a three-year period, a relevant change can occur as a result of a combination of events (see examples below).

Because only 5% shareholders whose percentages of stock ownership increase over the course of the testing period are taken into account, a shareholder who is not a 5% shareholder or whose ownership in the corporation decreases or remains the same will be disregarded for purposes of the ownership change analysis.[182]

> **Example 1:** Corporation X is a loss corporation with 100 shares outstanding. A owns 60 shares and B owns 40 shares. On January 1, 2008, B sells all of his X shares to C. Because the sale affects the percentage of stock owned by a 5% shareholder, the sale constitutes an owner shift requiring a determination of whether an ownership change occurred. As of the close of the testing date (January 1), the only 5% shareholder whose ownership interest increased is C. However, the percentage of stock owned by C increased by fewer than 50 percentage points over the lowest percentage of stock owned by C during the testing period (from 0 to 40%). As a result, the owner shift does not result in an ownership change triggering the Code Sec. 382 limitation.

> **Example 2:** The facts are the same as in Example 1. In addition, on January 15, 2009, X issues an additional 20 shares to each of D and E. The

---

[180] T.D. 8149, 08/11/1987. The distinction did initially matter for purposes of the statute's effective date.

[181] Treas. Reg. § 1.382-2T(a)(2)(i)(B).

[182] Ownership is determined on the basis of value, rather than number of shares. Because shares with the same material rights are considered to have the same value, however, factors such as control premiums or minority discounts are disregarded. Code Sec. 382(k)(6)(C), Treas. Reg. § 1.382-2(a)(3)(i).

3-year testing period ending on January 15, 2009, includes increases in the ownership of three 5% shareholders: C, D and E. The total increase in the ownership of all three shareholders is 57.2 percentage points, resulting in an ownership change (from 0 to 28.6 for C [40/140] and from 0 to 14.3 for each of D and E [20/140]).

Example 3: A owns all of the stock of Corporation X, a loss corporation. Corporation Y is owned 60% by B and 40% by C. On June 1, 2009, Corporation X merges into Corporation Y in a reorganization described under Code Sec. 368(a)(1)(A). Following the merger, Corporation Y is owned 20% by A, 50% by B and 30% by C. As of the June 1, 2009 testing date, B and C are both 5% shareholders who collectively increased their ownership in the loss corporation by more than 50 percentage points (from 0 to 50% for B and 0 to 30% for C). As a result, Corporation Y is a new loss corporation and the pre-change losses of Corporation X are subject to the limitation under Code Sec. 382.

Example 4: Corporation X is a loss corporation with 500 shares outstanding. A owns 300 shares, while B and C each own 100 shares. On February 1, 2009, A sells 200 shares of X stock to B. The sale constitutes an owner shift, but does not result in an ownership change, since B's interest only increases by 40 percentage points (from 20% [100/500] to 60% [300/500]). On July 15, 2010, A purchases all of C's shares. As of the July 15, 2010 testing date, A's interest in X has increased by 20 percentage points from its lowest point (from 20% [100/500]following A's sale to B to 40% [200/500] on the testing date). Coupled with B's 40 percentage point increase, the two transactions cause an ownership change, even though A's interest in X has actually decreased compared to his ownership interest at the beginning of the three year testing period.

(e) Five Percent Shareholders

In order to determine whether an ownership change occurred as of a particular testing date, the loss corporation must identify each 5% shareholder whose ownership increased immediately following the close of the testing date and compare such shareholder's ownership interest to the lowest percentage of stock owned by such shareholder during the testing period.[183]

A 5% shareholder includes any holder who, either directly or indirectly, owns at least 5% of the stock of the loss corporation. Because the rule considers both direct and indirect ownership interests, an individual cannot avoid 5% shareholder status by, for example, holding stock of the loss corporation indirectly through a wholly owned entity.

Additionally, all of the shareholders of the loss corporation who own less than 5% of the corporation's stock are aggregated together as a group and considered as one 5% shareholder (generally referred to as the corporation's "public group"). As a result, the stock of a widely held corporation is generally treated as being owned by

---

[183] A shareholder is allowed to tack the holding period of the transferor of stock acquired during the testing period by death, gift or divorce. Code Sec. 382(l)(3)(B). As a result, stock transfers pursuant to such circumstances are effectively ignored.

a single 5% shareholder and transactions among such corporation's shareholders will not generally result in an ownership change.

(i) *Constructive Ownership*

For purposes of determining ownership interests, the constructive ownership rules of Code Sec. 318 apply, with certain modifications. For example, stock owned separately by certain family members, such as a husband and wife, will be considered owned by a single shareholder (thus sales between such family members will be disregarded).

One important modification of the Code Sec. 318 rules is that stock held by an entity is attributed to its owners without regard to the 50% ownership limitation under Code Sec. 318(a)(2)(C). Further, stock attributed from an entity to its owners is not also treated as being owned by the entity. As a result, any amount of stock of a loss corporation owned by an entity will be considered to be owned by such entity's individual owners for purposes of identifying 5% shareholders.

(ii) *Types of Ownership Interests*

When considering the ownership interests of a loss corporation, all varieties of stock are generally included, except for certain non-voting, non-convertible preferred stock described in Code Sec. 1504(a)(4). Additionally, the owner of an option, warrant, convertible debt or other similar instrument that is convertible into stock will generally be treated as owning the underlying stock if such treatment results in an ownership change.

(iii) *Administrative Rules*

On any given testing date, a loss corporation is only required to calculate changes in the stock ownership of the following shareholders: (i) individual shareholders with direct ownership interests of 5% or more; (ii) individual shareholders with indirect ownership interests of 5% or more through either a first tier entity or a higher tier entity; and (iii) the public groups of the loss corporation and any first tier entity or higher tier entity.

For purposes of the foregoing, a "first tier entity" is defined as any entity shareholder with a direct ownership interest in the loss corporation of 5% or more, while a "higher tier entity" is any entity shareholder with an indirect ownership interest of 5% or more.

As a result of these rules, a loss corporation would have no obligation to consider an indirect individual shareholder if, for example, the entity in which he owned an interest owned less than 5% of the loss corporation (in that case, the less than 5% interest of the entity would be aggregated with the loss corporation's public group). This is the case even if the individual also holds a direct interest in the corporation of less than 5%, which, together with the indirect interest, exceeds 5%.

> **Example:** Individual A owns a 30% interest in Corporation X, which in turn owns a 4% interest in Corporation Z, a loss corporation. A also directly owns a 4% interest in Corporation Z. A is not a 5% shareholder for purposes of Code Sec. 382 even though he collectively owns 5% of Corporation Z ((([A's 30% ownership of X] x [X's 4% ownership of Z]) + A's 4% interest in Z).

¶903.04(e)(iii)

On the other hand, the shareholder's interests must be aggregated if he owns an interest in a first tier or higher tier entity (which, by definition, owns 5% or more of the loss corporation).

> *Example:* Individual A owns a 4% interest in Corporation X, which in turn owns a 30% interest in Corporation Z, a loss corporation. A is a 5% shareholder for purposes of Code Sec. 382 (([A's 4% ownership of X] x [X's 30% ownership of Z]) + A's 4% interest in Z).

(iv) *Public Groups*

As mentioned above, all of the shareholders of a loss corporation who own less than a 5% interest are aggregated together and treated as a single 5% shareholder. In addition, all of the shareholders of a first tier or higher tier entity that do not indirectly own 5% or more of the loss corporation are aggregated together as a public group of such first tier or higher tier entity.

A public group of a first tier or higher tier entity that indirectly owns a 5% or greater interest in the loss corporation is treated as a 5% shareholder. If the public group of a higher tier entity does not indirectly own more than 5% of the loss corporation, the group must be dropped down to the next lower tier entity and aggregated with that entity's public group for purposes of the analysis.

> *Example:* Corporation X, a loss corporation, is owned 20% by Individual A, 20% by Corporation Y, 10% by Corporation Z and 50% by a public group (individual shareholders, none of whom own an interest of 5% interest more). Corporation Y is owned 20% by Individual B and 80% by a public group. Corporation Z is owned 60% by Corporation V and 40% by Corporation W. Corporation W is publicly owned, while Corporation V is owned 85% by Individual C and 15% by a public group. The ownership structure is illustrated by the following chart:

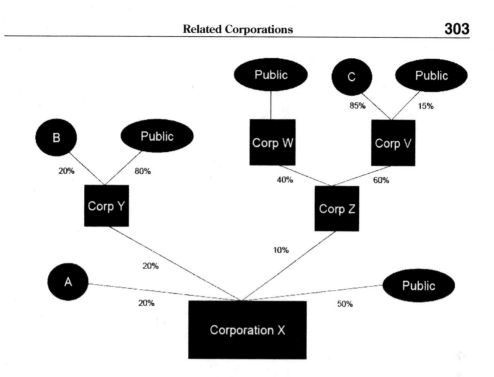

As noted above, for purposes of the ownership change analysis, a loss corporation must identify (i) individual shareholders with direct ownership interests of 5% or more; (ii) individual shareholders with indirect ownership interests of 5% or more through either a first tier entity or a higher tier entity; and (iii) the public groups of the loss corporation and any first tier or higher tier entity. In this case, Individual A is a direct 5% shareholder of Corporation X. The public group of Corporation X, which collectively holds a 50% interest in Corporation X, is considered a single direct 5% shareholder (this would be the case even if the public group owned less than a 5% interest in Corporation X). Corporation Y and Corporation Z, each of which owns a direct ownership interest in Corporation X of 5% or more, are first tier entities. Individual B owns more than a 5% interest in Corporation Y (a first tier entity), but is considered to indirectly own only 4% of Corporation X (B's 20% interest in Corporation Y x Corporation Y's 20% interest in Corporation X). As a result, B is not a 5% shareholder of Corporation X, but will instead be considered a member of the public group that owns the remaining 80% of Corporation Y. Together, B and the Corporation Y public group are treated as a single shareholder that indirectly owns a 20% interest in Corporation X. Corporation W indirectly owns a 4% interest in Corporation X (Corporation W's 40% interest in Corporation Z x Corporation Z's 10% interest in Corporation X). As a result, Corporation W is not considered a higher tier entity, but will be considered a member of Corporation Z's public group. Corporation V indirectly owns a 6% interest in Corporation X and is therefore a higher tier entity (Corporation V's 60% interest in Corporation Z x Corporation Z's 10% interest in Corporation X). C indirectly owns a 5.1% interest in Corporation X and is therefore a 5% shareholder (C's 85% interest in Corporation V x Corporation V's 60% interest in

¶903.04(e)(iv)

Corporation Z x Corporation Z's 10% interest in Corporation X). Corporation V's public group indirectly owns 0.9% of Corporation X and therefore is not considered a 5% shareholder (15% interest in Corporation V x Corporation V's 60% interest in Corporation Z x Corporation Z's 10% interest in Corporation X). However, the 0.9% interest must be added to the other members of the public group of the next lowest tier entity (Corporation Z), which also includes Corporation W's 4% interest. Because Corporation Z's public group indirectly owns less than 5% of Corporation X (Corporation W's 4% interest + 0.9% interest of Corporation V's public group), such shareholders are not considered in the analysis. Accordingly, the 5% shareholders of Corporation X include A, C, Corporation X's public group and Corporation Y's public group (which includes B).

It is easy to see from the above example how quickly the exercise of merely identifying 5% shareholders becomes cumbersome, even before calculating the changing ownership interests of such shareholders over the three-year testing period for purposes of determining whether an ownership change occurred.

In an attempt to ease the burdens of Code Sec. 382, the regulations permit a loss corporation to rely on the existence or absence of filings under Schedules 13D and 13G (required to be filed with the Securities and Exchange Commission when a shareholder acquires a 5% or greater interest in a public corporation); or a statement, signed under penalties of perjury, by a first tier or higher tier entity that no change in such entity's owners occurred as of the testing date. These rules will predictably not apply if the loss corporation has reasonable knowledge to the contrary.

(f) Code Sec. 382 Limitation

Once it is determined that an ownership change has occurred, the loss corporation will be limited in the amount of losses from a pre-change taxable year that can be used to offset taxable income in a post-change year. This "Section 382 limitation" is applied annually and is calculated by multiplying the loss corporation's value immediately before the ownership change by a prescribed rate.

The rate used is the long-term tax-exempt bond rate, which is published each month by the Internal Revenue Service. The applicable rate is the highest long-term tax-exempt bond rate in effect during the 3-month period ending with the month in which the ownership change occurs.

The value of the loss corporation is measured by the value of all of the loss corporation's stock immediately before the ownership change. The price paid for the stock generally determines its value, although price is not necessarily determinative.[184] Importantly, if one of the triggering events that caused the ownership change includes a redemption or other corporate contraction (which results in fewer outstanding shares), the value of the loss corporation is determined after taking into account such contraction.

---

[184] H.R. Rep. No. 841, 99th Cong., 2d Sess. II-187.

¶903.04(f)

Example: Corporation X undergoes an ownership change during a month when the applicable rate is 5%. At the time of the ownership change, the value of all of the outstanding stock of X is $1000. As a result, the annual limitation on the amount of taxable income that can be offset by NOL carryforwards from a pre-change taxable year is $50.

(i) *Excess Limitation*

The Code Sec. 382 limitation is permanent for the life of the pre-change losses held by the loss corporation at the time of the ownership change. However, the limitation for a single taxable year can be increased by the realization of certain built-in gains in the loss corporation's assets (discussed in more detail below). Additionally, if the Code Sec. 382 limitation for any post-change year exceeds the taxable income of the corporation for that year, the excess can be carried forward one year to increase the Code Sec. 382 limitation applied in the subsequent post-change year.

Example: The annual Code Sec. 382 limitation of Corporation X is $50. In Year 1, Corporation X earns $30 of taxable income and applies $30 of pre-change NOL carryforwards to offset this income. In Year 2, Corporation X earns $100 of taxable income. The $20 excess limitation from Year 1 is added to the annual $50 limitation, allowing X to offset $70 of taxable income in Year 2.

(ii) *Anti-Stuffing Rules*

Because the Code Sec. 382 limitation is based upon the price paid for the loss corporation's stock, the higher the price paid, the more pre-change losses will be available for use on an annual basis following the ownership change. If, however, the pre-change losses of the old loss corporation are significant compared to value, the Code Sec. 382 limitation may prevent all or some of the losses from being used before they expire under Code Sec. 172.

Because a higher value results in a higher Code Sec. 382 limitation, a loss corporation may be tempted to engage in transactions to increase its value prior to an anticipated ownership change. Predictably, Code Sec. 382 includes certain "anti-stuffing rules" that disregard such transactions.

For example, Code Sec. 382(l)(1) provides that pre-change capital contributions will be disregarded if the contributions are "part of a plan the principal purpose of which is to avoid or increase" the Code Sec. 382 limitation.

Additionally, if a loss corporation has an excess amount of "passive" assets (i.e., nonbusiness, investment assets) at the time of the ownership change, the value of the loss corporation can be reduced by the value of such assets.

(g) Mid-Year Ownership Changes

As a practical matter, ownership changes often do not occur on the last day of the taxable year. As a result, Code Sec. 382 includes rules for pro rating the Code Sec. 382 limitation based on the change date.

¶903.04(g)

If the ownership change occurs during a profitable year for the corporation, income earned prior to the change date can be offset with pre-change NOL carryforwards without limitation.[185] Income earned after the change date, however, is limited by a pro rata portion of the Code Sec. 382 limitation, calculated based on the number of days remaining in the year following the change date.

> **Example:** Corporation X undergoes an ownership change on July 1, resulting in an annual Code Sec. 382 limitation of $150. Only $75 worth of pre-change losses can be used to offset income earned after July 1 ([183/365] * 150)

If the ownership change occurs during a loss year, only the pre-change portion of losses incurred during the year will be subject to the Code Sec. 382 limitation. Losses that arise after the change date are not subject to the Code Sec. 382 limitation. In any subsequent taxable year in which the corporation has income that may be offset by both a pre-change loss subject to the Code Sec. 382 limitation and losses not subject to such limitation, income will be treated as having first been offset by the limited pre-change losses. This rule allows a corporation to use up losses subject to the Code Sec. 382 limitation, even though the corporation may be able to offset income in any given taxable year in excess of the limitation by applying additional post-change losses.

As an alternative to the pro rating rules described above, a corporation may elect to close its books as of the date of the ownership change.

(h) Built-In Gains and Losses

(i) *Built-In Losses*

The discussion above focused mainly on the operating losses of a corporation. However, a corporation may also have losses inherent in its assets, which have not yet been realized because the assets have not been sold (referred to as "built-in losses"). Code Sec. 382 also restricts the use of these built-in losses following an ownership change.

In general, if a corporation sells an asset for less than its adjusted basis, the corporation will realize a loss. Such realized loss can generally offset income of the corporation in the same manner as other operating losses. As a result, a corporation's built-in losses are treated as being economically equivalent to its NOLs and are similarly restricted under Code Sec. 382 following an ownership change.

If, at the time of an ownership change, the loss corporation holds non-cash assets with a total aggregate adjusted basis in excess of the aggregate fair market value, the corporation has a net unrealized built-in loss (NUBIL). The NUBIL will be subject to Code Sec. 382 if it exceeds a certain threshold amount (i.e., the lesser of $10,000,000 or 15% of the fair market value of assets prior to the ownership change).

---

[185] Taxable income is allocated ratably to each day of the taxable year for purposes of calculating the income earned before and after the change date.

If a corporation with a NUBIL recognizes a pre-change built-in loss within the five-year period following the ownership change (referred to as a "recognized built-in loss," or "RBIL"), the loss will be treated as a pre-change loss subject to the Code Sec. 382 limitation.

The rationale for this rule is that if the built-in loss had been recognized prior to the ownership change, it would have been a net operating loss at the time of the ownership change and would therefore have been subject to the Code Sec. 382 limitation.

> *Example:* Corporation X undergoes an ownership change in Year 1, at a time when it owns non-cash assets with an aggregate fair market value of $500,000 and an aggregate adjusted basis of $850,000. In Year 3, Corporation X sells one of the assets with an adjusted basis of $20,000 for $15,000. The $5000 RBIL will be added to the losses subject to the Code Sec. 382 limitation.

(ii) *Built-In Gains*

If, at the time of an ownership change, the aggregate fair market value of the corporation's non-cash assets exceeds the aggregate adjusted basis by more than the threshold amount, the corporation has a net unrealized built-in gain (NUBIG).

If a corporation with a NUBIG realizes a pre-change built-in gain within the five-year recognition period (a "recognized built-in gain," or "RBIG"), the Code Sec. 382 limitation for that year will be increased by the amount of the gain.

The rationale for increasing the Code Sec. 382 limitation is that if the gain had been recognized before the ownership change, it could have been used to offset the corporation's losses without limitation.

Because it can be difficult to determine whether built-in gains and losses of a corporation existed prior to or following an ownership change, the IRS has issued guidance to assist corporations in calculating NUBIG and NUBIL and identifying RBIG and RBIL.[186]

(i) Continuity of Business Enterprise Test

Notwithstanding the calculations described above, if a loss corporation does not meet a continuity of business enterprise test during the two-year period following a change of ownership, the corporation's NOL carryforwards will be disallowed completely (except to the extent of any recognized built-in gains or Code Sec. 338 gains). The concept of business continuity is the same as that used for purposes of qualifying a reorganization under Code Sec. 368 and generally requires the new loss corporation to continue the historic business of the old loss corporation or use a significant portion of the loss corporation's assets in a business.

Business continuity is generally not an issue if the change in ownership is triggered by transfers of stock of a single corporation, but can be an issue in the case of a merger or other reorganization where the new loss corporation differs from the old loss corporation.

---

[186] Notice 2003-65.

(j) Reporting Requirements

A loss corporation must file an information statement with its income tax return for each taxable year in which an owner shift or equity shift occurs, setting forth the dates on which such shifts occurred, the dates on which any ownership changes occurred, and the current losses of the corporation. This information statement is also used to make the election to close the books of the corporation as of the date of an ownership change, rather than allocate income and losses to periods before and after the ownership change.

.05 Code Sec. 383

(a) Generally

Code Sec. 382 limits the utilization of pre-acquisition losses. But acquisitions could also be motivated by a desire to take advantage of otherwise unusable tax credits. Code Sec. 383 complements Code Sec. 382 by addressing use of credits and net capital losses after an acquisition. Not surprisingly, the limitations imposed by Code Sec. 383 and many of the key definitions are modeled on the rules in Code Sec. 382.[187]

Under Code Sec. 383, if an ownership change takes place as to a loss corporation, for post-change years (1) the Code Sec. 382 limitation limits the amount of tax liability and (2) the Code Sec. 383 limitation limits the amount of regular tax liability, that may be offset by the new loss corporation's pre-change credits and capital losses.[188]

(b) Limitation as to Credits

The tax liability of a loss corporation for a post-change year can be offset by pre-change credits only up to the Code Sec. 383 credit limitation for the post-change year.[189] As is true with respect to net capital losses as well, this limitation is applied only after all other limitations in the Code are taken into account.[190]

The Code Sec. 383 credit limitation for a post-change year of a new loss corporation is an amount by which the corporation's regular income tax liability would be reduced if its taxable income for the year were reduced by the remainder of its section 382 limitation after subtracting use of pre-change losses.[191]

Pre-change credits subject to limitation under Code Sec. 383 include all of the following:

- excess foreign taxes under Code Sec. 904(c) of the old loss corporation, which are carried forward to the tax year ending on the change date or which are carried forward to the tax year that includes the change date, to the extent the credit is allocable to the period in the year ending on or before the change date;[192]

---

[187] The terms used in Code Sec. 383 have the same respective meanings as in Code Sec. 382, with appropriate adjustments to context. Code Sec. 383(e).

[188] Treas. Reg. § 1.383-1(b).

[189] Treas. Reg. § 1.383-1(d)(1).

[190] Treas. Reg. § 1.383-1(d)(3)(i).

[191] Treas. Reg. § 1.383-1(b) & (c)(6).

[192] Treas. Reg. § 1.383-1(c)(3)(i); see also Code Sec. 383(c).

- credits under Code Sec. 38 of the old loss corporation, which are carried forward to the tax year ending on the change date or which are carried forward from a tax year that includes the change date to the extent the credit is allocable to the period ending on or before the change date;[193] and

- available minimum tax credits of the old loss corporation under Code Sec. 53 to the extent they are attributable to periods ending on or before the change date.[194]

Example: Logres Corporation is a new loss corporation that uses the calendar year. For year 1, Logres has taxable income (before use of any pre-change loss) of $100,000. Logres has a Code Sec. 382 limitation of $25,000, a pre-change NOL of $12,000, a pre-change minimum tax credit of $50,000, and no pre-change capital losses. Logres's Code Sec. 383 credit limitation is the excess of its regular tax liability computed after allowing a $12,000 NOL deduction (taxable income of $88,000; assumed regular tax liability of $18,170), over its regular tax liability computed after allowing an additional deduction in the amount of Logres's Code Sec. 382 section limitation remaining after application of Code Sec. 383, or $13,000 (taxable income of $75,000; assumed regular tax liability of $13,750). Logres's Code Sec. 383 credit limitation is $4,420 ($18,170 minus $13,750).[195]

(c) Limitation as to Capital Losses

Code Sec. 383 treats capital loss carryovers after an ownership change in a manner like the Code Sec. 382 rules applicable to NOL carryovers. Any net capital loss used in a post-change year reduces the Code Sec. 382 limitation applied to pre-change losses under Code Sec. 382 for the year.[196]

Example: Laramie Corporation is on the calendar year. It has an ownership change on December 31 of Year 1 and becomes a new loss corporation. Before application of carryovers, Laramie has $60,000 of capital gains, $100,000 of ordinary taxable income, and a $100,000 Code Sec. 382 limitation for its first post-change year after the change date. Laramie's only carryovers are an $80,000 capital loss carryover and a $100,000 NOL carryover, both of which are from tax years before the change date.

Laramie first uses $60,000 of its pre-change capital loss carryover to offset its capital gain. This use reduces its Code Sec. 382 limitation to $40,000 ($100,000 minus $60,000). Laramie's pre-change NOL carryover can be used only to the extent of $40,000. Laramie's remaining $20,000 pre-change capital loss carryover and remaining $60,000 pre-change NOL carryover are carried to later years to the degree allowed by Code Secs. 172, 382, 383, and 1212.[197]

---

[193] Treas. Reg. § 1.383-1(c)(3)(ii); *see also* Code Sec. 383(a)(2)(A).

[194] Treas. Reg. § 1.383-1(c)(3)(iii); *see also* Code Sec. 383(a)(2)(B). The business credit and the minimum tax are discussed in Chapter 3.

[195] Treas. Reg. § 1.383-1(c)(6)(ii).

[196] Code Sec. 383(b).

[197] Treas. Reg. § 1.383-1(f) Example 1. The same regulation sets out two additional, more complex examples.

(d) Special Rules

What if the ownership change occurs, not conveniently on the first of last day of the loss corporation's tax year, but instead at some point during the year? In that case, the Code Sec. 383 tax attributes must be pro-rated between the pre-change and the post-change portions of the year. This allocation is made via the same principles that govern allocation of pre-change losses under Code Sec. 382.[198]

Both the tax attributes covered by Code Sec. 382 and those covered by Code Sec. 383 can reduce a loss corporation's tax liability in a post-change year. Thus, they need to be coordinated in their effect and application. The regulations do so. They prescribe the following order of application: (1) pre-change capital losses recognized during the year and subject to Code Sec. 382, (2) capital loss carryovers subject to Code Sec. 383, (3) pre-change ordinary losses recognized during the year and subject to Code Sec. 382, (4) NOL carryovers, (5) excess foreign taxes carried over under Code Sec. 904(c), (6) unused general business credits carried over under Code Sec. 39, and (7) unused minimum tax credits under Code Sec. 53.[199]

Any part of the Code Sec. 382 limitation unused in one year is available for carryover to later years.[200] The amount so available is the excess of the remaining Code Sec. 382 limitation for the post-change year over the "section 383 credit reduction amount" for the post-change year.[201] The Code Sec. 83 credit reduction amount is the sum of each dollar of taxable income that leads to a dollar of income tax liability that was offset by pre-change credits. The liabilities are divided by the effective marginal rate of tax that is imposed.[202]

Code Sec. 383 rules apply in the consolidated groups context in the same way as the Code Sec. 382 rules do.[203]

.06 Code Sec. 384

(a) Generally

Like Code Sec. 382, Code Sec. 384 limits the use of NOLs. Unlike Code Sec. 382, Code Sec. 384 applies to pre-acquisition NOLs of all parties to the acquisition. Code Sec. 384 was enacted in 1987 and substantially amended in 1988 – shortly after the 1986 amendments to Code Secs. 382 and 383.

Code Sec. 384 applies when either (1) one corporation acquires control of another corporation, (either directly or through another corporation) or (2) one corporation acquires the assets of another corporation in an A, C, or D reorganization.[204] In addition, for Code Sec. 384 to apply, at least one of the corporations must be a gain corporation, that is, it must have net unrealized built-in gain.[205]

When Code Sec. 384 applies, income for any recognition period tax year (to the extent attributable to recognized built-in gains) may not be offset by any

---

[198] Code Sec. 383(d).
[199] Treas. Reg. § 1.383-1(d)(2).
[200] Code Sec. 382(b)(2).
[201] Treas. Reg. § 1.383-1(e)(1).
[202] Treas. Reg. § 1.383-1(e)(2). The marginal rate is computed under stated modifications. The regulation sets

out an example of the computation of the Code Sec. 383 credit reduction using 1988 tax rates. *See* Treas. Reg. § 1.383-1(e)(3).
[203] Treas. Reg. § 1.1502-98.
[204] Code Sec. 384(a)(1).
[205] Code Sec. 384(a)(2) & (c)(4).

preacquisition loss, except a preacquisition loss of the gain corporation.[206] Similar rules apply in the case of any excess credit or net capital loss.[207]

Example: Calvert Corporation has an NOL carryover of $16,000. Calvert acquires all the assets of Erasmus Corporation in a transaction that satisfies Code Sec. 368(a)(1)(C). Those assets have a fair market value of $10,000 with an aggregate adjusted basis of $1,000. Accordingly, there is $9,000 net unrealized built-in gain as to the assets of Erasmus. Calvert sells the Erasmus assets, realizing $9,000 of gain. This $9,000 is Calvert's only income for the year, and it has no loss for the year. Calvert cannot use any of its $16,000 preacquisition loss to offset the $9,000 of recognized built-in gain.

There is an exception. The prohibition does not apply to preacquisition losses of a corporation if it and the gain corporation were members of the same controlled group throughout the five-year period ending on the date of acquisition.[208] "Controlled group" has the same meaning as in Code Sec. 1563 except that ownership of 50% (not 80%) of both (not either) the value and the voting power suffices.[209] The five-year period is relaxed if either of the corporations did not exist throughout the whole period.[210]

(b) Definitions

Code Sec. 384(c) contains extensive definitions, which effectively impose further requirements. The more important of those provisions include the following.

Recognized built-in gain: The Code Sec. 384(a) limitation operates with respect to income "to the extent attributable to recognized built-in gain." Such gain is any gain recognized during the five-year period beginning on the change date on disposition of any asset unless the gain corporation establishes that either (1) the asset was not held by the gain corporation on the acquisition date or (2) the gain is greater than the excess of the fair market value of the asset on the acquisition date over the asset's adjusted basis on that date.[211]

However, the recognized built-in gains for any year may not exceed the net unrealized built-in gain reduced by the recognized built-in gains for prior years within the five-year period that would have been offset by preacquisition losses had it not been for Code Sec. 384.[212] "Net unrealized built-in gains" is the extent to which the assets' fair market value immediately before the change exceeds the assets' aggregate adjusted basis at that time.[213]

Preacquisition Loss: Under Code Sec. 384(a), what may not be used to offset income are preacquisition losses (except those of the gain corporation). Such losses include NOL carry forwards to the year of the acquisition, NOLs for the year

---

[206] Code Sec. 384(a).

[207] Code Sec. 384(d). "Excess credit" has the same meaning as in Code Sec. 383(a)(2), that is, unused general business credits under Code Sec. 39 and unused minimum tax credits under Code Sec. 53.

[208] Code Sec. 384(b)(1).

[209] Code Sec. 384(b)(2). In addition, the determination of controlled group status is made without regard to Code Sec. 1563(a)(4).

[210] Code Sec. 384(b)(3).

[211] Code Sec. 384(c)(1)(A).

[212] Code Sec. 384(c)(1)(C).

[213] Code Sec. 384(c)(8) (incorporating Code Sec. 382(h)(3)(A)(i)).

of the acquisition to the extent allocable to the part of year on or before the acquisition date, and recognized built-in losses of corporations that had net unrealized built-in losses.[214]

Control: Under Code Sec. 384(a)(1)(A), one of the triggering events for the Code Sec. 384 limitation is when a corporation acquires "control" of another corporation. Control is achieved by ownership of stock constituting at least 80% of the total voting power and total value of the corporation.[215]

(c) Special Rules

Carryover and Ordering Rules: If Code Sec. 384 prevents utilization of any preacquisition loss, excess credit, or net capital loss, the item may be carried forward to future years.[216] If a preacquisition loss for any year is limited by Code Sec. 384 but an NOL from that year is not limited, the taxpayer's taxable income is treated as having been offset first by the loss subject to limitation.[217] Thus, as a practical matter, the acquiring corporation with limited preacquisition losses uses up its own losses before those of the acquired corporation.

Members of the Same Group: Above, we noted the exception to Code Sec. 384(a) when the corporations both were members of the same controlled group (as defined under modified Code Sec. 1563 principles) through the five-year period ending on the acquisition date. Outside of that exception, all corporations that are members of the same affiliated group (under modified Code Sec. 1504 principles) immediately before the acquisition date are treated as a single corporation.[218]

Predecessors and successors: The Code Sec. 384 limitations apply to any predecessor or successor corporations. In the case of successor corporations, the limitations continue to apply for the remainder of the five-year recognition period.[219]

Things to watch for: Congress has authorized Treasury to promulgate regulations "as may be necessary to carry out the purposes of [section 384]." This includes regulations to ensure that the purposes of Code Sec. 384 are not circumvented through either "(1) the use of any provision of law or regulations (including subchapter K [as to partnerships]), or (2) contributions of property to a corporation."[220] The IRS has announced its intention to develop regulations under this authority.[221] Thus far, however, regulations have not been issued under Code Sec. 384.

¶ 904 Consolidated Returns: Code Secs. 1501 to 1504

Large businesses often conduct operations through many specialized units. When such units are divisions, no special problems arise – the division is not a separate entity for tax purposes, so its operations are simply part of those of the larger corporation.

---

[214] Code Sec. 384(c)(3). For this purpose, NOLs generally are allocated ratably to each day of the year.

[215] Code Sec. 384(c)(5) (incorporating Code Sec. 1504(a)(2)).

[216] Code Sec. 384(e)(1).

[217] Code Sec. 384(c)(2).

[218] Code Sec. 384(c)(6).

[219] Code Sec. 384(c)(7).

[220] Code Sec. 384(f).

[221] *e.g.,* IRS Notice 90-27, 1990-1 C.B. 336 (regulations to be developed to preclude avoidance of Code Sec. 384 via installment sales of built-in gain assets).

Often, however, the units are other corporations: subsidiaries. Since each corporation is a separate juridical entity, without a special rule all corporations – regardless of their degree of relation – would have to file separate returns. Especially when related corporations engage in substantial transactions with each other, separate filing and separate calculation of tax liability can produce artificial outcomes.

Accordingly, Congress has granted closely related corporations – generally those having at least 80% common ownership – the option to file consolidated returns. Consolidated treatment is elective, not mandatory. However, if the election is made, all corporations which are part of the affiliated group must join in the consolidated return.[222]

.01 Overview

(a) Regulatory Authority

The importance of the consolidated return regime is indexed by the fact that there are over 60,000 consolidated groups.[223] Congress, however, has left the regulation of this key area largely to Treasury and the IRS. Indeed, this area is perhaps the largest specific delegation of lawmaking power in the Internal Revenue Code. Although the statutes establish a few threshold rules, the regulations are the source of nearly all the applicable requirements.

Code Sec. 1501 provides that "[a]n affiliated group of corporations" has "the privilege" of filing a consolidated income tax return instead of separate returns. Code Sec. 1503(a) directs that, whenever a consolidated return is made or required to be made, tax is "determined, computed, assessed, collected, and adjusted in accordance with the regulations . . . prescribed before the last day prescribed . . . for the filing of such return."

The regulations are prescribed under the authority of Code Sec. 1502. The scope of authority under Code Sec. 1502 is broad. Usually, delegations under other Code sections permit Treasury to promulgate regulations to enforce or carry into effect statutory provisions.[224] Rulemaking under such delegations is interstitial, filling in gaps.

In contrast, the delegation under Code Sec. 1502 is much broader, giving Treasury the power both to create the operative rule in the first place (the primary rule, not mere matters of detail) and to alter rules prescribed by other Code sections. Specifically, Code Sec. 1502 authorizes Treasury to:

> [P]rescribe such regulations as [it] may deem necessary in order that the tax liability of any affiliated group of corporations making a consolidated return and of each corporation in the group, both during and after the period of the affiliation, be [determined and collected] in such manner as clearly to reflect . . . liability . . . and in order to prevent avoidance of such tax liability. [Treasury]may prescribe rules that are different from the [Code] provisions . . . that would apply if such corporations filed separate returns.

---

[222] Code Secs. 1501 & 1504(a).

[223] *See* Don Leatherman, *Why Ride Aid Is Wrong*, 52 Am. U.L. Rev. 811, 813 n. 5 (2003).

[224] *e.g.* Code Sec. 7805(a).

In addition, Code Sec. 1504(a)(5) authorizes Treasury to issue regulations to implement the definition of "affiliated group." Treasury has used its delegated authority to promulgate over 90 final and temporary regulations in the consolidated return area.

Practice Tip: Formerly, courts and commentators sometimes distinguished between general authority tax regulations promulgated under Code Sec. 7805(a) and specific authority regulations promulgated under express delegations in other, more particular sections. Inaccurately, the former were equated with interpretive regulations and the latter with legislative regulations. Moreover, again inaccurately, specific authority regulations were thought to be entitled to greater deference from the courts than were general authority regulations. The consolidated return regulations are specific authority regulations.

However, the traditional view has now been authoritatively rejected. In a 2011 case, the Supreme Court held that general authority tax regulations are no less entitled to deference under the *Chevron* standard than are specific authority regulations.[225]

In any event, recognizing the sweeping power delegated to Treasury in this area, the courts far more often than not uphold consolidated return regulations when taxpayers contest their validity. Nonetheless, challenges to such regulations have succeeded in some cases.[226]

(b) Conceptual Bases

Subchapter K of the Code does not rigidly adhere to either an entity or an aggregate concept of partnerships. Similarly, the Code Sec. 1502 regulations do not rigidly use either a separate or consolidated approach to treatment of affiliated corporations. Sometimes the regulations treat a consolidated group as a single entity; other times they treat them as a collection of separate entities.

Example 1: As described in greater detail below, the single entity approach is applied at the ultimate computational level. All items of income, gain, loss, deductions, and credits of all members of the group are aggregated to calculate the group's consolidated taxable income. In addition, at the constituent levels, the single entity approach is used to determine many components of consolidated taxable income, such as net capital gains and losses, charitable deductions, and dividends received exclusion.[227]

Example 2: The separate entity approach is used for many purposes at the constituent levels of computation. For instance, there is no requirement that all group members use the same method of accounting; each member

---

[225] *Mayo Foundation for Medical Education & Research v. United States*, 131 S. Ct. 702, 714 (2011). For discussion of *Mayo*, see Steve R. Johnson, *Mayo and the Future of Tax Regulations*, Tax Notes, Mar. 28, 2011, p. 1547. *See generally Chevron U.S.A., Inc. v. Natural Resources Defense Council, Inc.*, 467 U.S. 837 (1984) (establishing a two-part test for determining whether a regulation validly implements the authorizing statute).

[226] *e.g., Rite Aid Corp. v. United States*, 255 F.3d 1357 (Fed. Cir. 2001); *Comm'r v. General Machinery Corp.*, 95 F.2d 759 (6th Cir. 1938); *Joseph Weidenhoff, Inc. v. Comm'r*, 32 T.C. 1222 (1959).

[227] Treas. Reg. §§ 1.1502-22, 1.1502-24 & 1.1502-26.

¶904.01(b)

corporation chooses its own method of accounting.[228] Moreover, subject to limiting rules, acquired members retain their pre-consolidation tax attributes.[229]

This hybridization is the result of two causes. First, as previously noted, Congress chose 80% ownership as the benchmark for eligibility for consolidation. This means that affiliated corporations may have some shareholders that are not members of the group. Separate corporation principles are sometimes needed to properly account for the interests of non-group shareholders.

Second, the regulations reflect two policies of tax neutrality: (1) the group should neither benefit nor suffer in a tax sense from forming a new member or transferring assets among members and (2) the group should neither benefit nor suffer in a tax sense from acquiring a new member or disposing of a current member. These policies are sometimes better advanced by a single entity approach and other times by a separate entities approach.[230]

(c) Major Tax Effects

Consolidation for income tax return purposes is elective. Thus, taxpayers must carefully consider the benefits and burdens that will flow from a choice to file a consolidated return.

Most corporate groups that are eligible to file consolidated returns choose to do so because consolidation can afford significant tax advantages. Some of the major considerations are noted here, then are developed in greater detail in subpart C below.

- In general, ordinary losses sustained by one group member may be offset against income generated by other members of the group. Similarly, capital losses of one may generally be offset against capital gains of others.

- Gains realized on transactions between members of the group are not subject to income tax in the year of gain but are deferred.

- Some tax benefits (such as the corporate charitable contribution deduction[231]) are capped by taxable income or other measures. Generally, when a consolidated return is filed, these limits are based on the aggregated income or other characteristics of the entire group, not just that of the particular corporation. This can result in larger or more rapid deduction or other tax benefit.

- Dividends paid by one member corporation to another do not enter into consolidated income and thus are not taxed.

Despite these and other tax advantages, filing a consolidated return is not always the right choice. Sometimes the benefits of consolidation can be achieved in

---

[228] *Id.* § 1.1502-17(a). This right is limited by an anti-abuse rule in subsection (c) of that regulation.

[229] Corporate tax attributes are discussed above in ¶ 903

[230] *See* Leatherman, *supra* n.223, at 815; *see also United Dominion Industries, Inc. v. United States*, 532 U.S. 822, 837 (2001).

[231] Code Sec. 170(b)(2)(A) (limiting this deduction to 10% of the corporation's taxable income for the year).

other ways.[232] Moreover, there can be disadvantages, as well as advantages, from consolidation. For instance, the advantage of deferring gain on intercompany transactions becomes a disadvantage when the transactions produce losses instead of gains – taxpayers typically want to use losses as rapidly as possible but losses on transactions between members of the same consolidated group are not immediately usable and must be deferred. Thus, whether consolidation is desirable always must be evaluated based on the specific facts and circumstances of the particular companies involved.

.02 Eligibility and Election

(a) Eligibility

The privilege of making consolidated returns is available to "affiliated groups." In general, an affiliated group consists of "1 or more chains of includible corporations connected through stock ownership with a parent corporation that is an includible corporation," as long as both of two conditions are satisfied. These conditions are (1) the common parent directly owns stock representing at least 80% of the voting power *and* at least 80% of the total value of at least one of the other includible corporations and (2) one or more of the other includible corporations directly owns stock meeting the above 80% control test in each of the includible corporations other than the common parent.[233]

(i) *Control Test*

> *Practice Tip:* The 80% test may seem familiar from other corporate tax contexts, but the statutes must be read carefully. 80% control does not mean the same thing in the various contexts. For example, Code Sec. 1563 defines "controlled group of corporations" by reference to voting power or value,[234] not voting power and value as in Code Sec. 1504. Similarly, an 80% test is used for reorganization and Code Sec. 351 purposes, but that standard adverts to control,[235] not control and value as in Code Sec. 1504.

The voting power prong of the dual 80% test involves voting stock. In general, voting stock is any stock that participates in electing of the corporation's directors. However, if substantial restrictions exist on the ability of the directors to act, the right to elect shareholders alone may not be conclusive and the effect of the restrictions should be taken into account.[236] Voting common stock and voting preferred stock both are taken into account.

> *Example:* The common parent owned all of the common stock and half of the voting preferred stock of a subsidiary. The holders of the preferred stock were entitled to elect three of the subsidiary's eight directors. The holders of the common stock had the right to elect the other five. Thus, the preferred shareholders had 37.5% of the total voting power, and the common sharehold-

---

[232] For example, under Code Sec. 243, at an 80% level of ownership, a corporation receiving dividends from another corporation generally is entitled to exclude 100% of the dividend from its taxable income, achieving the same benefit that exists as to dividends between members of a group filing a consolidated return.

[233] Code Sec. 1504(a)(1) & (2).

[234] Code Sec. 1563(a)(1).

[235] Code Sec. 351(a) & 368(c).

[236] *e.g., Alumax Inc. v. Comm'r*, 109 T.C. 135 (1997), *aff'd*, 165 F.3d 822 (11th Cir. 1999).

ers had 62.5%. The IRS ruled that the common parent owned 81.25% of the total voting power in the subsidiary (100% of 62.5% plus 50% of 37.5%). Thus, the voting power component of the 80% test was met.[237]

---

[237] Rev. Rul. 69-126, 1969-1 C.B. 218.

Chapter 10

Procedural Aspects

¶ 1001   **Filing Returns and Paying Associated Liabilities**
¶ 1002   **Examination of Returns**
¶ 1003   **Litigation and Assessment**
¶ 1004   **Collection of Tax**
¶ 1005   **Capacity and Identity Issues**

This chapter addresses rules of federal tax procedure that are of particular importance to corporations. The chapter discusses the rules governing (1) filing returns and paying associated tax liabilities, (2) examination of returns by the IRS, (3) litigation and assessment, (4) collection of taxes not "voluntarily" paid, and (5) issues of capacity and identity. In the main, the rules in these areas are the same for corporate and non-corporate taxpayers. However, there are a number of key differences, both as to the rules themselves and their practical effects. In the main, this chapter will not rehearse the features common to both corporate and non-corporate taxpayers. Instead, it will emphasize aspects particularly relevant to corporations and their shareholders.

¶ 1001 Filing Returns and Paying Associated Liabilities

This part discusses (1) general rules as to the filing of corporate tax returns, (2) disclosures that may be required in or included with the return, (3) reporting as to tax shelters, and (4) payment of the tax liabilities shown or to be shown on the return.

.01 *Filing Corporate Returns*

Every corporation subject to the tax is required to file federal income tax returns.[1] With a few exceptions,[2] S corporations are not subject to income tax. Thus, S corporations' 1120S forms are largely information returns.[3] The 1120 forms filed by C corporations are tax returns. As discussed in detail in Chapter 9, affiliated corporations may elect to file consolidated returns.

Corporate income tax returns are due, for calendar year corporations, on or before March 15 following the close of the tax year. They are due, for fiscal year corporations, on or before the fifteenth day of the third month following the close of the tax year.[4] The IRS is authorized to grant reasonable extensions of time to file.[5]

---

[1] Code Sec. 6012(a)(2).

[2] Such as the built-in gains tax of Code Sec. 1374 and the excess passive investment income tax of Code Sec. 1375.

[3] Code Sec. 6037(a).

[4] Code Sec. 6072(b).

[5] Code Sec. 6081(a).

The IRS may grant a three-month extension to a corporation if the corporation pays properly estimated tax, but the IRS may terminate the extension at any time by mailing the corporation a notice of termination at least ten days before the termination date set out in the notice.[6]

Failure to timely file the return can lead to imposition of a penalty under Code Sec. 6651(a)(1). In general, the penalty rate is 5% of the tax required to be shown on the return for each month (or portion of a month) of the delinquency, capped at 25% in the aggregate. The penalty is excused if the taxpayer shows that the "failure is due to reasonable cause and not due to willful neglect."

> **Practice Tip:** "Reasonable cause" includes reliance on the substantive (albeit erroneous) advice of a competent tax advisor, erroneous written advice by the IRS, and casualty or natural disaster beyond the taxpayer's control. "Reasonable cause" does not include forgetfulness, time or business pressures, reliance on an invalid extension, unavailability of records, or ignorance of the law.[7]

> **Example:** In a leading case, a taxpayer relied on an attorney to file the return on time. The attorney knew the correct filing date but failed to timely file because of forgetfulness and/or the demands of other work. The Supreme Court found that reasonable cause did not exist, thus upheld imposition of the Code Sec. 6651(a)(1) penalty. The duty to timely file is nondelegable. However, the Court acknowledged that reasonable cause would have existed if the advisor had erroneously advised the taxpayer that, under the law, the return either was not required to be filed or was required to be filed at a later date.[8]

.02 Return Disclosure

(a) Generally

Built into Form 1120 are over a dozen schedules providing detailed information to the IRS about the corporation and its tax items for the year. For large corporations, one important schedule is Schedule M-3 "Net Income (Loss) Reconciliation for Corporations with Total Assets of $10 Million or More." This schedule asks questions about the corporation's financial statements, and it reconciles financial statement net income or loss to the corporation's net income or loss for federal income tax purposes.

> **Things to watch for:** As described below, the IRS is refining a return disclosure regime for uncertain tax positions ("UTP"). As the IRS does so, there may be modifications of other features of corporate tax returns. For example, in a speech on September 25, 2010, Commissioner of Internal Revenue Douglas Shulman announced that the IRS is establishing a working group to review whether Schedule M-3 can be scaled back as the IRS begins to receive the information it needs from other sources, including UTP disclosures.

---

[6] Code Sec. 6081(b).
[7] E.g., Treas. Reg. §301.6404-3; IRM 20.1.1.3.
[8] *United States v. Boyle*, 469 U.S. 241 (1985).

(b) Uncertain Tax Position ("UTP") Disclosure

The IRS has concluded that it needs better ways to identify potential audit issues. An important and controversial recent change involves the UTP disclosure regime. The IRS estimates that, during audits of large businesses, it spends about a quarter of its time identifying issues, time which could be better spent examining those issues or auditing other taxpayers. The UTP program was created to identify issues more readily.

The original version of the UTP regime was set out in a series of IRS Announcements in the early months of 2010. On January 26, 2010, the IRS released Announcement 2010-9, which stated the IRS's intention to require business taxpayers to disclose their UTPs on their returns.[9] That Announcement was modified on March 29, 2010 by Announcement 2010-17.[10] Then, Announcement 2010-30, published on May 10, 2010, provided a draft Schedule UTP accompanied by draft instructions for the schedule.[11]

On September 9, 2010, the government published a Notice of Proposed Rulemaking inviting public comment on the proposed rules. The regime was modified again on September 24, 2010 via Announcement 2010-75, which released the final version of Schedule UTP and its instructions.[12] Below, we discuss the originally proposed UTP regime, the comments received by the IRS, then the changes to the original version which are reflected in the current version of the regime.

Under the original three Announcements, UTP disclosure would have been required if the business has over $10 million of assets and if the business or a related party "determines its 'United States federal income tax reserves' under Fin 48,[13] or other accounting standards relating to uncertain income tax positions involving United States federal income tax."[14] A "related party" for UTP purposes is any entity that is related to the taxpayer under the rules of Code Secs. 267(b), 318(a), or 707(b).

UTPs were to be disclosed as to which (i) the taxpayer or related entity has recorded a reserve on its financial statements, (ii) no reserve has been recorded because the taxpayer has concluded that, if the IRS had full knowledge of the position, a settlement would be unlikely to be reached, or (iii) no reserve has been recorded because the taxpayer believes the IRS's practice is not to examine the position.

The disclosure is effected by attaching a new schedule (Schedule UTP) to the Form 1120. Schedule UTP would include a concise description of each UTP and state "the maximum of potential federal tax liability attributable to each uncertain tax position (determined without regard to the taxpayer's risk analysis regarding its likelihood of prevailing on the merits)."

---

[9] 2010-7 I.R.B. 408.

[10] 2010-13 I.R.B. 515.

[11] 2010-19 I.R.B. 515.

[12] 2010-41 I.R.B. 1 (and related IRS news release IR-2010-98). As is true of most IRS forms, schedules, and instructions, Schedule UTP and its instructions can be downloaded from the IRS's website: *www.irs.gov*.

[13] Financial Accounting Standards Board ("FASB") Interpretation No. 48, currently set out in FASB ASC 740-10.

[14] 2010-7 IRB 408, 409.

¶1001.02(b)

The concise description would contain sufficient detail that the IRS could ascertain the nature of the issue in light of "the taxpayer's particular facts and the nature of the underlying transaction." The description would also include the taxpayer's rationale for its position and "the reasons for determining that the position is an uncertain tax position." The description would also contain all of the following:

- Up to three Internal Revenue Code sections that may be implicated by the position,

- identification of the tax year(s) to which the position relates,

- indication of whether the position involves an item of income, gain, loss, deduction, or credit,

- statement of whether the position entails permanent inclusion/exclusion of the item, or timing as to the item, or both,

- indication of whether the position relates to valuation, and

- statement whether the position involves basis computation.

The original version caused substantial concern on the part of corporations and their advisors and representatives. The principal criticisms centered on: the IRS's authority to impose the new approach; the relationship of the new approach to the IRS's policy of restraint as to seeking tax accrual workpapers; the effect of the new rule on privileges; burdens imposed on corporations; and effects on relationships between the IRS and taxpayers and among corporations, their advisors, and their independent auditors.

The revised version responds to many of these concerns and received widespread praise. The IRS made nearly a score of changes and clarifications, including the following:

(1) Fearing that it was moving too far too fast, the IRS modified the original requirement that all taxpayers with of at least $10 million of assets and with audited financial statements file Schedule UTP for 2010. Instead, the regime will be phased in. Only corporations with assets of $100 million or more will be required to file for 2010. The threshold will decrease to $50 million for 2012 returns and $10 million for 2014 returns.

(2) The IRS dropped the highly controversial requirement that taxpayers list the maximum tax exposure as to each UTP. Instead, corporations need only rank the items from largest to smallest based on amounts recorded in the tax reserves for accounting purposes. The amounts of the reserves would not have to be disclosed at any point, but all UTPs for which the reserve exceeds 10% of the aggregate amount of total tax reserves would have to be listed.

(3) The IRS abandoned the requirement that the rationale and nature of the uncertainty be included in the description of the item. IRS Commissioner Shulman has stated that the IRS is seeking information, not legal analysis of risk.

¶1001.02(b)

(4) The IRS abandoned the requirement that corporations report positions for which they have not recorded a reserve because the IRS does not have an administrative practice of auditing that type of issue. The related trigger dealing with expectation of litigation was modified.

(5) The IRS clarified that federal income tax positions –but not foreign or state tax positions – must be reported.

(6) The IRS clarified that an item is to be reported once a reserve is recorded.

(7) The IRS provided that corporations must report their own positions on their Schedules UTP, but not the positions of related parties.

(8) The IRS clarified that positions taken before 2010 need not be reported even if a reserve is recorded for financial statement purposes in 2010 or a later year.

(9) The IRS clarified the reporting of recurring positions taken in multiple years.

(10) The IRS clarified that worldwide assets are used to ascertain whether a corporation that files a Form 1120-F is required to file Schedule UTP.

(11) The IRS clarified the meanings of "audited financial statement" and "record a reserve" as elements of required filing.

(12) To reduce duplicative paperwork, the IRS clarified that an adequate Schedule UTP will constitute adequate disclosure for Code Sec. 6662 penalty purposes.

(13) The IRS provided assurances that it would not automatically share UTP disclosures with revenue authorities in other countries and that such sharing would likely be rare.

(14) In light of the new UTP information source, the IRS reaffirmed and expanded its policy of restraint as to seeking certain kinds of information from taxpayers.[15]

Practice Tip: The IRS says that it will not routinely request documents given to outside auditors and that it will not assert that disclosures waive the attorney-client privilege, the Code Sec. 7525 privilege, or work product doctrine protection. However, such restraint will not apply as to tax shelters the IRS considers abusive.

Things to watch for: (1) The IRS will consider whether to extend UTP-like reporting for 2011 or later years to some noncorporate entities, such as pass-through and tax-exempt entities.

(2) There has been speculation as to whether UTP reporting will affect the number of whistleblower awards paid by the IRS. Some think that the number

---

[15] IRM 4.10.20. For discussion of this policy and other issues as to the revised UTP regime, see J. Richard "Dick" Harvey Jr., Schedule *UTP Guidance – Initial Observations,* Tax Notes, Oct. 4, 2010, p. 115.

¶1001.02(b)

will decrease because potential information will already have been disclosed to the IRS. Other commentators disagree.[16]

(3) Additional revisions to UTP reporting are likely. In comments on proposed rules, practitioners have requested a number of additional changes. The Large Business and International Division has issued a directive outlining how the IRS plans to handle UTP disclosures.[17] The IRS contemplates special UTP training for field personnel and established a special unit, known as a "triage team," to centralize processing of UTP Schedules in order to check for compliance, identify trends, and select issues and returns for examination. Yet more guidance could come in a variety of modalities, including Internal Revenue Manual revisions and other internal guidance. In March 2011, the IRS posted on its website frequently asked questions as to Schedule UTP.

(c) Disclosure to Obviate Penalties

In addition to required disclosures, corporations and other taxpayers may voluntarily disclose other information as part of or along with their returns. Disclosure of potentially controversial tax reporting positions sometimes obviates imposition of penalties with respect to the item in question. The main disclosure form is Form 8275 "Disclosure Statement." It is supplanted by Form 8275-R "Regulation Disclosure Statement" when the taxpayer is disclosing a return position that is inconsistent with a Treasury Regulation.

The principal use of Forms 8275 and 8275-R is in connection with the accuracy-related penalty in Code Sec. 6662. As relevant to corporations, that penalty equals 20% of the portion of a tax underpayment attributable to any of five stated conditions: (1) negligence or intentional disregard of tax rules and regulations, (2) substantial understatement of income tax, (3) substantial income tax valuation misstatement, or (4) substantial overstatement of pension liabilities.[18] The penalty rate is raised to 40% in the event of gross valuation misstatements as to conditions (3) and (4).[19]

In general, the taxpayer can avoid liability under conditions (1) and (2) if the position in question is adequately disclosed and, in some cases, has at least a reasonable basis.[20] However, disclosure does not obviate penalties in the case of corporate tax shelter transactions.[21] A disclosure statement is adequate if it reasonably apprises the IRS of the nature and amount of the potential controversy. If it fails to do so, if it misrepresents the facts, or if the disclosure is too general, the statement will be inadequate and the disclosure exception to penalties will not apply.[22]

> ***Practice Tip:*** Disclosure can help the corporation's return preparer or other advisor as well as the corporation itself. Adequate disclosure can prevent

---

[16] *See* Jeremiah Coder, *UTP Reporting May Affect Whistleblower Claims,* Tax Notes, Sept. 6, 2010, p. 1027.

[17] Directive from Steven T. Miller to All Large Business & International Division Personnel, 2010 Tax Notes Today 186-70 (Sept. 24, 2010).

[18] Code Secs. 6662(a) & (b).

[19] Code Sec 6662(h).

[20] Code Sec. 6662(d)(2)(B), Treas. Reg. §§ 1.6662-3(c)(1), 1.6662-4(e)(2) & 1.6662-7.

[21] Code Sec. 6662(d)(2)(C).

[22] *e.g., Schirmer v. Comm'r,* 89 T.C. 277, 285-86 (1977); *Dibsy v. Comm'r,* T.C. Memo. 1995-477.

imposition of the penalty under Code Sec. 6694(a) as to negligence by a preparer or advisor.[23]

.03 Reporting as to Tax Shelters

The federal government has employed a multi-faceted strategy in its war against corporate and other "high end" tax shelters. One facet involves reporting and disclosure. Both "material advisors" and taxpayers themselves may have reporting requirements.

Material advisors are persons who provide, for compensation, "any material aid, assistance, or advice with respect to organizing, managing, promoting, selling, implementing, insuring, or carrying out any reportable transaction."[24] Materials advisors are required to file reports describing the purported tax benefits of the plan or arrangement. They also must maintain lists of persons whom they advised as to the transaction.[25]

Taxpayers participating in reportable transactions must file Form 8886. The form identifies the type of transaction involved, states whether the investment or participation was through a corporation or pass-through entity, and gives the name and address of persons paid a fee for promoting, soliciting, or recommending participation in the transaction or providing tax advice with respect to the transaction. The form also directs the taxpayer to describe the facts of the transaction and the types and estimated amounts of the anticipated tax benefits.

Under the regulations, reportable transactions include the following:[26]

- *Listed transactions*: transactions identified by the IRS as tax-avoidance transactions as well as transactions that are substantially similar to the identified tax avoidance transactions.

- *Confidential transactions*: transactions offered under conditions of confidentiality and for which the taxpayer paid the advisor a minimum fee.

- *Transactions with contractual protection*: transactions in which the fee paid is wholly or partly refundable if the expected tax benefits are not realized; also includes transactions in which the amount of the fee paid is contingent on the taxpayer receiving the expected tax benefit.[27]

- *Loss transactions*: transactions in which the taxpayer claims a Code Sec. 165 deduction over a stated amount. For corporations, this amount usually is $10 million in a single year or $20 million in a combination of years.

- *Transactions involving a brief asset holding period*: transactions that involve claimed tax credits over $250,000 in which the taxpayer held for 45 days or less the assets giving rise to the credits.

- *Transactions of interest*: transactions that are substantially similar to a type of transaction the IRS has identified as potentially abusive by public notice.

---

[23] Code Sec. 6694(a)(2).

[24] Code Sec. 6111(b)(1)(A). The compensation must exceed a threshold amount – currently $250,000 for reportable transactions as to corporations. Code Sec. 6111(b)(1)(B).

[25] Code Sec. 6112.

[26] Treas. Reg. §1.6011-4.

[27] Exceptions are set out in Rev. Proc. 2007-20, 2007-1 C.B. 517.

These typically are transactions about which the IRS lacks sufficient information to ascertain whether they should be reportable transactions.

The reporting regime is supported by two penalty sections. First, section 6707A imposes a penalty for failure to report information required to be disclosed as to a reportable transaction. For corporations, the penalty is $200,000 as to transactions of interest and $50,000 as to other types of reportable transactions.

Second, Code Sec. 6662A is an accuracy-related penalty for understatements of tax attributable to participation in reportable transactions "if a significant purpose of such transaction is the avoidance or evasion of Federal income tax."[28] The usual penalty rate is 20%, but the rate rises to 30% if the relevant facts are not disclosed as required by Code Sec. 6011.

A statute of limitations rule provides further incentive for disclosure. If a taxpayer does not include on a return or other statement any information required by the reportable transaction rules, the assessment limitations period as to the transaction will not expire earlier than one year after the date the information is provided to the IRS or, if earlier, the date a material advisor satisfies the list maintenance requirement of Code Sec. 6112.[29]

.04 Corporate Estimated Tax Payments

Corporations are required to "prepay" their federal income tax liabilities by making estimated tax payments throughout the year. If they fail to do so and if no exception applies, they are liable for a penalty under Code Sec. 6655.

To avoid the penalty, the corporation must pay a percentage of its estimated tax liabilities. The penalty is essentially an interest charge, based on the interest rate on underpayments of corporate estimated tax under Code Sec. 6621(a)(2).[30] In general, the period for which the penalty is imposed is determined by reference to quarterly periods starting with the date of the underpaid installment and ending with the date the underpayment is satisfied or, if earlier, the due date of the corporation's return for the year.[31]

To determine the estimated tax due each quarter, the corporation estimates its income for the tax year involved, then computes its tax liability based on that income, then subtracts any allowable credits.[32] The tax liabilities to which the estimated tax applies include the corporate income tax under Code Sec. 11, the alternative minimum tax under Code Sec. 55, the environment tax under Code Sec. 59A, the gross transportation income tax under Code Sec. 887, and the 30% withholding tax under Code Sec. 881 on U.S.-source income not connected with a United States trade or business.[33]

There is no "reasonable cause" defense against the Code Sec. 6655 penalty. There are, however, several escape valves. The penalty is not imposed if the tax owed by the corporation is under $500.[34]

---

[28] Code Sec. 6662A(b)(2).

[29] Code Sec. 6501(c)(10); Treas. Reg. § 301.6501(c)-1(g).

[30] Code Sec. 6655(a)(1); Treas. Reg. § 1.6655-1(a).

[31] Code Sec. 6655(b)(2); Treas. Reg. § 1.6655-1(c).

[32] Code Sec. 6655(g)(1)(B).

[33] Code Sec. 6655(g)(1); Treas. Reg. § 1.6655-1(g).

[34] Code Sec. 6655(f).

More importantly, four safe harbors exist as to calculation of the amount of estimated tax due each quarter. If the corporation's installments are computed under any of the safe harbor methods, no underpayment exists, so no penalty is imposed. There are many modifications and special rules. In general, however, the corporation is not liable for the penalty if it pays at least the smallest of the following amounts:

(1) 100% of the tax shown on the corporation's current year return.[35]

(2) 100% of the tax shown on the corporation's return for the prior taxable year.[36] This method is not available if the corporation filed no return for the year, it filed a return but the return showed zero liability, or the year was less than a twelve-month year. Also this method is available to large corporations only for the first quarterly installment.[37]

(3) The tax due for the year calculated by putting the corporation's income for the part of the year preceding the due date of the installment on an annualized basis.[38]

(4) An adjusted seasonal installment, if the corporation has seasonal income.[39]

¶ 1002 Examination of Returns

This part discusses two topics of particular significance to corporations during IRS audit or examination. They are (1) examination of corporate returns generally and (2) privileges that may be asserted against IRS attempts to obtain additional information from corporate taxpayers under audit.

.01 Examination of Corporate Returns Generally

Currently, the IRS Examination Division is organized functionally. Audits of the returns of small corporations (usually those whose assets do not exceed $10,000,000) are conducted by the Small Business and Self-Employed Division. Audits of larger corporations are conducted by the Large and Mid-Size Business Division (recently renamed the Large Business and International Division in order to emphasize the IRS's current priority as to transnational transactions). This Division is organized into industry segments, reflecting the notion that similar companies have similar tax issues. These segments include Communications, Technology, and Media; Financial Services; Heavy Manufacturing and Transportation; Natural Resources and Construction; and Retailers, Food, Pharmaceuticals, and Healthcare.

> ***Things to watch for:*** As part of its increasing emphasis on transnational issues, the IRS is forging closer relationships with revenue authorities in other countries, to cooperate on matters of mutual interest. In Fall 2010, IRS Commissioner Shulman announced that the IRS is conducting some joint audits

---

[35] Code Sec. 6655(d)(1)(B)(i); Treas. Reg. § 1.665-1(d)(1)(i).

[36] Code Sec. 6655(d)(1)(B)(ii); Treas. Reg. § 1.6655-1(d)(1)(ii).

[37] Code Sec. 6665(d)(2)(A); Treas. Reg. § 1.6655-1(e)(1), (2). A corporation is "large" for this pur-

pose if it, or a predecessor corporation, had at least $1 million of taxable income during a three-year testing period. Code Sec 6655(g)(2); Treas. Reg. § 1.6655-4.

[38] Code Sec. 6655(e)(1) & (2).

[39] Code Sec. 6655(e)(1) & (3).

with such foreign authorities. As of that time, one joint audit was already underway and another, with Australia, was being planned.

It is in the interests of both taxpayers and the IRS to conduct examinations efficiently. The IRS has developed a number of initiatives, at both the audit and administrative appeals levels, to promote efficiency without unduly comprising the accuracy of determinations. These initiatives change frequently, some being dropped or modified while new alternatives are created. The following are examples of measures currently or recently in use.

Audits of large corporations are often conducted as part of the Coordinated Examination Program ("CEP"). CEP exams are performed by the Examination Division's top revenue agents, aided by industry-specific position papers and audit programs developed by the Industry Specialization Program, Market Segment Specialization Program, and the like. CEP also can entail early involvement by IRS Chief Counsel attorneys and accelerated IRS Appeals Office consideration.

The Limited Issue Focused Examinations ("LIFE") program is a targeted audit program for very large corporations. Based on materiality benchmarks, audits under the LIFE program emphasize the most significant issues. The IRS and the corporation agree as to the process to be followed and the time frame.

Mechanisms exist at both the examination and IRS Appeals levels for early resolution of potentially or actually disputed issues. These mechanisms include Prefiling Agreements for certain, principally factual issues, and Advance Pricing Agreements for Code Sec. 482 issues.

In addition, to facilitate large case audits, the IRS has developed the Compliance Assurance Program ("CAP") to identify and resolve significant recurring issues. Under CAP, a corporation can seek agreement with the IRS – as to one or more particular issues – before filing the return. The IRS also has developed the Industry Issue Resolution Program ("IIRP") for reviewing intricate issues common to many corporations. Both the IRS and taxpayers may propose issues to be included in the program.

In some instances, early access to the Appeals Office may be helpful. It sometimes is available to taxpayers, including corporations, under the Early Referral Program. To expedite resolution at Appeals, the Fast Track Settlement Program was developed. It is available in some instances to both large and small corporations. Related procedures include a variety of alternative dispute resolution mechanisms, including mediation in some instances.

Things to watch for: The IRS is committed to efforts such as the above. It is examining various ways to resolve issues faster, and it is augmenting resources dedicated to efforts that hold the promise of accomplishing this end. As examples, the IRS announced the following steps in late 2010. (1) CAP has been in pilot status with limited taxpayer participation. The IRS intends to make CAP permanent and broaden participation in it. (2) The IRS also intends to make greater use of IIRP, including issuing guidance as to tax issues affecting telecommunications, electrical utilities, and other industrial sectors. (3) Approximately 80% of the issues that are assigned to Fast Track settlement

¶1002.01

are in fact settled. The IRS is endeavoring to get more cases into Fast Track settlement postures.

.02 Privileges Against IRS Information Gathering

Knowledge is power, and the effectiveness of IRS examinations often depends upon the expedition and thoroughness with which the IRS can gather the facts relevant to the return positions under consideration. Key decisions for the taxpayer entail how fully to comply with IRS requests for information and how to resist those requests the taxpayer wishes to oppose.

There are many strategies.[40] Most of them may be pursued with equal success (or lack of success) by corporate and non-corporate taxpayers. However, there are several nuances particular to corporate taxpayers as to privileges that may be opposed against IRS requests for information.

The principal privileges available to taxpayers are the Code Sec. 7525 "federally authorized tax practitioner" privilege, the attorney-client privilege, and the work product doctrine.[41] The Code Sec. 7525 privilege was enacted in 1998 and was designed to extend privilege to communications between taxpayers and non-attorney tax advisors[42] when comparable communications between taxpayers and their attorneys would be protected from disclosure by the attorney-client privilege.

> ***Practice Tip:*** The Supreme Court has held that, not just individuals, but corporations as well may avail themselves of the attorney-client privilege when the elements of that privilege are present.[43] However, the utility to taxpayers of both the attorney-client privilege and the Code Sec. 7525 privilege is limited and, in many situations, unsettled.[44] In part, this is because both privileges are lost if the ring of confidentiality as to the communications is broken, which happens often.[45] Also, some communications occurring in the process of preparation of tax returns are not privileged.[46]

A wrinkle of particular significance to corporations is found in Code Sec. 7525. That privilege does "not apply to any written communication between a federally authorized tax practitioner and a director, shareholder, officer, or employee, agent, or representative of a corporation in connection with the promotion of the direct or

---

[40] These are discussed in David M. Richardson, Jerome Borison & Steve Johnson, Civil Tax Procedure, Ch. 4 (2d ed. 2008).

[41] For discussion of these privileges, in the context of tax controversies, see Martin J. McMahon, Jr. & Ira B. Shepard, *Privileges and the Work Product Doctrine in Tax Cases*, 58 Tax Law. 405 (2005).

[42] The non-attorney advisors covered by this privilege are individuals authorized to practice before the IRS if their practice is subject to regulation under 31 U.S.C. § 330. Code Sec. 7525(a)(3)(A).

[43] *Upjohn Co. v. United States*, 449 U.S. 383 (1981).

[44] *See generally* Robert M. Moise, *Do We Really Have Privilege?*, Tax Adviser, Oct. 2010, at 716; Danielle M.

Smith & David L. Kleinman, *What Remains of the Federal Tax Practitioner Privilege Under Internal Revenue Code Section 7525?*, Daily Tax Rep., June 9, 2006, at J-I.

[45] *See, e.g.*, Amandeep S. Grewal, *Selective Waiver and the Tax Practitioner Privilege*, Tax Notes, Sept. 26, 2006, at 1139.

[46] *e.g., United States v. Frederick*, 182 F.3d 496 (7th Cir. 1999), *cert. denied*, 528 U.S. 1154 (2000); *Lawless v. United States*, 709 F.2d 485 (7th Cir. 1983); *KPMG LLC v. United States*, 237 F. Supp. 2d 35 (D.D.C. 2002). For discussion of these limitations, *see* Claudine V. Pease-Wingenter, *Does the Attorney-Client Privilege Apply to Tax Lawyers?*, 47 Washburn L.J. 699 (2008).

indirect participation of such corporation in any tax shelter."[47] The scope of this limitation has yet to be fully defined and has generated considerable controversy.[48]

> ***Practice Tip:*** In general, the party asserting the privilege – typically the taxpayer – bears the burden of proof as to it. However, there is authority for the view that, once the taxpayer establishes the preliminary facts tending to show that the Code Sec. 7525 privilege applies in the situation, the burden of going forward shifts to the IRS to establish that the tax shelter exception applies and defeats the privilege.[49]

A major area of dispute in recent years as to the work product doctrine has been the extent to which the doctrine can be used to defeat IRS efforts to obtain corporations' tax accrual workpapers. These documents are financial audit workpapers, prepared by a corporation itself or the corporation's independent auditor, which relate to the tax reserve the corporation maintains against current, deferred, contingent, or potential tax liabilities. These workpapers relate to footnotes disclosing such liabilities on audited financial statements.[50]

The controversy has been brewing for at least three decades. In the late 1970s and early 1980s, the IRS sought via summonses tax accrual workpapers maintained by the Arthur Young accounting firm for its client Amerada Hess. The Supreme Court ultimately upheld the summonses, holding that – although the privilege exists in some states – federal law does not recognize an accountant-client privilege.[51]

During the controversy, the IRS became concerned that seeking tax accrual workpapers routinely during tax examinations could chill relations between outside financial auditors and their corporate clients and could undermine cooperation between revenue agents and taxpayers. Accordingly, the IRS announced in 1981 a policy of restraint as to seeking access to tax accrual workpapers.[52]

In July 2002, as part of its war against corporate and high-end tax shelters, the IRS modified the policy of restraint. The IRS announced it would require taxpayers to produce all tax accrual workpapers if they entered into and failed to disclose their participation in "listed transactions" viewed by the IRS as potentially abusive tax shelters.[53]

> ***Practice Tip:*** The IRS has used inconsistent language in describing the current policy under Announcement 2002-63 as to tax accrual workpapers and listed transactions. Deborah Nolan, then-commissioner of the LMSB Division,

---

[47] Code Sec. 7525(b). "Tax shelter" has the same meaning as in Code Sec. 6662(d)(2)(c)(ii), which refers to any "plan or arrangement" which has as "a significant purpose . . . the avoidance or evasion of Federal income tax.".

[48] *See, e.g.*, Tax Trends, Tax Adviser, Aug. 2009, at 558. *Compare Countryside Limited Partnership v. Commissioner*, 132 T.C. 347 (2009) (rejecting application of the tax shelter exception and upholding the privilege) *to Valero Energy Corp. v. United States*, 569 F.3d 626 (7th Cir. 2009) (holding the exception applicable and rejecting the availability of the privilege.

[49] *Countryside Limited Partnership, supra*, 132 T.C. at 350.

[50] Such workpapers also are called tax contingency analysis, tax contingency reserve analysis, tax cushion analysis, and tax pool analysis. For additional discussion, see Michael M. Lloyd, Mark T. Gossart & Garrett A. Fenton, *Understanding Tax Reserves and the Situations in Which They Arise*, Tax Notes, July 6, 2009, at 66.

[51] *United States v. Arthur Young & Co.*, 465 U.S. 805 (1984).

[52] IRM 4.10.20.3(2).

[53] Announcement 2002-63, 2002-2 C.B. 72.

¶1002.02

stated that a request for such workpapers is "mandatory" when a taxpayer claims tax benefits as a result of a listed transaction. However, the Announcement itself states that the IRS "may" request workpapers in that context (although it also states that the IRS will then "routinely request" workpapers). On the basis of the "may" language, the corporation may seek to persuade the revenue agent performing the audit that he or she need not seek tax accrual workpapers.

Despite (or consistent with) the policy of restraint, the IRS has issued summonses for tax accrual workpapers a number of times. Often, corporations have resisted these summonses on the ground of the work product doctrine, claiming that the workpapers were prepared in anticipation of litigation, thus are privileged.

The courts are split as to the contours of the work product doctrine,[54] and the results of the litigation have been mixed.[55] Two highly prominent and well publicized decisions – *Textron*[56] and *Deloitte*[57] – involving the issue have been decided recently. These cases also split, *Textron* being decided for the IRS and *Deloitte* for the taxpayer.

> **Practice Tip:** The tax accrual workpapers controversy also has significance in contexts other than the federal income tax. In states imposing their own corporate income taxes, there has been controversy about whether the work product doctrine shields state income tax accrual workpapers from discovery by state revenue authorities.[58] In addition, the controversy may have securities law ramifications. The SEC has indicated that it intends to rely on Textron in some cases to try to obtain attorney work product material shared with financial auditors.[59]

> **Practice Tip:** An experienced practitioner recommends that the corporation and its advisors take five steps in managing tax accrual workpapers in the post-Textron environment: (1) recognize that the legal battle as to the work product doctrine is not over, (2) recognize that disclosure of such workpapers to the IRS is a possibility, (3) make greater use of inside or outside counsel, (4) segregate analysis into multiple workpapers, and (5) define ownership of the workpapers.[60]

> **Things to watch for:** More chapters remain to be written in the controversy about the work product doctrine and tax accrual workpapers. The future of the issue is hard to predict. It likely will be formed by the interaction of

---

[54] *See generally* Peter A. Lowy & Juan F. Vasquez, Jr., *When Is the Work of a Tax Professional Done in Anticipation of Litigation and Thus "Work Product"?*, J. Tax'n, Mar. 2003, at 155.

[55] *Compare United States v. El Paso Co.*, 682 F.2d 530 (5th Cir. 1982) (holding for the IRS), *cert. denied*, 466 U.S. 944 (1984), *to Regions Financial Corp. v. United States*, 101 AFTR2d 2008-2179 (N.D. Ala. 2008) (holding for the taxpayer), appeal dismissed, No. 08-13866 (11th Cir. Dec. 30, 2008).

[56] *United States v. Textron Inc.*, 560 F.3d 513 (1st Cir. 2009) (en banc), *aff'g in part & vacating in part* 507 F. Supp. 2d 138 (D.R.I. 2007), *cert. denied*, 130 S. Ct. 3320

(2010). For discussion of *Textron*, see Steve R. Johnson, The Work Product Doctrine and Tax Accrual Workpapers, Tax Notes, July 13, 2009, at 155.

[57] *United States v. Deloitte LLP*, 610 F.3d 129 (D.C. Cir. 2010).

[58] *See* Marc A. Simonetti & Richard C. Call, *The Work-Product Doctrine and State Tax Accrual Workpapers*, State Tax Notes, Nov. 3, 2008, at 327.

[59] *See* Yin Wilczek, *Securities Lawyers Warn "Textron" May Hurt Communications with Attorneys and Auditors*, Tax Management Weekly Rep., June 7, 2010, at 764.

[60] Stuart J. Bassin, *Managing Tax Accrual Workpapers After Textron*, Tax Notes, May 4, 2009, at 571, 579-80.

several phenomena. First, the IRS has reaffirmed its general policy of restraint.[61] Second, the degree of future tax shelter activity will significantly influence the issue; the IRS's interest in tax accrual workpapers will wax or wane as shelter activity grows or shrinks. Third, the new UTP reporting rules, described earlier in this part, may reduce the need for the IRS to seek tax accrual workpapers.[62]

¶ 1003 Litigation and Assessment

Assessment consists of the formal recordation on the IRS's records of a particular tax liability of a particular taxpayer. Although purely formal, the act is essential – the IRS may not engage in enforced collection actions until it has made an assessment.

The IRS may immediately assess amounts reported as due and owing on the tax return,[63] amounts paid by the taxpayer,[64] amounts resulting from mathematical or clerical error on the return,[65] amounts pursuant to a waiver of restriction on assessment by the taxpayer,[66] taxes to which the deficiency procedures do not apply,[67] and amounts subject to jeopardy and termination assessments.[68]

Several expedited assessment mechanisms are of particular significance to corporations. For example, if a corporation files with the IRS a statement as to an expected net operating loss carryback for a year, the time for payment of the corporation's federal income tax for the immediately preceding year is extended.[69] However, if the IRS believes there is jeopardy as to collection of the amount to which the extension relates, the IRS can immediately terminate the extension, notify the taxpayer, and demand payment.[70]

Another example involves the regime created by Code Secs. 1291 and 1298 for the income taxation of passive foreign investment companies ("PFICs"). The PFIC may elect to extend the time for payment of tax on undistributed PFIC earnings.[71] However, if the IRS believes collection of tax is in peril, the IRS again may end the extension, notify the taxpayer, and demand payment.[72]

If the IRS wishes to assess additional tax liabilities not falling under the above provisions, it will be compelled to resort to the deficiency procedures set out in Code Secs. 6211 to 6213. That is, the IRS will have to issue a statutory notice of deficiency setting out its determinations, afford the taxpayer the opportunity for pre-assessment Tax Court review, and defer assessment until expiration of the ninety-day Tax Court petition period or, if a petition is timely filed, until finality of the Tax Court proceedings.

---

[61] IRM 4.10.20; *see* Michael Joe, *IRS to Continue Policy of Restraint on Tax Accrual Workpapers*, Tax Notes, June 8, 2009, at 1187.

[62] *See, e.g.*, AM 2007-0012 (Mar. 22, 2007) (IRS generic legal advice taking the position that documents produced under FIN 48 to substantiate a taxpayer's UTPs should be treated as tax accrual workpapers).

[63] Code Sec. 6201(a)(1).

[64] Code Sec. 6213(b)(4).

[65] Code Sec. 6213(b)(1) & (g)(2).

[66] Code Sec. 6213(d).

[67] Code Sec. 6201(e). Such as employment taxes.

[68] Code Sec. 6851 & 6861.

[69] Code Sec. 6164(a).

[70] Code Secs. 6164(h) & 6864.

[71] Code Sec. 1294(a).

[72] Code Sec. 1294(c)(3); Reg. §1.1294-IT(e)(5). The IRS has discretion as to the amount of undistributed earnings with respect to which it will terminate the extension.

If the taxpayer believes it has overpaid its tax liabilities, the taxpayer may file a timely claim for refund with the IRS then, after the IRS denies or fails to act on the refund claim, file a refund suit in federal district court or the Court of Federal Claims.[73]

Below, we discuss four aspects of the deficiency and refund litigation processes that are of particular relevance to corporate taxpayers: (1) the burden of proof rules as to the Accumulated Earnings Tax ("AET"), (2) accuracy-related penalties and defenses to them, (3) interest with respect to underpayments and overpayments of tax, and (4) means-tested provisions.

.01 Burden of Proof as to the AET

The substantive rules governing the AET are discussed in detail in Chapter 3. When AET issues are litigated, several special burden of proof rules apply. They are described below.

There are two aspects of the burden of proof: the risk of nonpersuasion and the burden of production (also called the burden of going forward). The risk of nonpersuasion does not shift; it is on one party (usually, in civil tax litigation, the taxpayer) from the beginning to the end of the case. The burden of going forward may shift between the parties once or several times as the case progresses.

The AET is imposed when a corporation is formed or availed of for the purpose of avoiding shareholder-level income tax "by permitting earnings and profits to accumulate instead of being divided or distributed."[74] During audit, before it issues the statutory notice of deficiency including the AET adjustment, the IRS may mail the corporation notification that an AET adjustment is intended.[75] The corporation may reply to this notification by submitting to the IRS the grounds on which the corporation relies to establish that earning and profits were not accumulated beyond the reasonable needs of the business.[76]

In a subsequent Tax Court case involving the AET issue, the burden of proof with respect to whether there was an accumulation beyond the reasonable needs of the business is on the IRS if the IRS failed to give the pre-statutory notice notification of the AET issue. The burden shifts to the corporation, however, if the IRS gave the notification and the corporation failed to reply thereto or the corporation's reply lacked sufficient detail.[77]

If the IRS initially bears the burden of proof as to "accumulation beyond the reasonable needs of the business" and the IRS meets that burden, the burden shifts to the corporation to show that, despite that fact, the corporation was not formed or availed of for the purpose of avoiding shareholder-level income tax.[78]

There is purpose behind this elaborate regime for allocating the burden of proof. AET cases are intensely fact-driven. The AET burden of proof rules are designed to encourage the IRS and the corporation to exchange information fully and early – during audit, well in advance of court proceedings. The more fully both

---

[73] Code Sec. 7422.
[74] Code Sec. 532(a).
[75] Code Sec. 534(b).

[76] Code Sec. 534(c).
[77] Code Sec. 534(a); Treas. Reg. § 1.534-2(b) & (d).
[78] Code Sec. 533(a); Treas. Reg. § 1.533-1(a) & (b).

¶1003.01

parties know the facts, the more likely will be settlement or concession of the issue, sparing the parties and the court the time, expense, inconvenience, and uncertainty of litigation.

Practice Tip: The above rules suggest that the best thing the corporation and its advisors can do to forestall an AET adjustment is to develop detailed, reasonable, and feasible plans and projections for the future use of accumulated funds. These plans and projections should be developed contemporaneously with the accumulation, to avoid suspicions that they are post-facto rationalizations.

Practice Tip: To provide greater certainty as to which party bears the burden of proof under the above rules, it is common for the corporation and the IRS, once the AET case has been docketed in the Tax Court, to submit cross motions asking the court to identify which party bears the burden. This is good practice. Often, the court will issue a ruling on the motions,[79] which often spurs settlement or at least provides clarity if the case does proceed to trial.

.02 Accuracy-Related Penalties

Accuracy-related penalties may be imposed when filed returns contain serious inaccuracies. Code Sec. 6662 is the most frequently asserted of such penalties. The penalty rate is 20%, raised to 40% in the case of gross valuation misstatements and undisclosed positions contrary to the economic substance doctrine.[80] The penalty may be imposed when any of six conditions is present. Five of them potentially apply to corporate taxpayers: negligence or intentional disregard of tax rules, substantial understatement of income tax, substantial income tax valuation misstatement, substantial overpayment of pension liabilities, and claiming tax benefits inconsistent with the economic substance doctrine under Code Sec. 7701(o).[81]

There are defenses built into various of the bases. For example, the substantial understatement of income tax basis usually is obviated if either substantial authority exists as to the item or the item was adequately disclosed on the return.[82] In addition, there is a global defense: the Code Sec. 6662 penalty is not imposed if there was reasonable cause for the underpayment.[83]

Three aspects of the Code Sec. 6662 penalty are particularly relevant to corporate taxpayers. First, a substantial understatement of income tax usually is an understatement that exceeds the greater of $5,000 or 10% of the tax required to be shown on the return for the year.[84] In the case of most corporations, however, the threshold is the lesser of 10% of the tax required to be shown on the return (or, if greater, $10,000) or $10,000,000.[85]

---

[79] *e.g., Gustafson's Dairy, Inc. v. Comm'r*, 69 T.C.M. 1639 (1995); *Iowa School of Men's Hairstyling, Inc. v. Comm'r*, 64 T.C.M. 1114 (1992).

[80] Code Sec. 6662(a), (h) & (i).

[81] Code Sec. 6662(b).

[82] Code Sec. 6662(d)(2)(B).

[83] Code Sec. 6664(c)(1). This defense is not available as to Code Sec. 6662(b)(6), the penalty base involving the economic substance doctrine.

[84] Code Sec. 6662(d)(1)(A).

[85] Code Sec. 6662(d)(1)(B).

Second, the substantial authority and adequate disclosure defenses to the substantial income tax understatement basis do not apply with respect to tax shelter items.[86] For this purpose, "tax shelter" means any plan or arrangement "if a significant purpose . . . is the avoidance or evasion of Federal income tax."[87]

Third, transfer pricing adjustments under Code Sec. 482 are major grounds of contention between the IRS and corporate taxpayers. Code Sec. 482 adjustments of sufficient magnitude can constitute substantial income tax valuation misstatements for both 20% and 40% penalty purposes.[88]

Reinforcing Code Sec. 6662 is Code Sec. 6662A, which provides a penalty with respect to certain tax shelter items. The Code Sec. 6662A penalty is imposed as a result of an underpayment of income tax attributable to listed and reportable transactions. The penalty rate is 20%, or 30% if the transaction is not properly disclosed.[89]

The reasonable cause defense is narrower as to Code Sec. 6662A than Code Sec. 6662. The defense is unavailable for Code Sec. 6662A purposes unless (1) the relevant facts as to the item have been disclosed, (2) there was substantial authority for the position, and (3) the taxpayer reasonably believed that the position was "more likely than not" correct.[90] In addition, reliance on the opinion of a tax advisor does not constitute good cause if the advisor had a financial interest in the transaction or if the opinion was based on unreasonable assumptions or representations or if it failed to consider all relevant facts.[91]

.03 Interest

In general, a taxpayer that pays part or all of its true tax liability after the last date prescribed for payment must pay interest on the underpayment.[92] A taxpayer that pays more than its true tax liability is entitled to receive interest on the overpayment.[93]

Four points about interest are of particular significance to corporations. First, the usual interest rate as to both underpayments and overpayments is 3% over the federal short-term rate.[94] However, corporations that have "large corporate underpayments" (underpayments over $100,000) qualify for this normal rate only up to the thirtieth day after the IRS issues the notice of deficiency or, if earlier, the thirtieth day after the first IRS letter as to which the corporation could receive administrative review. Thereafter, the interest rate on the underpayment rises to 5% over the federal short-term rate.[95]

Second, corporations often have underpayments and overpayments for different tax years outstanding at the same time. Formerly, these were treated separately for interest calculation purposes. Since 1998, however, the Code has allowed "global interest netting." That is, the interest rate is zero to the extent interest is

---

[86] Code Sec. 6662(d)(2)(c)(i).

[87] Code Sec. 6662(d)(2)(c)(ii).

[88] Code Sec. 6662(e).

[89] Code Sec. 6662A(a), (d).

[90] Code Sec. 6664(d)(2).

[91] Code Sec. 6664(d)(3)(B)(ii) & (iii).

[92] Code Sec. 6601(a).

[93] Code Sec. 6611(b)(2).

[94] Code Sec. 6621(a); *see* Code Sec. 1274 (rules for determining the federal rate).

[95] Code Sec. 6621(c).

payable on an underpayment and allowable on an overpayment, even if different kinds of taxes are involved and the underpayment and overpayment rates differ.[96]

Third, corporations receive a lower rate of interest on overpayments. That rate is 2% over the federal short-term rate as to the first $10,000 of the overpayment, then drops to .5% on any remaining portion of the overpayment.[97]

Fourth, tax attributes such as net operating loss, net capital loss, and certain tax credit carrybacks affect the amount of underpayments and overpayments for normal purposes. They do not do so, however, for interest computation purposes.[98]

.04 Means-Tested Litigation-Related Provisions

Most Code provisions relating to the determination of tax liability are available to taxpayers of all types. However, a growing number of provisions are available to small corporations but not larger corporations. As described below, the first such means-tested provisions involved shifting of attorney's fees and related costs. More recently, means-tested has been incorporated into a variety of other federal tax procedural rules.

(a) Attorney's Fees and Other Costs

In 1980, Congress enacted the Equal Access to Justice Act ("EAJA"), which allows parties successful in litigation against the federal government to recover their attorney's fees and other costs from the government under certain conditions.[99] However, the EAJA made certain entities and high-net-worth individuals categorically ineligible for such recoveries. Among the ineligible are corporations whose net worth exceeds $7 million or which have over 500 employees.[100]

The EAJA applies in federal district court, but not in the Tax Court, where most tax liability cases are tried. Accordingly, in 1982, Congress added Code Sec. 7430 to the Internal Revenue Code. Under Code Sec. 7430, prevailing taxpayers may, if stated conditions are met, recover reasonable administrative and litigation costs from the IRS. However, Code Sec. 7430 incorporates the EAJA net-worth requirements,[101] so corporations above the stated thresholds are ineligible for cost-shifting.

(b) Other Provisions

Congress has grafted the EAJA/Code Sec. 7430 means-testing approach onto a number of other Code provisions. Specifically:

- Code Sec. 6404 gives the IRS authority to abate certain kinds of tax assessments, including assessments of interest under some circumstances. Taxpayers may challenge in Tax Court IRS decisions not to abate interest. However, such actions may be brought only by taxpayers whose net worths do not exceed the EAJA/Code Sec. 7430 limits.[102]

---

[96] Code Sec. 6621(d).

[97] Code Sec. 6621(a)(1).

[98] Code Sec. 6601(d)(1) & (3), 6611(f).

[99] 28 U.S.C. § 2412.

[100] 28 U.S.C. § 2412(d)(2)(B).

[101] Code Sec. 7430(c)(4)(A)(ii).

[102] Code Sec. 6404(h)(1).

- Code Secs. 7431 to 7435 provide damages remedies for taxpayers injured by some kinds of IRS actions. Both the Code Sec. 7431 and Code Sec. 7433 damages provisions, however, are available only to taxpayers under the EAJA/section ceilings.[103]

- Code Sec. 7436 gives the Tax Court jurisdiction to hear disputes about employment status (i.e., employee versus independent contractor classification). Successful private litigants in such cases may recover costs and fees, but again subject to the EAJA/Code Sec. 7430 eligibility limits.[104]

- Although numerous exceptions exist, the burden of proof in civil tax litigation usually is on the taxpayer.[105] Code Sec. 7491 purports to shift the burden to the IRS if a number of conditions are met. Taxpayers cannot take advantage of Code Sec. 7491, however, if their net worth exceeds the EAJA/Code Sec. 7430 ceilings.[106]

- Code Sec. 6656 provides for a failure-to-deposit penalty. The IRS is empowered to waive that penalty in some cases. Such waiver cannot be made, however, in favor of taxpayers with net worths above the EAJA/Code Sec. 7430 limits.[107]

¶ 1004 Collection of Tax

When a pass-through entity such as a partnership or an S corporation is used, the owners of the entity are responsible for reporting and paying tax on the entity's profits. Correlatively, if a deficiency is determined, the deficiency is assessed against and collected from the owners.

In contrast, C corporations are separate taxpayers from their owners. Accordingly, if a deficiency is determined as to a corporation's tax returns, the IRS will assess the deficiency against the corporation itself and will demand payment from the corporation. If the corporation does not "voluntarily" pay this assessment, the IRS will use its techniques of enforced collection (liens, levies, and administrative or judicial sale of seized property) against the assets of the corporation.

In general, the IRS may not go against the assets of the shareholders to collect any unpaid liabilities of the corporation. There are two exceptions to this, two main secondary liability mechanisms by which shareholders (or others) may be made to answer for the unpaid tax debts of their corporations: (1) the trust fund recovery "penalty" of Code Sec. 6672 and (2) transferee liability under Code Sec. 6901. These, and mechanisms related to them, are discussed below.

.01 Trust Fund Recovery "Penalty" and Related Mechanisms

(a) Code Sec. 6672

Every tax professional with business clients sooner or later encounters the so called Trust Fund Recovery Penalty under Code Sec. 6672 (also known in some

---

[103] Code Secs. 7431(c)(3) & 7433(e)(2)(B)(i).

[104] Code Sec. 7436(d)(2).

[105] *See* Steve R. Johnson, *The Dangers of Symbolic Legislation: Perceptions and Realities of the New Burden-of-Proof Rules,* 84 Iowa L. Rev. 413 (1999).

[106] Code Sec. 7491(a)(2)(C).

[107] Code Sec. 6656(c)(1).

¶1004.01(a)

quarters as the "civil penalty" or the "100% penalty"). This mechanism is used by the IRS to collect unpaid "trust fund" taxes that should have been paid over to the IRS by corporations and other employers. The mechanism makes the "responsible persons" in the corporation personally liable for those taxes.

> *Example:* Acme corporation has employees. It is supposed to collect and pay over to the IRS three types of taxes with respect to the employees. The first type is income taxes of the employees collected by Acme through withholding under Code Sec. 3402. The second is Federal Insurance Contribution Act ("FICA"). FICA liability is divided between the employer and the employee. Acme is liable for half the FICA tax. Each employee is liable for the other half, which Acme collects through withholding under Code Sec. 3121. The third type is Federal Unemployment Tax Act ("FUTA"). Acme is solely responsible for FUTA.

> The term "trust fund taxes" refers exclusively to income tax withholding and the employee's share of FICA. If Acme corporation fails to collect and pay over to the IRS the trust fund taxes, the IRS may assert Code Sec. 6672 liability against Acme's "responsible person(s)."

In general, there are two elements, both of which must be satisfied for Code Sec. 6672 liability to attach: (1) the person in question was a "responsible person" within the sense of the section and (2) that person must have willfully failed to collect, truthfully account for, and pay over the trust fund taxes.

The touchstones of "responsible person" classification involve the person's "status, duty, and authority" within the corporation. Typically, a responsible person is one who had the authority to decide which creditors of the corporation to pay and when to pay them.[108] There may be more than one responsible person in the corporation, and the IRS frequently pursues multiple targets simultaneously.

"Willfulness" for Code Sec. 6672 purposes "means a voluntary, conscious, and intentional decision to prefer other creditors over the government."[109]

These elements have many nuances. Thousands of Code Sec. 6672 cases have been litigated, and their results are not always easy to reconcile.[110]

> *Practice Tip:* Code Sec. 6672 cases are one of the few types of civil tax litigation in which juries are commonly used. Jury trial may be a good option for a client who has a weak case on the law but whose situation entails compelling or sympathetic facts.

> *Practice Tip:* Code Sec. 6672 is really a collection device, not a true penalty. The IRS can never collect more than the total of the unpaid trust fund taxes although it may collect them in whatever proportions from multiple responsible officers.

---

[108] *e.g., Mazo v. United States*, 591 F.2d 1151, 1153 (5th Cir. 1979); IRM 5.7.3.3.

[109] *Muck v. United States*, 3 F.3d 1378, 1381 (10th Cir. 1993).

[110] For detailed discussion of Code Sec. 6672 and alternatives to it, *see* Richardson, Borison & Johnson, *supra* n. 40, ch. 14.

¶1004.01(a)

Example: Baker Corporation has $20,000 in unpaid trust fund taxes. Each of two persons, Russel and Rhonda, could be held liable under Code Sec. 6672. The IRS is not compelled to collect proportionately, that is, $10,000 from Russel and $10,000 from Rhonda. The IRS may collect all $20,000 from Russel and zero from Rhonda, all $20,000 from Rhonda and zero from Russel, or any mix between the two.

If the IRS does collect disproportionately from one of the potentially liable persons, that person has a remedy. Under Code Sec. 6672(d), she may bring a suit for contribution in federal district court against the other potentially liable persons.

(b) Alternatives to Code Sec. 6672

Code Sec. 3505 may also create liability for unpaid trust fund taxes for businesses or persons who are not the employers of the employees. Code Sec. 3505(a) imposes liability on lenders, sureties, and others who directly pay the wages of another and fail to appropriately withhold taxes. Code Sec. 3505(b) establishes a 25% penalty when funds have been supplied to pay wages without accounting for the trust fund taxes.

Practice Tip: The IRS can assess and collect Code Sec. 6672 liabilities administratively although judicial review is available. In contrast, the government must bring suit in federal district court to collect Code Sec. 3505 liabilities.[111]

.02 Transferee Liability and Related Mechanisms

(a) Transferee Liability

Assume that the Charlie Corporation owes taxes but Charlie's shareholders would rather have the funds themselves than pay them over to the IRS. Can IRS collection be defeated by Charlie distributing all its assets to the shareholders perhaps followed by liquidation of Charlie? No. In such a case, the shareholders would become personally liable to the IRS by virtue of the transferee liability mechanism.[112]

Code Sec. 6901 defines the procedural aspects of transferee liability, but the substantive basis of liability must be found in some body of law outside the Internal Revenue Code.[113] Typically, in the corporate context, that basis is found in (1) state statutes prescribing treatment of corporate liabilities in the event of organic changes such as mergers, consolidations, liquidations, or bulk sales of assets or (2) state or federal fraudulent conveyance statutes.[114]

---

[111] *e.g., Jersey Shore State Bank v. United States*, 479 U.S. 442 (1987); *United States v. Fred A. Arnold, Inc.*, 573 F.2d 606 (9th Cir. 1978).

[112] For detailed discussion of transferee liability and alternatives to it, *see* Richarson, Borison & Johnson, *supra* n. 40, ch. 15.

[113] *Comm'r v. Stern*, 357 U.S. 39 (1958).

[114] Subpart D of the Federal Debt Collection Procedures Act of 1990 is a federal fraudulent conveyance statute. Title XXXVI, Crime Control Act of 1990, Pub. L. No. 101-647, 104 Stat. 4789, 4933.

> *Practice Tip:* Code Sec. 6901(a)(1)(B) also makes fiduciaries liable for unpaid federal taxes. However, shareholders have been held not to be fiduciaries of their corporations for this purpose.[115]

(b) Alternatives to Transferee Liability

When applicable, the transferee liability device renders the shareholder-distributee (or other transferee) personally liable for the unpaid tax liabilities of the corporation-transferor (usually capped at the value of the transferred assets, plus interest). Alternatively, the IRS may ask the Department of Justice to bring a fraudulent conveyance suit in federal district court. If successful, such a suit causes the transferred property to be reconveyed to the transferor, and the IRS can then effect collection against the transferor. In some cases, under the Uniform Fraudulent Transfer Act, the IRS may, among other remedies, recover a money judgment against the transferee.[116]

Transferee liability should be distinguished from IRS nominee and alter ego liens and levies. The IRS resorts to the latter mechanisms when the IRS already has assessments against the primary taxpayer (the corporation in our example) and that taxpayer's property is being held by another without formal conveyance of legal title. Such liens and levies also may be used when there is no genuine separate existence, such as when a sole shareholder routinely ignores corporate formalities, hopelessly blurring any distinction between the two.

> *Practice Tip:* Transferor-transferee cases usually stay civil. However, in extreme cases of egregious and contumacious transfers of assets among related persons for the purpose of defeating tax collection by the IRS, the participants may be criminally prosecuted under a variety of statutes, including Code Secs. 7201 (tax evasion) and 7212 (corrupt interference with tax administration), and 18 U.S.C. § 371 (conspiracy).[117]

¶ 1005 Capacity and Identity Issues

Corporations, as merely juridical entities, must act by and through natural individuals. Moreover, corporations' identities are altered by organic changes such as reorganizations and dissolutions. These facts raise questions in some instances about the validity of actions taken purportedly by and for a corporation. This part illustrates these questions in two areas: (1) execution of consents to extend the statute of limitations and (2) conducting litigation.

.01 Extending the Statute of Limitations

In general, if the IRS believes a corporation owes more tax than reported, the IRS must assess the additional tax (or issue a statutory notice of deficiency) within three years of the later of when the return was filed or was due to be filed.[118] Many events and conditions alter the normal three-year limitations period, however.[119]

---

[115] *Grieb v. Comm'r*, 36 T.C. 156 (1961).

[116] *See* Steve R. Johnson, *Using State Fraudulent Transfer Law to Collect Federal Taxes*, Nevada Law., June 2006, at 14.

[117] *e.g.*, *United States v. Krasovich*, 819 F.2d 253 (9th Cir. 1987).

[118] Code Sec. 6501(a). Issuance of a notice of deficiency suspends the running of the statute of limitations. Code Sec. 6501(a)(1).

[119] For example, as particularly relevant to corporations, the limitations period does not expire as to certain items until three years after the taxpayer files with the

A major modification exists under Code Sec. 6501(c)(4), which provides that the limitations period is enlarged by the timely execution by both the taxpayer and the IRS of a consent to extend the period. When the taxpayer is a corporation, who is empowered to execute such an extension on the corporation's behalf?

Code Sec. 6061 provides that any return, statement, or document made under the tax laws must be signed in accordance with the applicable forms or regulations. However, neither Code Sec. 6501(c)(4) nor the regulations thereunder specify who may sign consents on behalf of a corporation. This gap is filled by IRS practice. In general, the IRS applies the rules applicable to execution of returns to consents to extend the limitations period.[120]

In the case of an active corporation,

> a corporation's income tax returns must be signed by the president, vice-president, treasurer, chief accounting officer or any other officer duly authorized to act. The fact that an individual's name is signed on the return is prima facie evidence that the individual is authorized to sign the return. Accordingly, any such officer may sign a consent, whether or not that person was the same individual who signed the return.[121]

In the case of a dissolved corporation,

> in states in which a dissolved corporation continues in existence for purposes of winding up its affairs, any authorized officer of the corporation may sign a consent during the period the corporation continues in existence under state law. In states in which a corporation's existence is terminated by dissolution, however, no one may sign a consent for the corporation.[122]

A consent executed by another corporation acting as agent of the taxpayer corporation can be valid.[123] A technically defective consent may be given effect if ratified by the corporation or if the corporation is equitably estopped from denying its validity.[124] A consent signed by an authorized officer of a corporation's successor-in-fact will validly extend the limitations period for the former corporation.[125]

.02 Conducting Litigation

When the IRS issues a notice of deficiency to a corporation, the corporation may contest the IRS's determinations by filing a timely petition with the Tax Court. A Tax Court "case shall be brought by and in the name of the person against whom the [IRS] determined the deficiency."[126] However, the mere fact that the caption of the petition bears a name other than that of the corporation to which the IRS issued

---

(Footnote Continued)

IRS information required by Code Sec. 6038 as to foreign corporations, by Code Sec. 6038A about foreign-owned corporations, by Code Sec. 6038B as to transfers to foreign persons, by Code Sec. 6046 about the organization and ownership of foreign corporations, or by Code Sec. 6046A about reorganization of or acquisition of stock in foreign corporations. Code Sec. 6501(c)(8).

[120] Rev. Rul. 84-165, 1984-2 C.B. 305, amplifying Rev. Rul. 83-41, 1983-1 C.B. 349.

[121] *Id.; see also* Code Sec. 6062.

[122] Rev. Rul. 84-165, 1984-2 C.B. 305; *see also* Rev. Rul. 71-467, 1971-2 C.B. 411. In such a case, the IRS's recourse would be to pursue the shareholder-distributee(s) of the corporation under a transferee liability theory. Transferee liability is discussed in subpart ¶1004.02(a). A shareholder-distributee may sign a consent to extend the statute as to his or her own liabilities. Rev. Rul. 84-165, 1984-2 C.B. 305.

[123] *e.g., Lone Star Life Ins. Co. v. Comm'r*, 74 T.C.M. 904 (1997).

[124] *e.g., Benoit v. Comm'r*, 25 T.C. 656 (1955), vacated, 238 F.2d 485 (1st Cir. 1956).

[125] *e.g., San Francisco Wesco Polymers, Inc. v. Comm'r*, 77 T.C.M. 1945 (1999).

[126] Tax. Ct. R. 60(a)(1).

the deficiency notice is not sufficient ground for dismissal of the petition. The taxpayer typically is given the opportunity to amend the petition to correct the caption.[127]

However, the corporation must have the legal capacity to pursue the litigation, whether in the Tax Court or another forum. Whether a corporation has such capacity is determined by the law of the state or other jurisdiction in which the corporation was organized.[128] Thus, the mere fact that the IRS has authority to issue a notice of deficiency to a corporation whose existence has been terminated does not necessarily cloak the Tax Court with authority to entertain a petition filed to contest that notice. The capacity of the corporation to commence and continue the case depends on state law.[129]

> **Example 1:** A corporation filed a Tax Court petition more than two years after it was dissolved, but state law provided that a corporation lost its capacity to sue two years after dissolution. The Tax Court petition was dismissed for lack of jurisdiction. It was irrelevant that the notice of deficiency was issued more than two years after dissolution.[130]

> **Example 2:** A dissolved corporation had capacity to file a Tax Court petition. Florida law provides that a dissolved corporation retains the ability to litigate indefinitely to the extent needed to wind up the corporation's affairs.[131]

> **Example 3:** The IRS audited a return filed by Corporation A, and Tax Court litigation ensued. The case was settled pursuant to a stipulated decision. Before the Tax Court petition was filed, Corporation A merged with Corporation B. The merged corporation filed a motion to vacate the decision. The motion was denied. Under Oklahoma law, a claim against a corporation may be litigated as if no merger had occurred. Thus, Corporation A had capacity to commence, continue, and conclude the Tax Court case.[132]

---

[127] *e.g., Fletcher Plastics, Inc. v. Comm'r,* 64 T.C. 35 (1975).

[128] Tax Ct. R. 60(c).

[129] *e.g., Great Falls Bonding Agency, Inc. v. Comm'r,* 63 T.C. 304 (1975).

[130] *Dillman Bros. Asphalt Co., Inc. v. Comm'r,* 64 T.C. 793 (1976).

[131] *Starvest U.S., Inc. v. Comm'r,* 78 T.C.M. 475 (1999).

[132] *Brannon's of Shawnee, Inc. v. Comm'r,* 71 T.C. 108 (1978).

¶1005.02

343

Table of Internal Revenue Code Sections

References are to paragraph (¶) numbers.

Index

References are to paragraph (¶) numbers.